Rainer W. Schlegelmilch

Hartmut Lehbrink

Jochen von Osterroth

KÖNEMANN

Wartburg Motorwagen   36   Dixi 3/16 PS
BMW 326 Cabriolet   80   BMW 328 Roadster
Veritas RS   132   BMW 502 Cabriolet
BMW 700LS   178   BMW 3200CS
BMW 2002 turbo   216   BMW 2500

Contents · Inhalt · Sommaire

BMW 325iX touring   278   BMW 318i Cabrio
BMW 850i   312   BMW 318i Cabrio
BMW 740i   346   BMW 540i
BMW 328i   384   BMW M3 CSL
Mini Cooper   420   BMW Z4

Foreword by Albrecht Graf Goertz

To be allowed to write a foreword at an age when I may be suspected of soon needing an obituary is sufficiently stimulating for me to put my ancestors on hold for a while before following in their footsteps. Allow me to take the opportunity presented by this book, with its impressive photos by Rainer Schlegelmilch and the texts by Hartmut Lehbrink and Jochen von Osterroth, to cast an eye back over my career as a designer, which was significantly influenced by BMW.

On a cold January day in 1914, a certain Count Albrecht Rudolf Moritz Eustach Friedrich-Wilhelm Alex Eduard von Schlitz, known as von Görtz, was born on the Brunkensen estate south of Hanover which had been in the family's possession since 1272. What a burden of a name I had been saddled with! In contrast to my elder brother, Eberhard, I was not so interested in country life. I had fallen in love with cars, and at ten years old I duly drew my first automobile, an Adler.

Since my effort at schooling had exhausted itself with secondary school, my mother — my father had died at a young age — apprenticed me to a bank as a clerk, first in Germany, then in England. From there I emigrated to the USA in 1936 in the search for creative freedom far from the pressures of national socialism.

The American GI Albrecht Goertz saw action in the islands of the Pacific, only to get stuck in Honolulu as the only one of 40,000 soldiers returning to the front. Chance?

And chance stepped in for a second time. Back in New York, I parked my home-built car, designed as early as 1938, in front of the Waldorf-Astoria hotel. The car caught the eye of a man standing in front of me. This was none other than the "Frenchman" Raymond Loewy, a genius at PR and all-round designer who could package more or less anything into a streamlined shape.

I became Loewy's pupil, yet neither the master's textbook, *Ugliness does not sell well,* nor the theory taught in a Brooklyn design institute brought me much further forwards. Making use of Loewy's Studebaker connections, I started a period of helpful practical training with this automobile company which was so rich in tradition. Loewy tolerated this for two-and-a-half years before throwing me out with the "kind" words: "Goertz, you will never become a designer. You would do better to find yourself a rich wife."

In 1953 I opened my own studio in New York. One day, Maxie Hoffman, importer of European sports cars, told me that he would like to have a BMW sports car for the US market. The problem was, he said, winking at me, that it still had to be designed. I should make two sketches for BMW and send them to Hanns Grewenig, the sales director of the works. A prototype already presented by Loof did not accord with his ideas.

I sent the sketch off and after only 12 days received a telegram asking when I would come to Munich. With the next plane of course! A hectic time ensued, particularly as the first 1:5 model had to be reworked completely. As well as the roadster, to be called 507, BMW also wanted a spacious four-seater coupé/convertible, the 503.

Things were achieved which are only possible with a well-motivated team which is also prepared to work at weekends. And even for the head of development, Fritz Fiedler, it was — as so often — "no problem" when I just wanted to lower the engine a little in the 1:1 layout of the new 507 six months before the launch.

In the autumn of 1955 — we worked up to the last moment — BMW presented the 503 and the 507 in Frankfurt; I personally find the coupé the more beautiful car of the two. The 507 celebrated its New York launch in the spring of 1956.

In einem Nachruf-verdächtigen Alter noch ein Vorwort schreiben zu dürfen, ist Stimulans genug, meine Vorfahren noch etwas warten zu lassen, bis ich ihnen nachfahre. Gestatten Sie mir, die Veröffentlichung des vorliegenden Buches mit eindrucksvollen Fotos von Rainer Schlegelmilch sowie den Texten von Hartmut Lehbrink und Jochen von Osterroth zum Anlass zu nehmen, mein von BMW entscheidend mitgeprägtes Designerleben ein wenig Revue passieren zu lassen.

1914 wird an einem kalten Januartag auf dem seit 1272 im Familienbesitz befindlichen Gut Brunkensen südlich von Hannover ein gewisser Albrecht Rudolf Moritz Eustach Friedrich-Wilhelm Alex Eduard Graf von Schlitz genannt von Görtz geboren. Welch eine Namensbürde, die man mir da auferlegt hat. Im Gegensatz zu meinem älteren Bruder Eberhard interessiert mich das ländliche Ambiente weniger. Ich bin in Autos verliebt, und als Zehnjähriger male ich mein erstes Mobil, einen Adler. Da sich meine schulischen Leistungen auf die Mittlere Reife beschränken, steckt mich meine Mutter — mein Vater war früh verstorben — in eine Banklehre, erst in Deutschland, dann in England. Von dort aus emigriere ich 1936 in die USA auf der Suche nach kreativen Freiräumen, fern nationalsozialistischer Zwänge.

Der amerikanische Infanterist Albrecht Goertz kommt auf den Inseln des Pazifik zum Einsatz und bleibt dann in Honolulu hängen, als einziger von 40 000 Soldaten, die wieder an die Front sollen. Zufall?

Noch einmal kommt mir der Zufall zu Hilfe. Zurück in New York parke ich meinen bereits 1938 entworfenen Eigenbau vor dem Waldorf-Astoria. Das Auto findet einen vor mir stehenden Interessenten. Es ist kein geringerer als der gebürtige „Franzose" Raymond Loewy, ein PR-Genie und Allround-Designer, der fast alles in Stromlinienförmiges verpacken kann. Ich werde Loewys Schüler, doch weder das Lehrbuch des Meisters *Hässlichkeit verkauft sich schlecht* noch die theoretische Ausbildung in einem Brooklyner Design-Institut bringen mich weiter. Loewys Kontakte zu Studebaker nutzend, mache ich bei dieser traditionsreichen Automobilfirma ein hilfreiches Praktikum, das Loewy zweieinhalb Jahre lang duldet. Dann schmeißt er mich raus mit den „netten" Worten: „Goertz, Sie werden nie ein Designer. Heiraten Sie doch lieber eine reiche Frau."

1953 eröffne ich in New York mein eigenes Studio. Eines Tages sagt mir Maxie Hoffman, Importeur europäischer Sportwagen, dass er gern einen BMW-Sportwagen für den US-Markt hätte. Allerdings müsse der Wagen — mit einem Augenzwinkern zu mir — noch entworfen werden. Ich solle doch für BMW zwei Skizzen machen und diese Direktor Hanns Grewenig, dem kaufmännischen Vorstand des Werkes schicken. Ein bereits von Loof präsentierter Prototyp entspreche nicht seinen Vorstellungen. Ich schicke die Skizzen ab, und bereits nach 12 Tagen werde ich telegrafisch gefragt, wann ich nach München komme. Mit dem nächsten Flugzeug natürlich! Es folgt eine hektische Zeit, zumal das erste 1:5-Modell völlig überarbeitet werden muss. Außerdem will BMW neben dem Roadster, der 507 heißen soll, auch noch ein geräumiges viersitziges Coupé/Cabriolet, den 503.

Es werden Dinge möglich, die nur mit einer gut motivierten Truppe, die auch an den Wochenenden arbeitet, machbar sind. Und selbst für Entwicklungschef Fritz Fiedler ist es — wie so oft — „kein Problem", wenn ich auf dem 1:1-Layout des neuen 507 mal gerade den Motor weiter nach unten rücke — ein halbes Jahr vor der Premiere. Im Herbst 1955 — wir haben noch bis zur letzten Minute gearbeitet — präsentiert BMW in Frankfurt den 503 und den 507, den ich persönlich als Coupé schöner finde. In New York feiert der 507 im Frühjahr 1956 Premiere. Ich ernte viel Lob, und die Presse sieht im 507 gar ein „formgestalterisches Wunderwerk". Ganz im Vertrauen — schöne Linien müssen nicht

À un âge presque canonique, l'invitation à écrire la préface de ce livre est assez stimulante pour faire patienter mes ancêtres avant de les rejoindre. Permettez-moi de profiter de la publication du présent livre avec d'impressionnantes photos de Rainer Schlegelmilch ainsi que les textes de Hartmut Lehbrink et Jochen von Osterroth pour passer rapidement en revue ma vie de designer au cours de laquelle BMW a joué un rôle déterminant.

En 1914, par une froide journée de janvier, au manoir de Brunkensen, au sud de Hanovre, patrimoine familial depuis 1272, naît un certain Albrecht Rudolf Moritz Eustach Friedrich-Wilhelm Alex Eduard von Schlitz, comte de son état, de la lignée des von Görtz. Quel nom lourd à porter! Contrairement à mon frère aîné Eberhard, l'agriculture n'était vraiment pas ma tasse de thé. J'étais amoureux des voitures et, à l'âge de dix ans, j'ai peint ma première automobile, une Adler. Comme ma scolarité s'est arrêtée au brevet, ma mère — mon père étant décédé très jeune — me fit effectuer mon apprentissage dans une banque, en Allemagne et en Angleterre. De là, j'ai rejoint les États-Unis en 1936, à la recherche d'espaces créatifs, loin des contraintes imposées par le national-socialisme.

Le fantassin américain Albrecht Goertz est envoyé en mission dans les îles du Pacifique et reste abandonné à Honolulu, le seul parmi les 40 000 soldats devant retourner au front. Un hasard?

Le ciel devait me venir en aide une deuxième fois. De retour à New York, je gare la voiture que j'avais construite moi-même en 1938 devant le Waldorf-Astoria. Elle attire l'attention d'un passant. C'est le « Français » Raymond Loewy, génie des relations publiques et styliste touche-à-tout, capable de doter les produits les plus divers d'une beauté fonctionnelle. Je deviens l'élève de Loewy. Mais ni son livre *La laideur se vend mal* ni l'enseignement théorique dispensé dans un institut de design de Brooklyn ne me permettent de progresser. Mettant à profit les relations de Loewy avec Studebaker, je fais un stage qui me sera très utile dans cette firme automobile aux longues traditions. Un stage que Loewy tolère pendant deux ans et demi. Puis, il me renvoie en me disant « gentiment » : « Vous ne ferez jamais un bon designer, épousez plutôt une femme riche. »

En 1953, j'ouvre mon propre studio à New York. Un jour, Maxie Hoffman, importateur de voitures de sport européennes, me confie qu'il aimerait lancer une BMW sportive sur le marché américain. Le problème, m'avoue-t-il en me faisant un clin d'œil, c'est que cette voiture n'est pas encore dessinée. Il me suggère de réaliser deux esquisses et de les faire parvenir à Hanns Grewenig, directeur des ventes de la firme BMW. En me précisant qu'un prototype avait été présenté par Loof mais il ne correspondait pas à ses attentes.

J'envoie les esquisses et, douze jours plus tard, je reçois un télégramme me demandant de me rendre à Munich. Évidemment, je pris le premier avion! Il s'ensuit une période de grande agitation, d'autant que la première maquette à l'échelle 1:5 doit être totalement revue. En outre, en plus du roadster qui s'appellera 507, BMW souhaite développer un spacieux coupé/cabriolet à quatre places, la 503.

Ainsi deviennent possibles des choses grâce à une équipe très motivée, travaillant aussi les week-ends. Et, même pour le chef du développement, Fritz Fiedler, la réponse est toujours : « Pas de problème » lorsque, sur le plan grandeur nature de la nouvelle 507, je souhaite simplement que l'on abaisse légèrement le moteur — six mois avant le lancement.

À l'automne 1955 — nous avons travaillé jusqu'à la dernière minute —, BMW présente à Francfort la 503 et la 507, que je trouve plus jolie en coupé. À New York, le lancement de la 507

I was much praised in the press, which considered the 507 to be a "miracle of design". Just between you, me and the gatepost: beautiful lines do not have to be invented, they simply have to be put in the correct relationship to one another. For me it is an expression of emotion.

In terms of aerodynamics, too, I am reluctant to lump everything together. With the 507 I did not have to bow to the influence of the wind tunnel, which exercises a decisive effect on automobile design today, although I did of course take aerodynamic considerations into account. Consider it rather as "streamlining" with the premise that the car should be able to do 136 mph (220 kph) with the appropriate transmission. This test was undertaken on a closed motorway – with the required result.

It is no coincidence that the BMW 700 was created in cooperation with Michelotti. I recommended my colleague over coffee in Geneva, and today I can reveal why: my fee was a little too high for the company, which was somewhat battered at the time.

While BMW blossomed in the 1960s, creative unrest drew me to the land of the lotus blossom. Just imagine, a "German-American" applying to design cars in Japan. The result is no secret: my design, the Datsun 240Z, is considered to be the best-selling sports car in the world. Like Loewy, I designed many things; even – for the government – the inside of Mexican classrooms. But before becoming sidetracked to Fissler cooking pots and Constructa washing machines, and Rowenta lighters and irons, let me turn my attention again to the subject of BMW and thus this magnificent book.

Apologies for this small diversion away from BMW! After all, I always took a great interest in the development of the white and blue marque and never allowed the connection to break off. I have often exchanged experiences with Dr. Wolfgang Reitzle, for many years Head of Development and Design. I will never forget my many meetings with proud 507 owners. 40 of these cars united on the old market place in Siena – an uplifting feeling.

A private letter from former BMW Chairman, Bernd Pischetsrieder, gave me particular pleasure. He had finally succeeded in buying a 507, a memorial to me, as it were. Long live nostalgia! And this you can indulge to the full with the present book. After all, Goertz drove an Isetta – in New York. Thanks to BMW of course!

When I venture on to the highway today in my M3 (living in Brunkensen again since 1990), I see much automotive monotony. On the other hand I am always surprised by the trends that are being set with nuances of design. I do not know whether my taste always corresponded to contemporary taste, but the multitude of cars which I cannot identify until I see their name on the trunk is disturbing. With BMW, everything forms an integrated whole, "corporate design", some of it of classic beauty.

In conclusion, allow me to add an afterword to the foreword in this impressive book. There is no point in hoarding the money I have earned with my designs. On the contrary, I want to pass on the experience I have gained over the years – and they are many – to young talent. The Goertz Foundation supports up-and-coming designers in worldwide competitions.

I hope that this BMW book – a splendid volume with its many illustrations – gives you much pleasure.

erfunden werden, man muss sie nur in das richtige Verhältnis setzen. Bei mir ein Ausdruck der Emotion.

Auch aerodynamisch will ich nicht gleich alles über einen Kamm scheren. Dem Einfluss des Windkanals, der heutzutage das Autodesign entscheidend prägt, muss ich mich beim 507 nicht beugen, wenngleich ich natürlich aerodynamische Gegebenheiten berücksichtigt habe. Betrachten Sie es eher als ein „Streamlining" aus der Hand mit der Prämisse, dass der Wagen mit entsprechender Übersetzung auch 220 „Sachen" fahren kann. Dieser Test erfolgt dann auf einer gesperrten Autobahn – mit dem geforderten Resultat.

Dass der BMW 700 in Zusammenarbeit mit Michelotti entsteht, ist kein Zufall. Ich habe den Kollegen bei einem Kaffee in Genf empfohlen und darf heute verraten, warum: Meine Honorarforderung ist für das damals etwas gebeutelte Unternehmen zu hoch.

Während BMW in den sechziger Jahren aufblüht, treibt mich die schöpferische Unruhe in das Land der Lotosblüten. Stellen Sie sich vor, da bewirbt sich ein „Deutsch-Ami" in Japan und will Autos entwerfen! Das Ergebnis ist bekannt: Mein Design, der Datsun 240Z, gilt als meistverkaufter Sportwagen der Welt. Wie Loewy entwerfe ich Verschiedenes, sogar das Interieur mexikanischer Schulklassen – als Staatsauftrag. Doch ehe ich von Fissler-Kochtöpfen und Constructa-Waschmaschinen auf Rowenta-Feuerzeuge und -Bügeleisen komme, möchte ich mich wieder dem Thema BMW und diesem prächtigen Buch widmen.

Sehen Sie mir bitte diesen kleinen Exkurs nach. Schließlich habe ich die Entwicklung der weißblauen Marke stets verfolgt und die Kontakte nie abreißen lassen. Mit Dr. Wolfgang Reitzle, lange Jahre Chef für Entwicklung und Konstruktion, habe ich oft Erfahrungen ausgetauscht. Unvergessen bleiben mir die vielen Treffen stolzer 507-Besitzer. 40 dieser Wagen auf dem alten Marktplatz von Siena vereint – für mich ein erhebendes Gefühl.

Besonders habe ich mich über ein privates Schreiben des ehemaligen BMW-Vorstandsvorsitzenden Bernd Pischetsrieder gefreut. Es sei ihm endlich gelungen, einen 507 zu kaufen, sozusagen mein Denkmal. Es lebe die Nostalgie! Und diese dürfen Sie im vorliegenden Buch in vollen Zügen genießen. Schließlich bin ich Fahrer einer Isetta gewesen – und das in New York. Dank BMW natürlich!

Wenn ich mich heute (seit 1990 wieder in Brunkensen) mit meinem M3 auf die Autobahn begebe, sehe ich viel automobiles Einerlei, bin aber andererseits überrascht, dass auch mit designerischen Nuancen Akzente gesetzt werden. Ich weiß nicht, ob ich mit meinem Geschmack immer richtig liege, doch die große Anzahl von Autos, die ich erst am Namen auf der Heckklappe erkenne, ist bedenklich. Bei BMW wirkt alles wie aus einem Guss, „corporate design", teilweise klassisch schön.

Zum Schluss möchte ich in diesem großartigen Buch ein Nachwort im Vorwort anbringen. Es ist müßig, dass ich das Geld zähle, das ich mit meinen Designs verdient habe. Vielmehr möchte ich meine im Laufe der Jahre – es sind nicht wenige – gesammelten Erfahrungen an junge Talente weitergeben. Die Goertz-Stiftung engagiert sich für den Designer-Nachwuchs in weltweiten Wettbewerben.

Viel Freude an diesem BMW-Buch – einem prächtigen Bildband zum Genießen – wünscht Ihnen

au printemps 1956 est un succès. Je croule sous les éloges et la presse voit même dans la 507 un « chef-d'œuvre du design ». Soit dit entre nous : il n'est pas nécessaire d'inventer de belles lignes, il faut seulement leur donner les bonnes proportions. Pour moi, c'est l'expression de mon émotion.

Sur le plan aérodynamique, je ne veux pas tout mettre dans le même panier. Pour la 507, je n'ai pas besoin de me plier au diktat de la soufflerie qui, aujourd'hui, influence l'ensemble du design automobile. Cela ne m'a pas empêché de prendre en considération certaines lois de l'aérodynamique. Considérez plutôt ceci comme un « streamlining » dessiné par intuition avec un cahier des charges qui veut que la voiture puisse aussi rouler à 220 km/h avec la démultiplication correspondante. Ce test est alors réalisé sur une autoroute fermée à la circulation – et le résultat escompté est obtenu.

Si la BMW 700 est réalisée avec le concours de Michelotti, ce n'est pas le fruit du hasard. Buvant un café avec quelques collègues à Genève, je le leur ai recommandé. Je me permets de vous confier aujourd'hui pourquoi : mes prétentions étaient trop élevées pour l'entreprise alors moins florissante qu'aujourd'hui.

Alors que BMW connaît un vif essor dans les années 1960, mon impétuosité créatrice me fait partir pour l'empire du Soleil-Levant. Imaginez un « Germano-Américain » qui veut dessiner des voitures au Japon ! Le résultat est connu : Mon enfant, la Datsun 240Z, est considérée comme la voiture de sport la plus vendue dans le monde. Comme Raymond Loewy, je dessine beaucoup, et même – sur commande de l'État – l'aménagement intérieur de salles de classe au Mexique notamment. Mais avant de passer des Cocotte-Minute Fissler et machines à laver Constructa aux briquets et fers à repasser Rowenta, je préfère me consacrer à BMW et, donc, à ce magnifique ouvrage.

Pardonnez-moi cette petite digression. J'ai, en effet, toujours suivi l'évolution de la marque à l'emblème bleu et blanc et je n'ai jamais perdu mes contacts. J'ai souvent échangé mes points de vue avec le Dr Wolfgang Reitzle, longtemps chef du développement et de la construction. Je n'oublierai jamais les rencontres de fiers propriétaires de 507. Voir réunies 40 de ces voitures sur la vieille Place du Marché de Sienne – quelle émotion !

Je me suis particulièrement réjouis d'une lettre que m'a envoyée, à titre privé, Bernd Pischetsrieder, ancien président du directoire de BMW. Il a enfin réussi, écrit-il, à acheter une 507, mon chef-d'œuvre ! Vive la nostalgie ! Et c'est dans cette nostalgie que vous pouvez plonger grâce à ce présent livre. Savez-vous que j'ai possédé et construit une Isetta – et ce à New York. Grâce à BMW, naturellement !

Quand je circule aujourd'hui (depuis 1990, je réside de nouveau à Brunkensen) avec ma M3 sur l'autoroute, je croise une multitude de voitures qui se ressemblent toutes. Je suis surpris que quelques touches de design permettent néanmoins de leur donner une touche particulière. Je ne sais pas si mon goût répond toujours aux attentes, mais le grand nombre de voitures que je ne reconnais que lorsque je lis leur nom sur la malle arrière me donne matière à réflexion. Avec BMW, tout semble couler de source, le « corporate design », parfois d'une beauté classique.

Enfin, j'aimerais conclure cette préface par ceci. Il serait fastidieux de compter l'argent gagné avec mes réalisations. Je préfère léguer mes expériences accumulées au fil du temps – et elles sont légion – aux jeunes talents. La Fondation Goertz s'engage pour la jeune génération des designers en organisant des concours à l'échelle mondiale.

Prenez donc plaisir à lire ce livre sur BMW – un magnifique ouvrage photographique –, c'est ce que je vous souhaite.

Albrecht Graf Goertz

Achievements in White and Blue
BMW in Retrospect

War, Peace and War Again (1916–1945)
Engines from Munich (1916–1928)

They say that the achievements of many individuals lie behind any success story, but that the names of most fade into obscurity. The story of the origins of the Bayerische Motoren Werke (BMW) tends to lend support to this view, though it is hard to be sure in the absence of messages from the hereafter. And these are, as we all know, somewhat thin on the ground. On the other hand, the here and now offers messages of great reliability in the form of official records and notarized documents. In fact, as regards the birth of BMW, there is an embarrassment of riches in this respect, with no less than three relevant official documents in existence. Unfortunately, in our search for the truth, this situation turns out to be as much a hindrance as a help.

The first document is dated 7 March 1916 and is to be found in the Munich Register of Companies. It states that the Bayerische Flugzeugwerke AG (Bavarian Airplane Works, or BFW) had just been founded. Its purpose was to be "the manufacture and commercial distribution of airplanes and any related machinery, equipment and other objects, and further, in the pursuit of this purpose, the founding of other enterprises in any legally permissible form, or participation therein, and also the running of companies of any sort". The clerk noted that the capital stock amounted to one million marks.

The new company was very much following the trend of the times. The First World War had reached the halfway mark without any sign of a let-up, and anything related to aviation was booming. One of the founders was a certain Gustav Otto, son of the inventor Nikolaus August Otto. As the clerk's punctilious handwriting notes, he brought "the Otto plants, previously his property, along with all assets and liabilities" to the new company, receiving 432,782.44 marks in exchange. BFW's base of operations was the premises at Lerchenauer Straße 76, not far from Oberwiesenfeld – now a historic BMW site.

A second find, also in the Munich Register of Companies, dates from 21 July 1917. Here we read that Rapp Motorenwerke GmbH, of Schleißheimer Straße 288, had been renamed the Bayerische Motoren Werke GmbH, but only after the previous managing director, Karl Rapp, had left the company. The new managing director, Franz-Joseph Popp, made an entry on 5 October of the same year at the Imperial Patent Office to the effect that the company purpose was to produce "land, air and water vehicles, automobiles and bicycles, automobile and bicycle accessories, vehicle parts, stationary engines for solid, liquid and gaseous fuels, and their replacement and accessory parts" – a truly ambitious and diversified range of products. At the same time Popp registered the company's trademark, which still remains today – the stylized whirl of a rotating propeller surmounted by the

Krieg, Frieden und wieder Krieg (1916–1945)
Motoren aus München (1916–1928)

Der Erfolg, so heißt es, hat viele Väter, nur dass sich mancher Anspruch und so manche Zuweisung im dunkeln verliert. Das Bild lässt sich mit den üblichen Retuschen auf die Ursprünge der Bayerischen Motoren Werke übertragen, zumal Rückmeldungen aus dem Jenseits bekanntlich ausgesprochen rar sind. Dafür hat das Diesseits ungemein verlässliche Dokumente zu bieten in Gestalt des amtlich Niedergelegten und des notariell Beglaubigten. In bezug auf die Geburtsstunde von BMW schafft allerdings der Plural Verwirrung, denn gleich drei Urkunden erweisen sich bei der Wahrheitssuche als ebenso hilfreich wie hinderlich.

Die erste, datiert mit 7. März 1916, findet sich im Münchener Handelsregister. Sie hält fest, man habe gerade die Bayerische Flugzeugwerke AG (BFW) ins Leben gerufen. Ihr Zweck und Ziel sei „die Herstellung und der gewerbsmäßige Vertrieb von Flugzeugen und allen damit im Zusammenhang stehenden Maschinen, Geräten und sonstigen Gegenständen, ferner im Rahmen dieses Zwecks auch die Errichtung anderer Unternehmungen in jeder rechtlich zulässigen Form oder die Beteiligung hieran und überhaupt der Betrieb von Gesellschaften jeder Art". Das Stammkapital, notiert der Schreiber, betrage eine Million Mark.

Die neue Marke liegt voll im Trend. Der Erste Weltkrieg verzeichnet Halbzeit ohne Pfiff und Pause, und alles boomt, was mit der Fliegerei zu tun hat. Unter den Gründern wird Gustav Otto genannt, Sohn des Erfinders Nikolaus August Otto. Er habe, so ist in pingeliger Handschrift vermerkt, in die neue Gesellschaft „die ihm bisher gehörenden Otto-Werke samt allen Aktiva und Passiva" eingebracht und dafür 432 782,44 Mark erhalten. Standort der BFW ist die Liegenschaft Lerchenauer Straße 76, unweit des Oberwiesenfelds – historischer BMW-Boden.

Zum zweiten Mal wird man am 21. Juli 1917 fündig, wieder im Handelsregister der Stadt München. Die bisherige Rapp Motorenwerke GmbH in der Schleißheimer Straße 288, steht da zu lesen, habe man umgewidmet zur Bayerische Motoren Werke GmbH, allerdings erst nachdem der alte Geschäftsführer Karl Rapp ausgeschieden sei. Der neue, Franz-Joseph Popp, lässt am 5. Oktober des gleichen Jahres beim Kaiserlichen Patentamt eintragen, die Firma habe es sich zum Anliegen gemacht „Land-, Luft- und Wasserfahrzeuge, Automobile und Fahrräder, Automobil- und Fahrradzubehör, Fahrzeugteile, stationäre Motoren für feste, flüssige und gasförmige Betriebsstoffe und deren Ersatz- und Zubehörteile" herzustellen, eine wahrlich ambitionierte und breit gefächerte Produktpalette. Zugleich meldet Popp das bis heute bestehende Markenzeichen an, das stilisierte Wirbelfeld eines Propellers mit den Lettern BMW im Kopfende sowie zwei weißen und zwei blauen Viertelkreisen als Verneigung vor der bayerischen Heimat.

D'une guerre à l'autre (1916–1945)
Les moteurs de Munich (1916–1928)

Le succès, dit-on, a de nombreux pères, mais il est parfois difficile de le revendiquer ou, inversement, d'en attribuer le mérite à quelqu'un. Ce dicton s'applique tout à fait aux origines de Bayerische Motoren Werke (BMW), car il est rare que des voix se fassent entendre d'outre-tombe. En revanche, on dispose aujourd'hui de documents fiables, qui ont été rédigés officiellement et authentifiés par un notaire. Quant à la date de naissance de BMW, la prolifération d'informations sème toutefois la confusion. En effet, pas moins de trois actes officiels simultanés existent, tous aussi utiles que déroutants dans cette recherche de la vérité.

Le premier, daté du 7 mars 1916, se trouve dans le registre du commerce de la ville de Munich. Il établit la création, ce jour-là, des Bayerische Flugzeugwerke AG (BFW). Activités déclarées de la société : « la fabrication et la distribution commerciale des avions et de toutes les machines, appareils et objets s'y afférant ; dans le cadre de ses activités, elle peut également créer d'autres entreprises sous une forme juridique légale ou participer à celles-ci et exploiter des sociétés en tout genre. » Le capital social, a même ajouté le greffier, était d'un million de marks.

La nouvelle marque a le vent en poupe. La première mi-temps de la Première Guerre mondiale s'achève sans coup de sifflet ni interruption. Et tout ce qui touche au secteur de l'aviation connaît un essor sans précédent. Parmi les fondateurs figure Gustav Otto, le fils de l'inventeur du moteur à quatre temps, Nikolaus August Otto. Il a, est-il précisé d'une écriture d'expert-comptable, apporté dans la nouvelle société « les usines Otto, dont il est jusque-là propriétaire, avec tous les actifs et passifs » et a reçu pour cela 432 782,44 marks. La BFW siège dans une propriété située au 76 de la Lerchenauer Strasse, non loin de l'Oberwiesenfeld – un lieu historique pour BMW.

Le 21 juillet 1917, on fait une deuxième découverte dans le registre du commerce de Munich. La Rapp Motorenwerke GmbH, sise au 288 de la Schleissheimer Strasse, peut-on y lire, a été rebaptisée Bayerische Motoren Werke GmbH, mais seulement après que Karl Rapp, l'ancien administrateur-gérant, a démissionné. Le nouveau, Franz-Joseph Popp, fait enregistrer le 5 octobre 1917, auprès de l'Office impérial des brevets, que la firme s'est donné pour objectif de fabriquer « des véhicules terrestres, aéronautiques et amphibies, automobiles et bicyclettes, accessoires d'automobile et de bicyclette, pièces de véhicules, moteurs stationnaires pour combustibles solides, liquides et gazeux et leurs pièces de rechange et accessoires ». Une gamme de produits véritablement ambitieuse et très diversifiée. Simultanément, Popp fait breveter l'emblème de la marque, le tourbillon stylisé d'une hélice avec les lettres BMW sur la circonférence letters BMW, plus two white and two blue quadrants, in homage to his Bavarian homeland.

Thus the production facilities, name and emblem were all in place, albeit as yet in the hands of different owners. Nevertheless things were afoot behind the scenes, though the marriage of the two companies would not come till later. There was to be no wedding night or honeymoon for the not-so-young couple, however, for in 1922 the Bayerische Motoren Werke moved lock, stock and barrel into the premises of the ailing Bayerische Flugzeugwerke, and the latter was promptly dissolved.

Up to that point, the BMW ship had always had to chart stormy waters. Karl Rapp, erstwhile employee of the Daimler-Motoren-Gesellschaft and survivor from the pioneering days of the automobile industry, was a resilient character and a fighter, but luck always seemed to be against him and by the end, he was simply too tired and too ill to continue. When in 1912 the first "Kaiserpreis für aeronautische Apparate" (Imperial Prize for Aeronautical Devices) was announced, he entered the competition with his biplane, powered by a 90 bhp four-cylinder overhead camshaft engine. However, the plane only succeeded in attracting derision and ridicule as it failed to become airborne, managing no more than a few clumsy kangaroo hops down the airfield. For the second "Kaiserpreis" in autumn 1914, he planned to enter a 125 bhp six-cylinder machine, but unfortunately this time the First World War intervened. However, the war did also create a demand for airplanes, but Rapp's aviation engines were plagued by vibration problems and fell into disrepute with the Prussian and Bavarian authorities, as complaints about it were practically a daily occurrence.

However, in the meantime the Viennese banker and entrepreneur Camillo Castiglioni had appeared on the scene. He seemed entirely unconcerned by Rapp Motorenwerke's dubious reputation. Castiglioni was an enigmatic figure. He was the head of a wide-ranging business empire of almost

Registration of the BMW trademark at the Imperial Patent Office in Munich. The year is 1917.

Eintrag des BMW-Firmenzeichens beim Kaiserlichen Patentamt München. Man schreibt das Jahr 1917.

Inscription de l'emblème de la marque BMW à l'Office impérial des brevets de Munich en 1917.

Produktionsstätte, Name und Firmenzeichen sind damit vorhanden, wenn auch im Besitz verschiedener Personen. Schon spinnen sich Fäden hinüber und herüber, aber zur Ehe kommt es erst später. Allerdings bleiben dem nicht mehr ganz jungen Paar Hochzeitsnacht und Flitterwochen verwehrt, denn 1922 ziehen die Bayerischen Motoren Werke mit Sack und Pack in das Anwesen der maroden Bayerischen Flugzeugwerke um, die somit aufhören zu existieren.

Bis dahin muss sich das Schifflein BMW jedoch noch in aufgewühltem Fahrwasser behaupten. Das war schon immer so. Karl Rapp, als einstiger Kostgänger der Daimler-Motoren-Gesellschaft ein Stück Treibgut aus der Phase des automobilen Urknalls, ist zwar ein Stehaufmännchen, aber auch ein glückloser Kämpfer und daher am Ende krank und müde. Als 1912 der erste "Kaiserpreis für aeronautische Apparate" ausgelobt wird, bewirbt er sich mit einem Vierzylinder mit 90 Pferdestärken, bei deren Erzeugung eine oben liegende Nockenwelle im Spiel ist. Der Doppeldecker, der sich mit diesem Triebwerk in die Lüfte erheben soll, zieht mit ein paar neckischen Hüpfern lediglich Hohn und Spott auf sich. Beim zweiten Kaiserpreis im Herbst 1914 gedenkt man mit einem Sechszylinder mit 125 PS anzutreten. Aber diesmal kommt der Erste Weltkrieg dazwischen. Er erzeugt zugleich jedoch Nachfrage und Aufträge kommen herein. Aber Rapps Flugmotoren geraten bei den zuständigen preußischen und bayerischen Behörden ins Gerede und in Verruf, denn sie werden von Vibrationen gebeutelt. Reklamationen sind an der Tagesordnung.

Gänzlich unbeirrt vom schlechten Leumund der Rapp Motoren Werke bleibt der Wiener Bankier und Kommerzialrat Camillo Castiglioni, ein schillernder Zeitgenosse und Herrscher über ein gleichermaßen heimliches wie unheimliches Imperium. Wegen seines unbekümmerten Jonglierens mit vielstelligen Zahlen wird er im Volksmund auch Castimillioni genannt. Er erwirbt eine massive Portion der Rapp-Anteile und sorgt dafür, dass das Stammkapital im Herbst 1916 auf 1,2 Millionen Mark angewachsen ist. Natürlich geschieht dies nicht um Gottes Lohn. Castiglioni sitzt im Aufsichtsrat von Austro-Daimler in Wiener Neustadt und ist auch dort Teilhaber. Die einstige österreichische Daimler-Dependance ist voll ausgelastet. Ein Lizenzauftrag über 224 Flugmotoren mit einem Volumen von zehn Millionen Mark winkt daher einer Firma mit ähnlicher Struktur – gegen deftige Provision, versteht sich. Als Mann der Tat schafft Castiglioni die Voraussetzungen kurzerhand selbst.

Während der umtriebige Bankier eher die Mehrung seines Besitzstandes im Sinn hat, geht es einem anderen Österreicher vor allem um Kompetenz. Franz-Joseph Popp ist Oberleutnant der Reserve bei der österreichisch-ungarischen Marine und Diplomingenieur und hält sich als Sachverständiger des kaiserlich-königlichen Kriegsministeriums für Flugmaschinen überall auf dem laufenden, bei Benz etwa oder der NAG (Neue Automobil Gesellschaft). Den Großauftrag knüpft die Wiener Behörde an eine Bedingung: Mit Popp müsse ein Mann ihrer Wahl und ihres Vertrauens die Fertigung der 224 V12-Triebwerke, jedes 350 PS stark, in München überwachen.

Am 29. Oktober 1916 trifft der Dreißigjährige in der bayerischen Metropole ein und ahnt nicht, dass sich der Job zur Berufung auswachsen wird. Persönlich hat er mit Rapp-Motoren keine schlechten Erfahrungen gemacht. Verblüfft zeigt er sich indessen über die bescheidenen Räumlichkeiten des Unternehmens und die desolate Verfassung seines Maschinenparks. Gleichwohl investiert er Vertrauen, und das zahlt sich aus, zumal er die Anstellung des fähigen ehemaligen Daimler-Ingenieurs Max Friz unterstützt. Der hat sich

On 29 November 1916, Franz-Joseph Popp made his approach to the Rapp Motorenwerke.

Am 29. November 1916 wird Franz-Joseph Popp bei den Rapp Motorenwerken vorstellig.

Le 29 novembre 1916, Franz-Joseph Popp se présente aux usines de moteurs Rapp.

ainsi que des quarts de cercle respectivement blancs et bleus en hommage à la Bavière, sa patrie.

Unité de production, nom et emblème existent donc déjà, mais ils appartiennent à différents propriétaires. Ceux-ci commencent toutefois à tisser les liens qui vont les rapprocher. Le mariage ne sera malgré tout célébré que bien plus tard. Le couple, alors plus très jeune, n'aura malheureusement jamais le plaisir de savourer sa lune de miel. En effet, en 1922, les Bayerische Motoren Werke prennent possession, avec tambour et trompette, des terrains de Bayerische Flugzeugwerke qui disparaît.

En attendant, BMW aura encore dû surmonter de nombreuses tempêtes. Mais ce n'était pas la première fois. Karl Rapp, autrefois salarié de la Daimler-Motoren-Gesellschaft et, en tant que tel, survivant de la phase du Big Bang automobile, est un homme qui retombe toujours sur ses pieds. Mais c'est aussi un battant, qui n'a pas la chance à ses côtés et, à la fin, il est malade et fatigué. Lorsque, en 1912, on annonce que sera décerné le premier « Kaiserpreis für aeronautische Apparate » (prix impérial pour des appareils aéronautiques), il fait acte de candidature avec un quatre-cylindres de 90 ch muni d'un arbre à cames en tête. Le biplan, que l'on espérait voir prendre les airs propulsé par ce moteur, se contente de quelques bonds de cabri qui en font la risée générale. Lors de la deuxième édition du prix impérial, à l'automne 1914, il espère faire mieux avec un six-cylindres de 125 ch. Mais, cette fois-ci, c'est la Première Guerre mondiale qui fait capoter ses plans. En revanche, elle génère aussi une demande et cela lui vaut des commandes. Les moteurs d'avion de Rapp font toutefois l'objet de critiques de la part des autorités prussiennes et bavaroises et ont mauvaise réputation. Les vibrations qu'ils émettent sont un véritable handicap. Les réclamations sont monnaie courante.

Le banquier et conseiller commercial viennois Camillo Castiglioni, un personnage énigmatique et maître d'un empire mystérieux aux ramifications multiples, ne se laisse pas impressionner par la réputation douteuse des Rapp Motorenwerke. Il est habitué à jongler sans complexe avec les millions, et c'est la raison pour laquelle il a été surnommé Castimillioni.

Byzantine complexity, and his casual juggling with multi-figure sums had earned him the popular nickname "Castimillioni". He had acquired a major slice of Rapp stock, thus ensuring that the company's capital stock had grown to 1.2 million marks by autumn 1916. Castiglioni was both a stockholder and member of the supervisory board of Austro-Daimler in Wiener Neustadt. The erstwhile Austrian Daimler subsidiary was working at full capacity, and as a result, a license contract for the manufacture of 224 airplane engines, worth ten million marks, was up for grabs for a firm of similar structure – in return for a hefty commission, naturally. Ever the man of action, Castiglioni set the whole deal up himself at short notice.

While the go-getting banker was chiefly interested in increasing his holdings, another Austrian was more concerned about competence. This was Franz-Joseph Popp, a Lieutenant in the reserves of the Austro-Hungarian marines, and a graduate engineer. As an aviation expert attached to the Royal Imperial War Ministry, his business was to keep himself up-to-date with the latest developments on the ground, whether at Benz, for example, or at NAG (Neue Automobil Gesellschaft: New Automobile Company). Accordingly, the authorities in Vienna made the award of this large contract conditional on Popp and a man of their choice keeping a close eye on the production of the 224 V12 power units, each developing 350 bhp, in Munich.

The thirty-year old Popp arrived in the Bavarian capital on 29 October 1916 with absolutely no idea that the job in hand was to become his life's work. He personally had not had any negative experiences with the Rapp engines. However, he was shocked at the company's cramped premises and the desolate state of its machinery and equipment. Despite this he put his faith in the company, and this was rewarded when he supported the appointment of the highly competent ex-Daimler engineer Max Friz. He had just applied for a position with Rapp, still smarting that his old boss Paul Daimler in Stuttgart had rejected out of hand his request for a raise of 50 marks a month.

On 1 January 1917, the Daimler renegade started work in Munich, against Karl Rapp's wishes, who saw his erstwhile colleague Friz as a potential rival. He was even more discontented that he now found himself working for a foreign power, and so he retired, a disappointed and disgruntled man. Franz-Joseph Popp became technical director. However, the company was still hindered by its poor reputation, and the only remedy was to create a new identity. And thus that fateful entry in the Munich Register of Companies, dated 21 July 1917.

Before long BMW had a successful Friz design to show, a six-cylinder airplane engine dubbed the IIIa. Friz's altitude-compensated carburetor meant that its 220 bhp at sea level was only reduced by half at 19,800 feet (6000 meters). Not without reservations, the War Ministry ordered 600 of them at a total cost of 13.2 million marks, and further orders followed. Schleißheimer Straße became a place of hectic activity, and in the end BMW itself was forced, due to insufficient capacity, to farm out some of the production on license, to Opel, Adler, the NAG, and MAN. The Prussian and Bavarian Ministry's misgivings that existing financial cover was too thin were quieted when the company went public on 13 August 1918, with capital stock of 12 million marks. Franz-Joseph Popp was appointed President. The BMW IV, which could generate 250 bhp even at 10,000 feet (3000 meters), was developed from the BMW IIIa. By autumn of that year BMW was providing gainful employment for a workforce of 3500.

gerade bei Rapp beworben, schäumend vor Wut, weil sein alter Chef Paul Daimler in Stuttgart seine Bitte um eine Gehaltserhöhung von 50 Mark im Monat schnöde zurückgewiesen hat.

Am 1. Januar 1917 tritt der Daimler-Renegat seinen Dienst in München an – gegen den Willen von Karl Rapp, der in seinem früheren Mitarbeiter Friz einen Rivalen wittert. Noch mehr ärgert es ihn, dass er sich in den Dienst einer fremden Sache zu stellen hat, und so zieht er sich verletzt aufs Altenteil zurück. Technischer Direktor wird Franz-Joseph Popp. Doch noch immer krankt die Firma an ihrem schlechten Image. Da bleibt dem Unternehmen nur noch der Ausweg, in eine neue Identität zu schlüpfen. Diese bezeugt der Eintrag im Münchener Gesellschaftsregister vom 21. Juli 1917.

Advertisement by the Rapp Motorenwerke Munich of 1916, with an indication of the client.

Inserat der Rapp Motorenwerke München von 1916 mit dem Hinweis auf den Auftraggeber.

Une publicité des usines de moteurs Rapp de Munich, en 1916.

Binnen kurzem kann BMW eine gelungene Friz-Konstruktion vorweisen, den Flugmotor IIIa, einen Sechszylinder. Dank Friz' Höhenvergaser sind von seinen 220 PS am Boden in 6000 Metern Höhe nur die Hälfte abgeschmolzen. Nicht ohne Skepsis ordert das Kriegsministerium 600 Exemplare im Gegenwert von 13,2 Millionen Mark. Weitere Aufträge folgen. Hektische Betriebsamkeit kehrt in der Schleißheimer Straße ein, und schließlich vergeben die Bayerischen Motoren Werke mangels Kapazitäten selber Lizenzen an Opel, Adler, die NAG und an MAN. Auf die Einwände der preußischen und bayerischen Ministerien, die Kapitaldecke sei zu dünn, reagiert man am 13. August 1918 mit der Umwandlung in eine Aktiengesellschaft. Das Grundkapital beläuft sich auf 12 Millionen Mark. Zum Generaldirektor wird Franz-Joseph Popp ernannt. Friz entwickelt aus dem BMW IIIa den BMW IV, der noch in 3000 Metern Höhe mit 250 PS aufwartet. Im Herbst jenes Jahres stehen bei BMW 3500 Mitarbeiter in Lohn und Brot.

Il acquiert une grande partie des actions de Rapp et veille à ce que le capital social soit majoré à 1,2 million de marks à l'automne 1916. Castiglioni est membre du conseil de surveillance d'Austro-Daimler, à Wiener Neustadt, dont il est également actionnaire. L'ancienne filiale autrichienne de Daimler tourne au maximum de ses capacités. Une commande sous licence pour 224 moteurs d'avions, d'un montant de dix millions de marks, devra donc être passée à une firme ayant une structure similaire – moyennant une commission juteuse, cela va de soi. Homme d'action, Castiglioni procède lui-même sans hésiter aux formalités nécessaires.

Pendant que l'infatigable banquier a surtout pour objectif de faire fructifier sa fortune, un autre Autrichien s'intéresse, lui, à ses compétences. Franz-Joseph Popp est lieutenant-colonel de réserve de la marine austro-hongroise, ingénieur diplômé et expert du ministère de la Guerre de la monarchie austro-hongroise, ce qui lui permet d'être informé de tout ce qui touche à l'aviation, chez Benz ou chez NAG (Neue Automobil Gesellschaft). Une clause conditionne toutefois la commande gigantesque de l'administration viennoise : avec Popp, un homme de son choix et de confiance devra surveiller la fabrication des 224 moteurs V12, chacun d'une puissance de 350 ch, à Munich.

Le 29 octobre 1916, le trentenaire arrive dans la métropole bavaroise. Il ne sait pas que son métier va devenir… une vocation. Personnellement, il n'a pas fait de mauvaises expériences avec les moteurs Rapp. En revanche, il est stupéfait lorsqu'il découvre la modestie des locaux et l'âge avancé du parc de machines. Il ne se laisse pas démonter et ne perd pas confiance : cela portera ses fruits, d'autant qu'il soutient le recrutement de Max Friz, un ancien ingénieur de Daimler très compétent. Il vient offrir ses services à Rapp, en colère contre son ancien chef Paul Daimler, à Stuttgart, qui a refusé d'un ton cassant sa demande d'augmentation de salaire de 50 marks par mois.

Le 1er janvier 1917, l'ancien «mercenaire» de Daimler prend ses fonctions à Munich, contre la volonté de Karl Rapp, qui voit dans son ancien collaborateur Friz un rival. Il est encore plus furieux de devoir se mettre au service d'une cause étrangère, si bien que, vexé, il décide de prendre sa retraite. Franz-Joseph Popp est ainsi nommé directeur technique. Et pourtant, la firme souffre encore de sa mauvaise réputation. La solution consiste donc à lui donner une nouvelle identité. Or cela implique une inscription au registre des sociétés de Munich. C'est chose faite le 21 juillet 1917.

En peu de temps, BMW peut présenter une création réussie de Friz, le moteur d'avion IIIa, un six-cylindres. Grâce au carburateur à haute altitude de Friz, qui peut atteindre les 6000 mètres, il ne perd que la moitié des 220 ch qu'il avait au sol. Non sans scepticisme, le ministère de la Guerre en acquiert 600 exemplaires pour un montant de 13,2 millions de marks. D'autres commandes vont suivre. L'activité de l'usine de la Schleissheimer Strasse est intense et, finalement, les Bayerische Motoren Werke doivent, par manque de capacités, attribuer des licences à Opel, Adler, NAG et MAN. Les ministères prussien et bavarois ayant trouvé l'envergure financière de la firme trop réduite, BMW réplique en devenant une société anonyme, le 13 août 1918. Le capital social s'élève à 12 millions de marks. Franz-Joseph Popp est nommé directeur général. À partir du moteur BMW IIIa, Friz développe le BMW IV, qui a encore une puissance de 250 ch à 3000 mètres d'altitude. À l'automne de cette année-là, BMW emploie quelque 3500 collaborateurs.

La guerre, proclame Héraclite, est la mère de toutes choses. Si l'on prend au pied de la lettre le philosophe grec, BMW devient orpheline à la fin de 1918 : le Traité de

War, according to Heraclitus, is the father of all things. Taking the ancient Greek sage's wise words literally, at the end of 1918 BMW suddenly found itself orphaned. The Treaty of Versailles robbed it of its livelihood at a stroke, as the victorious powers imposed a prohibition on the construction of aviation engines in Germany. Flexibility was called for, and once again Popp came up trumps. An order from the Berlin company Knorr-Bremse AG for 10,000 brake systems for the Bayerische Eisenbahnverwaltung (Bavarian Railway Authority) tided BMW over, though the job was carried out with no great enthusiasm.

However, the obligation to keep the show on the road did not lead Popp to forget the company's true direction. On 9 June 1919, despite the ban, the pilot Zeno Diemer soared in his DFW CIV over Oberwiesenfeld, after 87 minutes reaching the dizzy height of 32,208 feet (9760 meters) – a world record. The IV in the airplane's designation indicates that it belonged in the 200–300 bhp class. It was powered by a BMW IV engine – good publicity for the company. Unfortunately though, Diemer's feat was never recognized by the governing body FAI (Fédération Aéronautique Internationale), since Germany, as a defeated power, was not a member of the organization.

In the spring of 1922, Castiglioni purchased the Bayerische Flugzeugwerke's plant for BMW on Lerchenauer Straße and the Süddeutsche Bremsen AG (Southern German Brakes) moved into their previous premises.

Production now rested essentially on two products. First there was the 45/60 bhp engine, a rugged four-cylinder power unit with a cubic capacity of 8 liters, an overhead camshaft and weighing 11 hundredweight. It was known as the "Bayern-Motor" (Bavarian engine). It had truly universal applications: "The Bayern-Motor, a great success for the German automotive industry, ideal for motor boats, trucks, tractors, motorized plows and motorized bogies," as an advertisement in an automobile magazine proclaimed as early as 1921.

Secondly there was the M2B15 "Bayern-Kleinmotor" (Bavarian mini-engine), designed by the BMW works superintendent Martin Stolle. This was an air-cooled two-cylinder 494 cc boxer engine generating 6.5 bhp at 2800 rpm. It was most suited for use in motorcycles and the smallest automobiles, such as the droll two-wheeled car made by Mauser-Werke, though only 25 of these were ever made, aiming at low-income buyers. On the other hand, the BMW R32 motorcycle was the sensation of the 1923 Berlin and Paris Motor Shows. This was a milestone in motorcycle design with its tough and robust boxer power train, universal drive and double-tube frame.

At the same time, German aviation was getting back on to its feet after the restrictions of the Versailles Treaty were loosened a little in 1922. BMW made news with a number of spectacular publicity events. For example, on 18 December 1924 the Swiss Lieutenant Colonel Walter Mittelholzer embarked in his Junkers A-20 on the arduous flight from Zurich to Teheran, a flight that would take him over the 18,715 foot (5671 meters) peak Damavand in the Persian Elburz mountains. The heart of the machine was a BMW IV, once again bringing it to the attention of the decision-makers. After the specter of inflation had subsided, BMW capital stock was set at three million reichsmarks at the end of 1924. This figure was raised to five million reichsmarks in 1925, to ten million in 1927, and to sixteen million in 1928. From 1926 onwards Dr Emil Georg von Stauss joined the supervisory board of Bayerische Motoren Werke AG as a representative of Deutsche Bank, becoming its president in 1927. The number two was Camillo Castiglioni, but von Stauss had begun a

Der Krieg, lehrt Heraklit, sei der Vater aller Dinge. Nimmt man den alten Griechen beim Wort, werden die Bayerischen Motoren Werke Ende 1918 zur vaterlosen Gesellschaft. Der Versailler Vertrag entzieht ihnen durch die strikte Weisung der Siegermächte, den Bau von Flugmotoren einzustellen, die Existenzgrundlage. Flexibilität ist gefragt, Popp verfügt auch darüber. Ein Auftrag der Berliner Knorr-Bremse AG über 10 000 Bremsanlagen für die Bayerische Eisenbahnverwaltung hilft zunächst aus der Patsche, wird aber ohne Leidenschaft umgesetzt.

Über der Pflicht, die Geschäfte am Laufen zu halten, vergisst Popp nicht die Neigung: Am 9. Juni 1919 erhebt sich trotz des Verbots, Flugmotoren zu bauen Pilot Zeno

Agriculture, too, was rendered early services, as this advertisement from the magazine *Jugend* (Youth) of 1918 shows.

Auch um die Landwirtschaft macht man sich frühzeitig verdient, wie diese Anzeige in der Zeitschrift *Jugend* von 1918 zeigt.

BMW propose aussi très tôt du matériel agricole, comme le prouve cette publicité parue dans la revue *Jugend* (Jeunesse) en 1918.

Diemer mit seiner DFW CIV vom Oberwiesenfeld aus in die Lüfte und erreicht in 87 Minuten die lichte Höhe von 9760 Metern. Das ist Weltrekord. Die „IV" im Typensigel der Maschine besagt, dass sie in der Klasse 200–300 PS angesiedelt ist. Sie wird von einem BMW-IV-Motor angetrieben – das ist gute Werbung. Der Höhenflug Diemers erhält jedoch nie den Segen der Kontrollbehörde FAI (Fédération Aéronautique Internationale), da ihr das besiegte Deutschland nicht angehört.

Im Frühjahr 1922 ersteht Castiglioni für BMW das Anwesen der Bayerischen Flugzeugwerke in der Lerchenauer Straße. In die bisherigen Räumlichkeiten zieht die Süddeutsche Bremsen AG ein.

Die Produktion ruht nun im wesentlichen auf zwei Säulen. Da ist das Triebwerk 45/60 PS, ein knorriger Vierzylinder mit 8 Litern Hubraum, obenliegender Nockenwelle und 11 Zentnern Gewicht, genannt der „Bayern-Motor". Er ist universell verwendbar: „Der Bayern-Motor, ein großer Erfolg der deutschen Wärmewirtschaft, besonders geeignet für Motorboote, Lastwagen, Traktoren, Motorpflüge, Eisenbahnselbstfahrer", lockt schon 1921 ein Inserat in einer Autozeitschrift.

Um eine Konstruktion von BMW-Werksmeister Martin Stolle handelt es sich bei dem „Bayern-Kleinmotor" M2B15, einem luftgekühlten Zweizylinder-Boxer mit 494 ccm und 6,5 PS bei 2800 Umdrehungen pro Minute. Geeignet ist er vor allem für die Verwendung in Motorrädern und Kleinstautos wie dem skurrilen Einspur-Wagen der Mauser-Werke, der allerdings lediglich in einer Stückzahl von 25 Exemplaren unter die armen Leute gebracht wird. Zur Sensation der Pariser und Berliner Autosalons von 1923 wird die erste BMW-Maschine Typ R32, ein Meilenstein im weltweiten

Versailles la prive de toute existence, avec la stricte injonction des puissances victorieuses de cesser de fabriquer des moteurs d'avions. Il faut donc faire preuve de souplesse, ce qui est une autre qualité de Popp. Une commande passée par Knorr-Bremse AG, de Berlin, pour 10 000 circuits de freinage destinés aux chemins de fer bavarois permet de voir venir. Mais cette commande ne déclenche pas les passions.

Tenu de faire tourner l'entreprise, Popp n'en oublie pas pour autant son vieux penchant : malgré l'interdiction de fabriquer des moteurs d'avions, le 9 juin 1919, le pilote Zeno Diemer, aux commandes de son DFW CIV, décolle de l'aérodrome d'Oberwiesenfeld et atteint en 87 minutes l'altitude de 9760 mètres. Record du monde ! Le « IV » de la fiche signalétique du moteur symbolise qu'il s'inscrit dans la classe des 200 à 300 ch. L'avion est propulsé par un moteur BMW IV – une superbe publicité. Le record d'altitude de Diemer ne sera toutefois jamais homologué par l'autorité de tutelle, la Fédération aéronautique internationale (FAI), car l'Allemagne vaincue ne figure pas parmi ses membres.

Au printemps 1922, Castiglioni achète au nom de BMW les terrains des Bayerische Flugzeugwerke dans la Lerchenauer Strasse. La Süddeutsche Bremsen AG s'installe dans ses anciens locaux.

La firme a désormais deux fers au feu. L'un d'eux est le moteur 45/60 PS, un quatre-cylindres rugueux de 8 litres de cylindrée à un arbre à cames en tête qui pèse plus de 500 kg surnommé « le moteur de Bavière ». Il est très polyvalent : « le moteur de Bavière, un grand succès de l'industrie automobile allemande, est idéal pour les bateaux à moteur, les camions, les tracteurs, les charrues motorisées, les autorails », proclame, dès 1921, une publicité publiée dans une revue automobile allemande.

Le « petit moteur de Bavière », le M2B15, un bicylindre à plat refroidi par air de 494 cm³ et 6,5 ch à 2800 tr/min, est une réalisation de Martin Stolle, directeur d'usine chez BMW.

Il est surtout utilisé pour les motos et voiturettes comme l'étrange voiture monovoie des usines Mauser, qui fera le bonheur de 25 acheteurs seulement. Mais l'événement des Salons de l'Automobile de Paris et de Berlin, en 1923, c'est la première motocyclette BMW R32, qui est entrée dans les annales de la moto mondiale avec son indestructible moteur boxer, sa transmission à cardan et sa partie cycle à doubles tubes.

L'aéronautique allemande reprend de la vigueur dès que les conditions draconiennes du Traité de Versailles sont légèrement assouplies en 1922. BMW fait de la publicité *pro domo* avec des actions spectaculaires. Le 18 décembre 1924, par exemple, le lieutenant-colonel suisse Walter Mittelholzer, aux commandes de son Junkers A-20, s'attaque à l'épuisant vol Zurich–Téhéran à l'occasion duquel il doit franchir des sommets comme le Demavend, qui culmine à 5671 mètres dans le massif de l'Elbourz, en Iran. Le cœur qui bat dans l'appareil est le BMW IV qui, ainsi, se rappelle au bon souvenir des décideurs. Une fois le spectre de l'inflation dissipé, on majore le capital social de BMW à trois millions de reichsmarks à la fin de 1924. Une augmentation de capital est décidée en 1925, à cinq millions de reichsmarks, puis en 1927, à dix millions et, en 1928, à seize millions. À partir de 1926, le Dr Emil Georg von Stauss siège au conseil de surveillance de la Bayerische Motoren Werke AG en qualité de représentant de la Deutsche Bank et, en 1927, en tant que président. Le numéro deux est Camillo Castiglioni. Simultanément, comme dans une partie d'échecs, von Stauss commence, partout où cela lui est possible, à couper l'herbe sous le pied à l'influent mais intrigant Autrichien.

Veni, Vidi, Dixi

The Fahrzeugfabrik Eisenach (Eisenach Vehicle Factory) came into being in 1896. Its founding father Heinrich Ehrhardt, a Thuringian country boy, is said to have been multi-talented. One of his achievements was commemorated in his feudal-sounding nickname "Der kleine Kanonenkönig" (The little cannon king), reflecting the fact that he was accredited with the invention of the barrel recoil damper for artillery. He was also ambitious: he aimed to set up the third automobile company in Germany after Daimler and Benz via construction under license of the French make Décauville, with de Dion-Bouton engines under the seat.

Though 307 of Ehrhardt's Wartburg cars were produced at his tiny plant, expenses were greater than earnings, and in 1903 he unapologetically called it a day. His parting speech, an attempt to exonerate himself from all guilt, was a testament to his erudite classical education. It is said to have ended with the word "dixi", the standard closing formula of ancient Roman orators, meaning "I have spoken".

No sooner had he left than things began to look up. Without further ado, the product was named after Ehrhardt's parting shot, and the mysterious name had the desired effect. Between 1904 and 1929, 15,822 Dixis were sold. However, right from the start the name was applied to a bewildering variety of different models, from a 1.2-liter for the less well off, to a 5-liter, and culminating with "a huge 'Salonlimousine', a 7.3-liter luxury model (author's note), also available as a sports car or landaulet", as the glib promotional Dixi literature of the time put it. Among a number of features which were ahead of their time was the ingenious modular assembly system.

Business was so good that the loss-making parent company in Gotha was kept going by the Eisenach business. By 1926, though, ruin was staring them in the face. But then the speculator Jakob Schapiro incorporated both companies into his hydra-like organization. New problems were soon to rear their ugly heads. The car factory at Eisenach was required to take over production of a 2.3-liter six-cylinder 40 bhp car from Zyklon, another Schapiro acquisition which in the view of his experienced team of engineers, was an automotive catastrophe. They responded with an alternative design, a 3.5-liter 65 bhp machine which blithely ignored market realities and duly flopped as surely as the cuckoo's egg from the Zyklon camp in Mylau, Saxony.

The fate of the Dixi appeared to be sealed. But then Schapiro had a cunning plan. The most popular small car in Great Britain was the Austin Seven, from the Austin Motor Company in Birmingham. This was a Spartan driving machine, but despite that, as popular as darts. An agreement for its construction under license was quickly reached, and in June 1927, 100 Austin Sevens arrived in Eisenach, still with their original right-hand drive. In no time at all 7000 of the Dixi 3/15 PS had been sold – a point in their favor which did not escape Franz-Joseph Popp's attention any more than the discrete charm of this compact British machine did. However some things, he immediately saw, would have to be changed.

Motorradbau mit ihrem robusten Boxer-Triebwerk, Kardanantrieb und Doppelrohrrahmen.

Doch auch die deutsche Fliegerei fasst wieder Tritt, nachdem die Beschränkungen des Versailler Vertrags schon 1922 ein wenig gelockert worden sind. BMW macht mit spektakulären Aktionen von sich reden. Am 18. Dezember 1924 etwa begibt sich der eidgenössische Oberleutnant Walter Mittelholzer mit seiner Junkers A-20 auf den beschwerlichen Flug von Zürich nach Teheran und muss dabei Gipfel wie den 5671 Meter hohen Demawend im persischen Elbursgebirge

Dixi-land: 3/15 Dixis, lined up in front of the administration building of the BMW works in Eisenach.

Dixi-Land: Dixi-Wagen vom Typ 3/15, aufgereiht vor dem Direktionsgebäude der BMW-Werke Eisenach.

Au pays de Dixi : des Dixi 3/15 alignées devant le bâtiment des usines BMW à Eisenach.

überwinden. Das Herz der Maschine ist der BMW IV, der sich damit erneut der geneigten Aufmerksamkeit der Entscheidungsträger empfiehlt. Nachdem der Spuk der Inflation verflogen ist, setzt man das BMW-Aktienkapital Ende 1924 auf drei Millionen Reichsmark fest. Erhöhungen folgen 1925 auf fünf Millionen, 1927 auf zehn Millionen und 1928 auf sechzehn Millionen. Ab 1926 sitzt Dr. Emil Georg von Stauss als Repräsentant der Deutschen Bank im Aufsichtsrat der Bayerischen Motoren Werke AG, ab 1927 als Vorsitzender. Zweiter Mann ist Camillo Castiglioni. Zugleich beginnt von Stauss, in einem klugen und zähen Schachspiel den Einfluss des wendigen und windigen Österreichers zu unterbinden, wo immer das möglich ist.

Gleichwohl zieht man gelegentlich an einem Strang, wenn auch aus unterschiedlichen Motiven. Die Zukunft von BMW, darüber herrscht Konsens, liege im Bau von Automobilen. Allerdings denkt man nicht an einen Start aus dem Stand, sondern sucht nach einem real existierenden Partner, vorzugsweise mit einem guten Namen, der dennoch in Nöten ist. Castiglioni, inzwischen mit dem pompösen, aber ziemlich unverbindlichen Ehrentitel „Präsident der Bayerischen Motoren Werke" bedacht, fungiert als Mittelsmann gegenüber dem Management der Eisenacher Fahrzeugfabrik, einer Filiale der Gothaer Waggonfabrik. Dieser kauft man den Zweigbetrieb im Schatten der Wartburg am 14. November 1928 ab, gegen 200 000 Reichsmark bar auf die Hand und BMW-Aktien im Nennwert von 800 000 Reichsmark. Zugleich übernehmen die Bayern Verbindlichkeiten der thüringischen Adoptivtochter in Höhe von elf Millionen Reichsmark.

Parfois, les deux hommes font cause commune, même si leurs motifs sont profondément différents. L'avenir de BMW – là-dessus, les deux hommes sont d'accord – réside dans la construction d'automobiles. Ils n'envisagent toutefois pas de partir de zéro et se mettent donc en quête d'un partenaire déjà bien établi, qui jouisse d'une bonne réputation et se trouve néanmoins en difficultés. Castiglioni, qui se pare entre-temps du titre honorifique et pompeux, mais sans signification réelle, de « Président des Bayerische Motoren Werke », joue les intermédiaires auprès de la direction de la Eisenacher Fahrzeugfabrik, une filiale de la Gothaer Waggonfabrik. Il lui rachète sa filiale qui se trouve à l'ombre de la Wartburg, le 14 novembre 1928, contre 200 000 reichsmarks versés en espèces et des actions de BMW pour une valeur nominale de 800 000 reichsmarks. Parallèlement, les Bavarois reprennent les dettes de leur filiale de Thuringe, qui s'élèvent à 11 millions de reichsmarks.

Carrière entre crise et catastrophe (1928–1945)

Les débuts de BMW en tant que constructeur automobile sont modestes, mais le cap choisi est le bon. La monoculture est de règle puisque le seul modèle construit est, pour l'instant, la 3/15 PS. Jusqu'à la mi-1929, l'anglaise naturalisée allemande continue d'être produite dans sa version de Thuringe, sauf qu'elle a le volant à gauche, en tant que Dixi 3/15 PS DA1 (DA pour Dixi-Austin ou, aussi, pour Deutsche Ausführung – fabrication allemande). À la fin du mois de juillet 1929, la presse attentive et un public très intéressé découvrent dans les nouveaux salons d'exposition de BMW, au 5 de la Gutenbergstrasse à Berlin, la BMW 3/15 PS DA2 que Popp a adaptée au goût allemand grâce à de discrètes et justes retouches. Il l'a également rendue plus sûre. En un paradoxe subtil, la publicité proclame que la nouvelle voiture est « plus grande à l'intérieur qu'à l'extérieur ». En publicité, la marque n'a, dès cette époque, jamais fait preuve de modestie : « BMW pense aux voitures de demain », peut-on lire ailleurs.

Alors que, sur la première Dixi, l'effet du frein à main sur les roues avant et du frein à pédale sur les roues arrière était des plus souples, un freinage à câble sur les quatre roues confère à la DA2 une décélération digne de ce nom. La calandre a une forme différente et l'emblème bleu et blanc bien connu a supplanté le logo de la Dixi, un centaure au galop avec la crinière flottant dans le vent.

La petite BMW est tout d'abord proposée au prix de 2500 reichsmarks dans une version berline avec une carrosserie tout acier sans marchepied fabriquée par Ambi-Budd à Berlin. Pour son esthétique, BMW s'est inspirée de Lucien Rosengart, à Neuilly-sur-Seine, qui commercialise lui aussi des répliques sous licence de l'Austin Seven – traitées à la française. Elle possède des vitres à manivelle et non coulissantes dans les portières, une lunette arrière plus grande et des sièges avant réglables. À cela s'ajoutent deux variantes décapotables, une voiture de tourisme à quatre places et une biplace allégée avec un châssis en bois recouvert de similicuir, le tout vendu au prix défiant toute concurrence de 2200 reichsmarks. BMW ne manque pas d'arguments face à ses concurrents sur le marché des voiturettes : l'Opel « Grenouille » toujours livrée en vert comme il se doit, sa concurrente directe, qui représente un tiers de la production automobile allemande en 1928 avec 42 741 exemplaires produits, coûte sensiblement le même prix. Une autre rivale, cunning and dogged tactical battle aimed at reducing the influence of the slippery Austrian wherever possible.

However, over some matters they could work in unison, albeit acting from very different motives. The general consensus, for example, was that the future of BMW lay in the construction of automobiles. They did not intend to start from scratch though, aiming rather to enter into partnership with a pre-existing manufacturer with a good reputation but running into difficulties. Castiglioni, now with the impressive-sounding but fairly meaningless honorary title "President of the Bayerische Motoren Werke" acted as an intermediary to the management of Eisenacher Fahrzeugfabrik (Eisenach Automobile Factory), a subsidiary of Gothaer Waggonfabrik (Gotha Railway Wagon Factory). On 14 November 1928, the subsidiary, located in Thuringia, eastern Germany, was duly sold to BMW in return for 200,000 reichsmarks in cash plus BMW shares to a nominal value of 800,000 reichsmarks. The Bavarian company also took on the Thuringian subsidiary's liabilities, amounting to eleven million reichsmarks.

Success During Crisis and Catastrophe (1928–1945)

BMW's first efforts as an automobile manufacturer were modest, but in the right direction. Initially they limited themselves to manufacturing the 3/15 PS. This native English machine continued to be built until mid-1929 in the Thuringian version, but now with the steering wheel on the left and designated the Dixi 3/15 PS DA 1 (DA standing for Dixi Austin or Deutsche Ausführung meaning German construction). By the end of July of that year, the BMW 3/15 PS DA 2 was introduced to an attentive press and to great public interest in BMW's new showrooms in Berlin's Gutenbergstraße 5. The car had been cleverly restyled by Popp to suit German taste, and its safety had also been improved. The new model was, according to the somewhat paradoxical advertising, "bigger inside than out". Even in those days they were never short of a snappy slogan or two: "BMW has a vision for the world of tomorrow," was another.

While the Dixi's brakes were comparatively feeble, with just a handbrake for the front wheels and a foot brake for the rear ones, the model DA 2's cable-actuated four-wheel braking system provided a respectable amount of stopping power. The radiator grill had been redesigned, and the famous blue-and-white trade mark had replaced the Dixi emblem, a galloping centaur with a flowing head of hair.

This diminutive BMW was initially on sale from Ambi-Budd in Berlin at a price of 2500 reichsmarks, firstly as a sedan with all-steel bodywork and no running boards. For the styling, BMW had availed itself of the services of Lucien Rosengart of Neuilly-sur-Seine, who specialized in the construction under license of Austin Seven reproductions *à la française*. It was fitted with winding windows in place of the previous sliding ones, and with a larger rear windscreen and adjustable front seats. There were also two open-top versions, a four-seater tourer and also a lightweight construction two-seater with artificial leather coverings over a wooden frame, available at the give-away price of 2200 reichsmarks. This put BMW in a good position in the competitive small car market. Its direct competitor, the Opel "Laubfrosch" ("greenback"), which left the factory a grass-green color, was responsible for over a third of all German automobile production in 1928, manufacturing a total of more than 42,741 cars, and costing roughly the same as the BMW. The much less threatening rival, the Hanomag 3/16 PS, would set you back 2800 reichsmarks.

A legend in its own lifetime: the R 32, the first motorcycle of the Bayerische Motoren Werke.

Schon zu Lebzeiten eine Legende: die R 32, das erste Motorrad der Bayerischen Motoren Werke.

Une légende dès sa création : la R 32, la première moto de Bayerische Motoren Werke.

Karriere zwischen Krise und Katastrophe (1928–1945)

Die Anfänge der Bayerischen Motoren Werke als Hersteller von Automobilen sind bescheiden, aber die Richtung stimmt. Zunächst beschränkt man sich auf die Herstellung des 3/15 PS in Monokultur. Noch bis Mitte 1929 wird der naturalisierte Engländer in der thüringischen Version weitergebaut, nun mit dem Lenkrad auf der linken Seite als Dixi 3/15 PS DA 1 (für Dixi-Austin oder auch Deutsche Ausführung). Ende Juli jenes Jahres wird in den neuen Schauräumen der Bayerischen Motoren Werke in der Berliner Gutenbergstraße 5 der aufmerksamen Presse und einem höchst aufgeschlossenen Publikum der BMW 3/15 PS DA 2 präsentiert, den Popp durch geschickte Retuschen dem deutschen Geschmack angepasst und sicherer gemacht hat. Der Neue, so verheißt die Werbung in subtiler Paradoxie, sei „innen größer als außen". Um flotte Sprüche ist man schon damals nicht verlegen: „BMW denkt an die Zeit von morgen", heißt es an anderer Stelle.

Während im Dixi die Handbremse vergleichsweise milde auf die Vorderräder und die Fußbremse auf die Hinterräder einwirkt, sorgt am Modell DA 2 eine Seilzug-Vieranlage für eine passable Verzögerung. Anders geformt ist die Kühlermaske, und das bekannte weißblaue Markenzeichen hat das Dixi-Emblem verdrängt, einen Zentauren in vollem Galopp mit flatterndem Haupthaar.

Für 2500 Reichsmark ist der kleine BMW zunächst als Limousine mit einer Ganzstahlkarosserie ohne Trittbretter von Ambi-Budd in Berlin erhältlich. Was das Styling anbelangt, hat man bei Lucien Rosengart in Neuilly-sur-Seine Anleihen gemacht, der seinerseits Lizenz-Nachbauten des Austin Seven in die Welt setzt – à la française. Sie wartet mit Kurbelfenstern anstatt der bisherigen Schiebefenster in den Türen, einer größeren Heckscheibe und verstellbaren Vordersitzen auf. Dazu kommen zwei offene Varianten, ein Tourer mit vier Plätzen sowie ein Zweisitzer in Leichtbauweise mit einem Kunstlederbezug über dem Holzrahmen zum Spottpreis von 2200 Reichsmark. Damit liegt BMW gut im Rennen und im Wettbewerb der Winzlinge: Der grasgrüne Opel Laubfrosch als direkter Konkurrent, 1928 durch eine Verbreitung von 42 741 Einheiten mit über einem Drittel an der deutschen Automobilproduktion beteiligt, kostet ungefähr genausoviel. Die Anschaffung des weit weniger bedrohlichen Rivalen Hanomag 3/16 PS schlägt mit 2800 Reichsmark zu Buche.

moins menaçante celle-là, la Hanomag 3/16 PS, atteint déjà les 2 800 reichsmarks.

Pour le reste, le secteur de l'automobile a le vent en poupe. Naturellement, l'onde de choc du krach boursier du 25 octobre 1929 à Wall Street avec ses répercussions ébranle aussi BMW à Munich et à Eisenach. En 1928, le personnel comprenant 2600 collaborateurs réalise un chiffre d'affaires de 27 millions de reichsmarks, et de 34 millions en 1929 avec 3800 ouvriers (Eisenach compris). Le chiffre d'affaires passe à 36 millions de reichsmarks pour 3100 ouvriers en 1930 avant de retomber à 27 millions seulement pour 2900 collaborateurs en 1931. Le creux de la vague est atteint en 1932 lorsque BMW emploie 2800 ouvriers et que son chiffre d'affaires fond à 20 millions de reichsmarks.

Comparée à d'autres entreprises, la marque surmonte sans trop de dommages le cataclysme du «jeudi noir», ce qui est dû à plusieurs facteurs. D'une part, la 3/15 PS est la voiture prédestinée en période de crise. Le numéro de juin 1930 de la revue de l'entreprise munichoise *BMW Blätter* ne manque pas l'occasion d'en vanter les qualités au volant. Mais il loue aussi les atouts économiques de la «voiture de 15 ch»: elle ne donne «pas seulement du baume au cœur, elle représente aussi une économie financière considérable». Pour une moyenne annuelle de 30 000 km, calcule l'auteur avec précision, les coûts d'exploitation au kilomètre pour son propriétaire ne s'élèveront qu'à 5,11 pfennigs, ce qui est vraiment insignifiant.

Naturellement, le succès de cette petite voiture s'explique par la voiturette elle-même, dont on ne peut que tomber amoureux, ainsi que Franz-Joseph Popp le constate dès la présentation de l'original, à Eisenach. Dès 1929, le sport permet à la BMW 3/15 PS et à ses concepteurs de devenir célèbres lorsque trois compères – Max Buchner, Albert Kandt et Willi Wagner – au volant d'un modèle flambant neuf, gagnent la Coupe internationale des Alpes avec la moyenne remarquable de 42 km/h. Un autre argument percutant pour les vendeurs est le paiement à tempérament, introduit en avril 1929. De nombreux adeptes de BMW y recourent sans hésiter et payent leur DA 2 à raison de 24 mensualités de 107 reichsmarks chacune.

Pour le reste aussi, Popp et son équipe ont la chance de leur côté, par exemple lorsqu'ils complètent leur gamme de motocyclettes, en 1931, avec la monocylindre R 2 de 200 cm³. Un autre pilier sur lequel la maison BMW repose en toute sécurité, ce sont ses moteurs d'avions, par exemple le neuf-cylindres en étoile Hornet de 525 ch, copyright Pratt & Whitney. Un cinq-cylindres de 50 ch à l'origine, puis de 54 ch, qui est né sur la planche à dessin de l'ingénieur en chef Max Friz et qui est destiné aux avions de sport.

Popp travaille d'arrache-pied pour agrandir et réorganiser le réseau de concessionnaires et le service après-vente, notamment les points de vente, chargés jusque-là des motocyclettes de la marque. Quelques concessionnaires de Mercedes sont également de la partie. Leurs programmes se complètent parce que, durant cette crise économique, les voitures de chez Daimler-Benz, toutes beaucoup plus coûteuses, sont plus difficiles à vendre et puis on entretient des relations amicales. De 1926, année de la fondation, à 1945, Franz-Joseph Popp est membre du conseil de surveillance de Daimler-Benz tandis que, de 1932 à la fin de la guerre, le Dr Wilhelm Kissel – jusqu'en 1942 président du directoire de la firme à l'étoile de Stuttgart – siège au conseil de surveillance de BMW.

BMW relève le défi, dans les années 1930, sur trois fronts : les motocyclettes, les automobiles et les moteurs d'avion. Cette dernière branche prend toutefois une telle

All in all fate smiled on BMW. Of course the Wall Street Crash of 25 October 1929 and its long-term aftershocks did not spare BMW's home territory in Munich and Eisenach. In 1928 a workforce of 2600 achieved a turnover of 27 million reichsmarks, while in 1929, 3800 produced 34 million (including the Eisenach plant). In 1930 a workforce of 3100 were responsible for sales of 36 million reichsmarks, figures which fell in 1931 to 2900 and 27 million respectively. The low point was reached in 1932, when BMW's workforce fell to 2800, and their turnover to 20 million reichsmarks.

The fact that BMW survived Black Friday relatively unscathed, compared with other businesses, is due to several factors. Firstly, the 3/15 PS could have been tailor-made for the slump. The June 1930 edition of the Munich in-house publication *BMW Blätter* did not refrain from extolling the virtues of the lady at the wheel of the 15 bhp automobile, but was also quick to praise the money-saving virtues of the car itself, proclaiming that it represented "not just spiritual balm, but at the same time an outstanding financial saving". The meticulous author has calculated that, with an annual mileage of 18,645 miles (30,000 km), the owner's running costs come to a modest 5.11 pfennigs per kilometer.

Naturally the character of the car itself was responsible for a good deal of its success. It was a car that you just had to fall in love with, as Franz-Joseph Popp himself had observed when first viewing the original in Eisenach. As early

Back against the wall: the postal service does not want to do without the Dixi either. The spare wheel is fixed to the roof.

Mit dem Rücken zur Wand: Auch die Reichspost mag auf den Dixi nicht verzichten. Der Reservereifen ist auf dem Dach befestigt.

En rang d'oignon: la Poste impériale ne veut pas se passer de la Dixi. Le pneu de secours est fixé sur le toit.

as 1929 the BMW 3/15 PS and its creators made names for themselves via the motor sport successes of Max Buchner, Albert Kandt and Willi Wagner, who drove a brandnew 3/15 to victory in the International Alpenfahrt (Alpine Race) with an outstanding average speed of 26 mph (42 kph). Furthermore, the introduction of an installment plan in April 1929 proved to be a potent selling point, the offer being taken up by many BMW fans, who paid for their DA 2 in 24 monthly installments of 107 reichsmarks.

In other respects, too, Popp and his team held a strong hand, for example their range of motorcycles, which they rounded off in 1931 with the single-cylinder 200 cc R2. A third mainstay of the BMW marque was its airplane engines, including the nine-cylinder radial engine Hornet, developing 525 bhp, manufactured under license from Pratt & Whitney. There was also a five-cylinder 50 bhp (later 54 bhp) engine, aimed at the sports airplane market, from the drawing-board of chief designer Max Friz.

Popp worked energetically on expanding and overhauling his distribution and service networks, in particular the centers

Veni, Vidi, Dixi

Die Fahrzeugfabrik Eisenach wird im Jahre 1896 ins Leben gerufen. Gründungsvater Heinrich Ehrhardt, Sohn eines thüringischen Waldbauern, gilt als Multitalent. Eine seiner Facetten spiegelt sich in seinem feudal-militanten Spitznamen „der kleine Kanonenkönig" wider: Man schreibt ihm die Erfindung der Rohrrücklaufbremse an Geschützen zu. Ehrgeizig ist er auch: Mittels Lizenzbauten des französischen Fabrikats Décauville mit de-Dion-Bouton-Triebwerken unter dem Sitz möchte er sich nach Daimler und Benz als dritte Marke auf dem deutschen Markt einrichten. Obwohl 307 von Ehrhardts Wartburg-Wagen das winzige Werk verlassen, übersteigen die Ausgaben entschieden die Einnahmen. 1903 nimmt er seinen Hut. Seine Abschiedsrede – ein Versuch, sich von Schuld reinzuwaschen – zeugt von humanistischem Feinschliff. Sie soll mit „dixi" geendet haben, der stereotypen Schlussformel römischer Redner: „Ich habe gesprochen."

Kaum ist er weg, geht es bergauf. Kurzerhand benennt man das Produkt nach Ehrhardts Schlusswort. Der dynamisch-mysteriöse Begriff verfehlt seine Wirkung nicht. Zwischen 1904 und 1929 werden 15 822 Dixis unter das fahrende Volk gebracht. Dabei deckt der einheitliche Name von Anfang an eine strotzende Vielfalt von Varianten ab, vom 1,2-Liter für die weniger Betuchten unter den Freunden der Marke über einen 5-Liter bis hin zur „Salonlimousine (mit 7,3 Litern, Anm. d. Verf.) in Luxusausführung, auch als Sportwagen und Landaulet zu haben", wie es in der Dixi-Werbung voller Eigenlob heißt. Seiner Zeit weit voraus ist unter anderem ein ausgeklügeltes Baukastensystem.

Das Geschäft läuft so gut, dass das verlustträchtige Mutterhaus in Gotha von den Eisenachern mitgeschleppt werden muss wie ein sicher Greis. 1926 droht der Ruin. Dennoch verleibt der Spekulant Jakob Schapiro beide Unternehmen seiner Vielfirmen-Hydra ein. Neue Probleme erheben drohend ihr Haupt. Der Fahrzeugfabrik Eisenach wird zur Auflage gemacht, einen 2,3-Liter-Sechszylinder mit 40 PS von Zyklon zu übernehmen, einer anderen Schapiro-Erwerbung, in den Augen ihres erfahrenen Ingenieursteams eine automobile Katastrophe. Man antwortet mit einem Gegenentwurf, einem 3,5 Liter mit 60 PS, souverän am Markt vorbei geplant und deshalb ebenso ein Flop wie das Kuckucksei aus der Zyklon-Garnison Mylau in Sachsen.

Unabwendbar scheint das „Dixi" am Ende der Grabrede auf Dixi. Da hat Schapiro eine clevere Idee. Großbritanniens Kleinwagen mit der größten Verbreitung ist der Seven der Austin Motor Company in Birmingham – eine spartanisch karge Fahrmaschine und dennoch populär wie der Dart-Sport. Über einen Lizenzbau hat man sich schnell geeinigt, und im Juni 1927 treffen 100 Austin Seven in Eisenach ein, noch im Urzustand mit Rechtslenkung. Im Nu sind 7000 Exemplare als Dixi 3/15 PS verkauft – ein Argument, dem sich Franz-Joseph Popp ebenso wenig entziehen kann wie dem diskreten Charme des britischen Winzlings. Einiges jedoch, das weiß er sofort, wird man wohl ändern müssen.

Trotz allem lacht BMW die Gunst der Stunde. Natürlich erschüttern die Schockwelle und die lang anhaltenden Nachbeben des Wall Street Crashs vom 25. Oktober 1929 auch das BMW-Territorium in München und Eisenach. 1928 erwirtschaftet eine Belegschaft von 2600 Mitarbeitern einen Umsatz von 27 Millionen Reichsmark. 1929 sind es 3800 bei 34 Millionen

Piggyback: Dixis being loaded in the works yard in Eisenach.

Huckepacksystem: Dixi-Verladung auf dem Werkhof in Eisenach.

En route: chargement de Dixi dans la cour de l'usine à Eisenach.

ampleur que l'on doit vite créer une firme spécifique, la BMW Flugmotorenbau Gesellschaft mbH, à Munich, avec un capital social de 7,5 millions de reichsmarks, le 31 décembre 1934. La filiale d'Eisenach, qui reçoit aussi de nombreuses commandes des Forces aériennes, devient indépendante.

Le catalogue des appareils propulsés par des moteurs BMW ressemble à un « Who's who » de l'aéronautique. On y trouve le légendaire Junkers 52, qui semble éternel, au même titre que le Dornier Wal et l'« avion rapide » He70 de Heinkel. Grâce aux mains expertes de l'ingénieur en chef Max Friz, le moteur Hornet de Pratt & Whitney, produit sous licence, donne bientôt naissance au BMW 132, auquel les 28 litres de cylindrée confèrent une puissance permanente de 625 ch à 3800 mètres d'altitude. En 1934, l'année de la scission, les motos BMW sont disponibles en 200, 400 et 750 cm³. Dans le même registre, BMW propose aussi les triporteurs F76 et F79, à l'apparence spartiate comme il se doit en période de crise, qui bénéficient d'une exonération d'impôts et peuvent être conduits sans permis.

Avec la construction automobile, la branche la plus jeune de la maison prend de plus en plus d'importance. Un point décisif sera l'arrivée à expiration du contrat de licence signé avec Austin, le 1er mars 1932. À cette occasion, avec leur nouveau modèle 3/20 PS, appelé officiellement 0,8 Liter/20 PS, les Bavarois prouvent au monde entier que leurs véhicules sont maintenant moins gourmandes en carburant. Leur seul et unique point commun avec leur prédécesseur est l'archaïque ressort à lames transversal à l'avant – mais désormais dépourvu de son essieu rigide. Comme il est de règle à l'époque, le design cultive la religion de l'angle droit. Les commentateurs apprécient à l'unanimité les lignes séduisantes avec lesquelles la première série de la 3/20 PS est habillée à l'usine de carrosseries de Mercedes-Benz, à Sindelfingen. Elle est suivie, deux ans plus tard, par la 309. On ignore aujourd'hui encore le pourquoi et le comment du « 3 » dans sa dénomination. Mais les deux derniers chiffres indiquent déjà, comme cela allait devenir une coutume chez BMW, la cylindrée de ses quatre chambres de combustion : 845 cm³, arrondis à 0,9 litre.

Inversement, on a aujourd'hui le plus grand mal à interpréter le nom de la première six-cylindres de la marque, la 303 présentée au Salon de l'Automobile de Berlin en février 1933. Sous son capot aux multiples fentes latérales se dissimule, avec 1173 cm³, le plus petit moteur du marché à présenter une telle architecture. Et voilà encore une première : la 303 fend déjà la bise avec une ligne que l'on ne peut pas confondre et qu'afficheront les BMW des générations which had hitherto dealt with the marque's motorcycles. This even included a few Mercedes dealers. During the Great Depression the much more expensive Daimler-Benz products were far harder to shift, and in any case relations between the two companies were cordial in those days. From the year of its formation in 1926 until 1945, Franz-Joseph Popp was a member of Daimler-Benz's supervisory board, and from 1932 until the end of the War, Dr Wilhelm Kissel, until 1942 President of Daimler-Benz's executive board, also sat on BMW's supervisory board.

BMW confronted the challenges of the 1930s on three fronts: motorcycles, automobiles and aviation engines. This latter division had in the meantime grown to such an extent that, with effect from 31 December 1934, it was hived off to Munich as BMW Flugmotorenbau Gesellschaft mbH (BMW Aviation Engine Construction Ltd), with capital stock of 7.5 million reichsmarks. And the branch in Eisenach, where intensive development work for the "Luftwaffe" was being undertaken, was soon trading as an independent entity.

The catalog of airplanes fitted with BMW power units reads like a "Who's Who" of aviation history. The legendary Junkers 52, along with the Dornier Wal and the Heinkel He 70 plane, are among its entries. Among the products to stem from the expert hands of chief designer Max Friz was the BMW 132, developed from the Pratt & Whitney engine the Hornet, which BMW had been constructing under license. This engine's 28 liter cubic capacity gave it a continuous output at 12,540 feet (3800 meters) of 625 bhp. In 1934, the year of the split, BMW's range of motorcycles included 200, 400 and 750 cc models, while the three-wheeler delivery vans F 76 and F 79, their moderate fuel consumption ideal for the Depression years, were powered by motorcycle components and could be purchased tax-free and driven without a driver's license.

However, the company's most recent division, automobile construction, was becoming ever more important. A turning point here was the ending of the license agreement with Austin on 1 March 1932, which coincided with the introduction by BMW of the 3/20 PS, officially known as the 0,8 Liter/ 20 PS, bearing witness for all to see that their automobiles had now flown the nest. The only thing it had in common with its predecessor was the archaic front transverse leaf spring, but without the old rigid axle. The car's angular lines were in tune with contemporary style trends. The reviewers praised the appealing bodywork with which the 3/20 PS was fitted at the Mercedes-Benz body plant at Sindelfingen. Its successor, the 309, appeared two years later. The origin of the "3" as a model designation remains unclear. However, in what was to

Streamlined: Ernst Henne in 1931 during a world record drive on the Neunkirchner Allee between Vienna and Wiener Neustadt.

Stromlinie: Ernst Henne 1931 bei seiner Weltrekordfahrt auf der Neunkirchner Allee zwischen Wien und Wiener Neustadt.

Aérodynamique: Ernst Henne, en 1931, lors de son record du monde sur la Neunkirchner Allee entre Vienne et Wiener Neustadt.

Umsatz (einschließlich Eisenach). 1930 erwirtschaften 3100 Kostgänger 36 Millionen Reichsmark und 1931 sind es nur noch 2900 bei 27 Millionen Umsatz. Die Talsohle ist 1932 erreicht, als BMW 2800 Werktätige beschäftigt und der Umsatz auf 20 Millionen Reichsmark zusammengeschmolzen ist.

Dass man aus dem Schatten des Schwarzen Freitags im Vergleich zu anderen Unternehmen relativ ungeschoren heraustritt, lässt sich auf mehrere Faktoren zurückführen. Zum einen wirkt der 3/15 PS wie maßgeschneidert für die Krise. Die Juni-Ausgabe der Münchener Hauspostille *BMW Blätter* von 1930 versäumt nicht, in gewinnorientierter Galanterie eine Lanze für die Qualitäten der Dame am Lenkrad zu brechen. Sie preist aber auch die Qualitäten des 15-PS-Wagens als mobiles Sparschwein: Er stelle „nicht nur eine geistige Entlastung dar, sondern zugleich eine außerordentliche finanzielle Erleichterung". Bei einem Jahresschnitt von 30 000 Kilometern, errechnet der Autor penibel, komme der Eigner mit moderaten 5,11 Pfennigen Betriebskosten pro Kilometer hin.

Verantwortlich für den Erfolg des Zwergs ist natürlich zunächst einmal das Wägelchen selbst, in das man sich einfach verlieben müsse, wie Franz-Joseph Popp bereits bei der Besichtigung des Originals in Eisenach feststellt. Schon 1929 gereicht dem BMW 3/15 PS und seinen Erzeugern der Sport zum Ruhme, als Max Buchner, Albert Kandt und Willi Wagner in einem brandneuen Exemplar die internationale Alpenfahrt mit dem bemerkenswerten Schnitt von 42 Stundenkilometern gewinnen. Als Verkaufsargument erweist sich darüber hinaus die Möglichkeit der Teilzahlung, eingeführt im April 1929. Viele BMW-Anhänger machen bereitwillig davon Gebrauch und stottern ihren DA 2 in 24 Raten à 107 Reichsmark ab.

Auch sonst haben Popp und seine Männer eine glückliche Hand, zum Beispiel als sie 1931 das Motorradprogramm mit dem Einzylinder-Modell R 2 mit 200 ccm nach unten abrunden. Weitere Säulen, auf denen das Haus BMW sicher ruht, sind seine Flugmaschinen, etwa ein Neunzylinder-Sternmotor Typ Hornet mit 525 PS, Copyright Pratt & Whitney. Für Sportflugzeuge gedacht ist ein Fünfzylinder mit zunächst 50 PS und später 54 PS, der am Reißbrett des Chefkonstrukteurs Max Friz entsteht.

Energisch kümmert sich Popp um Ausweitung und Umgestaltung des Betriebs- und Servicenetzes, vor allem der Stützpunkte, die sich bislang um die Motorräder der Marke gekümmert haben. Auch ein paar Mercedes-Händler sind dabei. Die Programme ergänzen sich – während der Weltwirtschaftskrise lassen sich die durchweg weit teureren Produkte von Daimler-Benz viel schwerer absetzen – und überdies ist man einander freundschaftlich verbunden. Vom Gründungsjahr 1926 bis 1945 sitzt Franz-Joseph Popp im Aufsichtsrat von Daimler-Benz und Dr. Wilhelm Kissel, bis 1942 Vorstandsvorsitzender der Stuttgarter Firma mit dem Stern, sitzt von 1932 bis Kriegsende im Aufsichtsrat von BMW.

Den Herausforderungen der dreißiger Jahre begegnen die Bayerischen Motoren Werke dreispurig mit den Produktlinien Motorrad, Auto und Flugmotor. Letzterer Zweig erlangt indessen solche Bedeutung, dass man ihn mit Wirkung vom 31. Dezember 1934 kurzerhand als BMW Flugmotorenbau Gesellschaft mbH zu München mit einem Stammkapital von 7,5 Millionen Reichsmark ausgliedert. Auch die Filiale in Eisenach, wo man intensive Entwicklungsarbeit für die Luftwaffe leistet, firmiert bald mit einer selbständigen Identität.

Der Katalog der Maschinen, die durch BMW-Triebwerke beflügelt werden, liest sich wie ein „Who's who" der Lüfte. Die unsterbliche Legende Junkers 52 findet sich ebenso darunter wie die Dornier Wal und das Heinkel-„Schnellflugzeug" He 70. Unter den kundigen Händen von Chefkonstrukteur

La Fahrzeugfabrik Eisenach (usine de voitures) est fondée en 1896 par Heinrich Ehrhardt, un fils de sylviculteur de Thuringe talentueux. Son surnom, « le petit roi du canon », est déjà révélateur : c'est à lui que l'on attribue l'invention du frein de recul des canons d'artillerie. Qui plus est, il est ambitieux : à l'aide de Decauville françaises à moteur de type de Dion Bouton sous le siège, produites sous licence, il veut devenir la troisième marque sur le marché allemand, après Daimler et Benz. Bien que 307 Wartburg d'Ehrhardt quittent la petite usine, les dépenses dépassent largement les recettes. En 1903, il jette l'éponge sans prévenir. Son discours d'adieu témoigne de son éducation humaniste. Selon la légende, ce discours se serait terminé par « dixi », la formule utilisée par les tribuns romains : « Dixi, j'ai parlé. »

À peine est-il parti que l'entreprise se redresse. Spontanément, on baptise le produit du dernier mot prononcé par Ehrhardt. Ce terme, aussi dynamique que mystérieux, ne manque pas son effet. Entre 1904 et 1929, 15 822 Dixi trouvent preneur. Dès le début, ce nom unique est apposé sur nombre de modèles, le programme allant d'une 1,2 litre pour les moins riches à une 5 litres et même une « limousine de salon » (de 7,3 litres, note de l'auteur) en version luxe, « disponible tant en voiture de sport qu'en landaulet », vante la publicité pour la Dixi. Son système de construction modulaire bien pensé, notamment, est très en avance sur son temps.

Les affaires marchent si bien que le groupe de Gotha, auquel appartient Dixi et qui n'engrange que des pertes, doit être soutenu à bout de bras par la firme d'Eisenach. En 1926, la faillite menace. Ceci n'empêche pas le spéculateur Jakob Schapiro d'intégrer les deux entreprises à la nébuleuse de ses firmes. De nouveaux problèmes surgissent. L'usine de voitures d'Eisenach se voit contrainte de reprendre de Zyklon – une autre acquisition de Schapiro – une six-cylindres de 2,3 litres de 40 ch, une voiture qui est, aux yeux de son équipe d'ingénieurs expérimentés, un modèle sans avenir. Ils répliquent avec leur propre projet, une 3,5 litres de 60 ch qui ne répond absolument pas aux besoins du marché et qui est par conséquent un échec retentissant, comme l'œuf de coucou de Zyklon, sorti de l'usine de Mylau, en Saxe.

Le sort de la Dixi semblait scellé. C'est alors que Schapiro a une idée lumineuse. La voiturette la plus vendue de Grande-Bretagne est la Seven, fabriquée à Birmingham par l'Austin Motor Company, un engin austère et, pourtant, aussi populaire que le jeu de fléchettes. Il en obtient rapidement la licence d'exploitation et, en juin 1927, 100 Austin Seven arrivent à Eisenach, dans leur état d'origine, avec le volant à droite. En un rien de temps, il en vend 7000 exemplaires sous le nom de 3/15 PS – un argument auquel Franz-Joseph Popp peut tout aussi peu résister qu'au charme discret de cette minuscule voiture britannique. Une chose lui vient toutefois immédiatement à l'esprit. Quelques modifications vont s'avérer nécessaires.

13 cylinders: a Junkers 52 with nine combustion chambers flies nimbly over the BMW four-cylinder in 1983.

13 Zylinder: Eine Junkers 52 mit neun Verbrennungs-einheiten überfliegt 1983 behäbig den BMW-Vierzylinder.

13 cylindres : un Junkers 52 doté d'un moteur à 9 cylindres survolant le bâtiment de BMW « à quatre cylindres » en 1983.

become standard future BMW usage, the two final digits indicate the capacity of each of its four cylinders: 845 cc, generously rounded up to 0.9 liters.

In contrast, the numbers 303 as the designation for the first BMW six-cylinder are difficult to interpret today. This model was launched in February 1933 at the Berlin Motor Show. Beneath its notched hood lay an 1173 cc engine, making it the smallest six-cylinder on the market. On top of this, the 303 was the first BMW with the unmistakable BMW front end, which would be familiar to future generations: the kidney shape, topped by the famous blue and white propeller. If you find the right street, a contemporary test driver enthused, the six-cylinder engine would enable you to "revel in the breathtaking feel of 100 kph (62 mph) speed". The men behind this machine were Fritz Fiedler, who had done outstanding work for Horch in the design of their eight and twelve-cylinder engines, and Rudolf Schleicher, who, after a period with Horch at the beginning of the 1930s, had returned to BMW. The engine's essential character was superb. From the start it was subject to a continual development process involving several increases in cubic capacity, by the end of which it had grown in size to around two liters. The culmination of the earlier 3 series was the 326 of 1936. With sales of 15,936 cars between 1936 and 1941 it became the best-selling BMW of its era. As early as 1935, a construction license had been granted to Frazer-Nash of Isleworth, in the English county of Middlesex, supplying them with some 319 right-hand drives plus running gear, to which the British partner added its own coachwork.

The 328, the most successful 2-liter sports car of the 1930s, made a suitably dramatic debut when Ernst Henne achieved victory in his class at the Eifel race at the Nürburgring on 14 June 1936. His average speed of 63 mph (101.5 kph) brought the small white BMW into the midst of the big super-charger cars.

Like John Surtees, Mike Hailwood or Johnny Cecotto in the postwar era, Henne was equally at home on two wheels or on four. On an icy November day in 1937, he flashed down the highway outside Frankfurt on a 500 cc motorcycle with streamlined fairing, reaching a record speed of 279.503 kph (174 mph). Henne's reaction to this showed unrivaled cool: "Pretty good, huh?" After the 1933 German Motorcycle Grand Prix, the papers had a triple BMW triumph to report: in the 500 cc class, the old warhorse Peppi Stelzer took the honors, in the 1000 cc class Eduard Kratz won, while Theodor Schoth took the sidecar title. In the 1938 Mille Miglia, the two British drivers Alfred Fane and William James

Max Friz entsteht aus dem Pratt & Whitney-Lizenzprodukt Hornet der BMW Typ 132, dessen 28 Liter Hubraum ihn auf 3800 Metern Höhe zu einer Dauerleistung von 625 PS befä-higen. 1934, im Jahr der Spaltung, sind BMW-Zweiräder mit 200, 400 und 750 ccm erhältlich. Auf Kraftradkomponenten stützen sich die Dreirad-Lieferwagen F76 und F79, mit kri-sengerecht spartanischem Erscheinungsbild, steuerfrei und ohne Führerschein zu fahren.

Immer mehr an Bedeutung aber gewinnt der jüngste Spross des Hauses – der Automobilbau. Ein wichtiges Datum ist in dieser Hinsicht die Beendigung des Lizenzvertra-ges mit Austin am 1. März 1932. Zugleich zeigen die Bayern mit der Neuentwicklung 3/20 PS – offiziell 0,8 Liter/20 PS genannt – der Welt, dass ihre Autos flügge geworden sind. Nur noch die archaische vordere Querblattfeder teilt die Neu-entwicklung mit dem Vorgänger – nun aber ohne die bishe-rige Starrachse. Das Design schwelgt im Stil der Zeit in rech-ten Winkeln. Die Rezensenten preisen die ansprechende Form, in welche die erste Serie des 3/20 PS im Mercedes-Benz-Karosseriewerk Sindelfingen gekleidet wird. Der Nach-folger 309 erscheint zwei Jahre später. Die Ursprünge der „3" in der Typenbezeichnung bleiben im Zwielicht. Aber die beiden letzten Ziffern erteilen analog zu künftigen BMW-Usancen Auskunft über den Hubraum seiner vier Verbren-nungseinheiten: 845 ccm, aufgerundet zu 0,9 Litern.

Kaum entwirren lässt sich hingegen das Zahlenknäuel 303 als Bezeichnung für den ersten Sechszylinder der Marke, der auf der Berliner Autoausstellung im Februar 1933 debü-tiert. Hinter seiner seitlich vielfach aufgebrochenen vorderen Haube verbirgt sich mit 1173 ccm der in dieser Konfiguration kleinste Motor des Markts. Und noch eine Premiere: Der 303 streckt bereits das unverwechselbare BMW-Gesicht späte-rer Generationen in den Fahrtwind, die Niere, gekrönt vom bekannten weißblauen Propellerkreis. Wer die richtige Straße finde, frohlockt ein zeitgenössischer Tester, könne mit dem neuen Sechszylinder „das Gefühl des berauschenden Tempo 100 auskosten". Die Männer hinter dieser Maschine sind Fritz Fiedler, der sich bei Horch um die Acht- und Zwölfzylinder ver-dient gemacht hat, und Rudolf Schleicher, der ebenfalls nach einem Intermezzo bei Horch zu Beginn der dreißiger Jahre zu BMW zurückgekehrt ist. Die Substanz des Motors ist glän-zend. Zugleich setzt ein kontinuierlicher Reifeprozess ein, in den sich etliche Hubraumvergrößerungen einlagern, bis bei rund zwei Litern ein Ende des Wachstums angezeigt scheint. Die frühen 3er kulminieren im 326 von 1936, denn mit 15 936 verkauften Exemplaren zwischen 1936 und 1941 wird er seiner Zeit zum BMW mit der größten Verbreitung. Schon 1935 vergibt man eine Lizenz an Frazer-Nash in Isle-worth in der englischen Grafschaft Middlesex und lässt etliche 319 mit Rechtslenkung sowie rollende Chassis für eigene Aufbauten des britischen Partners folgen.

Team prize for the BMW 315/1 in the 1934 International Alpine Race from Nice to Munich.

Mannschaftspreis für den BMW 315/1 bei der Internationalen Alpenfahrt 1934 von Nizza nach München.

Prix d'équipe pour la BMW 315/1 lors de la Coupe internationale des Alpes 1934 de Nice à Munich.

futures, les naseaux couronnés du célèbre emblème bleu et blanc. À condition de trouver la bonne route, se réjouit un essayeur contemporain, on peut, avec la nouvelle six-cylindres, « succomber à l'ivresse du 100 km/h ». Qui sont les hommes qui se cachent derrière cette voiture ? Fritz Fiedler, qui a effectué un travail remarquable chez Horch avec les huit et douze-cylindres, et Rudolf Schleicher, qui, après un passage chez Horch est revenu chez BMW au début des années 1930. Les caractéristiques de ce moteur sont remar-quables. Tout de suite, un processus de développement se met en place au cours duquel de nombreuses majorations de cylindrée s'effectueront jusqu'à atteindre les deux litres. Les ventes de la première « série 3 » culminent avec la 326 en 1936. Avec 15 936 exemplaires fabriqués entre 1936 et 1941, ce sera la BMW la plus produite de son époque. Dès 1935, une licence est accordée à Frazer-Nash, à Isleworth, dans le comté britannique du Middlesex, licence qui est suivie de la production d'innombrables 319 à conduite à droite ainsi que de châssis roulants pour les propres carrosseries du partenaire britannique.

Avec la 328, la voiture de sport de deux litres qui a remporté le plus de succès durant les années 1930, BMW défraye la chronique lors de son lancement en obtenant une victoire de prestige signée Ernst Henne lors de la course de l'Eifel, sur le Nürburgring, le 14 juin 1936. Avec une moyenne de 101,5 km/h, la petite BMW blanche marche effrontément sur les traces des grosses voitures à compresseur.

À l'instar de John Surtees, Mike Hailwood et Johnny Cecotto, Henne est aussi à l'aise sur deux roues que sur quatre. Par une glaciale journée de novembre 1937, au volant d'une moto de 500 cm³ à carénage aérodynamique, il signe un record de vitesse avec 279,503 km/h sur autoroute près de Francfort. Le premier commentaire de Henne témoigne de sa gouaille légendaire : « C'est pas mal, non ? » À l'issue du Grand Prix d'Allemagne pour motocyclettes de 1933, les manchettes des journaux annoncent un triomphal triplé BMW : en 500 cm³ avec le vieux renard de la course, Peppi Stelzer, avec Eduard Kratz en 1000 cm³ et avec Theodor Schoth en side-car. Aux Mille Miglia de 1938, les deux Britanniques Alfred Fane et William James remportent la victoire avec leur 328 inscrite dans la catégorie des deux-litres et terminent même 8e au classement général. En 1940, le rapide baron Huschke von Hanstein, accompagné de son copilote Walter Bäumer, ne se contente pas de ces résultats : ils remportent la victoire au volant d'une 328 à carrosserie en aluminium de Touring lors de la même manifestation, mais sur le circuit triangulaire Brescia–Crémone–Mantoue, qui, cette année-là, remplace la gigantesque boucle à travers l'Italie. Et ce ne sont là que quelques exemples.

« Racing improves the breed », disent les Anglais : la course anoblit la race. Mais pas seulement. À cette époque, BMW acquiert aux yeux du public la notoriété qui la démarque positivement des autres marques. Elle se fait ainsi connaître de ses clients, dont certains deviendront des passionnés – en proposant des modèles innovants, sportifs et indémodables, qui ont en main les choses de la vie, pour une conduite ferme et décontractée.

Temporairement, alors que la Seconde Guerre mondiale éclate, le 1er septembre 1939, le gouvernement interdit la vente et la livraison de toute automobile à des particuliers. Sous le manteau, mais non sans avoir l'accord tacite des autorités compétentes, la production de voitures de tourisme chez BMW se poursuit néanmoins au compte-gouttes pendant un certain temps. Jusqu'à la fin de 1939, BMW pro-duira respectivement 480 exemplaires des 321 et 326. À l'automne 1940, elle n'aura vendu que 201 voitures.

took the 2-liter title in their 328, also achieving eighth place in the overall classification. And in 1940 the racing Baron Huschke von Hanstein, accompanied by co-driver Walter Bäumer, was not to be fobbed off with a mere class victory: he won the overall victory in a 328 with a light alloy body from Touring at the same event, though this time on the triangular route Brescia-Cremona-Mantova, which that year replaced the usual giant circuit of whole of Italy. These are just a few examples of BMW's racing success.

"Racing improves the breed," as the English say. And that is not all; BMW's public image received just the boost it needed to make it stand out from its rivals. It sent out a message to the clientele and BMW devotees: BMWs are fresh, sporty and forever young, for people who keep a relaxed but firm hold on their lives.

Immediately after the start of the Second World War on 1 September 1939, the sale and delivery of motor vehicles to private individuals was prohibited. However, BMW's production of private cars somehow lingered on for a while, by a combination of underhand means and the blind eye turned by the authorities. By the end of that year, 480 cars of both the 321 and 326 models had been produced. By autumn 1940 just 201 cars had found owners. A few privileged people managed to have a wood carburetor fitted on the roof – an oven-like device which burned wood to produce fuel – and even succeeded in getting hold of an increasingly scarce tire for the spare wheel. However, the writing had been on the wall for a long time, and by May 1941 the production lines finally fell silent.

Motorcycles, though, were still in demand and continued to be manufactured in some quantity. The heavy R 75, ideal for off-road use, became a legend for its all-round ruggedness. And of course the organized machinery of death and destruction demanded airplanes: in 1939 BMW acquired the Brandenburgische Motorenwerke in Berlin-Spandau, previously part of the Siemens group, and with a long tradition of aviation engine construction. Here and at BMW's other manufacturing plants in Munich and Eisenach, tens of thousands of aviation engines were produced between then and 1945. The 003 jet engine was essentially a technological nicety, of no real relevance to the outcome of the conflict of that time and at best of some value as a defiant gesture. The He 162 "Volksjäger" (people's fighter) – production start on 24 September 1944, maiden flight on 6 December 1944 – fitted with the 003, reached a speed of 522 mph (840 kph) at a height of 19,800 feet (6000 meters).

Meanwhile BMW itself had become a target for British and American bombers. As a shrewd precaution, certain branches of production had already been relocated to innocent-seeming rural locations such as Immenstadt, Kempten or Kaufbeuren, before the bombs began to fall thick and fast. Nevertheless, between 9 March 1943 and 22 September 1944, Plant I in Oberwiesenfeld was hit ten times and on 12 July 1944, 1117 bombers dropped more than 10,000 bombs, containing a total of 2727 tons of explosives. The chroniclers of the 8th and 15th American air fleets kept meticulous records, also noting that BMW Plant II in Allach was bombed nine times in 1944 alone.

By the time the unconditional surrender was signed in Reims on 7 May 1945, BMW had, like so much else, suffered severely as a result of the war. A third of the plant lay deserted in a wasteland of rubble and twisted steel. Hordes of plunderers fell like locusts on the mortally injured imperium and made off with yet more of its assets. On 1 October 1945 the American deputy garrison commander Lieutenant Colonel Eugene Keller issued an order for the entire Munich plant to

Einen standesgemäß dramatischen Einstand gibt der 328 – erfolgreichster 2-Liter-Sportwagen der dreißiger Jahre – durch einen Klassensieg von Ernst Henne beim Eifelrennen auf dem Nürburgring am 14. Juni 1936. Mit seinem Schnitt von 101,5 Stundenkilometern bricht der kleine weiße BMW in die Domäne der großen Kompressorautos ein.

Wie später ein John Surtees, Mike Hailwood oder Johnny Cecotto ist Henne auf zwei wie auf vier Rädern zu Hause. An einem eisigen Novembertag des Jahres 1937 huscht er auf einer stromlinienförmig verkleideten 500er mit dem Rekordtempo von 279,503 Stundenkilometern über die Autobahn bei Frankfurt. Hennes erster Kommentar zeugt von unnachahmlicher Gelassenheit: „Das ist doch sehr gut, oder?" Nach dem Großen Preis von Deutschland für Motorräder 1933 melden die Gazetten einen BMW-Dreifach-Triumph: Bei den 500ern gewinnt der alte Haudegen Peppi Stelzer, bei den 1000ern Eduard Kratz, bei den Gespannen Theodor Schoth. Bei der Mille Miglia 1938 landen die beiden Briten Alfred Fane und William James mit ihrem 328 einen Sieg bei den 2-Litern und arbeiten sich bis auf Rang acht im Gesamtklassement vor. 1940 begnügt sich der rasende Baron Huschke von Hanstein in Begleitung von Copilot Walter Bäumer nicht mehr mit solchen Almosen des Erfolgs: Gesamtsieg in einem von Touring in Leichtmetall gewandeten 328-„Innenlenker" bei der gleichen Veranstaltung, allerdings auf dem Dreieckskurs mit den Eckpunkten Brescia–Cremona–Mantua, der in jenem Jahr die Riesenrunde durch Italien ersetzt. Dies sind nur einige Beispiele für den Erfolg der Marke im Motorsport.

„Racing improves the breed", sagen die Engländer: Rennen veredeln die Rasse. Nicht nur das: Das BMW-Bild in der Öffentlichkeit erhält damals jenen Kick, der es aus dem Markeneinerlei positiv heraushebt. Dies teilt sich zugleich den Kunden mit, unter denen auch BMW-Jünger sind: frisch, sportiv und dauerhaft jung; Menschen, die die Dinge des Lebens locker, aber unerbittlich im Griff haben.

Pünktlich zum Beginn des Zweiten Weltkriegs am 1. September 1939 werden der Verkauf und die Auslieferung von Kraftfahrzeugen an Privatleute untersagt. Unter der Hand und mit der heimlichen Billigung der zuständigen Behörden plätschert die PKW-Produktion bei BMW noch eine Zeitlang weiter. Bis zum Ende jenes Jahres entstehen jeweils 480 Exemplare der Typen 321 und 326. Im Herbst 1940 bringt man nur noch 201 Wagen an den Mann. Einige wenige Privilegierte haben ihrem Auto einen Holzvergaser auf den Buckel gepackt und einen der immer rarer werdenden Reifen für ihr Reserverad ergattert. Doch im Mai 1941 kommen die Bänder endgültig zum Stillstand.

Motorräder haben noch Konjunktur und werden weiter hergestellt. Die schwere geländegängige R 75 wird in ihrer knorrigen Solidität an allen Fronten zur Legende. Auch nach Flugzeugen verlangt die Maschinerie des organisierten Todes: 1939 hat BMW die damals zum Siemens-Konzern zählenden Brandenburgischen Motorenwerke in Berlin-Spandau erworben, die auf eine lange Tradition im Flugmotorenbau zurückblicken. Hier und in den anderen BMW-Fertigungsstätten in München und Eisenach werden bis 1945 Zehntausende von Flugmotoren gebaut. Eine technische Delikatesse, wenn auch nicht mehr von Bedeutung für die stattfindenden Kampfhandlungen und allenfalls noch als Drohgebärde tauglich, ist das Turbinenstrahltriebwerk 003. Der „Volksjäger" Heinkel He 162 (Konstruktionsbeginn 24. September 1944, erster Flug 6. Dezember 1944) erreicht damit in 6000 Metern Höhe 840 Stundenkilometer.

Unterdessen sind die Bayerischen Motoren Werke selbst in das Visier der angloamerikanischen Bombergeschwader geraten. In weiser Voraussicht hat man bestimmte Produk-

Quelques privilégiés ont fait équiper leur voiture d'un gazogène et sont même parvenus à se procurer pour leur roue de secours l'un de ces pneumatiques de plus en plus rares. Mais les choses ont depuis longtemps pris un cours inéluctable. En mai 1941, les chaînes s'arrêtent.

Seules les motocyclettes ont encore la cote et se fabriquent toujours. Sa solidité à toute épreuve, sur tous les fronts, élève la lourde R75 tout-terrain au rang de légende. La machine d'extermination allemande organisée a également besoin d'avions : en 1939, BMW a acquis les Brandenburgische Motorenwerke, à Berlin-Spandau, qui appartenaient alors au groupe Siemens et qui pouvaient se prévaloir d'une longue tradition en matière de construction de moteurs d'avions. Ici et dans les autres unités de fabrication de BMW à Munich et à Eisenach, on fabriquera des dizaines de milliers de moteurs d'avions jusqu'en 1945. Le réacteur 003 représente le nec plus ultra de la technologie, mais il ne jouera plus aucun rôle car les hostilités s'achèvent et il n'est donc plus qu'un tigre de papier. Le « chasseur du peuple », le Heinkel He162 (dont la construction débute le 24 septembre 1944 et qui fait son premier vol le 6 décembre 1944), atteint ainsi la vitesse de 840 km/h à 6000 mètres d'altitude.

Pendant ce temps, BMW est elle-même devenue la cible des escadrilles des bombardiers alliés. Par prudence, on a transféré certains pans de la production dans des sites d'une tranquillité trompeuse comme Immenstadt, Kempten ou Kaufbeuren. Mais les représailles n'en seront que plus sévères. Entre le 9 mars 1943 et le 22 septembre 1944, l'Usine I d'Oberwiesenfeld est bombardée à dix reprises. Au cours de la seule journée du 12 juillet 1944, 1117 appareils déversent plus de 10000 bombes contenant 2727 tonnes d'explosifs. Les chroniqueurs de la 8e et de la 15e escadrille américaine tiennent leurs comptes avec une précision de bénédictins et relèvent aussi que l'Usine II de BMW, à Allach, a été neuf fois la cible d'attaques ennemies rien qu'en 1944.

Lorsque les Allemands signent leur capitulation sans condition, le 7 mai 1945 à Reims, la guerre a laissé de profondes blessures chez BMW aussi. Un tiers des installations est à l'abandon dans un désert de pierre et d'acier. Des hordes de pilleurs s'abattent comme un nuage de criquets sur l'empire à l'agonie et le vident de sa substance. Le 1er octobre 1945, l'adjoint au commandant de la garnison américaine, le lieutenant-colonel Eugene Keller, donne l'ordre « d'emballer dans des caisses de bois et d'expédier par bateau » tous les équipements des usines de Munich, avant de les raser.

Ernst Henne on 14 June 1936 on the way to victory at the Nürburgring.

Ernst Henne am 14. Juni 1936 auf dem Weg zum Sieg auf dem Nürburgring.

Ernst Henne, le 14 juin 1936, sur la route de la victoire au Nürburgring.

BMW motorcycles were used not just for peaceful purposes: parade on Hitler's birthday on 20 April 1936.

Nicht nur friedlichen Zwecken wurden BMW-Motorräder zugeführt: Parade zu Hitlers Geburtstag am 20. April 1936.

Les motos BMW n'étaient pas utilisées qu'à des fins pacifiques : ici, la parade pour l'anniversaire d'Adolf Hitler, le 20 avril 1936.

The BMW Allach works, which escaped destruction, became a US Army supply and transport depot under German management.

Das unzerstört gebliebene BMW-Werk Allach wird unter deutscher Leitung ein Nachschub- und Fahrzeugdepot der US Army.

L'usine BMW d'Allach, épargnée par les bombardements, sera transformée en un entrepôt de ravitaillement de l'armée américaine, sous administration allemande.

be "packed in crates in preparation for shipment and subsequent destruction of the buildings".

Fortunately not everything was as black as it was painted, especially since the Allach plant was converted into a repair center for US military airplanes, the largest US spare parts storage facility on German territory. The Eisenach plant survived relatively unscathed, initially being confiscated "in the interests of the people of Thuringia", and then taking on a legally dubious identity under the aegis of the Soviet state-owned joint-stock company Avtovelo. The rise and fall of the Bayerische Motoren Werke had encompassed less than 30 years.

tionszweige bereits an unverfängliche ländliche Standorte wie Immenstadt, Kempten oder Kaufbeuren ausgelagert. Dann aber kommt es dennoch knüppeldick. Zwischen dem 9. März 1943 und dem 22. September 1944 wird Werk I im Oberwiesenfeld zehnmal heimgesucht. Allein am 12. Juli des vorletzten Kriegsjahres laden 1117 Maschinen über 10 000 Bomben mit 2727 Tonnen Sprengstoff ab. Die Chronisten der 8. und 15. amerikanischen Luftflotte führen darüber pedantisch Buch und vermerken auch, dem BMW-Werk II in Allach habe man allein im Jahre 1944 neun Besuche der feindseligen Art abgestattet.

Als am 7. Mai 1945 in Reims die bedingungslose Kapitulation unterzeichnet wird, hat der Krieg auch BMW schlimme Wunden geschlagen. Ein Drittel der Anlagen liegt verödet in einer Wüste aus Stein und Stahl. Horden von Plünderern fallen wie Heuschrecken über das waidwunde Imperium her und entziehen ihm weitere Substanz. Am 1. Oktober 1945 ergeht die Anweisung des stellvertretenden amerikanischen Standortkommandanten Oberstleutnant Eugene Keller, die verbleibenden Münchener Maschinen „in Lattenverschläge zur Verschiffung zu verpacken" und die Werksanlagen zu schleifen.

Zum Glück wird nicht alles so heiß gegessen, wie es gekocht wird, zumal das Werk Allach zum Reparaturzentrum für amerikanische Militärfahrzeuge und zum größten US-Ersatzteillager auf deutschem Territorium umgewidmet wird. Die Filiale Eisenach ist relativ glimpflich davongekommen und wird, zunächst „zugunsten des thüringischen Volkes" enteignet, unter der sowjetischen staatlichen Aktiengesellschaft Awtowelo weitergeführt. Zwischen Aufstieg und Fall der Bayerischen Motoren Werke lagen knapp 30 Jahre.

Par bonheur, selon un dicton allemand, « on ne mange pas la soupe aussi chaude qu'on la cuit » et l'usine d'Allach est transformée en centre de réparation pour les camions militaires américains et devient le plus grand entrepôt de pièces détachées des États-Unis en territoire allemand. La filiale d'Eisenach s'en est tirée relativement bien et, après avoir été confisquée « en faveur du peuple de Thuringe », est placée sous la tutelle de la société anonyme étatique soviétique Avtovelo. À peine trente ans se seront écoulés entre l'essor et la chute de Bayerische Motoren Werke.

Finding Their Feet (1945–1962)
Of Kitchen Accessories and Prodigal Sons (1945–1952)

The plan of the American Finance Minister Henry Morgenthau Junior was to return the Germans to stone age status as farmers and ranchers living in a fertile landscape unsullied by any dark satanic mills. The simple range of BMW products during the immediate postwar years would have warmed the cockles of his heart: cooking pots, baking sheets and whisks, for example, as well as bicycles and agricultural machinery for sowing and harrowing.

The head of the works police in Allach was Georg Meier, known to all as "Cast-iron Schorsch". His name was one of some renown, the robust Bavarian having won the Isle of Man Tourist Trophy for BMW in 1939. Meier urged that they should find their feet amidst all the chaos and confusion by returning to the manufacture of motorcycles, bearing in mind their previous success in this sector. The beginnings were modest but nevertheless impressive: the R24, with a single 250 cc cylinder and a four-speed foot gearshift, was launched at the Geneva Motor Show in March 1948, albeit in the form of a hastily cobbled-together dummy machine. However, by the end of 1949 alone 9459 were sold, providing their proud owners with a basic set of motorized wheels, and at the Milbertshofen plant a workforce of 2600 was once again on the payroll.

When the quarter-liter cubic capacity limit imposed by the occupying powers was lifted in 1950, production quickly switched to the long-planned 500 cc R51, a gem of a machine with telescopic rear forks and a two-cylinder boxer

Orientierungsstufe (1945–1962)
Von Küchenzubehör und reuigen Satelliten (1945–1952)

Nach den Plänen des amerikanischen Finanzministers Henry Morgenthau junior sollen die Deutschen in den Steinzeit-Status von Ackerbauern und Viehzüchtern zurückgeführt werden, wohnhaft in blühenden und von keinerlei qualmenden Schloten verschandelten Landschaften. Das BMW-Sortiment der unmittelbaren Nachkriegsjahre hätte ihm gewiss zur hellen Freude gereicht: Kochtöpfe, Backbleche und Schneebesen, Fahrräder, Landmaschinen zum Säen und Eggen.

Chef der Werkspolizei in Allach ist Georg Meier, den alle Welt „Gusseiserner Schorsch" nennt. Sein Name hat einen guten Klang: Der kernige Bayer hat 1939 für BMW die Tourist Trophy auf der Isle of Man gewonnen. Meier mahnt, man solle inmitten des Chaos Tritt fassen und den Bau von Motorrädern wieder aufnehmen, angesichts früherer Erfolge auf diesem Sektor. Die Anfänge sind bescheiden und dennoch eindrucksvoll: die R24 mit einem Zylinder von 250 ccm und Viergang-Fußschaltung wird auf dem Genfer Salon im März 1948 vorgestellt, wenn auch noch als zügig zusammengeschusterte Attrappe. Allein bis Ende 1949 verhelfen 9459 Exemplare ihren stolzen Besitzern zu elementarer Motorisierung, während im Werk Milbertshofen schon wieder 2600 Mitarbeiter auf den Gehaltslisten stehen.

Als die von den Besatzungsmächten verhängte Hubraumbeschränkung auf einen Viertelliter aufgehoben wird, rüstet man 1950 umgehend mit der längst geplanten R51 mit 500 ccm auf, einem Schmuckstück mit Teleskop-Hinterradfederung und einem Zweizylinder-Boxertriebwerk von ein-

Changement de cap (1945–1962)
Articles ménagers et fils prodigues (1945–1952)

Si les projets du ministre américain des Finances, Henry Morgenthau junior, étaient devenus réalité, les Allemands seraient revenus à l'âge de pierre et seraient devenus un peuple de paysans et d'éleveurs vivant dans un paysage rural où n'aurait plus fumé la moindre cheminée d'usine. Le nouvel assortiment de produits fabriqués par BMW dans l'immédiat après-guerre lui aurait assurément réchauffé le cœur : casseroles, plaques de four et fouets, bicyclettes, machines agricoles, etc.

Le chef des vigiles de l'usine d'Allach est Georg Meier, que tout le monde connaît sous le nom de « Schorsch ». Et il le porte bien : ce robuste Bavarois a remporté pour BMW, en 1939, le Tourist Trophy organisé sur l'Île de Man. Meier insiste pour que l'on reprenne conscience de ses origines, malgré le chaos, et que l'on se remette à construire des motocyclettes en s'inspirant des succès remportés jadis dans ce domaine. Les débuts sont modestes mais impressionnants : il s'agit de la R24 monocylindre de 250 cm³ à commande à quatre vitesses au pied, présentée au Salon de Genève de mars 1948, qui n'était, en réalité, qu'un modèle d'exposition. Fin 1949 déjà, 9459 exemplaires permettent à leurs fiers propriétaires de se déplacer de façon rudimentaire alors qu'à l'usine de Milbertshofen, les effectifs grimpent à 2600 collaborateurs.

En 1950, lorsque les puissances d'occupation suppriment le plafonnement de cylindrée à 250 cm³, BMW peut lancer immédiatement la R51 de 500 cm³ depuis longtemps dans les cartons, un véritable bijou de la mécanique avec power unit producing a highly pleasing engine note. Soon after this came the 600 cc R 67, and then the R 68 sports version, which with a top speed of 99 mph (160 kph) was the fastest production machine on the German market, as BMW themselves stressed with understandable pride. In 1954, motorcycle production reached its peak for the time being, with a production of 29,699 machines. Then came an abrupt turnaround, as the motorcycle boom subsided, a victim of the growing confidence of the "Wirtschaftswunder" years. Two-wheel vehicles were still stigmatized as a poor man's means of transport, and everyone was now looking to the sunlit uplands of the private sedan car.

From 1945 to 1947 the executive board consisted of Kurth Donath, Hanns Grewenig and Heinrich Krafft von Dellmensingen. Representations were regularly made to this triumvirate to produce a new BMW car, but they always rejected them out of hand. The marque's four-wheel tradition did live on to some extent, in exile and incognito, in mutant form. As part of the war reparations, H. J. Aldington, the managing director of the Bristol airplane works in Filton, England, received the plans for the BMW 327/28. Until 1948, its designer Fritz Fiedler was involved in the deal, not least due to the old friendship that existed between the two. In the spring of 1947, the Bristol 400, a blatant copy of the 327 coupé, was launched. Its successors, however, rapidly departed from the original design.

The fates of two prodigals who left the BMW fold for a period before receiving a generous welcome back were strikingly similar. The first of these was Ernst Loof of Bad Godesberg, once the head of styling at BMW, who left to manufacture racing and sports cars based on the 328 under the name Veritas from 1948 onwards. He gained a modest reputation in motor sport, and at the German Grand Prix of 1950 Tony Ulmen even achieved fourth place driving a Veritas. However, there was never enough money and things soon began to go downhill, and at the end of his freedom flight in 1953, Loof ended up back in the BMW styling department in Munich. Then there was Alex von Falkenhausen, at the end of the war head of the design office, who also went off to seek his fortune via the construction of sporty cars with a strong element of 1930s BMW incorporated into the design. However, the market niche identified by his firm AFM (short for Alexander von Falkenhausen, Munich) proved not to be sufficiently lucrative, and in 1954 the wiry nobleman returned to the Munich fold and once again did sterling service for the company as head of its racing division, where, over the years, he slowly took on the mantle of a gray eminence.

A Bristol 400 with Count G. Lurani and Frazer-Nash boss H. J. Aldington at the 1949 Mille Miglia.

Ein Bristol 400 mit dem Grafen G. Lurani und Frazer-Nash-Boss H. J. Aldington bei der Mille Miglia 1949.

Une Bristol 400 avec le comte G. Lurani et le chef de Frazer-Nash, H. J. Aldington, lors des Mille Miglia de 1949.

Prototype of the R 24 at the Hanover Export Fair in May 1948. The machine turned into a big seller.

Prototyp der R 24 bei der Exportmesse in Hannover im Mai 1948. Die Maschine wird ein Renner.

Le prototype de la R 24 à la Foire des Exportations de Hanovre en mai 1948. Cette moto sera un best-seller.

schmeichelndem Klang. Bald darauf wird die R 67 mit 600 ccm angeboten, schließlich die Sportversion R 68, mit 160 Stundenkilometer Spitze die schnellste deutsche Serienmaschine, wie man in wohlverstandenem Eigenlob herausstellt. 1954 erreicht die Motorradfertigung mit 29 699 Exemplaren einen vorläufigen Höhepunkt, der gleichzeitig den Umschwung bringt. Angekratzt von der Tischleindeckdich-Mentalität des Wirtschaftswunders, flaut der Boom ab, denn am Zweirad klebt noch immer das Odium des Vehikels für arme Leute, und jedermann trachtet nach den höheren Weihen überdachter Fortbewegung.

Der Vorstand besteht in den Jahren 1945 bis 1947 aus den Herren Kurth Donath, Hanns Grewenig und Heinrich Krafft von Dellmensingen. Immer wieder wird an dieses Triumvirat der Wunsch nach einem neuen Auto von BMW herangetragen und dennoch stets verworfen. Die Vierradtradition des Hauses blüht gewissermaßen im Exil weiter, inkognito und in der Form von Mutanten. Als Reparationsleistung erhält H. J. Aldington, Generaldirektor der Bristol-Flugzeugwerke im englischen Filton, die Pläne des BMW 327/28. Konstrukteur Fritz Fiedler ist bis 1948 in dem Deal inbegriffen, nicht zuletzt aus alter Freundschaft zwischen den beiden Männern. Im Frühjahr 1947 stellt man den Bristol 400 vor, eine unverhohlene Raubkopie des Coupés 327, dessen Nachfolger sich indessen rasch vom Original entfernen.

Verblüffend ähnlich verlaufen die Schicksale zweier Satelliten, die sich eine Zeitlang aus der BMW-Atmosphäre lösen und schließlich in diese zurückkehren, ohne zu verglühen. Da ist der Bad Godesberger Ernst Loof, einst Styling-Chef, der unter dem Namen Veritas ab 1948 Renn- und Sportwagen auf der Basis des 328 herstellt. Er bringt es in der Tat zu mäßigem sportlichem Ruhm, und beim Großen Preis von Deutschland 1950 belegt Veritas-Pilot Toni Ulmen sogar den vierten Platz. Überall fehlt es jedoch an Geld und bald geht es bergab. Nach dem Ende seines emanzipatorischen Ausflugs landet Loof 1953 wieder in der Styling-Abteilung in München. Da ist außerdem Alex von Falkenhausen, bei Kriegsende Leiter des Konstruktionsbüros, der ebenfalls mit dem Bau von sportiven Autos mit BMW-Ingredienzien der dreißiger Jahre sein Glück versucht. Die von seinem Unternehmen AFM (für Alexander von Falkenhausen, München) angepeilte Marktlücke erweist sich indes als wenig ergiebig. 1954 kehrt auch der drahtige Edelmann in den Schoß der Münchener Mutter zurück. Er macht sich als Leiter der Rennabteilung erneut um die Firma verdient und erlangt im Laufe der Zeit den Rang einer grauen Eminenz.

suspension arrière télescopique et bicylindre à plat au ronronnement mélodieux. Elle est bientôt suivie de la R67, de 600 cm³, puis de la version sport R68, qui est la plus rapide allemande des motos de série avec une vitesse de pointe atteignant les 160 km/h, comme le proclame la publicité de BMW, avec une fierté toute compréhensible. En 1954, la production de motos culmine à 29 699 exemplaires, ce qui est un record à cette époque. Quand soudain la tendance s'inverse : BMW est victime des nantis, rassasiés du miracle économique et le soufflé retombe. En effet, les deux-roues font figure de véhicules du pauvre et chacun aspire légitimement à posséder une voiture.

De 1945 à 1947, le directoire se compose de Kurth Donath, Hanns Grewenig et Heinrich Krafft von Dellmensingen. Ce triumvirat reçoit toujours les mêmes doléances – BMW devrait fabriquer une nouvelle voiture – et les rejette toujours. C'est à l'étranger, en catimini et sous une forme revue et corrigée que renaît la tradition des voitures à quatre roues de la maison. Au titre des réparations de guerre, H. J. Aldington, directeur général des usines d'avions Bristol à Filton, en Angleterre, a reçu les plans de la BMW 327/28. Jusqu'en 1948, l'ingénieur Fritz Fiedler fait partie de la transaction et travaille à ses côtés, ce qui est aussi dû en partie à la vieille amitié qui lie les deux hommes. Au printemps 1947, on assiste à la présentation de la Bristol 400, un plagiat éhonté du coupé 327, les modèles qui suivront vont toutefois rapidement se démarquer du design original.

Le destin des deux fils prodigues qui se dissocient un certain temps de la nébuleuse de BMW avant de finir par la rejoindre présente une similitude frappante. Le premier est Ernst Loof, de Bad Godesberg, jadis chef styliste de BMW, qui, sous le nom de Veritas, produit à partir de 1948 des voitures de course et de sport sur la base de la 328. Il acquiert même une certaine notoriété puisque, lors du Grand Prix d'Allemagne de 1950, Toni Ulmen, pilote de Veritas, décroche la quatrième place. Mais l'argent vient à manquer et les affaires périclitent, si bien qu'à l'issue de sa tentative d'émancipation, Loof revient au bureau de style de Munich, en 1953. Le second fils prodigue est Alex von Falkenhausen, directeur du bureau d'études à la fin de la guerre, qui tente sa chance en construisant des voitures sportives à partir d'éléments BMW des années 1930. Le marché visé par sa société AFM (pour Alexander von Falkenhausen, Munich) s'avère vite peu rentable. En 1954, cet aristocrate à la silhouette élancée revient dans le giron de la maison mère, à Munich, et recommence à y gagner ses galons comme directeur du département Compétition où, au fil du temps, il devient une éminence grise.

Rounded: this 600 experimental car from 1950 with its air-cooled two-cylinder engine never received its passing-out certificate.

Rundling: Dieser Versuchswagen Typ 600 von 1950 mit luftgekühltem Zweizylinder erhält nie das Reifezeugnis.

Tout en rondeurs: cette voiture expérimentale, une 600 de 1950 à bicylindre refroidi par air, ne sera jamais fabriquée en série.

Of Chubby-Cheeked Cherubs and Eggs on Wheels (1952–1962)

On the borderline between the past and the future, half conservative, half innovative, the BMW 501 was launched at the 1951 Frankfurt Motor Show. In itself, the car was a success, and met with enthusiastic acclaim from all sides, rapidly being given the affectionate nickname the "baroque angel". Even Pinin Farina, whose own body design for the 501 was rejected by BMW's executive board, was fulsome in his praise of the design team responsible, Alfred Böning and Peter Szimanowski. A mood of optimism reigned, but in fact the car proved to be a false dawn. The sumptuous curves of the four-door sedan, which was supplied exclusively in black, were a financial liability: just pressing the front wing, for example, involved three or four different production stages. The asking price of 15,150 marks was exorbitant when set against an average monthly income of 350 marks, and had to be steadily reduced in later versions. The original 65 bhp developed by the 2-liter six-cylinder engine at 4400 rpm had to lug around a dead weight of 2955 lbs (1340 kg). What is more, the 501 was up against the Mercedes 220, while the eight-cylinder 502, produced from 1954 onwards, was in competition with the Mercedes 300, and despite the clear quality of these automobiles, they were not much more than a Bavarian article of faith in the war of prestige with their Stuttgart rivals.

Count Goertz's two beautiful creations, the 503 and 507, failed to achieve anything like the expected response from the American market in 1955, where they had been hoping to spark a hectic stampede to the dealers. With sales of 412 of the 503 and just 252 of the 507, they ended up as pricy rarities and monuments to an ill-thought-out models policy, as did the 3200CS of 1961. Seductively styled by star couturier Nuccio Bertone, the big coupé, with sales of just 603 cars, did BMW's image no harm but emptied its coffers. A total of 23,120 six and eight-cylinder BMWs were sold in what was practically an act of charity by the company, as they were sold at a total loss of 76 million marks, or 3250 marks per car.

In a tightrope act between two extremes, to prevent the company bleeding to death at the top end of the automobile market, BMW's policy was to introduce mini cars at the other end of the market. From 1955 onwards, the Isetta "Motocoupé", a modish, whimsical and disarmingly practical car, provided meager profits. It was very much targeted at the less well off: "For just 5.80 marks two adults and a child can travel about 230 kilometers (143 miles)", as the advertisement proudly proclaimed. The "rolling egg" or "cuddle box" was not even spared the rigors of motor sport, being entered in the 1955 Mille Miglia. From 1957 onwards the "large" Isetta BMW 600 offered more car for your money, while the various members of the BMW 700 family, introduced from 1959, almost looked like real cars.

Meanwhile, the 1959 financial year had eaten up the last of the company's reserves. An injection of 15 million marks from the Bremen wood entrepreneur Hermann Krages in 1957 had disappeared like snow in the spring sunshine, and the company appeared incapable of surviving under its own steam. The management and major banks saw no other way out than affiliation to their arch-rival Mercedes-Benz. However, at a memorable annual meeting of shareholders on 9 December 1959, the 39th in the history of the company, the workforce, dealers and minor stockholders joined forces to battle for the company's independence amid tumultuous

Von rundlichen Engeln und rollenden Eiern (1952–1962)

Auf dem Grenzstreifen zwischen gestern und morgen, halb konservativ, halb innovativ, wird der BMW 501 auf der IAA 1951 präsentiert, eine runde Sache, allerdings nur im eigentlichen Sinne des Wortes. Gewiss, allenthalben wird ihm begeisterte Akklamation zuteil. Bald stellt sich der freundliche Spottname „Barockengel" ein. Sogar Pinin Farina, dessen eigener Karosserie-Entwurf für den 501 vom BMW-Vorstand verschmäht wurde, zollt dem zuständigen Team Alfred Böning und Peter Szimanowski hohes Lob. Aufbruchstimmung macht sich breit, aber der Start führt direkt in eine Sackgasse. Die üppigen Kurven des ausschließlich in vornehmem Schwarz gelieferten Viertürers schlagen teuer zu Buche: Die vorderen Kotflügel zum Beispiel müssen in drei bis vier Arbeitsgängen gepresst werden. Der Preis von 15 150 Mark ist angesichts eines Durchschnittseinkommens von 350 Mark saftig und wird in späteren Versionen schrittweise reduziert. Die ursprünglich 65 PS bei 4400 Umdrehungen pro Minute des 2-Liter-Sechszylinders haben ein massives Stück Eisen mit 1340 Kilo Leergewicht zu bewegen. Wie sich zuvor der 501 am Mercedes 200 messen lassen musste, so muss sich der Achtzylinder 502 ab 1954 den Vergleich mit dem Mercedes 300 gefallen lassen – trotz unzweifelhafter Qualitäten doch eher ein bayerischer Glaubensartikel im Prestigeduell gegen die Stuttgarter.

Die beiden schönen Geschöpfe des Grafen Goertz namens 503 und 507 lösen 1955 keineswegs den erhofften Widerhall und die erwartete ungestüme Kauflust auf dem amerikanischen Markt aus. Sie werden mit 412 gefertigten Exemplaren des 503 und lediglich 252 des 507 zu kostbaren Raritäten und prächtigen Monumenten einer unbedachten Modellpolitik, ebenso wie der 3200CS von 1961. Verführerisch eingekleidet von Star-Couturier Nuccio Bertone, pflegt das große Coupé in der schwachen Verbreitung von 603 Stück zwar das Image, leert aber die Kassen. Insgesamt werden 23 120 Sechs- und Achtzylinder unter das fahrende BMW-Volk gebracht, ein Akt von geradezu mildtätigem Charakter, denn er wird mit einem Verlust von 76 Millionen Mark – 3250 Mark pro Auto – verkauft.

Der misslichen Situation begegnet das Werk mit einem Hochseilakt zwischen den Extremen: Damit die Bayerischen Motoren Werke in den oberen Segmenten der Wagenhierarchie nicht verbluten, sollen Automobilzwerge die Kassen füllen. Ab 1955 fährt das „Motocoupé" Isetta – poppig, drollig und entwaffnend praktisch – magere Gewinne ein. Es ist fürwahr ein Angebot für schmale Geldbeutel: „Für ganze 5,80 DM fahren zwei Erwachsene und ein Kind rund 230 Kilometer weit", frohlockt die Werbung. Sogar gegen Sporteinsätze wie bei der Mille Miglia 1955 ist das „rollende Ei" oder die „Knutschkugel" nicht gefeit. Ab 1957 bietet die „große Isetta", der BMW 600, mehr Auto für das gleiche Geld, und beinahe schon wie richtige Autos sehen schließlich die Mitglieder der BMW-700-Familie ab 1959 aus.

Das Geschäftsjahr 1959 hat indes die letzten Reserven des Unternehmens aufgezehrt. Eine Finanzspritze des Bremer Holzkaufmanns Hermann Krages 1957 in Höhe von 15 Millionen Mark ist verpufft wie Spucke auf einer glühenden Herdplatte. Eine Sanierung aus eigener Kraft scheint nicht möglich. Verwaltung und Großbanken sehen keinen anderen Ausweg als die Anlehnung an den alten Rivalen Mercedes-Benz. Aber in der denkwürdigen Hauptversammlung vom 9. Dezember 1959, der 39. in der Geschichte des Hauses, kämpfen Belegschaft, Händler und Kleinaktionäre in tumultartigen Szenen um die Eigenständigkeit ihrer Firma. Ihr Feuer weckt

L'histoire de la Bavaroise plantureuse et de l'œuf à roulettes (1952–1962)

À la frontière entre les voitures d'hier et celles de demain, la BMW 501, aussi conservatrice qu'innovante, est présentée au Salon de l'Automobile de Francfort de 1951 avec ses rondeurs rassurantes. Elle reçoit de toutes parts un accueil enthousiaste et elle est vite surnommée l'« ange baroque ». Pinin Farina en personne, dont le prototype de carrosserie pour la 501 a été refusé par le directoire de BMW, ne tarit pas d'éloges envers ses concepteurs, l'équipe réunie autour d'Alfred Böning et Peter Szimanowski. L'ambiance est à l'optimisme, mais le départ sur les chapeaux de roue mène vite dans une impasse. Les courbes plantureuses de la quatre-portes commercialisée exclusivement en noir coûtent trop cher : les ailes avant, par exemple, doivent être embouties en trois ou quatre étapes. Son prix de 15 150 marks est astronomique comparé au revenu mensuel moyen allemand de 350 marks. À tel point que, pour les versions suivantes, il sera progressivement diminué. Les 65 ch (à 4400 tr/min) que développe à l'origine le six-cylindres de deux litres doivent traîner un poids mort imposant de 1340 kg. De même que la 501 est comparée à la Mercedes 220, la 502 huit-cylindres de 1954 sera comparée à la Mercedes 300, qui restera, malgré ses qualités, un article de foi de la Bavière dans la guerre de prestige contre Mercedes.

Les deux magnifiques réalisations du comte Goertz, baptisées 503 et 507, ne déclenchent pas, en 1955, l'enthousiasme escompté et la déception est grande lorsque l'on constate que le marché américain ne se les arrache pas. Commercialisées à raison de 412 exemplaires pour la 503 et de seulement 252 pour la 507, elles resteront des objets rares et des témoins arrogants d'une politique commerciale insuffisamment réfléchie, au même titre que la 3200 CS de 1961. Habillée d'une robe séduisante par le designer vedette Nuccio Bertone, le gros coupé diffusé à seulement 603 exemplaires redore le blason de BMW, mais vide ses caisses. Au total, 23 120 six et huit-cylindres feront le bonheur de quelques heureux propriétaires, véritable œuvre de bienfaisance pour la firme, car elles sont vendues à perte : 76 millions de marks, soit 3250 marks par voiture.

BMW est sur la corde raide. Pour que la firme, au bord de la faillite, ne disparaisse pas du haut de gamme de l'industrie automobile, des petites cylindrées à quatre roues vont devoir sauver la situation. À partir de 1955, l'Isetta « Motocoupé » – irrésistible, drôle et désarmante par son caractère pratique – permet d'engranger de maigres bénéfices. C'est une aubaine pour les petites bourses : « Pour 5,80 marks en tout et pour tout, deux adultes et un enfant peuvent parcourir 230 km », proclame la publicité. Il y en a même qui font courir les Mille Miglia de 1955 à « l'œuf à roulettes » ou encore au « pot de yaourt », c'est ainsi qu'on l'a surnommée. À partir de 1957, la « grosse Isetta », la BMW 600, vous en donne plus pour votre argent, et les versions suivantes de la famille BMW 700, apparues en 1959, ressemblent déjà presque à de véritables voitures.

1959 a, en revanche, englouti les dernières ressources de l'entreprise. Le négociant en bois brêmois Hermann Krages injecte, en 1957, 15 millions de marks, qui ont fondu comme neige au soleil. Tout redressement financier sans intervention extérieure semble exclu. La direction et les grandes banques évoquent le rachat par Mercedes-Benz, l'ennemi de toujours. Mais, lors de la mémorable assemblée générale du 9 décembre 1959, la 39e dans l'histoire de la maison, personnel, concessionnaires et petits actionnaires scenes. Their stand awakened the interest of major stock-holder Dr Herbert Quandt, and he took over a large slice of BMW stock. A new executive board was appointed, and a team of experts and an active works council also made a positive contribution. This time the direction was right, as they returned to once-familiar terrain: the middle ground. Aviation engine business also began to pick up. Rock bottom had been reached, and recovery was finally under way.

das Interesse des Großaktionärs Dr. Herbert Quandt, der eine große Anzahl der BMW-Anteile übernimmt. Ein neuer Vorstand wird eingesetzt, sachkundige Spezialisten und ein aktiver Betriebsrat helfen mit. Die Richtung stimmt und führt sogar auf altvertrautes Terrain: Der Mittelweg ist der richtige. Das Flugzeugtriebwerksgeschäft belebt sich ebenfalls. Die Talsohle ist durchmessen.

en viennent presque aux mains pour préserver l'indépendance de BMW. Leur enthousiasme suscite l'intérêt du grand actionnaire, le Dr Herbert Quandt, qui rachète alors une grande partie des actions BMW. Un nouveau directoire est constitué, des experts et un comité d'entreprise actif y mettent aussi leur grain de sel. Le cap choisi est le bon, on revient sur un terrain de pleine confiance : le moyen de gamme. Le segment des moteurs d'avions s'envole à son tour. Le creux de la vague est bientôt dépassé.

New Horizons (1962–1999)
The "New Class" (1962–1972)

When production of the new mid-range BMW 1500 began in February 1962, BMW had finally found its way home after all the errors and confusion of the postwar reconstruction period, and was back on the territory it had successfully occupied during the 1930s. Acclaimed as the star of the 1961 Frankfurt Motor Show, the straightforward no-frills lines of the 1500 subscribed to the old Prussian ideal of unassuming solidity, a value system that places content before style. The reaction of the trade press was one of fulsome praise: "Deeply hidden, but all the more deeply felt for that, the heart of the German car buyer yearns for a quality, which cannot be entirely satisfied by economical mass production cars," and the BMW 1500 was tailor-made to satisfy just that yearning, as *auto motor und sport* observed, clearly in a reflective mood at the time. Initially, BMW was barely able to meet the demand it had stirred up; with a production of 50 cars a day, supply was far less than worldwide demand. However, the company responded rapidly and energetically. While stockpiles of unsold 700 series cars faced an uncertain future, production facilities for the "New Class" were being expanded, development capacity was being increased and a special sales organization was being set up. True to Goethe's dictum that all isolation is despicable, the range of models was extended to suit a variety of tastes. It extended from the original 1500 to the 1800 TISA in 1964, a special edition of 200 aimed at sporting drivers, right up to the 2000tii in 1969.

1966 saw the birth of the compact two-door 1600-2, a car where BMW strategists were partially responsible for inventing and developing a new dimension for the automobile. By 1975 the 1600-2, with its attractively sturdy appearance, had shattered all previous BMW production records with total sales of 252,786. At the end of the 1960s, BMW also returned to its six-cylinder tradition, this time with greater success: the three big 1968 models, the 2500 and 2800 sedans and the 2800CS coupé immediately met with a rave reception, being hailed in reviews as a crowning achievement of European automobile construction.

All in all, BMW now had a program in place which left it excellently equipped to face the future. Over the next few years production and sales records tumbled with monotonous regularity. Motorcycle sales were also recovering, as the two-wheeler came to be viewed not as an alternative but as a supplement to the motor car. In 1969 just 5000 motorcycles were sold, but after the launch of the R50/5, R60/6 and R75/5 in 1970, sales rose sharply to more than 12,000, and just two years later production had risen to more than 21,000.

By the beginning of the 1970s the lean years of tough lessons and reconstruction were history, and years of plenty

Zu neuen Ufern (1962–1999)
„Neue Klasse" (1962–1972)

Mit dem Produktionsbeginn des Mittelklassewagens Typ 1500 im Februar 1962 findet das Unternehmen nach den Irrungen und Wirrungen der Wiederaufbauphase zu seinen Domänen zurück, die seit den späten dreißiger Jahren brachliegen. Als Star der IAA 1961 gefeiert, huldigt der schlicht und schnörkellos geformte Bayer gleichsam dem preußischen Imperativ der gehaltvollen Bescheidenheit: „Mehr Sein als Schein". Fast hymnisch schallt auch das Echo der Fachpresse zurück: „Tief versteckt, aber um so sicherer geborgen, befindet sich im Herzen des deutschen Autokäufers eine Sehnsucht nach Gediegenheit, die von preiswerten Großserienwagen nur unvollkommen erfüllt werden kann." Und just dieser Sehnsucht komme der BMW 1500 entgegen, merkt etwa *auto motor und sport* nachdenklich an. Anfangs kann man die Nachfrage, die man geweckt hat, kaum befriedigen: Mit 50 Einheiten am Tag ist das Angebot weitaus geringer als die weltweite Nachfrage. Die Reaktion erfolgt rasch und energisch. Während noch ganze Halden von 700ern unverkauft einer ungewissen Zukunft entgegendämmern, werden bereits die Produktionsanlagen für die „Neue Klasse" erweitert, die Entwicklungskapazitäten aufgestockt, eine gezielte Verkaufsorganisation geschaffen. Getreu der Goetheschen Devise, alle Vereinzelung sei verwerflich, fächert man die Baureihe filigran auf, um vielen unterschiedlichen Geschmäckern gerecht zu werden. Sie spannt sich vom Ur-Typ 1500 über den 1800 TISA anno 1964, einem Angebot nach Maß für den Sportfahrer in einer Kleinauflage von 200, bis hin zum 2000tii von 1969.

In das Jahr 1966 fällt die Geburtsstunde des kompakten zweitürigen 1600-2, mit dem die Strategen im Zeichen der Niere gewissermaßen eine weitere Dimension des Automobils erfinden und erschließen. Von gedrungen-attraktiver

Single cylinder and V8 – this combination proved unpalatable in the 1950s.

Einzylinder und V8 – dieser Spagat erweist sich in den fünfziger Jahren als wenig bekömmlich.

Monocylindre et V8 – dans les années 1950, ce grand écart s'avérera peu favorable au constructeur.

Vers d'autres horizons (1962–1999)
La « Nouvelle Classe » (1962–1972)

En lançant la production de la 1500 du segment intermédiaire, en février 1962, l'entreprise revient, après les errements de la phase de reconstruction, à son domaine de prédilection qu'elle avait négligé depuis la fin des années 1930. Célébrée comme la grande vedette du Salon de l'Automobile de Francfort en 1961, la Bavaroise, avec ses lignes sobres et sans fioritures, répond à l'idéal prussien dont la devise est « être plus que paraître ».

La presse spécialisée rivalise de commentaires élogieux : « Profondément ancrée se trouve au cœur de l'acheteur de voiture allemand une soif de confort et de luxe que les voitures de grande série bon marché ne peuvent totalement assouvir », et ce serait précisément à ces acheteurs que s'adresse la BMW 1500, note *auto motor und sport* sur un ton pensif.

Dès le début, BMW a le plus grand mal à satisfaire les besoins qu'elle a elle-même suscités : avec 50 unités par jour, l'offre est loin de suffire à la demande qui émane du monde entier.

La réaction ne se fait pas attendre, et elle est d'autant plus percutante. Alors que des parkings entiers sont encombrés de 700 invendues dont l'avenir est plus qu'incertain, les chaînes de production s'agrandissent déjà pour la « Nouvelle Classe », les capacités sont augmentées et un réseau de distribution efficace est mis en place. Selon la devise de Goethe, selon laquelle il peut être fatal de se concentrer sur une seule action, la gamme s'enrichit rapidement pour satisfaire les goûts les plus divers. Elle va de la 1500 d'origine à la 2000tii produite en 1969, en passant par la 1800 TISA de 1964, construite en seulement 200 exemplaires pour le bonheur des amateurs de conduite sportive.

1966 est l'année de naissance de la compacte 1600-2 à deux portes, avec laquelle les commerciaux réunis sous le signe des « naseaux » ont, en quelque sorte, donné à l'automobile une nouvelle dimension. Avec ses lignes puissantes, mais attrayantes, elle va, jusqu'en 1975, avec 252 786 exemplaires, battre tous les records de production dans l'histoire de la marque. À la fin des années 1960, BMW fait en outre revivre sa tradition du six-cylindres. Et, cette fois-ci, cela en vaut la peine : les trois grosses BMW de 1968, les berlines 2500 et 2800 ainsi que le coupé 2800 CS, récoltent immédiatement les commentaires enthousiastes et les éloges des milieux spécialisés, qui les considèrent comme les meilleures représentantes de la construction automobile européenne.

Avec un tel programme, BMW est parfaitement armée pour l'avenir. Au cours des années suivantes, elle bat record sur record pour la fabrication et la vente. Le segment de la moto, lui aussi, redémarre, d'autant que les deux-roues ne

Collected works: the first BMW 1500s being delivered to the dealers in 1963. Light colors were preferred.

Gesammelte Werke: Die ersten BMW 1500 werden 1963 an die Händler ausgeliefert. Man bevorzugt helle Farben.

Œuvres réunies : les premières BMW 1500 sont remises aux concessionnaires en 1963. Les couleures claires ont la cote.

beckoned. BMW's new pride was reinforced by a string of motor sport triumphs, and racetrack success was consciously used as a marketing tool. Slightly modified production sedans won the Spa 24-hour race in 1965, and in 1968 the Touring Cars Grand Prix at the Nürburgring, driven by Dieter Quester and Hubert Hahne, who also achieved considerable success in the 1970 Formula 2 season. A powerful visual symbol of the new BMW identity came in the form of the four-cylinder administrative building which soared heavenwards from 1972 on Munich's Petuelring, facing the similarly avant-garde Olympiapark, constructed that same year, providing it with a counterpart, and at the same time offering a certain counterpoint. In 1972, annual sales exceeded two billion marks for the first time; a further major investment was the expansion of the Dingolfing works, purchased from Glas in 1967.

Crisis Management and Breaking New Ground (1972–1980)

With the launch of the 520 in 1972, the Milbertshofen car manufacturer began, after a four-year development period, to open up new territory to the industry, without departing from its existing credo: the car was sporty, but with a generous portion of comfort and discreet luxury, created to a certain extent for the heads of expanding families, an intention underlined by the new designation. The new car soon came to be known as the "fiver" (5 series). It later became part of an all-round numbering system, as the compact cars came to be known as the 3 series from 1975, the big coupés from 1976 as the 6 series and the top-of-the-range BMWs from 1977 as the 7 series, while from 1989 onwards the 8 series heralded the coming golden age of the touring sports sedan. As in the 1930s, additional digits after the initial 3, 5 or 7 give information about the cubic capacity of each model.

The opening of the new administrative headquarters and of the low-slung BMW museum right next door were not the only causes for celebration in 1973; it also marked the 50th anniversary of BMW motorcycle production. Half a million machines had been manufactured to date, 21,122 of them the previous year alone. And that same year, Dingolfing began production under the sign of the whirling blue and white propeller, and the 100,000th BMW would roll off the production line there on 7 November 1975. By 1973 the new plant

Anmut, wird er bis 1975 mit einer Stückzahl von 252 786 alle bisherigen Produktionsrekorde der Marke in den Schatten stellen. Ende der sechziger Jahre nimmt BMW zudem seine Sechszylindertradition wieder auf, und diesmal lohnt es sich: Die drei großen Achtundsechziger, die Limousinen 2500 und 2800 sowie das Coupé 2800 CS, werden als Spitzenerzeugnisse europäischen Autobaus begeistert aufgenommen und erhalten überaus wohlwollende Rezensionen.

Mit diesem Programm ist man trefflich gerüstet. In den nächsten Jahren erzielt man immer neue Fertigungs- und Absatzrekorde. Auch das Motorradgeschäft belebt sich, als das Zweirad nicht mehr als Alternative, sondern als Ergänzung zum Auto in die Garage gestellt wird. Nachdem 1969 nur knapp 5000 Maschinen verkauft werden konnten, bringt das Jahr 1970 mit den neuen Modellen R50/5, R60/6 und R75/5 die Wende. Die Produktion steigt auf über 12 000 Exemplare, schon zwei Jahre später sind es mehr als 21 000.

Anfang der siebziger Jahre ist die Lehr- und Aufbauphase Vergangenheit und Herrenjahre sind angesagt. Der neue Stolz bei BMW gründet nicht zuletzt auf eine Unzahl von Trophäen im Sport, den man durchaus als Marketingmedium versteht. Seriennahe Limousinen erringen Siege beim 24-Stunden-Rennen von Spa 1965 oder 1968 beim „Großen Preis der Tourenwagen" auf dem Nürburgring unter Dieter Quester und Hubert Hahne, die 1970 auch für Erfolge in der Formel 2 sorgen. Als symbolträchtig-sichtbarer Ausdruck der neuen BMW-Identität reckt sich seit 1972 das vierzylindrige Verwaltungsgebäude am Münchener Petuelring gen Himmel, in bevorzugter Panoramalage gegenüber dem gleichermaßen avantgardistischen Olympiapark aus dem gleichen Jahr – Pendant und zugleich auch ein bisschen Kontrapunkt zu diesem. Der Jahresumsatz überschreitet 1972 erstmals zwei Milliarden Mark. Schwerpunkt weiterer Investitionen ist der Ausbau des Werks Dingolfing, das 1967 von Glas erworben wurde.

Krisenmanagement und Abschied von der Nische (1972–1980)

Mit dem 520 von 1972 beginnen die Milbertshofener Automacher nach vier Jahren Entwicklungszeit, dem Markt Neuland abzugewinnen, ohne mit ihrem bisherigen Credo zu brechen: Sportlich gibt er sich, aber versetzt mit einem guten Schuss Komfort und dezentem Luxus, sozusagen wie geschaffen für die Vorstände expandierender Familien. Diese Intention besiegelt der neue Name. Volkes Stimme nennt den Novizen bald salopp den „Fünfer". Er wird künftig Teil eines sinnträchtigen Systems, denn die Kompakten, das sind ab 1975 die 3er, die großen Coupés ab 1976 die 6er und die Oberklassen-BMW ab 1977 die 7er, während man mit dem 8er von 1989 die Beletage des kommoden Reisesportwagens betritt. Als Zusatzinformation sind der Statuszahl, wie gelegentlich schon in den dreißiger Jahren, Hinweise auf das Volumen der jeweiligen Maschine beigegeben.

Gründe zum Feiern liefert 1973 nicht nur der Einzug in den „Vierzylinder" und in das einer Schüssel ähnelnde BMW-Museum gleich nebenan, sondern auch ein Jubiläum der besonderen Art: Seit einem halben Jahrhundert fertigt man Motorräder. Eine halbe Million waren es bisher insgesamt, im Jahr zuvor allein 21 122 Stück. Zugleich nimmt Dingolfing im Zeichen des weißblau wirbelnden Propellers die Produktion auf. Am 7. November 1975 wird dort der 100 000. BMW vom Band laufen. Schon 1973 sorgt der neue Standort für

sont plus considérés comme une alternative, mais bel et bien comme un complément à la voiture qu'ils côtoient parfois dans le garage. Alors que, en 1969, à peine 5000 motos ont été vendues, l'année 1970 marque un changement de cap avec les nouveaux modèles R50/5, R60/6 et R75/5. La production grimpe à plus de 12 000 et atteint les 21 000 deux ans plus tard.

Au début des années 1970, les années d'apprentissage et de démarrage appartiennent depuis longtemps à une époque révolue. Des années de vaches grasses sont annoncées pour l'avenir. La nouvelle fierté de BMW s'appuie aussi et surtout sur la multitude de trophées remportés en compétition, que l'on conçoit comme un instrument de marketing. Des berlines proches de la série remportent, par exemple, des victoires aux 24 Heures de Spa en 1965 ou 1968 ainsi qu'au « Grand Prix des voitures de tourisme » du Nürburgring avec Dieter Quester et Hubert Hahne, qui sont aussi une garantie de succès en Formule 2 en 1970. Visible de loin et très symbolique de la nouvelle identité de BMW, le siège social dont l'architecture représente quatre cylindres, qui longe le grand boulevard du Petuelring, s'élève depuis 1972 dans le ciel de Munich, à un emplacement prestigieux. Il se situe en face du Parc olympique construit la même année, un autre symbole d'avant-garde auquel il fait écho. En 1972, le chiffre d'affaires annuel dépasse, pour la première fois, le seuil des deux milliards de marks. Un autre temps fort en matière d'investissements est l'agrandissement de l'usine de Dingolfing, rachetée à Glas en 1967.

Gestion de crise et nouvelle percée sur le marché (1972–1980)

Avec la 520, dévoilée en 1972, le constructeur automobile de Milbertshofen commence prudemment, après quatre années de développement, à défricher de nouvelles terres sans renier son cœur de métier : sportive, mais avec un soupçon de confort et de luxe discret, c'est le modèle tout désigné pour les pères de famille aisés de sa clientèle. Ce nouveau nom matérialise bien cette intention. En Allemagne, la nouvelle voiture est rapidement surnommée « la Cinq ». À l'avenir, elle fera partie intégrante d'une hiérarchie bien définie. En effet, les compactes, ce seront à partir de 1975 les série 3, les gros coupés seront à partir de 1976 les série 6 et les BMW catégorie luxe, à partir de 1977, les série 7. Alors que la vocation de la série 8, à partir de 1989, sera de représenter BMW dans le segment des voitures de grand tourisme de luxe. À titre d'information supplémentaire, la combinaison de chiffres révèle, comme dans les années 1930 déjà, la cylindrée du moteur qui se trouve sous le capot.

En 1973, BMW a plusieurs raisons de se réjouir : l'inauguration de son bâtiment en forme de « quatre-cylindres », du musée BMW en forme de coupelle à toit plat, tout proche, mais aussi elle fête un anniversaire à la saveur toute particulière : on fabrique des motos depuis un demi-siècle. Un demi-million, jusqu'à ce jour, et pas moins de 21 122 exemplaires rien que pour l'année 1972. Simultanément, Dingolfing was already responsible for massive growth as the workforce increased by 12 percent and production by 8 percent.

The shockwaves from the energy crisis – one quarter real, three quarters skilfully engineered – did not have a major impact on BMW, and merely led to a minor setback during 1974, when a workforce of 25,805 produced 188,965 cars, achieving a turnover of 2492 million marks. The corresponding figures for 1973 were 27,737 employees producing 197,446 automobiles and a turnover of 2608 million marks, and for 1975 28,989 employees producing 221,298 vehicles and a turnover of 3,254,500 million marks.

The new-found awareness of energy-related issues that the crisis sparked did not sit easily with BMW's sporty image, and many viewed powerful cars such as the 2002 turbo with its bulging flared fenders as an affront to public taste. In the teeth of all this, however, BMW Motorsport GmbH, the subsidiary set up in 1972, was making an indelible mark under its quietly efficient boss Jochen Neerpasch. The CSL coupés with their mighty spoilers powered from victory to victory throughout 1973, as BMW drivers won 11 of the 16 Formula 2 races that season, with the inevitable 2-liter four-cylinder machines

massive Zuwächse mit 12 Prozent mehr Mitarbeitern und einem Produktionsplus von 8 Prozent.

Die Ausläufer der zu einem Viertel realen, zu drei Vierteln geschickt eingefädelten Energiekrise erreichen die Bayerischen Motoren Werke nur in abgeschwächter Form, mit einem kleinen Einbruch 1974. Zu diesem Zeitpunkt beschäftigt man 25 805 Mitarbeiter, baut 188 965 Autos und erzielt einen Umsatz von 2492 Millionen Mark. 1973 waren es 27 737 Kostgänger, 197 446 Automobile, 2608 Millionen Mark Umsatz. 1975 wird sich eine Belegschaft von 28 989 um 221 298 Fahrzeuge und 3254,5 Millionen Mark Umsatz verdient machen.

Dabei verträgt sich das just entdeckte Energiegewissen kaum mit dem sportiven BMW-Image. Manch einer empfindet Kraft-Wagen wie den Typ 2002 turbo mit seinen schwellenden Kotflügelverbreiterungen geradezu als Affront. Gleichwohl macht die 1972 ins Leben gerufene BMW Motorsport GmbH unter ihrem stillen, aber effizienten Chef Jochen Neerpasch unüberhörbar auf sich aufmerksam: Die mächtig geflügelten CSL-Coupés driften 1973 von Sieg zu Sieg, und 11 von 16 Formel-2-Läufen gewinnen BMW-Piloten, im

entame sa production sous l'emblème bleu et blanc. Le 7 novembre 1975, la 100 000e BMW sortira de la chaîne. Dès 1973, la nouvelle unité de fabrication est rentabilisée avec des augmentations satisfaisantes : 12 % pour les effectifs et 8 % pour la production.

Les répercussions d'une crise énergétique pour un quart bien réelle, mais pour les trois quarts mise en scène avec adresse, n'atteignent que relativement BMW et se traduisent par une légère baisse de la production en 1974. La firme emploie alors 25 805 collaborateurs, construit 188 965 voitures et réalise un chiffre d'affaires de 2492 millions de marks. En 1973, ces chiffres étaient de 27 737 personnes pour les effectifs, 197 446 véhicules pour la production et 2608 millions de marks pour le chiffre d'affaires. En 1975, les effectifs atteignent 28 989 personnes, qui produisent 221 298 voitures et enregistrent un chiffre d'affaires de 3254,5 millions de marks.

Et pourtant, l'image sportive de BMW est peu conciliable avec la prise de conscience selon laquelle les réserves énergétiques s'épuisent. Nombreux sont ceux qui considèrent alors comme un affront le lancement de la 2002 turbo avec la

The Discreet Charm of the Niche

Paul Georg Hahnemann, born in 1912 in Strasbourg, was the man of action and power before Eberhard von Kuenheim. Anyone looking for visible evidence of his influence need only take a look at the Munich skyline: Hahnemann's monument, just half a meter shorter than the Frauenkirche, is the BMW administrative building, called the "Vierzylinder" (four cylinder), or simply "der Turm" (the tower). He successfully championed the design of Vienna professor Karl Schwanzer in 1970 in the teeth of general opposition, victorious here as he had been in so many battles since autumn 1961, with his sleeves rolled up and with the ready garrulousness of an itinerant preacher, always ready with a pithy saying or an earthy anecdote, the right man at the right time.

When he responded to the call from the BMW major shareholder Quandt to become head of the sales department, Hahnemann was head of marketing at Auto Union in Düsseldorf. He found the Bayerische Motoren Werke in a terrible state. In 1962 a workforce of 9189 managed to knock up 52,934 automobiles for an annual turnover of 295 million marks. When Hahnemann resigned on 27 October 1971, BMW's workforce numbered 23,307, the turnover had risen to 1.9 billion marks and production to 164,701 units.

Hahnemann later identified four main factors behind this dramatic turnaround. Firstly, he totally rationalized the product range. At the bottom of the range, the Isetta 600 and 700 were scrapped, as were the prestigious flops, the 501 and 502, and also the Bertone coupé at the top end. In their place he introduced the "New Class", comprising the 1500 (production of which commenced on 25 August 1962), the 1800 (1963), the 2000 (1966), and their respective variants. Hahnemann incessantly preached the wisdom of the niche. This was a psychological variable, vaguely defined via notions such as youthful, sporty, maneuverable or classy, not least designed to differentiate BMW products from those of big brother Daimler-Benz. Bavarian politician Franz-Josef Strauß christened the go-getting manager "Nischen-Paul" ('Paul the niche') at a celebration to mark Strauß's 50th birthday in 1965, and "Nischen-Paul" he remained. The ranks of journalists, always looking for a good catchphrase, were particularly fond of using the BMW chieftain's nom de guerre. For all that,

the 1968 six-cylinder 2500 and 2800 seemed tantamount to a head-on attack on the Stuttgarters. Hahnemann, though, performed verbal somersaults in his attempts to justify their introduction in terms of his philosophy of the niche.

The second factor cited by Hahnemann was the acquisition of Bavaria's other automobile manufacturer, the struggling firm Glas of Dingolfing. The company changed hands on 10 November 1966 for a purchase price of 9.1 million marks; BMW also took on the firm's debts of 50 million marks. The claustrophobic confines of the original Munich plant at Milbertshofen were by then working at full capacity, with a daily production of 450 units. The Glas deal meant more space and labor, and thus new capacity. The third factor stressed by Hahnemann was the network of BMW dealerships, which the competition initially dismissed contemptuously as "puncture repair men". "The other half of BMW is out there, in distribution, in repairs and in aftersales care," he would monotonously repeat like a religious mantra. And the final factor: the construction of the "Turm", a symbol for all that had been achieved, and a vehicle for the long-term promotion of the company.

Despite all his achievements, Paul G. Hahnemann left BMW full of anger. Too often, he had crossed swords with Herbert Quandt, and "Nischen-Paul's" habit of viewing the sales division as the measure of all things just did not fit in with the business climate at the beginning of the 1970s. Furthermore, his familiar and robust relations with the executive board went too much against the board leadership principle Quandt was seeking to introduce. Hahnemann and von Kuenheim's personalities were just too different; on 1 January 1970, von Kuenheim had become president of BMW's executive board, and intended to be one in more than just name.

What would Hahnemann do after the parting of the ways? As an ex-member of BMW's upper echelons, Hahnemann's pension was more than sufficient to keep body and soul together, but at the tender age of 60 he felt far too young to resign himself to long walks along the banks of the Isar in the company of his dog Sonja. The advice of friends that he should amuse himself and keep in shape with regular skiing was rejected out of hand. As a younger man he had always

been a winner in sport and he was not about to give anyone the opportunity to say: "Look at the old fool trying to pretend he's a teenager."

The suggestion in 1972 of the Transport Minister of the time, Georg Leber, that company rescuer Paul G. Hahnemann could turn around the ailing Bundesbahn as its President, was also little to his liking. For one thing, Hahnemann knew that within such a complex set-up he would be able to achieve little. Instead he took on the office equipment firm Pohlschröder, and between 1972 and 1976 wiped out its bank debts of 50 million marks and brought it back into profit. He persuaded the Hamburg salvage ship owner Ulrich Harms to acquire the ailing enterprise, and then talked him into giving the firm up again once it had recovered, thus allowing two giants of the sector, Strafer of Strasbourg and Steelcase of the USA, to each buy 50 percent of Pohlschröder. When these two companies merged to form a group at the beginning of the 1980s, it was rumored that Hahnemann had played the role of go-between and marriage broker for the two. He denied this with a twinkle in his eye, insisting that he had just been the personal adviser of Strafer's boss, Henry Lachman.

Not all of the professional rescuer's lesser enterprises went according to plan. For example, his effort to get the body-conscious Germans interested in the Singaporean wonder ointment "Tiger Balm" was not the greatest of successes. Notwithstanding this, right up until 1990 Hahnemann, now in his late 70s, was still putting in a solid 35-hour week at his Pohlschröder desk in his offices in Munich-Bogenhausen. When not occupied in safeguarding or proliferating his holdings, he took a keen interest in the academic careers of his two daughters Carolin and Suzan, both gifted philology students at the University of Munich. At the end he too achieved a philosophical peace of mind, his search for harmony extending even to his views on the contemporary automobile industry. Here Hahnemann felt considerable empathy for Daimler-Benz boss Edzard Reuter. In terms of achievements, he greatly admired Eberhard von Kuenheim.

Paul G. Hahnemann passed away in January 1997. "Nischen-Paul" had long since given way to an older and wiser man.

breathing down their necks, Alex von Falkenhausen having produced a small run of 50 of these. Jean-Pierre Jarier became European champion in his March 732, one of six to use a BMW power unit between then and 1982.

BMW had long since started thinking on a global scale: in France, Italy and Belgium distribution and customer service had been taken over by BMW subsidiaries. Suitably-sized networks of dealerships and garages were set up, while in South Africa the importer's existing assembly facility was converted into an autonomous production plant. The United States had long since become the most important export market, and no less than 80 BMW clubs bespoke the car's virtual cult status among its faithful following there. In 1974, for example, 35,877 BMWs were shipped to the States, and in November that year BMW of North America became a Bavarian bridgehead in the spiritual home of the motorcar.

The addition to the range in January 1975 of the BMW 1502 proved to be more than just a nostalgic last hurrah for the legendary 02 model range. Over the next two years more than 70,000 of this classic were shifted, despite the fact that

Rücken den unvermeidlichen 2-Liter-Vierzylinderrennmotor, von dem Alex von Falkenhausen eine kleine Serie von 50 Exemplaren aufgelegt hat. Europameister wird Jean-Pierre Jarier auf dem March 732 – einer von sechs Titeln mit BMW-Triebwerken bis 1982.

Längst denkt man bei BMW global: In Frankreich, Italien und Belgien übernehmen eigene Tochtergesellschaften Vertrieb und Kundendienst. Das Händler- und Werkstättennetz wird passgerecht auf die notwendige Größenordnung zugeschnitten. In Südafrika baut man den bisherigen Montagebetrieb des Importeurs zum autarken Fertigungsort aus. Zum wichtigsten Exportmarkt haben sich längst die Vereinigten Staaten entwickelt, wo nicht weniger als 80 Markenklubs zu Stätten kultischer Verehrung der bayerischen Technik geworden sind. 1974 beispielsweise werden 35 877 BMW nach Übersee verfrachtet, und im November konstituiert sich „BMW of North America" als bajuwarischer Brückenkopf im Autoland Nummer eins.

Dass ab Januar 1975 der Typ 1502 angeboten wird, erweist sich als mehr als nur ein nostalgisches Ausklingen der legendären Modellreihe 02. In den nächsten beiden Jahren

démesure de ses ailes élargies et son aileron avant agressif. Parallèlement, la BMW Motorsport GmbH, créée en 1972, se propulse sur le devant de la scène sous la conduite de son chef aussi discret qu'efficace, Jochen Neerpasch. En 1973, les coupés CSL aux imposants ailerons aérodynamiques volent de victoire en victoire et les pilotes BMW gagnent 11 des 16 manches de Formule 2 de la saison, avec l'incontournable quatre-cylindres de deux litres, dont Alex von Falkenhausen a produit une petite série de 50 exemplaires. Jean-Pierre Jarier, sur une March 732, est sacré champion d'Europe, l'un des six titres que remporteront les moteurs BMW jusqu'en 1982.

La stratégie est internationale depuis longtemps: en France, en Italie et en Belgique, des filiales BMW assurent la distribution et le service après-vente. Le réseau de concessionnaires et d'ateliers est conçu spécifiquement, en fonction des besoins. En Afrique du Sud, l'ancienne unité de montage de l'importateur se transforme en un site de production indépendant. Il y a des lustres que les États-Unis sont devenus le principal marché d'exportation et l'on n'y compte pas moins de 80 clubs de passionnés qui s'adonnent au culte de la marque bavaroise. En 1974, 35 877 BMW prennent la

Vom scheuen Charme der Nische

Paul Georg Hahnemann, 1912 in Straßburg geboren, ist der Macher und Motor vor Eberhard von Kuenheim. Wer nach sichtbaren Spuren seines Wirkens sucht, wird im Stadtbild von München fündig. Hahnemanns Denkmal ist einen halben Meter niedriger als die Frauenkirche: das BMW-Bürogebäude, auch „Vierzylinder" oder schlicht „Der Turm" genannt. Er boxt den Entwurf des Wiener Professors Karl Schwanzer 1970 gegen den allgemeinen Widerstand durch, so wie er seit Herbst 1961 vieles durchgeboxt hat: hemdsärmelig, von der rüden Beredsamkeit eines Wanderpredigers und immer für starke Sprüche und pralle Anekdoten gut – der richtige Mann zur richtigen Zeit.

Als ihn der Ruf von BMW-Großaktionär Quandt ereilt, zukünftiger Leiter des Verkaufs zu werden, ist Hahnemann Marketingchef bei der Auto Union in Düsseldorf. Die Bayerischen Motoren Werke sind in miserabler Verfassung. 1962 klempnern 9189 Mitarbeiter an 52 934 Automobilen und einem Jahresumsatz von 295 Millionen Mark. Als Hahnemann am 27. Oktober 1971 kündigt, stehen 23 307 Mitarbeiter auf der BMW-Gehaltsliste. Der Umsatz wird sich auf 1,9 Milliarden Mark belaufen, die Produktion bei 164 701 Einheiten liegen.

Die Ursachen für diese reife Leistung ordnet Hahnemann später vier Feldern zu. Zum einen entrümpelt er die Modellpalette. Die Einstiegsmodelle Isetta 600 und 700 am unteren Ende des Spektrums fliegen ebenso heraus wie die Prestige-Flops 501 und 502 und das Bertone-Coupé am oberen Ende. Dafür setzt er die „Neue Klasse" auf die richtige Schiene – den 1500 (die Bänder laufen am 25. August 1962 an), den 1800 (1963) und den 2000 (1966) mit ihren verschiedenen Varianten. Unablässig predigt Hahnemann die Lehre von der Nische. Das ist eine psychologische Größe, vage definiert durch Werte wie jugendlich, sportlich, handlich oder gediegen, nicht zuletzt, um die BMW-Produkte gegen die des großen Bruders Daimler-Benz abzugrenzen. „Nischen-Paul" nennt Franz-Josef Strauß den umtriebigen Manager 1965 anlässlich einer Feier zu Strauß' 50. Geburtstag, und „Nischen-Paul" bleibt ihm auf den Leib geschrieben wie eine Tätowierung. Vor allem die auf dergleichen begierige Zunft der Journalisten lässt sich den Kriegernamen des BMW-

Häuptlings genüsslich auf der Zunge zergehen. Die Sechszylinder 2500 und 2800 von 1968 kommen allerdings schon einer frontalen Attacke auf die Untertürkheimer gleich. Hahnemann scheut indes keine rhetorische Mühe, sie in seine Ideologie der Nische einzubeziehen.

Zum zweiten setzt Hahnemann den Erwerb des ins Schlingern geratenen bayerischen Autoherstellers Glas in Dingolfing durch. Die Übergabe findet am 10. November 1966 statt. Der Kaufpreis beträgt 9,1 Millionen Mark, außerdem übernimmt BMW die Schulden des Unternehmens in Höhe von 50 Millionen Mark. In der klaustrophobischen Enge des Stammwerks München-Milbertshofen hat man mit einer Tagesproduktion von 450 Einheiten das Ende der Fahnenstange erreicht. Der Glas-Deal bedeutet Areal und Arbeitskräfte und somit Kapazität. Zum dritten bringt Hahnemann das BMW-Händlernetz auf Vordermann, das die Konkurrenz anfänglich hämisch als die „Schlauchflicker" abqualifiziert hat. „Die andere Hälfte von BMW findet draußen statt, beim Vertrieb, in Wartung und Pflege", wiederholt er mit der einprägsamen Mechanik einer Gebetsmühle. Zum vierten errichtet er den „Turm", Sinnbild für Erreichtes, Vehikel wohl auch für eine Selbstdarstellung über den Tag hinaus.

Dennoch verlässt Paul G. Hahnemann die BMW im Zorn. Zu oft ist er mit Herbert Quandt aneinandergeraten. Zu wenig passt Nischen-Pauls Gepflogenheit, das Verkaufsressort zum Maß aller Dinge zu machen, Anfang der siebziger Jahre in die Landschaft. Zu sehr reibt sich sein kumpelhafter Umgang mit dem Vorstand am Direktorialprinzip, das Quandt anstrebt. Zu verschieden sind die Persönlichkeiten Hahnemanns und von Kuenheims, der seit dem 1. Januar 1970 BMW-Aufsichtsratsvorsitzender ist und es nicht nur dem Namen nach sein möchte.

Was nach dem Bruch kommt? Als ehemaligem Mitglied der BMW-Spitze steht Hahnemann ein Ruhegehalt zu, mit dem sich Butter, Brot und Bier gewiss bestreiten lassen. Im zarten Alter von knapp 60 Jahren fühlt sich der Frührentner indes noch zu jung für ausgedehnte Spaziergänge am Isarufer in Begleitung seines Hundes Sonja. Den Rat von Feunden, sich mit reichlich Skifahren bei Laune und bei Kondition zu halten, tut er ab: Als junger Mann habe er im Sport stets zu

den Besten gezählt, und niemand solle jetzt lästern: „Schau mal, der alte Knacker, wie der sich abrackert."

Auf mangelnde Gegenliebe stößt 1972 auch das Angebot des damaligen Verkehrsministers Georg Leber, der gelernte Profi-Sanierer Paul G. Hahnemann solle als Präsident die marode Bundesbahn aus den roten Zahlen fahren. Als Einzelner, weiß dieser, wird er in einem so komplizierten Apparat wenig ausrichten können. Dafür steuert Hahnemann den Büroausstatter Pohlschröder, der mit 50 Millionen Mark bei den Banken in der Kreide steht, zwischen 1972 und 1976 wieder in die schwarzen Zahlen. Er überredet den Hamburger Bergungsreeder Ulrich Harms zum Erwerb des maroden Unternehmens, luchst diesem jedoch den inzwischen wieder intakten Havaristen wieder ab. So können sich zwei Branchenriesen mit jeweils 50 Prozent bei Pohlschröder einkaufen, Strafer in Straßburg und Steelcase in den USA. Als sich diese beiden zu Beginn der achtziger Jahre zu einer Gruppe zusammenfinden, munkelt man, Hahnemann habe sich als Postillon d'amour und Heiratsvermittler um diesen Bund fürs Leben verdient gemacht. Er winkt da in augenzwinkernder Bescheidenheit ab, er sei lediglich der persönliche Berater von Strafer-Boss Henry Lachman.

Nicht immer von einem Happy-End gekrönt sind kleinere Aktivitäten des Berufssanierers, etwa der Versuch, den körperbewussten Deutschen für die Wundersalbe „Tiger Balm" aus Singapur zu erwärmen. Die ungebrochene Erwerbstätigkeit des Spätsiebzigers erfordert 1990 eine stramme 35-Stunden-Woche am Pohlschröder-Schreibtisch in seinem Büro in München-Bogenhausen. Wenn er nicht um Wahrung und Mehrung seines Besitzstandes bemüht ist, verfolgt er mit lebhaftem Interesse die akademische Laufbahn seiner Töchter Carolin und Suzan, begabten Philologiestudentinnen an der Münchener Universität. Auch er selbst betrachtet die Dinge am Ende abgeklärt, philosophisch, auf Harmonie bedacht, selbst was die zeitgenössische Autoszene betrifft. So fühlt sich Hahnemann menschlich Daimler-Benz-Boss Edzard Reuter verbunden. Was den Erfolg anbelangt, bewundert er Eberhard von Kuenheim.

Längst leise und weise geworden, stirbt Paul G. Hahnemann im Januar 1997.

Admired and scolded: "Nischen-Paul" Hahnemann.

Viel bewundert und viel gescholten:
„Nischen-Paul" Hahnemann.

Très admiré mais souvent en proie aux critiques :
Paul Hahnemann, surnommé « Paul la niche ».

sales head Hans-Erdmann Schönbeck had introduced a two-door 3 series model, a new compact automobile with pleasingly contemporary lines and technology to match. The BMW range was becoming ever larger, offering a glittering array of different models. At the 1976 Geneva Spring Motor Show, the stars of the show were the two new coupés, the 630CS and 633CSi, allowing head of development Bernhard Osswald and designer Paul Bracq to leave BMW on an impressive high note.

Equally spectacular was the R 100 RS, which came with full fairing and an integrated cockpit as standard, and blasted to 62 mph (100 kph) in 4.6 seconds. Since January of that year BMW Motorrad GmbH (BMW Motorcycle) of Berlin had become an organizationally independent entity. In the benign and publicity-friendly presence of West German President Walter Scheel, the cornerstone was laid in 1977 for modern motorcycle manufacture in the former and future capital of Germany, though this was overshadowed by the sensation created by the launch of the 7 series in January. The range of six-cylinder power units was extended downwards with the addition of a small 2-liter engine, not without some rhetorical allusions to old traditions and the glorious past.

That past was in the foreground in any case, since BMW was now celebrating its 50th anniversary as a car manufacturer, marking the occasion with a string of records: almost five billion marks in turnover, and production figures of 31,515 motorcycles and 290,236 automobiles. Executive board president von Kuenheim's belief that a figure of 350,000 was feasible by 1982 proved in reality to be less than optimistic, as the actual figure was 378,769. In 1978 half of all BMW engines had six cylinders, a number which in Munich had practically achieved the status of a tenet, and which was greeted in the trade press with great acclamation; devotees of the straight six held that nothing was quite as good or as smooth as this tried-and-tested power unit. 50 percent of all cars and 75 percent of all motorcycles went for export.

lassen sich über 70 000 Exemplare dieses Klassikers absetzen, obwohl Verkaufsleiter Hans-Erdmann Schönbeck im Juli mit dem zweitürigen 3er den neuen Kompakten in zeitgemäß-gefälliger Linienführung und entsprechender Technik vorstellt. Doch das BMW-Spektrum vergrößert sich weiter und erglänzt in bunter Vielfalt. Schon auf dem Frühjahrssalon in Genf 1976 werden neue Begehrlichkeiten durch die beiden Coupés 630CS und 633CSi erweckt, mit denen sich Entwicklungschef Bernhard Osswald und Designer Paul Bracq eindrucksvoll von BMW verabschieden.

Ebenso spektakulär ist die R100RS mit ihrer serienmäßigen Vollverkleidung und Integral-Cockpit, die in 4,6 Sekunden auf Tempo 100 spurtet. Seit Januar 1976 hat sich die BMW Motorrad GmbH in Berlin organisatorisch emanzipiert. Im wohlwollenden und werbewirksamen Beisein von Bundespräsident Walter Scheel wird 1977 in der alten und künftigen Hauptstadt der Grundstein für eine moderne neue Zweiradmanufaktur gelegt, überstrahlt gleichwohl vom Aufsehen, das das Erscheinen des 7ers im Januar erregt. Die Bandbreite der Sechszylindertriebwerke wird nach unten durch einen kleinen 2-Liter erweitert, nicht ohne rhetorische Anspielungen auf alte Gepflogenheiten und die glorreiche Vergangenheit.

Diese Vergangenheit rückt ohnehin ins Blickfeld, denn auch der Autohersteller BMW wird 50 und würdigt dieses Ereignis mit Rekordzahlen: fast fünf Milliarden Mark Umsatz, 31 515 Motorräder, 290 236 Automobile. Die Vision des Vorstandsvorsitzenden von Kuenheim, 1982 seien 350 000 machbar, wird von der Wirklichkeit korrigiert – nach oben: de facto sind es 378 769. Anno 1978 weist die Hälfte aller BMW-Motoren sechs Zylinder auf, eine Zahl, die in München fast in den Rang eines Dogmas erhoben wird und unermüdlichen Applaus durch die Fachpresse erhält: In weitem Umkreis gebe es nichts Besseres und Geschmeidigeres als dieses Reihentriebwerk. 50 Prozent aller Wagen und 75 Prozent aller Zweiräder werden dem Export zugeführt.

Überhaupt: 20 Jahre nach dem fast letalen Siechtum des Unternehmens sonnt man sich im Zauber der großen Zahlen,

Eberhard von Kuenheim, Chairman of the board of BMW AG in 1989.

Eberhard von Kuenheim, Vorstandsvorsitzender der BMW AG, anno 1989.

Eberhard von Kuenheim, président du directoire de BMW AG, en 1989.

Full of ideas: Jochen Neerpasch.

Unerschöpflicher Ideenreichtum: Jochen Neerpasch.

Jamais à court d'idées : Jochen Neerpasch.

direction des États-Unis où, en novembre, se constitue « BMW of North America » : une tête de pont bavaroise dans l'eldorado de l'automobile.

Le lancement de la 1502, en janvier 1975, est plus qu'un simple clin d'œil nostalgique à la légendaire gamme 02. Les deux années suivantes, BMW vend plus de 70 000 exemplaires de cette classique bien que le directeur des ventes, Hans-Erdmann Schönbeck, avec la nouvelle série 3 à deux portes, lance une nouvelle compacte aux lignes séduisantes tout à fait dans l'air du temps et avec des caractéristiques techniques inégalées. La gamme de BMW ne cesse de s'enrichir et brille par sa diversité. Au premier Salon du Printemps, à Genève en 1976, les deux coupés 630CS et 633CSi font sensation. On les doit au chef du développement, Bernhard Osswald, et au designer Paul Bracq, tous deux sur le départ.

Une autre création aussi spectaculaire est la R100RS, équipée en série d'un carénage intégral et d'un cockpit d'origine, qui abat le 0 à 100 km/h en 4,6 secondes. Depuis janvier 1976, la BMW Motorrad GmbH, qui a son siège à Berlin, s'est émancipée pour devenir une entité indépendante bien organisée. En présence du Président fédéral Walter Scheel est posée, en 1977, à Berlin, la première pierre d'une future usine de deux-roues. L'événement est très médiatique, la manifestation est toutefois empreinte de la stupéfaction qu'a suscitée la sortie de la série 7 en janvier. La gamme des six-cylindres est complétée par un petit deux-litres qui n'est pas sans rappeler une époque depuis longtemps révolue et un passé glorieux.

Celui-ci se rappelle d'ailleurs au bon souvenir de tous, puisque BMW constructeur automobile, elle aussi, fête son cinquantenaire, un événement marqué par de nombreux records : près de 5 milliards de marks de chiffre d'affaires, 31 515 motos produites et 293 236 voitures construites. Les prévisions du président du directoire, Eberhard von Kuenheim, qui prétend que 350 000 voitures fabriquées est un chiffre réaliste en 1982, sont rattrapées par la réalité. Une correction s'impose – à la hausse : de facto, ce nombre sera de 378 769. En 1978, la moitié des moteurs de BMW sont des six-cylindres, un résultat qui lui confère une légitimité à Munich et suscite les félicitations incessantes de la presse spécialisée : les amateurs de six-cylindres prétendent que rien n'égale ce bloc-moteur à la fois souple et à toute épreuve. La moitié des voitures et les trois quarts des motos sont destinées à l'exportation.

D'ailleurs vingt ans après les difficultés qui ont failli être fatales à l'entreprise, les Bavarois rosissent de fierté à la lecture des chiffres qui sont autant de records tandis que la croissance et l'augmentation des ventes sont toujours au rendez-vous, même à une période où d'autres se débattent

Le charme discret du marché de niche

Paul Georg Hahnemann, né en 1912 à Strasbourg, est l'homme d'action à qui Eberhard von Kuenheim a succédé. Quiconque recherche un témoignage de son œuvre se tournera vers Munich et regardera vers l'horizon. Le monument de Hahnemann est 50 cm moins élevé que la « Frauenkirche » : il s'agit des tours de bureaux de BMW, que l'on appelle aussi le « quatre-cylindres » ou, tout simplement, « la tour ». En 1970, il impose le projet du professeur viennois Karl Schwanzer envers et contre tout, de même que, depuis l'automne 1961, il a imposé bien d'autres projets, en parlant avec l'élocution d'un prédicateur itinérant, les manches retroussées, toujours connu pour ses bons mots et ses anecdotes inénarrables. *The right man at the right time.*

Hahnemann est chef du marketing chez Auto Union, à Düsseldorf, lorsqu'il apprend que le grand actionnaire de BMW, Herbert Quandt, l'a choisi comme futur directeur des ventes. BMW est dans un état lamentable. En 1962, 9189 ouvriers « bricolent » 52 934 voitures pour un chiffre d'affaires annuel de 295 millions de marks. Au moment de la démission de Hahnemann, le 27 octobre 1971, 23 307 salariés sont employés par BMW. Le chiffre d'affaires est passé à 1,9 milliard de marks et la production s'élève à 164 701 voitures.

Hahnemann donnera plus tard quatre explications à ce résultat flatteur. Dans un premier temps, il élague le programme. Les Isetta 600 et 700, voitures d'entrée de gamme, sont mises au placard au même titre que, à l'autre bout de la gamme, les 501 et 502 de prestige à l'échec retentissant, ou le coupé Bertone. En revanche, il met la « Nouvelle Classe » sur les rails, la 1500 (dont la production débute le 25 août 1962), puis la 1800 (1963) et la 2000 (1966) dans leurs différentes versions. Infatigablement, Hahnemann prône le marché de niche. Il s'agit d'un paramètre, vaguement défini par des notions comme jeune, sportif, maniable ou luxueux, qu'il utilise surtout pour différencier les modèles BMW de ceux de Daimler-Benz. En 1965, lors des cérémonies pour le cinquantenaire de Franz-Josef Strauss, celui-ci surnomme l'infatigable manager « Paul la niche », un surnom qui lui collera à la peau tel un tatouage. Pour la gent toujours avide de sensations que sont les journalistes, le nom de guerre du chef de BMW est une information bienvenue pour fleurir leurs reportages. Niche ou pas, les six-cylindres 2500 et 2800 de 1968 sont bel et bien une attaque de front dirigée contre Untertürkheim. Hahnemann pourtant ne

néglige pas ses efforts pour développer sa philosophie de niche.

Dans un deuxième temps, Hahnemann impose la reprise du constructeur automobile bavarois Glas, à Dingolfing, au bord de la faillite. L'entreprise change de main le 10 novembre 1966 et le prix d'achat est de 9,1 millions de marks. Pourtant, BMW accepte de régler les dettes de l'entreprise s'élevant à 50 millions de marks. Dans l'étroitesse de l'usine mère de Munich-Milbertshofen, BMW était finalement confrontée à une limite incompressible de sa production à 450 exemplaires par jour. La transaction avec Glas lui apportera de l'espace et de la main-d'œuvre, autrement dit des capacités de production supplémentaires.

Troisième coup de théâtre, Hahnemann donne un sérieux coup de balai dans le réseau de concessionnaires de BMW – ironiquement surnommés par la concurrence « bidouilleurs de chambres à air ». « 50 % des effectifs de BMW travaille à l'extérieur, dans la distribution, l'entretien et le service après-vente », se plaît-il à répéter avec la régularité d'un moulin à prières.

Quatrième fait d'armes, il édifie la « tour », symbole du chemin qui a été parcouru et qui a, sans doute pour objectif d'être la fierté de l'entreprise à long terme.

Et pourtant, Paul G. Hahnemann quittera BMW sur un coup de tête. Ses conflits avec Herbert Quandt auront été trop fréquents. Au début des années 1970, la volonté de « Paul la niche » de faire des ventes l'aune à laquelle doit être mesuré tout le reste est inconciliable avec les idées de l'époque. Au directoire, son style « fort en gueule » entraîne trop de frictions avec la ligne directoriale à laquelle aspire Herbert Quandt. Trop différentes sont aussi les personnalités de Hahnemann et de von Kuenheim, qui, depuis le 1er janvier 1970, officie comme président du conseil de surveillance de BMW et entend ne pas l'être uniquement sur le papier.

Que se passe-t-il après la rupture ? En tant qu'ancien membre de la direction de BMW, Hahnemann a droit à une pension qui permet sans aucun doute de financer aisément la bière, le pain et, aussi, le beurre pour le tartiner. Mais à 60 ans, le préretraité s'estime encore trop jeune pour se contenter de longues promenades sur les rives de l'Isar en compagnie de sa chienne Sonja. Il ne suit pas les conseils que lui donnent ses amis de conserver sa bonne humeur et sa santé en pratiquant le ski à haute dose : jeune, il a

toujours été un excellent sportif et il n'entend pas laisser quiconque se moquer de lui maintenant qu'il a vieilli : « Regarde le vieux croulant qui se prend pour un ado. »

En 1972, l'offre du ministre des Transports de l'époque, Georg Leber, qui veut recruter Paul G. Hahnemann, reconnu comme sauveur professionnel d'entreprises, et le nommer président de la Bundesbahn alors déficitaire, suscite tout aussi peu d'enthousiasme. Il sait que lui seul ne pourrait guère obtenir de résultats dans une structure aussi compliquée. En revanche, de 1972 à 1976, Hahnemann reprend en main le fabricant de meubles de bureau Pohlschröder, dont la dette auprès des banques avoisine les 50 millions de marks, redresse ses comptes et renoue avec les bénéfices. Il convainc l'armateur hambourgeois Ulrich Harms, spécialisé dans le sauvetage de navires, d'acquérir l'entreprise qui bat de l'aile avant de la lui racheter entre-temps lorsqu'elle est de nouveau en plein essor. Ainsi deux géants de ce secteur peuvent-ils reprendre respectivement 50 % de Pohlschröder, Strafer à Strasbourg et Steelcase aux États-Unis. Lorsque ces deux firmes fusionnent, au début des années 1980, on murmure que Hahnemann aurait joué le rôle d'entremetteur dans cette union. Il nie, par modestie, et rétorque qu'il a seulement été le conseiller personnel de Henry Lachman, le p.-d.g. de Strafer.

Mais tous les sauvetages de ce professionnel ne connaissent pas toujours une fin heureuse. C'est par exemple le cas pour sa tentative de faire découvrir aux Allemands soucieux de leur condition physique les bienfaits de la pommade miracle le « Baume du tigre » de Singapour. Quoi qu'il en soit, en 1990, toutes ces activités imposent encore à ce septuagénaire avancé une semaine qui dépasse largement les 35 heures à son bureau de Pohlschröder, dans sa société de Munich-Bogenhausen. Lorsqu'il n'est pas occupé à faire fructifier sa fortune, il suit attentivement la carrière universitaire de ses filles Carolin et Suzan, étudiantes douées en philologie à l'Université de Munich. À la fin de sa vie, lui-même voit les choses avec philosophie et sa recherche de l'harmonie modifie même son point de vue sur l'industrie automobile contemporaine. Ainsi, sur le plan humain, Hahnemann se sent-il très proche d'Edzard Reuter, le p.-d.g. de Daimler-Benz. Et il admire Eberhard von Kuenheim.

Paul G. Hahnemann meurt en janvier 1997. Cela fait longtemps déjà que « Paul la niche » est devenu silencieux – et sage.

To sum up, just 20 years after the company's near-terminal illness, BMW found itself in the sunlit uplands where growth and increased sales had become the norm, even in times when others were struggling against a stagnant economic situation. In autumn 1979, BMW could look back on a postwar production of three million automobiles, 90,000 of the 7 series alone had been produced and sold since its introduction, taking BMW into the heart of Mercedes-Benz territory; BMW had long since lost all fear of its arch-rival.

Meanwhile, the Motorsport GmbH was launching its latest masterpiece – the 535i. Possessing all the charisma of its rivals from the Via Emilia, the mid-engine M1 coupé embarked on a glittering career on roads and racetracks, at the Procar races for example, a Grand Prix sideshow in which amateur drivers pit their skills against the exclusive ranks of the Grand Prix drivers, taking on those with the fastest times from the training sessions.

werden Wachstum und Steigerung zur Norm, sogar in Zeiten, in denen andere im Gestrüpp einer unerquicklichen Wirtschaftslage straucheln. Im Herbst 1979 blicken die Bayerischen Motoren Werke auf die lange Reihe von drei Millionen gefertigten Autos seit Kriegsende zurück. Seit ihrer Einführung sind allein 90 000 7er produziert und abgesetzt worden – mitten hinein ins Mercedes-Benz-Land, vor dem man längst jegliche Schwellen- und Berührungsängste verloren hat.

Mit dem 535i legt die Motorsport GmbH ihr neuestes Meisterstück vor. Das mit dem vollen Charisma seiner Konkurrenten von der Via Emilia ausgestattete Mittelmotor-Coupé M1 beginnt seine glanzvolle Karriere auf Straße und Piste, etwa bei den Procar-Rennen im Rahmen der Grand Prix, wo die Trainingsschnellsten aus dem exklusiven Feld der Formel-1-Piloten sich mit Horden von ehrgeizigen Privatfahrern raufen.

dans une situation économique difficile. À l'automne 1979, BMW peut se prévaloir d'avoir fabriqué trois millions de voitures depuis la fin de la guerre. Depuis la création de cette gamme, elle a produit et vendu pas moins de 90 000 série 7, marchant ainsi sans vergogne sur les plates-bandes de Mercedes-Benz, à l'égard de laquelle la firme a depuis longtemps perdu tout sentiment d'appréhension et toute inhibition.

Avec la 535i, la Motorsport GmbH apporte une nouvelle fois la preuve de son incomparable savoir-faire. Le coupé M1 à moteur central, dont le charisme n'a rien à envier à ses concurrents de la Via Emilia, commence son impressionnante carrière sur routes et sur pistes, notamment lors des courses de Procar en lever de rideau des Grands Prix de Formule 1. Les pilotes choisis parmi les mieux classés aux essais sont alors confrontés à des hordes de concurrents privés qui ne sont pas disposés à s'en laisser compter.

The Motorrad GmbH returned to motor sport with the R 80 GS, immediately taking second place in the European motocross championship and winning both the German and World championships in the 750 cc class. In Steyr, Austria, the first sod was cut for the engine plant there, after the signing a year earlier of an agreement with Steyr-Daimler-Puch AG worth two billion Austrian Schillings, for the development and production of diesels.

Die Motorrad GmbH meldet sich mit der R 80 GS im Rennsport zurück, belegt gleich den zweiten Platz in der Gelände-Europameisterschaft und stellt sowohl den Weltmeister als auch den deutschen Meister in der Klasse über 750 ccm. Im österreichischen Steyr tut man den ersten Spatenstich für das dortige Motorenwerk: Schon ein Jahr früher wurde mit der Steyr-Daimler-Puch AG ein Abkommen getroffen über die Entwicklung und den Bau von Dieselmotoren, Volumen: zwei Milliarden Schillinge.

Avec la R 80 GS, Motorrad GmbH revient en compétition motocycliste et remporte d'emblée la deuxième place au championnat d'Europe d'enduro, fournissant aussi « accessoirement » le champion du monde et le champion d'Allemagne dans la catégorie des plus de 750 cm³. Dans la ville autrichienne de Steyr, le premier coup de pioche de la future usine de moteurs est donné : un an plus tard, un accord avait été passé avec Steyr-Daimler-Puch AG concernant le développement et la construction de moteurs diesel. Montant de la transaction : deux milliards de schillings.

Firing on all Cylinders, from Two to Twelve (1980–1990)

While the flying Swiss Marc Surer secured the fifth European Formula 2 championship for BMW in 1980, in Munich they were already reviewing the continued use of the production four-cylinder block in motor sport. The only mountain in motor sport yet to be climbed by BMW was the blue riband event, Formula 1. This job fell to Paul Rosche. Within the company he became known as "Camshaft Paul". Before very long the serried ranks of skeptics and know-it-alls had been silenced as Nelson Piquet secured a first victory for Brabham BMW at the Canadian Grand Prix in Montreal on 13 June 1982, and in 1983 the piercing-eyed Brazilian secured the world title. Like the Brabham BMW Formula 1 car, the aristocratic but nimble 745i sedan, BMW's flagship since 1980, was powered by an exhaust supercharger and supplied with fuel by the L-Jetronic electronically controlled injection system, as were its sister cars, the 728i, 732i and 735i.

In June 1981, a thoroughly revised 5 series consigned its predecessor to well-deserved retirement, and 16 months later the 1,000,000th car of the series rolled off the Dingolfing production line. In the meantime, BMW Iberica S.A. of Madrid had become the 12th foreign distribution company, and a daring attempt had been made to gain a foothold in a precarious market with the setting up of BMW Japan. By 1982, 3800 new BMWs were traversing the dusty roads of Spain, while 5300 had made the long journey to the land of the rising sun. This was to be the prologue to a success story, as Japanese BMW registrations multiplied sixfold over the following eight years. The launch of the new 3 series was set against the exotic backdrop of Morocco, and production of the 2,000,000th of these now not-so-compact BMWs was already in sight. Milbertshofen had long since reached its full capacity of 500 cars a day, and so a new plant was set up at Regensburg. On

Feuer aus allen Rohren: von zwei bis zwölf Zylindern (1980–1990)

Als der rasende Eidgenosse Marc Surer 1980 die fünfte Europameisterschaft in der Formel 2 an die BMW-Fahnen heftet, macht man sich in München bereits Gedanken um die weitere Verwendung des serienmäßigen Vierzylinderblocks im Rennsport. Als Steigerung und Krönung bleibt nur noch die Formel 1. Mit dieser Aufgabe betraut ist Paul Rosche, in firmeninterner Analogie zur einstigen Verkaufsikone „Nischen-Paul" Hahnemann salopp „Nocken-Paul" genannt. Binnen kurzem bringt er den nörgelnden Chor der Skeptiker und Besserwisser zum Verstummen: Am 13. Juni 1982 siegt Nelson Piquet erstmals mit dem Brabham BMW beim Großen Preis von Kanada in Montreal, und 1983 gewinnt der feueräugige Brasilianer zudem auch noch die Weltmeisterschaft. Wie der Brabham zwangsbeatmet durch einen Abgasturbolader, wird die großbürgerlich-agile Limousine 745i, die seit Mitte 1980 die BMW-Hierarchie krönt, ebenso von dem elektronisch geregelten Einspritzsystem L-Jetronic gespeist wie ihre Schwestern 728i, 732i und 735i.

Im Juni 1981 schickt der umfassend retuschierte 5er seinen Vorgänger aufs verdiente Altenteil. 16 Monate später wird das Werk Dingolfing das 1 000 000. Exemplar der Baureihe insgesamt melden. In der Zwischenzeit hat man mit der BMW Iberica S.A. in Madrid die 12. Auslandsvertriebsgesellschaft ins Leben gerufen und sich mit der Tochter BMW Japan keck auf einen prekären Markt vorgewagt. 1982 verkehren bereits 3800 neue BMW auf den Straßen Spaniens, während 5300 den langen Weg ins Land der aufgehenden Sonne gefunden haben. So liest sich der Prolog zu einer Erfolgsstory: Die Zulassungszahlen dort werden sich in den folgenden acht Jahren versechsfachen. Von exotischem Ambiente umfächelt ist die Vorstellung des neuen 3ers in Marokko, just als die Produktion von Numero 2 000 000 des nun nicht mehr ganz so kompakten BMW in Sicht ist. In Milbertshofen sind mit der Produktion von 500 Autos täglich längst die Grenzen jeglichen Wachstums erreicht, und so besiedelt man Neuland in Regensburg. Am 17. November 1986 werden die ersten 3er das dortige Werk 6 verlassen, gefragt wie eh und je trotz des Herausforderers Mercedes-Benz 190, mit dem die Untertürkheimer ihrerseits auf Kollisionskurs zu den Bajuwaren gegangen sind.

Als gewinnorientiertes Unternehmen verlieren die Bayerischen Motoren Werke auch die wirtschaftlich denkenden potentiellen Kunden nicht aus den Augen. 1983 erscheinen der 525e (eta-Konzept) und der 524td im Programm. Der Turbodiesel, mit fast acht Millionen Testkilometern auf dem Buckel, ist das Produkt der BMW Motoren Gesellschaft mbH in Steyr, inzwischen eine reine BMW-Enklave auf österreichischem Terrain. Zu den Aufgaben dieses Triebwerks zählte von Anfang an, das traditionelle Image vom rachitisch lahmenden und dennoch ruppigen Selbst-

Faire feu de tout bois : de deux à douze cylindres (1980–1990)

Lorsque le rapide Helvète Marc Surer remporte, en 1980, le cinquième titre de champion d'Europe de Formule 2 sous les couleurs de BMW, on réfléchit depuis longtemps déjà sur l'utilisation ultérieure du bloc quatre-cylindres de série en compétition automobile. Seule la catégorie reine, la Formule 1, entre encore en ligne de compte. C'est l'affaire de Paul Rosche, surnommé familièrement « Paul la came », en référence à « Paul la niche » Hahnemann, l'ancien roi de la vente. En peu de temps, Paul Rosche fait taire les sceptiques et ceux qui croient toujours tout savoir mieux que les autres : le 13 juin 1982, Nelson Piquet, au Grand Prix du Canada organisé à Montréal, décroche la première victoire avec la Brabham BMW et, en 1983, le Brésilien aux yeux de lynx enfonce le clou en coiffant la couronne de champion du monde. Alimentée comme la Brabham par un turbocompresseur, la grosse et luxueuse limousine 745i couronnant la hiérarchie BMW depuis la mi-1980, est animée d'un système d'injection à commande électronique L-Jetronic au même titre que ses sœurs, les 728i, 732i et 735i.

En juin 1981, la série 5, totalement revue, condamne le modèle précédent à une retraite bien méritée. Seize mois plus tard, l'usine de Dingolfing annonce la fabrication du 1 000 000ᵉ exemplaire de cette gamme. Entre-temps, avec la BMW Iberica S.A., à Madrid, la 12ᵉ société de distribution à l'étranger a été créée. Les Bavarois se lancent, avec courage, sur un marché incertain, avec leur filiale BMW Japon. En 1982, 3800 nouvelles BMW circulent déjà sur les routes d'Espagne alors que 5300 ont pris la (longue) direction de l'empire du Soleil-Levant. C'est le début d'une « success story » : au cours des huit années suivantes, le nombre des immatriculations dans ce pays va être multiplié par six. La présentation de la nouvelle série 3, au Maroc, a lieu dans un cadre exotique juste au moment où le cap du 2 000 000ᵉ exemplaire d'une BMW, qui n'est plus aussi compacte qu'à l'origine, est en passe d'être atteint. À Milbertshofen, avec 500 voitures par jour, on a depuis longtemps dépassé les capacités de production de l'usine et il faut en construire une nouvelle. Elle verra le jour à Ratisbonne. Le 17 novembre 1986, les premières série 3 quittent cette Usine 6, toujours aussi demandées et appréciées malgré la 190 de sa concurrente Mercedes-Benz. Avec ce modèle, le constructeur de Untertürkheim entend croiser le fer avec les Bavarois.

Dans une économie de marché, BMW ne perd pas des yeux les clients potentiels qui ont le sens de l'économie. En 1983, la 525e (concept eta) et la 524td font leur apparition. La turbodiesel, qui a accompli près de huit millions de kilomètres en essai, est le produit de la BMW Motoren Gesellschaft mbH sise à Steyr, qui est entre-temps devenue une enclave de BMW

They called him "Camshaft Paul": racing car engineer Rosche.

Sie nannten ihn „Nocken-Paul": Rennmotoreningenieur Rosche.

Il était surnommé « Paul la came » : l'ingénieur et motoriste Paul Rosche.

17 November 1986, the first 3 series cars left Regensburg's Plant 6, and as always they were in great demand despite the challenge from the Mercedes-Benz 190, signaling the Stuttgart company's intention of competing with the Bavarians head-on in this market niche.

As an economically-oriented enterprise, BMW never lost sight of those potential purchasers who themselves think along economical lines, thus the appearance in 1983 of the 525e (eta concept) and the 524td. The turbo-diesel, which incidentally had almost five million test miles (eight million kilometers) under its belt, was produced by BMW Motoren Gesellschaft mbH in Steyr, which had now become a pure BMW enclave within Austrian territory. Right from the start, one of the top priorities was to get away from the traditional image of the diesel as a rickety, rough-sounding crawler; this six-cylinder engine went about its business with the discretion of an English butler. On top of that, with 115 bhp at 4800 rpm, it was not short of power, albeit hardly in the same class as the mighty M 635CSi which came out a few months later, developed from the power unit of the M1, which from 1985 onwards was also to give the M5 a helping hand.

1983 also saw the market launch of a whole new generation of motorcycles, the K 100 with its water-cooled electronically-controlled four-cylinder engine. And bowing to the contemporary demand for all-wheel drive vehicles, the 325iX with its permanent four-wheel drive was introduced in 1985, and the three-cylinder K 75 was added to the motorcycle range that same year. Falling export sales due to the unfavorable exchange rate with the dollar were compensated for by increased domestic demand, not least due to falls in the price of crude oil.

The 100th anniversary of the invention of the automobile in 1986 was an emotive date for arch-rival Daimler-Benz more than anyone else, but BMW turned the occasion to their advantage by launching the new 7 series in all its glory. The highly-respected trade journal *auto motor und sport,* regarded by many readers as having a pronounced leaning towards Mercedes-Benz, put the 735i ahead of the Mercedes S class in a comparative test. The development of the new top-of-the-range model had cost a cool one-and-a-half billion marks, with 480 7 series sedans being put through the most arduous of paces during more than two million miles (three million kilometers) of testing. But the labor of love had not been in vain, and the first year's production sold out before you could say 'electronic fuel injection'.

The launch of the sleek new M3, a 195 bhp high-performance sedan fitted with spoilers and a four-cylinder four-valve engine set the course for future production-car based motor sport. Also quite an achievement was the production of 5000

Top motorcycle K 1, launched at the IFMA Motor Show in Cologne in September 1988.

Top-Zweirad K 1, vorgestellt auf der IFMA in Köln im September 1988.

Un deux-roues très haut de gamme: la K 1 présentée à l'IFMA, à Cologne, en septembre 1988.

zünder zu beheben: Der Sechszylinder versieht seinen Dienst mit der Diskretion eines englischen Butlers. Er steht überdies mit 115 PS bei 4800 Umdrehungen pro Minute gut im Saft, wenn auch weit entfernt von der ungestümen Potenz des M 635CSi ein paar Monate später, hervorgebracht vom Triebwerk des M1, das ab 1985 auch dem M5 auf die Sprünge helfen wird.

Ebenfalls 1983 bringt man eine völlig neue Generation von Motorrädern auf den Markt, die K 100 mit einer wassergekühlten, elektronisch gesteuerten Vierzylindermaschine. Ein artiger Knicks vor dem allradelnden Zeitgeist: der 325iX mit seinem permanenten Vierradantrieb anno 1985, als das Zweiradspektrum um die Dreizylindermaschine K 75 ergänzt wird. Einbußen beim Export wegen des ungünstigen Wechselkurses zum Dollar lassen sich durch eine erhöhte Nachfrage im Inland ausgleichen, nicht zuletzt weil die Rohölpreise zurückgegangen sind.

Den 100. Geburtstag des Automobils 1986, ein emotionsträchtiges Datum vor allem für den Dauerrivalen Daimler-Benz, nutzt BMW zu einem kraftvollen weißblauen Akzent. Der neue 7er kommt glänzend an. Das angesehene Fachblatt *auto motor und sport,* von vielen Lesern einer ausgeprägten Affinität zum Stuttgarter Stern bezichtigt, siedelt in einem Vergleichstest den 735i vor der Mercedes S-Klasse an. Lohnende Liebesmüh, denn 1,5 Milliarden Mark zehrte die Entwicklung des neuen Großen auf. 480 Exemplare einer Vorserie des 7ers durchlitten auf drei Millionen Testkilometern schwere Autoschicksale. Dafür ist die erste Jahresproduktion im Nu verkauft.

Mit der Vorstellung des pausbackigen geflügelten M3, einer 195 PS starken, flinken Hochleistungslimousine mit einem Vierzylinder-Vierventiler, stellt man die Weichen für den künftigen seriennahen Motorsport. Ein Kunststück auch dies: Zur Homologation bei der Legislative FISA muss eine Verbreitung von 5000 Stück in 12 aufeinanderfolgenden Monaten nachgewiesen werden. Die Europameisterschaft der Tourenwagen gewinnt der Venezianer Roberto Ravaglia auf dem 635CSi. Das BMW-Zweirad erringt ebenfalls einen höchst willkommenen Sieg, als die K 100RS vom Fachjournal *Motorrad* zum vierten Mal hintereinander zur Maschine des Jahres erkoren wird.

Ähnlich Vergnügliches widerfährt dem Zwölfzylinder 750iL, der auf dem Genfer Salon im Frühjahr 1987 seinen Einstand gibt. Als einhelliges Urteil über den Kandidaten braust es durch die abgebrühte Zunft der Motor-Schreiber wie Donnerhall: summa cum laude. Als Kontrapunkt wird dem neuen Flaggschiff der BMW-Flotte auf der IAA im Herbst der Z1 zur Seite gestellt, eine eigenwillige Interpretation der 1986 gegründeten BMW Technik GmbH zum Thema Roadster. Novitäten gibt es auch bei den Motorrädern mit den Enduros R80GS und R100GS. Deren hervorstechendstes Merkmal ist die neue, patentierte Doppelgelenkschwinge, BMW Paralever genannt. Der M3 sammelt bereits emsig Siege und Meisterschaften. Als Dienstwagen seiner Piloten hat er häufig auch abseits der Piste seine Robustheit unter Beweis zu stellen. Nach mehreren ebenso spektakulären wie glimpflichen Unfällen im Straßenverkehr schließen sich die Betroffenen, wie zum Beispiel der Italiener Ivan Capelli, schelmisch zu einer „M3 Destruction League" zusammen.

Da der real existierende 5er ein wenig in die Jahre und aus der Mode gekommen ist, findet 1988 die fällige Wachablösung statt. So gut ist der Neue gelungen, dass er sogar dem 3er aus dem gleichen Hause ein wenig das Wasser abgräbt. Mit der K 1 präsentiert die BMW Motorrad GmbH anlässlich der IFMA ein ungemein sportliches Instrument und wartet mit der willkommenen Innovation Zweirad-ABS auf.

Flawless: BMW K 100 – with a seat height of 30 inches (76 cm) it was suitable also for smaller people.

Tadellose Figur: BMW K 100, mit einer Sitzhöhe von 76 cm auch für kleine Leute geeignet.

Silhouette irréprochable : la BMW K 100 est aussi à la portée des petits gabarits avec une hauteur de selle de 76 cm.

en terre autrichienne. Le cahier des charges était exigeant : balayer l'image traditionnelle de moteurs qui manquaient de reprise, bruyants et sales, qui nuisait au moteur diesel. Le six-cylindres accomplit sa tâche avec la discrétion d'un serviteur britannique. Qui plus est, avec 115 ch à 4800 tr/min, il ne manque pas de vigueur même si, naturellement, il est à des années-lumière de la puissance époustouflante de la M635 CSi, par exemple, qui sortira quelques mois plus tard et qui est propulsée par le moteur de la M1, moteur qui fera aussi de la M5, en 1985, une star parmi les voitures routières.

Toujours en 1983, BMW lance sur le marché une génération inédite de motocyclettes, la K100 avec un moteur à quatre cylindres à refroidissement liquide et gestion électronique. Pour répondre à la demande du public, la 325iX à quatre roues motrices est donc lancée en 1985, et la K75, avec son moteur à trois cylindres, est ajoutée à la gamme des deux-roues la même année. Une baisse des exportations en raison du taux de change défavorable face au dollar est compensée par l'augmentation de la demande en Allemagne, aussi et surtout parce que les prix du pétrole brut ont chuté.

BMW profite du centenaire de l'automobile, en 1986, une année riche en émotions pour son éternelle rivale Daimler-Benz, pour mettre en avant la marque à l'emblème bleu et blanc. La nouvelle série 7 est accueillie à bras ouverts par les clients. La célèbre revue spécialisée *auto motor und sport,* que nombre de ses lecteurs accusent d'avoir des affinités avec l'étoile de Stuttgart, place la 735i avant la Mercedes classe S lors d'un essai comparatif. BMW voit ses efforts récompensés : elle a investi 1,5 milliard de marks dans le développement de son nouveau navire-amiral. 480 série 7 de pré-série ont enduré trois millions de kilomètres d'essais et de tortures, un destin que l'on ne souhaite à aucune voiture. La première année de production est vendue instantanément.

Avec la présentation de la M3, une berline rapide à hautes performances dont les arches de roues joufflues et les ailerons trahissent la sportivité et qui est propulsée par un quatre-cylindres à quatre soupapes de 195 ch, BMW pose des jalons pour la future production d'une série sportive. Autre performance : pour son homologation par la FISA, il est nécessaire d'en avoir produit 5000 exemplaires en douze mois consécutifs. Le Vénitien Roberto Ravaglia, sur une 635CSi, gagne le championnat d'Europe des voitures de tourisme. Sur deux roues, les BMW remportent aussi une victoire chaleureusement accueillie lorsque la K100 RS est sacrée « moto de l'année » pour la quatrième fois consécutive par la revue spécialisée *Motorrad.*

vehicles within 12 consecutive months, as required by the governing body FISA's race regulations. The European Touring Car Championship was won by the Venetian Roberto Ravaglia in a 635CSi. BMW motorcycles also achieved a noteworthy success when the K100RS was chosen as motorcycle of the year for the fourth year in succession by trade journal *Motorrad*.

The reception of the twelve-cylinder 750iL was similarly pleasing. At its launch in 1987 at the Geneva Spring Motor Show, the acclaim of the assembled trade journalists was unanimous and enthusiastic: it passed the test with flying colors. As a counterpoint to the new flagship of the BMW marque, in autumn that year the Z1 was introduced at the Frankfurt Motor Show. This somewhat idiosyncratic variation on the roadster theme was the work of the subsidiary BMW Technik GmbH, which had been founded in 1986. In the motorcycle sector there were also a couple of novelties: the endurance machines R80GS and R100GS. Their most noteworthy characteristic was the new patented double joint swinging fork. The M3 was soon busy accumulating victories and championships. Also serving as the driver's off-circuit company car, the M3 had many opportunities to demonstrate its robustness, and after several spectacular but minor accidents on public roads, those involved, including the Italian Ivan Capelli, declared themselves, tongue-in-cheek, founders of the "M3 Destruction League".

The existing 5 series was getting a little outmoded and long in the tooth, and in 1988 the changing of the guard duly came. The new model was such a success that it even cut a little into sales of BMW's own 3 series. Meanwhile, at the IFMA Motor Show the BMW Motorrad GmbH launched the K1, a tremendously sporty machine incorporating the welcome innovation of two-wheel ABS.

While the 6 series coupé had complemented the first 7 series sedan, this time things were the other way round, with the larger number complementing the smaller: at the 1989 Frankfurt Motor Show the 850i was launched as an adjunct to the latest 7 series. With its feline coiled-spring looks, it bristled with character tempered by a velvety smoothness. The launch of the 850i overshadowed another important development: the introduction of the catalytic converter on all BMW turbo diesels.

The worldwide demand for the whole range of BMWs was so great that, for the first time in the company's history, the year's production and sales broke the half million barrier, with a total of 511,476, of which 332,658 were destined for export. The ever-increasing demand for BMWs, now exclusively fitted with injection engines, was met by introducing continued production during works holidays, first at Dingolfing and then later in Munich and Regensburg too. Driving for the Schnitzer team, Roberto Ravaglia won a coveted title for the fourth successive year when he took the German Touring Car Championship.

Although sales were very sluggish in the five new eastern German states after the Berlin Wall came down, BMW prepared logistically for brisker trade by expanding its network of dealerships. One of the first BMW support centers in the eastern states was the firm Heinz Melkus of Dresden established in 1990. At around the same time BMW was making headlines in the business press with the beginnings of a program of diversification. In the spring, they purchased the KHD Luftfahrttechnik (aviation technology) division from Klöckner-Humboldt-Deutz, and in the summer they founded BMW Rolls-Royce AeroEngines GmbH in Oberursel as a joint venture with Rolls-Royce, throwing in the new acquisition as part of the deal, never forgetting the symbolic message of the blue

Während einst das 6er Coupé auf die erste 7er Limousine einstimmte, handhabt man es diesmal umgekehrt: Auf der IAA 1989 erscheint der 850i als Pendant zum jüngsten 7er, katzenhaft geduckt und voll strotzenden Temperaments, das gleichwohl wie auf Samtpfötchen daherkommt. In seinem Schlagschatten – und dennoch wichtig – vollzieht sich die Einführung des Katalysators für alle BMW Turbodiesel.

Die Nachfrage nach dem Modellprogramm ist weltweit so stark, dass erstmals in der Geschichte des Unternehmens innerhalb eines Jahres mit 511476 Automobilen mehr als eine halbe Million Fahrzeuge produziert und abgesetzt werden. 332658 davon gehen ins Ausland. Der ständig steigenden Nachfrage nach den nur noch mit Einspritzmotoren ausgestatteten Bayern-Mobilen begegnet man schließlich damit, dass erst in Dingolfing, später auch in München und Regensburg während der Betriebsferien weitergearbeitet wird. Als

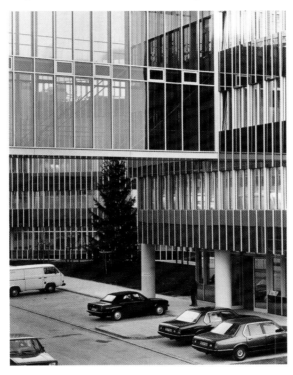

Seat in the glasshouse: BMW Research and Engineering Center (FIZ) in the North of Munich.

Sitz im Glashaus: BMW-Forschungs- und Ingenieurzentrum FIZ im Münchener Norden.

Dans la maison de verre : le centre de recherche et d'ingénierie (FIZ) de BMW, dans la banlieue nord de Munich.

Pilot des Schnitzer-Teams gewinnt Roberto Ravaglia mit der Deutschen Tourenwagen Meisterschaft zum vierten Mal hintereinander ein angepeiltes Championat.

Obwohl die Verkäufe unmittelbar nach dem Fall der Mauer in den fünf neuen Bundesländern nur schleppend anlaufen, bereitet man sich logistisch mit der Erweiterung des Händlernetzes auf mehr vor. Einer der ersten ostdeutschen BMW-Stützpunkte ist die Firma Heinz Melkus im Jahr 1990 in Dresden. Zu diesem Zeitpunkt versorgen die Bayerischen Motoren Werke die Wirtschaftspresse bereits durch beginnende Diversifikation mit Schlagzeilen. Im Frühjahr kauft man Klöckner-Humboldt-Deutz den Zweig KHD Luftfahrttechnik ab. Im Sommer gründet BMW in einem Joint Venture mit Rolls-Royce die BMW Rolls-Royce Aero Engines GmbH in Oberursel und bringt gleichsam als Morgengabe die Neuerwerbung mit in den Deal ein, immer vor dem Hintergrund der symbolischen Botschaft des weißblauen Emblems. Natürlich, sagt Eberhard von Kuenheim, erinnere er sich in diesem

La douze-cylindres 750iL, dont le lancement a lieu au Salon de Genève au printemps 1987, peut, elle aussi, être assurée d'un tel succès. Les journalistes spécialisés, qui en ont pourtant vu d'autres, rendent un verdict unanime sur le nouveau navire-amiral : il a passé le test haut la main. Aux antipodes de ce magnifique bâtiment de la flotte BMW est présentée au Salon de l'Automobile de Francfort de l'automne 1987, la Z1, une interprétation très personnelle de la société BMW Technik GmbH, fondée en 1986, sur le thème du roadster. Mais il y a aussi des nouveautés dans le segment des motos avec les enduros R80GS et R100GS. Leur principale caractéristique technique est la nouvelle fourche oscillante à double articulation que BMW a fait breveter sous le nom de « Paralever ». La M3, quant à elle, engrange sans répit victoires et titres de championnat. Voiture de fonction de ses pilotes en dehors des pistes, elle doit souvent apporter la preuve de sa solidité : après plusieurs accidents de circulation aussi spectaculaires que bénins, ces mauvais larrons, tel l'Italien Ivan Capelli, se regroupent ironiquement en une « M3 Destruction League ».

La série 5, quant à elle, commence à se démoder et n'est plus au top. La relève est assurée en 1988. La nouvelle voiture est si réussie qu'elle coupe même un peu l'herbe sous le pied de la série 3 de la même écurie. Avec la K1, la BMW Motorrad GmbH présente, à l'occasion de l'IFMA, un modèle ultrasportif qui se distingue par une innovation bienvenue, un ABS de moto.

Alors que, jadis, le coupé de la série 6 avait annoncé la première limousine de la série 7, cette fois-ci, les choses se passent à l'inverse : au Salon de l'Automobile de Francfort de 1989, la 850i est présentée comme une alternative à la dernière série 7, trapue comme un tigre prêt à bondir et pleine de tempérament, mais sans sortir ses griffes de ses pattes de velours. Elle en ferait presque oublier une innovation pourtant capitale : l'introduction du pot catalytique qui équipera toutes les BMW turbodiesel.

Le monde entier s'arrache les BMW, tous modèles confondus, si bien que, pour la première fois dans l'histoire de l'entreprise, l'entreprise produit et vend bel et bien plus d'un demi-million de voitures en un an : 511476, dont 332658 à l'étranger. La demande croissante pour ces voitures allemandes, qui ne sont plus équipées que de moteurs à injection, contraint finalement les usines à ne pas cesser la production pendant les vacances annuelles, tout d'abord à Dingolfing puis, plus tard, à Munich et à Ratisbonne. Roberto Ravaglia, pilote de l'équipe Schnitzer, avec le championnat d'Allemagne des voitures de tourisme, remporte pour la quatrième fois consécutive un championnat dont BMW avait fait son objectif avoué.

Bien que les ventes démarrent lentement dans les cinq nouveaux Länder après la chute du Mur de Berlin, BMW met en place la logistique nécessaire en développant rapidement son réseau de concessionnaires. L'une des premières antennes de BMW dans l'ex-Allemagne de l'Est est la société Heinz Melkus, à Dresde, qui est fondée en 1990. BMW annonce déjà à la presse économique sa diversification prochaine. Au printemps, BMW achète à Klöckner-Humboldt-Deutz sa filiale KHD Luftfahrttechnik (technique aéronautique). En été, en créant un joint-venture avec Rolls-Royce, BMW fonde la BMW Rolls-Royce Aero Engines GmbH, à Oberursel. BMW apporte à la nouvelle entité la notoriété de l'emblème bleu et blanc. Naturellement, Eberhard von Kuenheim fera savoir qu'il se rappela à ce moment là seulement des origines de BMW. Lorsque le *Sunday Times* annonce, en juillet 1992, que les Bavarois sont également and white emblems. Naturally, Eberhard von Kuenheim let it be known, this moment reminded him of BMW's origins. On the other hand, when the *Sunday Times* reported in July 1992 that BMW was interested in the automobile division of the historic English company, this was flatly denied.

BMW's latest subsidiary, BMW Fahrzeugtechnik (vehicle technology) GmbH is situated on land steeped in history. This plant, located in the Eisenach industrial district Deubachshof, has been producing large tools since 1992. On the occasion of BMW's first Research Day, the FIZ Forschungs- and Ingenieurzentrum (Research and Engineering Center) was opened on Hanauer Straße in Munich, creating jobs for more than 6000 scientists and engineers, plus their support teams.

Towards the end of the year the third generation 3 series was launched at the Istres test site in the South of France, initially in a four-door version fitted with the latest four-cylinder engine and the current four-valve straight six. Since 1988, BMW had been the sole motorcycle manufacturer to offer an anti-block braking system, fitting it to both the K 100 and the K 75. Now came a further first: a three-way catalytic converter for the models K 1 and K 100 RS. And there had also been the usual good news on the sporting front, for example victories in the 24-hour races at both the Nürburgring and in Spa.

BMW Worldwide (1990–2004)

On its 75th birthday in 1991, BMW was anything but a frail old-timer of a company, dreaming of days gone by. A judicious glance in the rear view mirror was accompanied by the more important act of reading the road ahead, with special reference to the technology of the future. At the Frankfurt Motor Show, a thoroughbred electric car bearing the famous blue and white emblem, called simply the E1, was waiting in the wings to make its noiseless entrance. A preview of the future is also to be found among the exhibits in the BMW Museum under the heading "Zeithorizonte" (time horizons), which in equal parts delves into the history of the car and looks ahead at the automobile world of tomorrow.

Once again, BMW emerged relatively unscathed from the global recession of the early 1990s. Falling export sales were more than made up for by increasing demand for BMW's products in the new eastern German states. As from September 1991, ABS was fitted as standard in all production BMWs. In autumn, along with a number of other social benefits, a new system of working hours was introduced at the Munich site, whereby personnel working hours were decoupled from production facility running times.

In 1992 a two-door model was added to the 3 series, which was immediately declared to be a coupé on the strength of its pleasingly sporting lines. In the dramatic and picturesque surroundings of the Monaco Grand Prix in May, the thoroughbred McLaren F1 was presented, a co-production with the English Formula 1 constructor, and a spectacular collection of sheer superlatives. These include the price tag of 1.5 million marks, rather tending to rule out the average salary earner as a potential customer. Similarly, opportunities to test this projectile's top speed of 231 mph (371 kph) tend to be limited, especially at rush hour in big cities. Even highly experienced car drivers can find this monster a little hot to handle, as McLaren boss Ron Dennis and future BMW boss Pischetsrieder demonstrated when they each managed the costly feat of writing off an F1.

The widest product range in the company's history was responsible for a new production record. When the factory

Augenblick der Ursprünge von BMW. Als hingegen die *Sunday Times* im Juli 1992 meldet, die Bayern seien am Autozweig der britischen Edelmarke interessiert, winken diese kühl ab.

Auf geschichtsgetränktem Boden begibt man sich auch mit der jüngsten Tochter BMW Fahrzeugtechnik GmbH. Im Eisenacher Gewerbeviertel Deubachshof fertigt dieses Werk ab 1992 Großwerkzeuge. Im Rahmen des ersten BMW Forschungstages wird das Forschungs- und Ingenieurzentrum FIZ an der Hanauer Straße in München eröffnet. Es schafft Arbeitsplätze für über 6000 Wissenschaftler und Ingenieure sowie ihre Teams.

Gegen Ende des Jahres wird auf dem Testgelände von Istres in Südfrankreich die dritte 3er Generation vorgestellt, zunächst ein Viertürer mit den neuesten Vierzylindern und den aktuellen Vierventil-Reihensechszylindern. Schon seit 1988 bietet BMW als einziger Zweiradhersteller ein Antiblockiersystem an, nun nicht mehr nur für die K 100, sondern auch für die K 75. Eine weitere Premiere: der geregelte Katalysator für die Modelle K 1 und K 100 RS. Auch im Sport hat man wie üblich Erfreuliches vorzuweisen, zum Beispiel Doppelsiege bei den beiden 24-Stunden-Rennen auf dem Nürburgring und in Spa.

Weißblau weltweit (1990–2004)

An ihrem 75. Geburtstag 1991 sind die Bayerischen Motoren Werke weit davon entfernt, als gebrechlicher Firmen-Senior längst Vergangenem nachzuträumen. Zum wohldosierten Blick in den Rückspiegel gesellt sich vor allem der nach vorn, hin zu den Technologien der Zukunft. Auf der IAA wartet ein reinrassiges Elektroauto mit dem weißblauen Sigel, schlicht E1 genannt, auf seinen lautlosen Einsatz. Eine Vorschau auf Künftiges decken auch die Exponate des BMW-Museums unter dem Motto „Zeithorizonte" ab, ein Ausflug in die Geschichte ebenso wie in die Zukunft zum Auto von morgen und seinem Umfeld.

Die globale Unruhe Anfang der neunziger Jahre lässt BMW wieder relativ ungeschoren. Einbußen auf den Exportmärkten lassen sich durchaus wettmachen, weil sich in den neuen Bundesländern die Nachfrage nach automobiler Markenware aus Bayern belebt. Ab September 1991 gehört ABS zur Grundausstattung aller serienmäßigen BMW. Im Herbst wird – neben anderen sozialen Segnungen im BMW-Land – ein neues Arbeitszeitmodell für den Standort München eingeführt, durch das die persönliche Dienstzeit der Werktätigen von der Laufzeit der Produktionsanlagen abgekoppelt werden kann.

1992 erweitert man das 3er Spektrum um einen Zweitürer, wegen seiner gefällig-sportiven Linie kurzerhand als Coupé deklariert. In das dramatisch-pittoreske Ambiente des Grand Prix von Monaco im Mai eingebettet wird die Präsentation des Vollbluts McLaren F1, entstanden in Koproduktion mit der britischen Monoposto-Manufaktur und spektakuläres Puzzle aus lauter Superlativen. Einer davon ist sein Preis von 1,5 Millionen Mark, der eine große Zahl von Erwerbstätigen aus dem Kreis der möglichen Kunden ausgrenzt. Auch lässt sich die Spitze des flachen Projektils – 371 Stundenkilometer – zumindest zu den Hauptstoßzeiten des Straßenverkehrs in Ballungsräumen selten ausfahren. Dass selbst kundige Autofahrer mit soviel Feuer ihre liebe Not haben, beweisen in Bälde sowohl McLaren-Boss Ron Dennis als auch der künftige BMW-Chef Pischetsrieder, indem sie je einen F1 zerstören.

intéressés par la branche automobile de cette marque britannique de prestige, Munich fait la sourde oreille.

Avec la dernière filiale, la BMW Fahrzeugtechnik GmbH, elle revient sur son terrain de prédilection. Dans la zone industrielle de Deubachshof, à Eisenach, cette usine fabrique, à partir de 1992, de grosses machines-outils. À l'occasion des premières Journées BMW de la Recherche, le centre de recherche et d'ingénierie FIZ est inauguré à la Hanauer Strasse, à Munich. Il emploie plus de 6000 scientifiques et ingénieurs ainsi que leurs équipes.

Vers la fin de l'année 1992, la troisième génération de la série 3 est présentée à Istres, dans le Midi de la France, tout d'abord sous la forme d'une quatre-portes avec le tout nouveau quatre-cylindres et les modernes six-cylindres en ligne à quatre soupapes. Depuis 1988, BMW est l'unique constructeur de motos à proposer un système antiblocage, non seulement pour la K 100, mais aussi pour la K 75. Autre première : le pot catalytique réglé pour les modèles K 1 et K 100 RS. En compétition aussi, BMW peut se prévaloir de nombreux succès : ainsi des doublés aux deux courses de 24 Heures, au Nürburgring et à Spa.

BMW dans le monde (1990–2004)

En 1991, année de son 75e anniversaire, BMW n'envisage pas une seconde de prendre sa retraite. Même si, nostalgique, elle jette un coup d'œil dans le rétroviseur, elle regarde devant elle, et l'avenir, ce sont les nouvelles technologies. Au Salon de l'Automobile de Francfort, une voiture à propulsion totalement électrique sous le logo bleu et blanc, sobrement baptisée E1, attend de prendre la route en silence. Les modèles exposés au musée BMW retracent l'histoire de l'automobile et présentent ce que sera la voiture de demain.

Une fois de plus, la crise économique mondiale du début des années 1990 épargne presque BMW. Le manque à gagner sur les marchés d'exportation est largement compensé par les achats des nouveaux Länder, où la demande d'automobiles en provenance de Bavière ne fait qu'augmenter. À partir de septembre 1991, l'ABS est monté en série de toutes les BMW. À l'automne – il ne s'agit que d'une mesure parmi tous les avantages sociaux existants outre-Rhin – un nouvel aménagement du temps de travail est mis en place sur le site de Munich : les horaires de travail des ouvriers s'adaptent au planning de fonctionnement des machines pour une meilleure productivité.

En 1992, la gamme de la série 3 s'enrichit d'une deux-portes que l'on qualifie sans hésiter coupé en raison de ses lignes sportives et séduisantes. Au Grand Prix de Monaco, en mai, a lieu la présentation d'un pur-sang baptisé McLaren F1, une coproduction réalisée avec le constructeur de monoplaces britannique, qui suscite une spectaculaire collection de superlatifs. Son prix, de 1,5 million de marks, en est un bon exemple. Celui-ci exclut d'office le salarié moyen des acheteurs potentiels. Par ailleurs, la vitesse de pointe de ce projectile sur route, 371 km/h, pourra rarement être atteinte, tout au moins aux heures de pointe dans les grandes agglomérations. Même des conducteurs aussi confirmés que Ron Dennis, le p.-d.g. de McLaren, ou le futur chef de BMW, Bernd Pischetsrieder, prouvent qu'il n'est pas aisé de dompter tant de tempérament : chacun d'eux détruira une F1.

gates were closed for the Christmas break on 23 December 1992, 598,000 automobiles had left the plants, including 100,000 3 series coupés. More than 35,000 motorcycles were sold during the same period, also a new record, suitably marking the 70th anniversary of two-wheeler production. After a meticulous search for an ideal location in the United States, BMW selected Greenville, near Spartanburg in South Carolina, and in September 1994 the first 318i rolled off the production line.

On 13 May 1993 Bernd Pischetsrieder became the new president of the executive board. Pischetsrieder, who hails from Munich, faced a double challenge. Firstly, he replaced the masterful Prussian Eberhard von Kuenheim, who turned BMW from a medium-sized car and motorcycle manufacturer into one of the 15 biggest business enterprises in Germany, also enjoying an excellent reputation on world markets. Secondly, the shockwaves of the global depression were now buffeting BMW. Despite this, the company remained in the black and had the satisfaction at the end of the year of having sold more units than Daimler-Benz, with figures of 534,000 as against 508,000. On top of this, BMW's showing at the Frankfurt Motor Show was a major talking point, as they put themselves forward as suppliers of mobility, under the slogan "Mobilität ist Leben" (Mobility is Life). Among other things, this new emphasis on mobility involved adding trekking and mountain bikes, manufactured by BMW themselves, to the company's range of products.

Right from the beginning of 1994 BMW went on the offensive on several fronts. On 31 January, it was announced that BMW had acquired Rover, and with it such desirable English brand names as Mini, Land-Rover and Range Rover, as well as the dormant legend MG. This welcome news came as a bolt from the blue, since the British company's links with the Japanese giant Honda had seemed stronger than ever. The reasons for this surprise acquisition were given by Bernd Pischetsrieder in the sober language of the official statement: "The product ranges of the two manufacturers complement each other almost perfectly. Our differing regional strengths will be reinforced. Our goal now is to lead two strong, independent automobile enterprises into the future, presenting a united front to our competitors". The year also saw the carefully orchestrated introduction of three new products: a short version of the 3 series, a new 7 series, now powered exclusively by eight and 12-cylinder engines, and a new 5 series of discrete and restrained appearance. BMW de Mexico S.A. in Toluca became the 16th BMW subsidiary, and in Peking a BMW agency rolled up its sleeves and got down to work.

The headlong rush towards internationalization once again made the headlines during 1995. BMW signed an agreement for the CKD (completely knocked down, i.e. delivered in parts) assembly of motorcycles in Indonesia, set up a subsidiary in Brazil, acquired Designworks (USA) as a BMW subsidiary, set up an automobile assembly facility in Vietnam and their first dealership on the Philippines, and yet more BMW subsidiaries were founded in Norway, Finland and South Korea. And with the Z3, a product of the Spartanburg plant, a BMW was launched that for the first time had not been produced in Germany. Hollywood provided invaluable free publicity when, in the latest James Bond film, the spy with the license to kill dispensed justice to the bad guys driving a Z3, in place of the speedy machines from Aston Martin and Lotus that had accompanied him in the past. Critics pointed out that the Z3 looked good but was underpowered. This was put right in 1996 by the introduction of a six-cylinder version and in 1997 by the appearance of the M roadster with its

Die bislang breiteste Produktpalette in der Geschichte des Unternehmens ist die Basis für einen neuen Produktionsrekord. Als am 23. Dezember 1992 die Fabriktore geschlossen werden, haben 598 000 Automobile die Werke verlassen, davon 100 000 3er Coupés. Mehr als 35 000 Motorräder waren es im gleichen Zeitraum, ebenfalls ein Bestwert pünktlich zum 70. Jubiläum der Zweiradfertigung. Am Ende einer sorgfältigen Standortsuche in den Vereinigten Staaten entscheidet man sich für Greenville bei Spartanburg in South Carolina, wo im September 1994 der erste 318i vom Band rollen wird.

Am 13. Mai 1993 bekommt das Unternehmen mit Bernd Pischetsrieder einen neuen Vorstandsvorsitzenden. Der Münchener blickt gelassen einer doppelten Herausforderung entgegen: Zum einen beerbt er den souveränen Ostpreußen Eberhard von Kuenheim, der die BMW AG von einem Auto- und Motorradhersteller im Mittelfeld zu einem der 15 größten Wirtschaftsunternehmen in Deutschland und zur Weltmarke von hohem Ansehen geführt hat. Zum anderen rütteln die Ausläufer der weltweiten Wirtschaftskrise nun auch an den Pforten von BMW. Gleichwohl bleibt man im schwarzen Bereich und wärmt sich an der Genugtuung, am Ende mit 534 000 Einheiten mehr hergestellt zu haben als Daimler-Benz mit 508 000. Für Gesprächsstoff sorgt der Auftritt auf der IAA in Frankfurt, wo sich BMW unter dem Slogan „Mobilität ist Leben" als Anbieter ebendieser Mobilität empfiehlt. Diese Mobilmachung neuen Stils bedeutet unter anderem, dass man nun auch Trekking- und Mountainbikes aus eigener Fertigung feilbietet.

Schon zu Beginn des Jahres 1994 gibt man sich offensiv auf etlichen Kriegsschauplätzen. Am 31. Januar wird bekannt, BMW habe Rover und damit englische Schmankerl wie den Mini, den Land-Rover und den Range Rover sowie die brachliegende Legende MG erworben. Die frohe Botschaft kommt aus heiterem Himmel, da die Bindungen der Briten an den japanischen Giganten Honda stärker zu sein schienen. Die Gründe für den Überraschungskauf erläutert Bernd Pischetsrieder in der strengen Sprache der offiziellen Statements: „Die Produktprogramme der beiden Hersteller ergänzen sich fast ideal. Unsere regional unterschiedlichen Stärken werden sich potenzieren. Unser Ziel ist es jetzt, zwei unabhängige starke Automobilunternehmen in Zukunft gemeinsam in den Wettbewerb zu führen." Im übrigen speist man in wohlüberlegter Dramaturgie drei Novitäten in den Markt ein: die Kurzversion des 3ers, einen neuen 7er, der nur noch von Acht- und Zwölfzylindern befeuert wird, und einen neuen 5er von dezent-zurückhaltendem Erscheinungsbild. Mit der BMW de Mexico S.A. in Toluca wird die 16. Tochtergesellschaft gegründet und in Peking krempelt eine BMW-Vertretung die Ärmel hoch.

Ein ungestümer Drang zur Internationalisierung spiegelt sich in den Schlagzeilen des Jahres 1995 wider: BMW schließt einen Vertrag ab über die CKD-Montage (für *completely knocked down,* d. h. in Teilen angeliefert) von Motorrädern in Indonesien, BMW ruft eine Tochtergesellschaft in Brasilien ins Leben, Designworks (USA) wird BMW-Tochter, BMW eröffnet einen Automobilmontagebetrieb in Vietnam und einen ersten Händlerbetrieb auf den Philippinen, BMW-Tochtergesellschaften werden in Norwegen, Finnland und Südkorea gegründet. Mit dem Z3, einem Produkt der Filiale Spartanburg, geht erstmals ein BMW-Auto an den Verkaufsstart, das nicht in Deutschland produziert wird. Hollywood leistet Schützenhilfe: Bei seiner jüngsten Schurken-Hatz rückt James Bond der organisierten Niedertracht mit einem Z3 zu Leibe wie früher schon mit flinken Erzeugnissen von Aston Martin und Lotus. Schön, aber zu schwach motorisiert sei der

Restrained optimism: Chairman of the board until January 1999, Bernd Pischetsrieder.

Verhaltener Optimismus: Vorstandsvorsitzer bis Januar 1999 Bernd Pischetsrieder.

Optimisme contenu: le président du directoire jusqu'en janvier 1999, Bernd Pischetsrieder.

La gamme est maintenant la plus diversifiée qu'il soit dans l'histoire de l'entreprise. C'est un tremplin idéal pour battre un nouveau record de production. Lorsque l'usine ferme ses portes, le 23 décembre 1992, 598 000 voitures sont sorties de chaîne, dont 100 000 coupés de la série 3. Plus de 35 000 motos ont été produites durant la même période, ce qui est également un record, qui arrive à point nommé pour le 70e anniversaire de la fabrication de deux-roues. À l'issue d'une longue recherche pour trouver le site idéal aux États-Unis, Greenville a fait l'unanimité. C'est donc près de Spartanburg, en Caroline du Sud, que la première 318i sortira de chaînes en septembre 1994.

Le 13 mai 1993, l'entreprise voit un nouveau p.-d.g. prendre les commandes avec Bernd Pischetsrieder comme président du directoire. Le Munichois ne se laisse pas impressionner par le double défi à relever: d'une part, il succède à Eberhard von Kuenheim, authentique aristocrate de Prusse orientale, qui a transformé BMW AG de constructeur de voitures et de motos de taille moyenne en l'une des 15 plus grandes entreprises économiques d'Allemagne et en une marque mondiale de grand prestige. D'autre part, les ondes de choc de la crise économique mondiale ébranlent maintenant aussi les fondations de BMW. Ceci n'empêche pas que les bilans soient toujours positifs et, à la fin de l'exercice, BMW peut se féliciter, avec 534 000 voitures, d'en avoir fabriqué plus que Daimler-Benz (avec 508 000). Au Salon de l'Automobile de Francfort, où BMW proclame que «La mobilité, c'est la vie», les Munichois font sensation en présentant ce qu'ils entendent par mobilité: la vente de vélos de trekking et de VTT de fabrication maison qui viennent s'ajouter à la gamme des produits existants.

Dès le début de l'année 1994, BMW passe à l'offensive sur tous les fronts: le 31 janvier, la marque annonce le rachat de Rover et, par la même occasion, de quelques modèles britanniques de grande réputation comme la Mini, la Land-Rover et la Range Rover ainsi que la légendaire MG à

Joachim Milberg: 1999–2001 chairman of the board of directors, moved to the company's supervisory board in 2002, becoming chairman in May 2004.

Joachim Milberg, 1999–2001 Vorstandvorsitzender, wechselt 2002 in den Aufsichtsrat und übernimmt im Mai 2004 dessen Vorsitz.

Joachim Milberg: président du directoire de 1999 à 2001, il a rejoint, en 2002, le conseil de surveillance, dont il a repris la présidence en mai 2004.

flared fenders. In the meantime, the BMW motorcycle division set a new record with sales of around 50,000.

Both production and turnover records tumbled once again in 1996 as car sales reached 1,150,000 (made up of 644,100 BMWs and 507,254 Rovers), augmented by motorcycle sales of 50,500, and the turnover rose to 52.3 billion marks, double the figure at the end of the 1980s. BMW and its satellites employed a workforce of 116,112. The 5 and 7 series were voted by the readers of *auto motor und sport* the best cars in the world. The BMW Rolls-Royce aviation engines received their international license. The decision over new production capacity fell in favor of an engine plant in Hams Hall, England and a joint enterprise with the Chrysler Corporation, which would produce small four-cylinder engines in South America.

Two very different exhibits at the Frankfurt Motor Show in 1997, the M coupé and the motorcycle one-off, the C1, had one thing in common: both protected their drivers from the elements with a roof. At the same time, BMW threw down the gauntlet to Daimler-Benz in motor sport's blue riband event as well, announcing their return to Formula 1 in the year 2000, as partners to the Williams team. The eye-catcher at the 32nd Tokyo Motor Show in October was the large Z07 convertible, in the long-neglected tradition of the 507. In 1999, it went into series production as the Z8, and 5700 of these magnificent retros were produced up to 2003.

In 1998 it turned out that the *Sunday Times* had been right all along in 1992. BMW AG really was interested in acquiring the automobile division of the blue-blooded Rolls-Royce marque. After a long and confusing wrangle with the Volkswagen group, BMW announced in a press release on 28 July that they had acquired the rights to the Rolls-Royce name for 40 million pounds sterling. Rolls-Royce Motor Cars was granted a license to manufacture and distribute Rolls-Royce cars until 31 December 2002.

Neue, mäkeln manche. Also schafft man mit der Sechszylindervariante von 1996 und mit dem ab 1997 bärenstark und mit üppigen Kotflügelverbreiterungen daherkommenden M roadster Abhilfe. Die BMW-Sparte Motorrad verbucht mit rund 50 000 Verkäufen einen neuen Bestwert.

Rekorde erzielen 1996 auch Produktion und Umsatz des Konzerns: 1,15 Millionen Automobile (644 100 BMW und 507 254 Rover im weiteren Sinne) sowie 50 500 Motorräder erreichen ihre glücklichen Kunden. Der Umsatz steigt auf 52,3 Milliarden Mark, doppelt soviel wie Ende der achtziger Jahre. 116 112 Mitarbeiter werken für BMW und seine Trabanten. Der 5er und der 7er werden von den Lesern von *auto motor und sport* zu den besten Autos der Welt gewählt. Die BMW-Rolls-Royce-Flugtriebwerke erhalten ihre internationale Zulassung. Die Entscheidung für neue Produktionskapazitäten fällt zugunsten eines Motorenwerks im englischen Hams Hall und eines gemeinsamen Unternehmens mit der Chrysler Corporation, das in Südamerika kleinere Vierzylindermotoren herstellen wird.

Die beiden ungleichen Exponate M coupé und Zweiradstudie C1 auf der Frankfurter IAA 1997 verbindet, dass ihre Fahrer ein festes Dach über dem Kopf vor den Unbilden der Witterung schützt. Zugleich wirft man Daimler-Benz den Fehdehandschuh auch im Spitzensport mit der Ankündigung hin, die Bayerischen Motoren Werke würden im Jahre 2000 in die Formel 1 zurückkehren – als Partner des Williams-Rennstalls. Blickfang auf der 32. Motor Show in Tokio im Oktober ist das große Cabriolet Z07 in der lange vernachlässigten Tradition des 507, wenn auch nur ein Unikat. Als Z8 ging es 1999 in Serie, und bis 2003 entstanden 5700 dieser prächtigen Retro-Exemplare.

1998 erweist sich, allerdings mit Verzögerung, dass die *Sunday Times* 1992 doch recht hatte: Die BMW AG interessiert sich in der Tat für die Abteilung Automobile der Nobelmarke Rolls-Royce. Am Ende eines verwirrenden Gerangels mit dem VW-Konzern erwirbt BMW, wie in einer Pressemitteilung vom 28. Juli ausgeführt wird, die Rolls-Royce-Namensrechte für 40 Millionen Pfund Sterling. Man erteilt Rolls-Royce Motor Cars eine bis zum 31. Dezember 2002 befristete Lizenz für die Fertigung und den Vertrieb von Rolls-Royce-Fahrzeugen.

Die britische Nobelmarke bekommt von der BMW Group in der Nachbarschaft der südenglischen Rennstrecke Goodwood ein neues Zuhause spendiert. Dort fertigen seit 2003 gut 300 hochmotivierte Mitarbeiter in einer harmonischen Synthese aus Handarbeit und Präzisionstechnik den Phantom. Im Frühjahr 2004, anlässlich des 100-jährigen Jubiläums von Rolls-Royce, wird auch die Cabrio-Studie 100 EX präsentiert. Den traditionellen Hubraum von 6,75 Litern respektierend, hat BMW einen neuen Motor für seinen automobilen Aristokraten entwickelt. Bereits bei 3500/min entfaltet der V12 mit 460 PS sein maximales Drehmoment von 720 Newtonmetern, und die Beschleunigung des gewichtigen Herren in 5,5 Sekunden von 0 auf 100 Stundenkilometer ist phänomenal. Trotz der nur 550 Kilo wiegenden Aluminium-Spaceframe-Karosserie aus dem BMW-Werk Dingolfing liegt das Gesamtgewicht bei zweieinhalb Tonnen. Die 60 Holzelemente der Innenverkleidung sind in bis zu 40 Schichten verleimt, und auch das aus Sachsen stammende Leder besitzt exklusiven Charakter: Es ist so durchgefärbt, dass es weder ausbleichen noch Risse bekommen kann.

Ein Riss anderer Art durchzieht noch vor der Jahrtausendwende die personelle Struktur des BMW-Vorstandes: Bernd Pischetsrieder und sein Vorstandskollege für Vertrieb und Entwicklung, Dr. Wolfgang Reitzle, werden verabschiedet.

l'agonie. Cette acquisition surprend tout le monde, car on croyait que les liens unissant le constructeur britannique au géant japonais Honda étaient plus forts que jamais. Bernd Pischetsrieder explique dans une déclaration officielle les raisons de cet achat inattendu : « Les programmes des deux constructeurs se complètent parfaitement. Nos points forts, bien que différents au plan régional, vont se compléter. Notre objectif maintenant consiste à devenir deux entreprises automobiles indépendantes et fortes, présentant un front uni face à la concurrence. » Pour le reste, selon une stratégie mûrement réfléchie, BMW lance sur le marché trois nouveautés : une version raccourcie de la série 3, une nouvelle série 7 désormais propulsée exclusivement par des huit et douze-cylindres, et une nouvelle série 5 au style discret qui est une grande réussite. Avec la constitution de BMW de Mexico S.A., à Toluca, la 16e filiale voit le jour et, à Pékin, une représentation de BMW s'attaque au marché chinois.

Les manchettes des journaux de 1995 confirment cette stratégie d'internationalisation : BMW passe un contrat pour un montage CKD (« completely knocked down », c'est-à-dire livrées en pièces détachées) de motos en Indonésie ; crée une filiale au Brésil, tandis que Designworks (aux États-Unis) devient une filiale de BMW ; inaugure aussi une chaîne de montage au Viêt-nam ; et ouvre sa première succursale aux Philippines ; des filiales BMW sont aussi fondées en Norvège, en Finlande et en Corée du Sud. Avec la Z3, qui est fabriquée dans la filiale de Spartanburg, la première BMW de l'histoire qui n'ait pas été produite en Allemagne apparaît sur le marché. Avec un coup de pouce de Hollywood : dans son dernier film, James Bond s'attaque au crime organisé avec une Z3, à l'instar de son prédécesseur au volant d'Aston Martin et de Lotus de légende. Certains critiquent cette Z3, certes, fort belle, mais pas assez musclée. On y remédie donc avec la version six-cylindres en 1996 et on fait taire toutes les mauvaises langues, en 1997, avec le M roadster aux passages de roues élargis. Les motocyclettes BMW signent, elles, un nouveau record avec quelque 50 000 motos vendues.

Autres records, en 1996, pour la production et le chiffre d'affaires réalisés par le groupe avec 1,15 million de voitures (644 100 BMW et 507 254 Rover) et 50 500 motos qui vont combler leurs heureux propriétaires. En hausse, le chiffre d'affaires passe à 52,3 milliards de marks, soit deux fois plus qu'à la fin des années 1980. 116 112 salariés travaillent pour BMW et ses filiales. Les lecteurs d'*auto motor und sport* consacrent la série 5 et la série 7 meilleures voitures du monde. Les usines de moteurs d'avions BMW/Rolls-Royce obtiennent leur agrément international. La décision d'accroître les capacités de production est prise en faveur d'une usine de moteurs sise à Hams Hall, en Angleterre, et d'un *joint-venture* avec la Chrysler Corporation, qui va fabriquer de petits moteurs à quatre-cylindres en Amérique du Sud.

Un point commun relie deux modèles aux antipodes, le M coupé et le prototype de scooter-moto C1, au Salon de l'Automobile de Francfort de 1997. Désormais un toit en dur protège leur conducteur des intempéries. Simultanément, Munich défie Daimler-Benz dans la catégorie reine de la compétition automobile, en annonçant que BMW fera son retour en Formule 1 en 2000 – en tant que partenaire de l'écurie Williams. La vedette sur le stand BMW au 32e Motor Show de Tokyo, en octobre, c'est le gros cabriolet Z07, reprenant la tradition longtemps négligée de la 507, bien qu'il ne s'agisse que d'un exemplaire unique. Elle a été commercialisée en série en 1999 sous le vocable Z8. 5700 exemplaires de cette magnifique voiture néo-rétro ont été produits jusqu'en 2003.

The BMW group provides the noble British mark with a new home in the neighborhood of the Goodwood racetrack in southern England. Since 2003, 300 highly motivated employees have produced the Phantom in a harmonious synthesis of craftsmanship and precision technology. The Cabriolet 100 EX is presented in the spring of 2004 to mark Rolls-Royce's 100 year anniversary. BMW have developed a new engine for its aristocratic automobile, respecting the traditional 6.75-liter capacity. The V12 with its 460 bhp unfolds its maximum 720 Newton meter torque at a mere 3500 rpm, while the weighty gentleman's acceleration from 0 to 62 mph (100 kph) in 5.5 seconds is phenomenal. Despite the aluminum space frame chassis from the BMW Dingolfing works weighing only 550 kilograms, the vehicle's total weight lies by two and a half tons. The wooden sections of the interior cladding are made of up to 40 layers glued together, and the leather from Saxony also possesses exclusive qualities: it is so thoroughly dyed that it neither fades nor does it become cracked.

Another kind of fissure runs through personnel structure of the BMW board ahead of the new millennium: Bernd Pischetsrieder and his board colleague responsible for sales and development Dr. Wolfgang Reitzle, take their leave. With them, BMW also rids itself of its British ballast – Rover. The takeover sum put up by the previous Rover boss John Towers for the "Phoenix" capital rescue group was more of a symbolic nature: ten Pounds Sterling. Land-Rover goes to Jaguar, where Reitzle is to be the new boss. Prof. Dr. Joachim Milberg, new chairman of the BMW board of directors since January 1999, receives the Mini brand to round off the production palette at the lower end. Mini then rises like a phoenix from the ashes!

The unexpected rise in the fortunes of the Mini follows the Rover investment debacle that for the last time in the 1999 business year manifests itself with a loss of a billion. In 2001, 42,395 vehicles are produced at the Mini works in Oxford, in 2002 it is 160,037, and in 2003 the works' manager Anton Heiss hits the capacity limit of the paint shop with 174,366 Minis. It could hardly keep up in applying the little cult vehicles' ecologically friendly – paint with a water-soluble base – war paint. Even so, Heiss prophesizes a further increase in production as the Mini receives a

Side entrance: the C1 concept car, a potential city vehicle for the next millennium.

Für Seiteneinsteiger: die Studie C1, ein potentielles Stadtgefährt für das nächste Jahrtausend.

Voiture ou scooter? Le prototype C1, l'engin urbain du prochain millénaire.

Well-known face: the Z07 roadster, available as the Z8 from spring 2000, is delightfully reminiscent of the legendary 507 from the 1950s.

Bekanntes Gesicht: Der Z07 Roadster, als Z8 lieferbar ab Frühjahr 2000, zitiert liebevoll die Legende 507 der fünfziger Jahre.

Visage connu: le roadster Z07, livrable à partir du printemps 2000, sous le nom de Z8, rappelle délicieusement le légendaire 507 des années 1950.

Mit ihnen entledigt sich BMW des britischen Ballasts namens Rover. Eher symbolisch, die Übernahme-Summe, die der frühere Rover-Chef John Towers für die Auffang-Kapital-gruppe „Phoenix" ausbaldowert hat: zehn Pfund Sterling. Land-Rover geht an Jaguar, wo Reitzle neuer Chef wird. Zur Abrundung der eigenen Produktpalette nach unten behält Prof. Dr. Joachim Milberg, seit Januar 1999 neuer Vorstandsvorsitzender von BMW, die Marke Mini. Und die steht auf wie Phoenix aus der Asche!

Nach dem Rover-Investitions-Debakel, das sich letztmalig im Geschäftsjahr 1999 mit einem Milliarden-Minus nieder-schlägt, folgt mit dem Mini ein ungeahnter Aufschwung. Im neuen Mini-Werk Oxford werden 2001 42 395 Wagen produziert, 2002 sind es bereits 160 037, und 2003 stößt Werkleiter Anton Heiss mit 174 366 Minis an die Kapazitäts-grenze – seiner Lackiererei. Die kommt mit der umweltfreund-lichen „Kriegsbemalung" (Lacke auf wasserlöslicher Basis) der kleinen Kultautos kaum noch hinterher. Dennoch pro-gnostiziert Heiss weitere Steigerungsraten, da 2004 dem Mini ein Cabrio zur Seite gestellt wird. Und damit dürfte er sich dann im siebenten Himmel befinden.

Mit positiven Bilanzen und erheblichen Zuwächsen auf dem Pkw- und Motorrad-Sektor sieht sich Milberg am Ziel seiner energischen Arbeit zur langfristigen Sanierung von BMW. Leider bleibt die eigene Gesundheit dabei auf der Strecke. Nach einer Bandscheiben-Operation hatte er sich weder geschont noch die verordnete Gymnastik betreiben können, stattdessen Dauerstress und viele längere Flug-reisen! Auf dringenden ärztlichen Rat, kürzer zu treten, verab-schiedet sich Milberg auf der Hauptversammlung im Mai 2001 und wechselt – seliger Rückfall – in den Aufsichtsrat, dessen Vorsitz er drei Jahre später übernimmt.

Milbergs Nachfolger, der promovierte Diplom-Physiker Helmut Panke, gilt als erfolgreicher Allrounder – zuletzt als Finanzvorstand – in der obersten BMW-Etage. Als neuer Chef balanciert er geschickt den Betriebsgewinn zwischen

En 1998, il s'avère après coup que le *Sunday Times* avait finalement raison en 1992: BMW AG s'intéresse au départe-ment Automobile de la prestigieuse marque Rolls-Royce. À l'issue d'une lutte acharnée, ponctuée de nombreux rebondissements, avec le groupe Volkswagen, BMW acquiert les droits pour exploiter le nom de Rolls-Royce pour la somme de 40 millions de livres sterling, comme l'annonce un communiqué de presse daté du 28 juillet. Rolls-Royce Motor Cars se voit accorder une licence temporaire, jusqu'au 31 décembre 2002, pour fabriquer et distribuer les somp-tueuses Rolls-Royce.

La prestigieuse marque britannique se voit offrir par le BMW Group un nouveau berceau à proximité du circuit auto-mobile de Goodwood, dans le sud de l'Angleterre. Dans cette usine, un peu plus de 300 ouvriers très motivés fabriquent, grâce à un savant dosage de travail manuel et de technique de précision, la Phantom. Au printemps 2004, à l'occasion du centenaire de la marque Rolls-Royce, l'étude de style du cabriolet 100 EX est présentée à Genève. Respectant la cylindrée traditionnelle de 6,75 litres, BMW a mis au point un nouveau moteur pour son automobile « aristo-cratique ». À 3500 tr/min, déjà, le V12 à la puissance de 460 ch développe son couple maximum de 720 Nm et permet à cet imposant carrosse d'accélérer de 0 à 100 km/h en 5,5 secondes, un résultat phénoménal pour une telle voiture. Malgré la carrosserie *spaceframe* en aluminium qui ne pèse que 550 kg et provient de l'usine BMW de Dingol-fing, son poids total excède 2,5 tonnes. Les soixante élé-ments en bois de l'habillage du cockpit sont collés (jusqu'à concurrence de quarante couches) et le cuir originaire de Saxe possède, lui aussi, un caractère exclusif: il est teinté dans la masse, il ne peut ainsi ni pâlir ni se fissurer.

C'est une fissure d'un tout autre genre qui survient, avant même la fin du millénaire, dans la structure du personnel du directoire de BMW: Bernd Pischetsrieder et son collègue du directoire responsable de la distribution et du développe-

The two BMW motor sport directors in question: Dr. Mario Theissen (left) and Gerhard Berger. Following a comprehensive test phase, BMW is since 2000 literally in the running once again, with the team surrounding the two experienced sport managers acquitting themselves most remarkably.

Die beiden BMW-Motorsport-Direktoren im Gespräch: Dr. Mario Theissen (links) und Gerhard Berger. Nach umfangreicher Erprobungsphase ist BMW seit 2000 im wahrsten Wortsinn wieder im Rennen, seither schlägt sich das Team um die beiden erfahrenen Sport-Manager mehr als beachtlich.

Conversation entre les deux directeurs de BMW Motorsport: Mario Theissen (à gauche) et Gerhard Berger. A l'issue d'une longue période de gestation, BMW est de nouveau dans la course au sens propre du mot. Et, depuis, l'écurie dirigée par les deux managers très au fait des arcanes de la course remporte des succès plus que respectables.

cabriolet for company in 2004. That will certainly be his seventh heaven.

In the face of a positive balance account and considerable increases in the automobile and Motorcycle sectors, Milberg considers himself to be at the winning line in his energetic struggle to secure BMW's long-term prospects – unfortunately at a cost to his health. Following a back operation, he had neither taken things easily nor performed the prescribed convalescence gymnastics, but had subjected himself to permanent stress and many long air flights! Urgently pressed by his physicians to take things easy, Milberg takes his leave at the General Meeting in May 2001 and moves on to the supervisory board – a blessed relapse – taking on the position of chairman three years later.

Milbergs successor, the diploma physicist Dr. Helmut Panke, is considered a successful all-rounder – latterly as financial director – on the BMW top floor. As new boss, he skillfully balances the company's finances ensuring a profit of 3.2 billion Euros between 2001 and 2003. Greater profitability in this hard fought branch is scarcely possible, taking into account the increased investment volume of the same period from 3.5 to 4.2 billion Euros. In accordance with its expansion strategy "production follows the market," BMW builds a plant in Shenyang, northern China. Since 2003, 30,000 BMW 3 and 5s leave the production halls of the capital of Liaoning province annually. There is obviously no

2001 und 2003 auf 3,2 Milliarden Euro ein. Profitabler geht es in dieser umkämpften Branche kaum, zumal das Investitionsvolumen im gleichen Zeitraum von 3,5 auf 4,2 Milliarden Euro wächst. Gemäß seiner Expansionsstrategie „die Produktion folgt dem Markt" errichtet BMW in Shenyang, Nord-China, ein Werk. Seit 2003 verlassen jährlich 30 000 3er- und 5er-BMW die Produktionshallen der Hauptstadt der Provinz Liaoning. An gut betuchten Chinesen mangelt es offenbar nicht, denn vom Topmodell der 7er-Reihe, dem 760Li, werden 2003 in China die meisten Exemplare verkauft. Zur 3er-Fertigung tragen hauptsächlich die Werke Regensburg, München und Rosslyn, Südafrika, bei. Ab 2005 startet auch an der Peripherie von Leipzig die 3er-Fabrikation – nach den neusten Erkenntnissen der Computertechnik.

Größte Einzelmärkte für die BMW Group sind 2003 mit je 25,1 Prozent Deutschland und die USA. In den Staaten hat sich der BMW-Umsatz innerhalb der letzten zehn Jahre vervierfacht. Zur positiven Entwicklung auf dem US-Markt trägt das BMW-Werk Spartanburg, South Carolina, bei, mit einer Produktion von 166 000 Z4 und X5 im Jahre 2003.

„Nie zuvor in der Geschichte unseres Unternehmens haben wir mehr neue Produkte hergestellt als 2003", resümiert Panke das Geschäftsjahr 2003. Aber auch neue Technologien feiern Premiere. Als einziger Automobilhersteller präsentiert BMW auf der IAA 2003 einen V12 als Wasserstoff-Triebwerk, das bivalent betrieben wird. Es läuft sowohl

ment, Wolfgang Reitzle, font leurs adieux. Avec eux, BMW se débarrasse du ballast britannique qui a pour nom Rover. Le montant du rachat, a imaginé l'ancien patron de Rover, John Towers, pour le groupe de capitaux «Phoenix» qui l'acquiert, est plutôt symbolique: 10 livres sterling. Land-Rover tombe dans l'escarcelle de Jaguar, dont le nouveau patron est Wolfgang Reitzle. Pour conserver dans sa gamme de produits un modèle plus bas de gamme, Joachim Milberg, promu nouveau président du directoire de BMW en janvier 1999, conserve la marque Mini. Et elle se remet à vivre, tel le phénix renaissant de ses cendres!

Après la débâcle financière qu'a été la reprise de Rover et qui s'est traduite pour la dernière fois, lors de l'exercice 1999, par un déficit de plusieurs milliards, un redressement inattendu se produit avec la Mini. Dans la nouvelle usine d'Oxford où naît la Mini, 42 395 voitures sont produites en 2001, mais déjà 160 037 en 2002 alors que, en 2003, le directeur de l'usine, Anton Heiss, avoue avoir atteint les limites de ses capacités – de sa ligne de peinture notamment – avec 174 366 Mini. Elle n'arrive pratiquement pas à assumer la demande pour les «peintures de guerre» de la petite voiture culte respectueuses de l'environnement avec des vernis solubles dans l'eau. Et pourtant, Anton Heiss pronostique une hausse de la production dès lors que la Mini va être rejointe par un cabriolet en 2004. Il a donc tout lieu d'être satisfait.

Avec des bilans positifs et une progression considérable des ventes de voitures de tourisme et de motos, le professeur Milberg voit enfin ses travaux récompensés et son objectif, atteint, à savoir l'assainissement financier à long terme de BMW. Malheureusement, il sacrifie pour cela sa propre santé. Après une opération à la colonne vertébrale, il n'a ni ménagé ses forces ni fait la gymnastique qui lui avait été ordonnée et il a enduré, au lieu de cela, un stress permanent et de nombreux et longs voyages en avion! Son médecin lui ayant intimé l'ordre de ménager ses forces, Joachim Milberg fait ses adieux lors de l'assemblée générale de mai 2001 et – «rétrogradation bienvenue» – passe au conseil de surveillance, dont il assumera la présidence trois ans plus tard.

Le successeur du professeur Milberg, le physicien diplômé et titulaire d'un doctorat Helmut Panke, est considéré comme un homme à tout faire couronné de succès – tout dernièrement membre du directoire en charge des finances – à l'étage supérieur de BMW. En tant que nouveau patron, il a le bonheur d'inscrire au bilan un bénéfice consolidé de 3,2 milliards d'euros entre 2001 et 2003. Pratiquement aucun constructeur automobile n'est aussi rentable dans ce secteur âprement disputé. D'autant plus que le volume d'investissements durant la même période a progressé de 3,5 à 4,2 milliards d'euros. Conformément à sa stratégie d'expansion selon la devise «la production suit le marché», BMW construit une usine à Shenyang, dans le nord de la Chine. Depuis 2003, 30 000 BMW Série 3 et 5 quittent chaque année les ateliers de production de la capitale de la province de Liaoning. Apparemment, les Chinois au portefeuille bien garni ne manquent pas. En effet, c'est la 760 Li, le modèle de haut de gamme de la Série 7, qui se vend le mieux en Chine en 2003. Ce sont les usines de Ratisbonne, Munich et Rosslyn, en Afrique du Sud, qui assument l'essentiel de la fabrication des Série 3. En 2005 débute aussi, à la périphérie de Leipzig, l'assemblage de la Série 3 – selon les enseignements les plus récents de la technique informatique.

Pris individuellement, les marchés les plus importants pour le BMW Group sont, en 2003, avec respectivement 25,1 %, l'Allemagne et les États-Unis. Aux États-Unis, le shortage of well-off Chinese, for the largest number of the top model of the 7 range, the 760Li, were sold in China in 2003. The BMW 3's production is mainly borne by Regensburg, Munich, and Rosslyn, South Africa. From 2005, fabrication of the BMW 3 is starting on the outskirts of Leipzig – utilizing all the latest developments in computer technology.

In 2003, the single largest markets for the BMW Group are Germany and the USA, both with 25.1 percent. BMW has quadrupled in the States over the last ten years. The BMW works at Spartanburg, South Carolina, have contributed significantly to this success with a production of 166,000 Z4s and X5s in 2003.

"We have never before in the history of our company produced as many new products as in 2003," Panke sums up the 2003 business year. New technologies have also celebrated a premiere. At the IAA in 2003, BMW presented, as the only automobile producer to do so, a hydrogen fuelled V12 that is operated in tandem. It can run equally on hydrogen or on gasoline. As Prof. Dr. Burkhard Göschel, director of development and purchasing puts it: "we will show with this engine that the potential of the combustion engine is not exhausted after one hundred years. The combination of combustion engine and hydrogen allow a new dimension in performance and emission reduction."

There is also technological innovation at the Berlin BMW motorcycle works, which delivered more vehicles in 2003 than ever before. With the F 650 CS and its combination of monolever fork and toothed pulley drive, a world novelty was presented in 2003. The straight four-cylinder engine of the K 1200 S, presented in June 2004, is a source of much power: this short-stroke engine releases 167 bhp at 10,250 rpm. An integrated six-gear transmission, electronically adjustable chassis – to be operated by button from the handlebars if desired – and ABS as standard belong to the characteristics of this bike which itself is similar to a racing machine.

BMW motor sport is moving toward the limits – in the widest but also in the highest category. Ralf Schumacher won third place in the Williams-BMW FW22 at the first Formula 1 comeback opportunity in 2000, and by the end of that season Ralf has secured fifth place, with the team taking third in the constructors' championship. Target achieved! The first victories follow in 2001, three from Ralf, and one contributed by Juan-Pablo Montoya, and again third place in the constructors' championship, while in 2002 the position of vice champion is secured. In 2003, motor sport director Dr. Mario Theissen goes on the offensive, almost succeeding. "We have experienced the emotional roller coaster, have fought right up until the final of the constructors' world championship, and have never been so near to our great target," the visibly disappointed Theissen admits. The BMW racing motor P83 did not let the team down once during the whole season. For victories and just as many pole positions may be a small consolation. BMW gains the mark title in its old domain, the Touring Car European Championship.

mit Wasserstoff wie auch mit Benzin. Dazu Prof. Dr. Burkhard Göschel, Vorstand für Entwicklung und Einkauf: „Wir werden mit diesem Motor zeigen, dass das Potential des Verbrennungsmotors nach über hundert Jahren noch nicht ausgereizt ist. Die Kombination aus Verbrennungsmotor und Wasserstoff ermöglicht eine neue Dimension an Leistung und Emissionsreduktion."

Technische Innovationen gibt es auch beim BMW-Motorradwerk in Berlin, das 2003 mehr Maschinen als je zuvor ausliefert. Mit der F 650 CS wird 2003 eine Weltneuheit, die Kombination von Einarmschwinge und Zahnriemenantrieb, vorgestellt. Viel Power steckt im Vierzylinder-Reihenmotor der im Juni 2004 präsentierten K 1200 S: 167 PS leistet dieser Kurzhuber bei 10 250/min. Integriertes Sechsgang-Getriebe, elektronisch einstellbares Fahrwerk – auf Wunsch per Knopfdruck vom Lenker aus zu betätigen – und serienmäßiges ABS gehören ebenso zu den Merkmalen dieses Zweirades, das einer Rennmaschine ähnelt.

Voll am Limit bewegt sich der BMW-Motorsport – in der Breite, aber auch in der höchsten Kategorie. Gleich beim ersten Einsatz des Formel-1-Comebacks 2000 ergattert Ralf Schumacher im Williams-BMW FW22 den dritten Platz, und am Ende jener Saison ist Ralf Fünfter und das Team in der Konstrukteurswertung Dritter. Soll voll erfüllt! 2001 folgen die ersten Siege, drei durch Ralf, und einen steuert Juan-Pablo Montoya bei. Wieder Dritter bei den Konstrukteuren, 2002 ist man bereits Vize-Meister. 2003 bläst Motorsport-Direktor Dr. Mario Theissen zum Großangriff, und beinahe hätte es geklappt. „Wir haben ein Wechselbad der Gefühle erlebt, haben bis zum Finale um die Weltmeisterschaft der Konstrukteure gekämpft, so nah waren wir unserem großen Ziel noch nie", gesteht der sichtlich enttäuschte Theissen. Während der gesamten Saison lässt der BMW-Rennmotor P83 die Truppe nicht im Stich. Vier Siege und ebensoviele Pole-Positionen mögen ein kleiner Trost sein. Den Marken-Titel erringt BMW in seiner alten Domäne, der Tourenwagen-Europameisterschaft.

chiffre d'affaires de BMW a quadruplé au cours des dix dernières années. L'usine BMW de Spartanburg, en Caroline du Sud, qui produit, en 2003, 166 000 Z4 et X5, contribue au bon développement sur le marché américain.

«Jamais auparavant dans l'histoire de notre entreprise nous n'avons fabriqué plus de nouvelles voitures qu'en 2003», résume Helmut Panke. Mais certaines technologies nouvelles fêtent aussi leur lancement. À l'IAA 2003, BMW est le seul et unique constructeur automobile à présenter un moteur V12 à hydrogène pouvant fonctionner sur un mode bivalent. Il brûle, en effet, aussi bien de l'hydrogène que de l'essence. Ce qui fait dire au professeur Burkhard Göschel, membre du directoire en charge du développement et des achats : «Avec ce moteur, nous allons montrer que le potentiel du moteur à combustion n'est toujours pas exploité à fond après plus d'un siècle. La combinaison moteur à combustion et hydrogène donne une nouvelle dimension en matière de puissance et de réduction des émissions de CO_2».

L'usine de motocyclettes BMW de Berlin, qui enregistre des ventes records, pour l'année 2003, n'est pas, elle non plus, avare d'innovations techniques. Avec la F 650 CS, elle présente cette année-là une nouveauté mondiale avec une combinaison de fourche monobras et d'entraînement par courroie dentée. Le quatre-cylindres en ligne, qui est présenté en juin 2004, pour la K 1200 S regorge de puissance : ce moteur à course courte développe 167 ch à 10 250 tr/min. Une boîte à six vitesses intégrée, une partie cycle à commande électronique – que l'on peut, sur demande, actionner depuis le guidon grâce à un bouton – et l'ABS en série figurent également parmi les caractéristiques de ce deux-roues qui ressemble à une moto de course.

BMW-Motorsport, quant à elle, ne recule pas devant les difficultés les plus insurmontables – aussi bien pour le sport à grande échelle que dans la catégorie suprême. Lorsque BMW fait son come-back en Formule 1 en 2000, dès la première course, Ralf Schumacher mène la Williams-BMW FW22 à la troisième place et, à la fin de cette saison-là, il termine cinquième au classement des pilotes et l'écurie arrive troisième pour la coupe des constructeurs. Objectif pleinement rempli! 2001 verra tomber les premières victoires, trois grâce à Ralf et une à porter à l'actif de Juan Pablo Montoya. De nouveau un troisième rang au championnat des marques et même déjà le titre de vice-champion du monde en 2002. En 2003, Mario Theissen, directeur de BMW Motorsport, sonne l'hallali, car il aurait quasiment atteint son but. «Nous avons connu une saison qui a été une véritable douche écossaise, nous nous sommes battus jusqu'à la finale pour décrocher le titre de champion du monde des constructeurs, nous n'avons jamais été aussi proches de notre objectif», concède, visiblement déçu, Mario Theissen. Pendant toute la saison, le moteur de course BMW, le P83, ne laisse jamais tomber l'écurie. Quatre victoires et un nombre identique de pole positions ne sont qu'une mince consolation. Le titre des marques, BMW le décroche dans ce qui est pratiquement son domaine réservé, le championnat d'Europe des voitures de tourisme.

Wartburg Motorwagen

On 3 December 1896, a bank consortium led by Privy Councilor and Group Chairman Dr Heinrich Ehrhardt founded the Fahrzeugfabrik Eisenach AG vehicle factory with the intention of building military vehicles and bicycles. Dr Ehrhardt with his Rheinmetall Group was a growing competitor of Krupp and was to pump 1.25 million goldmarks into the new company at Eisenach. The resourceful businessman had realized the potential of the Imperial Army as a profitable source of major orders. Ambulances and ammunition trucks, in addition to mobile kitchens, were all items appearing in large quantities on the commander's list of provisions.

There was another product intended for use outside the battlefield being sold in large quantities. This product was a bicycle with ratios designed for uphill cycling via a shaft drive, tailor-made for cycling up to the Wartburg castle. So the first mountain bike was named after the Landgrave of Thuringia's former seat and Martin Luther's refuge during the Reformation.

A new reformation was occuring, but this time Luther did not need to spill any ink to make Ehrhardt understand its consequences: he clearly saw the success that Daimler and Benz enjoyed with their volume-produced motorcars. To save both the time and money involved in an original development, Ehrhardt obtained the manufacturing license for the French Decauville-Voiturettes.

Like the bicycle, this car was also christened "Wartburg." Presented in Düsseldorf at the first German motor show in September 1898, it appeared alongside names such as Benz, Daimler, Opel and Dürkopp. Despite such stiff competition, it acquitted itself well.

This vehicle was also known as the "Wartburg motorized carriage" because of its carriage shape. Depending on how many people were sitting on the coach box and the opposite

bench, it could reach road speeds of up to 28 mph (45 kph). There were alternative two-cylinder engines available: an aircooled design (479 cc, 3.5 bhp) and a water-cooled motor delivering 5 bhp. Initially, the transmission only had two speeds, a third being introduced later.

The front suspension technology offered leaf-sprung comfort, recognizable today, but a lack of rear axle suspension meant that passengers' backs suffered. A single steering bar was employed, a conventional steering wheel was only introduced for the new generation of motorcars in 1902/03. This did not seem to affect the car's sporty characteristics. "Wartburg" cars gained excellent double victories in the major Dresden-Berlin and Aachen-Bonn car races of 1899. The carriage car won a total of 22 gold medals, including an award for elegance.

Of the six original cars remaining today, one is still capable of performing at competition level. This Wartburg, chassis number 88, had slumbered like Sleeping Beauty from 1903 to 1959 in Landsberg/Lech before being woken up by the Munich vintage car enthusiast Georg Schlautkötter.

Wiesloch 1964: Schlautkötter's Wartburg caused a sensation at the Bertha Benz memorial rally, demanding that the fire brigade leap into action. At the turn of the century, the local constabulary in Wiesloch stipulated that the fire brigade spray the streets with water whenever a motorcar was filled with petrol from a pharmacy. This is exactly what happened at the veteran event in which this car took part.

Den Bau von Militärfahrzeugen und Fahrrädern im Visier, gründet am 3. Dezember 1896 ein Bankenkonsortium unter Leitung des Geheimen Baurats Generaldirektor Dr.-Ing. e.h. Heinrich Ehrhardt die Fahrzeugfabrik Eisenach AG. 1,25 Millionen Goldmark pumpt der findige Unternehmer, der mit seinem Rheinmetall-Konzern bereits Krupp Konkurrenz macht, in das Eisenacher Werk, denn dicke Rüstungsaufträge winken. Sanitäts- und Munitionswagen sowie Feldküchen – allesamt in größerer Stückzahl – stehen auf der Beschaffungsliste des Berliner Kriegsministeriums.

Aber auch ein ziviles Nebenprodukt findet reißenden Absatz. Ein Fahrrad mit Bergübersetzung und Kardanantrieb – ideal für Fahrten hinauf zur Wartburg. Und so wird dieses erste „Mountain-Bike" nach dem ehemaligen Sitz der Landgrafen von Thüringen und Zufluchtsort Martin Luthers benannt.

Um Ehrhardt auf die bevorstehenden Umwälzungen des 20. Jahrhunderts vorzubereiten, bedarf es keines Reformators. Schwarz auf weiß gedruckt sieht Ehrhardt die Erfolge der Firmen Daimler und Benz im Bau serienmäßiger Motorwagen. Um die Kosten einer eigenen Entwicklung zu sparen und Zeit zu gewinnen, erwirbt er die Lizenz zum Nachbau der französischen Decauville-Voiturettes.

Wie das Fahrrad auf den Namen „Wartburg" getauft, stellt sich das Lizenz-Produkt im September 1898 auf der ersten deutschen Automobil-Ausstellung in Düsseldorf dem Vergleich mit Benz, Daimler, Opel und Dürkopp, und der fällt gut aus!

Wegen seiner Kutschenform auch „Wartburg-Kutschierwagen" genannt, läuft dieses Gefährt je nach Anzahl der Passagiere auf dem Kutschbock und dem gegenüber liegenden Kinderbänkchen bis zu 45 Stundenkilometer. Zwei Zweizylindermotoren stehen zur Auswahl: Ein luftgekühltes

Triebwerk (479 ccm, 3,5 PS) und ein wassergekühlter Motor, der 5 PS leistet. Das Getriebe beschränkt sich erst auf zwei, dann drei Gänge.

Während die Vorderradaufhängung geradezu modern anmutet, malträtiert die ungefederte Hinterachse die Bandscheiben der Passagiere. Gelenkt wird mit einer Kurbel. Erst die junge Motorwagen-Generation 1902/03 bekommt ein Lenkrad. Der Sportlichkeit tut es keinen Abbruch, denn in den großen Rennen Dresden–Berlin und Aachen–Bonn anno 1899 erringen die Wartburg Doppelsiege. Insgesamt 22 Goldmedaillen – darunter auch Edelmetall für seine Eleganz – heimst der Kutschwagen ein.

Von den sechs erhaltenen Exemplaren des Ur-Wartburg ist eines noch wettbewerbsfähig. Dieser Wagen mit der Chassis-Nummer 88 hatte von 1903 bis 1959 in Landsberg/Lech einen Dornröschen-Schlaf gehalten, ehe ihn der Münchner Oldtimer-Enthusiast Georg Schlautkötter weckte.

Wiesloch 1964: Der Wartburg Schlautkötters erregt bei der Bertha-Benz-Gedächtnis-Rallye Aufsehen und sorgt für einen Einsatz der Feuerwehr. Beim Betanken eines Motorwagens mit Benzin – aus der Apotheke (so eine Anordnung der Wieslocher Gendarmerie der Jahrhundertwende) – muss die Feuerwehr die Straße spritzen. So geschieht es auch bei dieser Veteranenveranstaltung.

Le 3 décembre 1896, un consortium bancaire dirigé par Heinrich Ehrhardt, ingénieur diplômé *honoris causa,* fonde la Fahrzeugfabrik Eisenach AG dans l'intention de construire des véhicules militaires et des bicyclettes. L'offensif industriel, qui se pose déjà en concurrent de Krupp avec son groupe Rheinmetall, injecte 1,25 million de marks or dans l'usine d'Eisenach, car il a en vue d'importantes commandes d'armes. Des ambulances, des transporteurs de munitions et des cuisines de campagne – le tout en quantité très importante – figurent dans les carnets de commandes des stratèges à Berlin.

On s'arrache aussi un produit qui s'utilise en dehors des champs de bataille. Il s'agit d'une bicyclette avec dérailleur pour la montagne et transmission à cardan – idéale pour monter sur la Wartburg. C'est ainsi que ce premier « vélo tout-terrain » est baptisé, du nom de l'ancien siège des Landgraves de Thuringe où Luther trouva refuge lors de la Réforme.

Mais une nouvelle Réforme se prépare et cette fois Luther n'a pas à intervenir pour que Ehrhardt en mesure les conséquences. Il observe les succès de Daimler et de Benz qui construisent en série des automobiles. Pour s'épargner les coûts de son propre développement et gagner du temps, il acquiert la licence de la voiturette française Decauville.

Baptisée, comme la bicyclette, du nom de « Wartburg », la voiture construite sous licence est exposée en septembre 1898 au premier Salon de l'Automobile d'Allemagne, à Düsseldorf, où on la compare aux Benz, Daimler, Opel et Dürkopp. La comparaison est flatteuse !

Surnommé « la calèche motorisée de Wartburg » en raison de sa forme rappelant celle d'une calèche, ce véhicule peut atteindre 45 km/h selon le nombre de personnes qu'il transporte sur le banc et sur la banquette opposée.

Pour les moteurs, on a le choix entre deux deux-cylindres : l'un refroidi par air (479 cm³, 3,5 ch), et l'autre refroidi par eau, qui développe 5 ch. La boîte a d'abord deux, puis trois vitesses.

Alors que la suspension avant présente un confort moderne, l'essieu arrière non suspendu maltraite la colonne vertébrale des passagers. La direction est à manivelle. Il faudra attendre la nouvelle génération de voitures à moteur de 1902–1903 pour voir apparaître un volant. Cela ne porte aucunement préjudice à la sportivité puisque, lors des grandes courses Dresde–Berlin et Aix-la-Chapelle–Bonn en 1899, les Wartburg signent un magnifique doublé. La voiturette rafle au total 22 médailles d'or, dont un prix d'élégance.

Des six exemplaires qui existent toujours, un seul est encore en mesure de courir. Cette Wartburg, numéro de châssis 88, avait sommeillé dans une grange de 1903 à 1959 à Landsberg/Lech avant d'être réveillée par Georg Schlautkötter, un Munichois fanatique de voitures de collection.

Wiesloch 1964 : lors du rallye commémoratif Bertha Benz, la Wartburg de Schlautkötter fait sensation, mais grâce à l'intervention des pompiers. Lors du ravitaillement d'une voiture à moteur en benzène de pharmacie – selon les instructions de la gendarmerie de Wiesloch à la fin du XIXe et du début du XXe siècle – les pompiers doivent inonder la route. Et c'est donc ce qu'ils ont fait lors de ce rassemblement de voitures anciennes.

A technically interesting vehicle: this delicate-looking motor vehicle, just over 4 feet (1.25 meters) wide, is steered by a hand crank via a rack-and-pinion and started with a hand wheel located alongside the driver's seat. During travel, the magneto ignition can be adjusted using two levers.

Ein technisch interessantes Fahrzeug: Der filigran wirkende, nur 1,25 Meter breite Motorwagen wird per Handkurbel über Zahnstangen gelenkt und mit einem Handrad, das sich neben dem Fahrersitz befindet, angeworfen. Während der Fahrt lässt sich die Magnetzündung an zwei Hebeln verstellen.

Une voiture intéressante sur le plan technique : cette automobile à l'aspect fragile, de seulement 1,25 m de large, possède une direction à manivelle via une crémaillère. Son moteur démarre à l'aide d'un volant placé à côté du siège du conducteur. Deux manettes permettent de régler l'allumage magnétique durant le voyage.

Dr. Götz, Pfarrki

Wartburg Motorwagen

The engine sits unprotected beneath the "coach-box", generating 3.5 bhp in the air-cooled version and 5 bhp in the water-cooled version. A feature that stands out is the linkage of the cam-adjusted rear wheel brakes. The front wheel suspension, with its encased helical springs and overhead transverse springs, is also ahead of its time.

Ungeschützt unter dem „Kutscherbock" arbeitet der Motor, der luftgekühlt 3,5 PS und wassergekühlt 5 PS leistet. Auffällig ist das Gestänge der mit Nocken verstellbaren Hinterradbremse. Die Vorderradaufhängung mit gekapselten Schraubenfedern und hochliegender Querfeder ist ebenfalls ihrer Zeit voraus.

Le moteur, d'une puissance de 3,5 ch dans la version à refroidissement par air et de 5 ch dans la version à refroidissement liquide, est exposé aux intempéries sous la banquette de cocher. Bien visible, la timonerie du frein arrière est réglable par cames. La suspension du train avant, avec ressorts hélicoïdaux protégés de la poussière et un ressort transversal surélevé, est également en avance sur son temps.

Dixi 3/15 PS

Strange but true: BMW cars are of British ancestry. Financially troubled, the Eisenach Dixi factory could not make use of the bank loan available for mass production of a small car as there was no own automotive design. The stock exchange speculator Jakob Schapiro, who had interests in several wagon and car companies, also controlled the Dixi factory. Without hesitation, Schapiro decided to buy the license to build the Austin Seven. This uncomplicated car with its 750 cc four-cylinder engine had sold strongly in Britain since 1922.

As well as the manufacturing license, Schapiro immediately obtained 100 Austin Sevens for the first Dixi 3/15 PS customers. These preliminary cars were sold with few alterations: even UK right-hand drive and braking only for the two rear wheels were retained.

In December 1927, the factory began producing its own Dixi 3/15 PS, type DA1. DA stood for Dixi Austin or "Deutsche Ausführung" meaning "German construction". A touring version of this diminutive car, just 970 lbs (440 kg), was created using the original plans and production documents from England. The 15 bhp were achieved at 3000 rpm, giving the vehicle a top speed of 47 mph (75 kph). Fuel consumption was correspondingly modest: 39.5 miles to the gallon (6 liters per 100 km). Just 42 tourers were built in December 1927, sales scheduled to begin in January 1928.

When BMW took over the busy but broke Dixi factory on 16 November 1928 for ten million reichsmark, production of the 3/15 initially continued unchanged. In 1928/29, 9308 Dixi DA1s left the factory in the shadow of Wartburg castle. The majority (4831 units) were tourers. The BMW-badged DA2, a considerable development of the basic Austin design, was mass-produced from summer 1929 onward. Thew DA2 saw Eisenach cars begin to carry the BMW name.

In the final months of production, the Dixi was available through special finance deals (discounts and 24 monthly installments). The DA1 was provided with a battery since the original magneto ignition was unreliable. No longer did customers gamble with the brakes ("they work more ... or less"), but BMW would improve this aspect.

As well as the tourer and limousine (for three large or four smaller passengers), the open-top two-seater was very popular. Dixi prices were between 2750 and 3200 reichsmark, a real market niche!

"It accords with the wishes of the sporting lady and the gentleman driver, who wish to drive a light two-seater vehicle with modern lines and elegant exterior", claimed BMW as it took over the Dixi legacy. What would "Grandfather" Austin say in the 1990s, now that BMW has again adopted British "grandchildren" at Rover and Rolls-Royce?

Eigentlich ist der Urahn aller BMW ein Brite. Die Eisenacher Dixi-Werke sind in finanziellen Schwierigkeiten, und dem Bankkredit für eine Serienfabrikation eines Kleinwagens steht keine brauchbare Entwicklung gegenüber. Börsenspekulant Jakob Schapiro, der an mehreren Waggon- und Fahrzeugfirmen beteiligt ist und auch die Dixi-Werke kontrolliert, besorgt kurzerhand eine Nachbau-Lizenz des Austin Seven. Dieser unkomplizierte Wagen mit einem 750-ccm-Vierzylindermotor verkauft sich auf der Insel seit 1922 prächtig.

Schapiro erwirbt nicht nur die Lizenz, sondern lässt auch gleich 100 Austin Seven kommen, um sie als erste Dixi 3/15 PS zu verkaufen. Diese „Vorabserie" geht fast unverändert – sogar noch mit Rechtslenkung – an die Kunden.

Im Dezember 1927 beginnt die Eigenproduktion des Dixi 3/15 PS, Typ DA1. Dabei steht „DA" als Kürzel für „Dixi Austin" oder für „Deutsche Ausführung". Nach Originalplänen und Fertigungsunterlagen aus England entsteht das 440 Kilo leichte Wägelchen in der Tourer-Version. Die 15 PS werden bei 3000 Umdrehungen pro Minute erreicht und beschleunigen das Gefährt auf bis zu 75 Stundenkilometer. Ähnlich bescheiden ist der Verbrauch: sechs Liter auf 100 Kilometer. 42 Tourer werden im Dezember 1927 gebaut, der Verkaufsbeginn wird auf Januar 1928 festgelegt.

Als BMW am 16. November 1928 für 10 Millionen Reichsmark die hochverschuldeten, aber emsig produzierenden Dixi-Werke übernimmt, wird der 3/15 erst einmal unverändert weitergebaut. 1928/29 verlassen 9308 Dixi DA1 das Werk in Sichtweite der Wartburg. Den Hauptanteil trägt die Produktion des Tourers mit 4831 Einheiten. Der DA2, eine erheblich weiterentwickelte Konstruktion, geht im Sommer 1929 parallel vom Band und trägt erstmals den Namen BMW.

Zurück zum Dixi, der in den letzten Monaten seiner Fertigung zu Sonderpreisen erhältlich ist – Rabatte und

Ratenzahlung in 24 Monaten. Dem DA1 wird eine Batterie eingebaut, da die Magnetzündung des Austin-Originals unzuverlässig arbeitet. Auch der Unsicherheitsfaktor Bremsen („they work more … or less") wird behoben.

Neben Tourer und Limousine (für drei große oder vier kleinere Passagiere) erfreut sich der offene Zweisitzer großer Beliebtheit. Die Dixi-Preise liegen zwischen 2750 und 3200 Reichsmark – eine echte Marktnische!

„Er entspricht dem Wunsche der sporttreibenden Dame und des Herrenfahrers, die ein leichtes zweisitziges Fahrzeug mit moderner Linienführung und elegantem Äußeren zu steuern wünschen." Mit dieser Werksaussage übernimmt der BMW das Erbe des Dixi. Was hätte „Großvater" Austin wohl gesagt, hätte er gewusst, dass BMW mit Rover und Rolls-Royce Jahrzehnte später wieder englische „Enkel" adoptieren würde?

L'ancêtre des BMW est en réalité une anglaise. Retour en arrière : les usines Dixi d'Eisenach rencontrent des difficultés financières et les crédits accordés par les banques pour la fabrication en série d'une petite voiture ne permettent pas de construire une automobile digne de ce nom. Un spéculateur, Jakob Schapiro, qui tire les ficelles de plusieurs entreprises de wagons et d'automobiles et qui contrôle aussi les usines Dixi, achète sans hésiter une licence pour produire une réplique de l'Austin Seven. Cette première voiture avec un petit moteur à quatre cylindres de 750 cm³ se vend comme des petits pains en Angleterre depuis 1922.

En plus de l'achat de la licence, Schapiro fait venir dans la foulée 100 Austin Seven pour pouvoir vendre à ses clients les premières Dixi 3/15 PS. Cette première série est vendue pratiquement sans modification – elles ont même conservé le volant à droite.

En décembre 1927 commence la production à Eisenach de la Dixi 3/15 PS, type DA1 (pour Dixi Austin et, à partir de 1928, pour « Deutsche Ausführung », fabrication allemande). Selon les plans originaux et les dossiers de fabrication en provenance d'Angleterre, cette voiturette de 440 kg est fabriquée en version tourer. Les 15 ch sont délivrés à 3000 tr/min et confèrent à l'engin une vitesse de 75 km/h. La consommation est modeste : 6 litres aux 100 km. Quarante-deux voitures de tourisme sont construites en décembre 1927 et la commercialisation est fixée à janvier 1928.

Quand BMW reprend pour 10 millions de reichsmarks les usines Dixi criblées de dettes, mais qui tournent à plein régime, le 16 novembre 1928, la 3/15 est, dans premier temps, usinée sans modification. En 1928–1929, 9308 Dixi DA1 quittent l'usine à un jet de pierre du château de la Wartburg. Avec 4831 exemplaires, la tourer se taille la part du lion de la production. La DA2, un modèle beaucoup plus perfectionné, est produite parallèlement à partir de l'été 1929. Et seule la DA2 porte le nom BMW.

Mais revenons à la Dixi qui, durant ses derniers mois de production, est vendue à un prix spécial (avec une ristourne et même payable en 24 mensualités). La DA1 est pourvue d'une batterie, car l'allumage magnétique de l'Austin d'origine n'est pas fiable. Le comportement des freins (« ils fonctionnent plus… ou moins ») est, lui aussi, revu et corrigé. Avec la tourer et la berline (pour trois grands ou quatre petits passagers), la biplace découverte jouit aussi d'une grande popularité. Les Dixi coûtent entre 2750 et 3200 reichsmarks. Une véritable niche !

« Elle répond aux besoins de la femme sportive et du gentleman qui veulent conduire une voiture biplace légère aux lignes modernes et à l'allure élégante », vante le slogan publicitaire de BMW lors de la reprise de l'exploitation de la Dixi. Qu'aurait dit le « grand-père » Austin dans les années 1990, s'il avait su que BMW, après Rover, tente encore, avec Rolls-Royce, d'adopter une autre « petite-fille » britannique ?

The galloping centaur – the symbol of the Dixi works at Eisenach – captured the hearts of motorists. It stands at the prow of the DA1, of which 9308 were produced during 1928 and 1929, under license to Austin. The tourer model depicted here accounted for the bulk of production.

Der galoppierende Zentaur – Symbol der Dixi-Werke Eisenach – stürmt mit dem DA1 in die Herzen der Automobilisten. 1928/29 werden 9308 Exemplare davon nach Austin-Lizenz gebaut. Der Hauptanteil der Produktion entfällt auf das hier abgebildete Tourer-Modell.

Le centaure au galop – emblème des usines Dixi d'Eisenach – a su conquérir le cœur des automobilistes avec la DA1. En 1928–1929, 9308 voitures de ce type sont construites sur licence Austin. Le modèle tourer représenté ici s'est taillé la part du lion de la production.

In the cockpit of the Dixi, instruments, switches and levers are reduced to a bare minimum. The fuel supply when idling is regulated by a lever fitted on the rim of the steering wheel. For the sake of simplicity, this also serves to bring the car to a standstill. The footbrake operates on the rear wheels and the handbrake on the front wheels.

Im Cockpit des Dixi sind Armaturen, Schalter und Hebel auf das Notwendigste reduziert. Das Standgas wird über einen Hebel auf dem Lenkradkranz reguliert. Er dient der Einfachheit halber auch gern zum Abstellen des Motors. Die Fußbremse wirkt auf die Hinterräder, während die Handbremse vorne greift.

Dans le cockpit de la Dixi, les cadrans, leviers et manettes se limitent au strict minimum. Un levier placé sur le volant permet de régler le ralenti. Astuce géniale : il sert aussi à couper le moteur. La pédale de frein agit sur les roues arrière alors que le frein à main agit sur le train avant.

Taking a look under the hood, the Dixi's engineering comes across as simple but functional: the Klaxon fitted above the 15 bhp engine with its laterally-mounted sidedraft carburetor may be a few decibels less loud than modern horns, but it is certainly more original.

Einfach, doch funktionell präsentiert sich die Dixi-Technik auch bei einem Blick unter die Haube: Die „Tröte" über dem 15-PS-Motor mit seitlich stehendem Flachstromvergaser ist heutigen Hupen zwar um einige Dezibel unterlegen, dafür aber umso origineller.

Simple et fonctionnelle : telle est la mécanique de la Dixi même sous le capot. La corne qui trône sur le moteur de 15 ch à carburateur horizontal placé sur le côté est, certes, beaucoup moins puissante que les klaxons d'aujourd'hui, mais nettement plus originale.

BMW Wartburg DA3

Mr W. from Munich is entitled to call himself the Croesus of veteran cars, for his stock of BMWs of the 3/15 PS category has been likened to a Dixi band with 20 soloists. The tone is set by a particularly beautiful Wartburg DA3. Machines such as the DA3 appear just six times in the archive lists of Jürgen Pollack, membership officer of the BMW Veteran Club.

On the subject of the DA3, Pollack defers to another expert: "I'm sure that Kasimirowicz in Düsseldorf will know more about that." Helmut Kasimirowicz, who has already assisted several BMWs to return to their old glory, including a rare express pick-up truck, knows more: "I know another three DA3 owners, I'm one of them."

The DA3 of Jürgen and Brigitte Klöckner possesses an original chassis with number and associated documentation which was only produced 150 times. Conversation about the refinements of the engine with copper suction pipe and double exhaust immediately turns to a special carburetor. Tested by the motor magazine Motor und Sport in 1930, the "Atmos carburetor" produced a performance increase of 1.4 bhp.

In the DA3, weighing no more than 904 lbs (410 kg) with its aluminium chassis, 18 to 19 bhp were sufficient to produce a car with "a full personality and spirit and all the signs of a thoroughbred sports car," wrote Motor und Sport.

On 17 April 1931, ADAC-Motorwelt added: "The low air resistance of the light and racy sports chassis contributes to the achievement of a good speed." When the windscreen – made of shatter-proof glass back then – was folded, the agile little DA3 neared 62 mph (100 kph).

Steering and handling of the small car surprised its contemporaries. A lowered front axle with transverse leaf-sprung suspension enabled a ride height reduction of almost 4 inches (10 cm) compared to the DA2, benefitting roadholding.

The sporting attributes also included the spare wheel fixed to the side of the bonnet, an absence of doors and the instruments. The latter were restricted to a roller speedo and an oil pressure gauge flanking the ignition switch.

In his Motor und Sport report of 1930, the author noted: "The Wartburg is a car for good drivers. Bad drivers do not deserve to own this automobile." Probably the best Wartburg driver was Robert "Bobby" Kohlrausch, born in Eisenach in 1904. Professionally, Bobby advanced from apprentice fitter in the Dixi works to engineer. The motorcycle which his father gave him as a reward for his hard work – modified as a racing machine by Bobby – earned him many cups, but also almost cost him his life. On the promise of never racing motorcycles again, his Dad gave him a BMW. So began an incredible career with 62 wins and four world records. Nobody had said anything about four-wheeler motor sports. Each year in May, when the "DA pilgrims" are engaged in their pilgrimage to Eisenach, one of the most beautiful Kohlrausch cups is reverently passed around.

Herr W. aus München darf sich Oldtimer-Krösus nennen, denn sein Bestand an BMW der 3/15-PS-Kategorie gleicht einer „Dixi-Band" mit 20 Solisten. Den Ton gibt freilich ein besonders schönes Exemplar des Typs DA3 Wartburg an. Solche DA3-Raritäten finden sich lediglich sechsmal in den Archiv-Listen von Jürgen Pollack, dem Mitglieder-Betreuer des BMW-Veteranen-Clubs.

Beim Thema DA3 verweist Pollack gern an einen Kenner: „Sicherlich weiß da der Kasimirowicz aus Düsseldorf noch mehr." Helmut Kasimirowicz, der schon einigen BMW, so auch einem seltenen Eil-Lieferwagen, zu altem Glanz verholfen hat, weiß tatsächlich mehr: „Ich kenne drei weitere DA3-Eigner, einer davon bin ich."

Der DA3 von Dr. Jürgen und Brigitte Klöckner verfügt über ein Originalfahrgestell mit Nummer und dazugehörigem Brief, wie er nur 150 Mal ausgestellt wurde. Angesichts des Motors – mit kupfernem Ansaugrohr und doppeltem Auspuff – kommt die Sprache sofort auf eine spezielle Vergaserbestückung. Solchermaßen exerziert von den Testern der Fachzeitschrift Motor und Sport im Jahre 1930, bringt ein so genannter „Atmos-Vergaser" einen Leistungszuwachs von 1,4 PS.

Bei dem nur 410 Kilo leichten DA3 mit Aluminium-Karosserie sorgen 18 bis 19 PS für „eine vollwertige Autopersönlichkeit mit Temperament und allen Anzeichen eines gutrassigen Sportwagens" (so Motor und Sport).

Und die ADAC-Motorwelt vom 17. April 1931 fügt hinzu: „Der geringe Luftwiderstand der leichten und schnittigen Sportkarosserie trägt zu einer guten Fahrgeschwindigkeit bei." Bei heruntergeklappter Windschutzscheibe, die bereits aus splitterfreiem Glas besteht, kommt das behände Wägelchen an die 100-km/h-Marke heran.

Lenkung und Handling des schmalen Wagens erstaunen die Zeitgenossen. Eine durchgekröpfte Vorderachse mit

Querfeder macht es nicht nur möglich, das Auto gegenüber dem DA2 um fast 10 Zentimeter tieferzulegen, sondern verbessert auch die Straßenlage.

Sportliche Attribute sind auch das seitlich neben der Motorhaube montierte Reserverad, der türlose Einstieg und die Instrumentierung, die sich auf einen Walzentacho, das Öldruckmanometer und das dazwischenliegende Schalt-Zündschloss beschränkt.

In einem *Motor und Sport*-Bericht von 1930 vermerkt der Autor: „Der Wartburg ist ein Wagen für gute Fahrer. Schlechte Fahrer verdienen nicht den Besitz dieses Automobils." Der wohl beste Wartburg-Lenker ist Robert „Bobby" Kohlrausch, 1904 in Eisenach geboren. Beruflich bringt es Bobby vom Schlosserlehrling in den Dixi-Werken bis zum Ingenieur. Das vom Vater als Lohn des Fleißes geschenkte Motorrad – von Bobby zur Rennmaschine umgebaut – fährt viele Pokale ein, kostet ihn aber auch fast das Leben. Gegen das Versprechen, nie mehr Motorradrennen zu fahren, spendiert der Papa einen BMW. Es ist der Beginn einer unglaublichen Karriere mit 62 Siegen und vier Weltrekorden. Von vier Rädern war ja nicht die Rede! Jedes Jahr im Mai, wenn die „DA-Pilger" gen Eisenach ziehen, wird einer der schönsten Kohlrausch-Pokale andächtig herumgereicht.

Monsieur W., de Munich, peut légitimement se considérer comme le Crésus des collectionneurs de voitures anciennes, car sa collection de BMW de la catégorie 3/15 PS ressemble à un « orchestre de Dixi » qui comprendrait 20 « solistes ». C'est toutefois un superbe exemplaire du type Wartburg DA3 qui donne le ton. Posséder une DA3 est exceptionnel puisqu'on en dénombre seulement six sur l'inventaire de Jürgen Pollack, qui gère le club des propriétaires de vieilles BMW.

Concernant la DA3, Pollack vous dirigera cependant volontiers vers un connaisseur : « Je pense que Kasimirowicz, de Düsseldorf, en sait encore plus. » Helmut Kasimirowicz, qui a déjà restauré de nombreuses BMW, dont une fourgonnette de livraison express assez rare, en sait plus en effet : « Je connais trois autres propriétaires de DA3, et je suis l'un d'eux. »

La DA3 du Dr Jürgen Klöckner et de son épouse Brigitte possède un châssis avec le numéro et la carte grise d'origine, qui n'a été délivrée qu'à 150 exemplaires. Quand on évoque les raffinements du moteur avec tubulure d'aspiration en cuivre et double pot d'échappement, on ne peut pas manquer de parler aussi des particularités de son carburateur. Lors d'un essai réalisé par la revue spécialisée *Motor und Sport* en 1930, le carburateur « Atmos » permet d'obtenir un gain de puissance de 1,4 ch.

Avec un poids de seulement 410 kg pour la DA3 à carrosserie aluminium, 18 ou 19 ch garantissent que « cet engin possède une identité et du tempérament, bref tous les ingrédients d'une voiture de sport racée », rapporte *Motor und Sport*.

L'*ADAC-Motorwelt* du 17 avril 1931 ajoute : « La faible résistance aérodynamique de la carrosserie sport, légère et racée, contribue à atteindre une bonne vitesse. » Avec son pare-brise rabattu, déjà en verre de sécurité, cette petite voiture rapide peut franchir les 100 km/h.

Le volant et le maniement de cet étroit engin étonnent ses contemporains. Un essieu avant galbé avec ressort transversal permet de la surbaisser de près de 10 cm par rapport à la DA2 ce qui entraîne une meilleure tenue de route.

D'autres caractéristiques permettent de la qualifier de voiture de sport : la roue de secours montée sur le côté du capot moteur, l'absence de portières et le tableau de bord constitué d'un tachymètre à tambour, d'un manomètre d'huile et d'une clé de contact entre les deux.

Dans un reportage de *Motor und Sport* de 1930, l'auteur souligne : « La Wartburg est réservée aux bons conducteurs. Un mauvais conducteur ne mérite pas de posséder une telle automobile. » Le meilleur conducteur de Wartburg est sans aucun doute Robert « Bobby » Kohlrausch, né en 1904 à Eisenach. Il commence sa carrière comme apprenti-ajusteur aux usines Dixi et finit ingénieur. Une fois transformée par Bobby en engin de compétition, la motocyclette que lui a offerte son père pour le récompenser de son travail gagne de nombreuses coupes, mais a failli lui coûter la vie. Contre la promesse de ne plus jamais courir en moto, son père lui offre une BMW : ce sera le début d'une incroyable carrière avec 62 victoires et quatre records du monde. Il n'avait, en effet, jamais promis de ne pas courir sur quatre roues ! Chaque année en mai, lorsque le « pèlerinage des DA » prend la direction d'Eisenach, on se transmet respectueusement de main en main l'une des plus belles coupes de Kohlrausch.

A motor magazine observed in 1930 that "the Wartburg is a car for good drivers." And apparently they were happy to crank up the 18 bhp engine in all weathers in order to get behind the wooden steering wheel and go for a spin. The folding windscreen was already made of shatter-proof glass and stays up "as an exception".

1930 heißt es in einer Fachzeitschrift: „Der Wartburg ist ein Wagen für gute Fahrer." Und die werfen den 18-PS-Motor offenbar bei jedem Wetter an, um sich hinter das dicke Holzlenkrad zu klemmen. Die umlegbare Windschutzscheibe besteht bereits aus splitterfreiem Glas und bleibt „ausnahmsweise" oben.

En 1930, une revue spécialisée proclame : « La Wartburg est réservée aux bons conducteurs » qui n'hésitent pas à mettre en marche le moteur de 18 ch par tous les temps pour se glisser derrière l'épais volant en bois. Le pare-brise rabattable est déjà en verre de sécurité et reste rarement à la verticale.

BMW Wartburg DA3   53

The tapering tail of the bodywork is a striking feature.
Its lightweight aluminium construction was the major factor
in keeping the car's weight down to a mere 904 lbs (410 kg).
The high power-to-weight ratio gave the car a top speed of
56 mph (90 kph).

Auffällig ist das spitz zulaufende Heck der leichten
Aluminiumkarosserie, die zu dem niedrigen Wagengewicht
von nur 410 Kilo entscheidend beiträgt. Das Leistungsgewicht ermöglicht stattliche 90 Stundenkilometer.

Une caractéristique de la carrosserie — en aluminium,
ce qui explique en grande partie le faible poids de la voiture,
seulement 410 kg — est son arrière boatstail. Son rapport
poids/performance avantageux lui permettait déjà à l'époque
d'atteindre la vitesse respectable de 90 km/h.

Max Friz, an engine designer who had left Daimler-Motoren-Gesellschaft due to unfulfilled salary expectations and a lack of interest in his project for high altitude flight-engines, was one of BMW's first pioneers. He was a genius in his field, capable of finding the engine to suit any purpose, especially to power planes, but also trucks, boats and motorbikes.

The BMW license agreement with Austin came to an end on 1 March 1932. As it had, in any case, been a thorn in his flesh, Friz, who had since become a company director, began to work on his own design for a two-stroke car engine with front-wheel drive transmission. Immersing himself in engine practice and suspension theory, Friz was forced to concede that the proposal of Eisenach staffers to adapt designs which were already in existence was a quicker means of achieving his objectives.

Transforming these designs to create the first proper BMW began with an engine whose stroke was lengthened by 80 mm while the original bore was retained. This extended stroke could deliver 20 bhp as opposed to the previous rating of 15 bhp, a fact mirrored by the new creation's name: 3/20 PS (PS is a German alternative measure of realistically rating horsepower). The modifications made to the crankshaft drive, cylinder head and side-mounted camshaft (now driven by a duplex chain instead of cast iron spur gears) meant that the design was effectively brand new.

One of the biggest departures from the British original could be seen in the chassis. The main features constituted a central frame (instead of U-section rails) and a propshaft extended right back to the swing axle. The front axle, one of the components most in need of updating, remained unaltered. Therefore, the driving characteristics continued to be somewhat less than driver-friendly, particularly since the new car's sturdy, but heavy body (from Daimler-Benz

at Sindelfingen) meant that it weighed 396 lbs (180 kg) more than the earlier 3/15 DA2.

Daimler-Benz built all four designs: limousine, tourer, convertible and roadster. What was even more confusing was the type designation AM1 for "1. Auto München" (1st Munich car). One of the special car bodies did, however, come from Munich: a cute roadster by Ludwig Weinberger. Some 7215 chassis (AM1–4) were manufactured from April 1932 to the end of 1934, all destined to cater for a wide variety of designs. 53 were destined for pick-up trucks.

Four of the 59 BMW 3/20s listed in the BMW Veteran Club Germany have the same owner: the lucky man is a Dutchman from Gouda. A Warsaw owner is even more fortunate: in addition to an AM4, he owns a truly rare model, the 1932 AM1 Roadster.

Die Daimler-Motoren-Gesellschaft hat er wegen unerfüllter Gehaltswünsche und allgemeinem Desinteresse an seinem Höhenflugmotoren-Projekt verlassen. Bei BMW ist der Motorenkonstrukteur Max Friz einer der Männer der ersten Stunde, ein genialer Kopf, der allem, was „kreucht und fleucht" – besonders Flugzeugen, aber auch Lastwagen, Booten und Motorrädern – die richtigen Triebwerke verpasst.

Der Lizenzvertrag mit Austin, der Friz ohnehin ein Dorn im Auge ist, wird zum 1. März 1932 gekündigt, und sofort macht sich Friz – inzwischen zum Direktor avanciert – an eine eigene Konstruktion. Das Ziel ist ein Zweitakter mit Frontantrieb. In Motorenpraxis und Fahrwerkstheorie tiefschürfend, muss Friz bald erkennen, dass der Vorschlag der Eisenacher, Vorhandenes umzukonstruieren, schneller zum Ziel führt.

Die Mutation zum richtigen BMW beginnt beim Motor, dessen Hub unter Beibehaltung der Bohrung auf 80 Millimeter verlängert wird. 20 statt 15 PS bringt die so erzielte Hubraumvergrößerung, und damit steht auch der Name des Debütanten fest: 3/20 PS. Änderungen an Kurbeltrieb und Zylinderkopf sowie der Antrieb der seitlichen Nockenwelle über eine Duplexkette anstelle der gusseisernen Stirnräder sprechen für eine „Fast-Neukonstruktion".

Noch mehr vom Insel-Original entfernt man sich beim Chassis. Wichtigste Merkmale sind der Zentralrahmen anstelle des U-Profils und eine bis nach hinten zur Pendelachse durchlaufende Kardanwelle. Ausgerechnet die Vorderachse, die eigentlich nach einer besseren Lösung verlangt, bleibt unverändert. Und so bleiben auch die Fahreigenschaften äußerst gewöhnungsbedürftig, zumal der Wagen mit seiner soliden, aber schweren Karosserie, gebaut im Daimler-Benz-Werk Sindelfingen, 180 Kilo mehr wiegt als der 3/15 DA2.

Daimler-Benz baut alle vier Aufbauten: Limousine, Tourer, Cabriolet und Roadster. Umso mehr verwirrt die Typen-

BMW 3/20 PS

bezeichnung AM1 für „1. Auto München". Immerhin stammt eine der Sonderkarosserien aus der Isar-Metropole: ein schnuckeliger Roadster von Ludwig Weinberger. Von April 1932 bis Ende 1934 werden 7215 Fahrgestelle (AM 1–4) für die verschiedensten Aufbauten gefertigt. Davon erhalten 53 einen Lieferwagenaufbau.

Von den 59 im BMW-Veteranen-Club Deutschland e.V. registrierten 3/20 befinden sich vier in einer Hand: Ein Holländer aus Gouda ist der Glückliche. Es gibt aber auch einen Überglücklichen, und der kommt aus Warschau: Ihm gehört neben einem AM4 eine echte Rarität, der AM1 Roadster von 1932.

Après avoir quitté la Daimler-Motoren-Gesellschaft qui avait refusé sa demande d'augmentation de salaire et ne s'intéressait pas à son projet de moteur d'avion, le motoriste Max Friz est, chez BMW, l'un des hommes de la première heure. C'est un génie qui dessine des moteurs qui s'adaptent à tous les engins – en particulier les avions, mais aussi les camions, les bateaux et les motos.

La licence d'exploitation accordée par Austin, la bête noire de Friz, est résiliée le 1er mars 1932 et, immédiatement, Friz – entre-temps promu directeur – s'attaque à son propre projet : un moteur à deux temps destiné à une traction avant. Parfait connaisseur de l'utilisation des moteurs et de la théorie des châssis, Friz doit admettre que la proposition des ingénieurs d'Eisenach consistant à adapter des plans déjà existants était un moyen plus rapide d'atteindre ses objectifs.

La transformation de ces plans pour créer la véritable première BMW commence avec le moteur, allongé à 80 mm pour un alésage inchangé. L'augmentation de cylindrée permet ainsi d'obtenir 20 ch au lieu de 15 et, par la même opération, donne son nom à la voiture : 3/20 PS. Des modifications sur l'embrayage et sur la culasse ainsi que sur la prise de force pour l'arbre à cames latéral à l'aide d'une chaîne duplex – et non plus d'engrenages en fonte – justifient le qualificatif de modèle quasiment nouveau.

Pour le châssis, on est encore plus éloigné de l'original. Les caractéristiques les plus importantes sont le cadre central (à la place de profilés en U) ainsi que la transmission par cardan allant jusqu'à l'essieu arrière oscillant. Quant à l'essieu avant, qui mériterait pourtant d'être amélioré, il reste en l'état. Sa conduite demande donc, pour le moins, une certaine accoutumance, d'autant que la voiture à la lourde mais solide carrosserie (fabriquée par l'usine

Daimler-Benz de Sindelfingen) pèse 180 kg de plus que la 3/15 DA2.

Daimler-Benz assemble chacun des quatre modèles : berline, tourer, cabriolet et roadster. La dénomination de AM1 pour « 1re Auto Munich » est d'autant plus troublante. Toujours est-il que l'une des carrosseries spéciales provient de Munich : il s'agit d'un joli petit roadster signé Ludwig Weinberger. D'avril 1932 à la fin de 1934 sont construits 7215 châssis (AM1–4) pour les carrosseries les plus diverses (dont 53 en version camionnette).

Sur les 59 BMW 3/20 enregistrées auprès du BMW-Veteranen-Club Deutschland e.V. (le club des collectionneurs de vieilles BMW), quatre se trouvent aux mains d'un seul homme : l'heureux propriétaire est un Hollandais de Gouda. Mais un propriétaire de Varsovie est encore plus chanceux : non seulement il possède une AM4 mais aussi un authentique roadster AM1 de 1932, ce qui est exceptionnel.

A "real" BMW, whose engine generated 20 bhp thanks to the increased cubic capacity.
59 of these BMW 3/20s are still on the BMW Veteran Club's lists.

Ein „richtiger" BMW, dessen Motor dank einer Hubraumvergrößerung 20 PS leistet.
Noch 59 dieser BMW 3/20 sind im BMW-Veteranen-Club registriert.

Une BMW véritable, dont le moteur développe 20 ch grâce à l'augmentation de cylindrée.
Le registre du club des collectionneurs de vieilles BMW fait encore état de 59 exemplaires
de ces BMW 3/20.

The body was mounted on the central box frame in Sindelfingen – by Daimler-Benz.

Auf den Zentralkastenrahmen werden in Sindelfingen die Aufbauten gesetzt –
von Daimler-Benz!

Les carrosseries sont montées sur le cadre à caisson central à Sindelfingen
– par Daimler-Benz!

BMW 3/20 PS

The BMW 3/20 PS is a rock-solid vehicle, but at 1430 lbs (650 kg) a relatively heavy one. Despite this, 7215 chassis were produced for a variety of different bodies, even including 53 pick-up trucks.

Der BMW 3/20 PS ist zwar ein grundsolides, aber mit 650 Kilo Gewicht doch ein relativ schweres Vehikel. Immerhin werden 7215 Fahrgestelle für verschiedene Aufbauten – darunter auch 53 Lieferwagen – gefertigt.

La BMW 3/20 PS est, certes, une voiture inusable, mais, avec ses 650 kg, tout de même relativement lourde. 7215 châssis seront néanmoins construits pour différents modèles – dont 53 camionnettes.

The dashboard is compact and well-designed. Underneath the hood, plenty of spare room is left by the small straight-cylinder engine with its laterally-mounted camshaft driven by a duplex chain.

Gebündelte Ordnung herrscht auf dem Amaturenbrett. Viel Platz unter der Haube lässt der kleine Reihenmotor, dessen seitliche Nockenwelle über eine Duplexkette angetrieben wird.

Tout est bien ordonné sur le tableau de bord. Le petit moteur en ligne dont l'arbre à cames latéral est actionné par une chaîne duplex est loin d'occuper la totalité du compartiment moteur.

BMW 303

The 3/20 formula delivered 5 bhp per cylinder. How do you get 30 bhp? Correct, install six cylinders. So a miniscule BMW engine was born; 1173 cc, meaning it was the smallest automotive six cylinder of all time. Like the whole BMW 303 car, it was an interim solution, but provided a basis for follow-up designs of the 1930s.

The six cylinders featured long stroke dimensions, measuring 56 x 80 mm, utilizing overhead valves. The pressurized lubrication now took a liter and a half more oil than a 3/20 and the carburation system had also been uprated with two Solex sidedraft carburetors.

The engineers from Eisenach developed a modern frame design with tubular steel longitudinal beams and four box-section cross beams. The 309, 315, 315/1, 319 and 329 models also followed this construction. New conscientious solutions had also been researched and developed for the suspension, which had previously been the car's Achilles' heel: control arms and transverse springs at the front, semi-elliptic springs at the live axle rear. This was an enormous technological advance on BMW's DA and AM predecessors.

Thanks to fine-tuning of shock absorbers and springs alongside direct rack and pinion steering, the 303 provided a completely new driving sensation. Pleasure in driving was disseminated and marketed by an advertising campaign involving a 1250 mile (2000 km) publicity trip through the German Reich.

Every fourth car of the 2300 BMW 303s built was a four-window convertible. The models on offer – only in production for a year – were completed by special designs, such as the Gläser sports convertible. Only two examples were manufactured of the tourer and the convertible limousine bodies.

The Wartburg area was still covered by the snow which fell in the winter of 1933/34: by then it was already clear that the 303 was old hat. In February, the exterior of the subsequent BMW 315 model was trimmed to give a final body style, one made unmistakable by six parallel cooling slots on each side of the hood. A 1.5 liter engine (to which the "fifteen" numeral after the "three" prefix refers in 315) was completed and installed from April onwards.

Theoretically, the increase in cubic capacity should, in percentage terms, produce 8 bhp more. That prediction was inaccurate, for an increase of only 4 bhp was achieved. This was, however, enough to enable the European 100 kph (62 mph) barrier to be breached.

Fünf PS pro Zylinder lautet die Gleichung beim 3/20. Wie kommt man also auf 30 PS? Richtig, indem man mit sechs Zylindern rechnet! So entsteht bei BMW mit 1173 ccm der hubraumschwächste automobile Sechszylinder aller Zeiten – eine Interimslösung wie das ganze Auto, aber eine Grundlage für die Folgekonstruktionen der dreißiger Jahre.

Über den sechs langhubigen Zylinderröhrchen mit je 56 x 80 mm liegen im Zylinderkopf hängende Ventile. Gegenüber dem 3/20 passen anderthalb Liter Öl mehr in den Druckumlauf, und auch das Vergasersystem wird der neuen Situation gerecht.

Die Ingenieure aus Eisenach entwickeln eine moderne Rahmenkonstruktion mit Stahlrohrlängsträgern und vier Kastenquerträgern. Auf dieser Basis entstehen auch die Modelle 309, 315, 315/1, 319 und 329. Für die Radaufhängungen, den bisherigen Schwachpunkt, gibt es ebenfalls durchdachte Lösungen: vorn mit Querlenkern und -feder, hinten mit halbelliptischen Blattfedern – ein enormer technischer Fortschritt gegenüber den DA- und AM-Vorgängern.

Dank der gefühlvollen Abstimmung von Stoßdämpfern und Federn und einer direkten Zahnstangenlenkung vermittelt der 303 ein völlig neues Fahrgefühl. Fahrfreude kommt auf, und die wird bei einer 2000 Kilometer langen Tour durch das Deutsche Reich werbewirksam vermittelt und vermarktet.

Jeder vierte der 2300 gebauten 303 ist ein Cabriolet mit vier Fenstern. Seltene Sonderaufbauten wie das Sport-Cabriolet von Gläser runden das Angebot dieser Baureihe, die nur ein Jahr lang in Produktion bleibt, ab. Vom Tourer und der Cabrio-Limousine werden jeweils nur zwei Fahrzeuge gefertigt.

Die Wartburg hüllt noch der Schnee des Winters 1933/34 ein, da ist schon klar, dass der 303 bereits Schnee von gestern ist. Im Februar wird das Outfit auf das

Nachfolgemodell BMW 315 getrimmt, leicht erkennbar an den sechs unterteilten Kühlschlitzfeldern auf jeder Seite der Motorhaube. Auch der 1,5-Liter-Motor, für den die 15 hinter der 3 steht, ist fertig und wird ab April eingebaut.

Die Rechnung, dass das neue Modell nun proportional zur Hubraumvergrößerung 8 PS mehr an die Räder bringen könnte, geht freilich nicht auf: Es sind lediglich vier Pferdestärken mehr, aber genug, um die „Schallgrenze" von 100 Stundenkilometern zu erreichen.

La BMW 3/20 développe 5 ch par cylindre. Comment obtenir 30 ch? Avec six cylindres bien sûr! C'est ainsi que naît chez BMW un minuscule moteur qui est, avec ses 1173 cm³, l'automobile six-cylindres la plus petite de tous les temps. Comme pour la BMW 303, cette voiture est une version intermédiaire mais qui jettera les bases des réalisations qui auront lieu dans le courant des années 1930.

Les six minuscules cylindres à longue course aux cotes respectives de 56 x 80 mm ont des soupapes en tête. Le circuit d'huile renferme un litre et demi de plus que celui de la 3/20 et le carburateur aussi est adapté à ce nouvel environnement.

Les ingénieurs d'Eisenach mettent au point un châssis-cadre moderne avec longerons longitudinaux en tube d'acier et quatre poutres transversales en caisson – un châssis en échelle que reprennent également les modèles 309, 315, 315/1, 319 et 329. Pour les suspensions, le talon d'Achille de ces voitures, on trouve également des solutions : des bras et ressorts transversaux à l'avant et des ressorts semi-elliptiques à l'arrière. C'est un énorme progrès qui est accompli sur le plan mécanique par rapport aux DA et AM de la génération précédente.

Grâce à la précision du réglage des amortisseurs et des ressorts ainsi qu'à une direction à crémaillère directe, la 303 donne des sensations absolument inédites à son conducteur. On ressent un réel plaisir de conduite – une campagne publicitaire effectuée sur 2000 km à travers le IIIe Reich en assure la promotion.

Près d'un quart des 2300 BMW 303 construites sont des cabriolets à quatre fenêtres. Les modèles proposés – qui ne seront fabriqués que pendant un an – dans cette gamme seront complétés de séries spéciales comme le Sport-Cabriolet de Gläser. Seulement deux exemplaires de la tourer et de la berline cabriolet seront fabriqués.

La Wartburg frissonne encore sous le manteau de neige de l'hiver 1933–1934, et il est clair que la 303 n'en est plus à son premier printemps. En février, son esthétique est alignée sur celle de la BMW 315, aisément reconnaissable par les six fentes de refroidissement disposées de chaque côté du capot moteur. Le moteur de 1,5 litre, symbolisé par le « quinze » derrière le « trois », est prêt techniquement et est lancé en avril 1934.

L'équation selon laquelle l'augmentation de cylindrée pourrait se traduire proportionnellement par 8 ch supplémentaires est fausse puisqu'ils ne sont qu'au nombre de quatre – mais cela suffit pour atteindre le « mur du son » de l'époque, les 100 km/h.

The BMW 303 saw the birth of the characteristic BMW kidney-shaped radiator grill and marked the launch of a completely new range of models. The first bodies were still produced in Sindelfingen, but mass production was at Ambi-Budd in Berlin.

Der BMW 303 markiert die Geburtsstunde der BMW-Nieren und den Beginn einer völlig neuen Baureihe. Die ersten Karosserien entstehen noch in Sindelfingen, der Serienbau erfolgt dann bei Ambi-Budd in Berlin.

La BMW 303 marque la naissance des « naseaux » chez BMW et le début d'une gamme de voitures encore inédites. Les premières carrosseries sont réalisées toujours à Sindelfingen, mais la construction en série a lieu chez Ambi-Budd à Berlin.

The new engine, with twin vertical carburetors and developing 30 bhp, was the smallest six-cylinder automobile of all time with its cubic capacity of 1.2 liters.

Der neue Motor, der mit seinen zwei Vertikalvergasern 30 PS leistet, ist mit 1,2 Litern Hubraum der kleinste automobile Sechszylinder aller Zeiten.

Le nouveau moteur de 1,2 litre, qui développe 30 ch avec ses deux carburateurs verticaux, est le plus petit six-cylindres de toute l'histoire de l'automobile.

For the 303 the engineers from Eisenach developed a modern frame incorporating tubular steel longitudinal beams and box-section cross members. The bodywork styling found great favor with motorists, as a promotional tour through the German Reich revealed, but the car's performance left something to be desired.

Für den 303 haben die Ingenieure aus Eisenach eine moderne Rahmenkonstruktion mit Stahlrohrlängsträgern und Kastenquerträgern entwickelt. Die Form der Karosserie findet bei den Automobilisten – wie sich bei einer Werbetour durch das Deutsche Reich herausstellt – großen Anklang. Die Leistung lässt indes noch Wünsche offen.

Pour la 303, les ingénieurs d'Eisenach ont conçu un châssis moderne à caissons avec des longerons longitudinaux creux en acier et des poutres transversales. Comme le clame une campagne publicitaire qui a traversé tout le IIIe Reich, sa carrosserie est tout à fait au goût des automobilistes, bien que sa puissance laisse encore à désirer.

BMW 303

The hinged windscreen ensures fresh air at the wheel and plenty of ventilation for the roomy interior. Just nine examples of the 56 mph (90 kph) BMW 303 are registered with the Veteran Club.

Für Frischluft am Steuer und Ventilation im geräumigen Innenraum sorgt die ausstellbare Windschutzscheibe. Von den 90 Stundenkilometer schnellen BMW 303 sind im Veteranen-Club lediglich noch neun Exemplare registriert.

Le pare-brise relevable permet de profiter de l'air frais au volant et d'aérer l'habitacle spacieux. À en croire le club des collectionneurs de BMW, il existe encore neuf exemplaires de cette BMW 303, capable d'atteindre les 90 km/h.

BMW 315/1 Sport-Zweisitzer

In 1933 a dramatic change took place. BMW abandoned its small-volume, four-cylinder baby engine and redesigned it as a six-cylinder. The result was an 1173 cc engine, which was the smallest in the world. It only took a few weeks before engineers at Eisenach recognized the engine's potential and increased the volume to 1490 cc. This motor move provided the basis for the BMW 315, which sold a total 9765 units to be highly successful. The bigger engine also laid the foundations for an attractive small sports car providing 40 bhp. It proved to be so successful in motor sport that the English company Frazer-Nash acquired the license to build it.

BMW engine size was increased again to achieve sporting success in the two-liter class. That 1911 cc development produced 55 bhp at 4000 rpm and an 81 mph (130 kph) top speed, 10 kph more than the smaller six-cylinder engine delivered.

Both sport two-seaters, the 315/1 and the 319/1, look almost identical. The "bigger brother" boasts three decorative strips on the grills on the side of the hood and features a small ventilator window, slightly reducing drafts around the necks of passengers. This sport two-seater should only be driven open-topped, for the raised fabric folding top gives a rather ugly appearance. A coupé top, designed by the Vereinigte Werkstätten München (workshop for car bodies and coach building) remained a short-lived oddity and was not a styling triumph.

In contrast to the 315 sport convertible and the 319/1 edition from the Munich BMW dealer and specialist bodywork producer, Ludwig Weinberger, the 315/1 Sport-Zweisitzer was notable for the delicate and refined style of its covered rear wheels.

All in all, the 315/1 was an uncomplicated vehicle with a simple chassis (at the front: lower control arm suspension,

transverse spring on top, plus rigid rear axle suspension via semi-elliptic spring). Interestingly, it already used an electric fuel pump for the 11-gallon (42-liter) tank. Maneuverability and a good power-weight ratio destined the 315/1 for motor sport, its only occasional drawback being the erratic drum brakes.

Both sport two-seaters correspond to the classic idea of a roadster, starting with the spartan cockpit. Two large round instruments dominate: the clock on the left and the speedometer with odometer on the right. Two smaller round instruments for water temperature and oil pressure, as well as many little levers and push-buttons (located above the glove compartment) are the only dashboard decorations. The small front windscreen with its parallel wipers is adjustable.

Even the doors, with their recessed armrests, are pure roadster: there are no handles to open them; a small lever inside works the mechanism. Of course there are no bumpers or external mirrors. One thing which is important, however, is the spare wheel, situated where you would expect the trunk to be.

Ein Umsturz vollzieht sich 1933: BMW wendet sich von seinem hubraumschwachen Vierzylindermotörchen ab und steigt auf sechs Zylinder um. Heraus kommt der mit 1173 ccm kleinste Sechszylinder der Welt. Welche Möglichkeiten in diesem Triebwerk stecken, erkennt man in Eisenach schon nach wenigen Wochen und vergrößert das Volumen auf 1490 ccm. Das ist die Basis des mit insgesamt 9765 Einheiten recht erfolgreich verkauften BMW 315, eine Baureihe, zu der auch ein attraktiv aussehender kleiner Sportwagen mit 40 PS gehört. Dieser ist im Motorsport so erfolgreich, dass die englische Firma Frazer-Nash das Recht zum Lizenzbau erwirbt.

Um auch in der 2-Liter-Klasse sportlich reüssieren zu können, wird der Motor nochmals vergrößert. Aus 1911 ccm werden bei 4000 Touren 55 PS geholt. Das bedeutet 130 Stundenkilometer Spitze – zehn mehr als mit dem kleineren Sechszylinder möglich sind.

Beide Sport-Zweisitzer, der 315/1 und der 319/1, unterscheiden sich optisch kaum. Der „große Bruder" protzt mit drei Zierleisten auf den seitlichen Motorhauben-Gittern und verfügt über ein kleines Ausstellfenster, das die Luftverwirbelung im Nackenbereich der Passagiere etwas reduziert. Diese Sport-Zweisitzer sollte man nur offen fahren, denn das geschlossene Stoffverdeck wirkt ziemlich ungehobelt. Ein Coupé-Aufsatz, entworfen von den Vereinigten Werkstätten in München, der stilistisch wenig gelungen ist, bleibt kurzlebiges Kuriosum.

Im Gegensatz zum 315 Sport-Cabriolet und der 319/1-Ausgabe des Münchner BMW-Vertreters und Sonderkarosserie-Herstellers Ludwig Weinberger wirkt der 315/1 Sport-Zweisitzer zierlich und mit seinen abgedeckten Hinterrädern elegant.

Insgesamt gesehen ist der 315/1 ein unkompliziertes, sportliches Fahrzeug mit simplem Fahrwerk – vorn verfügt er über einen Querlenker unten, eine Querfeder oben und hinten über eine starre Aufhängung mit Halbfedern. Interessant ist, dass er bereits eine elektrische Benzinpumpe für den 42-Liter-Tank aufweist. Wendigkeit und gutes Leistungsgewicht prädestinieren diesen Wagen zum motorsportlichen Einsatz, wo Freude und Erfolg nur ab und zu durch Schwächen der Trommelbremsen getrübt werden.

Beide Sport-Zweisitzer entsprechen den klassischen Roadster-Idealen, beginnend mit dem spartanischen Cockpit. Ins Blickfeld fallen zwei große Rundinstrumente: links die Uhr und rechts der Tachometer mit Kilometerzähler. Zwei kleinere Rundinstrumente für Wassertemperatur und Öldruck sowie einige Hebelchen und Zugknöpfe (selbst über dem Handschuhfach) sind die einzige Zierde des Armaturenbretts. Die knapp bemessene Frontscheibe mit den Parallelwischern ist verstellbar.

Aber auch die mit Armausschnitten versehenen Türen erinnern an einen Roadster: Griffe zum Öffnen fehlen, die Schlösser betätigt ein Hebelchen von innen. Natürlich sind auch keine Stoßstangen und Außenspiegel vorhanden. Wichtig ist allerdings das Reserverad, das sich dort befindet, wo man den Kofferraum vermutet.

En 1933, année révolutionnaire, BMW met au placard ses asthmatiques quatre-cylindres de petite cylindrée pour se tourner vers les six-cylindres. Avec 1173 cm³, c'est le plus petit six-cylindres du monde. Il n'a fallu que quelques semaines aux ingénieurs d'Eisenach pour s'en apercevoir et augmenter sa cylindrée à 1490 cm³. Il est l'âme de la BMW 315 qui connaîtra un succès enviable puisqu'elle sera vendue à 9765 exemplaires, une BMW 315 qui sera aussi épaulée par une séduisante petite voiture de sport de 40 ch. Celle-ci remporte tant de succès en compétition que la firme britannique Frazer-Nash achète une licence pour sa construction.

Pour lui assurer le succès sportif dans la catégorie deux litres également, la cylindrée de son moteur est encore majorée. Les 1911 cm³ délivrent 55 ch à 4000 tr/min : la vitesse de pointe est de 130 km/h, dix de plus qu'avec le petit six-cylindres.

Sur le plan esthétique, il est bien difficile de distinguer les deux biplaces de sport, la 315/1 et la 319/1. La « grande sœur » affiche trois joncs décoratifs sur les grilles d'aération latérales du capot moteur et possède un petit déflecteur qui réduit légèrement les courants d'air à hauteur de la nuque des passagers. On ne peut, en effet, conduire cette biplace de sport pratiquement qu'en décapotable, car la capote en toile fermée amoindrit la beauté des lignes. Un *hard-top* dessiné par les Vereinigte Werkstätten München (atelier de carrosserie et d'automobiles de Munich), qui n'est pas non plus une grande réussite esthétique, disparaîtra rapidement.

Contrairement à la 315 Cabriolet Sport et à la 319/1 carrossée par Ludwig Weinberger, un concessionnaire munichois de BMW qui fabrique aussi des carrosseries spéciales, la 315/1 Sport biplace affiche un style délicat et raffiné avec ses roues arrière carénées.

Globalement, la 315/1 est une voiture sportive et peu compliquée avec un châssis simple (bras transversaux inférieurs et ressort transversal supérieur à l'avant et, à l'arrière, suspension rigide à ressorts semi-elliptiques). Un détail intéressant est qu'elle possède déjà une pompe à essence électrique pour son réservoir d'une capacité de 42 litres. Maniabilité et un bon rapport poids/puissance prédestinent cette voiture à la compétition dont la seule faiblesse chronique provient des freins à tambour.

Les deux biplaces de sport correspondent au schéma classique du roadster, à commencer par leur cockpit spartiate. Deux gros cadrans circulaires sautent aux yeux : à gauche, l'horloge et, à droite, le tachymètre avec compteur journalier. Deux cadrans ronds de plus petit diamètre pour la température de l'eau et la pression d'huile ainsi que quelques petites manettes et boutons (même au-dessus de la boîte à gants) sont la seule décoration du tableau de bord. De petite dimension, le pare-brise à essuie-glaces parallèles est réglable.

Quant aux portières servant d'accoudoirs, elles sont dans le plus pur style des roadsters : il n'existe pas de poignées pour les ouvrir, un petit levier actionne le mécanisme de l'intérieur. Naturellement, il n'y a pas non plus de pare-chocs ni de rétroviseurs extérieurs. La roue de secours, en revanche, est indispensable et se trouve dans le coffre.

BMW 315/1 Sport-Zweisitzer

Sporty elegance and performance to match are the main features of the 315/1, which also had considerable success on the racetrack. The clock and speedometer, reading up to 93 mph (150 kph), are the dominant features of this roadster dashboard.

Sportliche Eleganz und ein ansprechendes Leistungspotential kennzeichnen den 315/1, der sich auch mit vielen rennsportlichen Meriten schmücken darf. Die Uhr und ein Tacho, der bis zu 150 Stundenkilometer anzeigt, sind die beherrschenden Rundinstrumente auf dem Roadster-Armaturenbrett.

Une élégance sportive ainsi qu'un potentiel intéressant caractérisent la 315/1 qui remportera de nombreuses victoires en compétition. Deux cadrans circulaires, la montre et le tachymètre gradué jusqu'à 150 km/h, trônent sur le tableau de bord du roadster.

LDK - SP 315

BMW 315/1 Sport-Zweisitzer

Harmony of form and function from all angles. The front windscreen of the stylish automobile is adjustable, the soft top is easy to operate, and the tapered "trunk" at the rear only has room for the spare wheel.

Harmonie von Form und Funktion aus jeder Perspektive. Die Frontscheibe des schnittigen Fahrzeugs ist verstellbar, das Verdeck leicht zu bedienen, und in dem auch nach hinten abgerundeten „Kofferraum" findet lediglich das Reserverad Platz.

Harmonie des formes et de la fonction quelle que soit la perspective : le pare-brise de cette élégante voiture s'ouvre et la capote s'escamote aisément, mais le « coffre » arrondi n'héberge que la roue de secours.

The elegant lines of the twin-seater 315/1, whose cladded rear wheels and long, sweeping wings accentuate the chic design.

Einfach chic ist die Linienführung des 315/1 Zweisitzers, dessen abgedeckte Hinterräder die elegante Note ebenso betonen wie die langgestreckten vorderen Kotflügel.

Elles sont d'un grand chic, les lignes de la 315/1 biplace dont les roues arrière carénées soulignent l'élégance au même titre que les interminables ailes avant.

BMW 326 Cabriolet

The 326 proved to be the most successful prewar BMW, despite the fact that it was thought to be somewhat conservative when it was presented in February 1936. This model had a 50 bhp six-cylinder engine, which fired the imagination of bodywork designers. Some 5500 convertibles were built in addition to more than 10,000 sedans, whose bodies were manufactured in Berlin-Johannisthal.

Coach builders Autenrieth in Darmstadt were a major player in the automotive sector and offered two-door as well four-door body designs. A 1938 prototype caused a sensation with its safety-conscious sliding doors. This was a beautiful car, one which is still in the best of health lovingly preserved to this day.

The convertible offered by the Vereinigte Werkstätten München for car bodies and coach building listed two doors, four seats, four windows. The two-seater convertibles by Drauz, Weinberger and Gläser were far sportier. Erdmann & Rossi's roadster appealed to the purists and could provide drivers with a wonderful slipstream sensation, one broken only by the windscreen.

The bumpers turned out to be a means by which the passage of each succeeding year could be determined: they appeared in pairs until 1938 and in a single blade from 1939. In the year of the car's "birth", the 326 had disc wheels, followed by perforated rims from 1937.

As already indicated, the "crowning glory" was the new six-cylinder engine, which had 1971 cc instead of 1911 cc and therefore took the two-liter class to the limit. This extremely long-stroke engine (66 x 96 mm equals a bore-to-stroke ratio of 1.45) made a compact cylinder block possible due to the small gaps between cylinders.

The crankshaft and the four-bearing camshaft with a duplex chain drive were correspondingly small. A pair of downdraft Solex 26 BFLV carburetors were part of the basic 326 equipment range. For reasons of cost, BMW decided to install just one carburetor in the 320 and 321 models, although this was at the expense of 5 bhp.

Depending on the version and equipment range, a 326 convertible cost between 5800 and 8000 reichsmarks. The chassis and engine alone cost 4450 reichsmarks. All in all, this mid-range convertible was relatively expensive, which made the strong sales figures even more surprising.

Als erfolgreichster BMW der Vorkriegsgeschichte entpuppt sich der 326, der bei seiner Vorstellung im Februar 1936 einen eher biederen Eindruck macht. Doch der 50-PS-Sechszylindermotor dieses Typs beflügelt offenbar die Phantasie der Karosserieschneider. Denn neben mehr als 10 000 Limousinen, deren Karosserien in Berlin-Johannisthal entstehen, werden auch 5500 Cabriolets gebaut.

Autenrieth in Darmstadt ist groß im Geschäft und bietet vier- und zweitürige Ausführungen an. 1938 wird ein vielbestaunter Prototyp mit Sicherheits-Schiebetüren vorgestellt, ein bildhübscher Wagen, der sich noch heute „bester Gesundheit" erfreut.

Zwei Türen, vier Sitze, vier Fenster, so lautet die Cabriolet-Offerte der Vereinigten Werkstätten für Karosserie- und Wagenbau in München. Weitaus sportlicher wirken die zweisitzigen Cabriolets von Drauz, Weinberger und Gläser. Erdmann & Rossis Roadster wendet sich an die Puristen und bietet ein nur von der Windschutzscheibe getrübtes Fahrtwind-Erlebnis.

Die Jahrgänge lassen sich an den Stoßstangen ablesen: Bis 1938 sind sie doppelt, ab 1939 nur noch einfach ausgeführt. Im „Geburtsjahrgang" sind die 326 mit Scheibenrädern ausgestattet, die ab 1937 durch Lochfelgen ersetzt werden.

Des „Pudels Kern" ist aber der neue Sechszylinder, der mit 1971 ccm (zuvor 1911 ccm) die 2-Liter-Klasse voll ausschöpft. Dieser extreme Langhuber (66 x 96 mm entsprechen einem Bohrung-Hub-Verhältnis von 1,45) ermöglicht wegen seiner kurzen Zylinderabstände einen kompakten Block.

Entsprechend kurz sind die Kurbelwelle und die vierfach gelagerte Nockenwelle mit Duplex-Kettenantrieb. Zwei Vertikalvergaser Solex 26 BFLV gehören zur Grundbestückung, während sich BMW aus Kostengründen bei den Modellen 320 und 321 auf einen Vergaser beschränkt und somit fünf PS „verschenkt".

Je nach Ausführung und Ausstattung müssen zwischen 5800 und 8000 Reichsmark für ein 326 Cabriolet bezahlt werden. Allein 4450 Reichsmark kostet das Fahrgestell mit Motor. Damit ist dieses Mittelklassecabriolet vergleichsweise teuer. Umso mehr überraschen die Verkaufszahlen.

La 326 sera la BMW produite en plus grand nombre durant l'avant-guerre bien que, lors de sa présentation en février 1936, elle fut perçue comme quelque peu conservatrice, mais le six-cylindres de 50 ch de cette version donne apparemment des ailes à l'imagination des constructeurs, car, en plus des plus de 10 000 berlines dont les carrosseries sont montées à Berlin-Johannisthal, BMW fabrique également 5500 cabriolets.

Autenrieth, à Darmstadt, fait également de bonnes affaires avec ses versions en deux et en quatre portes. En 1938, il présente un prototype à portières de sécurité coulissantes qui fait sensation, une magnifique voiture qui est aujourd'hui encore merveilleusement conservée.

Deux portes, quatre places, quatre fenêtres, telle est la formule choisie pour les cabriolets proposés par les Vereinigte Werkstätten München. Mais les cabriolets biplaces de Drauz, Weinberger et Gläser sont autrement plus sportifs. Le roadster d'Erdmann & Rossi est destiné aux puristes et offre les mêmes sensations qu'une décapotable que ne tempère qu'un petit pare-brise.

Les millésimes respectifs se distinguent par leurs pare-chocs : jusqu'en 1938, ils sont doubles, puis simples à partir de 1939. En 1936, l'année de leur mise sur le marché, les 326 possèdent des jantes à voile plein, puis des jantes perforées à partir de 1937.

Mais le chef-d'œuvre mécanique est le nouveau six-cylindres en ligne qui, avec une cylindrée de 1971 cm³ (contre 1911 cm³), exploite à fond la classe deux litres. Ce moteur à course extrêmement longue (66 x 96 mm donnent un rapport alésage/course de 1,45) autorise un bloc compact grâce aux faibles intervalles entre les cylindres.

D'autant plus courts sont donc le vilebrequin et l'arbre à cames à quatre paliers avec entraînement par chaîne duplex. Deux carburateurs verticaux Solex 26 BFLV font

partie de la dotation de série alors que, par souci d'économie, BMW se contente d'un seul carburateur, et renonce ainsi à 5 ch, pour les versions 320 et 321.

Selon la version et la finition choisies, une 326 Cabriolet coûte entre 5800 et 8000 reichsmarks. À lui seul, le châssis avec moteur coûte 4450 reichsmarks. Ce cabriolet du segment intermédiaire est finalement assez cher et son succès est donc d'autant plus surprenant.

The four seats, four side windows and two large doors of this BMW 326 Cabriolet make for a well-heeled mid-range car with a generously equipped interior offering plenty of passenger comfort.

Vier Sitze, vier Seitenfenster und zwei große Türen offeriert dieses BMW 326 Cabriolet: die gehobene Mittelklasse mit einem reich ausgestatteten Interieur und viel Fahrkomfort.

Cette BMW 326 Cabriolet offre quatre places, quatre vitres latérales et deux grandes portières : un certain luxe déjà, avec un habitacle richement équipé et un grand confort.

The driver's gaze is drawn over the large three-spoke steering wheel through the windscreen (no longer adjustable) to the free-standing headlamps. By the time the BMW 327 came along, these had been integrated into the wings.

Über das große Dreispeichenlenkrad fällt der Blick durch die nicht mehr ausstellbare Windschutzscheibe auf die freistehenden Lampen. Beim BMW 327 werden diese bereits in die Kotflügel integriert sein.

Derrière le grand volant à trois branches, le regard se dirige, à travers un pare-brise désormais fixe, vers les phares proéminents. Sur la BMW 327, ceux-ci seront déjà intégrés aux ailes.

BMW 326 Cabriolet

The six-cylinder engine developed 50 bhp. The striking double fenders of the 326 disappeared from the BMW range in 1939.

Der Sechszylindermotor mobilisiert 50 PS. Die geteilten, besonders markanten Doppelstoßstangen des 326 verschwinden 1939 aus dem BMW-Programm.

Le six-cylindres délivre 50 ch. Les doubles pare-chocs divisés de la 326, particulièrement marquants, disparaîtront du programme BMW en 1939.

BMW 326 Cabriolet

A successful model: more than 5500 of this attractive Cabriolet were sold, despite the price tag of almost 8000 reichsmarks. Apart from a few exceptions, Autenrieth of Darmstadt built the Cabriolet bodies.

Erfolgsmodell: Mehr als 5500 dieser attraktiven, nahezu 8000 Reichsmark teuren Cabriolets werden verkauft. Bis auf wenige Ausnahmen führt Autenrieth in Darmstadt den Cabriolet-Aufbau durch.

Un grand succès commercial : plus de 5500 exemplaires de ce joli cabriolet qui coûtait près de 8000 reichsmarks seront vendus. À quelques rares exceptions, les carrosseries seront l'œuvre d'Autenrieth, de Darmstadt.

BMW 328 Roadster

A feast for the eyes: slim fenders which extend full length, with elegantly integrated headlights. In sports tradition, no bumpers cover the small BMW kidneys at the front of the radiator of this roadster. The BMW 328 is not only a benchmark symbol of automotive esthetics but it also promises endless soft top fun.

Two leather belts secure the hood, which covers an engine capable of producing 80 bhp at 4500 rpm, a motor fed by three downdraft carburetors. To avoid developing a completely new engine, the existing six-cylinder unit was provided with a cylinder head whose brilliant design was worth a patent certificate in itself. Its tuning potential enabled power increases up to 120 bhp without difficulty, or 136 bhp for the final factory racing versions.

A consistently lightweight construction of only 1782 lbs (810 kg) and a balanced chassis ensured the best behavior even on the worst roads. This was a full-blooded sports car without any moodiness to spoil the fun. There is just one small fault: changing gear is like entering a labyrinth.

With the agility of a weasel, the 328 could outmaneuver many more powerful cars in the sports category, and on the racetrack it became a sporting legend in just three years with 405 wins and 154 second places. Indeed, races often featured internal BMW warfare, for there were starting grids made up exclusively of 328s.

The achievements of the racing version with the avant-garde aerodynamics of Carrozzeria Touring in Milan is worth a chapter in its own right. The series 328 also provided the basis for two streamlined versions built by the Wendler coachworks in Reutlingen, which reduced the drag coefficient and allowed very high maximum speeds.

Just 464 cars were built up to 1940. Frazer-Nash, British BMW importer since 1932, also built the 328 under license, converting it to right-hand drive.

The engine of the 328 experienced a comeback in postwar Britain and was used for several vehicles in the UK. Fritz Fiedler, one of the leading BMW designers, developed versions for Bristol and AFN. Last but not least, the Swiss automobile conversion company, Sbarro, contributed to the paeans of praise for the 328 with a replica in more recent times.

What was the 328? A classic or a vintage car? Perhaps a prestige badge for the company, a trendsetter of the 1930s for the sports cars of the postwar period? Maybe it was even a myth? Cult objects are a matter of taste. In the case of the 328, it is a fact that this timelessly elegant roadster has survived the era of automotive tin boxes and has remained forever youthful.

Eine Augenweide sind die schlanken, ganz nach hinten gezogenen Kotflügel mit den elegant integrierten Lampen. Keine Stoßstange verdeckt die sportlich schmalen BMW-Nieren vor dem Kühler dieses Roadsters. Der BMW 328 ist nicht nur ein Symbol automobiler Ästhetik, sondern verheißt auch schier endloses Cabriolet-Vergnügen.

Zwei Ledergurte sichern die Haube um das 80 PS bei 4500/min leistende Triebwerk, das von drei Fallstromvergasern beatmet wird. Um eine Neuentwicklung zu sparen, hat man den herkömmlichen Sechszylinder mit einem Zylinderkopf bestückt, dessen geniale Konstruktion eine Patenturkunde wert ist. Dieses Tuning erlaubt klaglos weitere Kraftschübe bis 120 PS und für die Rennversionen noch mehr.

Die konsequente Leichtbauweise (nur 810 Kilo) und ein ausgewogenes Fahrwerk sorgen für bestes Fahrverhalten selbst auf schlechtesten Straßen – ein Vollblutsportler ohne Launen. Kleines Manko: Die Schaltwege ähneln einem Labyrinth.

Mit der Wendigkeit eines Wiesels umkreist der 328 so manchen PS-Protz in der sportlichen Kategorie, und auf dem Rennparkett wird er mit 405 Siegen und 154 zweiten Plätzen in gerade mal drei Jahren zum Sportwagenmythos, wobei der Sieger oft als *primus inter pares* auftritt, denn letztlich gibt es Startfelder, die sich ausschließlich aus BMW 328 rekrutieren.

Das Ruhmesblatt der Rennversionen mit avantgardistischer Aerodynamik von Carrozzeria Touring in Mailand ist ein eigenes Kapitel wert. Aber auch auf Basis des serienmäßigen 328 werden von dem Karrosseriewerk Wendler in Reutlingen zwei Stromlinien-Exemplare gebaut, die den Luftwiderstandsbeiwert senken.

Bis 1940 werden 464 Exemplare gebaut. Frazer-Nash, seit 1932 britischer BMW-Importeur, führt die BMW 328 ein und baut sie auf Rechtslenkung um. Der Motor des 328 erlebt im Nachkriegs-England ein Comeback und beflügelt so manches Fahrzeug der Insel. Fritz Fiedler, einer der maßgeblichen BMW-Konstrukteure, entwickelt Derivate für Bristol und AFN. Last but not least stimmt der Schweizer Autoveredler Sbarro mit einer Replika in das Hohelied auf den 328 ein.

Was ist er nun eigentlich: ein Klassiker, ein Oldtimer, ein Firmenaushängeschild, ein Trendsetter der dreißiger Jahre für die Sportwagen der Nachkriegszeit oder gar ein Mythos? Kultobjekte sind Ansichtssache, aber beim 328 ist Tatsache: Dieser zeitlos elegante Roadster hat jede „Blechkultur" überlebt und wirkt noch immer jung.

Ces fines ailes élancées vers l'arrière et ses phares élégamment intégrés sont un véritable plaisir pour les yeux. Aucun pare-chocs ne couvre le radiateur de ce roadster aux naseaux d'une délicatesse et d'une sportivité sans conteste. La BMW 328 n'est pas seulement un symbole d'esthétique automobile, elle incarne aussi le plaisir infini de la conduite en cabriolet.

Deux courroies de cuir fixent le capot sous lequel ronronne un moteur qui délivre 80 ch à 4500 tr/min grâce à trois carburateurs inversés. Pour éviter de développer un moteur totalement nouveau, BMW a coiffé le six-cylindres conventionnel d'une culasse dont l'ingéniosité a mérité le dépôt d'un brevet. Son potentiel permet sans difficulté de faire monter la puissance jusqu'à 120 ch voire plus pour les versions course.

Une construction allégée de série (seulement 810 kg) et un châssis équilibré lui permettent d'offrir un comportement sans défaut même sur les plus mauvaises routes. Un pur-sang sans allure ! Elle n'a qu'un petit défaut : changer de vitesse est un véritable casse-tête.

Très maniable, la 328 rivalise avec des voitures de sport beaucoup plus puissantes. Elle s'impose sur les pistes du monde entier : avec 405 victoires et 154 deuxièmes places en trois ans, elle devient un mythe parmi les voitures de sport, une sorte de *primus inter pares* (le premier entre ses égaux). Dans certaines courses, les grilles de départ sont composées exclusivement de 328.

Le tableau de chasse des versions course à l'aérodynamique d'avant-garde signée par la Carrozzeria Touring à Milan mérite que l'on y consacre un chapitre spécifique. En s'inspirant de la 328 de série, le carrossier Wendler, à Reutlingen, construit deux exemplaires aérodynamiques qui en diminuent le C_x et qui permettent d'atteindre des vitesses maximales très élevées.

Jusqu'en 1940, 464 exemplaires seront produits. Frazer-Nash, importateur de BMW en Grande-Bretagne depuis 1932, importe des 328 et les transforme pour la conduite à gauche. Dans l'Angleterre de l'après-guerre, le moteur de la 328 fait un come-back et est utilisé sur plusieurs véhicules en Grande-Bretagne. Fritz Fiedler, l'un des grands ingénieurs de BMW, en développe les dérivés pour Bristol et AFN. *Last but not least,* le préparateur suisse Sbarro lui a rendu hommage récemment avec une admirable réplique.

Mais qu'est-ce qu'une 328 ? Une voiture classique ou un millésime ? Peut-être une carte de visite pour l'entreprise, un modèle des années 1930 à imiter par les voitures de sport de l'après-guerre, ou même un mythe ? Les avis sont partagés. Mais, pour la 328 une chose est acquise : ce roadster d'une élégance intemporelle a survécu à toutes les modes et reste indémodable.

A long slender kidney grill and sporting lines with no frills or flourishes and also no fender: the 328 is without doubt one of the most beautiful roadsters ever built. With its patented hood catch involving two leather straps to hold the engine hoods together, it has achieved cult status among BMW enthusiasts.

Eine schmale lange Niere und eine sportliche Linienführung ohne Schnörkel oder Stoßstangen: Der 328 ist zweifelsohne einer der schönsten Roadster, die je gebaut wurden. Mit den zwei Lederriemen, deren Patentverschlüsse die Motorhauben zusammenhalten, ist er ein automobilistisches Kultobjekt.

Des naseaux minces et étroits ainsi que des lignes sportives sans fioritures ni pare-chocs : la 328 est incontestablement l'un des plus jolis roadsters qui aient jamais été construits. Avec les deux courroies en cuir dont les fermetures brevetées maintiennent fermées les ailes du capot, c'est un objet de culte pour tout amateur d'automobiles.

DA-U 328

BMW 328 Roadster

The "legend on wheels" stood out for its excellent power-to-weight ratio and its superb handling.

Die „Legende auf Rädern" zeichnet sich durch ein günstiges Leistungsgewicht und exzellente Fahreigenschaften aus.

Cette voiture de légende se distingue par son excellent rapport poids/puissance et une parfaite tenue de route.

Based on the BMW 328, the bodywork designer baron Reinhard of König-Fachsenfeld came up with this streamlined body whose drag coefficient is 0.38, a remarkable figure for those days. The Fachsenfeld design, on the basis of a patent by Paul Jaray, was produced at the Wendler bodywork plant in Reutlingen. Two prototypes were built, one of which can be seen in the Deutsches Museum in Munich, while the other one, illustrated here, is in the hands of a private BMW collector from Nuremberg.

Auf Basis des BMW 328 entwirft der Formgestalter Reinhard Freiherr von König-Fachsenfeld diese Stromlinienkarosserie, deren Luftwiderstandsbeiwert bei 0,38 liegt und für damalige Zeiten recht beachtlich ist. Der Entwurf von Fachsenfeld nach einem Patent von Paul Jaray wird vom Karosseriewerk Wendler in Reutlingen realisiert. Zwei Prototypen werden gebaut, von denen einer im Deutschen Museum in München zu sehen ist. Dieser hier ist im Besitz eines privaten BMW-Sammlers aus Nürnberg.

Sur la plate-forme de la BMW 328, le designer Reinhard, baron de König-Fachsenfeld, dessine cette carrosserie aérodynamique dont le C_x – 0,38 – est vraiment remarquable pour cette époque. Le croquis de Fachsenfeld, selon un brevet de Paul Jaray, est réalisé par le carrossier Wendler, à Reutlingen. Deux prototypes seront construits, dont l'un est exposé au Deutsche Museum de Munich, celui-ci étant la propriété d'un collectionneur privé de Nuremberg.

Fachsenfeld did a huge amount of detail work to get the drag coefficient down, such as the curved windows and the flush door handles. Without the radiator ribs the drag coefficient would have been as low as 0.29.

Zur Reduzierung des Luftwiderstandsbeiwerts leistet Fachsenfeld enorm viel Detailarbeit, zu der abgerundete Scheiben und versenkte Türgriffe gehören. Ohne die Kühlrippen auf der Motorhaube hätte der C_w-Wert sogar nur bei 0,29 gelegen.

Pour obtenir un C_x optimal, Fachsenfeld n'a négligé aucun détail, telles les vitres arrondies et les poignées intégrées aux portières. Sans les ailettes de refroidissement sur le moteur, le C_x aurait été de 0,29 seulement.

BMW 327

Mr Reif from Chemnitz was one of the few fortunate people who were able to purchase the highly attractive BMW 327 convertible during the War. This stylish black design from Eisenach cost 7500 reichsmark. When Reif received the bill dated 12 May 1941, he could not know that his car, chassis and engine number 87306, would be the last of its kind to be made by BMW. Number 87307 was built in 1948 by the Soviet state company "Avtovelo" in a version identical to the 327 built before the War.

The 2+2 seater sports convertible was publicly unveiled in winter 1937. Initially it was difficult to target the right sales groups for the 327. Beauty and elegant lines, the capacity for storing a medium-sized case and a portable typewriter, and a rating of 55 bhp were not high priorities for buyers in this price category. Perhaps it was ideal for a traveling journalist with entourage?

Sales were therefore sluggish. When an 80 bhp version appeared in 1938 (327/28) to meet demands for performance and sportiness, strangely enough sales for the basic 327 also picked up. A total of 1124 convertibles and 179 coupés were built. In May 1941, the last coupé was supplied to the Brazilian consul-general de Louza-Ribeiro in Hamburg.

Like its predecessors, which were also equipped with a 2-liter engine (BMW 320, 321 and 326), the 327 had a low slung box-section chassis, on which car bodies manufactured by Ambi-Budd coachworks in Berlin-Johannisthal were used. Ambi-Budd and Autenrieth in Darmstadt were BMW's largest suppliers of car bodies in the 1930s.

Hurth and ZF supplied the four-speed transmission (with freewheel facility in first and second gear). The drive ratio was identical in both types, and the differences in the individual gears were minor. What was different was how the doors were hinged – at the front in the convertible and at the back in the coupé.

After the dismantling of Ambi-Budd, the BMW chassis tools of the 321, 326 and 327 types went to Avtovelo in East Germany. The Russians and East German successor EMW (Eisenacher Motoren Werk) manufactured 491 BMW 327 descendants between 1952 and 1954. The EMW 327-3, an attractive coupé with a large rear window, was also manufactured.

Just as it had many devotees amongst the leaders of the Third Reich, the 327 sports convertible became, in its postwar model, a status symbol for loyal and prominent Socialist Party comrades. Fans of veteran BMWs consider the 327 to be one of the most beautiful convertibles of its time.

Herr Reif aus Chemnitz gehört zu den wenigen Glücklichen, die in Kriegszeiten das äußerst attraktive Cabriolet BMW 327 erwerben dürfen. 7500 Reichsmark kostet dieser vornehmlich in Schwarz ausgelieferte Wagen aus Eisenach. Als Reif die am 12. Mai 1941 ausgestellte Rechnung erhält, weiß er noch nicht, dass sein Wagen mit der Fahrgestell- und Motornummer 87 306 der letzte aus der dortigen BMW-Produktion ist. Nr. 87 307 wird 1948 von der staatlichen sowjetischen Gesellschaft „Awtowelo" in unveränderter Vorkriegsausführung gebaut.

Ausgerechnet im Winter 1937 wird das 2+2-sitzige Sport-Cabriolet der Öffentlichkeit vorgestellt. Zunächst findet es nicht die richtige Zielgruppe, denn Schönheit und elegante Linienführung, die Möglichkeit, neben den Passagieren auch noch einen mittelgroßen Koffer und eine Reiseschreibmaschine unterzubringen sowie 55 PS Leistung sind in dieser Preiskategorie weniger gefragt – ideal höchstens für einen Reisejournalisten mit Anhang!

Der Verkauf läuft schleppend an. Als 1938 eine 80-PS-Version (327/28) kommt, um dem Verlangen nach Leistung und Sportlichkeit stattzugeben, beschleunigt sich seltsamerweise auch der Absatz des 327. Insgesamt werden 1124 Cabriolets und 179 Coupés gebaut. Das letzte Coupé wird im Mai 1941 dem brasilianischen Generalkonsul de Louza-Ribeiro in Hamburg ausgehändigt.

Wie seine ebenfalls mit dem 2-Liter-Motor ausgerüsteten Vorgänger (BMW 320, 321 und 326) hat der 327 einen Tiefbett-Kastenrahmen, auf den Karosserien vom Presswerk Ambi-Budd in Berlin-Johannisthal gesetzt werden. Ambi-Budd und Autenrieth in Darmstadt sind in den dreißiger Jahren die größten BMW-Karossiers.

Die Vierganggetriebe liefern Hurth (mit Freilauf im ersten und zweiten Gang) und ZF. Bei beiden ist die Antriebsübersetzung gleich und die Differenz in den einzelnen Gängen nur geringfügig. Unterschiedlich ist allerdings der Anschlag der Türen – beim Cabriolet vorn, beim Coupé hinten.

Awtowelo heißt die Firma, die bei der Demontage von Ambi-Budd den Zuschlag für den Erhalt der BMW-Karosseriewerkzeuge für die Typen 321, 326 und 327 erhält. Die Russen und der DDR-Nachfolgebetrieb EMW (Eisenacher Motoren Werk) fertigen zwischen 1952 und 1954 noch 491 Abkömmlinge des BMW 327. Unter der Bezeichnung EMW 327-3 entsteht auch ein hübsches Coupé mit großem Heckfenster.

Schon bei den Größen des Dritten Reiches beliebt, wird das Nachkriegsmodell des 327 Sport-Cabriolets zum Statussymbol linientreuer SED-Parteifunktionäre. BMW-Veteranen-Freaks gilt der 327 als eines der schönsten Cabriolets seiner Zeit.

Monsieur Reif, de Chemnitz, est l'un des heureux élus qui, durant la guerre, a eu le droit d'acheter une BMW 327, un cabriolet très réussi. Cette voiture fabriquée à Eisenach – livrée presque toujours en noir – coûtait 7500 reichsmarks. Lorsque Reif reçoit la facture le 12 mai 1941, il ignore encore que sa voiture avec le numéro de châssis et de moteur 87 306 est la dernière produite sous le label BMW. En 1948, la numéro 87 307 sera construite dans une version d'avant-guerre par la compagnie soviétique nationale Avtovelo.

Au cours de l'hiver 1937, le cabriolet sportif 2+2 est présenté au grand public. Mais il ne trouve pas d'emblée sa cible, car sa beauté et l'élégance de ses lignes alliées à la possibilité de transporter, outre les passagers, une valise de taille moyenne et une machine à écrire, et ses 55 ch sous le capot, ne sont pas les caractéristiques recherchées par les acheteurs d'automobiles dans cette catégorie de prix. Peut-être est-elle destinée à un journaliste en voyage ?

C'est pourquoi les ventes ne décollent pas. Lorsqu'apparaît, en 1938, une version de 80 ch (327/28) qui offre plus de puissance et de sportivité, les ventes de la 327 s'envolent curieusement elles aussi. Au total, 1124 cabriolets et 179 coupés seront construits. Le dernier coupé sera remis, en mai 1941, au consul général brésilien de Louza-Ribeiro à Hambourg.

Comme les BMW 320, 321 et 326 avant elle, également propulsées par un moteur de deux litres, la 327 possède un châssis à caisson surbaissé sur lequel est boulonnée la carrosserie montée par Ambi-Budd (emboutissage), à Berlin-Johannisthal. Durant les années 1930, Ambi-Budd et Autenrieth de Darmstadt seront les deux principaux carrossiers de BMW.

Les boîtes à quatre vitesses sont fournies par Hurth (avec moyeu de roue libre pour la première et la deuxième vitesse) et par ZF. Toutes les deux possèdent la même démultiplication et l'étagement est également assez proche. La différence se situe au niveau des portières – sur le cabriolet, elles sont articulées à l'avant, sur le coupé à l'arrière.

Après le démantèlement d'Ambi-Budd, la fabrication des carrosseries de BMW des versions 321, 326 et 327 est attribuée à Avtovelo en Allemagne de l'Est. De 1952 à 1954, les Russes et l'entreprise est-allemande EMW (Eisenacher Motoren Werk), qui prendra sa succession, créeront encore 491 dérivés de la BMW 327. Sous la dénomination EMW 327-3, ils créeront également un joli coupé avec une grande lunette arrière.

Déjà apprécié par les dirigeants du IIIe Reich, le modèle créé après-guerre pour succéder à la 327 Sport-Cabriolet deviendra un symbole de réussite pour les fonctionnaires du Parti socialiste. Les amoureux des BMW considèrent la 327 comme l'un des plus jolis cabriolets de son époque.

The elegant headlamps, mounted between the wings and the radiator hood, set the tone for the striking appearance of the BMW 327. Enthusiasts regard it as one of the most beautiful convertibles of the 1930s.

Die elegant in den Übergang von Kotflügel zu Kühlerhaube eingebetteten Scheinwerfer unterstreichen die ansprechende Optik des BMW 327. Kenner zählen ihn zu den schönsten Cabriolets der dreißiger Jahre.

Les phares élégamment positionnés à la césure entre les ailes et le capot soulignent l'esthétique réussie de la BMW 327. Les connaisseurs y voient l'un des plus jolis cabriolets des années 1930.

BMW 327

The option of having the 80 bhp engine of the BMW 328 fitted in the 327/28 meant the otherwise somewhat underpowered 327 Cabriolet had plenty of "oomph", and with a top speed of 78 mph (125 kph) it gave motorists a lot of car for their money.

Mit der Option auf den Einbau des 80-PS-Motors des BMW 328 (als 327/28) kommen auch die nicht so stark motorisierten 327 Cabriolets richtig in Fahrt – 125 Stundenkilometer bereiten wohl Vergnügen.

Avec la possibilité de faire monter le moteur de 80 ch de la BMW 328 dans la 327/28, même les 327 cabriolets moins puissamment motorisés « décoiffent » – 125 km/h suffisent amplement pour se faire plaisir.

The 327 Cabriolet with its 55 bhp, elegant white spoked steering wheel and matching horn ring is stylish rather than sporting.

Eher vornehm als sportlich lassen sich die 55 PS des 327 Cabriolets mit dem eleganten weißen Speichenlenkrad und dem passendem Hupring lenken.

Le fringant volant blanc à trois branches avec son klaxon circulaire incitera plutôt à conduire avec élégance que sur un rythme sportif cette 327 Cabriolet de 55 ch.

From October 1938 onwards, coupé versions of the 327 and the 327/28 were available. In contrast to the Cabriolet, the door is hinged at the rear.

Ab Oktober 1938 sind der 327 und der 327/28 auch als Coupé erhältlich. Im Gegensatz zum Cabriolet ist der Türanschlag beim Coupé hinten.

À partir d'octobre 1938, la 327 et la 327/28 sont également disponibles en version coupé. Contrairement aux cabriolets, les portes sont articulées à l'arrière.

Captivating lines and timeless beauty: the sweeping tail of the Coupé with a bulge where the spare wheel is housed. Only 179 coupés of the 327 and 86 of the 327/28 were produced by Autenrieth and Ambi-Budd.

Bestechende Linienführung und zeitlos schön: das gestreckte Heck des Coupés mit den spezifischen Rundungen, die sich der Reserveradausbuchtung im Kofferraumdeckel anpassen. Nur 179 Coupés des BMW 327 und 86 des BMW 327/28 wurden insgesamt von Autenrieth und Ambi-Budd gebaut.

Lignes irrésistibles et beauté intemporelle : la poupe élancée et un galbe racé épousent l'emplacement ménagé pour la roue de secours dans le couvercle de la malle. 179 coupés seulement de la 327 et 86 de la 327/28 ont été construits, au total, par Autenrieth et Ambi-Budd.

BMW 327

Available as an option: the 80 bhp straight-six engine with V-valves and three Solex downdraft carburetors.

Wahlweise erhältlich: der Sechszylinder-Reihenmotor (80 PS) mit V-förmig hängenden Ventilen und drei Solex-Fallstromvergasern.

Disponible en option : le six-cylindres en ligne de 80 ch à soupapes suspendues en V et trois carburateurs Solex inversés.

The 327/28 Cabriolet: stylish down to the last detail, from the indicator fitted flush with the door to the integrated headlamps, and the 327 chassis combined with the 80 bhp engine of the 328.

Das 327/28 Cabriolet ist chic bis ins kleinste Detail: der Einbauwinker vor der Tür, die integrierten Scheinwerfer und das Fahrwerk des 327, kombiniert mit dem 80-PS-Motor des 328.

Le cabriolet 327/28 est chic jusque dans les moindres détails : le clignotant à l'avant de la portière, les phares intégrés et le châssis de la 327 combiné au moteur de 80 ch de la 328.

BMW 327

BMW 327

With the partial cladding of the rear wheel usually present on the 327/28s removed, the perforated rims can be seen to good effect. The color-contrasted contours of the wings are another pleasing feature.

Ohne die Teil-Hinterradabdeckung, die beim 327/28 eigentlich üblich ist, kommen die Lochfelgen besonders gut zur Geltung. Auch die farblich abgesetzten Kotflügelkonturen treten so besser hervor.

Sans le carénage partiel des roues arrière, normalement utilisé sur les 327/28, les jantes perforées sont particulièrement bien mises en évidence. Les couleurs contrastées utilisées sur le contour des ailes sont une autre caractéristique plaisante de cette voiture.

The two-liter power unit: a straight-six engine with V-valves, timed by the laterally-mounted camshaft according to a simple principle, three downdraft carburetors and 80 bhp at 5000 rpm.

Die 2-Liter-Kraftquelle: 6 Zylinder in Reihe, V-förmig hängende Ventile, deren Steuerung über die seitlich liegende Nockenwelle nach einem überaus einfachen Prinzip erfolgt, drei Fallstromvergaser und 80 PS bei 5000/min.

Un coup d'œil sous le capot : six-cylindres en ligne de 2 litres, soupapes suspendues en V commandées par l'arbre à cames latéral selon un principe simple, trois carburateurs inversés et 80 ch à 5000 tr/min.

BMW 335

The "cake" consisting of the large cars with three to four liters cubic capacity was apparently already shared out by autumn 1938. A good half of that sales cake went to the Ford V8, whilst Opel received a large portion thanks to its Admiral. Add Daimler-Benz, Auto Union, Borgward and Stoewer to the picture, and the cake was virtually consumed. A small piece of cream was left over for the 140 bhp, extravagantly expensive Maybach SW38.

BMW aimed for their slice of the luxury cake with a 3.5-liter engine. Shortly after the test department moved from Eisenach to Munich, the six-cylinder motors, long-stroke engines displacing 3485 cc, were demonstrating the potential to deliver flagship performance of 90 bhp at 3500 rpm.

A mobile experimental lab, which was basically an extended BMW 326, aroused the interest of the Aldington brothers, owners of BMW's British partner and importer, Frazer-Nash. They presented this 335 prototype, equipped with right-hand drive, a lavish leather interior, and the Frazer-Nash BMW emblem, at the London Motor Show in October 1938.

This classy example of automotive technology stole the show from all its competitors, including the roomy US V8 limousines. Overjoyed, the Aldington brothers were able to keep this car, since BMW had already progressed with the development of the 335 to such an extent that it was ready for launch in volume production. Some adjustments were made to its physical appearance, since larger wheels made it necessary to widen the fenders.

Everything was ready on 17 February 1939. On that date, BMW presented the 335 as a limousine in Berlin, flanked by a convertible and a coupé. The 335 was praised both by experts and the public alike. With a power-to-weight ratio of 42.77 lbs/1 bhp (19.44 kg/1 bhp) – best value in this

category – the newcomer was just as accelerative as it was physically appealing.

Before the War forced BMW to change its priorities, just 415 examples of 335 were built. Their variety was astonishing, particularly amongst the convertibles, for 24 chassis were built with individual designs, mainly by Autenrieth. The Darmstadt company still managed to supply three coupés in 1945. At that time, Ernst Henne had the only works coupé built using Autenrieth components.

What was probably the most beautiful BMW of all was created by the Swiss chassis artist Herrmann Graber: a jewel of a car with a rear elegantly extended. As was Graber practice, this 335 was painted in stylish black and equipped with green leather seats, so this convertible was a BMW enthusiast's dream. The man for whom this dream came true was Dr Bernhard Knöchlein from Franconia, owner of this unique carriage.

Der „Kuchen" der großen Wagen mit drei bis vier Litern Hubraum scheint im Herbst 1938 verteilt zu sein. Die V8 von Ford machen gut die Hälfte aus, Opel sichert sich mit dem Admiral ein großes Stück, und mit Daimler-Benz, Auto Union, Borgward und Stoewer bleibt vom Kuchen so gut wie nichts übrig – nur ein kleines Sahnestück: der 140 PS starke, sündhaft teure Maybach SW38.

In diese PS-Klasse steigt BMW mit seinem 3,5-Liter-Motor ein. Und man beeilt sich. Schon kurz nach dem Umzug der Versuchsabteilung von Eisenach nach München lassen die Sechszylindertriebwerke, Langhuber mit 3485 ccm, ihr Leistungspotential (90 PS bei 3500/min) erahnen.

Ein rollendes Versuchslabor, im Prinzip ein verlängerter BMW 326, erregt das Interesse der Gebrüder Aldington, Herren über den britischen Partner und Importeur Frazer-Nash. Sie präsentieren diesen 335-Prototypen, versehen mit Rechtslenkung, üppigem Lederinterieur und Frazer-Nash-BMW-Emblem, im Oktober 1938 auf der London Motor Show.

Das edle Einzelstück stiehlt allen Konkurrenten, einschließlich den dicken V8-Limousinen aus den USA, die Show. Zu ihrem größten Glück dürfen die Aldington-Brothers diesen Wagen behalten, da BMW mit anderen Versuchsträgern in der Entwicklung des 335 schon zur Serienreife gelangt ist. Die Optik erfährt noch Korrekturen, da die größeren Räder Kotflügelverbreiterungen erforderlich machen.

Am 17. Februar 1939 ist es soweit. In Berlin stellt BMW den 335 als Limousine vor, flankiert von einem Cabriolet und einem Coupé. Fachwelt und Publikum sind begeistert. Mit seinem Leistungsgewicht von 19,44 Kilo pro PS – Bestwert in dieser Kategorie – glänzt der Neue mit seiner Technik ebenso wie mit dem schwungvollen Äußeren.

Obwohl nur 415 Wagen gebaut werden, ehe der Krieg auch bei BMW andere Prioritäten setzt, ist die Vielfalt –

gerade bei den Cabriolets – erstaunlich. Allein 24 Fahr-gestelle werden mit Einzelaufbauten, vornehmlich von Autenrieth, versehen. So liefert das Darmstädter Werk noch 1945 drei Coupés aus. Ernst Henne besitzt zu dieser Zeit das einzige Werks-Coupé, aufgebaut mit Teilen von Autenrieth.

Den wohl schönsten BMW überhaupt kreiert der Schweizer Karosseriekünstler Herrmann Graber: eine auto-mobile Preziose mit elegant nach hinten gestrecktem Heck. Vornehm schwarz lackiert und – wie bei Graber üblich – mit grünen Ledersitzen ausgestattet, ist dieses Cabriolet der Traum eines jeden BMW-Enthusiasten. Für einen BMW-Liebhaber ist er Realität: Dr. Bernhard Knöchlein aus Franken ist der Besitzer des einmaligen Gefährts.

À l'automne 1938, le marché des grosses voitures de trois à quatre litres de cylindrée semble être partagé entre les différents acteurs. Les Ford V8 en accaparent largement la moitié ; avec l'Admiral, Opel s'assure elle aussi une bonne part du gâteau tandis que Daimler-Benz, Auto Union, Borgward et Stoewer se partagent les miettes. Sans oublier la cerise sur le gâteau : la Maybach SW 38 de 140 ch dont le prix est astronomique.

Sans perdre de temps, BMW se lance sur ce marché avec son moteur de 3,5 litres. En effet, peu après que le service des essais a déménagé d'Eisenach à Munich, les six-cylindres, des moteurs à course longue de 3485 cm³, font une première démonstration de leur potentiel (90 ch à 3500 tr/min).

Une voiture expérimentale, en principe une BMW 326 allongée, suscite l'intérêt des frères Aldington, propriétaires du partenaire et importateur britannique Frazer-Nash. Ils présentent ce prototype 335 doté d'une direction à droite avec une superbe sellerie cuir et un emblème Frazer-Nash-BMW au Motor Show de Londres d'octobre 1938.

Cette somptueuse voiture vole la vedette à toutes ses concurrentes, y compris les grosses limousines V8 améri-caines. Comblés de bonheur, les frères Aldington peuvent même la conserver, car BMW a pratiquement mené à terme le projet de la 335 avec d'autres prototypes. Quelques modifications d'ordre esthétique auront lieu, notamment parce que les roues de plus grand diamètre exigent des ailes plus larges.

Le 17 février 1939, le jour J est arrivé. BMW présente la 335 en version berline, ainsi qu'un cabriolet et un coupé, à Berlin. Les professionnels et le grand public sont enthou-siastes. Outre son rapport poids/puissance de 19,44 kg par cheval (un record dans cette catégorie), la nouvelle venue est aussi puissante que ses lignes sont attrayantes.

Bien que 415 voitures seulement aient été construites chez BMW avant que la guerre n'éclate, leur diversité est étonnante, notamment pour les cabriolets. Pas moins de 24 châssis ont été habillés d'une carrosserie spéciale, le plus souvent signée Autenrieth. Ainsi l'usine de Darmstadt fournira-t-elle encore trois coupés en 1945. Ernst Henne possède, à cette époque, le seul coupé d'usine qui ait été monté à partir de pièces réalisées chez Autenrieth.

C'est incontestablement le carrossier suisse, Herrmann Graber, qui aura signé la plus belle BMW de tous les temps : un véritable bijou avec une poupe élégante aux lignes étirées vers l'arrière. D'une grande distinction avec sa peinture noire et – comme toujours chez Graber – ses sièges en cuir vert, ce cabriolet est le rêve de tous les amoureux de BMW. Il n'y a qu'une personne pour qui il soit une réalité : le Dr Bernhard Knöchlein, de Franconie, qui est le propriétaire de cette voiture unique dans tous les sens du terme.

BMW 335

In 1939 BMW entered the top end of the market with the launch of the 335. This one-off, built by Herrmann Graber in Switzerland, is in a class of its own. It is now in the possession of a German BMW enthusiast. Tilted slightly towards the back for reasons of space is the long 3.5-liter straight-cylinder power unit, with its two vertical staged dual-register carburetors, developed 90 bhp at 3500 rpm.

Mit dem 335 steigt BMW 1939 in die Oberklasse auf. Eine Klasse für sich ist dieses von Herrmann Graber in der Schweiz gefertige Einzelstück, das sich derzeit im Besitz eines deutschen BMW-Enthusiasten befindet. Aus Platzgründen leicht nach hinten geneigt ist das lange 3,5-Liter-Reihentriebwerk, das mit zwei Vertikal-Doppelregistervergasern 90 PS bei 3500/min leistet.

En 1939, avec la luxueuse 335, BMW monte en gamme. Ce spécimen, carrossé en Suisse par Herrmann Graber, est un modèle unique qui se trouve actuellement en possession d'un Allemand, fanatique de BMW. Par manque de place, le long 3,5 litres en ligne est légèrement incliné vers l'arrière. Avec ses deux doubles carburateurs verticaux à registre, il développe 90 ch à 3500 tr/min.

The 335 dashboard has an extravagant appearance, with its round instruments set in rounded-off rectangular housing. The steering wheel with four spokes instead of three is a new feature.

Extravagant gibt sich das Armaturenbrett des 335. Als ginge es um die Quadratur des Kreises, wurden die Rundinstrumente in abgerundete Rechteckfassungen gesetzt. Neu ist auch das Lenkrad mit vier anstelle von drei Speichen.

Le tableau de bord de la 335 est extravagant. Comme si l'on avait voulu résoudre la quadrature du cercle, les cadrans circulaires sont insérés dans un encadrement carré aux coins arrondis. Autre nouveauté : le volant possède maintenant quatre branches et non plus trois.

BMW 328 Mille Miglia & Touring

The success of the BMW 328 series from that Eifel race of June 1936, in which Ernst Henne came, saw and conquered, was overwhelming. But BMW wanted more than to win against itself, as had happened in the special race for 2-liter sports cars in the German Grand Prix of 1938.

Prepared for higher honors, an aluminium body was slipped over a tubular steel frame with box-section cross beams. This beautiful, lightweight roadster with its flowing side lines and rear wheel arches (covered if desired), was supplemented with a coupé by the Italian bodyshop Carrozzeria Touring.

This was more than fashion from Milan: the racing coupé corresponded to the aerodynamically favorable droplet form, but with a slightly raised rear end. The influence of Professor Wunibald Kamm, who was hired by BMW in his capacity as the founder of the motor vehicle and engine research institute at Stuttgart technical university, is unmistakeable. The so-called "Kamm tail" became famous in many subsequent performance cars.

Peace prevailed just for the 1939 edition of the "24 Heures du Mans". A trio of works BMWs fought the long-distance battle on the Sarthe circuit, including a Touring coupé with the number 26 and registration number IIA 58 116. For safety reasons the two leather belts over the hood are mandatory as was the extraordinary extra light. The small coupé was fast and tough, romping about among the larger-engined cars and racing to the finish. Its crew – Prince Max of Schaumburg-Lippe/Hans Wencher – was unexpectedly fifth in the overall rankings, including, of course, victory in its class with an average 83 mph (132.8 kph).

Then came the War. No reason for Italians to miss a race. Late in April in 1940, the "Gran Premio Brescia delle Mille Miglia" was held. Again the familiar registration number

IIA 58 116 made its way in the fastest time from the Piazza Vittoria in Brescia, via Crimona and Mantua, back to Brescia. A crazy average speed of 104 mph (166.7 kph) is set. That meant the Touring coupé – then driven by baron Fritz Huschke von Hanstein/Walter Bäumer – left their rivals comfortably behind. BMW also used three new roadsters, which came in third, fifth and sixth. A racing saloon with Kamm streamlining driven by count Lurani, retired.

Subsequently, the world was set on fire. As if nothing was happening, Carrozzeria Touring developed a new Spider on the basis of the 328. A delicious aerodynamic morsel, but one never to be enjoyed.

Die Erfolgsserie des BMW 328 seit jenem Eifelrennen 1936, als Ernst Henne kam, sah und siegte, ist überwältigend. Doch BMW will mehr als sich selbst besiegen, wie beim Sonderlauf der 2-Liter-Sportwagenklasse im Rahmen des Großen Preises von Deutschland 1938.

Um für höhere Weihen gewappnet zu sein, wird über einen Stahlrohrrahmen mit Kasten-Querträgern eine Aluminiumkarosserie gestülpt. Diesem hübschen Leicht-gewicht-Roadster mit seitlich fließenden Übergängen und wahlweise abdeckbaren Hinterradausschnitten stellt die italienische Karosserieschmiede Carrozzeria Touring ein Coupé zur Seite.

Es ist mehr als Mailänder Mode: Das Renncoupé ent-spricht der aerodynamisch günstigen Tropfenform, jedoch mit leicht hochgezogenem Heck. Der Einfluss von Professor Wunibald Kamm, der als Gründer des Forschungsinstituts für Kraftfahrwesen und Fahrzeugmotoren an der TH Stuttgart von BMW engagiert wird, ist unverkennbar. Das sogenannte „Kamm-Heck" prägt auch heutige Autogenerationen.

Noch ist Frieden! Unter den drei Werks-BMW, die 1939 die Langstreckenschlacht „24 Heures du Mans" an der Sarthe bestreiten sollen, ist auch ein Touring-Coupé mit der Startnummer 26 und dem Kennzeichen IIA 58 116. Aus Sicherheitsgründen dürfen die beiden Ledergurte über der Motorhaube ebensowenig fehlen wie ein voluminöser Zusatz-scheinwerfer. Das kleine Coupé erweist sich als schnell und hart im Nehmen, tummelt sich unter den Hubraum-Größen und hält brav durch. Die Besatzung Max Prinz zu Schaumburg-Lippe/Hans Wencher belegt einen unerwar-teten 5. Platz im Gesamtklassement, der natürlich den Klassensieg (Schnitt 132,8 km/h) beinhaltet.

Dann bricht der Krieg aus – für Italiener kein Grund, ein Rennen ausfallen zu lassen! In den letzten Apriltagen des Jahres 1940 steht der „Gran Premio Brescia delle Mille

Miglia" auf dem Plan. Und wieder bahnt sich der Wagen mit dem Kennzeichen IIA 58 116 am schnellsten den Weg von der Piazza Vittoria in Brescia über Cremona und Mantova zurück nach Brescia. Ein Wahnsinns-Schnitt von 166,7 km/h, mit dem das Touring-Coupé – diesmal von Baron Fritz Huschke von Hanstein (Beifahrer Walter Bäumer) pilotiert – die Konkurrenz hoffnungslos abhängt. BMW setzt außerdem drei neue Roadster ein, die die Plätze 3, 5 und 6 belegen. Eine Rennsportlimousine mit Kamm-Stromlinienform, vom Conte Lurani pilotiert, fällt aus.

Die Welt brennt, doch als sei nichts geschehen, entwickelt Carrozzeria Touring einen neuen Spider auf Basis des 328: ein aerodynamischer Leckerbissen, dessen Genuss den Automobilenthusiasten versagt bleibt.

La série de succès remportés par la BMW 328 depuis la fameuse course de l'Eifel de 1936 – où Ernst Henne est venu, a vu et a vaincu – est sans précédent. Mais BMW veut plus que se vaincre elle-même, comme ce fut le cas lors de la course spéciale pour les voitures de sport deux litres en marge du Grand Prix d'Allemagne de 1938.

Pour une plus grande consécration, un châssis en tube d'acier avec poutres transversales est coiffé d'une carrosserie en aluminium. Ce joli roadster allégé aux flancs fluides et avec carénages de roues arrière démontables est épaulé par un coupé signé par la Carrozzeria Touring, en Italie.

C'est plus que la mode de Milan : le coupé de course présente un aérodynamisme idéal en forme de goutte d'eau, mais avec un arrière légèrement surélevé. L'influence du professeur Wunibald Kamm, le fondateur de l'institut de recherche en automobiles et moteurs de véhicules à l'université technique de Stuttgart que BMW a recruté, est incontestable. L'arrière « Kamm » marque encore de son sceau les générations de voitures d'aujourd'hui.

Derniers jours de paix, 1939, 24 Heures du Mans : parmi les trois BMW d'usine sur la grille de départ pour la course d'endurance sur le circuit de la Sarthe figure aussi un coupé Touring avec le numéro 26 et la plaque minéralogique IIA 58 116. Pour des raisons de sécurité, les deux courroies de cuir sur le capot moteur doivent être présentes au même titre qu'un volumineux phare supplémentaire. Le petit coupé, rapide et endurant, se mêle même vaillamment aux plus grosses cylindrées. L'équipage, composé du prince Max zu Schaumburg-Lippe et de Hans Wencher, obtient une cinquième place inattendue au classement général, qui va évidemment de pair avec une victoire dans sa catégorie (avec une moyenne de 132,8 km/h).

La guerre éclate. Pour les Italiens, ce n'est pas une raison suffisante pour annuler les courses. Fin avril 1940, le

« Gran Premio Brescia delle Mille Miglia » figure au programme. Et c'est de nouveau la voiture immatriculée IIA 58 116 qui rejoint le plus vite la Piazza Vittoria à Brescia, après avoir bouclé la boucle par Crémone et Mantoue. Avec une moyenne fantastique de 166,7 km/h, le coupé Touring – piloté cette fois-ci par le baron Fritz Huschke von Hanstein et Walter Bäumer – écrase totalement la concurrence. BMW engage en outre trois nouveaux roadsters qui terminent en 3e, 5e et 6e place. Une berline sport-compétition à carrosserie aérodynamique Kamm, pilotée par le comte Lurani, doit en revanche déclarer forfait.

Le monde brûle. Comme si rien ne se passait, la Carrozzeria Touring met au point un nouveau Spider sur la base de la 328, un chef-d'œuvre d'aérodynamique dont les fanas d'automobile ne pourront jamais profiter.

The superb styling of the bodywork plus a number of engineering innovations from the racetrack would no doubt have been incorporated into the production cars before long. The War meant that all such plans had to be shelved.

Die herrliche Karosserieform sowie einige im Rennfahrzeug erprobte technische Innovationen wären sicherlich kurze Zeit später in Serie gegangen. Aufgrund des Krieges werden derartige Pläne ad acta gelegt.

La magnifique carrosserie ainsi que quelques innovations techniques testées sur les voitures de course auraient assurément fait leur apparition en série un peu plus tard, mais la guerre empêcha la réalisation de tels projets.

These three streamlined racing roadsters contested the 1940 Mille Miglia, ending up in third, fifth and sixth places. Overall victory went to a lightweight BMW Touring coupé. The Mille Miglia's aluminum bodywork considerably reduced its weight and also gave it a certain aerodynamic advantage.

Der Einsatz von drei dieser stromlinienförmigen Renn-Roadster bei der Mille Miglia 1940 endet mit den Plätzen drei, fünf und sechs. Der Gesamtsieg geht an ein BMW-Leichtbau-Coupé von Touring. Die Aluminium-Außenhaut des Mille Miglia bringt neben der erheblichen Gewichtseinsparung auch einige aerodynamische Vorteile.

L'inscription de trois roadsters de course aérodynamiques aux Mille Miglia de 1940 est récompensée par les 3ᵉ, 5ᵉ et 6ᵉ places. Une BMW coupé à carrosserie Touring allégée remporte la victoire au classement général. Outre une perte de poids non négligeable, la carrosserie en aluminium de la version Mille Miglia présente aussi des avantages aérodynamiques.

After the 328's success in the Mille Miglia, the Italian bodywork designer Carrozzeria Touring came up with this optimized racing Spider convertible with its uninterrupted beltline.

Auf Basis des 328 entsteht nach dem Erfolg bei der Mille Miglia bei der italienischen Karosserie-schmiede Carrozzeria Touring dieser optimierte Renn-Spider mit durchgehender Gürtellinie.

Après le succès de la 328 aux Mille Miglia, BMW fait réaliser chez le carrossier italien Carrozzeria Touring ce Spider de compétition optimisé, décapotable, avec ses contours ininterrompus.

BMW kidney grills and lamps are integrated into the rounded nose of this prototype of the Touring, causing virtually no turbulence.

BMW-Nieren und Lampen sind nahezu verwirbelungsfrei in den abgerundeten Bug des Prototypen von Touring integriert.

Les naseaux BMW et les phares sont parfaitement intégrés à l'avant galbé du prototype du Touring, afin d'éviter les prises d'air.

Some styling details from the "Superleggera", the shell of the Touring Spiders, which can be seen today in the BMW Museum in Munich.

Hier einige Styling-Details der „Superleggera"-Außenhaut des Touring Spiders, der heute im BMW-Museum in München steht.

Quelques détails du style de la carrosserie « Superleggera » du Spider Touring, qui est aujourd'hui exposé au musée BMW de Munich.

The racing version of the BMW six-cylinder was never short of power. The Mille Miglia Roadster of 1940 developed 130 bhp at 5750 rpm, and an altered compression and larger outlet valves allowed 136 bhp to be reached at 6000 rpm.

An Kraft mangelt es der kontinuierlich weiterentwickelten Rennversion des BMW-Sechszylinders nicht. Mit 130 PS bei 5750/min entspicht sie der Leistung des Mille-Miglia-Roadsters von 1940. Durch geänderte Kompression und größere Auslassventile werden dann sogar 136 PS bei 6000/min erzielt.

Le six-cylindres de la BMW dans sa version course, perfectionné en permanence, ne manque pas de puissance. Avec 130 ch à 5750 tr/min, il est aussi puissant que le roadster Mille Miglia de 1940. Un taux de compression supérieur et des soupapes d'échappement de plus grand diamètre permettent même d'obtenir 136 ch à 6000 tr/min.

By racing car standards the cockpit of the Touring looks positively comfortable. The large fuel tank was mounted directly behind the two-man crew.

Für ein Rennfahrzeug beinahe komfortabel mutet das Cockpit des Touring an. Der große Tank befindet sich direkt im Nacken der Besatzung.

Pour une voiture de course, l'habitacle de la Touring mérite presque le qualificatif de confortable. Le grand réservoir est placé dans le dos de l'équipage.

"One people, one Reich, one Führer … one chassis!" The propaganda slogans of the Third Reich might be extended thus in respect of the passenger vehicle for the German armed forces. The German army procurement office demanded a standard passenger vehicle in three weight classes. With exact instructions regarding the chassis, the order for the light version was awarded to Stoewer, Hanomag and BMW. No external changes were permitted. Emblems giving any indication of the manufacturer were forbidden.

As well as an engine of the manufacturer's choice – the only requirement was that it should fit under the bonnet and to the transmission – the profile of technical requirements specified permanent all-wheel drive, four limited slip differentials, and selectable, spindle-linked, four-wheel steering. Stoewer started production as early as 1936 and manufactured 7500 examples altogether, although not all of them had four-wheel steering. Hanomag produced 2000 units. BMW production started in April 1937 and carried on until summer 1940 and resulted in somewhere between 3225 and 3259 vehicles being produced, all called BMW 325.

A short wheelbase gave over-sensitive handling. Also, extremely complicated technology, and an unfavorable power-weight ratio, restricted the military usefulness of these vehicles. Transporting the 2.2 tons maximum permissible weight was hard work even for the strongest engine – BMW used its proven six-cylinders, achieving 50 bhp with two Solex updraft carburetors. The 325 was not suitable for the fabled German Blitzkrieg attacks, hobbled by a fuel tank range of just 150 miles (240 km). These standard specification military vehicles met their "Stalingrad" defeats well before the Russian campaign began. All were withdrawn from the arms supply programs before the winter of 1942.

Today the 325 is a real rarity. Only one roadworthy vehicle is known to exist, one which Udo Beckmann, a motor mechanic from Siegen, has saved from "death in action" by loving restoration. This 325, built in 1939 and supplied to the German army in May 1940, was provided with a large equipment box for communications purposes, in place of one seat and a door. This storage proved useful postwar, thus this 325 served years in Austria with the mountain rescue and fire brigade.

Driving skill is required to handle the all-wheel drive and steering systems, particularly in rough terrain and on winding roads. Beckmann's 325 rolls to the "front" today, without its radio equipment but with spade and searchlight. Then it does not head for the desert, as it did with Rommel, but to a BMW veterans' meeting. Once there, a photo of the Field Marshal in a 325 will be proudly passed around.

"Ein Volk, ein Reich, ein Führer … ein Fahrgestell!" So ließe sich die Propagandaparole des Dritten Reiches hinsichtlich der Personenkraftwagen für die Wehrmacht erweitern, denn das Heereswaffenamt setzt auf Einheits-Pkw, gestaffelt nach drei Gewichtsklassen. Mit genauen Chassis- und Fahrwerksvorgaben geht der Auftrag für die leichte Version an Stoewer, Hanomag und BMW. Äußerliche Abweichungen sind nicht erlaubt. Embleme, die auf den Hersteller schließen lassen, sind verboten.

Das technische Anforderungsprofil sieht neben Motoren eigener Wahl – sie müssen nur unter die Haube und an das Getriebe passen – permanenten Allradantrieb, vier Sperrdifferentiale und eine hinten abstellbare Vierrad-Spindellenkung vor. Stoewer beginnt bereits 1936 mit der Produktion und fertigt insgesamt rund 7500 Wagen, freilich nicht alle mit Vierrad-Lenkung. Hanomag produziert 2000 Einheiten. Bei BMW, wo der Produktionsstart im April 1937 erfolgt und bis zum Sommer 1940 gefertigt wird, entstehen zwischen 3225 und 3259 Wagen, genannt BMW 325.

Zu kurzer Radstand, empfindliche, da sehr aufwändige Technik und ein ungünstiges Leistungsgewicht schränken die Truppentauglichkeit dieses Fahrzeugs ein. Selbst für den stärksten Motor, den BMW-Sechszylinder, der mit zwei Solex-Steigstromvergasern 50 PS leistet, bedeutet das Bewegen von 2,2 Tonnen zulässigen Gesamtgewichts Schwerstarbeit – nichts für Blitzkriege, zumal der Tank im Gelände nach 240 Kilometern leer ist. So erleben die Einheits-Pkw ihr Stalingrad bereits in der Anfangsphase des Russlandfeldzugs. Noch vor dem Winter 1942 werden sie aus dem Rüstungsprogramm genommen.

Heute ist der 325 eine absolute Rarität. Bekannt ist nur ein fahrtaugliches Exemplar, das Udo Beckmann, ein Kfz-Meister aus Siegen, durch liebevolle Restaurierung vor dem „Heldentod" bewahrt hat. Dieser 325, der 1939 gebaut

BMW 325 Leichter Einheits-Pkw

und im Mai 1940 an die Wehrmacht ausgeliefert wurde, ist für Fernmeldezwecke mit einem großen Gerätekasten bestückt. Dafür fallen ein Sitz und eine Tür weg. Diese Konfiguration ist auch in Friedenszeiten brauchbar, und so dient dieser Wagen noch geraume Zeit in Österreich bei Bergwacht und Feuerwehr.

Fahrerisches Können ist beim Umgang mit dem Allradantriebs- und Lenkungssystem gefordert, besonders im Gelände und auf kurvenreichen Straßen. Wenn Beckmanns 325, ohne Funkgerät zwar, aber versehen mit Feldspaten und Suchscheinwerfer, heute wieder an die „Front" rollt, dann geht's nicht wie bei Rommel in die Wüste, sondern zum BMW-Veteranentreffen, wo dann stolz das Foto des Generalfeldmarschalls in einem 325 herumgereicht wird.

Un peuple, un Reich, un Führer … et un châssis ! » Ainsi pourrait-on résumer la devise du IIIᵉ Reich en matière de voitures particulières pour la Wehrmacht. En effet, le service des achats de l'Armée exige un seul type de voitures particulières dans trois catégories de poids. Avec un cahier des charges précis pour le châssis et les trains roulants, la commande de la version légère est attribuée à Stoewer, Hanomag et BMW. Aucun changement extérieur n'est autorisé. Tout emblème permettant d'identifier le constructeur est interdit.

Outre le moteur, au libre choix du constructeur – pourvu qu'il entre sous le capot et soit compatible avec la boîte de vitesses –, le cahier des charges prévoit une traction intégrale permanente, quatre différentiels autobloquants et une direction à broche sur les quatre roues, les deux roues arrière étant débrayables. Stoewer inaugure la production dès 1936 et fabrique environ 7500 voitures au total, mais toutes ne possèdent pas quatre roues directrices. Hanomag en produit 2000 exemplaires. Chez BMW (où la production débute en avril 1937 et où la fabrication durera jusque durant l'été 1940), entre 3225 et 3259 voitures sont construites, baptisées BMW 325.

Un empattement trop court, une technique peu fiable parce que trop sophistiquée et un rapport poids/puissance défavorable restreignent les possibilités d'utilisation par les troupes. Même pour le moteur le plus puissant – le six-cylindres BMW à deux carburateurs Solex verticaux développant 50 ch –, déplacer un poids total en charge autorisé de 2,2 tonnes représente un effort surhumain. La 325 ne correspond pas à ce que les Allemands attendent pour mener leurs fabuleuses attaques éclairs. D'autant plus que, en tout-terrain, le réservoir est à sec au bout de 240 km. Ainsi ces voitures vivent-elles leur « Stalingrad » avant même que ne soit entamée la campagne de Russie. L'hiver 1942 n'a

même pas commencé qu'elles disparaissent du programme des achats militaires.

Aujourd'hui, la 325 est une rareté. On ne connaît qu'un seul exemplaire apte à rouler, celui d'Udo Beckmann, un mécanicien de Siegen, qui l'a préservé de la « mort des héros » en la restaurant avec amour. Cette 325, construite en 1939 et livrée à la Wehrmacht en mai 1940, comporte un grand caisson pour les appareils de télécommunications (pour cela, il a fallu supprimer un siège et une portière). Après-guerre, cette voiture a encore longtemps été utilisée en Autriche par les secours en montagne et les pompiers.

Un certain savoir-faire est nécessaire pour rouler avec la traction intégrale et les quatre roues directrices, en particulier en tout-terrain et sur des routes sinueuses. Lorsque la 325 de Beckmann, sans appareil de transmission, mais avec sa pelle-bêche et son projecteur orientable, roule de nouveau « vers le front » aujourd'hui, elle ne part pas à la rencontre du désert comme au temps de Rommel, mais aux concentrations de vieilles BMW où l'on se passe alors de main en main la photo du maréchal des armées dans une 325.

Required by the German army procurement office: all-wheel drive and steering. The wheel suspension's double wishbone axles are each fitted with two helical springs.

Vom Heereswaffenamt gefordert: Allradantrieb und -lenkung. Die Doppel-Querlenker der Radaufhängungen sind mit je zwei dieser Schraubenfedern versehen.

Le cahier des charges de l'armée est exigeant : traction et direction intégrales. Les doubles bras transversaux des suspensions ont chacun deux ressorts hélicoïdaux.

BMW 325 Leichter Einheits-Pkw

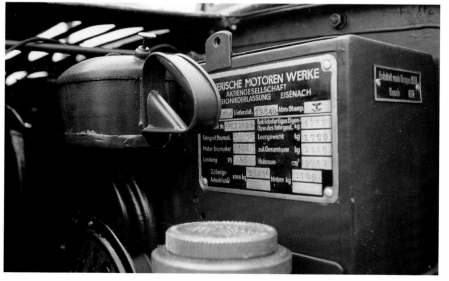

The BMW six-cylinder engine generates 50 bhp, which had to struggle to shift a two-tonner such as the version with a telecommunications equipment box shown here. The 325 is a great rarity, and this example is the only roadworthy one still in existence. After the War, it did service in the Austrian mountain rescue and fire departments.

50 PS leistet der BMW-Sechszylinder. Das bedeutet Schwerstarbeit beim Bewegen eines Zweitonners, der hier in der Ausführung mit einem Gerätekasten für Fernmelder gezeigt wird. Der 325 gilt als absolute Rarität, und fahrbereit ist offenbar nur noch dieses Exemplar, das nach dem Krieg der Bergwacht und Feuerwehr in Österreich gedient hat.

Le six-cylindres BMW développe 50 ch. Il est donc à la peine avec cette voiture qui pèse deux tonnes. Ici, un modèle avec la caisse réservée aux équipements de télécommunication. La 325 est un modèle rarissime. Seul cet exemplaire, utilisé par les secours en montagne et les pompiers en Autriche après-guerre, est encore en état de rouler.

Veritas RS

When an automotive development engineer, a businessman and a former world cycling champion decide to set up a company in the devastation that was postwar Germany, manufacture of a utilitarian vehicle immediately would seem likely. Perhaps a moped with a trailer? Or mini-vans, rubble-clearing vehicles or bicycles with passenger cars?

Completely wrong! The BMW engineer, Ernst Loof, the businessman, Lorenz Dietrich, and the ex-cycling star, Werner Miethe, wanted to build racing cars and sedan racers. This was supposed to happen in Munich-Allach, but the Americans did not give their consent, although Miethe also had US citizenship. The three moved instead to Meßkirch in Baden, because the French seemed to be more amenable to the project.

The hour of truth started with the name: Veritas. That was the name of the 1.5 and 2-liter cars built in factory ruins from remaining BMW components. However, winning cars were built as early as 1948 in the strangest of conditions, which demonstrated unbelievable powers of improvisation. The BMW motorbike legend and Auto Union Grand Prix driver Georg Meier brought BMW its first win in this period in a non-formula racing cars class.

Karl Kling, who was actually working for Daimler-Benz, also joined the unofficial BMW team. In 1949 – the small company's best year – Veritas headed the German racing scene. Helmut Glöckner and Karl Kling won both sports car classes at 1.5 and 2 liters. Toni Ulmen also performed well with Veritas racing cars.

Most of the 32 saloon racers were built in 1949. These Veritas RS had a lightweight, lattice-type chassis design with an aluminum skin. Because they were hand-made like all Veritas vehicles, each looked very different. The BMW from Carrozzeria Touring served as a model for the design.

Thanks to the modified crankshaft and a new cylinder head, ratings of 120 to 125 bhp were delivered from the basic engine (six-cylinder BMW 328). Depending on the ratio, the 2-liter RS could reach road speeds of up to 125 mph (200 kph). Coping with unexpected transverse accelerations required outstanding driver skills, since the RS was prone to slight instability.

The 1949 Veritas RS also attracted buyers from outside Germany. The alterations performed included body work, upgrading the electrical system and adding a fuel pump, but were generally minor. By the end of 1950, over 60 competition and motor sports Veritas were built.

Defeat in sporting events and lack of success in tests on road vehicles meant the graceful end for this vehicle marque. The upper echelons of motor sport witnessed the finale at the Nürburgring. Loof, after the split with his partners, launched a short production run in the buildings previously owned by Auto Union. Spohn from Ravensburg supplied him with the last of the line bodies. The Veritas type "Nürburgring" was to be Loof's last design, for he died shortly after the Veritas.

Wenn ein Automobil-Entwicklungsingenieur, ein Kaufmann und ein ehemaliger Radrenn-Weltmeister im zerbombten Nachkriegsdeutschland beschließen, eine Firma zu gründen, denkt man unwillkürlich an die Fertigung eines nützlichen Fahrzeugs: Mofa mit Anhänger, Kleinstlastwagen, Trümmer-Räumfahrzeug oder Fahrrad mit Beiwagen.

Völlig falsch! Der BMW-Ingenieur Ernst Loof, Kaufmann Lorenz Dietrich und Ex-Radstar Werner Miethe wollen Renn- und Rennsportwagen bauen. Das soll in München-Allach geschehen, doch die Amerikaner sind dagegen, obwohl Miethe sich auch als US-Bürger ausweisen kann. Die drei Herren weichen also nach Meßkirch im Badischen aus, da sich die Franzosen dem Projekt aufgeschlossen zeigen.

Die Stunde der Wahrheit beginnt mit der Namensgebung. Veritas – so heißen die zunächst in einer Fabrikruine zusammengebauten Wagen mit 1,5- und 2-Liter-Motoren aus BMW-Restbeständen. Unter abenteuerlichen Umständen und mit unglaublicher Improvisationskunst entstehen bereits 1948 Siegerwagen. Georg Meier, BMW-Motorrad-Legende und Grand-Prix-Fahrer der Auto Union, holt den ersten Erfolg in einer formelfreien Rennwagenklasse.

Der eigentlich in Daimler-Benz-Diensten stehende Karl Kling steigt ebenfalls in das Team ein. 1949 steht die kleine Firma auf dem Zenit ihrer Entwicklung: Veritas beherrscht die deutsche Rennszene. Mit Helmut Glöckner und Karl Kling gewinnt man in beiden Sportwagenklassen (1,5 und 2 Liter). Toni Ulmen hält sich bei den Rennwagen schadlos.

Die meisten der insgesamt 32 Rennsportwagen werden 1949 gebaut. Diese Veritas RS weisen eine leichte Gitterrohr-Rahmenkonstruktion mit einer Haut aus Aluminium auf, die – handgefertigt wie alles bei Veritas – recht unterschiedlich ausfällt. Optisches Vorbild ist der BMW von Carrozzeria Touring.

Dank einer geänderten Kurbelwelle und einem neuen Zylinderkopf werden aus dem Basis-Motor (Sechszylinder BMW 328) zwischen 120 und 125 PS herausgeholt. Je nach Übersetzung erreicht der 2-Liter-RS bis zu 200 Stundenkilometer. Höhere Querbeschleunigungen verlangen viel fahrerisches Können, da der RS nicht ganz verwindungssteif ist.

Der Veritas RS des Baujahres 1949 findet aufgrund seiner Erfolge auch Käufer im Ausland. Die Änderungen – Karosseriearbeiten, Umrüstung der Elektrik, zusätzliche Benzinpumpe etc. – sind meistens geringfügig. Bis Ende 1950 werden mehr als 60 Wettbewerbsautos und Sportwagen gebaut.

Sportliche Niederlagen und erfolglose Versuche mit Straßensportwagen führen letztlich zum Exitus der Marke. Dieser vollzieht sich an prominenter Stelle: am Nürburgring, wo Loof – nach der Trennung von seinen Partnern – in den ehemaligen Auto-Union-Hallen eine Kleinserie begonnen hat. Die Karosserie liefert ihm die Ravensburger Firma Spohn. Dieser Wagen, Typ „Nürburgring", ist Loofs letzte Konstruktion. Kurz nach dem Aus von Veritas stirbt er.

Quand un ingénieur automobile, un commercial et un ancien cycliste champion du monde décident, dans l'Allemagne bombardée de l'après-guerre, de créer une entreprise, la logique voudrait qu'ils fabriquent un quelconque véhicule utilitaire : un vélomoteur avec une remorque, une mini-camionnette, un camion pour déblayer les ruines ou un vélo avec un side-car.

Eh bien, pas du tout ! L'ingénieur de chez BMW, Ernst Loof, le commercial, Lorenz Dietrich et l'ex-vedette de la petite reine, Werner Miethe, veulent construire des voitures de course et de sport. Ils choisissent pour cela Munich-Allach, mais les Américains s'y opposent bien que Miethe puisse se prévaloir d'être un citoyen américain. Faisant contre mauvaise fortune bon cœur, les trois hommes optent pour Messkirch, dans la région de Bade, car les Français se montrent réceptifs au projet.

L'heure de vérité sonne au moment de baptiser la voiture. Veritas : tel est le nom qu'arborent d'abord les voitures à moteur de 1,5 et 2 litres assemblées dans une usine en ruines à partir de stocks de pièces BMW. Dans des circonstances abracadabrantes et avec un art consommé de l'improvisation, ils produisent déjà en 1948 des voitures qui remporteront des courses. Georg Meier, légende de la compétition motocycliste chez BMW et pilote de Grand Prix pour Auto Union, décroche la première place en catégorie voitures de course en formule libre.

Bientôt, Karl Kling, pourtant au service de Daimler-Benz, rejoint, lui aussi, l'écurie. En 1949 – la petite firme est alors à son apogée –, Veritas domine les milieux de la compétition en Allemagne : avec Helmut Glöckner et Karl Kling, la marque remporte les deux courses de voitures de sport (1,5 et 2 litres). Dans la catégorie voitures de course, Toni Ulmen défend avec honneur les couleurs de la marque.

La majorité des voitures de course, 32 au total, seront construites en 1949. Ces Veritas RS possèdent un léger châssis tubulaire recouvert d'une légère couche d'aluminium, toutes les carrosseries étant légèrement différentes parce que fabriquées à la main, comme tout chez Veritas. Qui s'inspire pour l'esthétique de la BMW de la Carrozzeria Touring.

Grâce à la modification d'un vilebrequin et à une nouvelle culasse, le moteur de base (le six-cylindres de la BMW 328) développe entre 120 et 125 ch. Selon la démultiplication, la RS de deux litres peut flirter avec le 200 km/h. Les accélérations transversales exigent beaucoup d'habileté de la part du pilote, car la RS manque de stabilité.

En raison de ses succès, la Veritas RS de 1949 trouve aussi preneur à l'étranger. Le plus souvent, les aménagements – travaux de carrosserie, modification du système électrique, pompe à essence supplémentaire, etc. – sont minimes. Jusqu'à la fin de 1950, plus de 60 voitures de course et de sport sortent des chaînes.

Des défaites sportives et l'échec des voitures de sport de route sonnent le glas de la marque. L'apothéose a lieu au Nürburgring où Loof – qui s'est séparé de ses associés – a commencé à produire une petite série dans les anciens ateliers d'Auto Union. La société Spohn, à Ravensburg, lui fournit les carrosseries. Cette voiture, le modèle « Nürburgring », est la dernière construction de Loof. Il décédera peu après l'arrêt de la production de la Veritas.

Beneath the adjustable windscreen the Veritas driver has an uninterrupted view of the rev counter, speedometer and oil pressure gauge, plus four other round instruments. With its three Solex carburetors, the two-liter six-cylinder engine developed 125 bhp.

Unter den verstellbaren Scheiben hat der Veritas-Pilot ständig Drehzahlmesser, Tacho, Öldruckmesser und vier weitere Rundinstrumente im Visier. Mit drei Solex-Vergasern entfaltet der 2-Liter-Sechszylinder 125 PS.

Sous le coupe-vent réglable, le pilote de la Veritas a constamment sous les yeux le compte-tours, le tachymètre, le manomètre d'huile ainsi que quatre autres cadrans. Avec trois carburateurs Solex, le six-cylindres de 2 litres développe 125 ch.

Veritas RS

Veritas RS

Veritas RS

The well-conceived and successful design of the RS made it a piece of high fashion on the racetrack. The headrests serve a purely aerodynamic purpose.

Durchdacht und gelungen: Form und Funktion des RS-Gewandes zählen 1949 zur Haute Couture im Rennwagenbau. Die Nackenstütze hat lediglich eine aerodynamische Funktion.

Bien conçue et réussie : le design de la RS relève de la haute couture si on le compare aux voitures de course de 1949. Le carénage de l'appuie-tête n'a qu'une fonction aérodynamique.

Bonjour Madame, please take your seat behind the ivorycolored wheel of the 22,000 mark BMW 502 Cabriolet. The advertising brochure for this noble car with the first German V8 engine of the postwar period totally ignored the man's world; only women, catching the admiring glances of men, were shown in this convertible. Indeed, the steering wheel with column shift gear lever, indicator and horn appeared to be made for delicate hands. The proper signal effect was produced by two Bosch musical horns behind the front bumper.

The wooden dashboard had a semi-circular speedo, which went up to 180 kph (112 mph), and the arrangement of the instruments gave a relaxed and light impression. The bias was defintely feminine: little levers and buttons below the Becker "Grand Prix" radio, ready to play *In the Mood* – Glenn Miller inviting the ladies out into the fresh country air. After all, the top was easy for ladies to operate, as the BMW advertising emphasized.

The purring of the 2.6-liter engine was drowned in the sound of the wind. The engine, with light alloy block, wet cylinder liners and five-bearing crankshaft, was thoroughly modern, a 100 bhp power source. The overhead valves were mounted in pairs to be activated by tappets, push rods and rocker arms. The camshaft was driven by a duplex roller chain.

Ladies, cruising down the boulevard with their 502 Cabriolet, were probably not particularly interested in recitations of technical engine data. Only fuel consumption, and thus opening a purse, was of interest: 16.3 miles to the gallon of Super and 0.25 pints of oil every 62 miles (14.5 litres Super and 0.15 litres oil per 100 km). The switch to the auxiliary tank had to be made after a good 250 miles (400 km). The coolant level for the radiator, too, needed to be inspected regularly.

Technical matters take over again with the ZF 4-speed manual transmission with full synchromesh on all forward gears, the gearbox itself being located under the front seats. A propshaft with two rubber joints linked the clutch to transmission. The connection to the final drive with hypoid bevel gears was by a secondary universal-joint propeller shaft, its joints on needle-roller bearings.

The excellent heating, once the radiator coolant had heated up to the proper temperature, and solid workmanship – the only draught came from the vents intended for that - purpose – made this convertible truly winter-proof. However, it was less advisable to use this 3090 lbs (1400 kg) car – up to 4365 lbs (1980 kg) when fully laden – on snow and ice. Altogether, Baur in Stuttgart built a little over 130 convertibles and coupés with the 2.6-liter engine. Autenrieth produced some 50 special tops for the 502, some of them varying significantly and even diverging from the BMW specifications, which earned them no favours with BMW when it came to placing new orders.

Bonjour Madame, nehmen Sie Platz hinter dem elfenbeinfarbenen Steuer des 22 000 Mark teuren BMW 502 Cabriolets. Die Werbebroschüre des edlen Wagens mit dem ersten deutschen V8-Motor der Nachkriegszeit negiert die Männerwelt völlig. Nur weibliche Personen, die bewundernden Blicke der Männer erhaschend, führen dieses Cabriolet vor. In der Tat sind das Lenkrad mit Gangschaltung, Blinker und Hupring wie geschaffen für zarte Hände. Für die richtige Signalwirkung sorgen zwei Bosch-Fanfaren hinter der vorderen Stoßstange.

Auch das holzgetäfelte Armaturenbrett mit dem halbkreisförmigen Tacho, dessen Anzeige bis zu 180 km/h reicht, und die Verteilung der Instrumente wirken locker und leicht – feminin eben wie auch die Hebelchen und Knöpfchen unterhalb des „Grand Prix"-Radios von Becker, das gerade *In the Mood* spielt. Glenn Miller lädt die Damen zu einem Open-Air-Ausflug ein. Schließlich ist das Verdeck für Damen leicht zu betätigen, wie es explizit in der BMW-Werbung steht.

Das Surren des 2,6-Liter-Motors geht im Fahrtwind unter. Eine moderne, 100 PS starke Kraftquelle ist dieses Triebwerk mit Leichtmetallblock, nassen Zylinderlaufbüchsen und fünffach gelagerter Kurbelwelle. Die Ventile hängen parallel und werden durch Stößel, Stoßstangen und Kipphebel betätigt. Über eine Duplex-Rollenkette erfolgt der Nockenwellenantrieb.

Damen, die mit ihrem 502 Cabriolet über den Boulevard flanieren, interessiert dieses Defilee technischer Motordaten wohl kaum. Nur der Verbrauch und der damit einhergehende Schwund im Portemonnaie spielen eine Rolle: 14,5 Liter Super und 0,15 Liter Öl auf 100 Kilometer dürfen es schon sein. Nach gut 400 Kilometern ist der Griff zum Reservehahn unumgänglich, und auch der Kühlwasserstand sollte ab und zu beobachtet werden.

BMW 502 Cabriolet

Technisch wird es wieder bei dem unter den Vordersitzen angeordneten ZF-Viergang-Zahnradgetriebe mit Sperrsynchronisation der Vorwärtsgänge. Von der Kupplung zum Getriebe läuft eine Kardanwelle mit zwei Gummigelenken. Eine Gelenkwelle mit nadelgelagerten Gelenken stellt die Antriebsverbindung zum Hinterachsgetriebe mit Hypoid-Kegelrädern her.

Die Heizung, die gut funktioniert, sobald das Kühlwasser die entsprechende Temperatur erreicht hat, und die solide Verarbeitung – es zieht nur über die dafür vorgesehenen Düsen herein – machen das Cabriolet wirklich winterfest. Sich mit dem 1400 Kilo schweren Wagen (beladen bis 1980 Kilo) auf Schnee und Eis zu bewegen, ist weniger ratsam. Insgesamt baut Baur in Stuttgart etwas mehr als 130 Cabriolets und Coupés mit dem 2,6-Liter-Motor. Autenrieth stellt etwa 50 Sonderaufbauten für den 502 her, teilweise recht verschieden und sogar abweichend von den BMW-Vorgaben – nicht gut für ein „Au revoir" bei der Vergabe von Werksaufträgen.

Bonjour madame, prenez donc place derrière le volant couleur ivoire de la BMW 502 Cabriolet qui coûte 22 000 marks.» Le prospectus de la prestigieuse voiture dotée du premier moteur V8 allemand de l'après-guerre fait totalement abstraction du monde masculin : seules de jolies femmes qui attirent les regards admirateurs des hommes conduisent ce cabriolet. De fait, le volant avec levier de changement de vitesses, clignotants et klaxon intégrés est conçu pour des mains de femmes. Deux klaxons Bosch situés près du pare-chocs avant signalent son arrivée à qui veut l'entendre.

Le tableau de bord en bois avec le tachymètre en demi-cercle gradué jusqu'à 180 km/h et la répartition des instruments évoquent, eux aussi, la décontraction et la légèreté. Tout aussi féminins sont les petits leviers et les boutons sous l'autoradio Becker « Grand Prix » qui joue *In the Mood*. Glenn Miller invite les dames à un concert en plein air. Enfin, la capote est facile à manier par la gent féminine, comme le vante la publicité BMW.

Le ronflement du moteur de 2,6 litres est couvert par le bruit du vent. Ce moteur d'un bloc en alliage léger, chemises humides et vilebrequin à cinq paliers est moderne et puissant (100 ch). Les soupapes suspendues sont parallèles et actionnées par des coupelles, des poussoirs et des culbuteurs. L'arbre à cames est entraîné par une chaîne à rouleaux duplex.

Les dames qui se plaisent à flâner sur les boulevards avec leur 502 Cabriolet ne prêteront qu'une oreille distraite à cette énumération de caractéristiques techniques. Elles s'intéresseront tout au plus à la consommation et, par conséquent, à leur porte-monnaie : la consommation est de 14,5 litres de super et de 0,15 litre d'huile aux 100 km. Tous les 400 km, le passage sur le réservoir de secours vous est signalé. Mais il ne faut pas oublier pour autant

de contrôler de temps à autre le niveau d'eau pour le refroidissement.

Pour la transmission, on retrouve la boîte ZF à engrenages à quatre rapports manuels avec synchronisation des rapports avant, qui se trouve sous les sièges avant. Un arbre intermédiaire court à deux joints élastiques relie l'embrayage à la boîte de vitesses. La liaison avec le pont arrière à couple hypoïde s'effectue au moyen d'un arbre à deux cardans à aiguilles.

Le chauffage performant, dès que l'eau du radiateur a atteint la température adéquate, et la grande qualité de finition – l'air ne pénètre qu'à travers les ouïes prévues à cet effet – font que ce cabriolet est réellement à l'épreuve de l'hiver. Il est toutefois peu conseillé de s'aventurer sur la neige et le verglas avec cette voiture qui pèse 1400 kg (et même jusqu'à 1980 kg en pleine charge). Au total, Baur, à Stuttgart, construit un peu plus de 130 cabriolets et coupés avec le moteur de 2,6 litres. Autenrieth assemble une cinquantaine de carrosseries spéciales de la 502, certaines divergeant fortement ou parfois même totalement des instructions de BMW, ce qui ne les plaça pas parmi les favoris au moment de passer les nouvelles commandes.

Portrait of a BMW 502. A total of more than 130 cabriolets and coupés, based on the 2.6-liter eight-cylinder 502, were built at the Baur bodywork plant in Stuttgart.

Konterfei eines BMW 502. Insgesamt werden von der Stuttgarter Karosseriefabrik Baur mehr als 130 Cabriolets und Coupés, basierend auf dem 502 mit 2,6-Liter-Achtzylinder, gebaut.

Portrait d'une BMW 502. Au total, le carrossier Baur, à Stuttgart, construira plus de 130 cabriolets et coupés, tous sur la plate-forme de la 502 à moteur huit cylindres de 2,6 litres.

The 15' 6" (4.7 meter) long convertible is based on a box-section frame with strong tubular cross members. The chassis and body are welded together. It was available in two and four-door models.

Das 4,7 Meter lange Cabriolet ruht auf einem Kastenrahmen mit starken Rohrquerträgern. Chassis und Aufbau sind miteinander verschweißt. Es ist zwei- oder viertürig lieferbar.

Le cabriolet de 4,7 mètres de long possède un châssis à caissons avec de solides poutres transversales. Le châssis et la carrosserie sont soudés l'un à l'autre. Deux versions sont disponibles : en deux ou en quatre portes.

The V proudly displayed on the trunk of this BMW indicates that this is the first German V8 engine of the postwar era. It developed 100 bhp at 4800 rpm.

Stolz trägt dieser BMW das V-Zeichen auf dem Kofferraumdeckel. Es steht für den ersten deutschen V8-Motor der Nachkriegszeit: Leistung 100 PS bei 4800 U/min.

Cette BMW arbore fièrement un V sur le couvercle de sa malle. Il trahit la présence du premier moteur V8 allemand de l'après-guerre. Puissance : 100 ch à 4800 tr/min.

BMW 502 Cabriolet

Ready to pounce: a rarity and an eyecatcher, this 106 mph (170 kph) coupé was manufactured in small numbers by Baur between 1955 and 1958. The Coupé roof with the drop-center rim stops short of the steel disc wheels, giving the tail of the car an elongated appearance.

Rarität und deshalb Blickfang: Das wie zum Sprung geduckt wirkende, 170 km/h schnelle Coupé wird von Baur zwischen 1955 und 1958 in kleiner Stückzahl gefertigt. Das noch vor den Stahlscheibenrädern mit Tiefbettfelge auslaufende Coupé-Dach streckt optisch die Heckpartie mit dem umgreifenden Stoßfänger.

Une rareté qui attire immanquablement le regard : ce coupé qui évoque un félin prêt à bondir est capable d'atteindre les 170 km/h et a été construit en nombre limité par Baur de 1955 à 1958. Le toit du Coupé, qui se termine avant les roues comportant des jantes ornées d'un disque d'acier, allonge la partie arrière dont les pare-chocs empiètent sur les ailes.

Stylish and contemporary: the white steering wheel and controls, plus a wood-paneled dashboard and leather seats. The engine is fitted with a dual-throat downdraft carburetor and a large air filter. The firing sequence 1-5-4-8-6-3-7-2 is conspicuous on the cylinder head cover.

Vornehm und zeitgemäß: Lenkrad und Bedienelemente in weiß, holzgetäfeltes Armaturenbrett und Ledersitze. Der Motor ist mit einem Doppel-Fallstromvergaser und großem Luftfilter bestückt, auffallend ist die Zündreihenfolge 1-5-4-8-6-3-7-2 auf dem Zylinderkopfdeckel.

Élégants et dans l'air du temps : volant et manettes de commande de couleur blanche, tableau de bord en bois et sièges en cuir. Le moteur est alimenté par un double carburateur inversé doté d'un grand filtre à air. L'ordre d'allumage – 1-5-4-8-6-3-7-2 – est affiché bien lisiblement sur le couvercle de la culasse.

BMW 502 3,2 Liter Super

The 501 and the 502, the first large postwar BMW sedans, had the unfortunate distinction of being nicknamed the "Bavarian baroque angels", although the rounded lines of these magnificent powerful limousines were extremely well-proportioned and, in aerodynamic terms, created relatively little turbulence.

The BMW 502 entered the annals of automotive history with its status of being the first German eight-cylinder car of the postwar era. It was based on the strong box-section frame with the tubular cross beams of the 501, welded to the solid steel body. The main visual difference from the 501 was the large panoramic rear window.

As the most powerful model in the range, the 502 3,2 Liter Super developed 140 bhp thanks to two dual-throat downdraft carburetors. This enabled the heavyweight carriage to attain road speeds of at least 109 mph (175 kph) and accelerate from 0 to 62 mph (0 to 100 kph) in a reported 14.5 seconds.

Undeniably the V8 with its light alloy engine block and wet cylinder lines marked the beginning of a new era of engine technology. Interestingly, the transmission was not directly flanged on to the engine. This resulted in a shorter secondary propshaft to the rear axle. The steering column was also abbreviated and was activated via a bevel gear, which enabled a steering wheel ratio of 3.5 turns lock-to-lock; the turning circle equalled that of today's 7 series.

The low numbers of the 3.2 Liter Super sold, which cost 20,000 marks when it was introduced, might have been acceptable on the grounds of prestige, but they were uneconomical. When all of the 502 3.2-liter cars produced between 1955 and 1964 are added together, the total comes to 3840. Not exactly a profitable business.

On the other hand, BMW could at last show the world that its products were worthy of competing with Mercedes-Benz. As a direct result of the 502, a variety of convertible and coupé versions were all individually produced by the car body manufacturers Baur of Stuttgart and Autenrieth of Darmstadt.

Thanks to its workmanlike and professional standards of finish, the prestigious external appearance and the high levels of driving comfort, the "baroque angels" truly earned the rating of "heavenly".

Bayerische Barockengel", mit dieser volkstümlichen Bezeichnung müssen die ersten großen Nachkriegs-limousinen von BMW – die Typen 501 und 502 – leben, obwohl die Rundungen der stattlichen Karossen durchaus gut proportioniert sind und aerodynamisch gesehen relativ wenig Verwirbelungen bilden.

Als erster deutscher Achtzylinderwagen der Nachkriegszeit geht der BMW 502 in die Annalen der Automobilgeschichte ein. Er basiert auf dem äußerst stabilen Kastenrahmen mit Rohrquerträgern des 501, mit dem die Ganzstahlkarosserie verschweißt ist. Vom 501 unterscheidet ihn optisch die große Panoramaheckscheibe.

Als stärkstes Modell der Serie entwickelt der 502 3,2 Liter Super dank zweier Doppel-Fallstromvergaser 140 PS. Damit kommt das schwere Gefährt auf rund 175 Stundenkilometer.

Dem bayerischen V8 mit seinem Leichtmetallblock und nassen Zylinderlaufbüchsen muss attestiert werden, eine neue Ära der Motorentechnik eingeleitet zu haben. Interessanterweise ist das Getriebe nicht direkt an den Motor angeflanscht. Daraus resultiert eine kürzere Kardanwelle zur Hinterachse. Auch die Lenksäule fällt kurz aus und läuft über ein Kegelrad, das dreieinhalb Lenkraddrehungen ermöglicht. Der Wendekreis entspricht dem der heutigen 7er Serie.

Die Stückzahlen des 3,2 Liter Super, der bei seiner Einführung knapp 20 000 Mark kostet, liegen in einer Größenordnung, die aus Prestigegründen akzeptabel sein mag, sich aber wirtschaftlich nicht rechnet. Die Summe aller von 1955 bis 1964 gebauten 502 3,2-Liter-Wagen beläuft sich auf gerade mal 3840 Fahrzeuge – ein Zuschussgeschäft!

Andererseits hat BMW dokumentiert, dass man Mercedes-Benz etwas entgegenzusetzen hat. Diverse Cabriolet-

und Coupé-Ausführungen der Karosseriehersteller Baur in Stuttgart und Autenrieth in Darmstadt ranken sich, individuell gefertigt, um den 502.

Für solide und saubere Verarbeitung, das repräsentative Äußere und den hohen Fahrkomfort verdienen die „Barockengel" jedenfalls das Prädikat „himmlisch gut"!

L'« ange baroque de Bavière » est le surnom qu'arborent les premières grandes berlines d'après-guerre de BMW, les 501 et 502, bien que leurs imposantes carrosseries tout en longueur affichent de belles proportions et soient d'une assez grande finesse aérodynamique.

La BMW 502 entrera dans les annales de l'histoire de l'automobile en tant que première huit-cylindres allemande de l'après-guerre. Elle reprend le châssis à caissons, extrêmement solide, à tubes transversaux de la 501 sur lequel la carrosserie en acier est soudée. Elle se distingue de la 501 par la grande lunette arrière panoramique.

Modèle le plus puissant de la série, la 502 3,2 Liter Super développe 140 ch grâce à ses deux carburateurs double corps inversés. Cela permet à la lourde voiture d'atteindre allégrement les 175 km/h et le 0 à 100 km/h en 14,5 secondes.

On doit reconnaître que le V8 bavarois à bloc en alliage léger et chemises humides inaugure une ère nouvelle dans la technique des moteurs. Détail intéressant, la boîte de vitesses n'est pas accolée directement au moteur. Cela se traduit par un arbre de transmission plus court jusqu'à l'essieu arrière. La colonne de direction, elle aussi, est courte et reliée à une roue conique qui autorise trois tours et demi de butée à butée. Le diamètre de braquage est sensiblement identique à celui de la série 7 d'aujourd'hui.

Le nombre d'exemplaires de la 3,2 Liter Super, qui coûte près de 20 000 marks, est insuffisant pour en assurer la rentabilité malgré son prestige. De 1955 à 1964, 3840 BMW 502 de 3,2 litres ont été construites au total. Une production déficitaire, donc !

En revanche, BMW a prouvé qu'elle pouvait répliquer à Mercedes-Benz. Diverses versions cabriolet et coupé signées par les carrossiers Baur, à Stuttgart, et Autenrieth,

à Darmstadt – fabriquées sur commande – sont venues compléter la gamme des 502.

Par la qualité de sa finition et sa solidité, son allure et son grand confort de conduite, l'« ange baroque » a incontestablement quelque chose de céleste.

Every porter's dream, the doors of the BMW 502 open at a flick of the wrist. The interior, with its sofa-like rear seat and sumptuously upholstered front seats, conveys the comfortable atmosphere of a cosy living-room.

Davon träumt jeder Portier: Der Einstieg zu diesem BMW lässt sich mit einem Handgriff öffnen. Das Interieur mit der couchähnlichen Rückbank und den gut gepolsterten Vordersitzen vermittelt eine behagliche Wohnzimmeratmosphäre.

Le rêve de tout voiturier : les portes de la BMW 502 s'ouvrent en un tour de main. L'habitacle, avec le véritable divan à l'arrière et les fauteuils avant aux épais coussins, lui confère une atmosphère de salon douillet.

The top model of the large type 501 and 502 BMW sedans, popularly known as the "Bavarian baroque angels", was the 3.2 Liter Super. The production version of this heavyweight cruiser had a maximum speed of 109 mph (175 kph), while the tuned engine of the sedan illustrated here was capable of 125 mph (200 kph).

Unter den großen BMW-Limousinen der Typen 501 und 502, volkstümlich „bayerische Barockengel" genannt, ist der 3,2 Liter Super das Spitzenmodell. Die Serienversion des schweren Gefährts kommt auf 175 km/h. Die hier gezeigte Limousine mit „frisiertem" Triebwerk erreicht die 200-km/h-Marke.

Parmi les grandes limousines BMW des séries 501 et 502, surnommées les « anges baroques de Bavière », la 3,2 Liter Super est la plus aboutie. La version de série de cette lourde voiture atteint les 175 km/h. La limousine présentée ici, dont le moteur a été préparé, flirte avec les 200 km/h.

BMW 502 3,2 Liter Super 151

The V8 engine, with its twin Zenith 32NDIX dual-throat downdraft carburetors, developed 140 bhp at 4800 rpm, while this version is capable of 160 bhp at 5600 rpm. Another non-standard feature of the 3.2 Liter Super is the Nardi sports steering wheel with its wooden rim.

Der V8-Motor leistet mit zwei Doppel-Fallstromvergasern der Marke Zenith 32NDIX 140 PS bei 4800/min, ist aber in dieser Version auf 160 PS bei 5600 U/min steigerungsfähig. Ebenfalls nicht Standard beim 3,2 Liter Super: das Nardi-Sportlenkrad mit Holzkranz.

Le moteur V8, avec ses deux doubles carburateurs inversés 32NDIX de marque Zenith, développe 140 ch à 4800 tr/min, mais atteint, dans cette version, jusqu'à 160 ch à 5600 tr/min. Le volant sport Nardi à couronne de bois n'est pas le volant de série de la 3,2 Liter Super.

BMW Isetta 300

The "cuddle box", as it was nicknamed, was a miniature car to fall in love with, a bench with a cabin on wheels: ideal for lovers! Desired by vintage car fans not just as an easy-to-park funmobile, this mini car with motorbike engine is officially called "Motocoupé Isetta".

Apart from the engine and numerous changes to details, the Isetta 250 outwardly reflected the prototype of the Italian company Iso, from which BMW bought the license plus bodywork tools. The engine already existed and came from the BMW R25 motorcycle, a four-stroke single-cylinder engine offering 12 bhp.

The original version, with wrap-round window at the rear, hinged windows and opening roof, looked like an aircraft cockpit. In 1956 the Isetta 250 was given a big sister with carlike characteristics, the Isetta 300. The figures show the progression in engine size from 245 to 298 cc. This produced a "powerful" jump in performance: just 1 bhp!

The tiny engine chugged and burbled along behind the passenger seat. The capacity of the petrol tank (3.5 gallons or 13 liters) was as modest as the fuel consumption (43 miles per gallon/5.5 liters per 100 km). The rear wheels, only 20 inches (52 cm) apart, were driven by a short transverse propshaft and a duplex chain bathed in oil. A little lever on the left-side panel was available for the driver to poke about mightily in the four-speed transmission: best operated by double declutching, for there was no synchronization.

Road holding – the Isetta was not a car which easily tipped over – was acceptable, and at 53 mph (85 kph) maximum speed, the Isetta could keep up with the traffic flow. A length of just over six feet (2.35 meters), a front-opening door, room for the beer crate in front of the passenger seat, and the shopping bags in the luggage space, are the attributes of this compact car. The Isetta has for more than 40 years been what the current Swatch Smart is still trying to attain.

Expectations were still modest in the 1950s. So an Isetta generally served as a car for all seasons: the drive to work as well as the holiday trip over the Alps to the Italian beaches.

As a classic car, the Isetta is still extremely serviceable in everyday use. That is particularly evident in city traffic and its lack of parking spaces. Have you ever tried parking a Corsa, Twingo or Polo at right angles to the traffic flow? Being able to get out forwards directly onto the pavement was also something appreciated by Prince Leopold of Bavaria on ice cream runs with the children. His Royal Highness, whose Isetta is painted in the Bavarian national colors, would not want to be without this midget of a car in his private family car fleet.

More than half of the 136,367 BMW Isettas built in Munich utilized the smaller engine, a question of the category of driver's license in Germany. The British imported the Isetta with just a single rear wheel owing to local laws which allowed three wheelers to be driven on a motorcycle license, with no requirement to take a separate car test.

Die „Knutschkugel", so der Volksmund, ist ein Kleinstwagen zum Lieben und Verlieben, eine Bank mit Kabine auf Rädern – ideal für Liebespaare! Das Mini-Auto mit Motorrad-Motor, von Oldtimer-Fans heute nicht nur als parkraumsparendes Spaßmobil gefragt, trägt die offizielle Bezeichnung „Motocoupé Isetta".

Vom Motor und zahlreichen Detailänderungen abgesehen entspricht die Isetta 250 dem Prototyp der italienischen Firma Iso, von der BMW die Nachbaulizenz samt Presswerkzeugen kauft. Der Motor ist ein alter Bekannter und stammt vom BMW-Motorrad R25, ein Viertakt-Einzylinder mit 12 PS.

Die Ur-Version der Isetta mit hinterer Panoramascheibe, Klappfenstern und Faltdach wirkt wie ein Flugzeug-Cockpit. 1956 bekommt die Isetta 250 eine große Schwester mit automobilen Zügen, die Isetta 300. Die Zahlen drücken den Hubraumzuwachs von 245 auf 298 ccm aus. Damit verbunden ist ein „gewaltiger" Leistungsschub: 1 PS!

Hinter dem Beifahrersitz tuckert und blubbert das kleine Motörchen. Bescheiden wie der Verbrauch (5,5 Liter) ist auch das Tankvolumen (13 Liter). Der Antrieb auf die nur 52 Zentimeter auseinanderstehenden Hinterräder erfolgt über eine quer liegende kurze Gelenkwelle und eine Duplex-Kette, die sich in einem Ölbad suhlt. Mit einem Hebelchen, links an der Seitenwand, darf in dem 4-Gang-Getriebe kräftig herumgerührt werden – am besten mit Zwischengas, denn eine Synchronisation existiert nicht.

Die Straßenlage – kein Umfaller-Wägelchen – ist passabel, und eine Höchstgeschwindigkeit von 85 Stundenkilometern reicht zu jenen Zeiten aus, um im Verkehrsfluss mitzuschwimmen. 2,35 Meter Länge, eine sich nach vorn öffnende Tür, Platz für den Bierkasten vor dem Beifahrersitz und die Einkaufsbeutel auf der Ablage sind Attribute eines gelungenen Kompaktfahrzeugs. Was der

Smart noch werden will, ist die Isetta schon seit mehr als 40 Jahren.

In den fünfziger Jahren sind die Ansprüche noch bescheiden, und die Isetta dient in den meisten Fällen als Auto für alle Fälle: für die Fahrt zur Arbeit ebenso wie für die Urlaubstour über die Alpen an Italiens Strände.

Als Oldtimer ist die Isetta noch äußerst alltagstauglich. Das zeigt sich besonders im von Parkplatznöten gebeutelten Großstadtverkehr. Versuchen Sie einmal, mit einem Corsa, Twingo oder Polo quer zur Fahrtrichtung einzuparken! Direkt nach vorn auf den Bürgersteig aussteigen zu können, schätzte auch Leopold Prinz von Bayern, wenn er mit seinen Kindern zur Eisdiele fuhr. Königliche Hoheit, dessen Isetta in den bayerischen Landesfarben lackiert ist, möchte den automobilen Winzling in seinem privaten Wittelsbacher Fuhrpark nicht missen.

Mehr als die Hälfte der 136 367 in München gebauten BMW Isetta begnügt sich mit dem Motor mit kleinerem Hubraum – in Deutschland eine Frage der Führerscheinklasse. Die Briten hingegen importieren die Isetta mit nur einem Hinterrad – ebenfalls eine Frage der Führerscheinklasse, denn in Großbritannien darf man die Dreiräder mit dem Motorradführerschein fahren.

Le « pot de yaourt », comme on l'a vite surnommée, est une micro-voiture au charme de laquelle on succombe aisément – un banc avec cabine sur roues, idéal pour les amoureux ! La mini-voiture possède un moteur de moto et n'a pas seulement la cote auprès des amateurs de voitures anciennes. Aussi compacte que ludique, elle porte officiellement le titre de « Motocoupé Isetta ».

À part le moteur et plusieurs détails techniques, l'Isetta 250 est, extérieurement, identique au prototype fabriqué par la firme italienne Iso, à laquelle BMW rachète la licence de construction et les presses d'emboutissage. Le moteur existe déjà. Il s'agit de celui de la moto BMW R 25, un monocylindre à quatre temps de 12 ch.

La version d'origine à lunette arrière panoramique, vitres entrebâillées et son toit ouvrant ressemble à un cockpit d'avion. En 1956, l'Isetta 250 est rejointe par sa « grande sœur » qui ressemble davantage à une véritable voiture, l'Isetta 300. Les chiffres traduisent la hausse de cylindrée de 245 à 298 cm³, laquelle va de pair avec un bond « gigantesque » en terme de puissance : 1 ch !

Le petit moteur ronronne derrière les sièges passagers. La consommation (5,5 litres) est aussi réduite que le volume du réservoir (13 litres). La transmission aux roues arrière, séparées l'une de l'autre par seulement 52 cm, est assurée par un court cardan transversal et une chaîne double immergée dans l'huile. Un petit levier accolé à la paroi latérale gauche permet de sélectionner les quatre rapports : de préférence avec double débrayage, car il n'existe pas de synchronisation.

La tenue de route est correcte – contrairement aux apparences, la voiturette tient la route – et, avec 85 km/h, l'Isetta se faufile dans la circulation comme un poisson dans l'eau. 2,35 m de long, une porte ouvrant vers l'avant, de la place pour une caisse de bière devant le siège du passager

et les sacs de courses sur la plage arrière : telles sont des caractéristiques de cette voiture compacte. Ce que la Smart veut devenir, l'Isetta l'est déjà depuis plus de quarante ans.

Dans les années 1950, on est encore modeste et l'Isetta sert, dans la majorité des cas, de voiture de tous les jours : pour se rendre au travail aussi bien que pour partir en vacances au-delà des Alpes, sur les plages d'Italie.

Aussi ancienne soit-elle, l'Isetta a encore parfaitement sa place dans la circulation de tous les jours. On le constate particulièrement dans les grandes agglomérations où l'on cherche souvent en vain une place de stationnement. Essayez donc de vous garer perpendiculairement à la circulation avec une Corsa, une Twingo ou une Polo ! Le prince Léopold de Bavière apprécie de pouvoir descendre par la porte avant directement sur le trottoir lorsqu'il emmène ses enfants manger une glace. Son Altesse Royale, dont l'Isetta est peinte aux couleurs nationales de la Bavière, ne se séparerait pour rien au monde de cette minuscule automobile qui appartient à son parc privé.

Plus de la moitié des 136 367 BMW Isetta qui ont été construites à Munich se contentent du moteur de plus petite cylindrée, ce qui s'explique par la catégorie de permis de conduire en vigueur en Allemagne. Si les Britanniques n'importent l'Isetta qu'avec une seule roue arrière, c'est parce qu'en Grande-Bretagne, il est possible de conduire un véhicule à trois roues avec un permis moto.

BMW Isetta 300

You get into the Isetta with its folding roof from the front. The "dashboard", which consists solely of a speedometer and the ignition lock, swings outwards with the door when it is opened. The gear lever for the four-speed transmission is fitted to the left-hand side wall. Top speed in fourth gear was 53 mph (85 kph), and 0 to 50 mph (0 to 80 kph) took around 40 seconds.

Von vorn erfolgt der Einstieg in die Isetta-Kabine mit Faltdach. Das „Armaturenbrett", lediglich aus Tacho und Zündschloss bestehend, schwenkt mit der Tür mit. Links an der Seitenwand befindet sich der Hebel für die Viergang-Schaltung des Klauengetriebes. Höchstgeschwindigkeit im vierten Gang: 85 Stundenkilometer, Beschleunigung auf 80 „Sachen" in rund 40 Sekunden!

L'accès à la cabine de l'Isetta à toit ouvrant s'effectue par l'avant. Le « tableau de bord », qui se compose uniquement d'un tachymètre et d'une serrure pour la clé de contact, est solidaire de la porte. À gauche, contre la paroi latérale, se trouve le levier de la boîte à quatre vitesses à crabots. Vitesse maximale en quatrième : 85 km/h, accélération de 0 à 80 km/h en 40 secondes environ.

Originally the Isetta had a glass dome, but in 1956 this was replaced by the roof design illustrated, with its sliding windows. The car was also fitted at that time with free-standing headlamps and a modified tail. The "trunk" was externally mounted.

Anfänglich besaß die Isetta noch eine Glaskuppel, die 1956 diesem Dachaufbau mit Schiebefenstern wich. Außerdem erhielt der Wagen freistehende Scheinwerfer und ein modifiziertes Heck. Der „Kofferraum" liegt extern.

À l'origine, l'Isetta possédait un toit en verre qui a fait place, en 1956, à ce type de toit ouvrant coulissant. En outre, la voiture a été dotée de phares proéminents et son arrière a été modifié. Le « coffre » se trouve à l'extérieur.

The tiny four-stroke, single-cylinder, forced-air-cooled engine developed 12 bhp in the Isetta 250, and one bhp more in the Isetta 300. Fuel economy was, not surprisingly, good, at around 43 miles per gallon (5.5 liters per 100 km).

Das von Gebläseluft gekühlte Viertakt-Einzylindermotörchen liefert 12 PS bei der Isetta 250 und ein PS mehr bei der Isetta 300 – sparsame Triebwerke, die 5,5 Liter auf 100 Kilometer verbrauchen.

Le petit monocylindre à quatre temps refroidi par turbine délivre 12 ch sous le capot de l'Isetta 250 et 13 ch sous celui de l'Isetta 300 – des moteurs économiques qui consomment 5,5 litres aux 100 km.

BMW Isetta 300

BMW 507

Otto von Schlitz was hereditary marshal of the archdiocese of Fulda in the year 1100. He was also the ancestor of the counts von Schlitz, known as von Goertz, a family who collected assorted honors for more than 800 years. Albrecht Count Goertz added a colorful image to the family history, for he had been resident in the US since 1936 and became a leading international design guru. For BMW's 507, first postwar pure sports car from BMW, creator Goertz built himself a monument.

Externally, the 507 would do honor to any Ferrari: an excitingly beautiful, harmoniously curved body line with an aggressive interpretation of the BMW kidney trademark styling cues, transformed into an appearance like the mouth of a shark. The aluminium skin of the car barely covers its technical elements, so there is nothing surplus to requirements. A small but unmistakable styling element is the grid with cooling slits and BMW symbol on the front wings. This only partly fulfils its task, since it barely covers the wheel.

A strong box frame, which offered excellent protection against side impacts, was the foundation of the Goertz-designed BMWs 507 and 503. The refined V8 engine with two Zenith dual-throat downdraft carburetors produces 150 bhp. Depending on the rear axle transmission ratio, this brought 123 to 138 mph (196 to 220 kph).

Space at the rear of the vehicle was constricted, containing a 29-gallon (110-liter) tank behind the seats. Probably for safety reasons, this large amount of fuel directly behind the backs of the passengers in the car was reduced to a 17-gallon (65-liter) tank surrounding the spare wheel.

"A car to set the pulse racing" was the contemporary comment in the influential magazine *ADAC-Motorwelt* (published by the German automobile club, ADAC). This referred primarily to the looks of the 507, but also covered the small difference between the unladen and the permitted maximum weight – a mere 375 lbs (170 kg). A well-built member of the affluent society with a little luggage was thus forced to find a "light" lady to take along for driving pleasure *à deux* in the 507.

Acceleration from 0 to 62 mph (0 to 100 kph), with a driver of normal weight at the wheel, of between 11 and 11.5 seconds is appropriate for a sports car of this caliber. Disc brakes, however, were only enjoyed by the last of the total 254 cars built.

The dream car of the 1950s – Elvis had a 507, too – and on the most wanted lists of classic car freaks today, the 507 could be supplied with a properly fitted hardtop. It could compare with the Mercedes 300 SL, for the latter was just a few marks cheaper in 1956.

A few details can be a nuisance in the 507. The distance of the steering column to the driver can be adjusted telescopically, but it can only be reduced: a blessing for people with short arms, but a nuisance for anyone of elongated build. The arrangement of various push buttons and levers on the dashboard is also far from ergonomic. A small windshield-wiped field and little possibility of adjusting the seats, are items one would put up with – if only one could count oneself among those happy people who can proudly call themselves BMW 507 owners.

Otto von Schlitz, um 1100 Erbmarschall des Hochstiftes Fulda, ist Urahn der Herren von Schlitz, genannt von Goertz, die 800 Jahre lang Meriten aller Art eingeheimst haben. Albrecht Graf Goertz fügt der Familiengeschichte eine farbige Metapher hinzu. Er lebt seit 1936 in den USA und ist Designer. Mit dem ersten Nachkriegssportwagen von BMW, dem 507, setzt sich Goertz ein Denkmal.

Das Äußere des 507 würde jedem Ferrari zu Ehre gereichen: eine aufregend schöne, harmonisch geschwungene Karosserielinie mit einer aggressiv wirkenden Interpretation der BMW-Niere, die eher einem Haifischmaul gleicht. Die Aluminiumschale des Wagens bedeckt so gerade den technischen Kern. Es gibt also keinerlei unnötige Überhänge. Kleines, aber unverwechselbares Stylingelement sind die Gitter mit Kühlschlitzen und BMW-Emblem in den vorderen Kotflügeln. Diese werden ihrer Bestimmung nur teilweise gerecht, da sie das Rad kaum abdecken.

Ein stabiler Kastenrahmen, der viel Schutz gegen seitlichen Aufprall bietet, ist das tragende Element der Goertz-Wagen 507 und 503. 150 PS leistet der kultivierte V8-Motor mit zwei Doppel-Fallstromvergasern von Zenith. Je nach Hinterachsübersetzung resultieren daraus 196 bis 220 Stundenkilometer.

Recht eng geht es im Fahrzeugheck zu, das zunächst ein 110-Liter-Tank hinter den Sitzen füllt. Wohl aus Sicherheitsgründen wird die große Benzinmenge direkt im Rücken der Fahrzeuginsassen zugunsten eines 65-Liter-Tanks, der das Reserverad umschließt, reduziert.

„Ein Herzklopfen erzeugendes Fahrzeug" – dieses eher auf die Optik des 507 bezogene zeitgenössische Statement der *ADAC-Motorwelt* gilt auch für die geringe Differenz zwischen Leer- und zulässigem Gesamtgewicht. Es sind lediglich 170 Kilo. Ein schwergewichtiger Wohlstandsbürger mit etwas Gepäck ist für das Fahrvergnügen zu zweit im 507 quasi gezwungen, eine zarte Frau mitzunehmen.

Die Beschleunigung von 0 auf 100 Stundenkilometer – mit einem normalgewichtigen Menschen am Steuer – zwischen 11 und 11,5 Sekunden, ist angemessen für einen Sportwagen dieses Kalibers. In den Genuss von Scheibenbremsen kommen allerdings nur die letzten der insgesamt 254 gebauten Wagen.

Das Traumauto der fünfziger Jahre (auch Elvis hatte einen 507) und der Oldtimer-Freaks von heute, lieferbar mit einem gelungenen und gut angepassten Hardtop, muss den Vergleich mit dem Mercedes 300 SL nicht scheuen, denn dieser ist 1956 sogar ein paar Mark billiger.

Beim 507 stören lediglich einige Details. So lässt sich der Abstand des Lenkrads zum Fahrer teleskopisch verstellen, aber nur in einem Bereich, der Menschen mit kurzen Armen entgegenkommt, während Fahrer mit großer „Reichweite" keine optimale Sitzposition finden. Auch die Anordnung diverser Zugknöpfe und Hebel des Armaturenbretts ist nicht glücklich gelöst. Kleines Wischerfeld und wenig Sitzverstellmöglichkeiten sind freilich Dinge, an die man sich gewöhnen könnte, würde man zu den Glücklichen gehören, die sich stolz Besitzer eines BMW 507 nennen dürfen.

Otto von Schlitz, qui dirigeait le diocèse de Fulda vers 1100, est l'ancêtre des seigneurs von Schlitz, nommés von Goertz, qui ont accumulé les honneurs en tout genre pendant plus de huit siècles. Le comte Albrecht von Goertz ajoute à la saga de la famille sa touche personnelle : depuis 1936, il vit aux États-Unis où il est designer. Avec le lancement de la première BMW de sport de l'après-guerre, la 507, son créateur, von Goertz, se construit lui-même sa réputation.

Les lignes de la 507 sont dignes d'une Ferrari : une carrosserie de toute beauté, aux galbes harmonieux et une interprétation agressive des naseaux de BMW, une proue qui ressemble plutôt à une gueule de requin. La carrosserie en aluminium de la voiture recouvre à peine sa mécanique. Il n'y a donc pas de superflu. Un élément de style, minuscule mais caractéristique, est la grille située dans l'aile avant, avec des fentes d'aération latérales et l'emblème BMW. Cette aile avant ne remplit d'ailleurs sa tâche qu'à moitié puisqu'elle couvre à peine la roue.

Un solide cadre à caissons, qui offre une bonne protection contre les collisions latérales, est « l'épine dorsale » des 507 et 503 de Goertz. Le velouté V8, à double carburateur inversé Zenith, développe 150 ch. Selon le rapport de pont, la vitesse de pointe oscille entre 196 et 220 km/h.

L'espace est plutôt compté à l'arrière, où un réservoir de 110 litres occupe beaucoup de place. Par sécurité, l'importante quantité d'essence logée directement dans le dos des passagers est réduite et va être stockée dans un réservoir de 65 litres qui encercle la roue de secours.

« Une voiture qui vous donne des battements au cœur » : ce constat de la revue ADAC-Motorwelt de cette époque, qui fait surtout allusion à l'esthétique de la 507, vaut aussi pour la faible différence entre le poids à vide et le poids total autorisé – seulement 170 kg ! Pour le plaisir de conduire

à deux en 507, tout conducteur aisé avec un tant soit peu d'embonpoint et quelques bagages est déjà contraint à emmener avec lui un passager « léger ».

Les accélérations de 0 à 100 km/h (avec un conducteur de poids normal au volant) sont dignes d'une voiture de sport de ce calibre puisqu'elles se situent entre 11 et 11,5 secondes. Seules les dernières voitures construites, sur 254 au total, bénéficieront de freins à disques.

La voiture de rêve des années 1950 (Elvis Presley avait lui aussi une 507) et des collectionneurs, qui était livrable avec un hard-top esthétique et bien étanche, a toujours été comparée à la Mercedes 300 SL qui, en 1956, coûte même quelques marks de moins.

Seuls quelques détails peuvent être reprochés à la 507. La distance qui sépare la colonne de direction – télescopique – du conducteur est réglable, mais elle peut seulement être diminuée : ce qui est une aubaine pour ceux qui ont de petits bras et un véritable casse-tête pour ceux qui sont dotés de long bras. De même, l'agencement des divers boutons et leviers sur le tableau de bord n'est pas parfaitement ergonomique. Un champ d'action réduit des essuie-glace sur le pare-brise et de faibles possibilités de réglage des sièges sont des détails auxquels on peut s'habituer et auxquels on s'habituerait volontiers – à condition de figurer parmi les heureux propriétaires d'une BMW 507.

BMW 507

The BMW 507, with its harmoniously flowing lines and aggressive version of the BMW kidney grill, is one of Count Goertz's most beautiful designs.

Sicherlich ist der BMW 507 mit seiner harmonisch geschwungenen Karosserielinie einerseits und der aggressiv wirkenden Interpretation der BMW-Niere andererseits eines der schönsten Designs des Grafen Goertz.

La BMW 507, avec sa carrosserie aux galbes élégants d'une part, et l'interprétation quelque peu agressive des naseaux de BMW d'autre part, est sans aucun doute l'une des plus belles réussites du comte von Goertz.

The sports steering wheel later added to the 507 cockpit by the German Nardi importer did nothing to detract from the roadster feeling, while the 4.50 E x 16 steel rims also contributed to the motor sport appearance.

Das nachträglich dem 507-Cockpit zugestandene Sportlenkrad des deutschen Nardi-Importeurs stört das Roadster-Feeling keineswegs. Motorsport-Optik auch bei den 4,50 E x 16 Stahlfelgen.

Le volant sport de l'importateur allemand Nardi, concédé ultérieurement au cockpit de la 507, ne porte en aucun cas préjudice à son style roadster. Les jantes en acier de 4,50E x 16 laissent aussi flotter un parfum de compétition.

BMW 507

This classic V8 engine with its light alloy block and twin dual-throat downdraft carburetors developed 150 bhp, rising to 165 bhp in the US version. This allowed top speeds of up to 138 mph (220 kph), depending on the rear axle ratio.

150 PS, in der US-Ausführung sogar 165 PS, leistet der klassische V8-Motor mit einem Leichtmetallblock und zwei Doppel-Fallstromvergasern. Damit sind je nach Hinterachs-übersetzung Geschwindigkeiten von bis zu 220 Stundenkilometern möglich.

Le moteur V8 classique à bloc en alliage léger et deux carburateurs double corps inversés développe 150 ch et même 165 ch dans sa version américaine. Il permet de rouler, selon le rapport de pont, jusqu'à 220 km/h.

The side air vents of the 507, reintroduced forty years later on the Z3, are unmistakable. The box-section frame, barely concealed by the bodywork, is painted black to make the belt line appear lower-slung.

Unverkennbar – beim Z3 40 Jahre später wieder aufgegriffen – sind die seitlichen Luftschlitze des 507. Der von der Außenhaut nur knapp bedeckte Kastenrahmen ist schwarz lackiert, damit die Gürtellinie niedriger wirkt.

Les fentes d'aération latérales de la 507 sont très caractéristiques de cette voiture et ont été reprises, quarante ans plus tard, pour la Z3. Le châssis à caissons qu'habille à grand peine la carrosserie est peint de couleur noire pour que la ligne de ceinture semble plus basse.

BMW 503

As well as the 507, Count Albrecht Goertz designed "an elegant luxury travel sports car from the stable of the large BMW eight-cylinder cars" (factory jargon). This design, outstanding owing to its long bonnet and the projecting BMW kidney grill at the front, made its debut as the 503 at the Frankfurt Motor Show during September 1955.

The engine, a light alloy V8 with wet cylinder liners and a separate transmission which was not directly bolted on to the engine, was taken from the 502. The same applied to the descriptive full protection frame. It was not until December 1957 that the transmission, which was situated under the front seats, was bolted to the engine. Then the gear change on the steering column was replaced with a lever on the transmission tunnel.

Convertible and coupé are designed for four passengers, always assuming that those in the rear seats are not too large. "The interior is designed for sporty but comfortable driving," as the 503 brochure put it. Today such coupés are described as having 2+2 seating, offering less accomodation in the rear than a 4-seater.

The 503 convertible folding mechanism was sophisticated. It was the first German automobile to have an electrically operated power-top; cranking the side windows up and down is also completed by electric motors.

The aluminium body, captivating with its neat, snugly-fitting manufacture, limited the weight of the car to 3300 lbs (1500 kg). At this kerb weight, 140 bhp manage to produce acceleration of 13 seconds from 0 to 62 mph (100 kph) and a top speed of 119 mph (190 kph). The petrol tank, situated behind the rear axle and with a space for the spare wheel, held 20 gallons (75 liters), sufficient for approximately 280 miles (450 km).

Like the 507, the last of the 503s enjoyed disc brakes on the front wheels. Also like the 507, the price – 29,500 marks for the convertible in 1956 – was within range of the Mercedes 300 SL. Only just over 400 of these noble 503 beasts, which needed to be subsidized by BMW, found a buyer. The 503 filled a market niche which was too small to make it economically viable. Today's owners of these flamboyant rarities therefore have all the more reasons to rub their hands together in glee.

Neben dem 507 entwirft Albrecht Graf Goertz „einen eleganten Reisesportwagen aus der Reihe der großen BMW-Achtzylinder" (Werks-Jargon). Dieses Fahrzeug, das durch seine lange Motorhaube und die wulstig nach vorn stehenden BMW-Nieren auffällt, wird als 503 auf der Frankfurter Automobilausstellung im September 1955 vorgestellt.

Das Triebwerk, ein V8 aus Leichtmetall mit nassen Zylinderlaufbüchsen und ein separates, nicht an den Motor angeflanschtes Getriebe, werden aus dem 502 übernommen, ebenso der so genannte Vollschutzrahmen. Erst im Dezember 1957 wird das unter den Vordersitzen liegende Getriebe mit dem Motor verblockt, die Lenkradschaltung von einem Hebel auf dem Kardantunnel abgelöst.

Cabriolet und Coupé sind für vier Passagiere ausgelegt, vorausgesetzt, dass die im Fond sitzenden von kleinerem Wuchs sind. „Der Innenraum ist auf sportliche wie bequeme Fahrweise ausgelegt", so der 503-Prospekt. Aus damaliger Sicht ist dieser Beschreibung nichts hinzuzufügen. Bequem ist sicherlich der Faltmechanismus des Cabrioletverdecks, der erstmalig bei einem deutschen Auto elektrisch betätigt wird, und auch die Kurbelarbeit zum Heben und Senken der Seitenscheiben übernehmen Elektromotoren.

Dank der Aluminiumkarosserie, die durch ihre saubere und passgenaue Fertigung besticht, kann das Wagengewicht auf 1500 Kilo beschränkt werden. Bei diesem Gewicht erreichen die 140 PS eine Beschleunigung von 0 auf 100 Stundenkilometer in 13 Sekunden und eine Höchstgeschwindigkeit von 190 Stundenkilometern. Der hinter der Hinterachse liegende und mit einer Ausbuchtung für das Reserverad versehene Kraftstofftank fasst 75 Liter. Das genügt für eine Strecke von rund 450 Kilometern.

Wie beim 507 kommen die letzten 503 noch in den Genuss von Scheibenbremsen an den Vorderrädern. Und wie beim 507 rangiert der Preis – 29 500 Mark für das Cabriolet 1956 – im Bereich dessen, was man für einen Mercedes 300 SL ausgeben muss. Nur etwas mehr als 400 dieser Edelstücke, bei denen BMW sogar noch ein paar Mark zuschießen muss, finden ihre Käufer. Der 503 füllt eine Marktnische, die zu klein für eine wirtschaftlich rentable Fertigung ist. Umso mehr reiben sich heute die Besitzer dieser extravaganten Rarität die Hände.

Outre la 507, le comte Albrecht von Goertz dessine « une élégante voiture de sport de voyage pour la gamme des grosses BMW huit-cylindres » (dans le jargon de l'usine). Cette voiture qui surprend par son long capot moteur et les proéminents naseaux BMW est présentée sous le nom de 503 au Salon de l'Automobile de Francfort en septembre 1955.

Le moteur, un V8 en alliage léger à chemises humides et avec boîte de vitesses séparée non accolée au bloc, est repris de la 502, tout comme le cadre à protection intégrale. Il faudra attendre décembre 1957 pour que la boîte de vitesses placée sous le siège avant rejoigne le moteur et que le sélecteur au volant soit remplacé par un levier sur le tunnel de transmission.

Le cabriolet et le coupé sont prévus pour quatre passagers à condition que les passagers arrière soient de petite taille. « L'habitacle est conçu pour un style de conduite sportif et décontracté », peut-on lire dans le prospectus qui vante la 503.

La commande de la capote, pour la première fois sur une voiture allemande, est électrique et les vitres latérales peuvent être descendues ou remontées grâce à des moteurs électriques.

Avec sa carrosserie en aluminium qui séduit par sa finition et l'exactitude de son montage, le poids de la voiture peut être limité à 1500 kg. Avec un tel poids, les 140 ch permettent des accélérations de 0 à 100 km/h en 13 secondes et une vitesse de pointe de 190 km/h. Le réservoir d'essence placé derrière l'essieu arrière, avec un espace pour la roue de secours, offre une capacité de 75 litres – assez pour parcourir quelque 450 km.

Comme pour la 507, la dernière 503 est équipée, elle aussi, de freins à disques sur les roues avant. Et, comme pour la 507, le prix – 29 500 marks pour le cabriolet de

1956 – concurrence celui de la Mercedes 300 SL. Un peu plus de 400 exemplaires de ces superbes voitures, qui coûtent même quelques marks à BMW, trouvent preneur. La 503 se situe sur un marché de niche trop étroit pour être rentable. Aujourd'hui, les propriétaires de cette voiture extravagante s'en frottent d'autant plus les mains.

BMW 503

BMW 503

Wolfgang Denzel, a technically-gifted man who was also a competent racing driver, was hungry for success as BMW's general importer for Austria. He dreamt of a really small, rear-engined BMW car for the middle class. What was so beautiful about the BMW 600 anyway? It was nothing more than a four-seater Isetta?

Denzel submitted his ideas to BMW in November 1957. The ideas received approval from the factory and, since the draft was conscientiously crafted, Denzel was asked that he should create a prototype with the Turin designer Michelotti. A few months later, the beautiful BMW 700 materialized. At the 1959 Frankfurt Motor Show, the 700 made its debut either as the coupé or a two-door sedan.

It caused a sensation and volume production was implemented immediately. The sedan, a value-for-money car designed for use by anyone, achieved a sales total which surpassed 60,000 units in the period 1959–62. Out of almost 30,000 coupés (1959–64), there were 9436 sport and CS versions alone.

The 700 coupé participated in motor racing on an impressively widespread basis. In 1959/60 alone, it had the distinction of winning 67 victories and being second 41 times. Drivers such as Hans Stuck senior (German champion at the age of 60) managed to keep competitors with larger engines at bay with the coupé. A further tuned 700 RS offered 70 bhp and a 125 mph (200 kph) top speed which put an end to the Fiat Abarth's domination of the winning positions in the smallest capacity classes. No less than 19 of these BMW motor racing open-top designs took victories, mainly at the great hill-climbing events such as Trento-Bondone, Gaisberg, Schauinsland and Roßfeld.

Meanwhile the sedan received a larger interior, achieved by adding 6.3 inches (16 cm) to the wheelbase. BMW extended the rear to accommodate a four-cylinder engine,

intended to vault the 700 (with an LS badge suffix) further into the middle class. The overall addition of 13 inches (32 cm) was of particular benefit to the rear passengers, because the planned change of engine was abandoned, resulting in a cavity between the boxer engine and rear bulkhead. A "workshop-friendly" layout improved access.

However, the proven two-cylinder's power was increased from 30 to 32 bhp in February 1963, although this had little impact on the car's driving performance. The trunk in the nose of the car was divided between the spare wheel – an additional crumple zone behind the bumper – and a 7.9-gallon (30-liter) tank, leaving just enough room for one large suitcase.

The combination of a pleasing interior – an effective dashboard layout with a 2-spoke steering wheel offering a good grip, a sporty gearshift and quality seats – and a tasteful exterior made this car a hit with customers. Great roadholding, 75 mph (120 kph) top speed and reasonable fuel consumption (31.5 miles per gallon of Super/7.5 liters per 100 km) were all contributing factors to its sales success. In three years some 92,416 LS sedans, in addition to 1730 LS coupés, were built.

Wolfgang Denzel – technisch begabt, als Rennfahrer ganz passabel und als BMW-Generalimporteur für Österreich erfolgshungrig – träumt von einem richtigen kleinen BMW-Mittelklassewagen mit Heckmotor. Was ist denn schon der BMW 600? Doch nicht mehr als eine viersitzige Isetta!

Denzel bringt seine eigenen Vorstellungen zu Papier und präsentiert diese im November 1957 im Werk. Den Münchnern ist es recht, und da die Entwürfe Hand und Fuß haben, schlagen sie Denzel vor, zusammen mit dem Turiner Designer Michelotti einen Prototypen auf die Räder zu stellen. Ein bildhübscher Wagen, der BMW 700, entsteht innerhalb weniger Monate. Auf der Frankfurter Automobilausstellung 1959 feiert der 700 als Coupé und zweitürige Limousine Premiere.

Die Resonanz ist gewaltig, und die Serienproduktion läuft sofort an. Die Limousine, ein preiswertes Gefährt für jedermann, wird von 1959 bis 1962 in mehr als 60 000 Einheiten verkauft. Auf knapp 30 000 Coupés (1959–64) kommen allein 9436 Sport- und CS-Ausführungen. Motorsport auf breiter Ebene wird eindrucksvoll praktiziert. Allein 1959/60 feiert das Coupé 67 Siege und 41 zweite Plätze. Fahrer wie Hans Stuck – mit 60 Jahren noch deutscher Meister – hängen mit dem Coupé sogar hubraumstärkere Konkurrenten ab, und mit dem Erscheinen des 700 RS, der mit 70 PS eine Spitzengeschwindigkeit von 200 Stundenkilometern erreicht, bricht BMW in die Domäne der siegesgewohnten Fiat Abarth ein. Gleich 19 dieser BMW-Rennsport-Spider werden auf die Siegerstraßen, vornehmlich bei großen Bergpreisen wie Trento-Bondone, Gaisberg, Schauinsland und Roßfeld, geschickt.

Mehr Innenraum durch 16 Zentimeter längeren Radstand sowie ein verlängertes Heck zur Aufnahme eines Vierzylindertriebwerks sollen den 700 mit dem Zusatz „LS" in die Mittel-

BMW 700LS

klasse heben. Die Gesamtverlängerung von 32 Zentimetern kommt vornehmlich den Fondpassagieren zugute, denn die vorgesehene Ummotorisierung erweist sich als Flop, so dass zwischen Boxermotor und Heckschürze ein Hohlraum entsteht. „Werkstattfreundlich" nennt man das.

Immerhin wird im Februar 1963 die Potenz des Zweizylinders von 30 auf 32 PS angehoben, was sich in den Fahrleistungen allerdings kaum bemerkbar macht. Den Kofferraum im Wagenbug teilen sich das Reserverad – als zusätzliche Knautschzone hinter dem Stoßfänger –, ein 30-Liter-Tank und obendrauf das restliche Volumen für einen großen Koffer.

Ein gefälliges Interieur – ein übersichtliches Armaturenbrett mit griffigem Zweispeichenlenkrad, sportlichem Schaltknüppel und guten Sitzen – sowie das ansprechende Äußere treffen den Geschmack der Kunden. Die ordentliche Straßenlage, eine Spitzengeschwindigkeit von 120 Stundenkilometern und ein vernünftiger Verbrauch (7,5 Liter Super) tragen zum Verkaufserfolg bei. In drei Jahren werden 92 416 LS-Limousinen gebaut, zu denen sich noch 1730 LS-Coupés gesellen.

Wolfgang Denzel, génie de la mécanique, bon pilote de course et, en tant qu'importateur exclusif de BMW pour l'Autriche, affamé de succès, rêve d'une vraie petite BMW du segment intermédiaire à moteur arrière. Et il voulait quelque chose de plus beau qu'une BMW 600, qui n'était finalement qu'une Isetta à quatre places.

Denzel réalise quelques croquis de son concept qu'il présente en novembre 1957 à l'usine. Celui-ci est du goût des Munichois et, comme ses plans semblent prometteurs, ils proposent à Denzel de réaliser un prototype conjointement avec le styliste turinois Michelotti. Une très jolie petite voiture, la BMW 700, naît quelques mois plus tard. Son lancement en tant que coupé et berline à deux portes aura lieu au Salon de l'Automobile de Francfort de 1959.

Le succès est immense et la production en série débute immédiatement. La berline, un engin à la portée de tous, est produite à plus de 60 000 exemplaires de 1959 à 1962. Sur près de 30 000 coupés (fabriqués de 1959 à 1964), pas moins de 9436 sont des versions sport et CS. Elles démocratisent en quelque sorte la compétition automobile. Rien qu'en 1959–1960, le coupé engrange 67 victoires et décroche 41 fois la deuxième place. Des pilotes comme Hans Stuck Senior (encore champion d'Allemagne à 60 ans) surclassent même des concurrentes de plus forte cylindrée avec le coupé qui bat en brèche les Fiat Abarth, pourtant abonnées à la victoire jusqu'à l'apparition de la 700RS (70 ch, 200 km/h en vitesse de pointe). Pas moins de 19 de ces Spider de compétition BMW remportent des victoires, notamment lors des Grands Prix qui ont lieu sur des routes de montagne comme Trento-Bondone, Gaisberg, Schauinsland et Rossfeld.

Un empattement allongé de 16 cm ainsi qu'une poupe plus longue pour recevoir un moteur à quatre cylindres

ont pour objectif de faire accéder la 700, désormais qualifiée de « LS », au segment intermédiaire. Cet allongement total de 32 cm bénéficie en premier lieu aux passagers de la banquette arrière, car le changement de motorisation est un échec. Le boxer (moteur à cylindres opposés à plat) original est si petit qu'il n'emplit même pas le compartiment moteur et évite ainsi des contorsions aux mécaniciens lors des révisions.

En février 1963, le deux-cylindres voit sa puissance passer de 30 à 32 ch, ce qui ne change toutefois pratiquement rien à ses performances. La roue de secours – avec un espace supplémentaire prévu derrière le pare-chocs –, un réservoir de 30 litres et assez d'espace pour une grosse valise se partagent le volume du coffre à l'avant.

Un habitacle séduisant (avec un tableau de bord bien agencé et un volant à deux branches, un levier de changement de vitesses sportif au centre et de bons sièges) ainsi que des lignes très réussies sont tout à fait du goût de la clientèle. Une tenue de route correcte, une vitesse de pointe de 120 km/h et une consommation raisonnable (7,5 litres de super aux 100 km) contribuent à son succès commercial. En trois ans, 92 416 berlines LS sont construites, auxquelles s'ajoutent encore 1730 coupés LS.

Encouraged by the success of the BMW 700, the Munich factory built the LS, an extra 13 inches (32 cm) in length, from 1962 onwards. This luxury was of particular benefit to the rear passengers and the trunk size.

Ermutigt durch den Erfolg des BMW 700 baut das Münchener Werk ab 1962 den 32 Zentimeter längeren LS. Dieser „Luxus" kommt besonders den Fondpassagieren und dem Kofferraumvolumen zugute.

Encouragée par le succès remporté par la BMW 700, l'usine de Munich construit, à partir de 1962, la LS dont l'empattement est allongé de 32 cm. Cet allongement bénéficie en particulier aux passagers de la banquette arrière et au volume du coffre.

The LS – a competitor of the DKW Junior de luxe – filled BMW's coffers: 92,416 of these small sedans were sold.

Mit dem LS – einem Konkurrenten des DKW Junior de luxe – füllt der Münchener Konzern durch den Verkauf von 92 416 dieser kleinen Limousinen seine Kassen.

Avec la LS – qui fait concurrence à la DKW Junior de luxe –, le groupe munichois remplit son tiroir-caisse en vendant 92 416 exemplaires de ces petites berlines.

Sober and functional: the cockpit of the 700LS with its two large round instruments – speedo and clock. The two-cylinder boxer engine with one downdraft carburetor left a lot of space in the rear. The 30 bhp unit was given an additional 2 bhp of performance in 1963.

Nüchtern und funktionell ist das Cockpit des 700LS mit zwei großen Rundinstrumenten – Tacho und Uhr. Der Zweizylinder-Boxermotor mit einem Fallstromvergaser lässt im Heck viel Platz. 1963 erhält der 30-PS-Triebling einen Leistungszuwachs von 2PS.

Sobre et fonctionnel : le cockpit de la 700LS avec ses deux grands cadrans – le tachymètre et l'horloge. Le bicylindre plat à carburateur inversé laisse beaucoup d'espace à l'arrière. En 1963, le petit moteur de 30 ch voit sa puissance augmenter de 2 ch.

When the attractive BMW 700 coupé and sedan were shown at the Frankfurt Motor Show in the autumn of 1959, the response was tremendous. BMW received sufficient advance orders for two whole production years.

Bei der Präsentation des attraktiven BMW 700 Coupé samt Limousine auf der Frankfurter Automobilausstellung im Herbst 1959 ist die Resonanz gewaltig. BMW erhält Vorbestellungen für zwei komplette Produktionsjahre.

Lors de la présentation de l'attrayante BMW 700 coupé aux côtés de la berline, au Salon de l'Automobile de Francfort de l'automne 1959, le succès est au rendez-vous. BMW enregistre des commandes correspondant à deux années complètes de production.

BMW 700LS

BMW 700LS

The spare wheel positioned behind the rounded nose – like a sort of bumper – and the fuel tank left little luggage space in the trunk of this rear-engined car. The small coupé scored undreamed-of success as the basic vehicle for motor sport, a success to which Hans Stuck, at the age of 60, contributed a German championship title.

Das hinter dem runden Bug – quasi als Puffer – stehende Reserverad und der Tank lassen dem Hecktriebler nur wenig Gepäckraum. Als Basisfahrzeug für den Motorsport erntet das kleine Coupé ungeahnte Erfolge, zu denen Hans Stuck im Alter von 60 Jahren einen deutschen Meistertitel beisteuert.

La roue de secours placée à la verticale derrière la proue arrondie – comme une sorte de butoir – et le réservoir ne laissent que peu de place pour les bagages dans le coffre de cette voiture à moteur arrière. Le petit coupé remportera des succès inouïs en compétition automobile, notamment avec Hans Stuck Senior au volant, qui y contribuera avec le titre de champion d'Allemagne… à l'âge de 60 ans.

BMW 3200CS

All of the designs coming from the pen of motorcar designer Nuccio Bertone were distinguished by timeless and therefore understated elegance. What was so attractive about the Maestro's work was his ability to unite clear lines and technical practicalities. The people in Munich believed that Bertone's reputation enhanced BMW's profile, as would a four-seater coupé, due to replace the slow-selling 503.

When the Italian creation made its debut at the Frankfurt Motor Show in September 1961, it was met with universal acclaim. The sturdiness of the car body was unmistakable and provided yet another example of Bertone's quality workmanship. The cars from Turin started arriving via Munich for sale at the start of 1962.

The fresh wind blowing through the nearby Alps seemed to lend the BMW V8 even more power. With a compression of 9:1, the light alloy engine equipped with two dual-throat downdraft carburetors delivered 160 bhp at 5600 rpm. Despite a corresponding increase in the torque figures, the specific fuel consumption values were more favorable than those of the 140 bhp 3200L. That meant 15 miles per gallon (16 liters per 100 km) of Super grade gas fuel consumption in normal use.

The combination of good taste and practicality proved to be just as successful in Bertone's cabin as it had been in the exterior. Large doors and the absence of a B-pillar facilitated access to the rear compartment. In addition to the steering column gear shift – with the scarcely audible meshing of gear teeth underneath the front seats – there was a stick shift for the propshaft center tunnel.

Like the 507, the frame consisted of a box section with tubular cross beams. This provided a strong foundation for Bertone's attractive solid steel body design. The chassis was also identical to the one used in the 507, following the American adage, "If it ain't broke, don't fix it."

Public roads were not graced with many production examples of the 3200CS. Only 602 coupés were made during the four years of its production run. Only one convertible variant was manufactured. It was intended for the man who wished to make BMW profitable once more – Dr Herbert Quandt, BMW's major shareholder.

Zeitlose und daher eher unauffällige Eleganz schwingt bei allen Entwürfen des Autodesigners Nuccio Bertone mit. Der Maestro besticht durch die klare Linienführung seiner Entwürfe, die sich stets an der Technik orientieren. Bertones Renommee, so findet man in München, steht BMW gut zu Gesicht, und ein viersitziges Coupé, das den schwer verkäuflichen 503 ablösen soll, ebenfalls.

Als die italienische Kreation im September 1961 auf der Frankfurter Automobilausstellung debütiert, erntet sie einhelliges Lob. Die Karosserie strahlt Solidität aus und unterstreicht Bertones Fertigungsqualität. Anfang 1962 treffen die ersten Wagen aus Turin in München ein.

Mit dem frischen Wind, der da über die Alpen weht, wird dem V8-Triebwerk noch mehr Kraft eingehaucht. Mit einer Verdichtung von 9:1 liefert der mit zwei Doppel-Fallstromvergasern bestückte Leichtmetallmotor 160 PS bei 5600 Umdrehungen ab. Trotz Anhebung der Drehmomentkurve fallen die spezifischen Verbrauchswerte günstiger aus als beim 140-PS-Motor des 3200L, was den Benzinverbrauch von 16 Litern Super auf 100 Kilometern Normalbetrieb jedoch nicht tangiert.

Gediegen und funktionell wie das Äußere präsentiert Bertone den Innenbereich. Große Türen und der Verzicht auf eine B-Säule erleichtern den Zutritt zum Fond. Neben der Lenkradschaltung – die Getriebezähne mahlen kaum hörbar unter den Vordersitzen – wird auch ein Schalthebel auf dem Kardantunnel angeboten.

Wie beim 507 besteht der Rahmen aus einem Kasten mit Rohrquerträgern – eine äußerst stabile Basis, über die Bertone seine hübsche Ganzstahlkarosserie gestülpt hat. Auch das Fahrwerk ist vom 507. Bewährtes soll man nicht neu erfinden!

Was die Produktionszahlen anbelangt, gehört auch der 3200CS zu den seltenen Erscheinungen im Straßenbild.

Nur 602 Coupés entstehen in vier Jahren Bauzeit. Die Produktion einer Cabrioletvariante beschränkt sich auf ein Unikat für den Mann, der BMW wieder schwarze Zahlen bescheren will: BMW-Großaktionär Dr. Herbert Quandt.

Une élégance intemporelle et, donc, plutôt discrète, marque de son sceau toutes les créations du « couturier » automobile Nuccio Bertone. Le maestro est célèbre pour son coup de crayon incisif qui allie lignes pures et prouesses techniques. La renommée de Bertone, estime-t-on à Munich, correspondrait fort bien à BMW, de même qu'un coupé à quatre places qui remplacerait la 503 difficile à vendre.

Lorsque la voiture de création italienne fait ses débuts en septembre 1961, au Salon de l'Automobile de Francfort, elle rencontre un succès fou. La carrosserie donne une impression de solidité et témoigne de la qualité des finitions qui a fait la réputation de Bertone. Début 1962, les premières voitures de Turin arrivent à Munich.

Dans son sillage, le moteur V8 gagne lui aussi en puissance. Avec un taux de compression de 9:1, le moteur en alliage léger à deux carburateurs double corps inversés développe 160 ch à 5600 tr/min. Malgré l'amélioration de la valeur de couple, les taux de consommation sont meilleurs que ceux de la 3200L avec 140 ch, ce qui n'affecte cependant en rien le prix à payer à la pompe avec 16 litres de super aux 100 km en conduite normale.

Bertone a réalisé un habitacle aussi luxueux et fonctionnel que la carrosserie. De grandes portières et l'absence de pied central facilitent l'accès à l'arrière. Outre le changement de vitesses au volant – presque silencieuse, la boîte se trouve sous les sièges avant – on peut aussi opter pour un levier sur le tunnel de transmission.

Comme pour la 507, le châssis est constitué d'une échelle avec des poutres transversales – une plate-forme d'une extrême solidité que Bertone a coiffée de sa jolie carrosserie tout acier. Les trains roulants, eux aussi, sont ceux de la 507. Pourquoi changer une équipe qui gagne ?

Les chiffres de la production font aussi de la 3200CS un modèle que l'on a rarement l'occasion de croiser sur sa route. 602 coupés seulement seront construits en quatre ans. La production de cabriolets se limite à un spécimen destiné à celui qui veut absolument faire sortir BMW du rouge : Herbert Quandt, l'actionnaire majoritaire de BMW.

BMW 3200CS

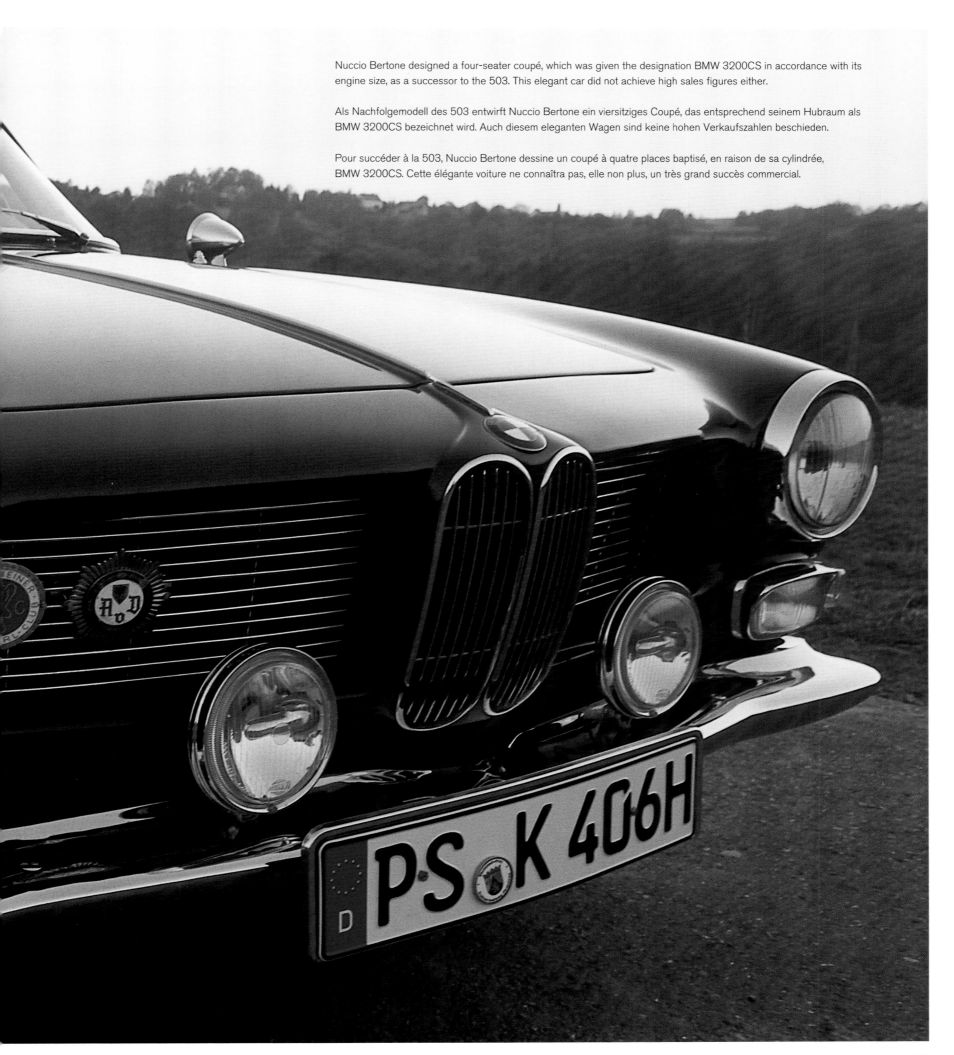

Nuccio Bertone designed a four-seater coupé, which was given the designation BMW 3200CS in accordance with its engine size, as a successor to the 503. This elegant car did not achieve high sales figures either.

Als Nachfolgemodell des 503 entwirft Nuccio Bertone ein viersitziges Coupé, das entsprechend seinem Hubraum als BMW 3200CS bezeichnet wird. Auch diesem eleganten Wagen sind keine hohen Verkaufszahlen beschieden.

Pour succéder à la 503, Nuccio Bertone dessine un coupé à quatre places baptisé, en raison de sa cylindrée, BMW 3200CS. Cette élégante voiture ne connaîtra pas, elle non plus, un très grand succès commercial.

BMW 3200CS

For the first time, the company emblem appeared on the C-pillar of a BMW. It represented the circular area of a propeller in the Bavarian state colors. The V8 engine had achieved 160 bhp by 1962. Bertone's all-steel BMW creation – with its lines typical of the maestro – was given large doors and retractable side windows but did not have the B-pillar which can be a nuisance when getting into a car. The attractive coupé had a top speed of 125 mph (200 kph).

Erstmals taucht das Firmenemblem auf – an der C-Säule eines BMW. Es stellt eine Propeller-kreisfläche in den bayerischen Landesfarben dar. Der V8 ist 1962 bei 160 PS angelangt. Bertones BMW-Kreation aus Ganzstahl – in der Linienführung typisch für den Maestro – verfügt über große Türen und versenkbare Seitenscheiben und verzichtet auf die beim Einsteigen störende B-Säule. 200 Stundenkilometer erreicht das schmucke Coupé.

L'emblème de la marque figure pour la première fois, à l'arrière, sur le montant du toit. Il représente une hélice et les couleurs de la Bavière. En 1962, le V8 délivre 160 ch. La carrosserie tout acier, dessinée par Bertone pour la BMW – dont les lignes trahissent la griffe du maître –, comporte de grandes portières et des vitres latérales descendantes sans montant de toit central, facilitant ainsi l'accès à la voiture. Cet élégant coupé tutoie les 200 km/h.

BMW 1500

Many motorsists awaited – the BMW drivers and owners amongst them with true longing – for BMW to build a middle-class car. Suddenly it appeared at the Frankfurt Motor Show in September 1961, as if born of the measures to return the company to profitability, measures which had been introduced so recently. The show BMW was still a prototype – one whose badge number, 1500, reflected the size of the four-cylinder engine in cubic centimeters. It was a plain type designation for a car which BMW described as a "new class".

The public and motoring press immediately placed the newcomer from Bavaria on a pedestal, and it rode back to the factory for fine-tuning on a wave of enthusiasm. It was above all the successful overall technical concept as well as its smart appearance which turned the car into a true alternative to the mid-range cars from American-owned multi-nationals Ford and Opel (GM), based at Cologne and Rüsselsheim.

The engine, initially rated at 75 bhp, had 80 bhp coaxed out of it at 5500 rpm by the time volume production started in October 1962. The small trick here was to raise the compression ratio from 8.2 to 8.8.

"Flexibility at lower engine speeds, phenomenal power at the higher ones," was the promise made by the BMW brochure. They had moved its performance – 94 mph (150 kph) and acceleration from 0 to 62 mph (0 to 100 kph) in 16.8 seconds – right into the sports car bracket.

While the Solex downdraft carburetors were changed for a more efficient version from the same manufacturer in 1964, the new transmission with Porsche locking synchronization was a "revelation". One which made the floor gear shift a pleasure to operate.

The beautifully shaped four-door monocoque steel body was based on a chassis which predicted the 4-wheel future at BMW. It was equipped with McPherson struts and coil springs at the front as well as trailing arms at the back.

Unfortunately the 1500, which was otherwise very solidly built, was prone to occasional technical hiccups. These kind of mechanical gremlins were eliminated in its successor, the BMW 1600.

The bare look behind the wheel – three circular instruments and the space for the radio – was no obstacle to sales. At a purchase price of something less than 9500 marks, the demand was considerably higher than the daily production output of 50 cars. By increasing capacity in 1963, a total of 23,807 cars were produced before the model was discontinued in 1964. By that time, the 1600 was already starting production, and a 1.8-liter model was selling well.

Viele Autofahrer – die markentreuen unter ihnen sogar sehnsüchtig – haben den Bau eines Mittelklassewagens von BMW erwartet. Auf der Frankfurter Automobilausstellung im September 1961 steht er plötzlich da, als sei er der jüngst erfolgten Sanierungsphase der BMW AG frisch entsprungen. Noch ist es ein Prototyp, dessen Zahlenkombination 1500 die Hubraumgröße des Vierzylindermotors widerspiegelt – eine schlichte Typenbezeichnung für ein Auto, das BMW als die „neue Klasse" bezeichnet.

Das Publikum und die Fachpresse heben den Neuling aus bajuwarischen Landen sofort auf einen Sockel, und eine Welle der Begeisterung trägt ihn zum Feinschliff zurück ins Werk. Vor allem das gelungene technische Gesamtkonzept sowie das adrette Erscheinungsbild lassen den 1500 als verlockende Alternative zu den Mittelklassewagen aus Köln und Rüsselsheim erscheinen.

Dem zunächst nur 75 PS starken Triebwerk werden bis zur Serienproduktion im Oktober 1962 80 PS bei 5500 Umdrehungen in der Minute entlockt. Der kleine Trick dabei ist die Anhebung der Verdichtung von 8,2 auf 8,8.

„Elastizität in den niederen, ungestüme Kraft in den oberen Drehzahlbereichen", verheißt der BMW-Prospekt und rückt die Fahrleistungen – 150 Stundenkilometer, Beschleunigung von 0 auf 100 in 16,8 Sekunden – in den Bereich von Sportwagenwerten.

Während die Solex-Fallstromvergaser 1964 gegen eine effizientere Version dieses Herstellers ausgetauscht werden, ist das neue Getriebe mit Porsche-Sperrsynchronisation eine „Offenbarung", in der man mit dem Mittelschalthebel gern herumrührt. Die formschöne viertürige Pontonkarosserie aus Stahl steht auf einem Fahrwerk, das mit McPherson-Federbeinen und Schraubenfedern vorn sowie Schräglenkern hinten bei BMW die technische Zukunft der rollenden Basis einläutet.

Leider befallen das an sich sehr solide gebaute Fahrzeug ab und zu kleinere technische „Hustenanfälle". Beim Nachfolger, dem 1600, plagen solche inneren Gebrechen den BMW-Fahrer nicht mehr.

Es ist für den Verkauf nicht hinderlich, dass das Armaturenbrett etwas dürftig aussieht – drei Rundinstrumente und die Aussparung für das Radio. Bei etwas weniger als 9500 Mark Kaufpreis ist die Nachfrage ungleich höher als die Produktionszahl von 50 Autos, die pro Tag vom Band rollen. Durch eine Kapazitätserhöhung 1963 werden letztlich bis 1964 23 807 Wagen gebaut. Da läuft der 1600 bereits an und das 1,8-Liter-Modell auf Hochtouren.

De nombreux automobilistes attendent – et même ardemment pour les fidèles de la marque – que BMW construise une voiture du segment intermédiaire. Au Salon de l'Automobile de Francfort de septembre 1961, elle est soudain là, comme si elle était née à l'issue des mesures prises et appliquées récemment par BMW AG pour renouer avec les profits. Il s'agit encore d'un prototype dont la combinaison de chiffres, 1500, trahit la cylindrée (quatre-cylindres), une dénomination sobre pour une voiture que BMW qualifie de « nouvelle classe ».

Le grand public et les professionnels accueillent immédiatement à bras ouverts la nouvelle petite Bavaroise et une vague d'enthousiasme l'accompagne jusqu'à son retour à l'usine pour une ultime mise au point. Le concept technique global réussi, surtout, ainsi que l'élégance de ses lignes en font une authentique alternative à ses concurrentes de Cologne et de Rüsselsheim.

Lors de sa production en série en octobre 1962, le moteur qui ne développait initialement que 75 ch en délivre 80 à 5500 tr/min. Clé de l'énigme : le taux de compression a été majoré de 8,2 à 8,8.

« Souplesse à bas régime, force irrésistible à haut régime », promet le prospectus de BMW qui met en exergue ses performances – 150 km/h, de 0 à 100 km/h en 16,8 secondes – lesquelles la situent dans le segment des voitures de sport.

Alors que les carburateurs inversés Solex disparaissent en 1964 en faveur d'une version plus performante de la même marque, la nouvelle boîte de vitesses à synchronisation Porsche est un chef-d'œuvre que l'on taquine volontiers avec le levier central. La jolie carrosserie ponton à quatre portes en acier trône sur un châssis qui augure, chez BMW, des futures quatre-roues. Elle est équipée des nouvelles plates-formes avec jambes élastiques Mc Pherson et ressorts hélicoïdaux à l'avant ainsi que de bras obliques à l'arrière.

Malheureusement, de petites « quintes de toux » viennent entraver de temps à autre la bonne marche de cette voiture en soi très solide. Avec sa remplaçante, la 1600, ce genre de malaise disparaîtra totalement.

Le fait que l'aménagement intérieur soit modeste – trois cadrans circulaires et le réceptacle de l'autoradio – ne fait absolument pas obstacle à son succès commercial. Pour un prix légèrement inférieur à 9500 marks, la demande est très nettement supérieure à la production quotidienne, qui est de 50 voitures. Une augmentation des capacités, en 1963, permet finalement de fabriquer 23 807 voitures jusqu'en 1964. Mais, à ce moment-là, la 1600 et la version à moteur de 1,8 litre se vendent déjà très bien.

BMW 1500

Its external appearance and four-cylinder engine, just under 1500 cc, as well as a modern chassis, made this car so popular that it exceeded the capacity of the BMW production lines.

Das äußere Erscheinungsbild und der Vierzylindermotor mit knapp 1500 ccm sowie ein fortschrittliches Fahrwerk machen diesen Wagen so beliebt, dass er die Fließbandkapazitäten von BMW übersteigt.

Son apparence extérieure, son moteur à quatre cylindres de près de 1500 cm³ ainsi que son châssis moderne rendent cette voiture si populaire que BMW doit accroître les capacités de ses chaînes de production.

Spaciousness, comfortable seating and details such as a padded horn button all reflected the "new class" in the interior of the BMW 1500. The only thing slightly out of character was the painted dashboard.

Geräumigkeit, Sitzkomfort und Details wie die Hupenknopfpolsterung spiegeln die „neue Klasse" auch im Interieur des BMW 1500 wider. Lediglich das lackierte Armaturenbrett stört hier ein wenig.

Habitabilité, confort et richesse des détails, comme le capitonnage du bouton de klaxon, reflètent la « nouvelle classe » également à l'intérieur de la BMW 1500. Seul le tableau de bord peint semble ici quelque peu déplacé.

The front section, with the headlights and BMW kidney aligned in the grill, made a welcome change from other mid-range sedans. This also applied to the consistent emphasis of the waistline, with a chrome strip around the car integrating door handles and front indicators.

Die Frontpartie mit den im Grill auf einer Ebene liegenden Lampen und BMW-Nieren hebt sich von anderen Mittelklasse-Limousinen wohltuend ab. Das gilt ebenso für die konsequente Betonung der Gürtellinie rundum durch eine Chromleiste mit integrierten Türgriffen und vorderen Blinkern.

La proue, avec les phares et les naseaux BMW intégrés sans cassure dans la calandre, se démarque avec bonheur de l'avant des autres berlines du segment intermédiaire. On peut en dire autant de sa ligne de ceinture, soulignée par un jonc chromé qui intègre les poignées de portières et les clignotants avant.

BMW 3200S Staatslimousine

After the memorable financial crisis AGM in winter 1959, BMW was well and truly on the road to recovery. The small 700 was selling very well, admittedly with a narrow profit margin, and success seemed to be just round the corner with the new middle-class BMW 1500.

Accompanying that boost in confidence, the company's thoughts turned to the large V8 limousines, whose production had fallen to 661 in 1960. They were due for an update, particularly since the official specifications now prohibited rear doors which opened towards the front.

The BMW chief designer, Wilhelm Hofmeister, implemented his proposed modifications on the solid technical basis of the 160 bhp aluminum V8 3200S: an extended roof to provide more headroom in the rear compartment, modified rear door hinges, an enlarged boot, and an additional headlamp on the fenders. Rear seat passengers were provided with fresh air by a large steel sunroof, which would become more and more important. However, matters did not progress beyond this prototype, simply because BMW stopped manufacturing large cars.

This car was initially used as a status symbol in the company car fleet. But BMW was soon to enjoy the kudos associated with having built a car for a state official. Alfons Goppel, premier of Bavaria since 1962, occasionally borrowed this flagship. The aforementioned steel sunroof proved to be particularly valuable for state visitors, who only had to stand in front of the rear seats to enjoy the spectator applause.

The attempt to intruduce this BMW to the politicians in Bonn proved a failure. Dr Konrad Adenauer's chauffeur was faithful to Mercedes. This also proved to be the case with the second launch in September 1965 in which the 505 was supposed to be BMW's answer to the Adenauer Mercedes 300. No more than two prototypes of this BMW Pullman limousine were manufactured. One of them ended its days in the BMW museum with the 3200Si prototype, and the other had to endure the indignities of commerce, advertising French fries, before the honor she deserved was restored to her by a BMW vintage car collector.

BMW ist seit der denkwürdigen Hauptversammlung im Winter 1959 auf dem Wege der Sanierung. Der kleine 700er verkauft sich – wenngleich mit geringer Gewinnmarge – recht gut, und mit dem neuen Mittelklassemodell BMW 1500 winkt der Erfolg.

Solchermaßen den Rücken gestärkt, macht sich das Unternehmen Gedanken über die Fortführung der großen V8-Limousinen, deren Stückzahl 1960 auf 661 gesunken ist. Die Modernisierung ist fällig, zumal Änderungen der Zulassungsvorschriften hinten angeschlagene Fondtüren verbieten.

Auf der soliden technischen Basis des 3200S mit seinem V8-Leichtmetallmotor mit 160 PS verwirklicht BMW-Designchef Wilhelm Hofmeister seine Modifikationsvorschläge: Strecken des Daches, um mehr Kopfraum im Fond zu erzielen, geänderter Türanschlag hinten, Vergrößerung des Kofferraums und Zusatzscheinwerfer in den Kotflügeln. Für die Frischluft auf der Rücksitzbank sorgt ein überdimensionales Stahlschiebedach, das noch Bedeutung erlangt. Es bleibt bei diesem Prototyp, denn BMW stellt die Produktion der großen Wagen ein.

Zunächst dient dieser Wagen zu repräsentativen Zwecken im Werksfuhrpark. Doch dann kann sich BMW den Orden, eine Staatskarosse gebaut zu haben, ans Revers heften. Bayerns Ministerpräsident Alfons Goppel, seit 1962 Landesvater, leiht sich des öfteren dieses einmalige Flaggschiff aus. Besonders bei Staatsbesuchen kommt das bereits erwähnte Stahlschiebedach zur Geltung. Wer auch immer bejubelt werden möchte, kann vor den Rücksitzen stehend die Ovationen entgegennehmen.

Ein Versuch, diesen BMW auch in Bonn zum Einsatz zu bringen, scheitert. Dr. Konrad Adenauers Chauffeur bleibt Mercedes treu. Das bestätigt sich auch beim zweiten Anlauf im September 1965, bei dem BMW mit dem 505 eine weitere Antwort auf den Mercedes 300 von Adenauer geben will. Es bleibt bei zwei Prototypen dieser Pullman-Limousine. Der eine wandert – wie auch der 3200Si Prototyp – ins BMW-Museum, der andere dient dem schnöden Mammon und wirbt für Pommes frites, ehe er von einem BMW-Oldtimer-Sammler den ihm gebührenden Ehrenplatz zugewiesen bekommt.

Depuis la mémorable assemblée générale de l'hiver 1959, convoquée à la suite d'une crise financière, BMW est de nouveau sur la voie de la guérison. La petite 700 se vend bien – même si elle ne génère pas des bénéfices extraordinaires – et le succès est garanti grâce au nouveau modèle du segment intermédiaire, la BMW 1500.

Maintenant qu'elle a les reins plus solides, l'entreprise songe aux futures grosses limousines V8, qui n'ont été produites qu'à 661 exemplaires en 1960. Une modernisation s'impose, d'autant que les normes bannissent désormais les portières arrière s'ouvrant dans le sens contraire de la marche.

Sur la solide base mécanique de la 3200S au V8 en alliage léger de 160 ch, le designer en chef de BMW, Wilhelm Hofmeister, concrétise les propositions de modifications qu'il avait faites : allongement du toit pour augmenter l'espace disponible pour la tête à l'arrière, modification des charnières des portières arrière, agrandissement du coffre et phares supplémentaires dans les ailes. Un toit coulissant en acier de grande dimension, qui allait plus tard prendre de l'importance, dégage l'horizon pour les passagers installés à l'arrière. Ce prototype restera un modèle unique, car BMW suspend la production des grosses limousines.

Cette voiture sert d'abord de véhicule de représentation dans la flotte de l'usine. Mais BMW finit, malgré tout, par se distinguer en construisant une limousine destinée aux personnages officiels. Le ministre-président bavarois Alfons Goppel, qui préside depuis 1962 aux destinées du Land, emprunte fréquemment ce navire-amiral exclusif. En particulier lors des visites officielles, où le toit coulissant sus-mentionné présente des avantages. Quel que soit celui qui veut se faire acclamer, il lui suffit de s'installer à l'arrière et de se lever pour recevoir les ovations du public.

BMW tente aussi de prendre pied à Bonn dans le fief de la marque à l'étoile – en vain. Le chauffeur de Konrad Adenauer est fidèle à Mercedes. La deuxième tentative de BMW, en septembre 1965, de répliquer à la Mercedes 300 d'Adenauer avec la BMW 505 se solde également par un échec. Il n'y aura que deux prototypes de cette limousine Pullman. Comme la 3200Si, un autre prototype, l'une passera sa retraite au musée BMW et l'autre sera sacrifiée sur l'autel du mercantilisme puisqu'elle fera de la publicité pour une marque de frites avant de reprendre la place qui lui revient, chez un collectionneur de BMW.

The Staatslimousine, based on the model 3200 Super, featured a slightly raised roof providing plenty of headroom for back seat passengers, an elongated tail and a modified rear door catch. It never got beyond a prototype version which saw sporadic service as an official car of the Bavarian State Government.

Leicht erhöhtes Dach mit viel Platz für die Passagiere im Fond, verlängertes Heck und geänderter Türanschlag hinten – so die Realisation der Staatslimousine, basierend auf dem Modell 3200 Super. Es bleibt bei einem Prototypen, der sporadisch der bayerischen Landesregierung dient.

Un toit légèrement surélevé avec beaucoup d'espace pour les passagers assis à l'arrière, une poupe allongée et une modification des charnières des portières arrière – voici comment obtenir une limousine d'apparat inspirée de la BMW 3200 Super. Il n'existera que ce prototype, qui sera utilisé de façon sporadique comme voiture officielle par le gouvernement régional de Bavière.

BMW 3200S Staatslimousine 201

The large supplementary headlamps and the pontoon-shaped trunk are striking features. The 160 bhp version of the 3.2-liter V8 engine powers the BMW, taking it up to a top speed of 118 mph (190 kph). Beneath the wood-paneled dashboard we see a large loudspeaker tastefully tucked away – perhaps for playing the national anthems.

Auffällig sind die größeren Zusatzscheinwerfer und die Pontonform des Kofferraums. Die 160-PS-Version des 3,2-Liter-V8-Motors bringt das „Flaggschiff" in Schwung und auf 190 km/h. Gediegen ist das holzverkleidete Armaturenbrett, unter dem ein großer Lautsprecher – wohl zum Abspielen der Nationalhymnen – montiert ist.

Différences frappantes : des phares d'appoint de plus grand diamètre et un coffre en forme de ponton. La version de 160 ch du V8 de 3,2 litres donne des ailes à ce navire-amiral et lui permet d'atteindre les 190 km/h. Luxueux : le tableau de bord en bois sous lequel se trouve un grand haut-parleur – peut-être prévu pour jouer les hymnes nationaux.

It was in total euphoria that BMW presented its chic coupé in the summer of 1965. This was characterized by its large windows and the absence of a center pillar. It was billed as "the reincarnation of the BMW 327". The most prominent features of the new look BMW were the flat wrap-around headlamps with integrated indicators. The oval reflectors earned the nickname of "slanted eyes" and were referred to inside BMW as "Asian eyes".

Technically, the coupé seemed to have been a prelude to the 2-liter sedans, which were launched in 1966. The 2000CS was already equipped with the 1990 cc engine capable of delivering 100 bhp with a single downdraft carburetor and 120 bhp with two double-barrel sidedraft carburetors. The chassis and the two-section propellor shaft were also taken from the sedan.

The majority of the 13,691 coupés leaving the Karmann works in Osnabrück over six years were fitted with a manually operated transmission and delivered 120 bhp (2000CS). The 100 bhp version (2000C), most of which were equipped with a ZF automatic transmission, was less popular.

To allow the 2-liter to run more smoothly, the chain drive of the overhead camshaft was equipped with sliding rails and an oil damped tensioning fixture. The transmission was also overhauled via wider stronger teeth and an expanding ring synchronizer. Accordingly, the diameter of the clutch was enlarged.

The car's "legs" were equipped with elastic mountings and, as was usual for that time, a special duct was fitted to allow cool air to reach the front brake discs. The dashboard and center console were given a businesslike and functional look. The four electric switches on the center console for window actuation were a nice and unfamiliar luxury toy for contemporary drivers.

Although the 2000CS was not the sportiest vehicle on the market, since it took 12 seconds to go from 0 to 62 mph (100 kph), but this acceleration figure was in keeping with the performance/weight ratio. The top speed of 115 mph (185 kph) was only slightly lower than that of the 1800TI/SA with 130 bhp.

The 2000CS was not expected to become a sporty machine. It was a four-seater which also had enough room for suitcases and bags – an apple for the pragmatist's eye, a medium-sized machine helping its drivers to see and be seen. To put it more simply: quite a lot of car for DM 17,000.

From February 1966, BMW offered a sporting four-door limousine (the 2000TI) identical with the 2000CS in engine, transmission and chassis. The former was replaced as early as 1968 by the tilux, which with its square headlights was compromised for contemporary taste.

Euphorisch präsentiert BMW im Sommer 1965 als „Wiedergeburt des BMW 327" ein schickes Coupé ohne Mittelpfosten und mit viel Fensterfläche. Auffälligstes Merkmal des neuen BMW-Gesichts sind die flachen, seitlich herumgezogenen Scheinwerfer mit integrierten Blinkern. Vom Volksmund bald „Schlitzaugen" genannt, findet man für die Ovalreflektoren auch in der werksinternen Terminologie einen sinnentsprechenden Begriff: „Asiatenaugen".

Technisch gesehen stellt das Coupé einen Vorgriff auf die 2-Liter-Limousinen des Jahrgangs 1966 dar. Es hat bereits den 1990-ccm-Motor, der mit einem Fallstromvergaser 100 PS und mit zwei Doppel-Flachstromvergasern 120 PS leistet. Auch das Fahrwerk und die zweigeteilte Kardanwelle werden von der Limousine übernommen.

Von den insgesamt 13 691 Coupés, die das Werk von Karmann in Osnabrück innerhalb von sechs Jahren verlassen, haben die meisten ein handgeschaltetes Getriebe und 120 PS (2000CS). Die 100-PS-Version (2000C), vornehmlich mit einer ZF-Automatik ausgerüstet, wird weniger gern gekauft.

Um das 2-Liter-Triebwerk zu mehr Laufruhe zu erziehen, wird der Kettenantrieb der oben liegenden Nockenwelle mit Gleitschienen und einer ölgedämpften Spannvorrichtung versehen. Auch das Getriebe mit verbreiterten Zahnrädern wird überarbeitet und erhält eine Spreizring-Synchronisierung. Analog fällt der Kupplungsdurchmesser größer aus.

Die „Beine" des Autos bekommen eine elastische Lagerung, und den Scheibenbremsen – wie damals üblich, nur vorn – wird durch einen Kunstgriff Kühlluft zugefächelt. Armaturenbrett und Mittelkonsole wirken aufgeräumt und funktionell. Ein schönes Spielzeug für die Zeitgenossen sind die vier Schalter der elektrischen Fensterheber auf der Mittelkonsole.

BMW 2000CS

Eine Beschleinigung von 0 auf 100 Stundenkilometer in 12 Sekunden entspricht nicht Sprinterwerten, aber dem Leistungsgewicht. Die Endgeschwindigkeit (185 km/h) liegt dagegen nur knapp unter der des 1800TI/SA mit 130 PS.

Sportliche Ambitionen werden mit dem 2000CS noch nicht verknüpft. Er ist ein Viersitzer, in dem auch einige Koffer und Taschen Platz finden, ein Beau für Pragmatiker, ein schickes Automobil zum Sehen und Gesehenwerden oder einfacher ausgedrückt – ziemlich viel Auto für 17 000 Mark.

In Motor, Getriebe und Fahrwerk mit dem 2000CS identisch, offeriert BMW ab Februar 1966 mit dem 2000TI auch eine sportliche viertürige Limousine. Diese wird bereits 1968 vom tilux – mit seinen Rechteck-Scheinwerfern ein Zugeständnis an den Zeitgeschmack – abgelöst.

Dans l'euphorie, BMW présente durant l'été 1965 la « réincarnation de la BMW 327 », un coupé d'un grand chic sans pied médian et avec de généreuses surfaces vitrées. La caractéristique de style la plus frappante du nouveau visage de la BMW est ses phares allongés qui mordent sur le côté avec leurs clignotants intégrés. Ces derniers sont rapidement surnommés les « yeux bridés » alors que chez BMW, en interne, les réflecteurs ovales possèdent un nom bien à eux : « yeux d'Asiatique ».

Sur le plan mécanique, le coupé annonce les berlines de 2 litres du millésime 1966. Il possède déjà un moteur de 1990 cm³ qui développe 100 ch avec un carburateur inversé et 120 ch dans la version à deux carburateurs double corps inversés. Les trains roulants et l'arbre de transmission en deux éléments, aussi, sont repris de la berline.

Sur un total de 13 691 coupés qui sortiront de l'usine Karmann à Osnabrück en six ans, la majorité possèdent une boîte manuelle et un moteur de 120 ch (2000CS). La version de 100 ch (2000C), la plus souvent équipée d'une boîte automatique ZF, ne fait pas l'unanimité.

Pour accroître la souplesse de fonctionnement du moteur de 2 litres, l'entraînement des chaînes de l'arbre à cames supérieur est assuré par des rails glissants avec un dispositif de tension baignant dans l'huile. La boîte de vitesses à engrenages élargis, elle aussi, est revue et reçoit une synchronisation à anneaux d'écartement. Logiquement, le diamètre de l'embrayage augmente lui aussi.

Les « jambes » de la voiture possèdent des paliers élastiques et les freins à disques – uniquement à l'avant comme cela était alors la tradition – sont refroidis grâce à une prise d'air spéciale. Le tableau de bord et la console médiane sont bien agencés et fonctionnels. Les quatre commandes des vitres électriques sur la console médiane sont un gadget apprécié des conducteurs de cette époque.

Les 12 secondes pour le 0 à 100 km/h ne sont pas un record spectaculaire, mais elles reflètent le rapport poids/ puissance. La vitesse de pointe (185 km/h) est, en revanche, proche de celle de la 1800TI/SA de 130 ch.

La 2000CS n'a pas encore d'ambitions sportives. Il s'agit d'une quatre-places qui peut aisément emmener quelques valises et quelques sacs – une belle voiture pour conducteurs pragmatiques, un véhicule de taille moyenne destiné à la promenade pour voir et être vu ou, tout simplement, choisi par beaucoup pour son prix de 17 000 marks.

Avec la 2000TI, identique à la 2000CS pour le moteur, la boîte de vitesses et le châssis, BMW propose, à partir de février 1966, une sportive berline à quatre portes. Dès 1968, celle-ci sera remplacée par la tilux qui, avec ses phares rectangulaires, fait une concession aux goûts de l'époque.

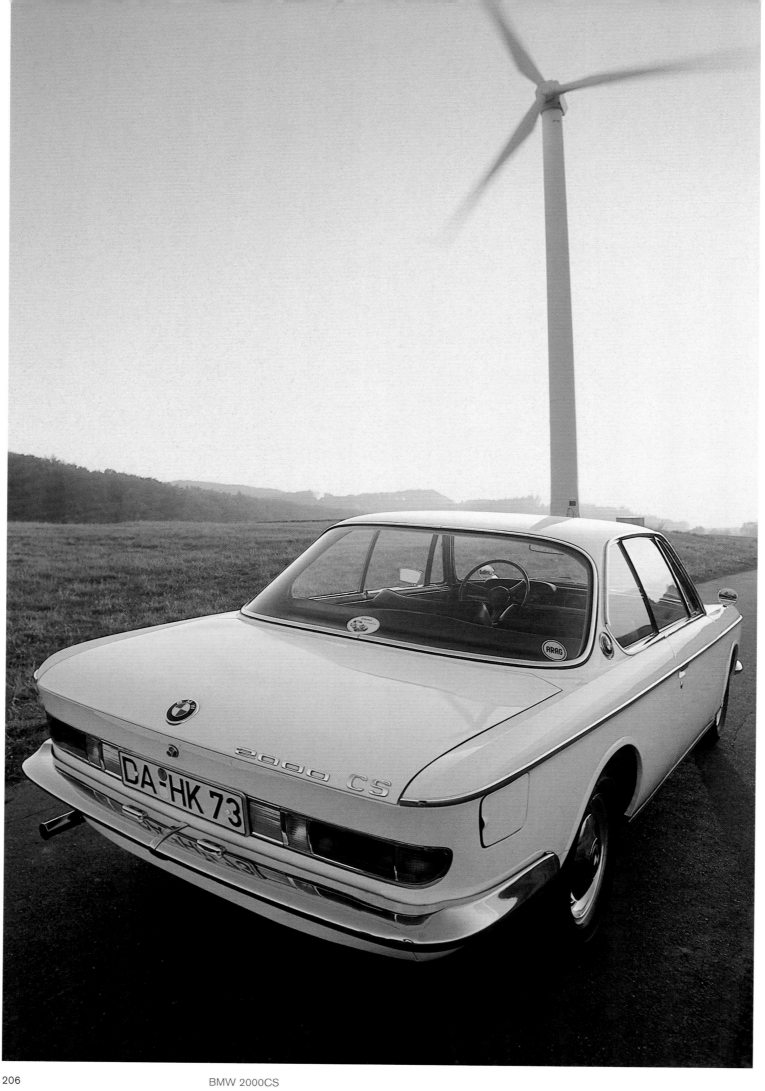

This coupé, with its strong appeal to contemporary taste, lacking a central pillar and with a great deal of window area, stood out particularly because of its headlights – also called "slanted eyes" – which were wrapped round to the side to integrate the indicators.

Das dem Zeitgeschmack stark angepasste Coupé ohne Mittelpfosten und mit viel Fensterfläche fällt besonders durch die seitlich herum- gezogenen Scheinwerfer – auch „Schlitzaugen" genannt – auf.

Le coupé, qui reflète fidèlement le goût de son époque avec l'absence de montant central et ses généreuses surfaces vitrées, se distingue particulièrement par les phares mordant sur les côtés.

BMW 2000CS

Dashboard and central console with their sensibly arranged instruments and controls – the four controls for the electrical windows in front of the gear lever could hardly be missed – were appropriate for the outfit of the coupé. The 1990 cc engine anticipated the 1966 two-liter sedan.

Armaturenbrett und Mittelkonsole mit sinnvoll angeordneten Instrumenten und Schaltern – die vier elektrischen Fensterheber vor dem Schaltknüppel sind nicht zu übersehen – passen zum Erscheinungsbild des Coupés. Der 1990-ccm-Motor ist bereits ein Vorgriff auf die 2-Liter-Limousine des Jahrgangs 1966.

Le tableau de bord et la console médiane avec les instruments et manettes agencés ergonomiquement – les quatre lève-vitres électriques devant le levier de vitesses sautent aux yeux – vont avec le style extérieur du coupé. Le moteur de 1990 cm³ annonce déjà la berline de deux litres du millésime 1966.

BMW 2000CS

BMW 2000CS

BMW 1802 & 2002tii

It requires special skills to cater for almost all tastes with a single model series. To put this ideal into practice, so that the product is also widely accepted, is the art of marketing. This is what happened between 1966 and 1977. BMW stretched the range of their "02 series" to extremes, from a 75 bhp economy model to the powerful 170 bhp turbo 2002. Commercial success proved this policy right: 863,203 cars were sold.

In the middle range there were two models which supplied optimum value for their price: the 1802 (90 bhp, 104 mph/167 kph) for 10,435 marks and the 2002tii (130 bhp, 119 mph/190 kph) which cost at least 2000 marks more.

The four-cylinder short-stroke engine (with 1766 cc for the 1802 and 1990 cc for the 2002tii) turned out to be an extremely reliable, lively engine. That the injection engine of the 2002tii with its 40 extra bhp only consumed 0.22 of a gallon (1 liter) more than the carburetor version may have been due to the efficient metering of the Kugelfischer injection pump. Both 02s had good roadholding, although it was worth installing the rollover bar in the 1802 which was standard in the 2002tii.

The 02 series went into the winter of 1973 with pepped-up looks – black radiator grill, rectangular instead of circular rear lights – and with safety equipment such as headrests and seatbelts. The rear-wheel drive of the tii proved powerful in the snow as was attested by contemporary test reports.

The normal production specification could be uprated in both versions: a sporty five-speed transmission was available as an option. Of course the brakes – discs at the front, drums at the rear – were larger for the 2002tii, and enlarged HR tires did justice to the greater loads encountered by the tii version.

The tii still had a good advantage over the 1802, sprinting from 0 to 62 mph (100 kph) in just 10 seconds. But that did not particularly worry the typical BMW 1802 buyer who might be lagging behind by two seconds. This was not the sportsman on the road, this was a man who wanted reliability, space and comfort from his vehicle at a reasonable price, whilst being able to keep up with the highway traffic flow.

From September 1973, BMW built larger tanks into the rear of the 1802 and 2002tii to increase the range. The bonus distance? Approximately 19 miles (30 km). With price increases of 33 per cent in four years, the cars reflected contemporary trends. The economic recession which was beginning to make itself sharply felt did not affect sales. Thus the 1802 achieved 83,351 and the 2002tii 38,703 units in the sales statistics, benchmarks to stand until the 3 series set new standards in July 1975.

Mit einer Modellreihe fast jeden Geschmack zu treffen, bedarf eines besonderen Riechers. Diese Idee dann so umzusetzen, dass das Produkt auch akzeptiert wird, ist die hohe Kunst des Marketings – so geschehen in den elf Jahren zwischen 1966 und 1977, in denen BMW mit den „02ern" eine Modellreihe in extreme Richtungen ausweitet – vom 75-PS-Sparmobil bis zum 170-PS-Turbo-Kraftpaket. Der Erfolg gibt dieser Modellpolitik recht: 863 203 verkaufte Autos.

Mittendrin liegen zwei Modelle, die für ihren Preis einen optimalen Gegenwert liefern: der 1802 (90 PS, 167 km/h) für 10 435 Mark und der gut 2000 Mark teurere 2002tii (130 PS, 190 km/h).

Der Vierzylinder-Kurzhubmotor (mit 1766 ccm beim 1802 und 1990 ccm beim 2002tii) erweist sich als ein äußerst zuverlässiges, temperamentvolles Triebwerk. Dass der 40 PS stärkere Einspritzmotor des 2002tii nur einen Liter Benzin mehr schluckt als der Vergaser, mag an der guten Dosierung der Kugelfischer-Einspritzpumpe liegen. Gut auf der Straße liegen beide, wobei sich beim 1802 der Einbau von Drehstabstabilisatoren, die beim 2002tii serienmäßig sind, empfiehlt.

Optisch aufgepäppelt – mit schwarzem Kühlergrill, eckigen statt runden Heckleuchten – und mit Sicherheitskomponenten wie Kopfstützen und Sicherheitsgurten ausgestattet, gehen die 02er in den Winter 1973. Dass auch der Heckantrieb des tii die Kraft in den Schnee bringt, attestieren ihm entsprechende Fahrberichte.

Der normale Gang der Dinge lässt sich bei beiden Ausführungen beschleunigen. Gegen Aufpreis gibt es ein sportliches Fünfganggetriebe. Natürlich sind die Bremsen, vorne Scheiben- und hinten Trommelbremsen, beim 2002tii größer dimensioniert, und HR-Reifen werden den größeren Belastungen gerecht.

Beim Sprint aus dem Stand auf 100 Stundenkilometer hat der tii mit 10 Sekunden die Nase vorn. Den typischen Käufer des BMW 1802 stört es aber nicht, dass er da zwei Sekunden hinterherhinkt. Er ist nicht der Sportler auf der Straße, sondern ein Mann, der von seinem Fahrzeug Zuverlässigkeit, Platz und Komfort zu einem günstigen Preis erwartet, und dennoch in der Lage sein will, im Autobahnverkehr gut im Fluss zu bleiben.

Zur Erhöhung der Reichweite stattet BMW ab September 1973 den 1802 und den 2002tii mit größeren Tanks aus. Der Distanzgewinn beträgt rund 30 Kilometer. Mit Preissteigerungen von 33 Prozent in vier Jahren liegen beide Wagen im Trend der Zeit, und die sich andeutende Wirtschaftsrezession tangiert den Absatz offenbar nicht. So bringt es der 1802 auf 83 351 und der 2002tii auf immerhin 38 703 Einheiten in der Verkaufsstatistik, ehe im Juli 1975 die 3er Reihe neue Maßstäbe setzt.

Satisfaire tous les goûts avec une seule gamme n'est pas à la portée de tout le monde. Mais réussir ce pari avec un produit qui est largement plébiscité relève du miracle marketing. C'est ce qui s'est passé entre 1966 et 1977, lorsque BMW a, avec les « 02 », décliné une gamme dans deux directions opposées – du modèle d'appel de 75 ch à la version sportive à moteur turbo de 170 ch. Le succès légitime a posteriori cette politique, puisque BMW en a vendu pas moins de 863 203 exemplaires.

Au cœur de cette gamme, il y a deux modèles d'un bon rapport qualité/prix : la 1802 (90 ch, 167 km/h) pour 10 435 marks et la 2002tii (130 ch, 190 km/h), qui coûte largement 2000 marks de plus.

Le quatre-cylindres à course courte (de 1766 cm³ pour la 1802 et de 1990 cm³ pour la 2002tii) se révèle être un moteur extrêmement fiable en dépit de son tempérament vif. Si le moteur à injection de la 2002tii, plus puissant de 40 ch, ne consomme qu'un litre de plus que la version à carburateur, cela est sans doute dû au bon réglage de la pompe d'injection Kugelfischer. Toutes les deux ont une bonne tenue de route, mais il est recommandé d'équiper la 1802 des barres de torsion stabilisatrices qui figurent en série sur la 2002tii.

Les 02 sont légèrement modifiées esthétiquement au cours de l'hiver 1973 – calandre noire, feux arrière rectangulaires et non plus ronds – et dotée d'éléments de sécurité comme des appuie-tête et des ceintures de sécurité. Les essais réalisés durant cette saison prouvent que la propulsion arrière de la tii ne connaît pas de problèmes de transmission même sur la neige.

Il est possible d'opter pour des options sur les deux versions : contre supplément, BMW propose une sportive boîte manuelle à cinq vitesses. Naturellement, les freins – à disques à l'avant et à tambours à l'arrière – sont de plus

grandes dimensions pour la 2002tii et des pneus HR répondent mieux à plus de sollicitations.

La tii ne perd pas son temps en route puisqu'il lui suffit de dix secondes pour passer de 0 à 100 km/h. La BMW 1802 demande deux secondes de plus, mais cela ne dérange en rien ses acheteurs. Le client type n'est pas un conducteur sportif sur route, mais un homme qui attend de sa voiture fiabilité, habitabilité et confort à un prix intéressant et qui soit malgré tout en mesure d'atteindre aisément la vitesse de circulation sur autoroute.

Pour augmenter l'autonomie de parcours, BMW installe à partir de septembre 1973 des réservoirs de plus grande capacité dans les 1802 et 2002tii. Gain : une trentaine de kilomètres. Avec une hausse du prix de 33 % en quatre ans, les deux voitures sont tout à fait dans l'air du temps et la récession économique qui se profile n'affecte en rien les ventes. Ainsi la 1802 se vend à raison de 83 351 exemplaires et la 2002tii à 38 703 unités, avant que la série 3 ne vienne ouvrir un nouveau chapitre en juillet 1975.

Outwardly, the two-door 02 series BMW gave a delicate and unassuming effect. But the 130 bhp performance of the 2-liter engine in the 2002tii, with Kugelfischer fuel injection, was enough to make an impression.

Äußerlich wirken die zweitürigen 02er BMW zierlich und unscheinbar. Aber mit den 130 PS, die der 2-Liter-Motor im 2002tii mit Kugelfischer-Einspritzpumpe leistet, lässt sich Staat machen.

Extérieurement, les BMW 02 à deux portes n'attirent pas le regard. Mais, avec les 130 ch que délivre le moteur de deux litres de la 2002tii à injection Kugelfischer, il ne faut pas se fier aux apparences.

A discreet hint of the 2-liter engine under the hood was provided by the radiator grill, black except for two ribs. The designation at the rear specified the model.

Ein dezenter Hinweis auf das 2-Liter-Triebwerk unter der Haube ist der bis auf zwei Rippen geschwärzte Kühlergrill. Die Bezeichnung auf dem Heck gibt den jeweiligen Typ an.

Une allusion discrète au deux-litres qui œuvre sous le capot : la calandre teinte en noir à l'exception de deux rainures chromées. Le logotype à l'arrière indique de quelle version il s'agit.

Of the 863,000 02 series cars which were built, the share in the sales statistics of the 119 mph (190 kph) 2002tii amounted to 38,703 units.

Von den 863 000 gebauten Wagen der 02er Reihe beträgt der Anteil des 190 Stundenkilometer schnellen 2002tii in der Verkaufsstatistik 38 703 Einheiten.

Sur les 863 000 exemplaires vendus de la série 02, 38 703 sont des 2002tii qui flirtent

At first it is just a slight whistling sound at 4000 rpm, which grows into the "sweet roll of thunder" when the performance potential arrives alongside 6400 rpm. In the 2002 turbo, BMW took account of the resolution of the international ruling body of motor sport (FISA = Fédération Internationale du Sport Automobile) in Paris that future rallies would only be open to production sedans.

Thus a very powerful machine was presented to the public at the Frankfurt Motor Show in 1973. A specific bhp per liter performance of 85 bhp outdid even the Porsche Carrera RS (80 bhp/liter). The magical letters "turbo" were an incentive to use the accelerator, but for some BMW shareholders, all this extrovert badging was like a red rag to a bull. They demanded that these "unreasonable" letters be removed from the cars, or at least from those supplied in Germany.

Assertive owners of the "turbo" were, of course, inclined to advertise to an even greater extent their four-wheeled power symbol, whose hot exhaust gases caused the vanes of the charger to whiz up to an almost unbelievable speed of 90,000 rpm. But it was not only the stripes of BMW Motorsport GmbH and the standard front spoiler which identified the 2002 turbo as the basis of a sporting car. Massive widening of the fenders and a rear spoiler gave the game away: here was the signal to attack in motor sport.

The interior transmitted a hint of sportiness: bucket seats, leather steering wheel and a speedometer which went to 150 mph (240 kph) with room for even higher speeds. This potential was restricted in the production version, and only really came into play beyond 4500 rpm. Power was shut off after mere moments of glory by a mundane contact breaker that was regulated by centrifugal force.

The understeering performance was a trait that a keen BMW driver, hitherto used to correcting sliding rear wheels during fast cornering, had to practice. However, drivers who were not averse to occasional excursions on to the north loop of the Nürburgring, quickly acclimatized to the effective brakes, which showed little fade. Back in 1973, internally ventilated discs with four-piston calipers at the front and enlarged brake drums at the rear represented state of the art technology. The same praise did not apply to fuel consumption at 12.5 miles per gallon or 19 liters per 100 km. Its thirst for petrol was such that the petrol tank, enlarged to 18.5 gallons (70 liters), was empty after only 250 miles (400 km) of driving.

But anyone who likes to enjoy his driving pleasure to the full, wants to overtake on country roads without difficulty, and gets his kicks from the swing of the turbocharger boost gauge needle will not be too bothered by the dictates of the petrol pump. They sound their horn for the chase – with turbo power.

Erst ist es nur ein leichter Pfeifton bei 4000 Umdrehungen, der sich zu einem „süßen Donnergrollen" erhebt, wenn das Leistungspotential vehement bis auf 6400 Touren ansteigt. Mit dem 2002 turbo hat BMW einem Beschluss der obersten internationalen Automobilsportbehörde FISA (Féderation Internationale du Sport Automobile) in Paris Rechnung getragen, wonach der Rallyesport künftig nur noch mit Serien-Tourenwagen zu bestreiten ist.

Was für ein Kraftpaket, das sich auf der IAA 1973 dem Publikum präsentiert! Mit einer spezifischen Literleistung von knapp 85 PS wird sogar der Porsche Carrera RS (80 PS/Liter) überflügelt. Der magische Schriftzug „turbo" reizt zum Gas geben. Für einige Aktionäre der BMW AG ist der „turbo" eher ein Reizwort. Sie fordern – zumindest für die in Deutschland ausgelieferten Wagen – ein Verbot der „unzumutbaren" Lettern.

Ambitionierte Besitzer des BMW turbo neigen zu noch größerer Plakatierung ihres vierrädrigen Kraftsymbols, dessen heiße Abgase die Schaufeln des Laders in die unglaubliche Rotationsgeschwindigkeit von nahezu 90 000 Umdrehungen pro Minute versetzen. Doch nicht nur das Streifendesign der BMW Motorsport GmbH und der serienmäßige Frontspoiler identifizieren den 2002 turbo als Basissportler. Wuchtige Kotflügelverbreiterungen und ein Heckspoiler verraten, dass hiermit auch im Motorsport zum Angriff geblasen werden soll.

Das Interieur vermittelt einen Hauch von Sportlichkeit: Schalensitze, Lederlenkrad und ein Tacho, der bis 240 km/h reicht – Spielraum für noch mehr Potential. Dieses ist in der Serienversion beschränkt, setzt erst jenseits von 4500 Touren richtig ein und wird nach Momenten der Kraft und Herrlichkeit durch einen banalen fliehkraftgeregelten Unterbrecherkontakt abgeriegelt.

BMW 2002 turbo

Gewöhnungsbedürftig ist das untersteuernde Fahrverhalten für einen BMW-Fahrer, der bislang gewohnt war, schnellen Kurvenpassagen mit dem Einfangen des Wagenhecks zu begegnen. Schnell gewöhnt sich der Freund gelegentlicher Ausritte auf die Nordschleife des Nürburgrings dagegen an die effektvoll – kaum Fading – arbeitenden Bremsen. Innenbelüftete Scheiben mit Vierkolbensätteln vorn und vergrößerte Bremstrommeln hinten sind 1973 modernster Stand der Technik. Vom Verbrauch (19 Liter bei Vollgas) kann man das weniger behaupten. Der Benzindurst ist so ausgeprägt, dass der auf 70 Liter vergrößerte Treibstofftank bereits nach 400 Kilometern normalen Fahrbetriebs leer ist.

Doch wer den Fahrspaß in vollen Zügen genießen will, auf Landstraßen problemlos überholen kann und sich am Ausschlag der Nadel des Ladedruckanzeigers Adrenalinstöße holt, den interessiert das Diktat der Zapfsäule wenig. Er bläst mit Turbo-Power zum Halali!

On ne perçoit tout d'abord qu'un léger sifflement à 4000 tr/min, qui se mue en un « délicieux coup de tonnerre » à 6400 tr/min lorsque l'on exploite tout le potentiel. Avec la 2002 turbo, BMW a tenu compte d'une résolution prise par la Fédération internationale du sport automobile (FISA), à Paris, qui exige que, désormais, seules les voitures de tourisme de série puissent participer aux rallyes.

Quelle puissante voiture est présentée au public du Salon de l'Automobile de Francfort en 1973 ! Avec une puissance au litre de près de 85 ch, elle bat même la Porsche Carrera RS (80 ch/litre). L'emblème magique « turbo » incite à écraser l'accélérateur. Quelques actionnaires de BMW AG sont choqués et ils exigent, tout au moins pour les voitures livrées en Allemagne, une suppression de cette mention jugée « provocante ».

Les propriétaires ambitieux de la « turbo » sont, au contraire, plutôt enclins à afficher encore plus visiblement les performances de leur engin dont les gaz d'échappement brûlants font tourner les ailettes du turbocompresseur au régime incroyable de près de 90 000 tr/min. Mais il n'y a pas que les bandes décoratives de la BMW Motorsport GmbH et l'aileron avant de série qui font de la 2002 turbo une excellente voiture pour la course. De massifs élargisseurs d'ailes et un aileron arrière trahissent aussi sa vocation : la compétition automobile.

Le cockpit confirme sa sportivité : baquets, volant cuir et un tachymètre gradué jusqu'à 240 km/h, avec de la marge pour encore plus de potentiel. Celui-ci est limité dans la version de série, qui ne commence vraiment à pousser qu'à partir de 4500 tours et où, après quelques instants de gloire et de splendeur, un banal rupteur actionné par la force centrifuge met un terme à cette débauche de puissance.

Le comportement du véhicule demande une certaine accoutumance de la part des pilotes de BMW, jusqu'ici habitués à franchir rapidement les virages en contrôlant le décrochement de l'arrière. L'amateur de courses folles sur la boucle Nord du Nürburgring s'est vite habitué à l'efficacité des freins pratiquement insensibles au fading : en 1973, les disques ventilés à quatre pistons à l'avant et les tambours de plus grande dimension à l'arrière sont le must. On ne peut pas en dire autant de la consommation (19 litres à plein gaz). Sa soif est telle que le réservoir de carburant agrandi à 70 litres est déjà à sec après 400 kilomètres de conduite normale.

Mais celui qui veut profiter du plaisir de conduire, doubler quand il le souhaite sur les petites routes de campagne et ressentir une poussée d'adrénaline chaque fois que l'aiguille du manomètre de pression atteint la butée ne s'intéresse guère à la facture de la pompe à essence. Il sonne l'hallali – turbo à fond.

The front spoiler with its BMW Motorsport stripes and widened
wings clearly indicated that this 02 series BMW was intended to be used as a basis
for motor sport.

Der Frontspoiler im BMW-Motorsport-Streifendesign und die Kotflügelverbreiterungen machen deutlich, dass dieser
02er BMW als Basisauto für den Motorsport gedacht ist.

L'aileron avant avec les bandes de couleur typiques de BMW Motorsport et les élargisseurs d'ailes joufflus indiquent
sans équivoque que cette BMW 02 est conçue à la base pour la compétition automobile.

BMW 2002 turbo

BMW 2002 turbo

From its roof to the tread of its 185/70HR tires, considered wide at the time, the 2002 turbo provided Bavarian power without compare. Sales were moderate due to the generally bad economic situation. No more than 1670 deliveries were made.

Vom Dach bis hin zur damals als breit geltenden 185/70HR-Sohle ist der 2002 turbo ein „Kraft-Bayer" sondergleichen. Aufgrund der allgemein schlechten wirtschaftlichen Lage läuft der Verkauf mäßig. Der Wagen wird insgesamt nur 1670 Mal ausgeliefert.

Du toit aux pneus de 185/70HR, ce qui n'était pas rien à l'époque, la 2002 turbo roule des mécaniques. Mais la conjoncture économique n'est pas favorable aux sportives de cet acabit et cette voiture ne sera, au total, produite qu'à 1670 exemplaires.

BMW 2002 turbo

Bucket seats, leather steering wheel, speedo up to 150 mph (240 kph) and gauge for the turbocharger: appropriate equipment for this eight-second sprinter from 0 to 62 mph (100 kph). The 2-liter unit unleashed a snarling 170 bhp.

Schalensitze, Lederlenkrad, Tacho bis 240 km/h und Druckanzeige für den Abgasturbolader: Dies sind die standesgemäßen Attribute des 8-Sekunden-Sprinters (von 0 auf 100 km/h). In dem 2-Liter-Aggregat werden 170 PS fauchend entfacht.

Baquets, volant cuir, compteur gradué jusqu'à 240 km/h et affichage de la pression du turbocompresseur, cette sprinteuse qui passe de 0 à 100 km/h en 8 secondes affiche fièrement ses attributs. Le moteur de deux litres délivre 170 ch, qui piaffent d'impatience.

BMW 2500

BMW wanted an upper mid-range car to invade Mercedes territory. The two new six-cylinder engines were designed accordingly: 2.5 liters at 150 bhp and 2.8 liters at 170 bhp. But equipment, dimensions and pricing were also aimed at their counterparts from Mercedes. "Heavy guns" in the form of a ride level device and a limited slip differential as standard equipment were used by the luxuriously equipped 2800 to go into battle against Mercedes. The battle of material goodies ended in withdrawal by BMW to a less costly position. Nevertheless, the limited slip differential continued to be available – albeit at extra cost.

The 2500 model got off to a better start: between September and Christmas 1968, 2560 of these four-door sedans came off the production line and at the end of the nine-year production period, it was almost 95,000, most of them with manual transmissions. Over 17,000 comfort-conscious BMW customers left the hard work to the ZF automatic transmission with hydraulic torque converter and three-speed planetary gears.

The new six-cylinder four-stroke in-line engine with a seven-bearing crankshaft and overhead camshaft had a compression ratio of 9:1 and turned out to be extremely refined. It was also an ideal foundation for engine derivatives up to 3.3 liters. It was not easy on the fuel, for the 20.5-gallon (78 liter) tank in the rear was insufficient for 310 miles (500 km), even when driven with fuel economy in mind.

The driving comfort which one expected from a BMW 2500 was taken care of by independent suspension with McPherson struts having lower control arms at the front and semi-trailing arms at the rear. As befits a luxury car, a servo-assisted hydraulic dual circuit brake system supported disc brakes all round. This spacious sedan was properly equipped: a functional dashboard with circular instruments and a broad central console. There was a manageable steering wheel, comfortable body-shaped seats (from 1973 also height-adjustable, provided with headrests), and sensibly organized compartments for odds and ends or maps.

Another practical detail awaited discovery on opening the trunk. On the inside was a large folding case with 30 tools to cover all eventualities. Whether the three spare spark plugs would have cured any breakdown was never put to the test. The engine was durable and deep-chested: it could accelerate a 2500 with two passengers – a total of around one-and-a-half tons – to 119 mph (190 kph). Not bad for a 1960s sedan.

Mit einem Wagen der gehobenen Mittelklasse will BMW auf Mercedes-Terrain vorstoßen. Entsprechend sind die beiden neuen Sechszylindertriebwerke ausgelegt: 2,5 Liter mit 150 PS und 2,8 Liter mit 170 PS. Aber auch Ausstattung, Abmessungen und das Preis-Leistungs-Verhältnis zielen auf die Pendants mit dem Stern. Mit „schweren Geschützen", nämlich serienmäßiger Niveauregulierung und einem Sperrdifferential, zieht der luxuriös eingerichtete 2800 ins Feld gen Untertürkheim. Die Materialschlacht endet mit dem Rückzug auf eine weniger aufwändige Basis. Immerhin kann das Sperrdifferential, nunmehr gegen Aufpreis, als Extra weiterhin bestellt werden.

Besser läuft die Produktion des 2500 an. Von September bis Weihnachten 1968 gehen 2560 dieser viertürigen Limousinen vom Band, und nach der neunjährigen Produktionszeit sind es nahezu 95 000, vornehmlich mit Schaltgetriebe ausgerüstet. Etwas mehr als 17 000 komfortbewusste BMW-Kunden überlassen die Hebelarbeit der ZF-Automatik mit hydraulischem Wandler und Dreigang-Planetengetriebe.

Der neue Sechszylinder-Viertakt-Reihenmotor mit siebenfach gelagerter Kurbelwelle und oben liegender Nockenwelle ist 9:1 verdichtet und erweist sich als äußerst kultiviert: ein ideales Basistriebwerk für Derivate bis zu 3,3 Litern. Sparsam ist er freilich nicht, denn der 78-Liter-Tank im Heck reicht selbst bei schonender Fahrweise nicht einmal für 500 Kilometer.

Für einen Fahrkomfort, wie man ihn vom BMW 2500 erwartet, sorgen die Einzelradaufhängungen mit Federbeinen – vorn an Quer-, hinten an Schräglenkern. Standesgemäß sorgt eine servounterstützte hydraulische Zweikreisbremse mit vier Scheibenbremsen für angemessene Verzögerung. Die geräumige Limousine ist ordentlich eingerichtet: funktionelles Armaturenbrett mit Rundinstrumenten und breiter Mittelkonsole, griffiges Lenkrad, bequeme, körpergerecht geformte Sitze (ab 1973 auch in der Höhe regulierbar und mit Kopfstützen versehen) und sinnvoll verteilte Ablagen für Kleinigkeiten und Atlanten.

Auch beim Aufklappen des Kofferraumdeckels entdeckt man ein praktisches Detail. An der Innenseite befindet sich ein großes Klappetui mit 30 Werkzeugen für alle Fälle. Ob die drei Reservezündkerzen einen Motorschaden „kurieren" können, ist nie ausprobiert worden. Das Triebwerk erweist sich als standhaft und bringt den Wagen mit zwei Passagieren – zusammen rund anderthalb Tonnen – auf 190 Stundenkilometer: recht passabel für eine Limousine der sechziger Jahre.

BMW veut concurrencer Mercedes avec une voiture du segment intermédiaire supérieur. Les deux nouveaux six-cylindres sont conçus en conséquence : 2,5 litres de 150 ch et 2,8 litres de 170 ch. Leur finition, leurs dimensions et leur rapport qualité/prix rivalisent avec ceux de la marque à l'étoile. D'une grande technicité, à savoir un correcteur d'assiette en série et un différentiel autobloquant, la luxueuse 2800 passe à l'attaque contre la marque d'Untertürkheim. La « bataille » se termine par le retrait de BMW qui opte pour une version moins coûteuse. Le différentiel autobloquant – maintenant proposé en option – est néanmoins toujours disponible.

La 2500 prend, elle, un meilleur départ : de septembre à Noël 1968, 2560 de ces limousines à quatre portes sortent des chaînes et, après neuf ans de production, on en compte 95 000, dont la quasi-totalité possède une boîte manuelle. Un peu plus de 17 000 acheteurs de BMW optent pour la boîte automatique ZF universelle à trois rapports et convertisseur hydraulique.

Le nouveau six-cylindres en ligne à quatre temps avec vilebrequin à sept paliers et arbres à cames en tête affiche un taux de compression de 9:1 et s'avère extrêmement perfectionné. Une excellente base, donc, pour monter en cylindrée jusqu'à 3,3 litres. Il n'est malheureusement pas économique puisque même le réservoir de 78 litres installé à l'arrière ne permet d'effectuer que 500 kilomètres en conduisant régulièrement.

Des suspensions indépendantes avec jambes élastiques McPherson – avec leviers transversaux à l'avant et bras obliques à l'arrière – garantissent le confort de conduite que l'on est en droit d'attendre d'une BMW 2500. Comme il se doit, le double circuit de freinage à assistance hydraulique est à disques sur les quatre roues. Spacieuse, la limousine est parfaitement « aménagée » : un tableau de bord

fonctionnel avec des cadrans circulaires et une large console médiane, un volant agréable à manœuvrer, des sièges confortables et ergonomiques (également réglables en hauteur et avec appuie-tête à partir de 1973) et des vide-poches bien placés.

Le couvercle de la malle possède un détail pratique : il comporte une mallette d'outillage intégrée avec une trentaine d'outils pour parer à toutes les éventualités. Quelqu'un aura-t-il jamais réussi à réparer une panne de moteur avec les trois bougies de réserve que l'on y trouve ? Le moteur s'avère endurant et, avec deux personnes à bord – soit au total un poids d'environ une tonne et demie –, il propulse cette voiture à 190 km/h, une performance vraiment remarquable pour une limousine des années 1960.

The imposing exterior of the 2500, with its double-headlamp front and slightly bulging tail. The car marked a deliberate attempt by BMW to encroach on Mercedes territory.

Wuchtige Doppelscheinwerferfront und ausladendes Heck: Der 2500, mit dem BMW 1968 gezielt auf Mercedes-Terrain vorstößt, hat auch repräsentativen Chrom zu bieten.

Une ligne agressive, des phares doubles et une poupe interminable : la 2500 avec laquelle BMW marche résolument sur les plates-bandes de Mercedes en 1968 ne manque pas d'atouts.

BMW 2500

The dashboard, center console and storage shelf are functional and well-designed. The six-cylinder in-line engine, with its block angled 30 degrees to the right, generated 150 bhp.

Klar gegliedert und funktionell angeordnet präsentieren sich Armaturenbrett und Mittelkonsole mit Ablagefach. 150 PS aktiviert der Sechszylinder-Reihenmotor mit einem um 30 Grad zur rechten Seite geneigten Block.

Bien agencés et fonctionnels, telles sont les caractéristiques du tableau de bord et de la console médiane avec vide-poches. Le six-cylindres en ligne, dont le bloc est incliné de 30° sur la droite, développe 150 ch.

BMW 2500

Almost 95,000 of this comfortable upper mid-range car were produced by BMW over a nine-year period.

Nahezu 95 000 dieser komfortablen Wagen der gehobenen Mittelklasse werden in neun Jahren bei BMW produziert.

Près de 95 000 de ces confortables voitures du segment supérieur seront produites chez BMW en neuf ans.

BMW 3.0CSi

Much admired at the Paris Motor Show in the autumn of 1968, BMW presented the 2800CS as a commitment to large sporty coupés. The chassis of this slim car without a B-pillar was simply the consistent further development of the 2000CS and was built by Karmann. Final assembly and the installation of the six-cylinder engine were at Dingolfing, a new BMW site in 1967. Here Hans Glas had failed in the construction of his top-of-the-range coupés and was forced to hand over his factory to BMW. The CS swiftly developed and soon the small "i" behind the CS indicated the transition to an injection engine. Simultaneously, the engine size was increased to 2985 cc – hence the 3.0 badge.

A strong 200 bhp engine catapulted the 3100 lbs (1400 kg) CSi to 135 mph (220 kph). As early as 1972, it was slimmed down by 285 lbs (130 kg) and the engine size was increased to 3003 cc for a special CSL version, the L standing for lightweight. CSL customers were rewarded with a tangible increase in acceleration from 0 to 62 mph (100 kph). The coupé's heart, that highly revving engine, remained refinement personified. But such refinement is expensive: 13.5 miles to the gallon (17.5 liters per 100 km) driven hard made frequent gas station stops inevitable, despite a 18.5-gallon (70 liter) tank. This at a time when European petrol prices rocketed.

Which coupé driver is going to allow an oil crisis to spoil his fun behind the wheel? BMW, believing that it had to respond to a period of economic challenge with a 2.5-liter economy version, produced a flop. The strange calculation of dropping 50 bhp, losing rapid acceleration and the top speed, all to save two-thirds of a gallon (3 liters) was hardly worth noting, so there were only 844 buyers. Even savings of about 4000 marks were insufficient. Some options, which came as standard on the CSi, had to be added on.

The opposite trend was indicated. The CSL coupé with huge front spoiler, wind splitters and rear spoiler was aimed at sporting activities, its luxury accessories removed for weight reasons. The sports package was supplemented by gigantic wing structures at the rear of the car and a roof spoiler. This fixed the outline of the racing coupé – except for widening the fenders.

The success story of the coupés (2800CS from 1968 to 1971, 3.0CS/CSi from 1971 to 1975) was reflected in healthy production figures. If the 844 "economy" 2.5 coupés are included, more than 30,000 cars were built, 8142 of them the CSi.

Auf dem Pariser Autosalon im Herbst 1968 viel bestaunt, stellt BMW den 2800CS als Bekenntnis zu großen sportlichen Coupés vor. Freilich ist die Karosserie des schlanken Wagens ohne B-Säule nichts anderes als eine konsequente Weiterentwicklung des 2000CS und wird bei Karmann gebaut. Die Endmontage und der Einbau des Sechszylindermotors erfolgen in Dingolfing. Hier ist Hans Glas am Bau solcher Oberklassecoupés gescheitert und hat sein Werk an BMW abtreten müssen. Der CS entwickelt sich rasant, und bald symbolisiert das kleine „i" hinter dem CS den Übergang zum Einspritzmotor. Gleichzeitig wird der Hubraum auf 2985 ccm vergrößert – deshalb 3.0.

200 PS wuchten den immerhin 1400 Kilo schweren Wagen auf 220 Stundenkilometer. Bereits 1972 wird der CSi um 130 Kilo abgespeckt, und das Triebwerk bekommt 3003 ccm Hubraum. Diese Ausführung wird CSL genannt. Mit einer deutlich besseren Beschleunigung von 0 auf 100 Stundenkilometer werden die Käufer des Coupés belohnt. Das Herzstück, der drehfreudige Motor, überzeugt durch seine Laufkultur. Aber diese Kultur kostet etwas: 17,5 Liter Super bei allzu scharfer Gangart machen trotz des 70-Liter-Tanks häufige Tankstopps unumgänglich und das bei rapide steigenden Benzinpreisen.

Doch welcher Coupéfahrer lässt sich schon das Fahrvergnügen durch eine sogenannte Ölkrise verderben? Im Glauben, den wirtschaftlich schweren Zeiten mit einer 2,5-Liter-Sparversion begegnen zu müssen, erlebt BMW einen Reinfall. Die Rechnung, auf 50 PS, eindrucksvolle Beschleunigungserlebnisse und Geschwindigkeiten um 220 Stundenkilometer verzichten zu können, um pro Tankfüllung läppische drei Liter zu sparen, begreifen nur 844 Käufer. Selbst die Ersparnis von rund 4000 Mark lockt nicht, da einige Extras, die beim CSi zum Serienumfang gehören, dagegen aufgerechnet werden müssen.

Der Trend geht genau in die andere Richtung. Das CSL-Coupé mit überdimensionalem Frontspoiler, Windsplits und Heckspoiler zielt auf sportliche Aktivitäten, zumal auf Luxusaccessoires aus Gewichtsgründen verzichtet wird. Ein gigantisches Flügelwerk für das Wagenheck und ein Dachspoiler ergänzen das Sportpaket. Damit steht das Outfit des Rennsport-Coupés bereits – bis auf Kotflügelverbreiterungen – fest.

Die Erfolgsstory der Coupés (2800CS von 1968 bis 1971, 3.0CS/CSi von 1971 bis 1975) schlägt sich in einer ansehnlichen Produktion nieder. Einschließlich der 844 „Sparbrötchen" werden mehr als 30 000 Wagen gebaut, 8142 davon sind CSi.

Au Salon de l'Automobile de Paris, à l'automne 1968, sous les yeux étonnés des nombreux visiteurs, BMW dévoile la 2800CS, qui se classe parmi les gros coupés sportifs. La carrosserie de l'élégante voiture sans montant central n'est toutefois rien d'autre qu'une juste extrapolation de la 2000CS. Elle est construite chez Karmann. Le montage final et l'installation du moteur six-cylindres ont lieu à Dingolfing. Dans cette ville, Hans Glas avait fait faillite en voulant construire de tels coupés du segment supérieur et avait dû céder son usine à BMW. La CS connaît un développement rapide et, bientôt, le petit «i» derrière le CS signale la présence d'un moteur à injection. Simultanément, la cylindrée passe à 2985 cm³ – d'où le 3.0.

Pas moins de 200 ch propulsent à 220 km/h cette voiture qui pèse tout de même 1400 kg. Dès 1972, elle est allégée de 130 kg et le moteur a une cylindrée de 3003 cm³. Cette version est appelée CSL. L'acheteur du coupé CSL appréciera, lui, les meilleures accélérations pour le 0 à 100 km/h. Le moteur, par sa spontanéité à monter en régime, séduit par sa perfection. Mais cette perfection a un prix : malgré un réservoir de 70 litres, les 17,5 litres de super consommés à bride abattue imposent des ravitaillements fréquents et ce, alors que le prix de l'essence augmente à vue d'œil.

Mais quel amateur de coupés accepterait de gâcher son plaisir à cause d'un soi-disant choc pétrolier ? BMW, croyant répliquer avec une version économique de 2,5 litres en période de crise économique, subit un échec cinglant : seuls 844 acheteurs se laissent séduire – renoncer à 50 ch, à l'ivresse des accélérations et à des vitesses d'environ 220 km/h pour économiser trois malheureux litres par plein d'essence. Même l'économie à l'achat d'environ 4000 marks n'est pas un argument suffisamment convaincant, car il

faut y ajouter quelques options qui font partie de l'équipement de série sur la CSi.

La tendance va exactement dans le sens contraire. Le coupé CSL, avec un imposant aileron avant, windsplits et becquet arrière, affiche effrontément sa sportivité, d'autant plus que des accessoires de luxe ont été supprimés pour l'alléger. Le kit sport est complété par un impressionnant becquet arrière et un aileron de toit. Les lignes du coupé compétition sont à la mesure de ses ambitions – à l'exception des élargisseurs d'ailes.

La «success-story» des coupés (2800CS de 1968 à 1971, 3.0CS/CSi de 1971 à 1975) s'est traduite par un succès commercial sans précédent – y compris les 844 exemplaires de la «version économique», plus de 30 000 voitures sont construites, dont 8142 CSi.

The type plate on the tailgate makes it abundantly clear that this is a CS with a 3-liter injection engine.

Unübersehbar verkündet das Typenschild auf der Heckklappe, dass es sich hier um einen CS mit dem 3-Liter-Einspritzmotor handelt.

L'inscription sur la malle arrière affiche fièrement qu'il s'agit ici d'une CS à moteur à injection de 3 litres.

Beneath the hood resides a six-cylinder engine with electronically-controlled Bosch fuel injection. It generates 200 bhp at 5300 rpm.

Unter der Haube macht sich ein Sechszylinder mit elektronisch gesteuerter Bosch-Benzin-einspritzung breit. Bei 5300 Umdrehungen werden 200 PS frei.

Un six-cylindres à injection électronique Bosch occupe le compartiment moteur.
Il délivre 200 ch à 5300 tr/min.

BMW 3.0CSL/3.0CSL (IMSA)

The commentator was left speechless and the spectators around the bumpy airfield track in Sebring in Florida shouted their approval: cheerful Hans Stuck from Germany's Bavarian state provided an interview featuring three pithy answers and a protracted mountain-country yodel. Such vocal gymnastics from deepest Bavaria graced many of the famous US racetracks in 1975, from East Coast Daytona and Watkins Glen to the sunny Californian tracks of Monterey, Riverside and Laguna Seca.

BMW hoped to be rewarded with extra exports as a result of its participation in the American IMSA (International Motor Sports Association) Championship. BMW Motorsport GmbH entered the 3.0CSL winged coupé – a great racing success in Europe ever since its 1973 debut. The sunshade on the CSL's windshield bore the legend in large capital letters: "Bavarian Motor Works". That prevented any misunderstanding of the BMW abbreviation in the States. Incredibly, newspapers had written "British Motor Works" as the translation of BMW. That was before the Munich CSLs raced in the New World, and nobody made that mistake again.

The core team of two white racing coupés with the Motorsport GmbH stripes included the Bavarian Stuck, the fast Swede Ronnie Peterson, British long distance specialist (formerly of Porsche and Ferrari) Brian Redman, and a youngster from the US by the name of Sam Posey. A strong and – as it turned out – a successful team. They certainly had no intention of lagging behind their winning European counterparts, including Hagen-born Siggi Müller, who drove a CSL owned by Rüdiger Faltz (Essen) to win the European touring car title.

The appearance of the IMSA coupé differed from the European CSL in its large air intakes for the transmission, rear axle and engine oil coolers, these being integrated within vast fender extensions. The rear fenders had to be huge to cover the 16 inch-wide Dunlop rollers with appropriate BBS wheels. These racing wheels were naturally equipped with central wheel studs to facilitate rapid wheel changes.

Magnesium wheel uprights, aluminum wheel hubs and the aluminum casings of the Bilstein gas shock-absorbers tubes reduced kerb weight. The adjustable top spring plates meant that the distance from the ground could be immediately controlled to suit each race circuit. Similarly suspension springs of many different poundage rates were also sent across the Atlantic from Munich to cater for the different racetrack characteristics.

To achieve better weight distribution, the trunk was filled up with the fuel tank, dry sump oil tank, brake bias control, an automatic fire-extinguisher system, battery, pioneering hydraulic system for the experimental ABS anti-lock braking and an alternator. Two large gas filler necks distinguished the trunk deck, under a large rear CSL wing.

The twin side exhaust pipes replicated a lion's roar when the 430 bhp engine – increased to at least 450 by the end of the season – ran flat out. Bavarian lions have a loud roar. Otherwise Stuck, with a talent as divine as opera star Caruso, would not have had anything to yodel about.

Dem Streckensprecher verschlägt es die Sprache, und die Zuschauer rund um die holprige Flugplatzpiste von Sebring in Florida johlen vor Begeisterung: Frohnatur Hans Stuck aus „Bavaria, Germany" hat gerade ein Interview gegeben – drei kurze, aber kernige Antworten und einen langen Jodler! Diese urbayerische Stimmbandverrenkung erschallt 1975 noch auf vielen bekannten US-Racetracks zwischen Daytona, Watkins Glen und den sonnigen kalifornischen Pisten von Monterey, Riverside und Laguna Seca.

BMW erwartet sich von dem Engagement in der amerikanischen IMSA-Serie (International Motor Sports Association) deutliche Exportimpulse. Und so setzt die BMW-Motorsport GmbH werkseitig die schon seit 1973 in Europa äußerst erfolgreichen 3.0CSL-Flügel-Coupés ein. Um eine Fehlinterpretation des Kürzels „BMW" in den Staaten auszuschließen, steht in großen Lettern auf der Windschutzscheibenblende des CSL „Bavarian Motor Works". Man sollte es nicht glauben, aber vor dem Auftauchen der Münchener in der Neuen Welt hatte ein Blatt tatsächlich „British Motor Works" geschrieben.

Die Stammcrew der beiden weißen Coupés mit den Streifen der Motorsport GmbH bilden neben dem Bayern Hans-Joachim Stuck der schnelle Schwede Ronnie Peterson, der britische Allround-Pilot und Langstreckenspezialist (auf Porsche und Ferrari) Brian Redman sowie der Amerikaner Sam Posey – eine starke Truppe und, wie sich herausstellt, erfolgreich obendrein. Was die Siege angeht, möchte man seinen Kollegen in Europa – der Hagener Siggi Müller holt auf einem CSL von Rüdiger Faltz (Essen) den Tourenwagen-Europameistertitel – in nichts nachstehen.

Optisch unterscheiden sich die IMSA-Coupés von den in Europa eingesetzten CSL durch große Luftschächte für die Ölkühler von Getriebe, Hinterachse und Motor in den hinteren Kotflügelverbreiterungen. Diese fallen gewaltig aus, denn sie müssen 16 Zoll breite Dunlop-Walzen mit ebenso großen BBS-Felgen abdecken. Natürlich sind diese Räder für schnelle Radwechsel mit Zentralverschlüssen versehen.

Für Gewichtsersparnis sorgen Magnesium-Radträger, Aluminiumradnaben und Alurohre in den Bilstein-Gasdruckstoßdämpfern. Über geschraubte Federteller lässt sich der Bodenabstand regulieren, und für die unterschiedlichen Rennstrecken-Charakteristika haben die Münchener Federn aller erdenklichen Härtegrade über den Teich geschippert.

Aus Gründen der besseren Gewichtsverteilung ist der untere Bereich des „Kofferraums" vollbepackt mit dem Tank sowie Ölsumpf, Bremskraftregler, Feuerlöschbombe, Batterie, Hydrauliksystem für das ABS und Lichtmaschine. Zwei große Einfüllstutzen zieren den „beflügelten" Kofferraumdeckel.

Der Sound der beiden seitlichen Auspuffrohre erinnert an das Gebrüll von Löwen, sobald sich die 430 PS – zu Saisonende sollen es gut 450 gewesen sein – voll entfalten. Es hat auch niemand bestritten, dass ein bayerischer Löwe gut brüllen kann. Sonst hätte der „Strietzel" Stuck ja nichts zum Jodeln.

Le commentateur en perd la parole et les spectateurs, massés aux abords de la piste autour de l'aéroport de Sebring, en Floride, hurlent de plaisir : Hans-Joachim Stuck, cet Allemand souriant originaire de la Bavière, vient d'accorder une interview – trois réponses brèves, mais percutantes, avant d'entamer une tyrolienne ! En 1975, ce chant montagnard typiquement bavarois résonnera sur de nombreux circuits américains prestigieux entre Daytona, Watkins Glen et les pistes ensoleillées de Monterey, Riverside et Laguna Seca, en Californie.

BMW espère que son engagement dans la série américaine IMSA (International Motor Sports Association) donnera un coup de fouet à ses exportations vers les États-Unis. Et c'est ainsi que la BMW Motorsport GmbH engage ses coupés à ailerons 3.0CSL, qui remportent déjà un très grand succès en Europe depuis 1973. Pour parer à toute interprétation erronée de l'abréviation BMW aux États-Unis, « Bavarian Motor Works » figure en lettres capitales sur le pare-soleil apposé sur le pare-brise des CSL. C'est incroyable mais avant l'arrivée des Munichois sur le Nouveau Continent, un journal avait déjà pris le nom de BMW pour l'abréviation de « British Motor Works ».

Outre le Bavarois Hans-Joachim Stuck, l'équipage des deux coupés blancs avec les banderoles bleues et rouges de la Motorsport GmbH est composé du rapide suédois Ronnie Peterson, du pilote britannique touche-à-tout et spécialiste de l'endurance (sur Porsche et Ferrari) Brian Redman, ainsi que de l'Américain Sam Posey. Une équipe de choc et, comme on allait le constater, une équipe gagnante. Côté victoires, ils veulent être à la hauteur de leurs collègues qui se battent sur les circuits européens, comme par exemple Siggi Müller, originaire de Hagen, qui coiffe la couronne de champion d'Europe des voitures de tourisme sur une CSL de Rüdiger Faltz (Essen).

Les coupés IMSA se distinguent des CSL engagées en Europe par de grandes prises d'air pour la transmission, le pont arrière et les radiateurs d'huile du moteur intégrés dans les ailes arrière élargies. Ces dernières sont gigantesques, car elles doivent héberger de larges pneus Dunlop de 16 pouces avec des jantes BBS de mêmes dimensions. Naturellement, ces roues comportent un moyeu de fixation central pour garantir un changement rapide de pneumatiques.

Par souci de poids, les paliers de roues sont en magnésium, les moyeux de roues et les tubes des amortisseurs à gaz Bilstein sont en aluminium. Des coupelles de ressort vissées permettent de modifier la garde au sol et, pour répondre aux différentes caractéristiques des circuits, les Munichois ont expédié outre-Atlantique un assortiment de ressorts.

Pour obtenir une meilleure répartition du poids, le « coffre » est rempli avec le réservoir à essence, la lubrification à carter sec, les répartiteurs de la puissance de freinage, l'extincteur réglementaire, la batterie, le système hydraulique pour l'ABS et l'alternateur. Deux grosses goulottes de remplissage décorent le couvercle de malle arborant un gigantesque aileron.

Le bruit émis par les deux énormes pots d'échappement latéraux rappelle les feulements d'un lion dès que vrombissent les 430 ch – qui sont même largement 450 à la fin de la saison. Les lions de Bavière savent se faire entendre. Sinon Stuck, avec un talent proche de celui du chanteur d'opéra Caruso, n'aurait pas pu pousser la tyrolienne.

1000-km-Nürburgring (D), 1975

During the 4-hour touring car classic race on the north loop of the Nürburgring in 1975, the Faltz-Alpina 3.0CSLs – here the car of Müller/Peltier who came second – were clearly dominant.

Beim 4-Stunden-Tourenwagen-Klassiker auf der Nordschleife des Nürburgrings 1975 dominieren die Faltz-Alpina-3.0CSL klar – hier der Wagen der Zweit-platzierten Müller/Peltier.

Lors des 4 Heures du Nürburgring pour voitures de tourisme, sur le circuit nord du Nürburgring, en 1975, la domination des Faltz-Alpina-3.0CSL – ici la voiture de Müller/Peltier qui finiront deuxièmes – est évidente.

Norisring (D), 1975

Hans-Joachim Stuck (left, at the Nuremberg 200 mile race) wrote motor sport history for BMW in Europe with the 3.0CSL, as he did with the IMSA version of the coupé with its prominent spoilers and his start number of 25.

Hans-Joachim Stuck (links beim 200-Meilen-Rennen von Nürnberg) schreibt mit dem 3.0CSL in Europa für BMW ebenso Motorsportgeschichte wie mit der IMSA-Ausführung des Flügel-Coupés mit „seiner" Startnummer 25.

Hans-Joachim Stuck (à gauche lors des 200 Miles de Nuremberg) écrit un chapitre de l'histoire de la compétition automobile pour BMW avec la 3.0CSL en Europe et fait de même aux États-Unis avec la version IMSA du coupé bardé d'ailerons arborant le n° 25.

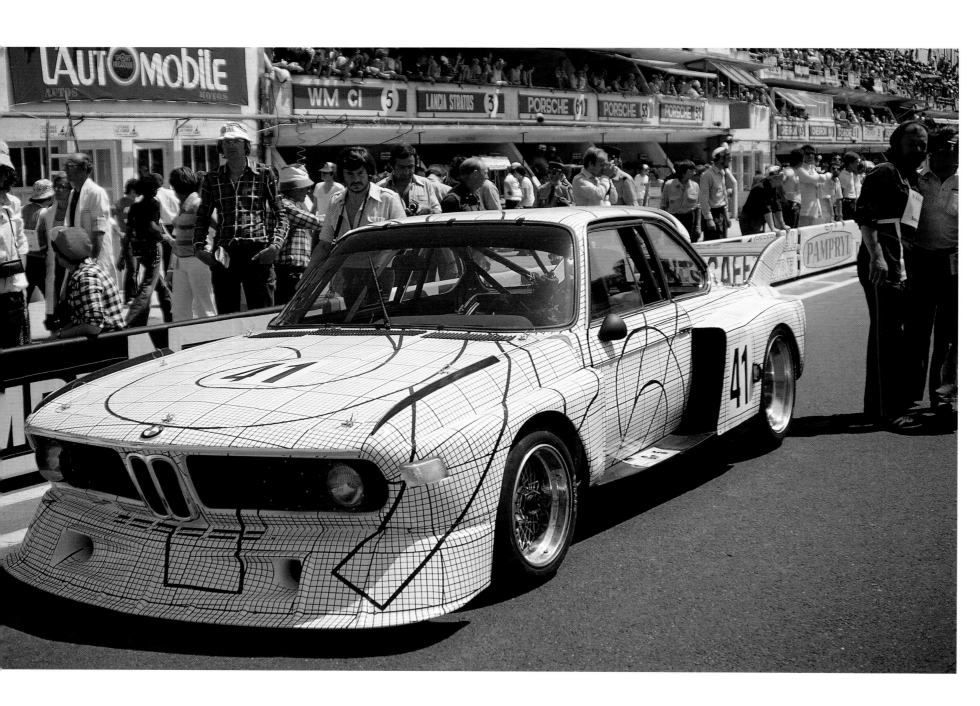

Art and motor sport: with his coordinate paper design, the American artist Frank Stella intended to depict high-tech precision on the works 3.0CSL. Unfortunately, the work of art on the "stage" of Le Mans 1976 only had a life of 2 hours 16 minutes.

Kunst und Motorsport: Mit den Linien auf dem Millimeterpapier will der amerikanische Künstler Frank Stella auf dem Werks-3.0CSL High-Tech und Präzision darstellen. Leider ist dem Kunstwerk auf der „Bühne" von Le Mans 1976 nur eine Lebensdauer von zwei Stunden und 16 Minuten beschieden.

Art et compétition automobile : ce papier millimétrique dessiné sur la 3.0CSL d'usine par l'artiste américain Frank Stella représente la haute technologie et la précision. Malheureusement, sur le podium de défilé du Mans en 1976, on ne pourra admirer l'œuvre d'art que pendant deux heures et seize minutes.

US safety regulations as demonstrated by the 3.0CSL (IMSA): the driver's door was welded shut – Stuck inserted his long frame through the net (replacing the side windows) – and there were additional brackets for the rear windscreen. In the 1975 season the six-cylinder produced 450 bhp. Pictured here, the automobile "High Priest" Paul Rosche and his masterpiece.

US-Sicherheitsvorschriften am Beispiel des 3.0CSL (IMSA): eine zugeschweißte Fahrertür – der Einstieg für den langen Stuck erfolgt durch das Netz (statt Seitenscheibe) – und die zusätzlich mit Klammern gehaltene Heckscheibe. Bis zu 450 PS gibt der Sechszylinder in der Saison 1975 ab. Rechts im Bild der „Motor-Papst" Paul Rosche und sein Meisterwerk.

Normes de sécurité à l'américaine à l'exemple de la 3.0CSL (IMSA) : une porte conducteur soudée – le longiligne Stuck doit se glisser à bord après avoir déplacé le filet (il n'y a plus de vitre latérale) – et une lunette arrière maintenue en place par deux brides. Le six-cylindres produit jusqu'à 450 ch au cours de la saison 1975. Paul Rosche, le « pape » de la construction automobile est photographié ici avec son chef-d'œuvre.

BMW 520

The first of a new BMW generation saw the light of an automotive day in September 1972: the 520. It heralded the start of the middleweight 5 series. Although this BMW partially owed its physical appearance to the planned six-cylinder engine, its heart was a four-cylinder engine. And this heartbeat was simply not enough for a vehicle at the top end of the middle class. This fact was only taken into account five years later, when all BMW 520s had a new six-cylinder implant.

The four-cylinder required some automotive surgery. Changing the combustion chambers to what are known as "3-sphere turbulence combustion chambers" prompted a compression ratio increase, therefore optimizing the mixture combustion and increasing both performance and fuel efficiency. More functional changes came for environmental reasons: the new Stromberg downdraft carburetor with automatic start improved emission control, particularly in cold starts.

The only problems encountered were related to the vehicle's performance. A 115 bhp engine required almost 13 seconds to bring a car weighing 2805 lbs (1275 kg) from 0 to 62 mph (100 kph); to make matters worse, there were 44 lbs (20 kg) extra with the automatic. At the top end, speeds of up to 109 mph (175 kph) were attained and the fuel injection car which delivered 130 bhp could reach 114 mph (183 kph).

The addition of longer wheelbases, wider track and anti-roll bars to the tried and tested chassis with McPherson struts at the front, and a triangulated trailing arm at the rear, was so effective that only a mild "pedicure" was required: fine-tuning the suspension. Helpful cornering characteristics – there were early signals of slight oversteer – and high levels of driving comfort were both 520 plus points.

The safe chassis with strengthened struts and special beam rigidity in the sub-frame were worthy of special note.

Computer calculations predicted what could be crumpled in an accident, and what should remain intact.

High standards were, of course, expected of a car which cost 15,000 marks without any extras in 1972. The efficient interior did not let anyone down. The dashboard lit up in impressive muted orange shades whenever the lights were switched on, but what was most striking was the volume of fresh or heated air which could be displaced every 60 seconds.

The 520 came with either a five-speed or an automatic transmission and options even included the seatbelts. Yet it offered so much for its price that over 45,000 new 5 series were sold in 1973 alone.

Die „Erstgeburt" einer neuen BMW-Generation erblickt im September 1972 das Licht der Autowelt: der 520, mit dem die 5er Reihe anfängt. Auch wenn er sich optisch ein wenig an den großen Sechszylindern orientiert, ist sein Herz ein Vierzylinder. Und das schlägt eigentlich zu schwach für ein Fahrzeug der gehobenen Mittelklasse. Erst fünf Jahre später trägt man diesem Umstand Rechnung und implantiert neue Sechszylinder in den BMW 520.

Einen kleinen „chirurgischen Eingriff" hat sich der Vierzylinder jedoch gefallen lassen müssen. Durch die Umwandlung der Brennräume in sogenannte „3-Kugel-Wirbelwannen" und somit durch die Vergrößerung des Verdichtungsverhältnisses wird die Verbrennung des Gemischs optimiert. Dazu kommt etwas „Umwelt-Kosmetik". Für eine bessere Abgasregulierung – besonders bei Kaltstarts – sorgen die neuen Stromberg-Fallstromvergaser mit Startautomatik.

Trotzdem hapert es bei der Fitness, denn der 115-PS-Motor benötigt nahezu 13 Sekunden, um das stattliche Gewicht von 1275 Kilo (bei der Automatik sind es 20 Kilo zusätzlich) von 0 auf 100 Stundenkilometer zu beschleunigen. Oben heraus geht es bis 175 Stundenkilometer weiter, und der Einspritzer mit 130 PS bringt es immerhin auf 183 km/h.

Verlängerter Radstand, verbreiterte Spur und Drehstabstabilisatoren kommen dem bewährten Fahrwerk mit McPherson-Federbeinen vorn und einer Schräglenkerachse hinten so entgegen, dass nur noch etwas „Pediküre" notwendig ist, nämlich Feintuning bei der Federungsabstimmung. Gutmütige Kurveneigenschaften – leichtes Übersteuern kündigt sich frühzeitig an – und hoher Fahrkomfort sind Pluspunkte des 520.

Besonderes Augenmerk verdienen die sicheren Chassis mit verstärkten Holmen und besonderen Flankenversteifungen in der Bodengruppe. Computer haben errechnet, was bei einem Unfall geknautscht werden soll und was intakt bleiben muss.

Natürlich werden an einen Wagen, der 1972 ohne Extras knapp 15 000 Mark ab Werk kostet, auch Ansprüche gestellt. In dieser Hinsicht gibt sich das Interieur keine Blöße. Dass die Armaturen bei eingeschaltetem Licht orangefarben leuchten, ist eher nebensächlich. Außergewöhnlich hoch ist das Volumen der Frisch- oder Heizungsluft, die pro Minute bewegt werden kann.

Der Wagen, der auch mit Fünfganggetriebe oder Automatik erhältlich ist, und zu dessen Extras unter anderem Sicherheitsgurte zählen, bietet für seinen Preis offenbar so viel, dass allein 1973 über 45 000 neue 5er verkauft werden.

Une nouvelle génération de BMW voit le jour en septembre 1972. Son premier « rejeton » est la 520. Elle inaugure par la même occasion la série 5. Même si, sur le plan esthétique, elle s'inspire assez étroitement des grosses six-cylindres, on trouve sous son capot un moteur à quatre-cylindres. Un moteur qui manque d'ailleurs d'un peu de nervosité pour une voiture du segment intermédiaire supérieur. Il faudra attendre cinq ans pour que ce petit défaut disparaisse et que la BMW 520 reçoive un six-cylindres.

Le quatre-cylindres a cependant dû subir bon gré mal gré une petite « intervention chirurgicale ». La combustion du mélange est optimisée par des modifications des chambres de combustion appelées « baignoires à tourbillons à trois sphères », ce qui permet d'augmenter le taux de compression. BMW en profite aussi pour faire un geste pour l'environnement. Les nouveaux carburateurs inversés Stromberg avec starter automatique régulent mieux les gaz d'échappement, en particulier lors des démarrages à froid.

Il n'y a que les muscles qui lui fassent défaut. Il faut près de 13 secondes au moteur de 115 ch pour faire passer de 0 à 100 km/h une voiture qui pèse 1275 kg (et même 20 kg supplémentaires dans la version à boîte automatique). La vitesse de pointe se limite à 175 km/h, la version à injection de 130 ch atteignant tout de même 183 km/h.

Un empattement allongé, des sillons plus larges et des barres de torsion stabilisatrices complètent si bien les trains roulants à jambes élastiques McPherson qui ont fait leurs preuves à l'avant tout comme l'essieu arrière à bras obliques qu'il suffit d'affiner les tarages de suspension pour obtenir un comportement parfaitement équilibré. Le comportement sécurisant en virage – le dérapage arrière ne surprend jamais – et le confort dynamique sont des atouts de la 520.

Une attention toute particulière a été apportée à la cellule passagers au niveau de la sécurité avec des longerons renforcés et des flancs plus rigides. Des ordinateurs ont calculé et programmé ce qui doit se déformer ou non en cas de collision.

Naturellement, une voiture qui coûte près de 15 000 marks départ usine sans options en 1972 ne doit pas décevoir. Et, de ce point de vue, le cockpit est assez réussi. Lorsque la lumière est allumée, les cadrans sont illuminés d'une couleur orange, mais ce détail est plutôt secondaire. En revanche, le volume d'air frais ou chaud par minute que brasse l'installation est inhabituellement élevé.

La voiture est disponible au choix avec une boîte manuelle à cinq vitesses ou une transmission automatique. La liste des options comprend même les ceintures de sécurité. Cette voiture en offre tant pour son prix que, rien qu'en 1973, plus de 45 000 nouvelles 520 seront vendues.

The launch of the BMW 520 in 1972 heralded a new generation: the 5 series. Safety, comfort and good handling were the distinguishing characteristics of this automobile, which bears a slight external resemblance to the large BMW six-cylinder.

Mit dem BMW 520 läuft 1972 eine neue Generation an: die 5er Reihe. Sicherheit, Komfort und gutes Fahrverhalten kennzeichnen dieses Fahrzeug, das sich äußerlich leicht an die großen Sechszylinder von BMW anlehnt.

La BMW 520 de 1972 marque l'arrivée d'une nouvelle génération : la série 5. Sécurité, confort et bonne tenue de route sont les qualités de cette voiture qui, sur le plan esthétique, s'inspire quelque peu des grosses BMW six-cylindres.

244   BMW 520

Vast quantities of fresh or heated air are forced into the car by the three controls on the center console. However, the car's engine was less impressive, being a four-cylinder affair developing 115 bhp.

Ein enormes Volumen an Frisch- und Heizungsluft wird von den drei Schaltern in der Mittel-konsole des Cockpits bewegt. Den Wagen selbst bewegt allerdings nur ein 115-PS-Vierzylinder.

Les trois commandes sur la console médiane brassent un volume énorme d'air frais ou réchauffé. Pour sa propulsion, la voiture se contente d'un quatre-cylindres de 115 ch.

BMW 323i

With its completely new six-cylinder injection engine, the 323i was the Bavarian muscle in the 3 series, which was launched in May 1975. Two exhaust pipes draw visible and aural attention to the fact that here the monotone of the 3 series palette – from the 316 to the 320 – was relieved by the sound of a 143 bhp engine. With inlet manifold fuel injection (Bosch K-Jetronic) the mixture was precisely prepared. The 2.3-liter engine smoothly delivered its power with minimal vibration from a crankshaft held in seven bearings and civilized by a dozen counterweights.

Driving pleasure – not just in a straight line at a top speed of 122 mph (196 kph) – was assisted by strengthened springs and stabilizers. This was a compact car that did not have to be wrestled into corners, for the servo-assisted steering worked with pleasant ease and extreme precision.

Four disc brakes, the front ones internally ventilated, rein in the free-running temperament of the 323i on request. Offering acceleration of just nine seconds from 0 to 62 mph (100 kph) the 323i was a class leader – always assuming efficient use of the five-speed transmission, installed from September 1979 onwards. Those who preferred a little less sportiness and wished to change gear without hassle were provided with a ZF automatic transmission that featured an hydraulic torque converter and three-speed planetary gears.

Using a relatively high compression ratio of 9.5:1, this 3 series consumed many a liter of Super. Yet an average of 17 miles to the gallon (14 liters per 100 km) represented efficient performance in 1978 when compared against the high bhp figure. The competition from Alfa Romeo and Daimler-Benz was thirstier, but after some 260 miles (420 km) the tank of the Bavarian was empty.

The first 3 series (designated E21 for internal use) lived until 1983 and presented the white and blue BMW badge

with a result previously thought impossible: 1.36 million cars sold, of which approximately 35 percent featured the six-cylinder engine.

As the top model, the 323i had collected a valuable cross-section of admiring customers: there were drivers with sporting ambitions, casual users of the accelerator, and people who valued reserves of power and effective brakes for everyday use.

Mit einem völlig neuen Sechszylinder-Einspritzmotor ist der 323i der „Kraftbayer" der im Mai 1975 aus der Taufe gehobenen 3er Serie. Zwei Auspuffrohre machen äußerlich, aber auch akustisch darauf aufmerksam, dass hier die „Eintönigkeit" der 3er Palette – beginnend mit dem 316 bis zum 320 – vom Sound eines 143 PS starken Triebwerkes unterbrochen wird. Mit einer Saugrohr-Benzineinspritzung (Bosch-K-Jetronic) wird das Gemisch gut dosiert aufbereitet. Laufruhig entfaltet das 2,3-Liter-Triebwerk seine Leistung: Keine Vibrationen, denn die siebenfach gelagerte Kurbelwelle weist ein Dutzend Gegengewichte auf.

Der Freude am Fahren – nicht nur geradeaus mit einer Spitzengeschwindigkeit von 196 Stundenkilometern – dienen verstärkte Federn und Stabilisatoren. Ein kompaktes Auto, das nicht mit Nachdruck in die Kurven gezogen werden muss, weil die Servolenkung angenehm leicht und äußerst präzise arbeitet.

Vier Scheibenbremsen – die vorderen innenbelüftet – zügeln bei Bedarf das Temperament des 323i, der mit einer Beschleunigung von knapp neun Sekunden von 0 auf 100 Stundenkilometer Primus in der Mittelklasse ist, gute Schaltarbeit mit dem ab September 1979 eingebauten Fünfganggetriebe vorausgesetzt. Wer es weniger sportlich mag und ohne Hakelei in die Gänge kommen will, dem steht eine ZF-Automatik mit hydraulischem Wandler und 3-Gang-Planetengetriebe zur Verfügung.

Mit einem relativ hohem Verdichtungsverhältnis von 9,5:1 stemmt dieser 3er eine ordentliche „Maß" Superbenzin. Doch 14 Liter im Schnitt sind 1978 gemessen an der PS-Zahl Bestwert. Die Konkurrenten von Alfa Romeo und Daimler-Benz schlucken mehr Benzin. Nach rund 420 Kilometern ist der Maßkrug des Bajuwaren jedenfalls leer.

Die erste 3er Reihe (werksintern E21 genannt) läuft bis 1983 und beschert der weißblauen Marke ein bis dahin nicht für möglich gehaltenes Ergebnis: 1,36 Millionen Wagen, davon etwa 35 Prozent mit einem Sechszylinder bestückt, werden ausgeliefert.

Als Topmodell dieser Erfolgsreihe schafft sich der 323i einen ansehnlichen Freundeskreis: sportlich ambitionierte Fahrer, lässige Gasgeber und Menschen, die im Alltagsbetrieb Kraftreserven und wirksame Bremsen für schnelles und sicheres Vorankommen schätzen.

Avec son nouveau six-cylindres à injection, la 323i est la « Bavaroise musclée » de la nouvelle série 3 qui voit le jour en mai 1975. Extérieurement, deux pots d'échappement attirent bruyamment l'attention sur le fait que la « monotonie » de la série 3, qui va de la 316 à la 320, est rompue par ce moteur de 143 ch. L'injection d'essence Bosch K-Jetronic dans les tubulures d'aspiration garantit un bon dosage du mélange. Le 2,3 litres se distingue par une montée en puissance régulière, sans vibration, car le vilebrequin à sept paliers comporte douze contrepoids.

Le plaisir de conduire – et pas seulement en ligne droite à la vitesse de pointe de 196 km/h – est intense grâce à la présence de ressorts et de stabilisateurs renforcés. Une voiture compacte qu'il n'est pas nécessaire de pousser dans les virages parce que la direction assistée est agréablement légère et extrêmement précise.

Quatre freins à disques, ventilés à l'avant, jugulent – si besoin est – le tempérament de la 323i, qui est la première de sa classe avec à peine 9 secondes pour les accélérations de 0 à 100 km/h, à condition de bien manier la boîte de cinq vitesses qui l'équipe à partir de septembre 1979. Celui qui préfère une conduite plus paisible a une excellente alternative avec une boîte automatique ZF à convertisseur hydraulique et boîte universelle à 3 rapports.

Avec son taux de compression relativement élevé de 9,5:1, cette série 3 ne dédaigne pas le super. Mais, en 1978, une consommation moyenne de 14 litres au 100 km est un résultat inégalé compte tenu de la performance. Ses concurrentes de chez Alfa Romeo et Daimler-Benz consomment davantage. Elle peut parcourir 420 km, avant de rejoindre la pompe à essence.

La première série 3 (nom de code interne E21) est construite jusqu'en 1983 et permet à la marque à l'hélice bleue et blanche de remporter un succès commercial inédit à ce jour : 1,36 million de voitures vendues, dont un bon tiers de six-cylindres.

Autour de la 323i, se constitue un enviable club d'amateurs : les automobilistes férus de conduite sportive, ceux qui aiment rouler vite et décontractés ainsi que ceux qui, dans la vie quotidienne, apprécient d'avoir de la puissance en réserve et des freins efficaces pour rouler vite en toute sécurité.

The top model of the new 3 series, designated E21 within the company, is immediately recognizable from the front thanks to the 323i type plate next to the double headlamps. It proved so lively that it was fitted with a five-speed gearbox in September 1979.

Das Top-Modell der werksintern E21 genannten neuen 3er Reihe, von vorn sofort an dem Typenschild 323i neben den Doppelscheinwerfern erkennbar, versprüht so viel Temperament, dass es im September 1979 mit einem Fünfganggetriebe belohnt wird.

Le top model de la nouvelle série 3, qui porte le nom de code E21, est reconnaissable immédiatement à l'inscription 323i qui figure à côté des doubles phares. Son tempérament est si débordant qu'il est récompensé, en septembre 1979, par une boîte manuelle à cinq vitesses.

BMW 323i

BMW 323i

A drive-free continuous fuel injection system supplies the smooth lively six-cylinder in-line engine, which develops 143 bhp, giving this mid-range model a 0 to 62 mph (100 kph) time of just under nine seconds.

Eine antriebslose, kontinuierliche Benzineinspritzung versorgt den drehfreudigen laufruhigen Reihensechszylinder, dessen 143 PS den flotten Mittelklassewagen in knapp neun Sekunden auf 100 Stundenkilometer beschleunigen.

Une injection d'essence continue sans entraînement mécanique alimente le six-cylindres en ligne souple et réactif dont les 143 ch permettent à cette rapide voiture de taille moyenne d'atteindre le 0 à 100 km/h en 9 secondes à peine.

BMW 728i

In accordance with the "law" governing series designations at BMW (3 series from 1975, 5 series from 1972 and 6 series from 1976), the new large sedan which appeared in May 1977 was designated the 7 series – right at the top of the BMW hierarchy. The objective was clear: to gain entry to territory occupied by the Mercedes-Benz S class. The 728i in particular, whose six-cylinder engine provided 184 bhp of performance, was unleashed on S class buyers in 1979. Its balanced cost-to-performance ratio determined that 33,700 marks had to be forked out for the luxurious one-and-a-half ton car.

The 2.8-liter engine materialized as flexible and willing, barely audible to the passengers. If the car was luxurious under the bonnet, the same was true of the interior with its armchair-like front seats and a back seat "sofa", on which just two headrests indicated that three should not try to squeeze inside. A quality interior and solid workmanship contributed to the good reputation of the sedan in the same memorable way as its performance.

From 0 to 62 mph (100 kph) with a manual transmission took 9.5 seconds and made the grade as "pretty speedy". The top speed of 125 mph (200 kph) corresponded to rival automotive upper-class standards. Chassis, brakes (discs all round), and the ball and nut type power steering gave this large car an amazing agility even on small country roads.

The 7 series was given four engines (170 to 218 bhp), and in 1984 the equipment was supplemented, as befitted its status, by ABS as standard. Armored 7 series cars for those "at risk", and a turbocharged 745i "Executive" for those with "ballistic salaries" concluded the range at the top. The 728 (with Bosch electronic fuel injection from 1979) achieved more than 100,000 units, if the production of BMW South Africa is included. In May 1986, BMW closed the initial and tasty 7 series chapter coded E23.

Nach dem BMW-spezifischen „Gesetz der Serie" (3er ab 1975, 5er ab 1972 und 6er ab 1976) wird die neue große Limousine, die im Mai 1977 erscheint, hierarchisch in der 7er Reihe – also ganz oben – angesiedelt. Die Zielrichtung ist eindeutig. Man will sich mit der S-Klasse von Mercedes-Benz messen. Besonders der 728i, dessen Sechszylindermotor 184 PS leistet, geht 1979 mit einem ausgewogenen Preis-Leistungs-Verhältnis auf die S-Klassen-Klientel los. 33 700 Mark sind für den luxuriösen Anderthalbtonner hinzublättern.

Das 2,8-Liter-Triebwerk erweist sich als elastisch und drehfreudig, kaum hörbar für die Passagiere. Kultiviert wie der Antrieb ist auch der Innenraum mit seinen fauteuilartigen Vordersitzen und der sofaähnlichen Rückbank, deren zwei Nackenstützen symbolisch andeuten, dass man sich hier nicht zu dritt hinzwängen sollte. Gediegenes Interieur und solide Verarbeitung tragen zum guten Ruf der Limousine ebenso bei wie die Fahrleistungen.

Die Beschleunigung in 9,5 Sekunden von 0 auf 100 Stundenkilometer (mit Schaltgetriebe) verdienen das Prädikat „recht flott". Auch die Spitze von 200 Stundenkilometern entspricht dem Niveau der automobilen Oberschicht. Fahrwerk, Bremsanlage – vorn und hinten Scheibenbremsen – und die Kugelmutter-Hydro-Servolenkung machen den großen Wagen auch auf kleinen Landstraßen recht beweglich.

Vier Motoren von 170 bis 218 PS werden der 7er Reihe spendiert, und 1984 kommt die standesgemäße Ausrüstung mit serienmäßigem ABS hinzu. Gepanzerte 7er für „Gefährdete" und ein 745i „Executive" für „unsinnig hoch Verdienende" runden die Palette nach oben ab. Der 728 (ab 1979 mit der elektronischen Benzineinspritzung von Bosch) bringt es einschließlich der Produktion von BMW Südafrika auf mehr als 100 000 Einheiten. Im Mai 1986 schließt BMW das erfreuliche Kapitel E23 ab.

Selon la loi des séries chez BMW (série 3 à partir de 1975, série 5 à partir de 1972 et série 6 à partir de 1976), la nouvelle grosse limousine qui fait son apparition en mai 1977 se situe, hiérarchiquement, dans la série 7 – autrement dit dans le haut de la gamme. L'objectif est sans équivoque : concurrencer la classe S de Mercedes-Benz. En particulier la 728i, dont le six-cylindres développe 184 ch, brigue les faveurs de la clientèle de la classe S, en 1979, avec un bon rapport qualité/prix. La luxueuse voiture de 1500 kg coûte 33 700 marks.

Souple, le moteur de 2,8 litres est friand de hauts régimes et reste pratiquement inaudible pour les passagers. Le « luxe » sous le capot se retrouve également dans l'habitacle avec des sièges avant comparables à des fauteuils et un véritable divan à l'arrière où deux appuie-tête indiquent qu'il est inutile de tenter d'y loger un troisième passager. Un intérieur soigné et une finition de qualité contribuent à asseoir la bonne réputation de la limousine au même titre que ses performances.

Dans cette catégorie, 9,5 secondes pour le 0 à 100 km/h (avec boîte manuelle) est un excellent résultat. La vitesse de pointe de 200 km/h, est, elle aussi, tout à fait à la hauteur dans cette catégorie de véhicules haut de gamme. Trains roulants, circuit de freinage (avec disques à l'avant et à l'arrière) et la direction hydraulique à écrou à billes confèrent une maniabilité inattendue à cette grosse voiture même sur des petites routes de campagne.

Quatre moteurs (170 à 218 ch) équipent la série 7 qui voit apparaître, en 1984, le montage en série d'un système ABS « digne de son rang ». Une série 7 blindée pour les hommes politiques et autres personnes « en danger » ainsi qu'une 745i « Executive » pour les « gros salaires » complètent la gamme vers le haut. La 728 (équipée d'une injection électronique Bosch à partir de 1979) est fabriquée à plus de 100 000 exemplaires, y compris la production de BMW Afrique du Sud. En mai 1986, BMW clos le passionnant chapitre E23.

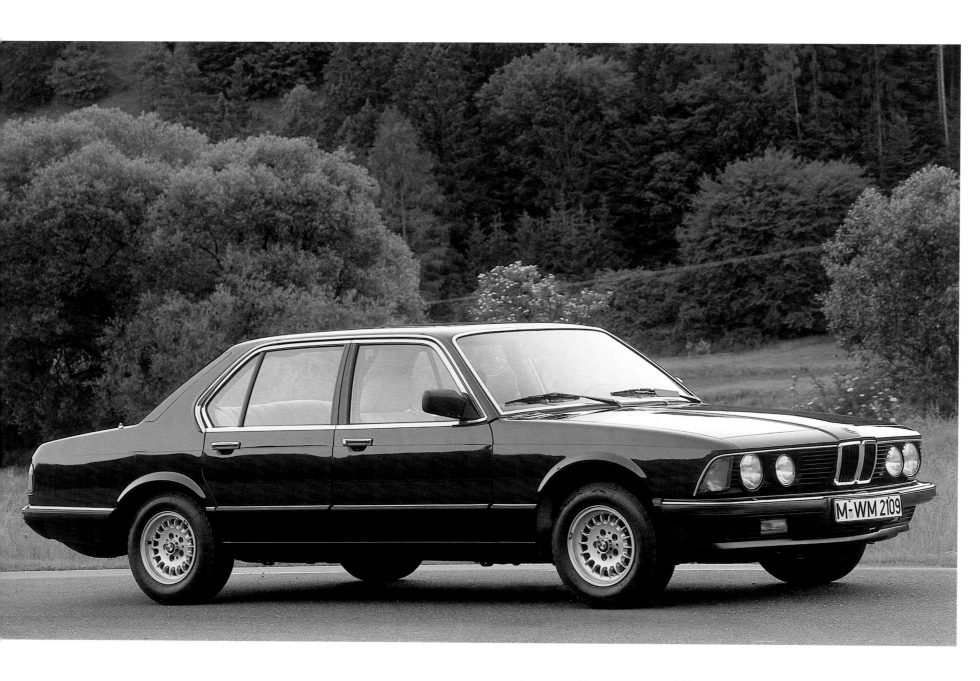

Launched in May 1977, the new BMW 7 series sedans were on an immediate collision course with the Mercedes-Benz S class. The 728i, which offered excellent value for money, was particularly successful. After a "learning process" in the 733i, the electronic fuel injection system, indicated on the type plate with the letter "i", was introduced to all 7 series models in 1979.

Die neuen Limousinen von BMW, die im Mai 1977 „vom Stapel gelassen" und als 7er eingestuft werden, schwimmen auf Kollisionskurs mit der S-Klasse von Mercedes-Benz. Besonders erfolgreich, da preiswert, ist der 728i. Die elektronische Benzineinspritzung, äußerlich dokumentiert durch das Kürzel „i" hinter der Typenbezeichnung, wird nach einem Reifeprozess im 733i ab 1979 in alle 7er Modelle implantiert.

Lancées en mai 1977, les nouvelles limousines de BMW, cataloguées série 7, viennent marcher sur les plates-bandes de la classe S de Mercedes-Benz. La moins chère, la 728i, est celle qui remporte le plus de succès. L'injection d'essence électronique, dont la présence est signalée par le « i » à l'arrière, équipe toutes les séries 7 à partir de 1979, après avoir fait ses preuves sur la 733i.

"Don't choose a special car, choose your own standpoint", was the BMW advertisement theme for the 6 series, which could be admired at the Geneva Motor Show in March 1976. The special car (coded E24) turned out to be an elegant 6 series coupé for the discriminating. This was a quality guarantee from BMW which its partner Karmann apparently failed to satisfy, since final assembly was transferred early in its production life to the BMW factory at Dingolfing. Karmann was left with the production of the bare body.

Once more it was clear that coupé buyers make sporting comparisons of engine performance. The 630CS (3-liter carburetor engine) and the 628CSi (2.8-liter injection engine) sold a total 9642 units between 1971 and 1987. The 633CSi, whose 3.2-liter unit delivered a more generous 197 bhp, earned 20,234 buyers. Plenty, but nothing when compared to the 635CSi: 51,564 examples were built with its 3.5-liter engine, rated from 211 bhp (catalytic converter) to 286 bhp (M version). German membership figures of the BMW 6 series club of Germany are correspondingly high.

Externally the CSi appearance was hardly spectacular and characterized more by classical lines, typical for a BMW coupé. Aerodynamic aids such as front and rear spoilers to cut lift at high speeds were probably appearance items, considering the original kerb weight of 3290 lbs (1495 kg).

The technical innovations were more convincing, particularly as far as the electronics were concerned. There were digital engine electronics with manual gear change down to 1000 rpm. Or there was the option of total electronic control of engine and transmission via a four-speed automatic transmission using electronics and hydraulics. Unfortunately, the entry of electronics to the dashboard could not be avoided either. There was an on-board computer which played along with an "SI Service Interval Indicator" and "EC Energy Control". At 16 miles to the gallon of Super (15 liters per 100 km) this was a joke.

Also mechanically there was progress to report for the CSi of the 6 series. The new coupés eventually combined the advantages of the 7 series' double-jointed transverse control arm front axle and new 13-degree trailing arm angles inherited from the 5 series. For a car of this price class the issue of an ABS system as standard was no longer worthy of comment as early as the 1980s. From 1987 onwards it was supplemented by a rear suspension self-leveling device.

The voluminous coupé proved surprisingly rapid in motor sport, and won the European touring car championships three times (1981, 1983 and 1986) as well as the German national title in 1983. There was no lack of power potential in the racing version of the 3.5-liter engine with two valves per cylinder, peaking at a best of 380 bhp, but frequently having to win against rivals with V12 motors or turbochargers.

"Entscheiden Sie sich nicht nur für ein besonderes Automobil, sondern auch für einen eigenen Standpunkt." Mit diesem Slogan wirbt BMW für die 6er Reihe, deren Vorbote auf dem Genfer Salon im März 1976 zu bestaunen ist. Das „besondere" Auto der Baureihe E24 entpuppt sich als elegantes Coupé für Anspruchsvolle. Für BMW ist dies eine Qualitätsverpflichtung, der Partner Karmann offenbar nicht genügt, denn die Endmontage wird ins BMW-Werk Dingolfing verlegt. Karmann bleibt die Fertigung der Rohkarosse.

Einmal mehr zeigt sich, dass Coupékäufer den Vergleich mit Sportwagen suchen, wenn es um die Triebwerksleistung geht. Der 630CS mit 3-Liter-Vergasermotor und der 628CSi mit 2,8-Liter-Einspritzmotor bringen es von 1971 bis 1987 zusammen auf 9642 verkaufte Einheiten. Der 633CSi, dessen 3,2-Liter-Aggregat mit etwas üppigeren 197 PS aufwartet, findet 20 234 Käufer. Dies sind große Absatzzahlen und doch nichts gegen den 635CSi: 51 564 dieser Coupés mit 3,5-Liter-Motoren, deren Leistung von 211 PS (mit Kat) bis 286 PS (M-Version) reicht, werden gebaut. Entsprechend hoch ist die Mitgliederzahl im „BMW 6er Club Deutschland e.V."

Das äußere Erscheinungsbild des CSi, kaum spektakulär und eher von klassischer Linienführung geprägt, ist typisch für ein Coupé. Aerodynamische Hilfen wie Front- und Heckspoiler für mehr Abtrieb bei höheren Geschwindigkeiten dürften angesichts von 1495 Kilo Leergewicht in erster Linie der Optik gedient haben.

Überzeugender sind die technischen Innovationen, besonders im Bereich der Elektronik: Digitale Motorelektronik mit Schubabschaltung bis hinunter zu 1000 Touren oder – auf Wunsch – eine elektronische Gesamtsteuerung für Motor und Getriebe durch eine Viergang-Automatik mit elektronisch-hydraulischer Arbeitsweise. Leider lässt sich

BMW 635CSi

der Einzug der Elektronik auch ins Armaturenbrett nicht vermeiden. Dort tobt sich ein Bordcomputer mit „SI Service Intervallanzeiger" und „EC Energie Control" aus – bei 15 Litern Super auf 100 Kilometer ein Witz!

Aber auch mechanisch gibt es beim CSi der 6er Reihe Fortschritte zu vermelden. Die neuen Coupés vereinen die Vorteile der Doppelgelenk-Federbeinvorderachse mit denen einer neuen 13-Grad-Schräglenkerhinterachse. Für einen Wagen dieser Preisklasse erübrigt sich schon in den achtziger Jahren die Frage nach einem serienmäßig eingebauten ABS-System. Ab 1987 kommt noch eine Niveauregelung hinzu.

Als erstaunlich wendig erweist sich das voluminöse Coupé im Motorsport. Dreimal immerhin holt es die Touren-wagen-Europameisterschaft (1981, 1983 und 1986) sowie 1983 den nationalen deutschen Titel. An Kraft mangelt es der Rennversion des 3,5-Liter-Motors mit zwei Ventilen pro Zylinder ohnehin nicht: 380 PS bringt er an die Hinterräder.

Ne choisissez pas une voiture spéciale, choisissez la vôtre », déclare le slogan publicitaire de BMW pour la série 6 dont on peut admirer le prototype au Salon de Genève en 1976. La voiture « spéciale », nom de code E24, se présente sous les traits d'un élégant coupé pour conducteur exigeant. Pour BMW, qualité oblige – une obligation à laquelle ne répond apparemment pas son partenaire Karmann, car le montage final est transféré à l'usine BMW de Dingolfing, Karmann conservant la fabri-cation de la carrosserie blanche.

Une fois de plus, on constate que les acheteurs de coupés ont les mêmes critères de jugement que les ache-teurs de voitures de sport en ce qui concerne la puissance des moteurs. La 630CS (moteur à carburateur de 3 litres) et la 628CSi (moteur à injection de 2,8 litres) ont été vendues à 9642 unités de 1971 à 1987. La 633CSi, dont le 3,2 litres, plus puissant, développe 197 ch fait 20 234 adeptes, ce qui est beaucoup mais peu comparé à la 635CSi : 51 564 de ces coupés à moteur de 3,5 litres, dont la puissance va de 211 ch (avec catalyseur) à 286 ch (version M), seront construits. Comme on peut l'imaginer, le nombre des adhérents au club allemand des BMW série 6 est élevé.

Rejetant le tape-à-l'œil et plutôt empreinte de classi-cisme, l'allure extérieure de la CSi est typique d'un coupé. Compte tenu d'un poids à vide de 1495 kg, les composants aérodynamiques tels que les becquets avant et arrière, censés générer la stabilité nécessaire à haute vitesse, n'auraient pas été d'une grande efficacité.

Les innovations techniques sont plus convaincantes, notamment dans le domaine de l'électronique : gestion moteur numérique avec coupure de l'alimentation jusqu'à moins de 1000 tr/min ou, sur demande, une gestion électronique globale du moteur et de la boîte de vitesses

grâce à une transmission automatique à quatre rapports avec commande électronique et hydraulique. Malheureuse-ment, l'omniprésence de l'électronique n'épargne pas le tableau de bord. Un ordinateur de bord, avec affichage des périodicités d'entretien et contrôle de la consommation, fait son apparition. À 15 litres de super aux 100 km, c'est une plaisanterie !

Mais, dans le domaine de la mécanique aussi, la version CSi de la série 6 peut se prévaloir d'avoir fait des progrès. Les nouveaux coupés allient les avantages d'un essieu avant à jambes élastiques à double articulation à ceux d'un nouveau train arrière à bras obliques inclinés de 13 degrés. Pour une voiture de cette catégorie de prix, la présence en série du système ABS dès les années 1980 s'impose. Un correcteur d'assiette s'y ajoute en 1987.

Le volumineux coupé s'avère étonnamment maniable en compétition et remporte trois fois le championnat d'Europe des voitures de tourisme (en 1981, 1983 et 1986) ainsi que le championnat d'Allemagne en 1983. La version course du moteur de 3,5 litres ne manque pas de chevaux avec ses deux soupapes par cylindre : elle a 380 ch sous le capot.

The orange dashboard illumination and displays are the outward signs that the computer age has dawned beneath the hood of the elegant 6 series coupé. 51,564 CSis were sold in total.

Armaturenbrett-Illuminierung in rot-orange und Displays signalisieren oberflächlich, dass unter der Haube des eleganten Coupés der 6er Reihe das Computerzeitalter Einzug gehalten hat. Vom 635 CSi werden 51 564 Wagen verkauft.

Les éclairages orange du tableau de bord et des écrans signalent au premier coup d'œil que l'ordinateur et les microprocesseurs commencent à se propager sous le capot de l'élégant coupé de la série 6. 51 564 exemplaires de la 635CSi seront vendus.

The 3.5-liter power unit generates 218 bhp without the catalytic converter. Including its auxiliaries, the engine fills the 635CSi's engine space, though leaving sufficient space for the ever-increasing electronics. The age of digital motoring is heralded by such features as total electronic control of engine and transmission.

Das 3,5-Liter-Triebwerk mit 218 PS ohne Kat und seine Nebenaggregate füllen den Motorraum des 635CSi, lassen aber genügend Platz für die zunehmende Elektronisierung, beginnend bei der digitalen Motorelektronik mit Schubabschaltung bis hin zur elektronischen Gesamtsteuerung von Motor und Getriebe.

Le moteur de 3,5 litres et 218 ch sans catalyseur emplit le compartiment moteur de la 635CSi avec ses organes, mais laisse assez de place pour l'électronique qui se généralise, de la gestion moteur numérique avec coupure de l'alimentation à la gestion électronique complète du moteur et de la boîte de vitesses.

The M 635CSi, launched at the 1983 Frankfurt Motor Show, is both sporty and lavishly appointed, as befits a 155 mph (250 kph) coupé costing more than a Porsche S. The variety of accessories is impressive, and ranges from automatic electric controls and firmly-upholstered adjustable leather seats, whose adjustment options include the actual length of the seating surface, to the three-spoke sports steering wheel, also individually adjustable.

Im M 635CSi – Premiere auf der IAA 1983 in Frankfurt – geht es sportlich und nobel zu. Schließlich kostet das 250 km/h schnelle Coupé mehr als ein Porsche S. Auffällig sind die vielen Accessoires, die elektrischen Bedienungshilfen und die straff gepolsterten Ledersitze, deren Einstellmöglichkeiten auch die Länge der Sitzfläche einschließen. Ebenfalls individuell einstellbar ist das Dreispeichen-Sportlenkrad.

La M 635CSi, dont le lancement a lieu au Salon de l'Automobile de Francfort en 1983, est aussi sportive qu'élégante. Ce coupé capable d'atteindre les 250 km/h coûte d'ailleurs plus cher qu'une Porsche S. Il se distingue notamment par ses nombreux accessoires, ses commandes électriques automatiques et des sièges cuir capitonnés et fermes, dont les coussins sont réglables. Le volant sport à trois branches se règle selon les besoins du conducteur.

BMW 635CSi

The M 635CSi power unit was borrowed from the M1. The six-cylinder four-valve engine with light alloy cross-flow cylinder heads generates a mighty 286 bhp at 6500 rpm, giving the one-and-a-half ton coupé stunning performance figures, for example 0 to 125 mph (200 kph) in just 30 seconds, a good 10 seconds less than the Mercedes 500 SEC.

Dem M1 entlehnt ist die Kraftquelle des M 635CSi. Der Sechszylinder-Vierventiler mit Querstromzylinderkopf aus Leichtmetall mobilisiert bei 6500/min stattliche 286 PS, die dem anderthalb Tonnen schweren Coupé zu beachtlichen Fahrleistungen verhelfen. Von 0 auf 200 km/h benötigt es knapp 30 Sekunden, gut 10 Sekunden weniger als ein Mercedes 500 SEC.

Le moteur de la M 635CSi s'inspire de celui de la M1. Le six-cylindres à quatre soupapes avec culasse cross-flow en alliage léger ne développe pas moins de 286 ch à 6500 tr/min qui confèrent de brillantes performances à ce coupé de 1500 kg : à peine 30 secondes pour le 0 à 200 km/h, 10 secondes de moins qu'une Mercedes 500 SEC !

BMW M1

Motor sport as a creative platform for engineers and the source of many innovative solutions for the series: that is how BMW Motorsport GmbH, founded in 1972, saw its task, which of course also had its commercial aspects. Ambitious plans, for the BMW personnel in Munich's Preußenstraße wanted more than simply to adapt production cars to the racetrack. With code E26, they certainly succeeded in proving their capabilities through a unique high-tech development.

This internal company code concealed a thoroughbred sports car. To use the car in motor sport, BMW had to prove that 400 road vehicles had been built within a two-year period. And that was their weak point. Due to a lack of capacity of their own, BMW trustingly turned to the sports car manufacturer Lamborghini, a thoroughly competent partner. But Lamborghini was hit by financial problems shortly after the first BMW prototype was completed.

BMW reacted quickly and switched the project to Baur coachworks in Stuttgart. As early as the Paris Motor Show of 1978, the E26 development, designed by Giorgio Guigiaro, was presented to the world as the M1. With the M1, BMW Motorsport GmbH created for itself a prestige visiting card for all subsequent products which utilized the prefix "M".

The M1, a mid-engine sports car without frills, was too functional for its target group. That certain something of a Ferrari was missing, although performance was adequate: six seconds from 0 to 62 mph (100 kph) and a top speed of 162 mph (260 kph). The four-valve M88/1 engine also proved itself durable, offering 277 bhp from a volume of 3.5 liters and 495 bhp for the racing version. Another technical treat was the chassis with independent suspension for each wheel and internally ventilated disc brakes.

Formula 1 had to provide this piece of BMW sports equipment with an adequate forum. Quickly – as always

when the financial conditions are right – the godfather of Grand Prix racing, Bernie Ecclestone, and the BMW sports boss, Jochen Neerpasch, came to an agreement. BMW M1 races were to be held on Saturdays before the Grands Prix in Europe.

It was compulsory for all F1 drivers (except Ferrari and Renault) that the first five in Friday's F1 qualifying participate in the prestigious BMW series, called Procar. This was "huge fun" (said Procar driver Hans Stuck), and in 1979 and 1980 sometimes made the pulses of the crowd beat faster than the premier league Grand Prix on Sunday.

Altogether 50 racing versions of the M1 were built, partly with the assistance of Project Four Racing and Osella. Then there was a beefy group 5 version with turbochargers and approximately 900 bhp. All in all, the minimum required by the world association was met, but this limited number is probably the reason why the M1 is traded nowadays at higher prices than its new car values back then.

Die 1972 gegründete BMW Motorsport GmbH definiert sich als kreative Bühne für Ingenieure und Ausgangspunkt vieler innovativer Lösungen für die Serie – eine hehre Aufgabe, die natürlich auch kommerzielle Aspekte hat. Die BMW-Mannen in Münchens Preußenstraße wollen mehr, als nur Serienwagen die Tauglichkeit für das Rennparkett zu verleihen. Dem selbstgestellten Anspruch, mit eigener High-Tech-Entwicklung einen eindrucksvollen Leistungsnachweis zu erbringen, ist die Abteilung mit dem E26 sicherlich gerecht geworden.

Hinter diesem firmeninternen Kürzel verbirgt sich ein reinrassiger Sportwagen. Um diesen im Motorsport einsetzen zu können, muss der Hersteller nachweisen können, dass er innerhalb von zwei Jahren mindestens 400 Straßenfahrzeuge dieses Typs gebaut hat. Und da liegt der Schwachpunkt. Mangels eigener Fertigungskapazitäten wendet sich BMW vertrauensvoll an den Sportwagenhersteller Lamborghini, einen durchaus kompetenten Partner, der jedoch kurz nach Fertigstellung der ersten Prototypen in wirtschaftliche Schwierigkeiten gerät.

BMW schaltet schnell und überträgt der Karosseriefabrik Baur in Stuttgart das Projekt. Bereits auf dem Pariser Autosalon 1978 wird der von Giorgio Guigiaro entworfene Wagen der Weltöffentlichkeit als M1 präsentiert. Mit dem M1 schafft sich die BMW Motorsport GmbH das Aushängeschild für alle Produkte, die sich hinter dem Buchstaben „M" verbergen.

Der M1, ein Mittelmotorsportwagen ohne Schnörkel, wirkt auf die Zielgruppe zu funktional. Das gewisse Etwas eines Ferrari fehlt, obwohl die Leistungen adäquat sind: sechs Sekunden von 0 auf 100 Stundenkilometer und eine Spitze von 260 Stundenkilometer. Auch in puncto Standfestigkeit bewährt sich das Vierventiler-Triebwerk vom Typ M88/1. Aus 3,5 Liter Hubraum werden 277 PS geholt und

495 PS für die Rennversion. Als technischer Leckerbissen erweist sich das Fahrwerk mit Einzelradaufhängungen und innenbelüfteten Scheibenbremsen.

Um diesem Sportgerät das angemessene Forum zu bieten, muss die Formel 1 herhalten. Schnell – wie immer, wenn die finanziellen Konditionen stimmen – werden sich Grand-Prix-Pate Bernie Ecclestone und BMW-Sportchef Jochen Neerpasch einig. An den Samstagen vor den europäischen Grand Prix soll ein BMW-M1-Rennen angesetzt werden. Bei der ohnehin hochkarätig besetzten Serie, genannt Procar, sollen jeweils die fünf Trainingsschnellsten aus dem Freitagstraining der Formel 1 starten. Ausgenommen sind lediglich die Fahrer von Ferrari und Renault. Diese Serie ist eine „Mordsgaudi", so Procar-Pilot Hans Stuck, und lässt 1979 und 1980 die Zuschauerherzen manchmal höher schlagen als der am Sonntag folgende Lauf der höchsten Klasse des Motorsports.

50 Rennversionen, teilweise unter Mithilfe von Project Four Racing und Osella, werden gebaut. Dazu kommt eine bullige Gruppe-5-Version mit Turboladern und rund 900 PS. Insgesamt wird das vom Weltverband geforderte Minimum gerade eben erfüllt, und deswegen liegt es wohl an dieser begrenzten Stückzahl, dass der M1 heute zu Preisen gehandelt wird, die weit über seinem damaligen Neuwert liegen.

La compétition automobile est un véritable espace créatif pour les ingénieurs et donne naissance à de nombreuses innovations pour les futures séries : pour la BMW Motorsport GmbH, fondée en 1972, cette stratégie comporte, naturellement, aussi des aspects commerciaux. Les hommes de BMW de la Preussenstrasse veulent plus que conférer à une voiture de série l'aptitude à la compétition. Avec la E26, ils sont assurément parvenus à apporter la preuve de leur savoir-faire avec une débauche de haute technologie.

Derrière ce nom de code se dissimule, en effet, une voiture de sport racée, un véritable pur-sang. Pour pouvoir l'engager en compétition, il faut en avoir construit 400 en version routière sur une période de deux ans. Et c'est là que le bât blesse. Ne possédant pas les capacités de production nécessaires, BMW se tourne en toute confiance vers le constructeur de voitures de sport italien Lamborghini, un partenaire compétent, mais qui, peu après la sortie des premiers prototypes, doit faire face à des difficultés économiques.

BMW n'hésite pas longtemps avant de confier le projet au carrossier Baur, à Stuttgart. Dès le Salon de l'Automobile de Paris en 1978, la M1 dessinée par Giorgio Guigiaro est présentée au monde entier. Avec la M1, la BMW Motorsport GmbH s'offre une belle carte de visite pour tous les produits qui arboreront plus tard le « M » magique.

La M1, une voiture de sport à moteur central sans fioritures, est trop fonctionnelle pour ses acheteurs potentiels. Il lui manque le « petit quelque chose en plus » d'une Ferrari bien que ses prestations n'aient rien à lui envier : 6 secondes pour passer de 0 à 100 km/h et une vitesse de pointe de 260 km/h. En termes de fiabilité, le quatre-soupapes M88/1 est, lui aussi, au-dessus de tout soupçon. Pour une cylindrée de 3,5 litres, il développe 277 ch, et même 495 ch dans la version course. Elle est aussi d'un grand raffinement technique : les trains roulants comportent une suspension à roues indépendantes et des freins à disques ventilés.

La seule scène digne de cette voiture de sport est la Formule 1. Rapidement – comme toujours lorsque les questions d'argent sont réglées –, le parrain de la Formule 1, Bernie Ecclestone, et le directeur de course de BMW, Jochen Neerpasch, se mettent d'accord. Une course de BMW M1 aura lieu le samedi, avant chaque Grand Prix de Formule 1 organisé en Europe. Tous les pilotes (sauf ceux de Ferrari et de Renault) doivent obligatoirement participer à cette course prestigieuse baptisée Procar dès lors qu'ils figurent parmi les cinq premiers des essais du vendredi. Pour le pilote Procar Hans Stuck, c'est une « partie de rigolade » et, en 1979 et 1980, cette course fait parfois plus frémir les spectateurs que la catégorie reine de la compétition automobile qui a lieu le dimanche.

Cinquante versions course, dont certaines avec l'aide de Project Four Racing et d'Osella, seront construites – sans compter une puissante version du groupe 5 à turbocompresseurs d'environ 900 ch. En fin de compte, BMW réussit tout juste à respecter les exigences de la Fédération mondiale et c'est bien en raison de ce nombre limité que, aujourd'hui, la M1 affiche une cote plus élevée que son prix de vente en tant que voiture neuve.

BMW M1

Italian bodywork man Giorgio Guigiaro was responsible for the design of the M1. The front of the M1 is reminiscent of Frenchman Paul Bracq's 1972 prototype.

Für das Design des M1 ist der italienische Karosserie-Künstler Giorgio Guigiaro verantwortlich. Die Front des M1 erinnert an den Prototypen des Franzosen Paul Bracq aus dem Jahr 1972.

Le carrossier italien Giorgio Guigiaro signe le design de la M1. L'avant rappelle le prototype du Français Paul Bracq de 1972.

The M1 allowed BMW to show its rivals a clean pair of heels. It provided BMW Motorsport GmbH with a mobile billboard for all its products bearing the letter "M" in their names. The mid-engine automobile is a no-frills machine, with form very much secondary to function. High tech, particularly in the chassis area, and the reliability of the power unit are the dominant factors. The four-valve straight-six M88/1 engine produces 277 bhp (as against the 495 bhp of the racing version). And the cockpit would warm the cockles of any sports car driver. What more could the enthusiast want?

Der Konkurrenz das Heck zu zeigen, ist BMW dank des M1 durchaus gelungen. Mit dem M1 schafft sich die BMW Motorsport GmbH ein Aushängeschild für all ihre Produkte, die sich mit dem „M" schmücken. Der Mittelmotorwagen hat rundum keine Schnörkel, da seine Form der Funktion untergeordnet ist. High-Tech, besonders beim Fahrwerk, und Zuverlässigkeit des Triebwerks dominieren. Der Vierventilmotor, ein Reihensechszylinder des Typs M88/1, aktiviert 277 PS – bei der Rennversion sind es 495 PS. Das Cockpit: Sportfahrer-Herz, was willst Du mehr?

Faire manger la poussière à la concurrence, BMW y est parfaitement arrivée avec la M1. Avec cette voiture, BMW Motorsport GmbH donne du prestige à tous les produits qui arboreront ultérieurement le célèbre « M ». La voiture à moteur central possède une carrosserie sans fioritures, fonctionnelle avant tout. La haute technologie, en particulier pour les trains roulants, et la fiabilité de son moteur sont les éléments prédominants. 277 ch – mais 495 ch pour la version course – sont libérés par le moteur à quatre soupapes, un six-cylindres en ligne du type M88/1. Le cockpit satisfait tous les amoureux de la compétition. Qu'espérer de plus ?

Kyalami, South Africa, 1983 Grand Prix: Alain Prost, Renault-Turbo, appears destined for the Formula 1 world championship. But the champagne mood of the French team goes up in a puff of turbocharger smoke. Not Renault, which pioneered Grand Prix turbo engine technology, but Brabham and BMW seized the prize as the "first Formula 1 turbo world champion" in motor sport history. Brazilian Nelson Piquet became the new world champion – if only by a narrow margin.

Piquet described the success of the Brabham-BMW cooperation: "A high level of technical expertise and professionalism. A team of such efficient mechanics that I consider them my life insurance, and a warm relationship between me, designer Gordon Murray, the team, and engine builder Paul Rosche."

Rosche, nicknamed "camshaft Paul" by insiders, had managed the impossible task of conjuring a standard four-cylinder block into an engine which in qualifying produced such performance that it went off the dial of the engine brake in Munich. That meant this M12/13 miracle engine produced more than 1280 bhp at full turbo-boost.

With newly developed electronic engine management for ignition and injection, Bosch contributed an innovation in monitoring which – a first – featured trackside telemetry. Yet no electronics help if the foundation is wrong. But quality was so solid from Rosche and his team that it could withstand 11,000 rpm and a temperature of 1100 degrees centigrade without complaint.

Special fuel from the BASF subsidiary Wintershall with a very high anti-knock value enabled the production of additional power. BMW also notched up a PR success: it took barely two years from the decision to develop a Formula 1 engine to the world championship title – an achievement hitherto never attained.

Murray and his collaborator David North had succeeded in building unusually effective "ground effect" aerodynamics. The BT52, developed from the BT49, assembled an homogenous unit of chassis layout, driver position, aerodynamics and fine detail. This was a great challenge for the suppliers. A small example: Murray commissioned not only one, but three companies (Weismann, Alfa Romeo and Getrag) to work on the development of the transmission on a Hewland base, to choose the best.

That only the best materials were up to Murray's standards is shown by the use of carbon fiber panels and a special aluminium alloy for the monocoque, plus driveshafts of high strength alloys, special steels and miniature components of durable light alloys.

The result was a "fantastic" engine with a perfect racing car, guided by a gifted driving talent. No one should have been surprised by the world championship.

Kyalami, Südafrika, Grand-Prix-Finale 1983: Alain Prost, Renault-Turbo, scheint der Titel sicher zu sein. Doch die Champagnerlaune der französischen Equipe verpufft in einem Turboladerschaden. Nicht Renault, Vorreiter der Turbo-Motorentechnik in der Formel 1, sondern Brabham und BMW ernten den Ruhm des ersten „Turbo-Weltmeistertitels" in der Motorsportgeschichte. Der Brasilianer Nelson Piquet ist – wenn auch mit knappem Vorsprung – neuer Champion.

Piquet skizziert den Erfolg der Brabham-BMW-Liaison folgendermaßen: „Hohes technisches Niveau und Professionalität, eine so gut aufeinander eingespielte Mechanikertruppe, dass ich sie als meine Lebensversicherung betrachte, und eine herzliche Beziehung zwischen mir, Konstrukteur Gordon Murray, dem Team und Motorenmacher Paul Rosche."

Rosche, von Insidern „Nocken-Paule" genannt, hat das Unglaubliche geschafft, aus einem Serien-Vierzylinderblock ein Triebwerk zu zaubern, das im Endstadium mehr leistet, als die Messskala der Motorbremse in München anzeigt. Das heißt, dass dieser M12/13-Wundermotor mehr als 1280 PS bei vollem Turbo-Boost freisetzt.

Mit einem neuentwickelten elektronischen Motormanagement für Zündung und Einspritzung steuert Bosch eine Innovation bei, die telemetrisch – ein Novum – überwacht wird. Doch alle Elektronik nützt nichts, wenn die Basis nicht stimmt. Diese ist bei Rosche jedoch derart solide, dass sie klaglos 11 000 Umdrehungen pro Minute und 1100 Grad Erwärmung aushält.

Spezialbenzin der BASF-Tochter Wintershall, dessen Klopffestigkeit weit über jener handelsüblicher Kraftstoffe liegt, ermöglicht die Entfaltung zusätzlicher Power. BMW verbucht auch einen PR-Erfolg: Knapp zwei Jahre verstreichen von der Entscheidung, ein Formel-1-Triebwerk zu

Brabham BMW BT52

entwickeln bis zum Weltmeistertitel – eine bis dahin unerreichte Glanzleistung.

Kongenial ist das Chassis. Murray und seinem Mitarbeiter David North ist ein ungewöhnlich gut funktionierendes „ground effect car" gelungen. Der BT52, konsequent aus dem BT49 weiterentwickelt, bildet eine homogene Einheit aus Chassis-Layout, Fahrerposition, Aerodynamik und Feinarbeit im Detail. Da sind natürlich auch die Zulieferer gefordert. Kleines Beispiel: Murray setzt gleich drei Firmen auf die Weiterentwicklung des Getriebes auf Hewland-Basis an – Weismann, Alfa Romeo und Getrag –, um aus dem Vollen schöpfen zu können.

Dass nur die besten Materialien seinen Ansprüchen genügen, bezeugt die Verwendung von so futuristischen Werkstoffen wie Kohlefaserplatten und einer speziellen Aluminiumlegierung beim Monocoque, Antriebswellen aus hochlegiertem Edelstahl und Kleinstteilen aus stabilem Leichtmetall.

Das Ergebnis ist ein „Bombenmotor" in einem perfekten Rennwagen, pilotiert von einem begnadeten Fahrertalent. Wen wundert da die Weltmeisterkrone?

Kyalami, Afrique du Sud, finale du championnat du monde 1983 : Alain Prost, sur Renault-Turbo, part favori pour remporter la victoire. Mais l'équipe française qui se voyait déjà sabler le champagne voit ses espoirs s'évanouir avec l'explosion d'un turbocompresseur. Ce n'est donc pas Renault, le pionnier de la suralimentation en Formule 1, mais Brabham et BMW qui reçoivent le premier titre de « champion du monde de l'ère des turbos » dans l'histoire de la compétition automobile. Le Brésilien Nelson Piquet est sacré champion du monde, mais avec une infime avance.

« Une technicité élevée et un grand professionnalisme, une équipe de mécaniciens parfaitement rodés à la tâche que je considérais comme mon assurance-vie et des rapports cordiaux entre moi-même, l'ingénieur Gordon Murray, l'équipe et le motoriste Paul Rosche, déclare Piquet, expliquent le succès du mariage Brabham-BMW. »

Paul Rosche, que les initiés surnomment « Paul la came » a réussi l'impossible : transformer un bloc de quatre-cylindres de série en un moteur qui, à son stade ultime, délivre plus de chevaux que le banc d'essai de Munich n'est capable d'en afficher. Cela signifie que ce merveilleux moteur M12/13 développe plus de 1280 ch à plein régime.

Bosch apporte son savoir-faire avec une toute nouvelle gestion électronique du moteur pour l'allumage et l'injection, qui – c'est une nouveauté – est surveillée par télémétrie. Mais toute l'électronique ne sert à rien si le moteur n'est pas bon. Or, avec Rosche, celui-ci est inébranlable, il supporte sans broncher 11 000 tr/min et 1100 degrés.

Un carburant spécial produit par Wintershall, une filiale de BASF, avec une limite de détonation très élevée permet d'obtenir quelques chevaux supplémentaires. Mais BMW remporte aussi un succès médiatique : il s'est écoulé à peine deux ans entre la décision de construire le moteur

de Formule 1 et l'accession au titre de champion du monde – une brillante performance jusqu'alors inégalée.

Tout aussi génial est le châssis. Murray et son collaborateur David North ont signé une « voiture à effet de sol » fonctionnant à la perfection. La BT52, développée à partir de la BT49, présente un châssis homogène, une position de conduite, des lignes aérodynamiques et des détails raffinés. Mais les sous-traitants ont aussi dû jouer le jeu. Un petit exemple : pour perfectionner la boîte de vitesses (à l'origine une Hewland), Murray fait simultanément appel à trois firmes – Weismann, Alfa Romeo et Getrag – afin de choisir la meilleure.

Seuls les meilleurs matériaux satisfont aux critères de Gordon Murray, ce que prouvent l'utilisation de panneaux de fibre de carbone et un alliage d'aluminium spécial pour la monocoque, des arbres de transmission en alliage spécial et de minuscules pièces en alliage léger indestructible.

Résultat : ce moteur est une « bombe » dans une voiture de course parfaite, conduite par un pilote béni des dieux. Qui s'étonnera donc qu'il remporte le titre de champion du monde ?

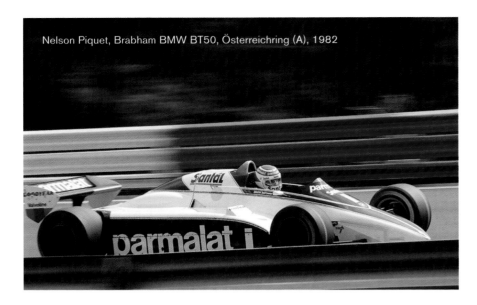

Nelson Piquet, Brabham BMW BT50, Österreichring (A), 1982

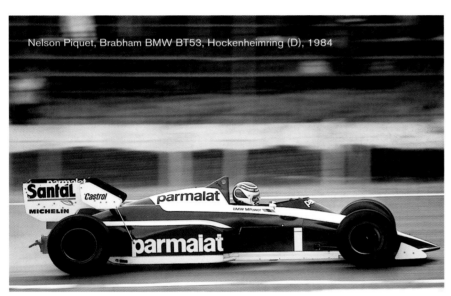

Nelson Piquet, Brabham BMW BT53, Hockenheimring (D), 1984

Nelson Piquet, Brabham BMW BT54, Paul Ricard (F), 1985

Brabham BMW BT52

Start number 1 for the first "turbo world champion" in the history of motor sport: Nelson Piquet in a Brabham BMW BT53 of 1984.

Startnummer 1 für den ersten „Turbo-Weltmeister" der Motorsportgeschichte: Nelson Piquet im Brabham BMW BT53 von 1984.

Le premier champion du monde de l'ère des turbos dans l'histoire de la compétition automobile : Nelson Piquet dans la Brabham BMW BT53 de 1984.

The exhaust system, consisting of V2A steel pipes with single KKK turbocharger and relief valve (left). This turbocharger can withstand 2.9 bar boost pressure and 1100° centigrade. The racing version of these 1.5-liter "miracle engines" can easily achieve 800 bhp. The actual top performance of this engine, based on a production four-cylinder, lies off the 1280 bhp scale of the BMW test unit.

Das Auspuffsystem aus V2A-Stahl mit dem KKK-Einfach-Turbolader und dem Abblasventil (links). 2,9 bar Ladedruck und 1100° Celsius hält dieser Turbolader aus. Die 1,5-Liter-„Wundermotoren" der Rennversion kommen locker auf 800 PS. Die tatsächliche Leistung des Triebwerks, basierend auf einem Serien-Vierzylinderblock, liegt jenseits der 1280-PS-Messskala der BMW-Motorbremse.

Le système d'échappe-ment en tubes d'acier inoxydable avec le turbo KKK à un étage et la soupape de décharge (à gauche). Ce turbo-compresseur résiste à une pression de suralimentation de 2,9 bars et à une température de 1100° C. En configuration course, les incroyables moteurs de 1,5 litre développent allègrement 800 ch. On ignore la puissance maximum développée par ce moteur dérivé d'un bloc quatre-cylindres de série, en tout cas elle dépasse les 1280 ch de l'échelle de mesure du banc d'essai des moteurs de BMW.

Brabham BMW BT52

With its touring designation, BMW really presented a station wagon in August 1987: not the blend of coupé with a rear hatch and station wagon sedan, as had been the case for the 1971 touring on an 02 base. The customer demand was there, and thus deliveries started in March 1988 with four engine variants. There was also a 325iX, a designation which was neither secretive nor arbitrarily chosen.

The "X" meant 4-wheel drive (4x4). BMW had previously introduced this 325 name once in their 1939 standard light military vehicle for the German Army. The principle of driving all four wheels, revived by BMW in 1985, made more sense in a station wagon than a sedan – unless, of course, it was for a motor sport application.

Like all touring models, the 325iX was equipped with double-tube shock absorbers, disc brakes all round, headlights with ellipsoid dipped beams and a catalytic converter. The 170 bhp of the six-cylinder engine were sufficient to give the car a top speed of 130 mph (208 kph).

At the core of the four-wheel drive principle was a central transfer case with planetary differential and visco-locks. The additional power to the front axle was transmitted by a side drive, via a sprocket chain, and secondary shaft. A total 63 percent of power went to the rear axle and the remaining 37 percent drove the front wheels.

The 4x4 drive equipment, at about 176 lbs (80 kg), weighed heavily on the purchase price. The "X" cost an additional 8500 marks. Unsurprisingly production of the 4x4 drive version accounted for less than three percent of the touring output, nevertheless 5273 "X"s were made. This is an indication of the success of the first station wagon from BMW.

In terms of equipment it was anything but your typical "workhorse". That is also why a loading rail directly above the bumper was left off. The rear lights only allowed sufficient opening for, say, golf bags, prams or a collapsible bicycle. Bulky chests, workmen's tools or building materials should kindly be transported by other means. That, at least, is how those who love this car see it – the speedy "three".

Mit dem touring stellt BMW im August 1987 einen echten Kombi vor, kein Verschnitt aus Coupé mit Heckklappe und Kombilimousine wie das gleichnamige Fahrzeug von 1971. Die entsprechende Nachfrage besteht, und so läuft im März 1988 die Auslieferung mit vier Motorvarianten an. Es gibt auch einen 325iX, eine Bezeichnung, die weder geheimnisvoll, noch x-beliebig gewählt worden ist.

Das „X" steht für Allradantrieb. Den hatte es bei BMW schon einmal gegeben: 1939 und ebenfalls bei einem 325er, dem leichten Einheits-Pkw für die Wehrmacht. Das von BMW 1985 wieder aufgegriffene Prinzip des Vierradantriebs macht bei einem Kombi eher Sinn als bei einer Limousine, es sei denn, man will diese im Motorsport einsetzen.

Wie alle Touringmodelle ist der 325iX mit Doppelrohr-Gasdruckdämpfern, Scheibenbremsen rundum, Scheinwerfern mit Ellipsoid-Abblendlicht und einem Katalysator ausgerüstet. Die 170 PS des Sechszylindertriebwerks reichen aus, um dem Wagen eine Spitzengeschwindigkeit von 208 Stundenkilometern zu verleihen.

Kernpunkt des Allradprinzips ist ein zentrales Verteilergetriebe mit Planetendifferential und Visco-Sperren. Der zusätzliche Antrieb zur Vorderachse wird durch einen Seitentrieb über Zahnkette und Nebenwelle erreicht. Zu 63 Prozent geht die Kraft an die Hinterachse, die restlichen 37 Prozent treiben die Vorderräder an.

Die rund 80 Kilo Allradtechnik liegen dem Käufer im wahrsten Sinne des Wortes schwer auf der Tasche: 8500 Mark Aufpreis kostet das „X". Kein Wunder also, dass der Produktionsanteil der Allradler unter den Tourings keine drei Prozent ausmacht. Absolut gesehen sind es immerhin 5273 „X". Daran lässt sich ermessen, wie erfolgreich der erste Kombi von BMW insgesamt ist.

BMW 325iX touring

Der Ausstattung nach ist er alles andere als ein typischer „Lastesel". Und deshalb wurde auch auf eine Ladekante direkt über der Stoßstange verzichtet. Die Heckleuchten lassen nur eine Durchreiche frei, etwa für Golfbags, Kinderwagen oder ein Klappfahrrad. Sperrige Kisten, Handwerkerzubehör oder Baumaterialien sollen gefälligst mit anderen Transportmitteln befördert werden. So sehen es jedenfalls diejenigen, die ihn lieben – den „flotten 3er".

BMW dévoile en août 1987 un authentique break : qui ne ressemble en rien à la première voiture du même nom présentée en 1971. Les commandes ne se font pas attendre et c'est ainsi que la commercialisation commence en mars 1988 avec quatre motorisations différentes. Il existe aussi une 325iX, une dénomination qui n'est pas fortuite.

Le « X » signifie traction intégrale. BMW avait déjà utilisé ce numéro 325 en 1939 pour une voiture militaire légère destinée à l'armée allemande. Reprendre, en 1985, le principe des quatre roues motrices a plus de sens avec un break qu'avec une berline, à moins que l'on ne veuille engager celle-ci en compétition.

Comme toutes les touring, la 325iX possède des amortisseurs à gaz bitube, des freins à disques sur les quatre roues, des feux de croisement ellipsoïdaux et un pot catalytique. Les 170 ch du six-cylindres suffisent pour donner à la voiture une vitesse de pointe de 208 km/h.

La clé de voûte de la traction intégrale est une boîte de distribution centrale avec différentiel universel et viscocoupleurs. La prise de force supplémentaire pour l'essieu avant s'effectue sur le côté à l'aide d'une chaîne dentée et d'un arbre secondaire. 63 % de la puissance dégagée sont dirigés vers l'essieu arrière, les 37 % restants entraînant les roues avant.

Les quelque 80 kg de traction intégrale pèsent aussi sur le prix d'achat : la « X » coûte 8500 marks de plus que la version normale. Rien d'étonnant, donc, à ce que les ventes de quatre roues motrices parmi les touring ne dépassent pas 3 %, ce qui se traduit tout de même par 5273 « X » vendues. Ces chiffres indiquent le succès remporté par le premier break de BMW.

Son aménagement est tout sauf banal. Et c'est d'ailleurs la raison pour laquelle on renonce au seuil de chargement placé directement au-dessus du pare-chocs. Les optiques arrière n'autorisent en effet qu'une découpe de coffre limitée – par exemple pour un équipement de golf, une poussette ou un vélo pliant. Pour le transport d'objets encombrants, vous choisirez un autre véhicule. Telle est en tout cas la philosophie de ceux qui l'adorent, cette rapide série 3.

BMW identified a market niche and, to fill it, constructed a pure estate car based on the 3 series. The 325iX touring is driven by a 170 bhp engine and a transfer gear providing power to all axles. The harmonious parallel roof and belt line give the touring an interesting appearance, while the BBS design alloy wheels lend a sporty note. The design of the tailgate adds to the torsional rigidity, but is a nuisance when it comes to loading the trunk.

Eine Marktlücke: BMW baut, basierend auf dem 3er, einen reinen Kombi. Der 325iX touring wird von 170 PS über ein zentrales Verteilergetriebe an allen Achsen angetrieben. Der harmonische „Parallelschwung" aus Dach- und Gürtellinie macht den touring auch optisch interessant, wobei die Leichtmetallräder im BBS-Design eine sportliche Note hinzufügen. Das Heck, dessen Rücklichter wie bei der Limousine angeordnet sind, dient der Verwindungssteifigkeit, ist beim Beladen aber eher hinderlich.

BMW découvre un marché de niche et, sur la base de la série 3, construit un authentique break : la 325iX touring de 170 ch possède une traction intégrale avec boîte de distribution centrale. Les lignes harmonieuses du toit et de la carrosserie donnent à la touring une esthétique intéressante, tandis que les jantes en alliage BBS lui confèrent une touche de sportivité. La découpe du coffre est favorable à la rigidité torsionnelle, mais n'est guère pratique.

BMW 318i Cabrio

"Decapitating" BMW bodies and adapting them to open cars was fashionable at Baur in Stuttgart. Installing a Targa rollbar, effectively as a replacement to the B-pillar, also was a practical Baur tradition. At the Frankfurt Motor Show in September 1985, BMW demonstrated its willingness to do its own "beheading" to produce a full convertible. This car, which was much more elegant than the equivalent Baur version, was initially available based on the 325i and 320.

It was only in 1990 – the new E36 3 series was poised on the brink of volume production – that the 318i was accompanied by a convertible version. The 318i with the new four-cylinder engine had a three-way catalytic converter and a lambda oxygen sensor. This was a sensible solution, particularly since the 113 bhp seemed to be perfectly capable of running for 21.5 miles on a gallon of normal lead-free petrol (11 liters per 100 km).

The price (less than 50,000 marks, back in 1993) was also attractive for those convertibles fans for whom a 325i was simply out of reach. The pleasure to be gained from driving under an open sky was never clouded with the four-cylinder engine. Employing the five-speed manual gearbox, acceleration from 0 to 62 mph (100 kph) came in just under 11 seconds, and with a top speed of 119 mph (190 kph), it was quite enough to lift your spirits without blowing your head off. Models with automatic transmission were almost as fast.

Narrow winding streets did not pose any problems to this convertible, provided that its driver had muscular arms, or spent the extra money and installed power-assisted steering. The convertible only encountered problems in extreme cases of hard driving. Situations in which the rear drum brakes – discs at the front – could not cope did not generally appear in normal street driving conditions.

The finish and the folding mechanism of the fabric hood were of top quality. For those who did prefer something more substantial over their heads in winter, BMW also offered a hardtop cover. This item admittedly did not make the appearance of this 3 series more beautiful.

Das „Enthaupten" von BMW-Karosserien für den Umbau in offene Autos gehört bei Baur in Stuttgart zum Pflichtprogramm. Und traditionell bei Baur ist auch die Installation eines Targabügels, quasi als B-Säulen-Ersatz. Im September 1985 jedoch zeigt BMW auf der Frankfurter Automobilausstellung, dass man gewillt ist, selbst zu „köpfen", und zwar so, dass ein Vollcabriolet dabei herauskommt. Dieses Cabriolet – eleganter als die Baur-Version – ist zunächst auf Basis des 325i und des 320 erhältlich.

Erst 1990 – die neuen 3er der Baureihe E36 stehen bereits kurz vor der Serienreife – gesellt sich dem 318i ebenfalls ein Cabriolet zu. Der 318i mit dem neuen Vierzylindermotor verfügt über einen Dreiwegekatalysator und eine Lambda-Sonde – eine vernünftige Lösung, zumal sich die 113 PS mit knapp 11 Litern normaler bleifreier Flüssignahrung zufriedengeben.

Attraktiv ist auch der Preis für die Cabriolet-Fans, denen der 325i ein zu „starkes Stück" ist, kostet der 318i doch selbst 1993 noch unter 50 000 Mark. Auch mit dem Vierzylindertriebwerk bietet der offene 3er ungetrübten Fahrspaß unter freiem Himmel. Mit dem Fünfgang-Schaltgetriebe ist eine Beschleunigung von 0 auf 100 Stundenkilometer in knapp 11 Sekunden möglich, und die Spitzengeschwindigkeit von 190 Stundenkilometer genügt für viel Kopffreiheit. Nur geringfügig langsamer geht es mit der Automatik voran.

Auf engen kurvenreichen Straßen erweist sich dieses Cabriolet als sehr wendig, vorausgesetzt man hat kräftige Arme oder sich gegen Aufpreis eine Servolenkung einbauen lassen. Verwindungsprobleme kennt das 3er Cabrio höchstens im Extremfall, und Situationen, denen die hinteren Trommelbremsen – vorn hat das Cabriolet Scheibenbremsen – nicht gewachsen sind, treten im normalen Fahrbetrieb nicht auf.

Verarbeitung und Faltmechanismus des Stoffverdecks sind erstklassig. Wer im Winter jedoch mehr über dem Kopf haben möchte, dem bietet BMW einen maßgeschneiderten Hardtop-Aufsatz, durch den der 3er jedoch nicht verschönert wird.

Chez Baur, à Stuttgart, « décapiter » des carrosseries de BMW pour en faire des décapotables fait partie de la routine. Chez Baur d'ailleurs, le montage d'un arceau Targa, qui remplace en quelque sorte le pied médian, est une tradition. En septembre 1985, au Salon de l'Automobile de Francfort, BMW veut montrer qu'à Munich aussi, on est parfaitement capable de « faire rouler des têtes » afin d'obtenir un cabriolet à part entière. Celui-ci – plus élégant que celui de Baur – est tout d'abord disponible en version 325i et 320.

Ce n'est qu'en 1990 – alors que la nouvelle série 3 de la gamme E36 va bientôt être dévoilée au grand public – que l'on voit également apparaître un cabriolet 318i. Cette 318i propulsée par un nouveau moteur à quatre-cylindres possède un catalyseur trois voies et une sonde lambda. Une solution raisonnable, d'autant plus que les 113 ch se contentent d'à peine 11 litres aux 100 km d'essence ordinaire sans plomb.

Le prix est aussi attrayant pour les amateurs de cabriolets (en 1993, inférieur à 50 000 marks) pour lesquels une 325i est hors de portée. Avec le quatre-cylindres sous le capot, rouler cheveux au vent sous les rayons du soleil est un aussi grand plaisir. La boîte manuelle à cinq vitesses permet d'accélérer de 0 à 100 km/h en 11 secondes à peine et la vitesse de pointe de 190 km/h est tout à fait suffisante pour vous libérer l'esprit sans vous arracher la tête. La version à boîte automatique est quasiment aussi rapide.

Sur les routes étroites et sinueuses, ce cabriolet s'avère très maniable à condition que l'on ait suffisamment de « biceps » ou que l'on s'offre, en option, une direction assistée. La décapotable de la série 3 ne connaît des problèmes de rigidité torsionnelle que dans des cas extrêmes. Dans des conditions de circulation normale, les freins à tambours à l'arrière et à disques à l'avant sont toujours fiables.

La finition et le mécanisme de fermeture de la capote sont haut de gamme. Quiconque souhaite une protection en dur au-dessus de la tête durant l'hiver peut faire appel à BMW qui propose un hard-top taillé sur mesure, mais qui ne contribue pas particulièrement à embellir la série 3.

BMW 318i Cabrio

BMW 318i Cabrio

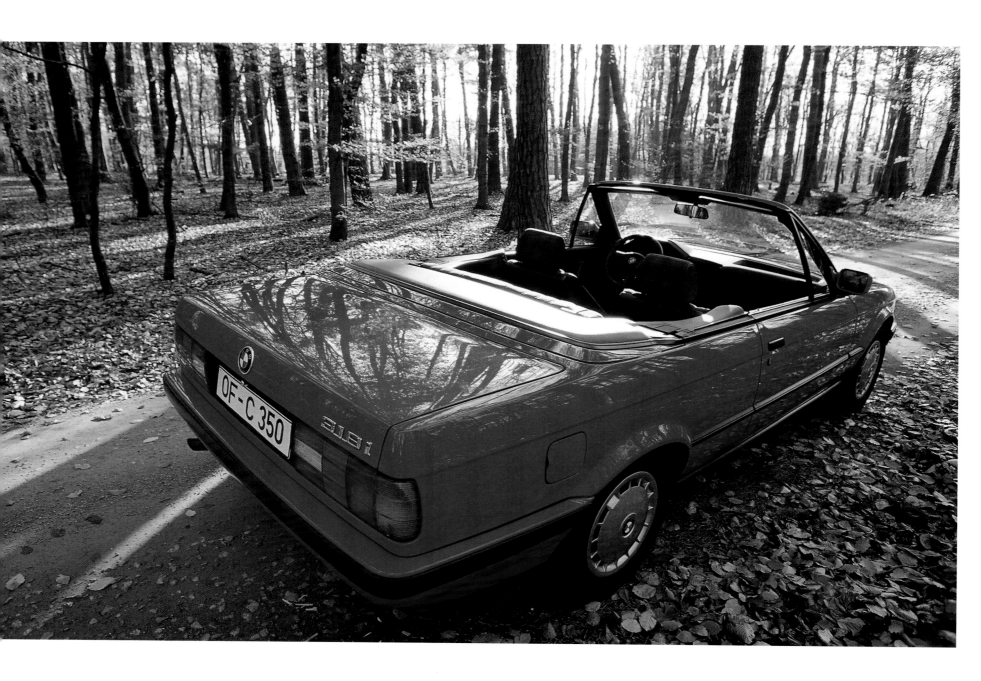

The convertible version of the 318i first arrived on the market in 1990. It is a highly economical convertible, its four-cylinder engine with three-way catalytic converter and lambda probe having a fuel consumption of around 21.5 miles per gallon (11 liters per 100 km).

Erst 1990 kommt der 318i auch „oben ohne" auf den Markt: ein äußerst preiswertes Cabriolet, dessen Vierzylindermotor mit Dreiwegekatalysator und Lambda-Sonde knapp 11 Liter Normalbenzin verbraucht.

Il faut attendre 1990 pour voir une 318i décapotable apparaître sur le marché : il s'agit d'un cabriolet au prix extrêmement intéressant, dont le quatre-cylindres à catalyseur trois voies et sonde lambda se contente de 11 litres d'essence ordinaire aux 100 km.

BMW 318i Cabrio 287

BMW M3 Sport Evolution

The 1987 touring car world championship was in the bag – a unique title – and the European championship of 1988 too, both with Roberto Ravaglia. Still the engineers at BMW Motorsport GmbH saw stars. To be precise, one star in particular – that of Mercedes in Stuttgart. To shine in the German touring car championship as well, BMW had to make the racing version of its successful M3 undergo evolutionary changes. That meant evidence of 500 identical vehicles had to be presented to the governing body, the FIA, in Paris. Such machines contained the latest in knowledge from competition, gathered on the track.

However, competitor Mercedes-Benz was one step ahead and had approved the 190E 2.5-16 Evolution, a multi-wing creation which produced a rapid reaction from BMW. Sales problems with the tuned road version of the M3 Evolution (E30) did not cause much of a headache in Munich. Although 20,000 marks more than the usual M3, the "Evo" immediately sold out.

The product of this technology transfer in both directions rubbed off on the road and racing "Evo". The racing car, with almost 360 bhp, was given a catalytic converter and lambda sensor. Both "Evos" now possessed sophisticated engine electronics, large-diameter disc brakes made of high-alloy steel, an exhaust system of highest quality steel, and a rear spoiler with an adjustable lip.

The chassis ride stiffness was adjustable; three levels could be electronically selected – "Sport" (here the "Evo" hugs the road), "Normal" and "Comfort". The latter was totally inappropriate for a stark racing platform chassis, one lacking electric windows and other normal refinements.

The bucket seats with guide slots for full harness seat belts befitted the sporty image of the "Evo". Why it was fitted with three-point inertia reel belts in red remains a BMW mystery. The warning tone which could be heard

when the driver pre-set maximum speed was exeeded was a curious feature of this "road-runner" which could manage 145 mph (248 kph).

The manual adjustment of the front and rear spoilers – here owners were expected to handle the screwdriver themselves, according to the manual – was a bit of a nuisance for normal use, but essential for making aerodynamic adjustments for the racetrack. After all, the racing "Evo" could manage a good 185 mph (300 kph), depending on the transmission.

The driver of the showroom M3 Evo was provided with more than enough in terms of road holding and acceleration. Hold tight: the "Evo" was catapulted from 0 to 62 mph (100 kph) in 6.3 seconds, and the standing kilometer was achieved after just 26.7 seconds. Any sweat at such explosive acceleration was absorbed by a suede steering wheel.

At the end of six years of racing the M3 and its Evolution, the "M team" could be satisfied with more than 1500 wins and 50 international titles.

Da ist man nun Tourenwagen-Weltmeister 1987 – eine einmalige Titelvergabe – und Europameister 1988 mit Roberto Ravaglia, und dennoch sehen die Techniker der BMW Motorsport GmbH Sterne, genauer gesagt: Stern aus Stuttgart! Um auch in der Deutschen Tourenwagen-Meisterschaft brillieren zu können, muss BMW den erfolgreichen M3 in Rennausführung einer Weiterentwicklung unterziehen. Das bedeutet, der Bau von 500 identischen Fahrzeugen, in die die neuesten Erkenntnisse aus dem Wettbewerb auf der Strecke einfließen, ist der obersten Automobilbehörde FIA in Paris nachzuweisen.

Doch mit eben diesem Schritt ist Konkurrent Mercedes-Benz zuvorgekommen und hat den 190E 2.5-16 Evolution homologieren lassen, eine mit viel Flügelwerk versehene Kreation, auf die BMW eilig reagiert. Über Absatzprobleme mit der aufgemotzten Straßenversion des M3 Evolution (E30) muss man sich in München keine Sorgen machen. Obwohl 20 000 Mark teurer als der „normale" M3, ist der „Evo" sofort vergriffen.

Das Produkt dieses Technologietransfers in beiden Richtungen färbt auf Straßen- und Renn-„Evo" ab. Das Rennauto, knapp 360 PS stark, bekommt Kat und Lambda-Sonde, und beide „Evos" verfügen jetzt über eine ausgefeilte digitale Motorelektronik, groß dimensionierte Scheibenbremsen aus hochlegiertem Stahl, eine Auspuffanlage aus Edelstahl sowie einen Heckspoiler mit verstellbarer Lippe.

Verstellbar ist auch das gesamte Fahrwerk. Elektronisch wählbar sind die Stufen „Sport" – da liegt der „Evo" richtig gut auf der Straße –, „Normal" und „Komfort". Letztere passt überhaupt nicht zu einer Fahrmaschine, bei der auf elektrische Fensterheber und sonstige Alltagshilfen verzichtet wird.

Zum sportlichen Image des „Evo" passen die Schalensitze mit Führungsrillen für Hosenträgergurte. Warum er dann mit Dreipunkt-Automatikgurten ausgerüstet wird, bleibt BMW-Geheimnis. Auch mutet bei einem „Straßenrenner", der 248 Stundenkilometer geht, der Piepton für selbst gesetzte Sollgeschwindigkeiten an wie das Geräusch einer Sirene beim Feueralarm.

Das manuelle Einstellen von Front- und Heckspoiler – hier darf man nach Betriebsanleitung selbst schrauben – ist für den Normalbetrieb eher lästig, für die aerodynamische Anpassung an eine Rennstrecke jedoch unerlässlich. Schließlich geht der Renn-„Evo" je nach Übersetzung gut 300 Stundenkilometer.

Dem Fahrer der zivilen Version wird in puncto Straßenlage und Beschleunigung schon genug geboten. Festhalten: In 6,3 Sekunden katapultiert sich der „Evo" von 0 auf 100 Stundenkilometer, und der stehende Kilometer wird bereits nach 26,7 Sekunden erreicht. Etwaige Schweißtropfen bei einem derartigen Adrenalinstoß saugt das Wildlederlenkrad auf.

Nach sechs Jahren Rennbetrieb des M3 und seiner Evolution dürfen sich die „M-Mannen" über 1500 Siege und 50 internationale Titel freuen.

Le titre de champion du monde des voitures de tourisme en 1987 dans la poche – un titre décerné une seule et unique fois – et celui de champion d'Europe 1988 aussi avec Roberto Ravaglia et, pourtant, les ingénieurs de BMW Motorsport GmbH ne voient que des étoiles : plus précisément, une étoile – celle de Mercedes à Stuttgart. Pour pouvoir briller également dans le championnat d'Allemagne des voitures de tourisme, BMW doit revoir et corriger la copie de sa M3 version course pourtant couronnée de succès. Et cela signifie la production de 500 voitures identiques intégrant les derniers enseignements de la compétition pour obtenir l'homologation des instances suprêmes de l'automobile, la FIA, à Paris.

Mais son concurrent Mercedes-Benz ne s'en laisse pas compter et a déjà fait homologuer une version plus sophistiquée, la 190E 2.5-16 Evolution. Une création dotée de nombreux accessoires aérodynamiques. Une stratégie à laquelle BMW réagit du tac au tac. À Munich, on ne perd pas de temps en conjecture sur les problèmes de vente de la version route « musclée » de la M3 Evolution (E30). Bien qu'elle coûte 20 000 marks de plus que la M3 de série, on se l'arrache jusqu'au dernier exemplaire.

Ce transfert de technologie profite tant à l'« Evo » de route qu'à l'« Evo » de circuit. La voiture de course, avec près de 360 ch, est dotée d'un catalyseur et d'une sonde lambda tandis que les deux « Evo » sont maintenant dotées d'une gestion électronique moteur numérique sophistiquée, de freins à disques de grandes dimensions en acier à alliage spécial, d'une ligne d'échappement en acier inoxydable ainsi que d'un becquet arrière à déflecteur réglable.

Réglable, ce qualificatif vaut aussi pour l'ensemble des trains roulants : on peut sélectionner électroniquement les niveaux « Sport » – l'« Evo » colle alors comme une ventouse à la route – « Normal » ou « Confort ». Ce dernier niveau ne

correspond absolument pas à un tel engin car il lui manque les lève-vitres électriques et autres gadgets de cet acabit.

Les baquets avec ouvertures pour les harnais correspondent en revanche fort bien à l'image sportive de l'« Evo ». Mais alors pourquoi l'équiper de ceintures automatiques à trois points ? Cela reste un mystère. Pour un bolide roulant à 248 km/h, l'émission d'un bip sonore en cas de dépassement de la vitesse que l'on s'est fixée est assez incongrue.

Le réglage manuel des ailerons avant et arrière – les conducteurs sont priés de se reporter au mode d'emploi pour les déplacer eux-mêmes – est quelque peu superflu en utilisation routière normale, mais, en revanche, absolument indispensable pour peaufiner les réglages aérodynamiques sur circuit. En effet, l'« Evo » version course atteint largement les 300 km/h selon son rapport de pont.

En termes de tenue de route et d'accélérations, les conducteurs de la version route en ont pour leur argent. Mais il faut bien se tenir : l'« Evo » est catapultée de 0 à 100 km/h en 6,3 secondes et abat le kilomètre arrêté en 26,7 secondes à peine. Heureusement les poussées d'adrénaline sont adoucies par un agréable volant gainé de daim.

Après six ans de compétition avec la M3 et son Evolution, l'équipe des « M » peut se prévaloir de plus de 1500 victoires et de 50 titres internationaux.

The road version of the M3 Sport Evolution has impressive handling and performance, with a top speed of 155 mph (248 kph) and a 0 to 62 mph (100 kph) time of 6.3 seconds. The racing version won more than 1500 races and captured 50 international titles over a six-year period.

Die „zivile" Version des M3 Sport Evolution beeindruckt durch ihr Handling und ihre Leistung: 248 km/h Spitze, in 6,3 Sekunden von 0 auf 100 km/h. In der Rennversion bringt es der M3 innerhalb von sechs Jahren auf 1500 Siege und 50 internationale Titel.

La version Sport Evolution pour la route de la M3 stupéfait par sa maniabilité et ses performances : 248 km/h en vitesse de pointe, 0 à 100 km/h en 6,3 secondes. Dans la version course, la M3 remporte en six ans 1 500 victoires et 50 titres internationaux.

The chassis beneath the "plump cheeks" of the M3, which is equipped to take wide tires in a variety of sizes, had three electronically-adjustable suspension settings: a stiff sporty set-up, normal or comfortable.

Das Fahrwerk unter den „dicken Backen" des M3, der für Breitreifen unterschiedlicher Dimensionen gerüstet ist, lässt sich via Elektronik sportlich straff oder komfortabel einstellen. Dazwischen liegt noch die Stufe „Normal".

Sous les « ailes joufflues » de la M3 conçue pour recevoir des pneus larges de différentes dimensions, le châssis peut être réglé électroniquement. Trois niveaux au choix : « Sport », « Normal » ou « Confort ».

Aerodynamic features such as spoilers with manually adjustable lips to increase downforce, so vital in motor sport, were here introduced into the small production run of 500 M3s – thus the name Sport Evolution. The super-functional cockpit features leather bucket seats with guide mechanisms for harness belts (though these do not come with the car) and a sports steering wheel with a suede grip area. Tests reveal a power output of 238 bhp at 7000 rpm for the four-valve four-cylinder engine with electronic fuel injection and a three-way catalytic converter.

Die im Motorsport erforderlichen aerodynamischen Attribute, wie Spoiler mit manuell verstellbarer Lippe für mehr Abtrieb, halten in der Kleinserie der 500 M3 Einzug – darum der Name Sport Evolution. In dem äußerst funktionellen Cockpit fallen die Lederschalensitze mit Führungen für Hosenträgergurte (die freilich nicht mitgeliefert werden) und das Sportlenkrad mit Wildleder-Griffzone auf. Das Power-Stenogramm des Vierventil-Vierzylinders mit elektronischer Benzineinspritzung und geregeltem Dreiwegekatalysator lautet 238 PS bei 7000/min.

Des accessoires aérodynamiques indispensables en compétition, comme l'aileron à arête réglable à la main pour obtenir plus de stabilité, font leur apparition dans la petite série de la M3 produite à 500 exemplaires et qui porte le nom de Sport Evolution. Dans l'habitacle extrêmement fonctionnel, on remarque les baquets en cuir avec ouvertures pour le harnais six points (qui n'est toutefois pas livré avec la voiture) et le volant sport partiellement gainé de daim. La puissance du quatre-cylindres à quatre soupapes à injection électronique et catalyseur réglé à trois voies culmine à 238 ch à 7000 tr/min.

BMW Z1

The roadster is focused, it embodies the core qualities of a BMW directly and unmistakably," was the comment of Dr Wolfgang Reitzle on the return of the BMW roadster in its most modern form. The Z1 was the surprise at the 1987 Frankfurt Motor Show. Pleasure could also be seen on the face of the rather distinguished and reticent BMW director for development and production as he invited the journalists for a test drive. Relaxed Reitzle wore a turtleneck pullover and a broad grin: "It might not be the most sensible car, but it's great fun."

This piece of fun was to cost more than 80,000 marks and was not originally planned as a production car, for it was designed and built as a high-technology demonstration vehicle for BMW Technik GmbH. So customer demand was all the more surprising. When the first Z1s went to the dealers, there were already 5000 orders. Assumed buyers' interest led to doubled and tripled production, reaching up to 18 Z1s per day. That was too much for a limited market. The Z1 could only be made affordable to roadster fans with discounts, and production ceased at 8000 cars in June 1991.

The marketing and pricing principle is missing from the Z1, and that was the crux of a roadster which was to serve as a test bed for new axles and trend-setting processed plastics in automotive construction. A galvanized sheet steel frame encloses the vehicle floor made of epoxy resin and PV plastics which were reinforced with glass fiber. This monocoque structure carried the external skin made of various thermoplastic compounds, and the relatively central, front engine, from the BMW 325i.

Virgin territory was entered with the doors: they retracted downwards. In view of the high sill, it is not easy for non-sporty people to get into the Z1, particularly when the folding top is closed. But anyone not of a sporty disposition has the wrong vehicle with the roadster anyway. Perfect handling,

even with extreme load changes, is due to the chassis with independent suspension and the Z-axle at the rear. The "Z" signifies a "centrally articulated, spherical double wishbone axle" in German. Got that?

That the Z1 did without the usual spoilers, was due to the turbulence-free underbody, and a diffuser which – together with a lip on the trunk – ensured sufficient downward aerodynamic air pressure, even at a top speed of 141 mph (225 kph).

Just as Reitzle said, the maneuverability and easy handling of this roadster, which is less than 13 feet long (4 meters), makes it incredible fun to drive. It can only be fully enjoyed when the top is folded down, even if this increases the drag coefficient from Cd 0.36 to Cd 0.43. The irrationality of this car is due less to the fact that there is insufficient luggage space for longer journeys, or that it offers drivers with sporting ambitions a meager 170 bhp, than to its price. 10,000 marks less and the Z1 would have been a big seller for a decade.

Der Roadster bringt die Sache auf den Punkt. Er verkörpert die Kerneigenschaften eines BMW direkt und unmissverständlich", so kommentiert Dr.-Ing. Wolfgang Reitzle die Rückkehr zum Roadster, wenngleich modernster Prägung. Der Z1 ist die Überraschung auf der IAA 1987. Und man merkt dem eher vornehm zurückhaltenden BMW-Vorstandsmitglied für Entwicklung und Produktion die Freude über den gelungenen Coup an, als er die Journalisten zu Testfahrten bittet. Reitzle mit Rollkragenpullover und breitem Lausbuben-Grinsen: „Er ist vielleicht etwas unvernünftig, aber er macht ungemein Spaß."

Der Spaß soll mehr als 80 000 Mark kosten und war ursprünglich nicht für die Serie vorgesehen, sondern konzipiert und gebaut als Technologieträger der BMW Technik GmbH. Umso mehr überrascht die Nachfrage. In der Phase der Erstauslieferungen an die Händler liegen bereits 5000 Bestellungen vor. Spekulatives Käuferinteresse führt zur Verdopplung und Verdreifachung der Produktion – bis zu 18 Z1 werden pro Tag gefertigt. Zuviel für einen begrenzten Markt. Nur mit Rabatten ist der Z1 letztlich an den Roadster-Fan zu bringen, und nach 8000 gebauten Wagen wird im Juni 1991 die Fertigung eingestellt.

Die Komponenten Marketing und Preispolitik haben bei der Konzipierung des Z1 keine Rolle gespielt, und das ist die Crux dieses Roadsters, der ursprünglich frei von Produktionszwängen zur Erprobung neuer Achsen und richtungsweisender Kunststoffverarbeitungsverfahren im Automobilbau dienen sollte. Ein Stahlblechgerüst, natürlich verzinkt, umschließt den Fahrzeugboden aus glasfaserverstärktem Epoxidharz und PV. Dieses „Monocoque" trägt die aus verschiedenen Thermoplast-Verbindungen bestehende Außenhaut und den relativ zentrierten Frontmotor des BMW 325i.

Bei den Türen werden neue Wege beschritten: Sie sind nach unten versenkbar. Angesichts der hohen Schwelle bietet der Z1 unsportlichen Menschen keinen leichten Einstieg, besonders bei geschlossenem Verdeck. Aber für Unsportliche ist der Roadster sowieso nicht das richtige Auto. Sein perfektes Handling selbst bei extremen Lastwechseln verdankt der Z1 dem Fahrwerk mit Einzelradaufhängungen und der Z-Achse hinten. Das „Z" steht für eine „zentralpunktgeführte sphärische Doppel-Querlenkerachse". Alles klar?

Dass der Z1 ohne das übliche Spoilerwerk auskommt, verdankt er dem verwirbelungsfrei gestalteten Unterboden und einem Diffusor, der zusammen mit einer Lippe auf dem Kofferraum für genügend Anpressdruck auch bei einer Höchstgeschwindigkeit von 225 Stundenkilometern sorgt.

Wendigkeit und Handlichkeit des nicht einmal vier Meter langen Roadsters machen, wie Reitzle richtig feststellt, wirklich ungemein Spaß – ein Vergnügen, das erst bei offenem Verdeck voll zu genießen ist, auch wenn dadurch der Luftwiderstandsbeiwert von c_w 0,36 auf c_w 0,43 steigt. Die Unvernunft des Wagens liegt weniger darin, dass er für längere Reisen nicht genügend Gepäckraum bereithält und sportlich ambitionierten Fahrern nur magere 170 PS bietet, sondern in seinem Preis. 10 000 Mark günstiger, und der Z1 wäre ein Renner für ein Jahrzehnt geworden.

Le roadster met les points sur les i, il incarne à la perfection les caractéristiques d'une BMW, de façon claire et nette », déclare l'ingénieur Wolfgang Reitzle pour commenter le retour du roadster dans sa version ultramoderne. La Z1 est « la » surprise du Salon de l'Automobile de Francfort en 1987. Reitzle, plutôt discret et réservé membre du directoire de BMW, au titre du développement et de la production, ne peut s'en cacher lorsqu'il invite les journalistes à essayer la voiture. Vêtu d'un pull à col roulé et arborant un large sourire, il déclare : « Ce n'est peut-être pas raisonnable, mais c'est un véritable plaisir. »

Le plaisir est censé coûter plus de 80 000 marks et n'était, à l'origine, pas prévu pour la série : il a été conçu et construit au départ pour servir de vitrine technologique à la BMW Technik GmbH. La demande des acheteurs est d'autant plus surprenante. Durant la phase des premières livraisons aux concessionnaires, 5000 commandes ont déjà été passées. La spéculation fait doubler puis tripler la production – jusqu'à 18 Z1 par jour sortent des chaînes de production. Ce qui est beaucoup trop pour un marché restreint. Au final, la Z1 ne trouve preneur parmi les fanas du roadster qu'avec une réduction de son prix et la production est suspendue en juin 1991 avec 8000 voitures sorties des chaînes.

Les composantes marketing et une stratégie commerciale font défaut à la Z1. C'est là le problème pour un roadster, libéré des contraintes de la production pour la mise à l'essai de nouveaux essieux et de matières plastiques novatrices dans la construction automobile. Un squelette d'acier, naturellement galvanisé, enserre la plate-forme en résine époxyde et PVC renforcés de fibre de verre. Cette « monocoque » est dotée d'une carrosserie en matériaux composites et matière thermoplastique et héberge le moteur avant de la BMW 325i en position presque centrale.

Innovation également pour les portières : elles sont escamotables vers le bas. Compte tenu de sa hauteur, l'accès n'est pas aisé pour un conducteur non sportif, *a fortiori* quand la capote est fermée. De toute façon, ceux pour qui le sport est un vain mot n'ont pas leur place dans le roadster. La Z1 doit son comportement parfait, même lors d'importants changements de charges, à son châssis à suspension à roue indépendante et à son essieu en Z à l'arrière. Le « Z » signifie « double essieu transversal sphérique à guidage central ». Tout est clair ?

Si la Z1 peut se passer des ailerons traditionnels, elle le doit à son soubassement qui ne provoque aucun tourbillon et à un diffuseur qui, conjointement avec une lèvre sur le couvercle du coffre, génère suffisamment de stabilité même à la vitesse maximum de 225 km/h.

La vivacité et la maniabilité de ce petit roadster de moins de quatre mètres de long sont, comme le disait Reitzle, vraiment amusantes et le plaisir est encore plus grand en décapotable même si, alors, le c_x passe de 0,36 à 0,43. Le caractère déraisonnable de la voiture, c'est son prix plutôt que le fait qu'il n'y ait pas suffisamment de place pour les bagages ou encore qu'avec 170 ch, elle ne peut guère satisfaire les pilotes amateurs de conduite sportive. Dix mille marks de moins, et la Z1 aurait été la vedette d'une décennie entière.

For the roadster fan, the Z1 with its 170 bhp and retractable doors represents pure motoring fun. For BMW, its main purpose was to test new technology in the form of innovative synthetic components, aerodynamic details and the new Z-axle (centrally articulated, spherical double wishbone axle). Softtop compartment and trunk above, a turbulence-free underbody: the Z1 tail is fitted with a diffuser whose airstream is directed over a reverse airfoil fitted between the flat exhaust pipes.

Für den Roadster-Fan ist der Z1 mit seinen 170 PS und den versenkbaren Türen ein „Spaßmobil". Für BMW ist er primär ein Technologieträger zur Erprobung innovativer Kunststoff-Komponenten, aerodynamischer Detaillösungen und der neuen Z-Achse (zentralpunktgeführte sphärische Doppel-Querlenkerachse). Klappverdeckfach und Kofferraum oben, verwirbelungsfreier Boden unten: Das Z1-Heck verfügt über einen Diffusor, dessen Luftstrom über ein umgekehrtes Flügelprofil zwischen den flachen Auspuffrohren abgeführt wird.

Pour les fanas du roadster, la Z1 de 170 ch aux portières escamotables est une véritable voiture d'agrément. Pour BMW, il s'agit surtout d'une vitrine technologique qui permet de tester des matières plastiques novatrices, des solutions aérodynamiques de détail et le nouvel essieu en Z (double essieu transversal sphérique à guidage central). Sous le compartiment où vient se loger la capote et sous le coffre se trouve un soubassement empêchant tout tourbillon : l'arrière de la Z1 comporte, en effet, un diffuseur dont le courant d'air est canalisé par un profil d'aile inversé entre les pots d'échappement aplatis.

BMW Z1

BMW 750iL

Count Hans von der Goltz, supervisory board chairman of BMW AG, and his equally blue-blooded managing director, Dr Eberhard von Kuenheim, know what is right: *"Noblesse oblige"*. BMW was to be among those who set the future tone in the highest sedan society, echoing Maybach in the 1930s. Expensive handbuilt labor, little high-tech and incredibly high prices handicapped the noble British conveyance of aristocracy, Rolls-Royce. They were no competition for BMW – except that the name has that ring of royalty about it. The real competition in terms of numbers of cars registered was the S class from Mercedes-Benz. Stuttgart was convinced the S class would not lose any buyers to Munich.

Wrong! The new 750i – the first German twelve-cylinder luxury car since the Second World War – overtook the S class in new cars registered in Germany as early as May 1987. It was almost unheard-of that the Bavarians should steal the show from Stuttgart's Swabians in the luxury class. The only sound from Rolls was a surprised whisper. One was clearly "not amused".

This miracle of Bavarian engine technology had a block and twelve cylinder heads made of aluminium. That is why the 2500 or so refined engine parts together did not weigh more than 530 lbs (240 kg). The crankshaft of the V-engine had seven bearings. Since the two halves of the V had their own drive units and catalytic converters, total engine failure was almost unthinkable.

The 5-liter engine could only be heard when it delivered all 300 bhp – something which happened at an engine speed of 5200 rpm, so it was nobly restrained but powerful. Simply majestic. The most modern engine management and four-speed automatic transmission with drive programs "Sport" and "Economy" belonged to the magnicent and splendid Bavarian aristocrat. The 1.8 tons of unladen weight

could be accelerated to 62 mph (100 kph) in less than eight seconds, and BMW was content to limit top speed electronically to 155 mph (250 kph). Higher speeds than that would reduce driving comfort. This, in any case, was equivalent to being carried in a sedan-chair due to automatic stabilization and electronic shock absorber controls.

Luxury reigned in the cabin, with five comfortable seats of the finest leather. And however hard you looked, not even the smallest technical refinement invented to make cars more comfortable was missing. Anyone wanting a drinks cabinet or a television would be advised to choose the 4 inches (11 cm) longer 750iL. In 1987 the 750i still cost a "modest" 102,000 marks, the stretched (L-badged) version demanded 17,000 marks more. The refined pleasure of being able to afford this ultimate limousine was enjoyed by almost 20,000 obviously well-heeled people in 1987/88.

Hans Graf von der Goltz, Aufsichtsratsvorsitzender der BMW AG, und sein ebenfalls blaublütiger Vorstand Dr.-Ing. h.c. Eberhard von Kuenheim wissen, was sich gehört: „Noblesse oblige!" BMW soll auch in der High society der Nobelkarossen künftig mit den Ton angeben – so wie Maybach in den dreißiger Jahren. Viel Handarbeit, wenig High-Tech und zu hohe Preise sind das Handicap der britischen Hochadels-Kutsche Rolls-Royce. Für BMW ist dieser Hersteller kein Konkurrent – nur der Name ist eben unvergleichlich vornehm. Die eigentliche Konkurrenz in der Zulassungsstatistik ist die S-Klasse von Mercedes-Benz. Und von der, so ist man zumindest in Stuttgart überzeugt, wird kein Käufer nach München abwandern.

Irrtum! Der neue BMW 750i – der erste deutsche Zwölfzylinder-Luxuswagen nach dem Zweiten Weltkrieg – überholt bereits im Mai 1987 die S-Klasse bei den Fahrzeugzulassungen in Deutschland. Ein unerhörter Vorgang, dass die Bayern in der Luxusklasse den Schwaben die Show stehlen! Von Rolls-Royce hört man nur erstauntes Raunen: Man ist sichtlich „not amused".

Motorblock und Zylinderköpfe dieses Wunderwerks bayerischer Motorenbaukunst bestehen aus Aluminium, und deshalb wiegen die rund 2500 edlen Motorenteile zusammengenommen nicht mehr als 240 Kilo. Die Kurbelwelle des V-Motors ist siebenfach gelagert, und da die beiden Sechszylinder, aus denen er sich zusammensetzt, ihre eigenen Antriebsaggregate und Katalysatoren aufweisen, ist ein völliger Motorausfall kaum denkbar.

Erst wenn dieses 5-Liter-Triebwerk die vollen 300 PS entfaltet – und das geschieht bei 5200 Umdrehungen pro Minute – ist auch der Sound vernehmbar: vornehm zurückhaltend, aber kraftvoll – majestätisch eben. Modernstes Motormanagement und eine Viergangautomatik mit den

Fahrprogrammen „Sport" und „Economy" gehören zur Standardausstattung dieses bayerischen Prunkstücks, und wenn dessen Fahrer es wünscht, katapultiert die Urgewalt dieses Motors die 1,8 Tonnen Leergewicht in weniger als acht Sekunden auf 100 Stundenkilometer. Um den Fahrkomfort nicht zu schmälern, beliebt man werksseitig die Höchstgeschwindigkeit elektronisch auf 250 Stundenkilometer zu begrenzen. Mehr soll es nicht sein. Dieser Fahrkomfort wird ohnehin durch eine automatische Stabilisierung und eine elektronische Dämpferkontrolle auf Sänftenniveau gehalten.

In der „Sänfte" mit fünf komfortablen Sesseln aus feinstem Leder regiert der Luxus, und solange man auch sucht, es fehlt nicht die geringste jener vielen technischen Raffinessen, die für die Bequemlichkeit von Fahrzeuginsassen erfunden worden sind. Wer den Einbau einer Bordbar oder eines Fernsehers wünscht, sollte sich für den 11 Zentimeter längeren 750iL entscheiden.

1987 kostet der 750i noch „bescheidene" 102 000 Mark, die Langversion 17 000 Mark mehr. Das hochnoble Vergnügen, dieses Nonplusultra einer Limousine zu fahren – oder standesgemäß fahren zu lassen – gönnen sich 1987/88 fast 20 000 entsprechend betuchte Menschen.

Le comte Hans von der Goltz, président du conseil de surveillance de BMW, et son collègue Eberhard von Kuenheim, noble lui aussi, docteur *honoris causa* en ingénierie, savent ce qu'il faut faire : « Noblesse oblige ! » À l'avenir, BMW donnera le ton sur le marché des limousines de très grand luxe – comme Maybach dans les années 1930. Beaucoup de travail encore réalisé à la main, peu de haute technologie et des prix trop élevés sont les handicaps de Rolls-Royce, cette noble marque de l'industrie automobile britannique : pour BMW, ce n'est pas un concurrent – seul son nom lui donne une connotation royale. Sa concurrente directe, selon les statistiques d'immatriculations, c'est la classe S de Mercedes-Benz. Et, à Stuttgart, chacun est convaincu que celle-ci ne perdra aucun acheteur. Ces derniers ne passeront pas dans le camp de Munich.

C'est une erreur ! La nouvelle BMW 750i – la première douze-cylindres de luxe allemande depuis la Seconde Guerre mondiale – double la classe S en termes d'immatriculations de voitures neuves en Allemagne dès mai 1987. Il est absolument stupéfiant que les Bavarois volent la vedette aux Souabes dans la catégorie des voitures de grand luxe. Rolls-Royce s'en étonne et n'est manifestement pas *amused*.

Le bijou de la technique bavaroise en termes de moteur possède un bloc et des culasses en aluminium. Ce qui explique que les quelque 2500 prestigieuses pièces du moteur ne pèsent pas plus de 240 kg. Le vilebrequin du moteur en V est à sept paliers. Comme chacun des deux « six-cylindres » du moteur comporte son propre groupe de transmission, il est pratiquement exclu que le moteur tombe totalement en panne.

Il faut que ce moteur de 5 litres libère la totalité de ses 300 ch – ce qu'il fait dès 5200 tr/min – pour que l'on en perçoive la présence, il est d'une retenue discrète

mais vigoureux. Majestueux, tout simplement. Une gestion moteur ultramoderne et une boîte automatique à quatre rapports avec comme programmes « Sport » et « Économique » équipent ce pur-sang digne des haras des rois de Bavière. Côté performance, il est tout à fait possible de catapulter les 1,8 tonne à vide de la voiture en moins de 8 secondes de 0 à 100 km/h et la vitesse maximum limitée électroniquement à 250 km/h laisse planer une ombre sur les possibilités réelles de la voiture. Cela suffit pour que l'on puisse profiter pleinement du confort. Grâce à un contrôle automatique de la stabilisation et électronique des amortisseurs, on a de toute façon l'impression de rouler sur un nuage.

Le luxe règne en maître dans ce carrosse aux cinq fauteuils en cuir confortables. Et même en cherchant bien, il ne manque aucun gadget technique inventé pour le confort des passagers. Celui qui souhaite faire installer un bar ou un téléviseur devra opter pour la version 750iL allongée de 11 cm.

En 1987, la 750i coûte encore la « modique » somme de 102 000 marks, ajoutez 17 000 marks pour la version à empattement long. En 1987–1988, 20 000 personnes peuvent se payer le luxe incomparable de posséder ce *nec plus ultra* de la technique automobile.

The renaissance of the German V12 engine (60°) – the 1929 Maybach 12, forerunner of the legendary "Zeppelin DS7", had one – was celebrated by BMW in 1987 with the introduction of the 750i/750iL. To mark this historic event, Niki Lauda was invited to test drive the blue-blooded Bavarian thoroughbred in Vienna.

1987 feiert BMW mit dem 750i/750iL die Renaissance des deutschen V12-Motors (60°). 1929 gab es ihn schon im Maybach 12, dem Vorläufer des legendären „Zeppelin DS7". Ein historisches Ereignis, das Niki Lauda zu einem Test des noblen Bayern in Wien bewegt.

BMW fait renaître un moteur V12 allemand (à 60°) en 1987 avec le lancement de la 750i/750iL – le précédent remontait à 1929 avec la Maybach 12, précurseur de la légendaire « Zeppelin DS7 ». Un événement historique qui incite Niki Lauda à essayer cette BMW de prestige à Vienne.

BMW 750iL

Four and a half inches (11 cm) more legroom than the 750i: triple world champion Niki Lauda enjoys the unaccustomed comfort of the back seat. Barely audible is the noise of the 300 bhp engine, whose two cylinder banks have their own separate aggregate running from the injection unit to the catalytic converter. Boeing pilot Lauda samples the sumptuous driver area of the 7 series.

11 Zentimeter mehr Beinfreiheit als im 750i: Dem dreifachen Weltmeister, der hier Fond-passagier ist, behagt dieser Komfort. Kaum hörbar ist die „12-Ton-Musik" des 300-PS-Triebwerks, dessen zwei Zylinderreihen von der Einspritzanlage bis zum Kat beide über eigene Aggregate verfügen. Dem Boeing-Piloten Lauda ist das Cockpit des 7ers eine Laudatio wert.

Onze cm de plus pour les jambes que dans la 750i : le triple champion du monde, installé sur la banquette arrière, apprécie ce confort. Le V12 de 300 ch est très silencieux ; de l'injection aux catalyseurs, chaque banc de cylindres possède son groupe de transmission. Lauda, le pilote de Boeing, ne tarit pas d'éloges sur l'habitacle de la série 7.

Just eight months after the launch of the 5 series (E34), the sporting version arrived in August 1988. It concealed, as always with BMW, massive performance behind a tiny abbreviation: M5. Externally, only the restrained aerodynamic aids on the lower body, the ventilated light alloy wheels and the badge indicated the M5. The power of the engine (315 bhp; from 1992 upped to 340 bhp) remained hidden.

Well then, raise the hood. "BMW M Power" stamped boldly on the valve cover could not be overlooked, and neither could the long funnels of the inlet tract with the unusual air intake. An electronically controlled flap was activated here in such an ingenious way that enhanced torque and performance were achieved right back in the intake area. "Resonance-tuned intake pressure charging" was BMW's name for this process.

Also at the back there were tell-tale signs that this engine was a powerful unit. After the catalytic converter, the exhaust gases exited by two mighty tail pipes. It is hardly necessary to mention that optimum combustion was achieved in the six cylinders with a total of 24 valves, and that the crankshaft with 12 counterweights was a metal-forging masterpiece.

A 25 bhp increase in power in 1992 boosted maximum torque from 360 Nm to 400 Nm at 4750 rpm, but had no effect on acceleration. This was powerful enough as it was, at 6.5 seconds from 0 to 62 mph (100 kph). That leaves the question of top speed. Not really relevant, for at 155 mph (250 kph) the Bosch Motronic intervened and prohibited further speed. This Motronic, initially the M1.2, and from 1992 the M3.3, managed the engine and regulated the lambda catalytic converter.

The M5 sat 0.7 inches (20 mm) lower than its brothers in the 5 series. Yet little adjustment was required to adapt the chassis to cope with the enhanced performance. Electronic shock absorber ride adjustment and hydro-pneumatic leveling were the magic technical words. As in the 750i, they stood for impressive roadholding and cornering, giving pleasure to those occupying the sporty and elegant cockpit. Whether a light inside the gearshift knob for the sporty five-speed transmission was really necessary is debatable.

In 1992, the year in which the M5 was upgraded again, including hot five-spoke star wheels, BMW also supplied its "M5 bullet" in a touring derivative. This sporting wagon cost 127,650 marks, and had particularly wide rear tires (255/40 ZR17).

To blow away a Porsche or a Chevy Corvette on the highway with a four-door station wagon is most certainly not part of any driving test. But – leaving all morals aside – this might well be an uplifting moment.

Nur acht Monate nach der Vorstellung der 5er Reihe (E34) folgt im August 1988 das „Muskelpaket". Und dieses verbirgt, wie bei BMW üblich, seine große Leistung hinter einem kleinen Kürzel: M5. Äußerlich deuten nur dezente aerodynamische Hilfen im unteren Karosseriebereich, die Leichtmetallräder mit Lüftereinsatz und das Kürzel auf den M5 hin. Die Kraft (315 PS, ab 1992 sogar 340 PS) liegt im Verborgenen.

Also Haube auf! „BMW M Power" steht unübersehbar auf dem Zylinderkopfdeckel. Unübersehbar auch die langen Trichter des Ansaugtrakts mit dem ungewöhnlichen Luftmengensammler, in dem eine elektronisch gesteuerte Klappe derart geschickt arbeitet, dass sie schon im Ansaugbereich für mehr Drehmoment und Leistung sorgt. „Resonanzaufladung" nennt BMW diesen Vorgang. Auch am hinteren Ende gibt es verräterische Anzeichen dafür, dass es sich bei diesem Motor um ein Kraftwerk handelt. Nach Passieren des Katalysators entweichen die Auspuffgase durch zwei gewaltige Endrohre. Dass in den sechs Zylindern mit insgesamt 24 Ventilen eine optimale Verbrennung erzielt wird und die Kurbelwelle mit 12 Gegengewichten ein Meisterstück der Schmiedekunst ist, braucht wohl nicht erwähnt zu werden.

Die Potenzsteigerung um 25 PS im Jahre 1992 hebt zwar das maximale Drehmoment von 360 Nm auf 400 Nm bei 4750 Touren, wirkt sich aber nicht auf die Beschleunigung aus, die mit knapp 6,5 Sekunden von 0 auf 100 Stundenkilometer ohnehin jenseits von Gut und Böse ist. Auch die Frage nach der Endgeschwindigkeit erübrigt sich, denn bei 250 Stundenkilometer greift die Bosch Motronic ein und untersagt weiteres „Speeding". Diese Motronic – zunächst die M1.2, ab 1992 die M3.3 – steuert den Motor und die Lambda-Regelung des Katalysators.

Der M5 liegt 20 Millimeter tiefer als die Serienbrüder der 5er Reihe. Doch sind für die Anpassung des Fahrwerks

BMW M5

an das neue Kräfteverhältnis nur geringe Einstellarbeiten erforderlich. Wie schon beim 750i heißen die technischen Zauberworte für gute Straßen- und Kurvenlage elektronische Dämpferkraftverstellung und hydropneumatische Niveauregulierung – zur Freude der Fahrer, die sich in dem sportlich-eleganten Cockpit betätigen dürfen. Über den Sinn des von innen angestrahlten Schaltknopfes des sportlich abgestimmten Fünfganggetriebes lässt sich streiten.

1992, im Jahre der nochmaligen Aufrüstung des M5, unter anderem mit „heißen" Fünfstern-Rädern, liefert BMW das M5-Geschoss auch als Touring aus. Dieser 127 650 Mark teure Wagen steht hinten auf besonders breiten Sohlen (255/40 ZR 17).

Mit einem viertürigen Kombi auf der Autobahn einen Porsche oder eine Chevy-Corvette zu „verblasen", gehört gewiss nicht zur Reifeprüfung eines Autofahrers, dürfte aber – mal ganz unpädagogisch betrachtet – ein erhebender Moment sein.

Huit mois seulement après la présentation de la série 5 (E34), BMW en dévoile, en août 1988, la version «musclée». Et, comme cela est la tradition chez BMW, celle-ci dissimule son immense potentiel derrière une simple abréviation : M5. Extérieurement, seuls de discrets artifices aérodynamiques le long des bas de caisse, des jantes en alliage léger ressemblant à des ailettes de turbine et l'abréviation indiquent qu'il s'agit bien de la M5. La puissance du moteur (315 ch et même 340 à partir de 1992) ne saute pas aux yeux.

Alors, ouvrons le capot ! «BMW M Power» peut-on lire en grandes lettres sur la culasse et les longues tubulures du collecteur d'aspiration avec l'immense boîtier du filtre à air. On sait tout de suite à qui on a affaire. Dans ce boîtier, une soupape à commande électronique agit avec tant d'ingéniosité qu'elle génère plus de couple et de puissance dès le collecteur d'aspiration. C'est ce que BMW appelle la «suralimentation par résonance».

À l'arrière aussi, certains signes trahissent que ce moteur n'est pas d'un gabarit courant. Après avoir franchi le catalyseur, les gaz brûlés s'échappent par deux énormes pots d'échappement. Point n'est besoin de signaler à ce propos qu'une combustion optimale est garantie dans les six-cylindres avec, au total, 24 soupapes et que le vilebrequin à 12 contrepoids est un chef-d'œuvre. L'augmentation de puissance de 25 ch en 1992 fait passer le couple maximum de 360 Nm à 400 Nm à 4750 tr/min, mais reste sans effet sur l'accélération : avec 6,5 secondes à peine pour le 0 à 100 km/h, elle est de toute façon suffisante. Reste la question de la vitesse de pointe. Elle n'est pas capitale. En effet, à 250 km/h, la gestion Bosch Motronic intervient et jugule efficacement les autres accélérations. Cette Motronic, tout d'abord la M1.2, puis la M3.3 à partir de 1992, gère le moteur et la régulation du catalyseur par une sonde lambda.

La M5 est surbaissée de 20 millimètres par rapport aux autre modèles de la série 5. Mais peu de réglages sont nécessaires pour adapter les trains roulants au nouveau rapport de forces. Des amortisseurs à réglage électronique et un correcteur d'assiette hydropneumatique comme pour la 750i sont la formule magique qui garantit une tenue de route à toute épreuve en ligne droite et dans les courbes, pour le plus grand plaisir de celui qui a l'opportunité et le bonheur de se glisser au volant. Les avis sont partagés quant au bien-fondé de l'éclairage intérieur du pommeau de changement de vitesses de la boîte manuelle à cinq rapports.

En 1992, année de la montée en puissance de la M5 – notamment avec de spectaculaires jantes en étoile à cinq rayons –, BMW commercialise également sa «bombe M5» en une version touring. Ce break de 127 650 marks est monté sur des pneus particulièrement larges à l'arrière (255/40 ZR 17).

Donner la réplique sur autoroute à une Porsche ou à une Chevrolet Corvette au volant d'un break à quatre portes n'est pas à la portée de tous les automobilistes, mais – faisons pour une fois abstraction de toute morale – ceci est sans aucun doute un moment inoubliable.

BMW M5

The extensively equipped cockpit of the M5 reflects well on this exclusive car. Its M-power means that a worthy "opponent" rarely appears in the aerodynamically shaped rear-view mirror.

So manchem Nobelgefährt zur Ehre gereicht das reichhaltig ausgestattete M5-Cockpit. Dank der M-Power taucht nur selten ein ebenbürtiger „Gegner" im aerodynamischen Rückspiegel auf.

L'habitacle richement équipé de la M5 est digne d'une voiture de sport de prestige. Avec le moteur M Power, peu de véhicules sont capables de rivaliser avec ses performances.

With the M5, the power – 315 bhp to begin with, then 340 bhp from 1992 – and the brilliance of a sports car are contained in a spacious sedan. The M5 touring perfectly combines a load capacity of 1058 lbs (480 kg) with extreme performance: a top speed of 155 mph (250 kph) and from 0 to 62 mph (100 kph) in 6.5 seconds. The discreet spoilers in the lower body area are essential because of the wide tires and emphasize the aerodynamic shape of the car.

Beim M5 stecken die Kraft – zunächst 315 PS, ab 1992 dann 340 PS – und die Herrlichkeit eines Sportwagens in einer geräumigen Limousine. Der M5 touring kombiniert perfekt eine Transportkapazität von 480 Kilo mit extremen Fahrleistungen: 250 km/h Spitze und von 0 auf 100 km/h in 6,5 Sekunden. Das dezente Spoilerwerk im unteren Karosseriebereich ist wegen der Breitreifen unabdingbar und unterstreicht die aerodynamische Form des Fahrzeugs.

Avec la M5, le ramage – tout d'abord 315 ch, puis 340 ch à partir de 1992 – vaut le plumage, une fougueuse voiture de sport se cache sous les traits d'une spacieuse familiale. La M5 touring combine à la perfection une capacité de transport de 480 kg à des performances extrêmes : une vitesse de pointe de 250 km/h et le 0 à 100 km/h en 6,5 secondes. Les discrets artifices aérodynamiques le long du soubassement sont indispensables en raison de la largeur des pneus et soulignent la forme aérodynamique de la voiture.

BMW M5

BMW 850i

In the 8 series coupé, BMW once and for all invaded the territory of the Mercedes-Benz luxury class. Launched in the autumn of 1989, it contained a synthesis of sportiness and comfort, advanced technology and all that is good and expensive. Opinions diverge as to whether this new upper-class car was exciting or just beautiful. Either way, it combined several styling elements which are typical of BMW.

Because of the extremely slim nose of the 850i, the BMW kidneys grills were made wider rather than high to remind us of the 1972 BMW Turbo study by Paul Bracq. The prominent lines of the fenders were borrowed from the M3 (E30), but both shape and height of the stub rear end are like those of other contemporary BMWs. Four exhaust pipes under a lip predict the power and splendor of a twelve-cylinder engine.

This V12 motor, shared by the 750i with aluminum engine block and cylinder heads, produced 300 bhp. That was increased in the 850CSi (from 1992 on) by a rise in cubic capacity from 4988 to 5578 cc to produce 380 bhp. The six-speed transmission is less popular than the optional automatic: a classic choice by the wealthy buyers of this coupé in favor of comfort. For sporty drivers, there are more agile models in the BMW range than this heavy coupé.

As far as maneuverability was concerned, the CSi entered a new dimension, for the wider back tire treads (265/40 ZR17) and unique rear axle were responsive to steering inputs. The cost-benefit calculation for these expensive, active rear axle kinematics was a matter of debate. Yet expensive things – particularly when they concern electronics – have their enthusiastic supporters. Measured against the sales figures (before the introduction of the Ci and CSi in 1992, some 16,000 coupés were sold), the price was probably not important. The CSi sold at 180,000 marks and more, but the demand was somewhat restrained.

The alarm bells rang immediately in BMW's marketing department: in 1993 the 840Ci appeared with an 286 bhp V8 engine, five-speed transmission and fewer electronics for 129,000 marks. This model did without the usual speed-limiting device at 155 mph (250 kph), for that was the actual top speed.

The sensual pleasure which BMW promises when driving the 8 series coupé is produced just by looking at the functional and extremely tasteful interior. It is quite simply "upper class", and the safety belts integrated into the seats are "safety first".

Eine Synthese aus Sportlichkeit und Komfort, Technik auf höchstem Niveau und allem, was gut und teuer ist, steckt im 8er Coupé, mit dem BMW im Herbst 1989 endgültig in die Pfründe der Mercedes-Benz-Luxusklasse eindringt. Die Meinungen darüber, ob das neue Nobelmobil aufregend oder nur schön ist, gehen auseinander. Immerhin vereint es mehrere BMW-typische Stylingelemente.

So erinnert die extrem flache Schnauze des 850i, dessen BMW-Nieren eher breit als hoch ausfallen, an die Turbo-Studie Paul Bracqs von 1972. Die ausladende Linienführung der Kotflügel ist dem M3 (E30) entlehnt, Form und Höhe der Abrisskante des Hecks gleichen den anderen Modellreihen. Vier wuchtige Auspuffrohre unter einer Lippe verkünden die Kraft und die Herrlichkeit eines Zwölfzylinders.

Dieses auch im 750i verwendete Kraftwerk mit Motorblock und Zylinderköpfen aus Aluminium bringt 300 PS und wird beim 850CSi ab 1992 durch eine Hubraumvergrößerung von 4988 ccm auf 5578 ccm auf 380 PS gesteigert. Das Sechsgang-Schaltgetriebe findet weniger Anklang als die wahlweise erhältliche Automatik – ein unmissverständliches Bekenntnis der wohlhabenden Käuferschicht dieses Coupés zum Komfort. Für eher sportliche Fahrer gibt es im Hause BMW wendigere Mobile als das schwere Coupé.

Das Thema Wendigkeit allerdings erfährt beim CSi eine neue Dimension, denn die breiten hinteren Sohlen (265/40 ZR17) lassen sich lenken. Über die Kosten-Nutzen-Rechnung dieser aufwändigen aktiven Hinterachskinematik lässt sich freilich streiten. Dennoch findet Aufwändiges, besonders im Bereich Elektronik, Liebhaber. Angesichts der Verkaufszahlen – vor Einführung des Ci und CSi 1992 wurden mehr als 16 000 Coupés verkauft – scheint in dieser Fahrzeugkategorie der Preis keine entscheidende Rolle zu spielen. Der CSi für 180 000 Mark ohne Extras findet ebenfalls Käufer, aber der Absatz ist verhalten.

In der Marketingabteilung läuten die Alarmglocken. 1993 erscheint der 840Ci mit 286-PS-V8-Motor, Fünfganggetriebe und etwas weniger Elektronik für 129 000 Mark. Dieses Modell benötigt keine Abriegelung bei 250 Stundenkilometer: Es ist seine Spitzengeschwindigkeit.

Der sinnliche Genuss, den BMW beim Fahren des 8er Coupés verheißt, kommt zumindest bei einem Blick auf das funktionelle, äußerst geschmackvoll gestaltete Interieur auf. Dieses ist einfach „upper class", und die in den Sitzen integrierten Sicherheitsgurte „safety first".

Une synthèse de sportivité et de confort, un summum de technicité et tout ce qui est bon et cher se dissimulent dans le coupé de la série 8 avec lequel BMW veut, à l'automne 1989, marcher définitivement sur les plates-bandes de la luxueuse Mercedes-Benz. Cette nouvelle voiture de prestige est-elle sensationnelle ou simplement belle ? Les avis sont partagés. Elle réunit toutefois plusieurs éléments de style typiques de BMW.

Ainsi le mufle extrêmement plat de la 850i, dont les naseaux BMW sont plus larges que hauts, rappelle-il le prototype qu'était la BMW Turbo de Paul Bracq en 1972. L'ample galbe des ailes s'inspire de la M3 (E30) tandis que la forme et la hauteur de l'arête de décrochement à l'arrière sont identiques à celles des autres gammes. Quatre imposants pots d'échappement sous un becquet trahissent la puissance débordante et la magnificence d'un douze-cylindres.

Ce moteur à bloc et culasses en aluminium aussi utilisé pour la 750i développe 300 ch et voit sa cylindrée passer, pour la 850CSi (à partir de 1992), de 4988 à 5578 cm³ pour une puissance de 380 ch. La boîte manuelle à 6 vitesses remporte moins de succès que la transmission automatique proposée comme une alternative : un choix classique de la part des acheteurs aisés de ce coupé en faveur du confort. Pour les amateurs épris de conduite sportive, il y a, chez BMW des engins autrement plus maniables que ce lourd coupé.

Le thème de la maniabilité prend une dimension nouvelle avec la CSi, car les larges pneus arrière (265/40 ZR 17) braquent. On peut toutefois se perdre en conjecture sur le rapport coût/utilité de cette sophistiquée cinématique d'essieu arrière actif.

La complexité, notamment dans le domaine de l'électronique, fait cependant des adeptes. Par rapport aux chiffres de ventes (avant le lancement de la Ci et de la CSi en

1992, le nombre de coupés avait déjà dépassé 16 000), le prix n'a apparemment aucune incidence. Et c'est ainsi que la CSi trouve preneur même à 180 000 marks et plus, mais la demande s'affaiblit quelque peu.

L'alarme se déclenche immédiatement chez les spécialistes du marketing : en 1993, BMW lance la 840Ci à moteur V8 de 286 ch, boîte manuelle à 5 vitesses et un peu moins d'électronique pour 129 000 marks. Ce modèle n'a pas besoin de rupteur à 250 km/h : c'est sa vitesse de pointe.

Le plaisir que BMW promet aux conducteurs des coupés de la série 8 transparaît rien qu'en jetant un coup d'œil sur l'habitacle fonctionnel, de bon goût. Il est tout simplement haut de gamme, et les ceintures intégrées aux sièges assurent une totale sécurité.

BMW 85oi

Beneath the hood of the 850i we see a familiar sight: as in the 750i, a mighty 5-liter V12 engine does the business. The dashboard is restrained, but well-illuminated and ergonomic, and the center console features a trip computer and air conditioning system as well as the radio.

Unter der Haube des 850i bietet sich ein vertrautes Bild: Wie beim 750i verrichtet hier der starke 5-Liter-V12 seine Arbeit. Nüchtern, gut beleuchtet und im Blickfeld: Die übersichtlichen Armaturen und die Mittelkonsole mit Bordcomputer, Radio und Klimaanlage.

Sous le capot de la 850i se trouve une « vieille connaissance » : le puissant V12 de 5 litres de la 750i. Sobre mais bien éclairé : le tableau de bord est bien agencé, il se prolonge par la console médiane avec ordinateur de bord, autoradio et climatisation.

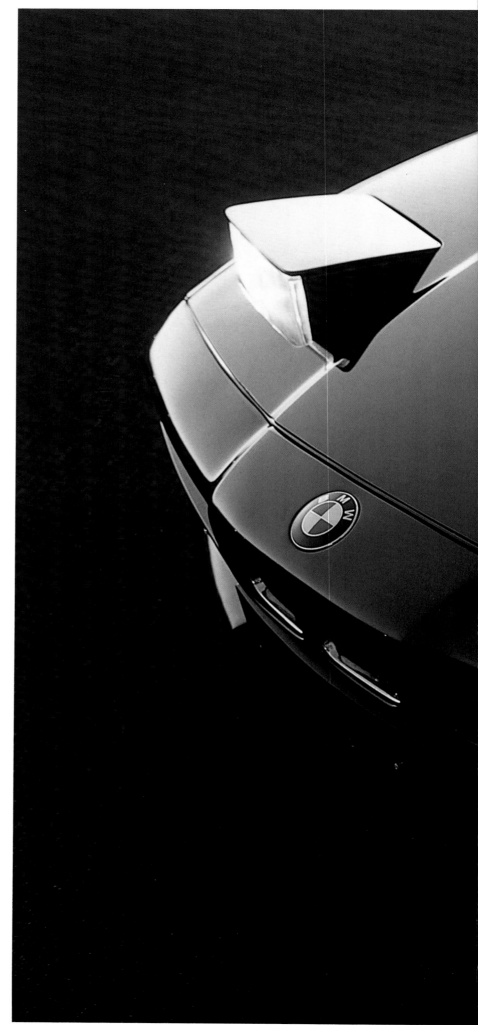

The 850i's retractable headlights incorporate low beam and fog lamps. The parking lights and high beam are integrated into the fender area. The trunk has ample space for two people's baggage. The tail of the coupé conceals a novelty: thanks to a suspension system with five wheel suspension arms, the multi-link suspension, the wide rear wheels steer along with the driver, so to speak.

Die „Schlafaugen" des 850i: Klappscheinwerfer mit Abblend- und Nebellampen. Stand- und Fernlicht erstrahlen aus dem Stoßfänger. Für das Gepäck von zwei Personen gut bemessen ist der Kofferraum. Das Coupé wartet mit einer Besonderheit im Heck auf. Dank einer räumlich wirkenden Radaufhängung mit fünf Lenkern, der Integralachse, lenken die breiten Hinterräder sozusagen mit.

Les phares escamotables de la 850i renferment les feux de route et de croisement. Les feux de position et les longues portées se trouvent dans le pare-chocs. Le coffre est suffisamment grand pour loger les bagages de deux personnes. Grâce à une suspension agissant comme un essieu intégral, les larges roues arrière ont un effet directionnel.

BMW 318i Cabrio

Even more elegant than its predecessor and full of technological gems, the E36 BMW 3 series convertible was unveiled in 1993. The aerodynamic wedge shape underlined the classic look of the open-top BMW which, according to its creators, was joy incarnated. From 1994, the advent of the 318i made this pleasure available to those with a more modest budget.

This tried and tested engine could deliver 115 bhp along with a few other innovations. For example, the maximum torque of 168 Nm could now be achieved at 3900 rpm. "DISA" was the name given by BMW to a new, high-tech component: the variable air intake unit controlled by the complex Digital Motor Electronics (DME). This unit delivered enhanced torque characteristics over the entire torque range by creating long intake tracts at low engine speeds, shortening as engine speed rises to develop full power at optimum revs. No distributor was left to interfere with radio and telephone reception, because the engine was controlled by the BMS 43 engine unit.

A reduction in fuel consumption to just under 29.5 miles per gallon (8 liters per 100 km) on the manual shift model was largely due to the introduction of the roller finger valve gear, which minimized friction between the camshaft and the fingers enormously. Despite the fun factor involved in driving convertibles, cost-effectiveness must be accorded high priority.

Although it was less nimble than its predecessor when accelerating, due to the extra 330 lbs (150 kg) of added technology carried, it had a higher top speed of 121 mph (194 kph). Overall, the four-cylinder convertible truly was value for money. The volume production model contained a plethora of goodies. Under the letter "A" alone, you could find safety components such as ABS, airbags and ASC+T (Automatic Stability Control + Traction).

The properly reinforced car body with the strong windscreen frame contributed to the safety of the vehicle's occupants. Additional rollover protection was provided by an extended roll bar system, which shot up automatically behind the rear seats in emergencies.

As an alternative to the five-speed manual gearbox, there was an electro-hydraulic automatic transmission with a special winter program for setting off in snow and slush. This was a very useful feature, as the Bavarians knew only too well, and would probably come in handy for the rest of the world, too. Experience favored the usual E36 central control-arm type of rear axle of 3 series with squat and dip compensation as well as anti-dive control.

Convertible drivers normally have an individualist streak, which BMW catered for with its individual program, naturally provided the customer was willing to pay. This meant that even the most extravagant combinations of colors and interior variants could be specially ordered, such as yellow leather with black piping on the seats, carbon fiber finishers, azure blue and titanium silver on the outside.

Noch eleganter als der Vorgänger und vollgepackt mit technischen Leckerbissen stellt sich 1993 das Cabrio der 3er Reihe (E36) vor. Die aerodynamisch günstige Keilform unterstreicht den Chic des offenen BMW, den seine Schöpfer als ein Stück Lebensfreude anpreisen. Diese ist ab 1994 auch weniger Betuchten in Form des 318i zugänglich.

115 PS leistet inzwischen das bewährte Triebwerk, das mit einigen Innovationen aufwarten kann. So wird das maximale Drehmoment von 168 Nm schon bei 3900 Umdrehungen pro Minute erreicht. „DISA" nennt BMW eine neue High-Tech-Komponente: die differenzierte Sauganlage, gesteuert durch eine komplexe digitale Motorelektronik. Sie gewährleistet einen verbesserten Drehmomentverlauf über das gesamte Drehzahlspektrum durch lange Ansaugwege bei niedrigen Touren und kurze zur vollen Leistungsausbeute im Bereich der Höchstdrehzahl. Kein Zündverteiler stört mehr den Radio- oder Telefonempfang, denn schließlich hat das Triebwerk die BMS-43-Motorsteuerung.

Einen wesentlichen Beitrag zur Senkung des Benzinverbrauchs der handgeschalteten Version auf knapp 8 Liter pro 100 Kilometer leisten die erstmalig verwendeten Rollenschlepphebel, die die Reibung zwischen Nockenwelle und Schlepphebel enorm reduzieren. Hoch lebe die Wirtschaftlichkeit, die bei allem Cabrioletspaß nicht außer Acht gelassen werden darf.

Mit rund 150 Kilo mehr Gewicht im Anzug behäbiger als sein Vorgänger, aber in der Endgeschwindigkeit schneller (Spitze 194 Stundenkilometer), ist das Vierzylindercabriolet sein Geld allemal wert. Es beherbergt serienmäßige Goodies in Hülle und Fülle. Allein unter dem Buchstaben „A" finden sich Sicherheitskomponenten wie ABS, Airbags und die automatische Stabilitätskontrolle ASC+T (Automatic Stability Control + Traction). Zur Sicherheit der Fahrzeuginsassen trägt auch die gut verstärkte Karosserie mit stabilem Windschutzscheibenrahmen bei. Für zusätzlichen Überrollschutz empfiehlt sich ein Bügelsystem, das im Falle des Überschlags automatisch hinter der Rücksitzbank nach oben schnellt.

Alternativ zum Fünfgang-Schaltgetriebe gibt es ein elektronisch-hydraulisches Automatikgetriebe mit einer speziellen Anfahrstufe für Schnee und Matsch – aus bayerischer Sicht sehr nützlich, für den Rest der Welt zumindest kein Nachteil. Bestens bewährt hat sich die Zentrallenker-Hinterachse mit Anfahr- und Tauchreduzierung sowie Bremsnickausgleich.

Cabrioletfahrer sind gewöhnlich Individualisten, und denen kommt BMW mit sogenannten Individualangeboten entgegen. Gegen entsprechendes Aufgeld dürfen Farben und Interieurvarianten wild kombiniert werden – zum Beispiel gelbes Leder mit schwarzen Paspelierungen auf den Sitzen, Kohlefaserverblendungen, Azurblau und Titansilber außen.

Plus élégant encore que celui de la génération précédente et truffé de détails techniques, le cabriolet de la série 3 (E36) apparaît en 1993. Ses lignes aérodynamiques mettent en évidence le chic de la BMW décapotable qui, pour ses créateurs, contribue à voir la vie en rose. Pour les portefeuilles moins bien garnis, cette voiture est disponible également, à partir de 1994, sous la forme d'une 318i.

Le moteur testé qui bénéficie de quelques innovations développe entre-temps 115 ch. Le couple maximum de 168 Nm est ainsi disponible dès 3900 tr/min. BMW a baptisé « DISA » un nouveau dispositif à haute technologie : le système d'aspiration différencié commandé par le complexe moteur électronique (Digital Motor Electronics). Il garantit une meilleure valeur de couple dans tous les régimes grâce à des tubulures d'aspiration longues à bas régime, mais plus courtes à haut régime pour exploiter totalement le potentiel. Il n'y a plus d'allumage qui puisse nuire à la qualité de réception de la radio ou du téléphone puisque le moteur possède une gestion électronique BMS 43.

Les culbuteurs à rouleau, qui diminuent considérablement la friction entre arbre à cames et culbuteurs, contribue de façon essentielle à faire baisser la consommation – 8 litres à peine aux 100 kilomètres pour la boîte manuelle. C'est une innovation qui génère des économies. Ce n'est pas parce que l'on est au volant d'un cabriolet qu'on doit jeter l'argent par les fenêtres.

Moins vif en reprise que son prédécesseur puisqu'il pèse environ 150 kg de plus, mais plus rapide en vitesse de pointe (194 km/h maximum), le cabriolet quatre-cylindres vaut vraiment son prix. Il renferme, en effet, une pléthore de raffinements proposés en série. Rien que sous la rubrique « A », on trouve des éléments de sécurité comme l'ABS, les airbags et l'ASC+T (Automatic Stability Control + Traction)

– un dispositif automatique de contrôle de stabilité et de traction. La carrosserie renforcée avec un solide pare-brise garantit également la sécurité des passagers. Un système d'arceau, qui se déclenche automatiquement derrière les appuie-tête arrière dès qu'une situation critique se présente, offre une protection supplémentaire en cas de tonneaux.

En alternative à la boîte manuelle à cinq vitesses, BMW propose une boîte automatique à commande électronico-hydraulique avec un rapport de démarrage spécial pour la neige et la boue – qui a fait ses preuves dans les rigueurs de l'hiver bavarois. Mais pour le reste du monde, cela n'est assurément pas vital. Le train arrière à guidage central avec dispositif limitant la plongée au freinage et le cabrage aux accélérations a, lui aussi, parfaitement fait ses preuves.

BMW va au-devant des désirs des conducteurs et des conductrices de cabriolets en leur proposant des options individuelles. Ils peuvent ainsi choisir à volonté – contre espèces sonnantes et trébuchantes, naturellement – toutes les combinaisons possibles de couleurs de carrosserie et de décoration intérieure : des sièges de cuir jaune avec liseré noir, des panneaux de fibre de carbone bleu azur et argent titane à l'extérieur.

BMW 318i Cabrio

The 318i Cabrio is visually very pleasing with its elegant and harmonious lines from the flat hood to the relatively low rear. It has 115 bhp at its disposal.

Das 318i Cabrio ist wegen der eleganten und harmonischen Linienführung von der flachen Motorhaube bis zu dem relativ niedrigen Heck optisch äußerst ansprechend. Es verfügt über 115 PS.

La 318i Cabrio est une très grande réussite esthétique en raison de l'élégance et de l'harmonie de ses lignes qui partent du capot moteur plat à l'arrière relativement bas. Elle est propulsée par un moteur de 115 ch.

BMW 318i Cabrio

The fuel efficiency of the proven four-cylinder engine does nothing to reduce the feeling that there are no "constraints".

Der sparsame Benzinverbrauch des bewährten Vierzylinders mindert gewiss nicht das Gefühl der grenzenlosen Freiheit.

Les économies prouvées de consommation du quatre-cylindres ne minorent en rien la sensation de liberté.

BMW M3

Chosen as "Car of the Century" by American journalists, BMW is convinced that there are few other cars which have collected so many laurels as the M3 of the E36 series. In all modesty, the later M3 has undergone a considerable metamorphosis – transformed from a pure piece of sporting equipment to a cultivated high-performance car.

However, there was a major E36 M3 change from the 286 bhp 3-liter engine to a 3.2-liter engine with 321 bhp in 1995. The new aluminum six-cylinder engine of the 328i served as the basis for this powerful machine which possessed all the technical delicacies of BMW's horse-power-generating kitchen: four valves per cylinder, continuously variable camshaft timing control of both intake and exhaust camshafts, plus the most modern digital electronic engine management with anti-knock control. The latter is, indeed, necessary as the M3 engine has such a high compression ratio that it demands Super-Plus fuel. On the other hand the top speed is electronically limited to 155 mph (250 kph). Petrol consumption is encouraging: average consumption above 19.7 miles per gallon (12 liters per 100 km) must be considered modest for a car which sprints from 0 to 62 mph (100 kph) in 5.5 seconds. The elasticity of engine power delivery is considerable and the explosive performance starts as low as 2000 rpm, beginning an almost endless stream of power. The engine power of the M3 is supported by a six-speed transmission with a long sixth gear, so that the tachometer shows just 6000 rpm at 155 mph (250 kph). Optionally, BMW offers a taste of the sequential gearboxes used in motor sport: clutch and the six forward gears are managed electro-hydraulically by computer. The gear lever has an automatic and a manual shift mode.

The chassis is optimized with a single-joint McPherson strut axle at the front and central trailing arm axle at the rear.

Directional stability, handling and cornering stability could hardly be bettered. Driving comfort too deserves a *par excellence* rating.

A large trunk and 17-gallon (65-liter) tank mean that long legs can only be accommodated across the rear seats of the M3. Both M3 variants, coupé and convertible, have a large front spoiler. Standard equipment covers airbags, ABS, leather steering wheel, steering column adjustment and light alloy wheels with varied tire widths (225/45 front and 245/40 ZR 17 rear).

The convertible, on the market since May 1994, is a little softer than the coupé. Open air fun and rapid acceleration fit as well together as an open top and the euphoria of a 155 mph (250 kph) maximum in the rear of an M3 convertible.

Von amerikanischen Journalisten wird er zum „Auto des Jahrhunderts" gekürt, und BMW ist überzeugt, dass kaum ein Auto in der Vergangenheit so viele Lorbeeren wie der M3 der Baureihe E36 eingeheimst hat. In aller Bescheidenheit wird davon gesprochen, dass der M3 mit seiner Wandlung vom reinen Sportgerät hin zum kultivierten Hochleistungsauto eine starke Metamorphose erfahren hat.

Stark ist tatsächlich die Wandlung vom 286 PS starken 3-Liter-Motor zum 3,2-Liter-Triebwerk mit 321 PS im Jahr 1995. Der neue Aluminium-Sechszylinder des 328i dient als Basis des Kraftpakets, das über alle technischen Leckerbissen der BMW-PS-Küche verfügt: vier Ventile pro Zylinder, variable stufenlose Nockenwellenspreizung, Steuerung der Ein- und Auslassnockenwelle und natürlich modernstes elektronisches Motormanagement mit Klopf-regelung. Letztere ist auch erforderlich, denn der M3-Motor ist derart hoch verdichtet, dass er nach Super-Plus-Benzin verlangt. Andererseits wird die Höchstgeschwindigkeit bei 250 Stundenkilometer elektronisch abgeriegelt. Tröstlich ist der Benzinverbrauch: Für einen Wagen, der in 5,5 Sekunden von 0 auf 100 Stundenkilometer sprintet, darf ein Durch-schnittsverbrauch, der unter 12 Litern liegt, als moderat gelten.

Die Elastizität des Motors ist beachtlich. Bereits bei 2000 Touren setzt der Schub mit Brachialgewalt ein, und es beginnt eine schier endlose Leistungsausbeute. Unterstützt wird die Durchzugskraft des M3 durch ein Sechsgang-getriebe mit langem sechsten Gang, so dass der Drehzahl-messer bei 250 Stundenkilometer gerade 6000 Umdrehun-gen pro Minute anzeigt.

Auf Wunsch bietet BMW sogar das im Motorsport verwendete sequentielle Getriebe an: die Kupplung und die sechs Vorwärtsgänge werden computergesteuert hydraulisch geschaltet. Dabei verfügt der Wählhebel über eine automatisierte und eine manuelle Schaltgasse.

Optimal abgestimmt ist das Fahrwerk mit Eingelenk-Federbeinachse vorn und Zentrallenkerachse hinten. Geradeauslauf, Handling und Kurvenstabilität sind kaum noch zu übertreffen. Auch dem Fahrkomfort muss ein „par excellence" attestiert werden.

Zugunsten des großen Kofferraums und des 65-Liter-Tanks lassen sich lange Beine im Fond des M3 nur quer verstauen. Beide M3-Varianten, Coupé und Cabriolet, haben einen großen Frontspoiler. Serienmäßig sind auch Airbags, ABS, Lederlenkrad, Lenksäulenverstellung und Leichtmetallräder mit Mischbereifung (225/45 vorn und 245/40 ZR 17 hinten).

Das Cabriolet, seit Mai 1994 auf dem Markt, ist etwas weicher abgestimmt als das Coupé. Frischluftvergnügen und Querbeschleunigung passen eben genausowenig zusammen wie offenes Verdeck und der genussvoll erlebte Rausch der Geschwindigkeit bei 250 Stundenkilometer.

Les journalistes américains l'ont sacrée «voiture du siècle» et pour BMW rarement une voiture aura remporté par le passé autant de lauriers que la M3 de la série E36. En toute humilité, elle déclare que la M3 a, en passant d'un pur engin sportif à une voiture perfectionnée et performante, subi une métamorphose sans pareille.

La mutation est en effet impressionnante du 3 litres de 286 ch en un 3,2 litres développant 321 ch en 1995. Le nouveau six-cylindres en aluminium de la 328i est la base de ce bolide qui contient tous les perfectionnements techniques connus des motoristes de chez BMW : quatre soupapes par cylindre, une distribution variable en continu des arbres à cames côté admission et échappement ainsi que, naturellement, une gestion moteur électronique ultramoderne avec une régulation antidétonation. Celle-ci est d'ailleurs absolument indispensable, car le moteur de la M3 a un taux de compression si élevé qu'il doit impérativement consommer du super plus. En contrepartie, la vitesse maximum est régulée électroniquement à 250 km/h. Sa consommation d'essence est une consolation : pour une voiture qui abat le 0 à 100 km/h en 5,5 secondes, une consommation moyenne inférieure à 12 litres peut légitimement être qualifiée de modeste.

La souplesse du moteur est remarquable, et, dès 2000 tr/min commence une montée en puissance qui semble ne jamais devoir finir. Les reprises de la M3 sont soutenues par une boîte à six vitesses à sixième longue, si bien qu'à 250 km/h, l'aiguille du compte-tours ne dépasse jamais les 6000 tr/min.

En option, BMW propose la boîte séquentielle utilisée en compétition : l'embrayage et les six rapports avant sont actionnés par une commande électronique. Le pommeau trône alors au centre d'une double grille : automatique et manuelle.

Les trains roulants sont réglés de façon optimale avec des jambes élastiques à articulation unique à l'avant et un essieu arrière à bras guidés au centre. La tenue de route, la maniabilité et la stabilité dans les courbes sont pratiquement inégalées et le confort de conduite mérite, lui aussi, un prix d'excellence.

Le coffre de grande capacité et le réservoir de 65 litres obligent celui qui a de longues jambes à s'asseoir en biais à l'arrière. Les deux variantes de la M3, le coupé et le cabriolet, possèdent un généreux aileron avant. L'équipement de série comporte aussi des airbags, l'ABS, un volant cuir, une colonne de direction réglable et des jantes alliage chaussées de pneus mixtes (225/45 à l'avant et 245/40 ZR 17 à l'arrière).

Le cabriolet commercialisé depuis mai 1994 est un peu plus souple que le coupé. Il ne faut naturellement pas chercher à concilier les plaisirs de la décapotable et ceux des accélérations transversales.

The 286 bhp 3-liter engine of the M3 was replaced in 1995 by a 3.2-liter engine with 321 bhp. It was based on the aluminum six-cylinder engine of the 328i. As the basis for motor sport, the coupé is the "racer" in the M3 family. The appropriate wheel design for the road is also supplied.

Der 3-Liter-Motor des M3 mit 286 PS wird 1995 von einem 3,2-Liter-Triebwerk mit 321 PS abgelöst. Er basiert auf dem Aluminium-Sechszylinder des 328i. Als Basisfahrzeug für den Motorsport ist das Coupé der „Renner" in der M3-Familie. Das passende Raddesign für die Straße wird mitgeliefert.

Le moteur de 3 litres de la M3, qui développe 286 ch, est remplacé par un 3,2 litres de 321 ch en 1995. Il s'est inspiré du six-cylindres en aluminium de la 328i. Comme voiture de base pour la compétition, le coupé est « la fusée » dans la famille des M3. Le design des jantes pour la route est à l'unisson.

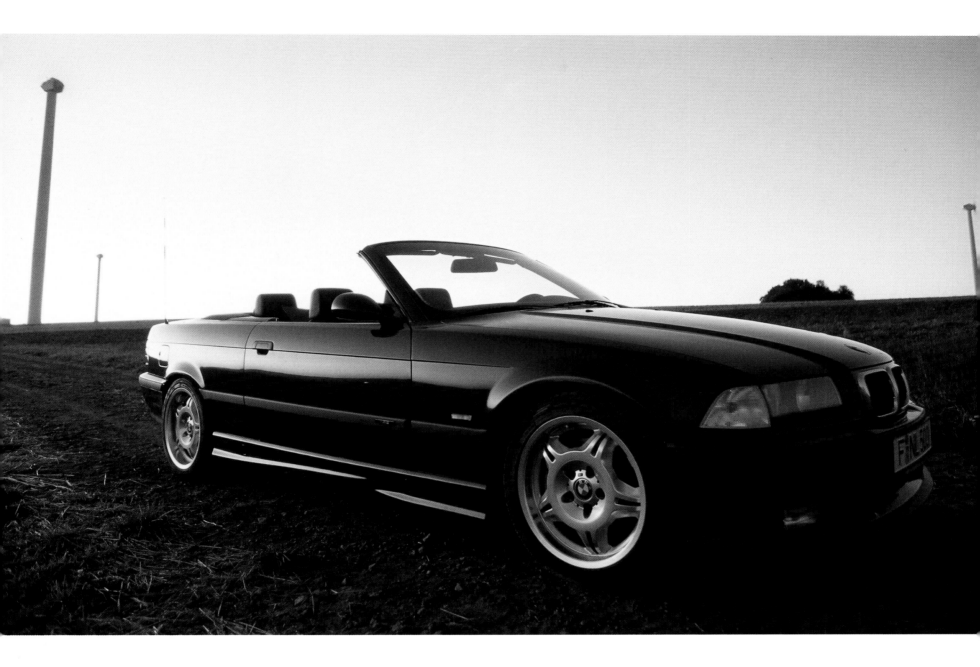

With acceleration almost as fast as the M3 coupé, the M3 convertible accelerates from a standing start to 62 mph (100 kph) in 5.5 seconds, turning a drive with the top down into an exceptional experience.

Fast so sprintstark wie das M3 Coupé beschleunigt das M3 Cabrio in 5,5 Sekunden aus dem Stand auf 100 Stundenkilometer und lässt das Fahren mit offenem Verdeck zu einem besonderen Erlebnis werden.

Avec presque d'aussi bonnes reprises que le coupé M3, la M3 Cabriolet abat le 0 à 100 km/h en 5,5 secondes. Dans cette voiture, rouler en décapotable fait éprouver des sensations exceptionnelles.

The large air intake on the M3 front spoiler is unmistakable;
it ensures the necessary pressure at high speeds.

Unverkennbar ist der große Kühllufteinlass des M3-Front-
spoilers, der in den hohen Geschwindigkeitsbereichen für
den nötigen Anpressdruck sorgt.

Reconnaissable entre mille : la grande prise d'air de
refroidissement dans l'imposant aileron avant de la M3
lui confère l'appui indispensable à haute vitesse.

The abbreviation "ti" (touring international) on a BMW badge symbolized from 1964 to 1975 the sportiness of a Porsche combined with space for a family. Drivers of a BMW "ti" or even a 130 bhp "tii" – the extra "i" denoted with fuel injection – had a youthful and dynamic image.

When BMW recalled these virtues in 1994, seeking its lost target customer group with the 318ti compact, those potential customers had largely swapped over to Volkswagen's Golf GTI. With spirited engine performance and driving manners, BMW became involved in the market of the GTI which was 1000 marks cheaper. Truly, the looks of the Bavarian with the short rear end compensated for the 7 mph (11 kph) missing at the top compared with the GTI.

Compared to other 3 series, 9 inches (23 cm) are missing from the rear end, but the large tailgate and individually folding rear seats provide excellent versatility on the inside. Those for whom this is not enough can allow themselves the open air variant – an electrically-operated fabric top, stretching the whole length of the roof.

Until 1996 the 318ti compact was powered by the four-valve engine from the 318ti coupé. This 1796 cc engine developed an unpleasant noise level at anything higher than 5000 rpm. BMW reacted with a larger capacity (1895 cc) to this single weakness. The alternative for power freaks was the 323ti compact: a six-cylinder of 170 bhp and 144 mph (230 kph) top speed.

That brings us back to the constant struggle of the "ti" with the GTI as to who is stronger, more maneuverable and faster, all whilst trying to achieve the most favorable consumption figures. Since dedicated BMW drivers resist any comparison with the products from VW at Wolfsburg, the rear drive BMW ti should be looked at in its own right, and not in comparison to a GTI front-wheel drive car.

The strengths of the compact car from Munich lie in its maneuverability, neutral cornering behavior complimented by extremely precise steering, and the effective ABS brakes. The gear-change too is satisfying. Unfortunately the fifth gear is a little too short for cruising comfort. Impact safety, exhaust values and economy are to best BMW standards.

Nostalgia for the 2000tii Touring of 1971, which was 4 inches (10 cm) smaller all round and produced a mere 10 bhp less, arises from design similarities of the ti compact as a two-door with a large tailgate. The difference lies in the numbers produced. In this respect the 2002tii Touring was a rarity compared to its compact descendant.

Die Abkürzung „ti" (touring international) auf dem Typenschild eines BMW symbolisiert zwischen 1964 und 1975 die Kombination aus der Sportlichkeit eines Porsche mit dem Platzangebot einer familientauglichen Limousine. Die Fahrer eines „ti" oder gar eines 130 PS starken „tii" – also mit Einspritzung – gelten als jung und dynamisch.

BMW besinnt sich 1994 wieder auf diese Tugenden und sucht mit dem 318ti compact die verlorene Zielgruppe, die in der Zwischenzeit größtenteils auf den Golf GTI umgestiegen ist. Mit temperamentvoller Motorleistung und Fahrkultur mischt sich BMW in das Segment des 1000 Mark günstigeren GTI. Und gewiss macht die Optik des Kurzheck-Bayern die gegenüber dem GTI um 11 Stundenkilometer geringere Spitzengeschwindigkeit wett.

Gegenüber den anderen 3ern fehlen am „Hintern" 23 Zentimeter, doch durch die große Hecktür und die einzeln umklappbaren Fondsitze ist eine gewisse Innenraumvariabilität gegeben. Wem diese nicht ausreicht, der kann sich die Open-Air-Variante genehmigen – ein Stoffverdeck, das elektrisch über die ganze Dachlänge geöffnet werden kann.

Bis 1996 wird der 318ti compact vom Vierventiler des 318ti Coupé angetrieben. Dieser Motor mit 1796 ccm Hubraum entwickelt bei mehr als 5000 Umdrehungen pro Minute einen unangenehm hohen Geräuschpegel – seine einzige Schwachstelle, die BMW mit einem größeren Hubraum (1895 ccm) korrigiert. Die Alternative für Powerfreaks lautet 323ti compact: Sechszylinder, 170 PS, 230 Stundenkilometer Spitze.

Damit sind wir wieder beim „Golf-Krieg", dieser ständigen Auseinandersetzung des „ti" mit dem GTI über die Frage, wer nun stärker, handlicher und schneller ist, und das bei möglichst günstigen Verbrauchswerten. Da ein-

BMW 318ti compact

geschworene BMW-Fahrer jeglichem Vergleich mit den Produkten aus Wolfsburg abhold sind, sollte der BMW ti so gesehen werden, wie er ist, und nicht im Vergleich mit dem Fronttriebler GTI.

Die Stärken des kompakten Autos aus München liegen in seiner Handlichkeit, seinem neutralen Kurvenverhalten, einer äußerst präzisen Lenkung und den wirksamen Bremsen mit ABS. Auch das Getriebe lässt sich mit der bei BMW üblichen Präzision schalten. Leider ist der fünfte Gang etwas zu kurz geraten. Aufprallsicherheit, Abgaswerte und Wirtschaftlichkeit entsprechen BMW-Standards.

Nostalgische Gefühle für den 2000tii Touring von 1971, der gerade 10 Zentimeter kleiner war und nur 10 PS weniger gebracht hat, kommen angesichts der ähnlichen Konzeption des ti compact als Zweitürer mit türähnlicher Heckklappe auf. Der feine Unterschied liegt in der Stückzahl. In dieser Hinsicht ist der alte tii Touring eine Rarität.

Avec l'abréviation «ti» (pour touring international) à l'arrière des voitures, BMW concilie, de 1964 à 1975, la sportivité d'une Porsche et l'habitabilité d'une limousine familiale. Les conducteurs de «ti», ou de la version à injection «tii» de 130 ch, sont considérés comme jeunes et dynamiques.

Lorsque BMW en prend conscience en 1994 et cherche à reconquérir sa clientèle cible qu'elle a perdu en lui proposant la 318ti compact, ses acheteurs potentiels ont, en majorité, rejoint sans tambour ni trompette le camp de la Golf GTI. Avec une motorisation qui a du tempérament et qui se conduit en douceur, BMW offre un véhicule de la catégorie des GTI, moins cher de 1000 marks. Et, assurément, l'esthétique de la BMW à l'arrière tronqué compense un peu les 11 km/h de vitesse de pointe qui lui manque face à la GTI.

Par rapport aux autres séries 3, elle a raccourci de 23 cm à l'arrière, mais le grand hayon et la banquette arrière fractionnée et rabattable lui permettent d'offrir une grande souplesse d'utilisation. Celui à qui cela ne suffit pas peut opter pour la variante «open air» – avec une capote électrique s'ouvrant sur toute la longueur du toit.

Jusqu'en 1996, la 318ti compact est propulsée par le quatre-soupapes de la 318ti coupé. À plus de 5000 tr/min, ce moteur de 1796 cm³ de cylindrée est bruyant. C'est son seul point faible, mais BMW réplique en augmentant la cylindrée à 1895 cm³. L'alternative pour les amateurs de performance a pour nom 323ti compact: six cylindres, 170 ch, une vitesse de pointe de 230 km/h.

Cela nous ramène à la confrontation permanente entre les «ti» et les GTI pour savoir lesquelles sont les plus puissantes, les plus maniables et les plus rapides et celles qui consomment le moins. Comme les inconditionnels de la BMW refusent toute comparaison avec son concurrent de Wolfsburg, il faut prendre la BMW ti comme elle est et ne pas la comparer à une traction avant baptisée GTI.

Les points forts de la voiture compacte de Munich sont sa maniabilité, sa stabilité dans les virages avec une direction extrêmement précise et ses freins efficaces avec ABS. La boîte de vitesses se laisse manœuvrer avec une précision propre à BMW. Malheureusement, la cinquième a une démultiplication un peu trop courte. La sécurité en cas de collision, un véhicule peu polluant, la sobriété et le prix sont les meilleurs atouts de BMW.

Compte tenu de la similitude entre la BMW ti compacte à deux portes, avec hayon, et la 2000tii Touring de 1971, que BMW avait raccourcie de 10 cm et qui développait seulement 10 ch de moins, on ne peut être que nostalgique. La seule différence, mais elle est de taille, réside dans les chiffres de production. La tii Touring est, en effet, très rare.

Younger buyers in particular value this compact zippy BMW without a "rear", which is 9 inches (23 cm) shorter than the other 3 series cars. The space in the two-door sedan with its sloping rear is quite acceptable. 930 lbs (422 kg) of additional load are allowed.

Besonders jüngere Käuferschichten schätzen den kompakten spritzigen BMW ohne „Hintern", der 23 Zentimeter kürzer ist als die anderen 3er. Das Platzangebot in der zweitürigen Schräg-heck-Limousine ist durchaus akzeptabel. 422 Kilo Zuladung sind erlaubt.

Les jeunes acheteurs, en particulier, apprécient la compacte et nerveuse BMW dont l'arrière mesure 23 cm de moins que les autres séries 3. L'habitacle de la berline deux portes, dont l'arrière est tronqué, est tout à fait acceptable. Elle peut transporter jusqu'à 422 kg.

Until 1996, the 318ti compact was powered by the 140 bhp four-valve four-cylinder engine of the 318ti coupé. Smart: the steering wheel with leather grip.

Bis 1996 wird der 318ti compact vom Vierventil-Vierzylinder mit 140 PS des 318ti coupé angetrieben. Schick ist das Lenkrad mit Ledergriffzone.

Jusqu'en 1996, la 318ti compact est propulsée par le quatre-cylindres à quatre soupapes de 140 ch de la 318ti coupé. Très chic : le volant en cuir.

BMW 318ti compact

BMW 320i touring

BMW has fond memories of the first Touring model, which as a two-door combination of estate car, sedan and coupé made a lively addition to the model range in 1971. The 3 series "touring" of the E36 generation, which was described by BMW as an "automobile for people who value individuality and have a mobile dynamic lifestyle," is more than a refined example of a four-door estate car.

The 320i, one of seven different engine configurations, has the now classic BMW format of the six-cylinder in-line 1991 cc engine. This power source with a three-way catalytic converter and a lambda sensor can deliver 150 bhp – exactly what could be expected from this "high-class beast of burden," which can take a load of half a ton. Laden only with the driver, the 320i can reach 132 mph (212 kph) and also does well in the sprint stakes, accelerating from 0 to 62 mph (100 kph) in approximately 10 seconds. The fuel tank has the same capacity for all touring variants of the 3 series: it only needs refueling every 375 miles (600 km) of mixed driving.

This sporting wagon's priority is a versatile compartment design which can accommodate the widest possible variety of loads. The loading volume of 1320 liters is enclosed by a large and retractable rear baggage cover. Practical hoops and other securing fixtures for loads ensure that nothing gets damaged when taking sharp corners. This sports wagon manages changes of direction and tight bends in an extremely smooth manner. Thanks to the Automatic Stability Control (ASC), wheel spin or sudden slides of the 320i touring's rear wheels are minimized. Like all models of the 3 series, the chassis is specified to optimum levels with the central control-arm rear axle.

Safety really does come first with this car: ABS, disc brakes (internally vented at the front), airbags including a side airbag for driver and front-seat passenger, plus impact absorption zones and the integrated side collision protection are all part of the standard equipment features.

In addition to those zones of passive and active safety, there are also extra features including some aimed specifically at the family. For example the 320i touring has electric circuit sockets that are integrated in the child seats at the rear of the car. Whether small children will use these plug-in points for reading lights or Walkman entertainment is another matter altogether.

The tasteful interior of the 320i displays a great deal of attention to practical details. In mass-produced automobiles, anything important appears exactly where you would expect. The answer to any extra individual requirements can be found in the BMW catalogs for special equipment, following their motto: "Anything developed and installed by us must be good."

Gern besinnt sich BMW auf den ersten Touring, der 1971 als zweitürige Mischung aus Kombi, Limousine und Coupé die Modellpalette belebte. Der 3er touring der heutigen BMW-Generation, von den Werbestrategen als „Automobil für Menschen, die auf Individualität Wert legen und einen mobilen dynamischen Lebensstil haben" beschrieben, ist mehr als ein viertüriger Kombi der besseren Art.

Der 320i, eine von sieben verschiedenen Triebwerkskonfigurationen, hat den mittlerweile schon klassischen Sechszylinder-Reihenmotor mit 1991 ccm Hubraum. Diese Kraftquelle mit Dreiwegekatalysator und Lambda-Sonde leistet 150 PS, genau das Richtige für einen „Edel-Lastesel", dem eine halbe Tonne Zuladung aufgebürdet werden kann. Nur mit dem Fahrer beladen, erreicht der 320i eine Spitzengeschwindigkeit von 212 Stundenkilometern und zieht mit einer Beschleunigung von rund 10 Sekunden von 0 auf 100 Stundenkilometer recht ordentlich an. Der Tankinhalt, bei allen touring der 3er Serie gleich groß, reicht im gemischten Betrieb für eine Fahrtstrecke von rund 600 Kilometern.

Bei einem Kombi ist die Umsetzung eines variablen Raumkonzeptes wichtig, das Freiraum für die verschiedensten Formen der Zuladung schafft. Beim 3er verschließt eine große Heckklappe das Ladevolumen von 1320 Litern. Praktische Ösen und sonstige Ladeguthalterungen sorgen auch bei extremen Kurvenfahrten für Ordnung. Schnelle Richtungswechsel und enge Kurven meistert dieser Kombi ohne Schwankungen, denn dank der automatischen Stabilitätskontrolle werden ein Durchdrehen der Räder oder die Gefahr eines plötzlichen Ausbrechens des Wagenhecks auf ein Minimum reduziert. Wie bei allen 3ern ist das Fahrwerk mit Zentrallenker-Hinterachse bestens nivelliert.

Das Thema Sicherheit wird großgeschrieben: ABS, Scheibenbremsen (vorn innenbelüftet), Airbags einschließlich

Seitenairbag für Fahrer und Beifahrer und Stoßabsorbie-
rungszonen gehören ebenso zum Standard wie der integrierte seitliche Aufprallschutz.

Neben diesen sinnvollen Bausteinen zur Verbesserung
der passiven und aktiven Sicherheit gibt es natürlich auch
viel Staffage und außerdem das sogenannte „Family"-
Konzept, bei dem Kindersitze mit Bordstromsteckdosen in
der hinteren Sitzbank integriert sind. Ob die Kleinen wohl
mit Leseleuchten oder dem Anschluss für einen Walkman
sehr viel anfangen können?

Viel Liebe zum praktischen Detail verrät das geschmack-
volle Interieur des 320i. Alles Wichtige ist in der serienmäßigen Ausgabe dort, wo man es sich wünscht. Darüber
hinaus gehenden individuellen Bedürfnissen setzen die
BMW-Sonderausstattungskataloge keine Grenzen, frei
nach dem Motto: Gut ist alles, was von uns entwickelt und
eingebaut wird.

Ce n'est pas sans une certaine nostalgie que BMW
se rappelle sa première Touring, lancée en 1971,
qui était un savant mélange de deux portes de
break, berline et coupé – un authentique élargissement de
sa gamme donc. La série 3 touring de l'actuelle génération
de BMW, que Munich qualifie d'«automobile pour les
conducteurs qui ont une personnalité et qui sont dynamiques», est plus qu'un break à quatre portes – elle est
« la » perfection.

La 320i, l'une de sept configurations de moteur différentes, possède le six-cylindres de 1991 cm³ qui est, entre-
temps, devenu un grand classique. Ce propulseur à catalyseur trois voies et à sonde lambda développe 150 ch, juste
ce qu'il convient pour une «bête de somme prestigieuse»
qui peut transporter une demi-tonne de bagages. «Chargée»
du seul conducteur, la 320i atteint 212 km/h et accélère
énergiquement puisqu'elle couvre le 0 à 100 km/h en
quelque 10 secondes. En conduite mixte, le réservoir de
carburant, dont la capacité est identique pour toutes les
touring de la série 3, octroie une autonomie de 600 km.

Un aspect important pour un break est la libre disposition de l'intérieur qui donne carte blanche à toutes les
formes de transport. Un grand hayon donne accès à un
coffre d'une capacité de 1320 litres. De pratiques œillets
de fixation et divers points d'arrimage garantissent que tout
reste bien en place même lorsque l'on franchit très rapidement les virages. Car ce break maîtrise parfaitement les
fréquents changements de cap et les virages serrés. Grâce
au contrôle de stabilité automatique, tout patinage des roues
ou dérapage brutal de l'arrière est pratiquement exclu.
Comme pour toutes les séries 3, le châssis est parfaitement
jugulé grâce à l'essieu arrière à guidage central.

Le thème de la sécurité n'a été négligé en rien : ABS,
freins à disques (ventilés à l'avant), coussins gonflables avec

airbags latéraux pour le conducteur et le passager avant et
zones d'amortissement des chocs font partie de l'équipement de série au même titre que la protection anticollision
latérale intégrée.

Outre ces éléments de sécurité passive et active, il en
existe naturellement bien d'autres qui vont du gadget au
concept « Family », selon lequel les sièges pour enfants
intégrés à la banquette arrière comportent une prise de
courant électrique. Mais que peuvent bien en faire nos
chères petites têtes blondes ?

Très bien conçu, le cockpit de la 320i fait place à de
nombreux détails pratiques. On trouve en série toutes les
choses indispensables là où on s'attend à les trouver. Le
catalogue d'options de BMW, qui ne connaît pratiquement
pas de limites (selon la devise « nous mettons au point et
nous construisons le meilleur »), répond aux besoins les
plus personnels.

BMW 320i touring

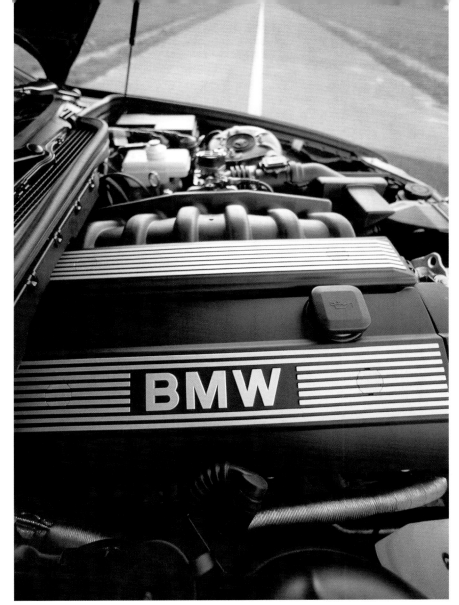

The 320i touring is well equipped with the 150 bhp 2-liter six-cylinder engine which can easily carry the burden of an extra half-ton load.

Mit dem 150 PS starken 2-Liter-Sechszylindermotor ist der 320i touring, dem ohne weiteres eine halbe Tonne Zuladung aufgebürdet werden kann, bestens ausgestattet.

Avec le six-cylindres de 2 litres et 150 ch, la 320i touring, qui peut transporter sans difficulté une demi-tonne, dispose d'un propulseur idéal.

BMW 320i touring

In 1989, Gordon Murray revealed a secret. The South African had been a successful Formula 1 designer with Brabham in the BMW turbo engine era. Now Gordon worked with McLaren. His secret? It was a sketch of a racing-inspired road car to put anything else in the shade. Gordon predicted, "with McLaren, I can make my dream come true and design the ultimate sports car. Ron Dennis, the head of McLaren, and his partner Mansour Ojjeh are planning to launch a small, exclusive production series of this design."

BMW was selected from an exotic range of candidates as engine supplier. The reason for this was that the new BMW V12 (type S70/2) could produce at least 550 bhp from a six-liter engine. Equally impressive was that this power rating was achieved in the form of a gradual performance curve, not by the sudden surges of turbo power. Murray's friendship with Paul Rosche, the "High Priest" of BMW engines, meant that this new alliance took place smoothly. After all, they had pulled off the first Formula 1 "turbo title" in 1983 together.

The prestigious Monte Carlo Sporting Club and the 1992 Monaco Grand Prix were worthy venues for the car's debut to be staged. The McLaren BMW was baptized "F1" with performance which outstripped this aspirant name. In keeping with Formula 1 racing tradition, the F1 driver sat in the middle of the cockpit. However, two passengers, sitting slightly behind and to either side of the driver, also had the privilege of experiencing the sensation of this road rocket in action.

The countdown to this driving experience started in early 1993. Jonathan Palmer who, as a Formula 1 driver was deemed fit to test the first F1 prototype, spoke of driving characteristics which were very similar to those exhibited by a Grand Prix car. A small difference: the aerodynamic body of the "F1 rocket" complete with its aerodynamic downforce configuration simply kept on accelerating past the 125 mph (200 kph) mark. The F1 reached – on a suitably long stretch of track and with no side winds – over 231 mph (370 kph).

One of the first to order the F1 (costing at least 1.6 million marks – then close to a million dollars) was former world champion Keke Rosberg, who was chauffeured around the Nürburgring by Ron Dennis in the supercar's first outing. Some 300 cars were planned, one a week from 1994. The chassis was just as elaborate as the 90 component concoction which made up the carbon fiber monocoque. One built to resemble a racing car, but adapted for the public highway. Preferably, a road without potholes was expected.

Unlike the racing version which won the 1996 GT Long Distance World Championship, the road version of the F1 did not need a spoiler. A rear flap was only electrically extended during braking. The normal F1 did not have the sequential gearshifts of the later racing F1 GTR; instead, shifts were in a six-speed H-gate. The rocker switches on the steering wheel only activated the headlights and the horn. Any remaining space contrasted with all the carbon, Kevlar and light-weight materials in the F1, for it was clad in deluxe leather, according to each customer's preferences. Anyway, there was little room left over for accessories.

Gordon Murray verrät 1989 ein Geheimnis. Der Südafrikaner, in Brabhams Diensten erfolgreicher Formel-1-Konstrukteur und seit der Auflösung des Teams bei McLaren tätig, skizziert einen Straßensportwagen, der alles bisher Dagewesene in den Schatten stellen soll. „Ich darf mir bei McLaren einen Traum erfüllen und konstruiere den ultimativen Sportwagen, mit dem McLaren-Chef Ron Dennis und sein Teilhaber Mansour Ojjeh eine exklusive Kleinserie geplant haben."

Unter den in Frage kommenden Motorenlieferanten fällt die Wahl auf BMW. Ausschlaggebend dafür ist, dass der neue BMW V12 (Typ S70/2) aus sechs Litern Hubraum locker 550 PS und mehr holt, und das in einer stetigen Leistungskurve, also nicht durch plötzlich einsetzende Turbo-Power. Da BMWs „Motoren-Papst" Paul Rosche ein guter Freund von Murray ist – man hat 1983 gemeinsam den ersten „Turbo-Weltmeistertitel" der Formel 1 geholt, wird das neuerliche „Let's get together" erleichtert.

Der vornehme Sporting Club von Monte Carlo und der dortige Grand Prix 1992 sind der würdige Rahmen, um einen Wagen zu präsentieren, der „F1" heißt und diesem Namen alle Ehre macht. Wie in einem Formel-Wagen sitzt der Fahrer in der Cockpitmitte. Aber auch zwei Passagiere, seitlich und etwas nach hinten versetzt, dürfen dabeisein, wenn die „Rakete" gezündet wird.

Der Countdown zum Fahrerlebnis läuft im Frühjahr 1993 an. Jonathan Palmer, der als Formel-1-Pilot für tauglich befunden wird, die ersten F1-Prototypen zu testen, erklärt, dass das Fahrverhalten dem eines Grand-Prix-Wagens sehr nahe kommt. Der Unterschied liegt darin, dass die aerodynamisch vollendet verkleidete F1-Rakete mit „Saugeffekt" auch jenseits der 200-km/h-Marke endlos weiterbeschleunigt und – eine entsprechend lange Gerade ohne Seitenwind vorausgesetzt – 370 Stundenkilometer erreicht.

McLaren F1

Unter den ersten Bestellern des immerhin 1,6 Millionen Mark teuren F1 ist auch der frühere Formel-1-Weltmeister Keke Rosberg, der sich beim ersten „Outing" mit dem Supersportwagen von Ron Dennis über den Nürburgring chauffieren lässt. 300 Wagen sollen gebaut werden, ab 1994 pro Woche ein Exemplar. Aufwändig wie das aus 90 Teilen zusammengesetzte Kohlefaser-Monocoque ist auch das Fahrwerk: reinrassige Rennwagentechnik, aber straßentauglich. Schlaglöcher sind allerdings nicht eingeplant.

Im Gegensatz zur Rennversion, die 1996 die GT-Langstreckenweltmeisterschaft gewinnt, kommt der Straßen-F1 ohne Spoiler aus. Nur beim Bremsen wird eine Heckklappe ausgefahren. Und statt der sequentiellen Schaltung des F1 GTR wird die Normalausgabe manuell in einer Sechsgang-Kulisse geschaltet. Die Wippen am Lenkrad betätigen lediglich das Fernlicht und die Hupe. Was zwischen Karbon, Kevlar und Leichtmetall an Freiräumen bleibt, wird nach individuellen Wünschen mit feinstem Leder kaschiert. Viel Platz für Gepäck bleibt ohnehin nicht.

En 1989, Gordon Murray dévoile un secret. Le Sud-Africain et ancien constructeur génial de Formule 1 au service de Brabham, qui travaille pour McLaren depuis la dissolution de l'écurie, a conçu une voiture de sport routière destinée à éclipser tout ce que l'on connu à ce jour. « Chez McLaren, j'ai le plaisir de réaliser un rêve en construisant une voiture de sport aux caractéristiques inédites. Le p.-d.g. de McLaren, Ron Dennis, et son associé Mansour Ojjeh ont projeté de réaliser une série confidentielle et exclusive. »

Parmi les fournisseurs de moteurs envisagés, le choix se porte sur BMW. Un facteur déterminant est que le nouveau V12 BMW (type S70/2) développe allégrement 550 ch et plus à partir de six litres – et ce avec une montée en puissance régulière, autrement dit sans les à-coups d'un turbo. Le fait que le « pape » des moteurs BMW, Paul Rosche, soit un bon ami de Gordon Murray – ils ont en effet remporté en commun, en 1983, le premier titre de champion du monde de Formule 1 de l'ère du turbo – facilite bien évidemment le nouveau « Travaillons ensemble ».

Le sélect Sporting Club de Monte-Carlo et le Grand Prix qui y est organisé en 1992 sont le cadre idéal pour présenter une voiture baptisée « F1 » et qui roule encore plus vite que les monoplaces. Comme dans une monoplace, le conducteur se trouve au centre du cockpit. Les deux passagers, placés de chaque côté et légèrement décalés vers l'arrière, ont le plaisir d'être témoins de l'allumage de la « fusée ».

Le compte à rebours pour sa commercialisation débute au printemps 1993. Jonathan Palmer, pilote de Formule 1 ayant la pointure nécessaire pour tester le premier prototype de la F1, parle d'un comportement très proche de celui d'une voiture de Grand Prix. Détail d'importance, la « fusée F1 » à l'aérodynamique parfaite et avec « effet de sol » accélère infatigablement même après avoir franchi le mur des 200 km/h et – à condition de se trouver sur une longue ligne droite et sans vent latéral – peut monter jusqu'à 370 km/h.

Parmi les premiers à passer commande de cette F1 qui coûte tout de même 1,6 million de marks figure aussi l'ancien champion du monde Keke Rosberg qui, pour les premiers tours de roue de la super voiture de sport, se fait piloter sur le Nürburgring par Ron Dennis. Il est prévu de construire 300 voitures, une par semaine à partir de 1994. Aussi sophistiqué que la monocoque en fibre de carbone composée de 90 pièces, le châssis est digne de celui d'une voiture de course, mais à l'épreuve de la route. Les nids de poule ne sont évidemment pas recommandés.

Contrairement à la version course qui remporte le Championnat du monde d'endurance des GT en 1996, la F1 de route ne comporte pas le moindre aileron. Il n'y a qu'au freinage que s'érige un becquet à l'arrière. Et, à la place de la commande séquentielle de la F1 GTR, l'édition destinée au commun des mortels offre une coulisse à six vitesses. Les manettes au volant n'actionnent que les feux de route et le klaxon. Ce qui reste d'espace libre entre la fibre de carbone, le Kevlar et l'alliage léger est, selon les désirs du client, drapé du cuir le plus luxueux. Il ne reste de toute façon pas beaucoup de place à bord pour les accessoires.

Getting into this unusual 1+2 seat cockpit of the McLaren F1, which can reach 230 mph (370 kph) on the appropriate track, in itself inspires the imagination of car freaks.

Bereits der Einstieg in das ungewöhnliche 1+2-Sitze-Cockpit des McLaren F1, der auf entsprechender Fahrbahn 370 Stundenkilometer erreichen kann, beflügelt die Phantasie jedes Autofreaks.

L'accès à l'extraordinaire cockpit 1+2 de la McLaren F1, capable d'atteindre 370 km/h lorsque les circonstances s'y prêtent, aiguise déjà l'imagination de tous les amoureux de l'automobile.

In the F1, diverse flaps hide a lot of high tech. The action of the brakes is supported by an extendable air flap when the car is in motion.

Unter diversen Klappen verbirgt sich viel High-Tech. Während der Fahrt wird die Bremswirkung von einer ausfahrbaren Heckklappe unterstützt.

Une multitude de capots dissimulent la haute technologie omniprésente. Un aérofrein escamotable vient épauler le système de freinage conventionnel à haute vitesse.

McLaren F1

Powerful: the exhaust system with its four metal catalytic converters and the added carbon air intake of the BMW 12-cylinder engine. It produces a performance of 550 bhp and more from a capacity of six liters.

Gewaltig ist die mit vier Metallkatalysatoren bestückte Auspuffanlage und der aufgesetzte Karbon-Luftsammler des BMW-12-Zylinders, der mit sechs Litern Hubraum 550 PS und mehr leistet.

Impressionnant : la ligne d'échappement à quatre catalyseurs métalliques et le collecteur d'air en carbone coiffant le douze-cylindres BMW qui développe 550 ch ou plus à partir de 6 litres de cylindrée.

Dynamic: the wedge-shaped body of the McLaren F1 makes do without any noticeable spoilers or fins. The aerodynamically formed underbody ensures the necessary "suction". Technical essentials are aesthetically implemented in the integration of various air intakes and outlets.

Dynamisch: Die keilförmige Karosserie des McLaren F1 kommt ohne auffälligen Spoiler oder Flossen aus. Für den gewünschten Saugeffekt sorgt der aerodynamisch geformte Unterboden. Bei der Integration diverser Lufteinlässe und -auslässe werden technische Notwendigkeiten ästhetisch umgesetzt.

Dynamique : la carrosserie de la McLaren F1 ne possède pas le moindre aileron ou becquet disgracieux. Le soubassement, à la forme aérodynamique calculée avec précision, garantit l'effet d'aspiration souhaité. Quand technique et esthétique se concilient, notamment avec l'intégration des diverses prises et sorties d'air.

This large BMW contains a multitude of useful small items with which BMW has done an excellent job. The 740i is a regal representative of the automotive upper class: technically perfect, luxuriously appointed, functionally thought through down to the smallest switch. Powered by the satin-smooth performance of the 4.4-liter V8 engine, whose long stroke characteristics mean the maximum torque peak for pulling power arrives at a remarkably low 3900 rpm.

What characterizes this latest generation of BMW eight-cylinder engines is not enhanced performance – 286 bhp does that job – but smoothness, a broad torque range and improved fuel economy. In figures, acceleration from 0 to 62 mph (100 kph) in 6.6 seconds says as much for the 740i as average fuel consumption of just 19 miles to the gallon of Super unleaded fuel (12.5 liters per 100 km). As usual for many bigger BMWs, top speed is electronically limited to 155 mph (250 kph).

In the manual transmission model, a sixth gear was added to the fifth to serve as an overdrive ratio, reducing engine revs by 17 percent and thus saving fuel. Anyone who loves luxury sedans will want to avoid straining his clutch foot, particularly as BMW offers an electro-hydraulically controlled five-speed automatic transmission as a popular optional extra. This is provided with technical refinements such as adaptive transmission control and Steptronic.

The BMW technical dictionary, which forms part of every 7 series brochure, reads at first sight like the manual for a space shuttle. There is reference to "Check Control", "Multi-Information Display" (MID), "On-Board Computer", "On-Board Diagnostics" and the optionally available satellite navigation system which calculates the car's position through a "Global Positioning System" (GPS).

It is no doubt reassuring for the normal car user to know that the 740i (like all new 5 and 7 series cars) is equipped as standard with a head airbag, which has been fitted into the roof frame and usefully supplements the effect of the side airbag in the door. Naturally this system of tubed bags also has a catchy designation: "Inflatable Tubular Structure" (ITS). In comparison to the Mercedes-Benz S420, BMW have consciously dotted the "i" of the 740.

Im großen BMW steckt eine Fülle nützlicher Kleinigkeiten, bei denen BMW Großartiges geleistet hat. Der 740i ist ein souveräner Vertreter der Oberschicht unter den Automobilen: technisch perfekt, luxuriös im Interieur und funktionell durchdacht bis zum kleinsten Schalter. Er verwöhnt seine Passagiere mit der samtweichen Laufkultur des V8-Motors mit knapp 4,4 Litern Hubraum. Dank der langhubigen Auslegung dieses Triebwerks wird das maximale Drehmoment bereits bei 3900 Umdrehungen pro Minute erreicht.

Die jüngste Generation der BMW-Achtzylinder kennzeichnet nicht mehr brachiale Kraft und Leistung – 286 PS genügen –, sondern Laufkultur, breiterer Drehmomentverlauf und gleichzeitige Senkung des Kraftstoffverbrauchs. In Zahlen ausgedrückt spricht eine Beschleunigung von 0 auf 100 Stundenkilometer in nur 6,6 Sekunden ebenso für den 740i wie ein durchschnittlicher Benzinverbrauch von 12,5 Litern Super. Wie bei BMW Usus, ist die Höchstgeschwindigkeit elektronisch auf 250 Stundenkilometer beschränkt.

Beim Schaltgetriebe wurde auf den fünften Gang noch ein sechster gesetzt – als Schongang, der die Motordrehzahl um 17 Prozent senkt und somit den Benzinverbrauch reduziert. Wer Luxuslimousinen liebt, schont meist den Kupplungsfuß, zumal BMW im Sonderausstattungspaket ein elektronisch-hydraulisch gesteuertes Fünfgang-Automatikgetriebe anbietet. Dieses ist natürlich mit technischen Raffinessen wie adaptiver Getriebesteuerung und Steptronic versehen.

Das BMW-Techniklexikon, Bestandteil jedes 7er-Prospekts, liest sich auf den ersten Blick wie das Handbuch eines Spaceshuttles. Da ist die Rede von „Check Control", „Multi-Informations-Display" (MID), „Bordcomputer", „On-Bord-Diagnose" und dem auf Wunsch

BMW 740i

erhältlichen Navigationssystem, das mit Hilfe des „Global Positioning System" (GPS) den jeweiligen Standort des Fahrzeugs errechnet.

Für den Normalverbraucher ist sicherlich beruhigend, dass der 740i (wie alle neuen 5er und 7er) serienmäßig mit einem Kopf-Airbag ausgerüstet ist, der, im Dachrahmen integriert, die Wirkung des in der Tür befindlichen Seiten-Airbags sinnvoll ergänzt. Natürlich trägt auch dieses Schlauchsystem eine werbewirksame Bezeichnung in unaussprechlichem Technikerslang: „Inflatable Tubular Structure" (ITS). Mit dem 740i hat BMW dem Mercedes-Benz S420 jedenfalls das bewusste „i"-Tüpfelchen aufgesetzt.

La grosse BMW regorge de multiples petits détails pour lesquels BMW n'a pas regardé à la dépense. La 740i incarne la voiture de luxe par excellence qui prend soin de ses passagers : parfaite sur le plan mécanique, avec un habitacle luxueux, fonctionnelle jusqu'au bout des manettes et animée d'un moteur V8 de 4,4 litres de cylindrée. Sa course longue permet à ce propulseur de délivrer son couple maximum dès 3900 tr/min.

Ce qui caractérise la dernière génération des huit-cylindres BMW n'est pas une débauche de puissance – 286 ch suffisent. Ses points forts sont en réalité la souplesse, la plage de couples et, simultanément, une moindre consommation de carburant. En chiffres, cela se traduit par des accélérations de 0 à 100 km/h en 6,6 secondes seulement ainsi que par une consommation moyenne de 12,5 litres de super aux 100 km. Comme il est de coutume chez BMW, la vitesse maximum est régulée électroniquement à 250 km/h.

La boîte manuelle a vu sa cinquième vitesse complétée par un sixième rapport – une démultipliée qui fait retomber le régime moteur de 17 % et donc aussi la consommation. Le véritable amateur de limousines de luxe ne manie pas volontiers l'embrayage, d'autant que, dans la liste des options, BMW propose une boîte automatique à cinq vitesses à commande électronico-hydraulique. Celle-ci comporte naturellement divers détails techniques comme une gestion adaptative et une commande Steptronic.

La notice de la mécanique d'une BMW, qui fait partie intégrante de tout prospectus de série 7, évoque à la première lecture le mode d'emploi d'une navette spatiale. On y parle de «Check Control», de «Multi-Information Display» (MID), d'«ordinateur de bord», d'«On-Board-Diagnostics» et du système de navigation proposé en option, qui indique l'endroit où l'on se trouve à l'aide du «Global Positioning System» (GPS).

Pour l'automobiliste lambda, il est assurément tranquillisant de savoir que la 740i (comme toutes les séries 5 et 7) comporte en série un airbag spécial intégré pour protéger la tête, complétant efficacement les airbags latéraux se trouvant dans les portières. Ce système de coussins gonflables porte le nom d'«Inflatable Tubular Structure» (ITS). En songeant à la Mercedes-Benz S420, BMW a attribué un «i» à la 740.

The aesthetics of top-of-the-range cars find expression in the elegant lines of the 740i:
a refined atmosphere with functional dashboard inside and a powerful eight-cylinder engine
under the hood.

Die Ästhetik der „Oberschicht unter den Automobilen" drückt sich in der eleganten
Linienführung des 740i aus: ein edles Ambiente mit funktionellem Armaturenbrett im
Inneren und einem kraftvollen Achtzylinder unter der Haube.

Le « grand chic automobile » se retrouve dans l'élégance des lignes de la 740i : le luxe avec
un tableau de bord fonctionnel à l'intérieur et un puissant huit-cylindres sous le capot.

BMW 740i

BMW 740i

As flagship of the fourth generation of the 5 series (E39), which entered the automotive spring of 1997 with seven engine options, the 540i has been given a beefy but very modern 4.4-liter unit. This V8 aluminum engine with electronic engine management develops 420 Nm torque at a remarkably low 3900 rpm and even at very low engine revs it is surprisingly flexible. The 286 bhp provides acceleration of 6.2 seconds from 0 to 62 mph (100 kph) and a top speed of 155 mph (250 kph).

With reasonably restrained driving, not always easy given the premium road holding, the 540i does a good 19.2 miles to the gallon of Super (12.3 liters per 100 km). With the touring model, the higher weight of 3737 lbs (1695 kg) instead of 3494 lbs (1585 kg) becomes apparent with additional consumption of one tenth of a gallon. A carefully calculated six-speed manual transmission is designed for drivers who like to use the gears. Those who do not are happier with the modern adaptively controlled automatic transmission with five gears.

This new member of the 5 series stands out by its lightweight construction; thus the rigidity of the body shell has been considerably increased while maintaining the same weight as the previous model. The lightweight construction chassis components, mostly of aluminum, were a world first for a production model. Aluminum wheels were also standard on the 540i.

The integral rear axle, spatially effective suspension with acceleration and braking anti-dive mechanism, is taken from the BMW 7 series. Optionally, the aluminum integral axle can be combined with a pneumatic self-leveling mechanism. That means that the suspension quality remains the same irrespective of the axle load.

ABS and ASC+T (Automatic Stability Control + Traction) are supplied as a matter of course for all members of the 5 series of this generation. And also present in this series is everything else necessary to provide safe and comfortable driving, even at high speeds.

Of course there is still room at BMW for a few special wishes such as automatic dip internal and external mirrors or a navigation system with TV monitor. Automatic air conditioning for the 540i became a standard part of 5 series equipment from the autumn of 1997 onwards.

The lines of this member of the 5 series can hardly be bettered in terms of aesthetics. Technical requirements and maximum interior space have been assembled in a shape to meet functional needs, which is seen as a trendsetter for further BMW models while producing good aerodynamic values.

Als Flaggschiff der vierten Generation der 5er Reihe (E39), die mit sieben Motorisierungsoptionen in den Autofrühling 1997 startet, ist der 540i mit einem bulligen, aber hochmodernen 4,4-Liter-Aggregat bestückt. Dieses V8-Aluminiumtriebwerk mit elektronischem Motormanagement entwickelt bereits bei 3900 Touren ein Drehmoment von 420 Newtonmetern und ist selbst bei ganz niedrigen Drehzahlen erstaunlich elastisch. Die 286 PS ermöglichen eine Beschleunigung von 0 auf 100 Stundenkilometer in 6,2 Sekunden und eine Spitzengeschwindigkeit von 250 Sachen.

Bei nicht allzu forcierter Fahrweise, die sich angesichts der optimalen Straßenlage allerdings gern aufdrängt, schlürft der 540i lediglich 12,3 Liter Super. Beim Touring macht sich das höhere Gewicht von 1695 (statt 1585) Kilo mit einem Mehrverbrauch von knapp einem halben Liter bemerkbar. Ein sorgsam abgestimmtes Sechsgang-Getriebe kommt schaltfreudigen Fahrern entgegen. Schaltfaule freuen sich über das moderne, adaptiv gesteuerte Automatikgetriebe mit fünf Gängen.

Der neue 5er glänzt durch seine Leichtbauweise. So kann die Steifigkeit der Rohkarosse bei gleichem Gewicht gegenüber dem Vorgängermodell erheblich vergrößert werden. Weltpremiere bei einem Serienmodell feiert das weitgehend aus Aluminium gefertigte Leichtbaufahrwerk. Da ist es nur sinnvoll, dass auch die Alufelgen zur Serienausstattung des 540i gehören.

Die Integralhinterachse, eine räumlich wirkende Radaufhängung mit Anfahr- und Bremsnickausgleich, wird der BMW-Oberklasse entnommen; auf Wunsch ist dieser technische Leckerbissen auch noch mit einem pneumatischen Niveauausgleich kombinierbar. Das bedeutet gleich bleibende Federungsqualität unabhängig von der Achslast. ABS und ASC+T (Schlupf- und Traktionsregelung) sind

BMW 540i

bei allen 5ern dieser Generation eine Selbstverständlichkeit. Auch sonst verfügt diese Klasse über alles, was sicherem und komfortablem Fahren dient – auch bei hohen Geschwindigkeiten.

Natürlich hat BMW noch Raum für ein paar Sonderwünsche gelassen, so zum Beispiel für automatisch abblendende Innen- und Außenspiegel oder ein Navigationssystem mit TV-tauglichem Monitor. Die Klimaautomatik indessen ist beim 540i ab Herbst 1997 bereits fester Bestandteil der Serie.

Die Linienführung dieser 5er ist an Ästhetik kaum zu überbieten. Technische Vorgaben und maximaler Innenraum werden funktionsgerecht in eine Form gebracht, die, neben guten aerodynamischen Werten, als richtungsweisend für künftige BMW-Modelle gilt.

En tant que navire-amiral de la quatrième génération de la série 5 (E39) qui inaugure le printemps automobile 1997 avec une gamme de sept moteurs, la 540i est propulsée par un vigoureux et ultramoderne 4,4 litres. Ce V8 en aluminium à gestion moteur électronique développe déjà un couple de 420 Nm à 3900 tr/min ; même à bas régime, il fait preuve d'une souplesse étonnante. Les 286 ch lui permettent d'accélérer de 0 à 100 km/h en 6,2 secondes et d'atteindre allégrement les 250 km/h.

Avec une conduite décontractée, qui ne met pas à contribution sa tenue de route exceptionnelle, la 540i consomme seulement 12,3 litres de super aux 100 km. Dans la version touring, le poids de 1695 kg, au lieu de 1585, se traduit par un supplément de consommation d'un demi-litre à peine. Une boîte à six vitesses bien étagée séduira les virtuoses du pommeau. Les adeptes de la boîte automatique se féliciteront de la moderne transmission automatique à cinq vitesses et de la commande adaptative.

La nouvelle série 5 brille par la légèreté de sa construction : ainsi la carrosserie blanche offre-t-elle, à poids identique, une bien plus grande rigidité torsionnelle que l'ancien modèle. Les trains roulants en alliage léger, pratiquement tout en aluminium, sont une première mondiale sur une voiture de série. Sur la 540i, les jantes alliage sont également de série.

L'essieu arrière intégral, une suspension dont la trajectoire est étroite, avec compensation des mouvements de caisse à l'accélération et au freinage, est le même que celui qui équipe les BMW série 7 et les coupés. Sur demande, l'essieu intégral en aluminium peut être combiné à un correcteur d'assiette pneumatique. Cela signifie que la qualité de la suspension reste identique quelle que soit la charge.

ABS et ASC+T (régulation antipatinage) vont bien sûr équiper toutes les séries 5 de cette génération. Et cette

gamme contient tout ce qui peut garantir une conduite sûre et confortable – aussi et surtout à haute vitesse.

Naturellement, BMW a aussi pensé à ceux qui ont des souhaits particuliers, par exemple des rétroviseurs intérieurs et extérieurs automatiques anti-éblouissement ou un système de navigation avec un écran de télévision. À partir de l'automne 1997, la climatisation automatique fait déjà partie de l'équipement de série pour la 540i.

L'esthétique de cette série 5 est difficile à dépasser. Les caractéristiques techniques et l'habitabilité maximum sont conciliés de façon fonctionnelle sous les traits d'une carrosserie qui, outre un bon coefficient aérodynamique, s'avérera innovante pour d'autres gammes de BMW.

Under the 540i's stylistically successful, forward-extending hood with the BMW kidneys, there slumbers the same power source as in the 740i: a 4.4-liter aluminum V8 engine.

Unter der stilistisch gekonnt nach vorn gezogenen Haube mit den BMW-Nieren schlummert beim 540i die gleiche Kraftquelle wie beim 740i: ein 4,4-Liter-V8 aus Aluminium.

Sous le capot esthétiquement réussi de la 540i, avec les traditionnels naseaux BMW, ronronne le même propulseur que pour la 740i : un V8 de 4,4 litres en aluminium.

BMW 540i

The monitor for on-board computer, navigation system and TV has been cleverly integrated into the central console of the stylishly thoroughbred 5 series.

Geschickt ist der TV-taugliche Monitor für Bordcomputer und Navigationssystem in die Mittelkonsole des schnittigen Edel-5ers integriert.

L'écran de l'ordinateur de bord, du système de navigation et de la télévision est parfaitement intégré dans la console médiane de la rapide série 5 de prestige.

The first press photos of the new BMW M5 were of symbolic character: they showed a miracle in blue – one available to drive from November 1998, at 400 bhp, 500 Nm torque and offering acceleration of 5.3 seconds from 0 to 62 mph (100 kph)!

The "ultimate performance machine" from Munich is outwardly unassuming. It is distinguished subtly from the usual 5 series by a larger air intake, oval fog lights, aerodynamically designed external mirrors which can be folded away, shiny chrome light alloy wheels with fat tires (245/40 ZR 18 and 275/35 ZR 18) and the four stainless steel exhausts of the eight-cylinder engine.

A special Bosch Motronic manages the throttle flaps, the temperature-sensitive lubrication oil supply, and fully automatic variable timing of the intake and exhaust camshafts. This increases torque at lower and middle engine speeds. As well as this double VANOS system, patented by BMW M GmbH, the accelerator action can also be electronically adjusted. Power with an instant "blast" or a comfortable power surge: the press of a button is all it takes.

Clever aerodynamic design of the subframe and a taut sporty chassis enable the M5 to achieve lateral acceleration loads of 1.2 g. When the color drains from drivers' faces in fast bends, the engine oil also experiences an unhealthy centrifugal force. Instead of a racing dry sump system, the M5 counters such oil surges with a lubrication system that reacts to lateral force.

Compound disc brakes, which BMW uses in motor racing, ensure better heat diffusion when braking through their "floating" construction. In addition, they are longer lasting than normal brakes. The conventional six-speed transmission has short precise shifts. Those who are averse to changing gear can console themselves with the fact that the M5 – rolling comfortably along in fourth gear – can

manage to spurt from 50 mph (80 kph) to 75 mph (120 kph) in less than 5 seconds.

Be it elegantly restrained or sporty and dynamic, there are no design limits for the M5 interior. Everything is simply perfected in this sporty five-seater 5-liter car. The only problem is being able to afford this superlative sedan. The M5 has had a firm customer base since 1985, and approximately 1000 automotive individualists acquire this wolf in sheep's clothing every year.

Die ersten Pressefotos des neuen BMW M5 haben Symbolcharakter: Zu sehen ist ein blaues Wunder, und das kann man seit November 1998 auch erleben – bei 400 PS, 500 Newtonmeter Drehmoment und einer Beschleunigung von 0 auf Tempo 100 in 5,3 Sekunden!

Das „ultimative Kraftpaket" aus München gibt sich äußerlich unaufdringlich. Vom normalen 5er unterscheidet es sich nur durch einen größeren Kühllufteinlass, ovale Nebelscheinwerfer, aerodynamisch gestaltete und elektrisch wegklappbare Außenspiegel, chromglänzende Leichtmetallräder mit dicken Puschen (245/40 ZR 18 und 275/35 ZR 18) und die vier Edelstahl-Auspuffrohre des Achtzylinders.

Eine spezielle Mototronic regelt die Drosselklappen, den thermischen Ölniveau-Geber und die vollautomatische Spreizung der Ein- und Auslassnockenwellen zur Drehmomentsteigerung im unteren und mittleren Drehzahlbereich. Neben diesem von der BMW M GmbH patentierten Doppel-VANOS-System lässt sich auch das Gaspedal elektronisch beeinflussen. Ob plötzliche Kraftentfaltung oder komfortables Anschwellen der motorischen Leistung – ein Druck auf den Schalter genügt!

Geschickte aerodynamische Gestaltung des Unterbodens und ein straffes sportliches Fahrwerk erlauben dem M5 Querbeschleunigungen von 1,2 g. Wenn einem Fahrer in schnellen Kurven die Farbe aus dem Gesicht weicht, verspürt auch das Motoröl den ungesunden Drang nach außen. Statt mit einem Trockensumpf begegnet der M5 solchen Strömungen mit einem querkraftgesteuerten Schmierungssystem.

So genannte „Compound-Scheibenbremsen", wie sie BMW im Motorsport verwendet, sorgen durch ihre „schwimmende" Bauweise für eine bessere Ableitung der Reibungswärme. Außerdem sind sie haltbarer als die üblichen Bremsen. Eher konventionell ist das Sechsganggetriebe mit

BMW M5

kurzen präzisen Schaltwegen. Schaltfaule können sich damit trösten, dass der neue M5 – gemütlich im vierten Gang dahinrollend – einen Zwischenspurt von 80 auf 120 Stundenkilometer in weniger als 5 Sekunden schafft.

Ob vornehm zurückhaltend oder sportlich dynamisch – der Gestaltung des M5-Interieurs sind keine Grenzen gesetzt. An diesem sportlichen 5-Liter-Wagen mit fünf Sitzen ist eben alles perfekt. Man muss sich diesen Superlativ einer Limousine nur leisten können. Doch der M5 hat seit 1985 eine feste Käuferschicht: Pro Jahr legen sich rund 1000 Individualisten diesen Wolf im Schafspelz zu.

Les premières photos parues dans la presse de la nouvelle BMW M5 sont symboliques : au diapason de la couleur de la carrosserie, du sang bleu coule dans les veines de cette voiture. C'est un cocktail détonant que l'on peut déguster depuis novembre 1998 : une puissance de 400 ch, un couple de 500 Nm et 5,3 secondes pour les accélérations de 0 à 100 km/h !

Extérieurement, la « nouvelle reine de la Bavière » est presque trop discrète. De la série 5 « normale » elle ne se distingue que par de plus grandes prises d'air, des phares antibrouillard ovales, des rétroviseurs extérieurs électriques plus fins, aérodynamiques et rabattables, des jantes alliage chromées avec des pneus larges (245/40 ZR 18 et 275/35 ZR 18) et les quatre sorties du pot d'échappement chromées du huit-cylindres.

Une gestion Mototronic spéciale orchestre la symphonie des vis papillon, du capteur de niveau d'huile thermique et de la distribution variable automatique des arbres à cames d'admission et d'échappement aux régimes inférieurs et intermédiaires qui augmente le couple. Outre ce système breveté par BMW M GmbH sous le nom de « double VANOS », elle régule aussi l'accélérateur électronique. Montée en puissance instantanée ou envol progressif et régulier de la performance : pour choisir, il suffit d'appuyer sur un bouton.

Une juste configuration aérodynamique du soubassement et un châssis sportif d'une fermeté de bonne qualité permettent à la M5 d'encaisser des accélérations transversales de 1,2 g. Quand le visage du conducteur commence à changer de couleur dans les virages, l'huile moteur a, elle aussi, la propension « malsaine » à succomber aux effets de la force centrifuge. En alternative à la lubrification à carter sec, la M5 combat un tel afflux d'essence avec un système de lubrification commandé par la force transversale.

Grâce à leur montage « flottant », les freins à disques en composites, utilisés par BMW en compétition, garantissent une meilleure évacuation de la chaleur de friction, ce qui leur donne accessoirement beaucoup plus d'endurance que les freins traditionnels. La boîte à six vitesses est, quant à elle, plutôt conventionnelle avec ses changements courts et précis. Que ceux qui n'aiment pas changer de vitesse se consolent, la nouvelle M5 – même si elle roule tranquillement en quatrième – peut toujours accélérer instantanément en moins de 5 secondes de 80 à 120 km/h.

Que l'on opte pour une élégance discrète ou une sportivité dynamique, on n'a que l'embarras du choix pour la décoration de l'habitacle de la M5. Avec cette sportive de 5 litres pour cinq passagers, tout est parfait – sauf que tout le monde n'a pas les moyens de se l'offrir. Depuis 1985, la M5 a son club d'amoureux : chaque année, environ 1000 d'entre eux s'offrent cette authentique grand tourisme aux allures de berline bourgeoise.

BMW M5

Tremendous power, discreetly packaged, speedy light alloy wheels, M sports seats and a well-built interior: the 400 bhp M5 is a high-performance sedan of that special type which sets new standards.

Gewaltige Power, diskret verpackt, rasante Leichtmetallräder, M-Sportsitze und ein gediegenes Interieur: Der 400-PS-M5 ist eine Hochleistungs-Limousine der besonderen Art, die neue Maßstäbe setzt.

Une puissance pléthorique, une allure de paisible familiale, de saisissantes jantes en alliage léger, des sièges sport M et un habitacle soigné : la M5 de 400 ch est une berline racée à hautes performances. Elle fera date, incontestablement.

BMW M5

BMW M roadster

Based on such beautiful two-seaters as the 328 and the postwar 507 and Z1 models, the first drawings for a new road sports car were created in Munich during 1989. It was to be a roadster, though not quite as spartan as in the originals. Modern technology, packaged in a sporting dress, with a touch of traditional BMW fashion at an affordable price: that is the profile of design priorities.

However, it is not in Bavaria's 1972 Olympic City, but near the site of the 1996 Olympic Games that the Z roadster begins to depart a production line. The newest BMW factory in America's Spartanburg, South Carolina, adjacent to Inter-state 85 to Atlanta, offers the Z3 with various engines: 115 bhp 1.8-liter four-cylinder, 140 bhp 1.9-liter four-cylinder and the 192 bhp 2.8-liter six-cylinder.

Real roadster driving required even more power. This was acquired around the BMW resources that ring Munich's river, the Isar. Thus the M model with 3.2 liters and 321 bhp (as for the European M3) was developed for the "ultimate driving experience," as BMW put it. But the M roadster has to power 265 lbs (120 kg) less than the M3. This difference does not, however, show up in the enormous acceleration from 0 to 62 mph (100 kph): recorded 5.4 seconds for both.

A slightly longer wheelbase and a wider track at the front and rear, as well as significantly wider tire dimensions differentiate the M roadster from the Z3, as do discreet spoilers. At the end of the side cooling grills – surely a reminder of the 507 – the "M" badge of speed is displayed proudly, instead of the BMW roundel.

A roadster aura is also transmitted by the round chrome instruments for the clock, external temperature and oil temperature on the wide transmission tunnel, under which a five-ratio gearbox, geared like the Z3 2.8, does its duty.

Dashboard and rich leather interior provide evidence of design imagination.

There is no spare wheel. The special shape of the light-alloy wheels is designed to prevent the tires coming off if there is a flat. Should a puncture occur, the driver operates an "M Mobility System" comprising a mini-compressor and quick sealant. If that does not help, nothing for it but a phone rescue: BMW breakdown service is famous for its good organization.

The electro-hydraulic activation of the fabric top comes as standard on the M, and as an extra on the four-cylinder models. The tonneau fabric must be manually buttoned over the folded top for that real roadster feeling.

The expensive chassis is not harsh, but well adjusted. Even under high acceleration this sports car dips only slightly. Performance, especially along roads with many bends and steering load changes, is a pleasure, for the steering stays precise. The vehicle amiably covers loose ground. The stunts which Pierce "James Bond" Brosnan did with the Z3 in the film *Golden Eye* do not require the driving skills of a Finnish rally star such as Rauno Aaltonen.

Given its enormous potential, the M roadster must have large-diameter ventilated disc brakes, measuring 12.4 inches (315 mm) front; the rears are 12.3 inches (312 mm). ABS braking and anti-dive mechanisms are BMW virtues of the 1990s.

Anknüpfend an so schöne Zweisitzer wie den 328 und die Nachkriegsmodelle 507 und Z1 entstehen 1989 in München erste Zeichnungen für einen neuen Straßensportwagen – ein Roadster, wenngleich die Ausstattung weniger spartanisch sein soll. Moderne Technik in sportlichem Anzug mit einem Hauch traditioneller BMW-Mode, dazu ein erschwinglicher Preis – so lautet das Anforderungsprofil.

Doch nicht in Bayerns Olympiastadt, sondern in der Nähe des Austragungsortes der Spiele von 1996 geht der Z roadster vom Band. Das jüngste BMW-Werk in Spartanburg, South Carolina (USA) ganz in der Nähe des Interstate Highway 85 nach Atlanta, bietet den Z3 in unterschiedlichen Motorisierungsvarianten an: 1,8-Liter-Vierzylinder mit 115 PS, 1,9-Liter-Vierzylinder mit 140 PS und 2,8-Liter-Sechszylinder mit 192 PS.

Richtiges Roadster-Running erfordert noch mehr Power, und die ist wiederum an der Isar zu haben. Dort gibt es für das „ultimative Fahrerlebnis", so BMW, die Variante „M" mit 3,2 Litern und 321 PS – analog zum M3. Allerdings wiegt der M roadster 120 Kilo weniger als der M3, was bei diesem Kraftpotential allerdings keine Rolle mehr spielt. In unglaublichen 5,4 Sekunden beschleunigen beide von 0 auf 100 Stundenkilometer.

Geringfügig längerer Radstand und die breite Spur vorn und hinten sowie wesentlich breitere Reifen und der dezente Spoiler unterscheiden den „M" vom „Z". Am Ende der seitlichen Kühlschlitze – sicherlich eine Reminiszenz an den 507 – prangt stolz statt des BMW-Emblems das „schnelle M".

Roadster-Feeling vermitteln auch die in Chrom gefassten Rundinstrumente für Uhrzeit, Außen- und Öltemperatur auf dem breiten Getriebetunnel, unter dem eine Fünfgang-Schaltung, abgestuft wie beim Z3 2.8, ihren Dienst verrichtet.

Armaturenbrett und reichlich Lederinterieur zeugen von Einfallsreichtum.

Diesen vermisst man hingegen beim Reserverad – es gibt keines! Die spezielle Form der Leichtmetallfelgen soll ein Abspringen des Reifens im Falle eines „Platten" verhindern. Kommt es doch dazu, greift der Fahrer zum „M Mobility System", einem Kleinkompressor und Schnelldichtmittel. Hilft das nicht, muss der BMW-Notdienst anrücken, der bekanntlich gut organisiert ist.

Die elektrohydraulische Betätigung des Stoffverdecks gehört beim „M" zum Standard, bei den Vierzylindermodellen zu den Extras. Hier muss die Persenning von Hand über das zusammengefaltete Verdeck geknöpft werden – ein Rest von Roadster-Feeling.

Keineswegs hart, sondern gut abgestimmt ist das aufwändige Fahrwerk. Selbst bei hoher Querbeschleunigung neigt sich dieser Sportwagen nur geringfügig. Das Fahrverhalten ist eine Wonne, besonders auf kurvenreicher Strecke mit vielen Lastwechseln; die Lenkung ist präzise. Gutmütig bewegt sich dieses Fahrzeug selbst auf lockerem Untergrund. Was James-Bond-Darsteller Pierce Brosnan im Film *Golden Eye* mit dem Z3 anstellt, bedarf nicht der Fahrkünste eines Rauno Aaltonen.

Angesichts des enormen Leistungspotentials kann der M roadster auf belüftete Scheibenbremsen großen Durchmessers – vorn 315, hinten 312 Millimeter – nicht verzichten. ABS, Brems- und Anfahrnickausgleich gehören zu den BMW-Ausstattungsmerkmalen der neunziger Jahre.

C'est dans la tradition des jolies biplaces telles que la 328 et les 507 et Z1 d'après-guerre que sont réalisées, en 1989 à Munich, les premières esquisses pour une nouvelle sportive de route. Ce sera un roadster, mais pas aussi modeste que les originaux. Technicité et modernisme, une allure sportive et les arguments esthétiques traditionnels de BMW, un prix attrayant – tel est le cahier des charges.

Ce n'est pas dans la ville olympique bavaroise, mais à proximité du site des jeux Olympiques de 1996 que la Z roadster sort des chaînes. La toute nouvelle usine de BMW à Spartanburg, en Caroline du Sud (États-Unis), près de l'Interstate Highway 85 qui mène à Atlanta, propose la Z3 avec trois motorisations : le quatre-cylindres de 1,8 litre et 115 ch, le quatre-cylindres de 1,9 litre et 140 ch, et le six-cylindres de 2,8 litres et 192 ch.

Mais pour obtenir un roadster digne de ce nom, il faut encore plus de puissance et le savoir-faire des équipes de Munich. C'est là qu'est assemblée, pour conduire « avec un maximum de plaisir » dit BMW, la variante « M » avec ce même moteur de 3,2 litres et 321 ch qui propulse la M3. Le M roadster pèse 120 kg de moins que la M3. Mais cela n'a aucune incidence sur les fantastiques accélérations de 0 à 100 km/h : 5,4 secondes pour toutes les deux.

Un empattement légèrement plus long et des voies plus larges à l'avant et à l'arrière, des pneus nettement plus volumineux et de discrets ailerons distinguent la « M » de la « Z ». À l'extrémité des ouïes de refroidissement latérales – une réminiscence de la 507 – s'affiche fièrement, à la place de l'emblème BMW, le « rapide M ».

Les cadrans circulaires cernés de chrome pour la montre, le thermomètre affichant la température extérieure et le thermomètre à huile sur le large tunnel de transmission sous lequel se trouve une boîte à cinq vitesses avec le même

étagement que pour la Z3 2.8 contribuent à faire de ce véhicule un authentique roadster. Le tableau de bord et le cuir à profusion dans l'habitacle sont le fruit de l'imagination des ingénieurs.

Ne cherchez pas la roue de secours – il n'y en a pas. La forme particulière des jantes en alliage est censée empêcher le pneu de se dégonfler en cas de crevaison. Si toutefois cela se produit, le conducteur dispose du « M Mobility System », un mini-compresseur et une bombe anti-crevaison. Si cela ne suffit pas, un appel téléphonique et le service de dépannage de BMW est toujours là, bien organisé.

La commande électro-hydraulique de la capote est de série pour le M et en option pour les quatre-cylindres. Le couvre-capote doit être fixé manuellement. N'est pas roadster qui veut !

Sophistiqués, les trains roulants sont souples, mais bien réglés. Même en cas de fortes accélérations transversales, cette voiture de sport ne prend pratiquement pas de roulis. Le comportement, notamment sur routes sinueuses avec de nombreux transferts de charges, est un délice et la direction est précise. Même sur revêtement peu adhérent, cette voiture ne perd rien de son tempérament. Pour ressembler à Pierce Brosnan qui a incarné James Bond dans le film *Golden Eye* au volant de la Z3, il n'est pas nécessaire d'être un virtuose du volant comme le pilote finlandais Rauno Aaltonen.

Vu son énorme potentiel, le M roadster ne peut pas se passer de disques ventilés de grand diamètre (315 mm à l'avant, 312 mm à l'arrière). ABS et dispositif antiplongée au freinage et à l'accélération font partie des avantages des BMW des années 1990.

With a display of consistency in the development of the BMW roadster tradition, the Munich company built the "ultimate driving machine": the M roadster – the 321 bhp power derivative of the US-built Z roadster.

In konsequenter Weiterführung der BMW-Roadster-Tradition bauen die Münchner das „ultimative Fahrerlebnis": den M roadster, der das 321-PS-Power-Derivat des in den USA gefertigten Z roadster ist.

Poussant à son paroxysme la tradition du roadster BMW, les Munichois offrent « un maximum de plaisir » à la conduite : le M roadster, qui est la version de 321 ch du Z roadster construit aux États-Unis.

A classic side profile with long hood and cooling vents. The front spoiler and a wide track with the corresponding tires clearly distinguish the M roadster from the basic version.

Klassisches Seitenprofil mit langer Motorhaube und Kühlschlitz. Der Frontspoiler und die breite Spur mit den entsprechenden „Walzen" heben den M roadster deutlich von der Basisversion ab.

Un profil classique au long capot moteur ponctué de fentes de refroidissement. L'aileron avant et les larges chapes avec les pneus correspondants distinguent le M roadster de la version de base. Il n'y a pas de confusion possible.

Open or closed, the driving characteristics of the M roadster with its sporty chassis and a power to weight ratio of 9.7 lbs (4.4 kg) per bhp are so convincing that many competitors see nothing but the rear end of the car.

Ob offen oder geschlossen: Die Fahreigenschaften des M roadsters sind angesichts des sportlichen Fahrwerks und einem Leistungsgewicht von 4,4 Kilo pro PS so überzeugend, dass viele Konkurrenten nur noch das Heck des Wagens sehen.

Que la capote soit ouverte ou fermée les performances du M roadster sont si exceptionnelles, compte tenu du châssis sport et d'un rapport poids/puissance de 4,4 kg par ch, que beaucoup de ses rivales ne voient cette voiture que de l'arrière.

BMW M roadster

The 3.2-liter in-line six-cylinder engine with 24 valves provides a convincing display of power with a torque of 350 Nm, which is achieved at a speed as low as 3250 rpm.

Der 3,2-Liter-Reihensechszylinder mit 24 Ventilen überzeugt neben seiner Kraft durch ein Drehmoment von 350 Newtonmetern, das bereits bei 3250 Umdrehungen pro Minute erreicht wird.

Outre sa puissance, le six-cylindres en ligne de 3,2 litres convainc aussi par son couple de 350 Nm déjà délivré à 3250 tr/min.

BMW M roadster

Success through performance! Together with the BMW emblem, the M symbol not only stands for success on the racetrack, but also on the road. The leather and chrome trim makes an essential contribution to the design of the cockpit, as can be seen on the wide central console above the five-speed transmission tunnel.

Erfolg durch Leistung! In Verbindung mit dem BMW-Emblem steht das M-Symbol nicht nur für Erfolg auf der Rennpiste, sondern auch auf der Straße. Dass Leder und Chromblenden zur Gestaltung des Cockpits wesentlich beitragen, zeigt die breite Mittelkonsole über dem Tunnel des Fünfgang-Schaltgetriebes.

Conjointement avec le logo BMW, le M emblématique est un symbole de succès tant sur les pistes des circuits que sur la route. La large console médiane sur la colonne hébergeant la boîte manuelle à cinq vitesses témoigne de ce que le cuir et les applications de chrome contribuent joliment à la sportivité de l'habitacle.

BMW Z3 coupé 2.8

Opinion is divided between "as ugly as sin" and "stunning", attributes which would seem to be mutually exclusive. Whether or not you like the look of the Z3 coupé, which was unveiled on a rotating pedestal at the 1997 Frankfurt Motor Show, is a matter of taste. Yet technically it is very tasty. From the front, this sports car has the dynamic and powerful appearance of a roadster. From the back, it looks like a new Touring wagon of the 3 series, its extended fenders allowing an almost chubby-cheeked look. From the side, it does not seem to fit into any category. Perhaps "unconventional" is the best way of describing it.

You cannot help making certain comparisons – the elegant BMW 328 Mille Miglia or the Touring Coupé, or perhaps the MGB in its 1965 GT guise. It also seems as if the 1971 Volvo P1800 ES sports wagon, transformed into the Volvo Coupé, has also provided some inspiration here.

This unmistakable Z3 coupé is offered only with powerful engines (2.8 liter, 192 bhp, and with the 321 bhp M-engine). Thanks to the fact that it is aerodynamically superior to the roadster, the 2.8-liter has a top speed of 144 mph (231 kph) and can reach 62 mph (100 kph) in less than 7 seconds from rest. The M version's power potential is phenomenal.

If you love unusual things, then price considerations normally take a back seat. Either you've got the cash, or you haven't! But even in terms of cost-effectiveness, BMW's Z3 2.8 coupé is worth every cent. Finding anything similar for 64,000 marks is difficult.

The chassis has a single-joint suspension taken from the 3 series at the front, and space-saving semi-trailing arms at the back with squat and anti-dip control. These are supported by ideal basic components: a long wheelbase with minimal body overhangs, a wide track and a relatively low center of gravity. Thanks to the ASC+T (Automatic

Stability Control plus Traction), and the direct servo-assisted rack and pinion steering, Alpine mountain passes become a pleasurable challenge to Z3 coupé drivers. This roadrunner is capable of high levels of lateral acceleration without being prone to unexpected skids, and the limit can be appreciated and controlled.

A roll bar has been incorporated in the roof for rollover accidents, and the Z3 coupé's occupants are protected in extreme situations by four airbags. BMW always displays its good taste when it comes to the car's interior. Even the standard trim contains high-quality materials. The 410 liters of space created by the estate car body can hold two complete sets of golfing equipment so easily that it appears custom-built.

"The Z3 coupé 2.8 produces extreme reactions – love it or leave it," was how the BMW head of design Christopher Bangle was quoted in the special edition of the 1997 BMW magazine on the Frankfurt Motor Show. Unconventionality often creates its own attraction – on a second look.

Die Meinungen divergieren zwischen „potthässlich" und „todschick" und anderen, ähnlich konträren Attributen. Das Z3 coupé, erstmals bei der IAA 1997 auf einer Drehscheibe zur Schau gestellt, ist zwar optisch Geschmacksache, in technischer Hinsicht aber ein Lecker-bissen. Von vorn wirkt dieser Sportwagen dynamisch und kraftvoll wie ein Roadster, von hinten wie ein neuer 3er Kombi mit etwas pausbäckig geratenen Kotflügelverbreiterungen und von der Seite irgendwie undefinierbar. Vielleicht ist „eigenwillig" der richtige Ausdruck.

Vergleiche drängen sich auf zwischen dem eleganten BMW 328 Mille Miglia und dem Touring Coupé oder dem MGB und seiner GT-Version von 1965. Es scheint, als habe auch das zum Sportkombi P1800 ES mutierte Volvo Coupé von 1971 in mancher Hinsicht Pate gestanden.

Der Unverwechselbare wird nur mit kraftvollen Trieb-werken (2,8 Liter, 192 PS und mit dem 321-PS-M-Motor) angeboten. Dank seiner im Vergleich zum Roadster besseren Aerodynamik erreicht er in der 2,8-Liter-Version 231 Stunden-kilometer und beschleunigt in weniger als 7 Sekunden aus dem Stand auf 100 Stundenkilometer. Das Leistungspoten-tial der M-Version ist schlichtweg gigantisch.

Hat man eine Vorliebe für Ungewöhnliches, spielt der Preis meistens eine untergeordnete Rolle. Man hat es – oder man hat es nicht! Doch gerade beim Preis-Leistungs-Vergleich bietet BMW mit dem Z3 2.8 ein Coupé, das Zoll für Zoll sein Geld wert ist. Ein vergleichbares Auto für 64 000 Mark muss man erst einmal finden.

Das Fahrwerk, vorn die Eingelenk-Federbeinachse aus dem 3er, hinten die raumsparende Schräglenkerhinterachse mit Anfahr- und Bremsnickausgleich, stützt sich auf ideale Basiskomponenten. Langer Radstand mit wenig Karosserie-überhängen, breite Spur und ein relativ niedriger Schwer-punkt tun ein übriges. Mit dem „Automatischen Stabilitäts-

und Traktionssystem" (ASC+T) und der direkten servounter-
stützten Zahnstangenlenkung werden Alpenpässe zur ver-
gnüglichen Herausforderung eines Z3-coupé-Fahrers. Auf
hohe Querbeschleunigungen reagiert dieser Roadrunner
mit wenig Seitenneigung, und im Grenzbereich bleibt er
stets kontrollierbar.

Ein im Dach integrierter Überrollbügel und vier Airbags
schützen die Fahrzeuginsassen im Extremfall. Geschmackvoll
hat BMW das Interieur gestaltet. Schon das Standardoutfit
beinhaltet edle Materialien. Das durch den Kombi-Anbau
erzielte Volumen von 410 Litern ist wie geschaffen für zwei
vollständige Golfausrüstungen.

„Die Formensprache des Z3 coupé 2.8 wirkt polari-
sierend – *love it or leave it*", wird BMW-Chefdesigner
Christopher Bangle im IAA-Special des BMW-Magazins
1997 zitiert. Eigenwilliges wirkt oft sehr anziehend – auf
den zweiten Blick!

Les avis sont partagés entre « horriblement laid » et
« absolument chic ». Le coupé Z3, dévoilé au Salon
de l'Automobile de Francfort en 1997, est très appé-
tissant sur le plan mécanique. Sur le plan esthétique, c'est
une question de goût. Vue de l'avant, cette voiture de sport
incarne dynamisme et énergie, comme un roadster, alors
que, vue de l'arrière, elle évoque un break de la nouvelle
série 3 avec des élargisseurs d'ailes un peu trop rebondis.
De profil, elle est indéfinissable. « Originale » serait sans
doute l'expression appropriée.

Des comparaisons viennent tout de suite à l'esprit –
avec l'élégante BMW 328 Mille Miglia et le Touring coupé
ou la MGB dans sa version GT de 1965. Mais le coupé
Volvo de 1971, métamorphosé en break de chasse
P1800 ES, pourrait aussi lui avoir servi de modèle.

En voiture particulière, elle n'est proposée qu'avec de
puissants moteurs (un 2,8 litres de 192 ch et le moteur M
de 321 ch). Grâce à une meilleure aérodynamique que
celle du roadster, la version de 2,8 litres atteint une vitesse
de pointe de 231 km/h et accélère de 0 à 100 km/h en moins
de 7 secondes. Le potentiel de la version M est immense.

Quand on aime les voitures qui sortent du commun, le
prix est souvent un argument secondaire. La passion prime
sur la raison ! Or, pour le rapport qualité/prix, justement,
avec le Z3 coupé 2.8, BMW propose une voiture qui vaut
son pesant d'or. Essayez de trouver son équivalent pour
64 000 marks.

Les trains roulants, avec l'essieu avant à jambes élastiques à une seule articulation de la série 3 et le train arrière
compact à bras obliques avec compensation de la plongée
à l'accélération et au freinage, sont montés sur une plate-
forme idéale : un empattement long avec des porte-à-faux
réduits, des chapes larges et un centre de gravité relativement bas. Avec le dispositif ASC+T – contrôle automatique

de la stabilité et de la traction – et la direction à crémaillère
directe avec assistance, escalader les cols alpins devient
un jeu d'enfant pour tout conducteur de coupé Z3. Ce *road-
runner* réagit avec une prise de roulis réduite à sa plus simple
expression face aux accélérations transversales élevées et la
limite d'adhérence est toujours aisément contrôlable.

Un arceau de sécurité intégré au toit et quatre airbags
protègent les passagers en cas d'accident. L'aménagement
de l'habitacle est de bon goût. La version standard, déjà,
comporte tous les matériaux nobles imaginables. Le volume
de 410 litres disponible pour les bagages dans le vaste
arrière break est capable de loger deux équipements de
golf complets.

Le coupé Z3 2.8 provoque des réactions extrêmes –
« *Love it or leave it* » (aimez-la ou laissez-la !), déclara
Christopher Bangle, le chef styliste de BMW, dans le numéro
spécial du magazine BMW de 1997 lors du Salon de l'Automobile de Francfort. Ce qui est original récolte souvent
l'amour – au second coup d'œil !

BMW Z3 coupé 2.8

The coupé body, with its echoes of a station wagon and its large hatch, is particularly striking from the rear. The 2.8-liter engine with 192 bhp gives the Z3 coupé a top speed of 144 mph (231 kph) – the ideal transport for golfers in a hurry offers enough space for two complete sets of golf equipment.

Der einem Kombi ähnliche und mit einer großen Ladeklappe versehene Coupé-Aufbau wirkt von hinten besonders markant. Der 2,8-Liter-Motor mit 192 PS beschert dem Z3 coupé eine Spitzengeschwindigkeit von 231 Stundenkilometern. Eigentlich ein ideales Gefährt für Golfer in Eile, da der Kofferraum für zwei vollständige Golfausrüstungen Raum bietet.

La version coupé, qui rappelle un break avec son grand hayon, est très caractéristique vue de l'arrière. Le moteur de 2,8 litres et 192 ch permet au Z3 coupé d'atteindre une vitesse de pointe de 231 km/h. C'est l'engin idéal, donc, pour les joueurs de golf pressés puisqu'il peut même héberger deux équipements de golf complets.

BMW Z3 coupé 2.8

BMW V12 Le Mans

oss of lubrication in the wheel bearings, something which was inexplicable and had not occurred during testing, made it impossible for the BMW V12 Le Mans to continue after only four hours in the 24-hour Le Mans classic race on the Sarthe. "I'm sorry for the whole team which put the BMW V12 Le Mans on its feet in a very short development time," Karl-Heinz Kalbfell, marketing boss of BMW AG and of BMW Motorsport Ltd. in England, commented.

The new sports racing car was created in the British former premises of Williams Grand Prix Engineering in Didcot (south of Oxford) in no time at all. It was an open two-seater with a 550 bhp V12 engine of 5990 cc, developed for the Le Mans Prototype Class 1 which prescribed a minimum weight of 1929 lbs (875 kg). Just try to imagine: in September 1997 the BMW engineers were standing in front of empty halls, waiting for their drawing boards and computers. Just nine months later their sports prototype started from the third row of the Le Mans grid.

This racing car with its carbon fiber chassis and aluminum honeycomb structure, as well as a crash-absorbent front section, possessed a potential which could not be exhausted in competition. The rear of the car also demonstrated modern and truly compact racing car design. The transmission, flange-mounted transversely at the rear of the engine to save space, also accommodated the engine oil tank. Engine and transmission were positioned together in a single sub-frame which was bolted to the chassis.

The center of gravity of the BMW was low and almost in the middle of the car. That is also where the driver sat. In place of the passenger seat – according to motor sport regulations, all that is required is an appropriate space – all

kinds of essential equipment filled the area to the left of the driver. The only driver comfort concession was the servo-assisted steering, for ABS, traction control or automatic transmission were not allowed. Imagine 24 hours of manual labor changing six gears – even if the gear change was not in a tricky H-pattern but sequential as with a motorcycle.

Constant running for 50 hours, including all the load alternations and the rpm loads occurring at Le Mans, were completed by the V12 on the Munich test beds without problems. The engine, consisting of 600 components and weighing only 474 lbs (215 kg), was simultaneously powerful and economical.

The aerodynamics, too, were sophisticated. According to factory information, downward thrust on the car more than doubles the car's weight when track speed exceeds 162 mph (260 kph). BMW could not resist adding: "With grip like this the BMW V12 Le Mans could theoretically drive upside down on the ceiling."

The first action at Le Mans brought BMW firmly down to earth again. Kalbfell: "Today we were disappointed because of a defective component, but there will be another 24-hour race in Le Mans in 1999, and we are looking forward to that."

Schmiermittelverlust an den Radlagern, unerklärlich und bei Testfahrten nie aufgetreten, macht eine weitere Teilnahme des BMW V12 „LM" am 24-Stunden-Klassiker an der Sarthe nach vier Stunden unmöglich. „Es tut mir leid für das gesamte Team, das den BMW V12 Le Mans innerhalb so kurzer Entwicklungszeit auf die Beine gestellt hat", erklärt Karl-Heinz Kalbfell, Marketingchef der BMW AG und der BMW Motorsport Ltd. in England.

In kürzester Zeit ist in den ehemaligen Hallen von Williams Grand Prix Engineering in Didcot südlich von Oxford der neue Sportwagen entstanden: ein offener Zweisitzer mit einem rund 550 PS starken BMW V12, entwickelt für die Le-Mans-Prototypenklasse 1, die ein Mindestgewicht von 875 Kilo vorschreibt. Man stelle sich das einmal vor: Da stehen die BMW-Techniker im September 1997 vor leeren Hallen und warten auf ihre Reißbretter und Computer und neun Monate später steht ihr Sport-Prototyp in der dritten Startreihe von Le Mans.

Dieses Rennfahrzeug mit Kohlefaserchassis, Aluminium-Wabenstruktur und einem Crash-absorbierenden Vorderwagen verfügt über ein Potential, das im praktischen Einsatz nicht ausgeschöpft werden kann. Auch das Wagenheck demonstriert modernen und deshalb kompakten Rennwagenbau. Das hinter dem Motor aus Platzgründen quer angeflanschte Getriebe beherbergt auch den Öltank des Motors. Motor und Getriebe sitzen zusammen in einem Rahmen, der mit dem Chassis verschraubt ist.

Der Schwerpunkt des BMW liegt tief und fast in der Fahrzeugmitte. Dort befindet sich auch der Arbeitsplatz des Piloten. Statt des Beifahrersitzes – nur der Platz dafür muss laut Reglement vorgesehen sein – füllen allerlei Steuergeräte den Raum links des Fahrers. Einziges Zugeständnis an dessen Komfortbedürfnis ist die Servolenkung, denn ABS, Traktionskontrollen oder gar Automatikgetriebe sind nicht erlaubt. Das bedeutet 24 Stunden lang Handarbeit beim Schalten, wenngleich nicht im H-Schema, sondern sequenziell wie beim Motorrad.

Einen 50-Stunden-Dauerlauf mit sämtlichen Lastwechseln und den in Le Mans auftretenden Drehzahlbelastungen absolviert der V12 auf dem Prüfstand in München klaglos. Das aus 600 Teilen bestehende, nur 215 Kilo schwere Triebwerk ist kraftvoll und sparsam zugleich.

Ausgefeilt ist auch die Aerodynamik. Laut Werksangaben übersteigt ab 260 Stundenkilometer der auf das Fahrzeug wirkende Anpreßdruck das Eigengewicht des Wagens. Man verkneift sich nicht den Zusatz: „Bei dieser Geschwindigkeit könnte der BMW V12 Le Mans theoretisch an der Decke fahren."

Der erste scharfe Einsatz in Le Mans hat die BMW-Mannen wieder auf den Boden der Tatsachen zurückgeholt. „Heute sind wir wegen eines defekten Einzelteils enttäuscht", meint Kalbfell, „aber es wird auch 1999 ein 24-Stunden-Rennen in Le Mans geben, und darauf freuen wir uns."

Lors des 24 Heures du Mans en 1998, une fuite de lubrifiant à hauteur des moyeux de roues, un incident inexplicable qui ne s'est jamais manifesté lors des essais privés, cloue aux stands la BMW V12 Le Mans au bout de quatre heures à peine. « Cela me fait de la peine pour toute l'équipe qui a construit en vraiment peu de temps la BMW V12 Le Mans », déclare Karl-Heinz Kalbfell, le chef du marketing de BMW AG qui coiffe simultanément la casquette de directeur de BMW Motorsport Ltd en Angleterre.

Une nouvelle voiture de sport est née en un très bref laps de temps dans les anciens ateliers de Williams Grand Prix Engineering, à Didcot (au sud d'Oxford) : il s'agit d'une biplace découverte propulsée par un V12 BMW d'environ 550 ch, mis au point pour les prototypes de la classe 1 du Mans qui prescrit un poids minimum de 875 kg. Imaginez la situation : en septembre 1997, les techniciens de BMW se tiennent dans des ateliers vides et attendent leurs planches à dessin et leurs ordinateurs. Neuf mois plus tard, leur prototype sport occupe la troisième ligne sur la grille de départ du Mans.

Cette voiture de course à châssis en fibre de carbone et à structure en nid d'abeille en aluminium avec une proue absorbant l'impact d'une collision possède un potentiel qui ne sera jamais exploité à fond en compétition. La partie arrière de la voiture, elle aussi, est une illustration du modernisme et de la compacité des voitures de course d'aujourd'hui. La boîte de vitesses, montée en position transversale derrière le moteur pour économiser de la place, renferme également le réservoir d'huile du moteur. Le moteur et la boîte de vitesses sont tous les deux hébergés dans un berceau auxiliaire boulonné au châssis.

Le centre de gravité de la BMW est très bas et se situe presque au centre de la voiture. C'est également là que se trouve le poste de pilotage. À la place du siège passager – d'après le règlement en vigueur, seule la place prévue à cet effet doit être respectée – se trouvent de multiples manettes de commande sur la gauche du conducteur. La seule concession au confort est la direction assistée puisque ni l'ABS, ni les contrôles de motricité ni les boîtes automatiques ne sont autorisées. Cela signifie 24 heures de changements de vitesses à la main, non pas avec une grille en H, mais avec une boîte séquentielle comme pour les motos.

Au banc d'essai, à Munich, le V12 a subi sans le moindre problème un test de longue durée de cinquante heures avec la totalité des transferts de charge et des changements de régime se produisant au Mans. Le moteur, qui se compose de 600 pièces et ne pèse que 215 kg, est à la fois puissant et sobre.

L'aérodynamique, elle aussi, est des plus élégantes. Selon ses constructeurs, la force qui agit sur la voiture à partir de 260 km/h dépasse son propre poids. On n'hésite pas à ajouter : « À cette vitesse, la BMW V12 Le Mans pourrait théoriquement rouler au plafond. »

Mais la première participation au Mans ramène l'équipe de BMW sur terre. « Aujourd'hui, déclare Karl-Heinz Kalbfell, nous sommes déçus en raison d'une pièce défectueuse, mais, en 1999 aussi, il y aura une autre course au Mans et nous nous en réjouissons déjà. »

The carbon fiber chassis, aerodynamically optimized in
the wind tunnel of Williams Grand Prix Engineering −
without rear lights during the tests − ensures a sufficient
level of downward thrust that the car could in theory
drive upside down on the ceiling at speeds faster than
162 mph (260 kph).

Die im Windkanal von Williams Grand Prix Engineering
aerodynamisch optimierte Kohlefaseraußenhaut − hier
bei den Tests noch ohne Rücklichter − sorgt für derart viel
Anpressdruck, dass der Wagen jenseits der 260 Stundenkilometer theoretisch auch an der Decke fahren könnte.

La carrosserie en fibre de carbone − encore sans feux arrière
lors des tests − qui a été optimisée aérodynamiquement dans
la soufflerie de Williams Grand Prix Engineering génère tant
d'appui que la voiture pourrait théoriquement rouler au
plafond dès qu'elle dépasse les 260 km/h.

Veni, vidi, vici: the BMW V12 LMR made its debut in 1999 in Le Mans, winning straight off with a 21 round lead for the pilot trio of Winkelhock-Martini-Dalmas over the second-placed Toyota team. Fifth position was taken by the BMW LM98 of the previous year, piloted by Bscher-Auberleen-Soper.

Veni, vidi, vici: der BMW V12 LMR debütierte 1999 in Le Mans und siegte auf Anhieb mit dem Fahrer-Trio Winkelhock-Martini-Dalmas, mit 21 Runden Vorsprung auf den zweitplatzierten Toyota. Fünfter wurde der Vorjahres-BMW LM98, pilotiert von Bscher-Auberleen-Soper.

Veni, vidi, vici : la BMW V12 LMR a fait ses débuts aux 24 Heures du Mans en 1999 et a remporté d'emblée la victoire avec la troïka de pilotes Winkelhock-Martini-Dalmas, avec 21 tours d'avance sur le deuxième, une Toyota. La BMW LM98 de l'année précédente, pilotée par l'équipage Bscher-Auberleen-Soper, a terminé cinquième.

"Errors are the rungs on the ladder to success. The trick is to detect them at an early stage of the design process, to eliminate them and to learn from them." That is what the American BMW design chief Christopher E. Bangle had to say about the development of the new 3 series. Five and a half years had elapsed between the first draft design and the car's market launch in April 1998.

Some 2.6 million working hours were invested in the E46, as it was referred to in-house. Over 2400 parts were completely redesigned and 130 prototypes handmade. The new model was to meet the highest standards of excellence right down to the last detail. The "small BMW" embodies the achievement of these exacting objectives.

"Corporate design" meant that this model had to bear at least some resemblance to the 5 series car, but on closer inspection, you can see that Chris Bangle has achieved stylistic high-precision work. The striking face of this car is characterized by the extended kidney-shaped grill on the hood, and the individually framed double round headlights. A harmonious effect is also created by the rear section, its rear lights wrapping around the trunk lid, surmounted by a wedge-shaped spoiler acting as an aerodynamic highlight.

Despite the high trunk compartment and the bulky appearance of the wide track body, the car does not seem to be out of proportion thanks to finely detailed artistic touches. For example, the elegant roof and beltlines are supported by horizontal grooves, lips and rubber strips all round – stylish elements which also have a function.

This wonderful outline conceals an optimum use of space and, most importantly, a great deal of technology. With 193 bhp, the 328i is the most powerful of the five engine

variants with which the E46 BMW 3 series begins. The torque characteristics of this in-line six-cylinder engine – already silky smooth anyway – have been enhanced still further. "Double VANOS" is the latest entry in BMW's technical dictionary, stating: "Depending on the accelerator's position and the engine speed, the valve activation times of the intake and exhaust camshafts are adapted to the operating conditions of the engine in an infinitely variable manner." The electro-mechanical control of the throttle valve allows the engine to idle tranquilly, and ensures power is delivered in a smooth surge during acceleration.

"Putting your foot down" with the new 328i is always a pleasure because the 62 mph (100 kph) mark is reached by the high-precision speedo after a mere 7 seconds, and top speeds of 150 mph (240 kph) are not too bad either. Hans-Joachim Stuck put it in a nutshell in the BMW magazine: "The roadholding and power are phenomenal." As for the statement of his racing partner Johnny Cecotto, no one could have summarized the aesthetically-pleasing harmonious lines any better: "There is a unique synthesis of sportiness and elegance and the standard of active and passive safety is no less impressive. It is wonderful that so many familiar developments from larger BMW models have been incorporated into the new 3 series sedan, and that they are not only reserved for people who can afford larger models. All in all, the very comfortable driving characteristics, despite the car's enormous power capacity, mean that it is a truly charismatic drive."

"Fehler sind die Sprossen auf der Leiter zum Erfolg. Die Kunst ist es, sie beim Designprozess frühzeitig zu erkennen, auszumerzen und aus Ihnen zu lernen", so BMW-Chefdesigner Christopher E. Bangle über die Entwicklungsphase des neuen 3ers. Zwischen dem ersten Entwurf und der Markteinführung im April 1998 sind fünfeinhalb Jahre vergangen.

2,6 Millionen Arbeitsstunden werden in den E46, wie er firmenintern heißt, investiert. 2400 Teile werden völlig neu konzipiert und 130 Prototypen von Hand gefertigt. Höchsten Qualitätsansprüchen soll der Neue genügen, und diese erfordern Perfektion bis ins letzte Detail. Dafür ist der „kleine BMW" ein Musterbeispiel.

Zwar verlangt das Corporate Design nach einer gewissen Ähnlichkeit zum 5er, aber bei näherer Betrachtung stellt sich heraus, dass Christopher Bangle stilistische Feinarbeit geleistet hat. Die verlängerte Nierennase der Motorhaube und die Doppelscheinwerfer mit den Augenringen prägen das markante Gesicht. Harmonisch wirkt auch die Heckpartie mit den in den Kofferraumdeckel gezogenen Heckleuchten, über denen sich eine Abrisskante als aerodynamisches Attribut wölbt.

Trotz des hohen Kofferraums und der wuchtigen Wirkung des Breitfahrwerks stimmen die Proportionen dank kleiner, aber gelungener Kunstgriffe. So unterstützen horizontale Sicken, Lippen und rundum geführte Gummileisten die elegante Dach- und Gürtellinienführung – Stylingelemente, die auch eine Funktion erfüllen.

Unter dieser herrlichen Silhouette verbirgt sich eine optimale Raumausnutzung und vor allem viel Technik. Unter den fünf Antriebsvarianten, mit denen die Baureihe startet,

BMW 328i

ist der 328i mit 193 PS die kraftvollste. Der Drehmomentverlauf dieses ohnehin seidenweichen Reihensechszylinders ist nochmals verbessert worden. „Doppel-VANOS" heißt der jüngste Eintrag ins BMW-Techniklexikon: „Die Ventilsteuerzeiten sowohl der Einlass- als auch der Auslassnockenwelle werden abhängig von der Gaspedalstellung und der Motordrehzahl stufenlos den Betriebsbedingungen des Motors angepasst." Eine elektromechanische Drosselklappensteuerung sorgt für einen butterweichen Leerlauf und sanftes Ansprechverhalten beim Gas geben.

Es macht Spaß, beim neuen 328i zu beschleunigen, denn bereits nach 7 Sekunden zeigt der präzise Tacho 100 km/h an, und eine Spitzengeschwindigkeit von 240 Stundenkilometer lassen keine Wünsche offen. Hans-Joachim Stuck bringt es im BMW-Magazin auf den Punkt: „Straßenlage und Power sind phänomenal". Dem Statement seines Rennfahrer-Kollegen Johnny Cecotto ist wohl nichts mehr hinzuzufügen, wenn er diesem 3er ästhetische Harmonie bescheinigt und zusammenfasst: „Die Synthese von Sportlichkeit und Eleganz ist einzigartig, der Standard der aktiven und passiven Sicherheit eindrucksvoll. Es ist toll, dass viele aus größeren Baureihen bekannte Entwicklungen in die neue 3er Limousine einfließen und nicht Menschen vorbehalten bleiben, die sich größere Modelle leisten können. Mein Fazit: Das trotz der Power sehr komfortable Fahrverhalten macht das Fahrzeug zu einem richtig sympathischen Wegbegleiter."

C'est en forgeant que l'on devient forgeron. L'art consiste à reconnaître ses erreurs à temps, lors du processus de design, à les éliminer et à en tirer les enseignements », déclare Christopher E. Bangle, chef styliste chez BMW, en évoquant les phases de développement de la nouvelle série 3. Avant sa commercialisation en avril 1998, cinq ans et demi se sont écoulés depuis le premier coup de crayon.

Quelque 2,6 millions d'heures de travail sont investies dans la E46, comme on l'appelle au sein de l'entreprise. 2400 pièces sont conçues à partir d'une feuille blanche et 130 prototypes sont fabriqués à la main. La nouvelle voiture doit satisfaire aux exigences de qualité les plus strictes et cela implique la perfection jusque dans les moindres détails. La « petite BMW » en est un exemple.

Certes, le *corporate design* exige une certaine similitude avec la série 5, mais, à y regarder de près, on constate que Christopher Bangle a réalisé un excellent travail esthétique. Le léger prolongement du mufle caractéristique de BMW et les phares doubles avec les « valises » sous les yeux lui donnent une allure caractéristique. Tout aussi harmonieuse est la poupe avec les phares empiétant sur le couvercle du coffre qui se termine sur un léger décrochement aérodynamique.

Malgré la hauteur du coffre et l'effet massif des larges trains roulants, les proportions sont parfaites grâce à des astuces à peine perceptibles, mais efficaces : des rainures horizontales, des arêtes et les bandeaux de caoutchouc cernant la voiture mettent en exergue l'élégance des lignes de toit et de ceinture – des éléments de style qui sont fonctionnels.

Sous cette silhouette magnifique se dissimule une utilisation optimale de l'espace disponible et surtout beaucoup de

technique. Des cinq série 3 qui sont lancées, la 328i est la plus puissante avec ses 193 ch. La courbe de couple de ce six-cylindres en ligne déjà réputé pour sa souplesse a encore été améliorée. « Double VANOS » est le nom de la dernière entrée au lexique de BMW : « Ce système permet d'adapter en continu la distribution des soupapes, aussi bien pour l'arbre à cames d'admission que pour l'arbre à cames d'échappement, en fonction de la position de l'accélérateur et du régime moteur et selon l'état de charge du moteur. » Une commande électromécanique de la vis papillon garantit un ralenti régulier et des réactions spontanées à l'accélérateur.

Quel plaisir à appuyer sur l'accélérateur de la nouvelle 328i, dont le tachymètre très précis indique 100 km/h au bout de seulement 7 secondes, et qui satisfait tout à fait avec une vitesse de pointe de 240 km/h. Dans le magazine de BMW, le verdict de Hans-Joachim Stuck tombe comme un couperet : « Tenue de route et puissance sont phénoménales. » Il n'est pas nécessaire d'ajouter le moindre commentaire à la déclaration de son collègue, le pilote de course Johnny Cecotto, qui confère à cette série 3 une harmonie esthétique qu'il résume ainsi : « La synthèse de sportivité et d'élégance est unique au monde ; le niveau de sécurité active et passive est impressionnant. Il est intéressant de voir que de nombreuses innovations apparues avec les gammes supérieures soient reprises par la nouvelle BMW de la série 3 et ne soient pas réservées aux conducteurs qui peuvent s'offrir les modèles haut de gamme. Pour conclure : le comportement très confortable malgré la puissance disponible fait de cette voiture un compagnon de route bien sympathique. »

BMW 328i

A typical feature of the new face of the 3 series is the flat hood pulled down around the BMW kidney, with a space left for the flanking double headlights.

Typisch für das neue Gesicht der 3er Reihe ist die flache, über die BMW-Niere heruntergezogene Motorhaube, flankiert von Doppelscheinwerfern mit nach unten ausgesparten Masken.

Le capot moteur aplati descendant au-delà des naseaux BMW et cerné par les phares doubles avec découpe inférieure est caractéristique du nouveau visage de la série 3.

F·NL 1046
BMW AG NIEDERLASSUNG FRANKFURT/M.

The coupé-like roof shape with the slight lip over the trunk is part of an overall aerodynamic concept which allows the 328i to achieve a top speed of 150 mph (240 kph) with 193 bhp.

Die Coupé-ähnliche Dachform mit leicht angedeuteter Abrisskante über dem Kofferraum ist Teil eines aerodynamischen Gesamtkonzepts, das den 328i mit 193 PS auf 240 Stundenkilometer bringt.

Le toit de style coupé, avec arête de décrochement légèrement esquissée au-dessus du coffre, fait partie d'un concept aérodynamique général qui permet à la 328i de 193 ch d'atteindre les 240 km/h.

BMW 328i

BMW M3 CSL

The BMW M3 CSL, presented as a concept car at the 2001 IAA, is said to possess such attributes as "pure driving dynamic, intelligent lightweight construction," or "unadulterated racing sport technology." High motor performance and drastic weight reduction result in a ratio of 7.7 lbs (3.5 kilogram) per bhp – 9.61 (4.36) for standard M3. The light construction concept considered more and more important by BMW M GmbH, contains several easily visible CFRP components: The flaps in the lower front panel with a massive air intake, exterior mirrors, and even the roof. Although lacquered, the lower front panel itself, the doors, the rear diffuser, and the trunk lid with its striking trailing edge, are also all made of carbon fiber. There are also many carbon fiber parts in the vehicles interior, in which two racing bucket seats are anchored. In addition, this orgy of lightweight but stable material also includes the aluminum engine hood and the magnesium instrumentation frame. The vehicle is given the necessary torsion stability by using a special steel for the body frame and a sandwich construction for the floor pan.

"With a driving time of distinctly less than eight minutes on the northern loop of the Nürburgring, the M3 CSL Concept Car beats its standard series counterparts by almost 30 seconds," according to a written BMW statement at the IAA. Quod erat demonstrandum! The specialist magazine *sport auto* performed this endurance test on this most demanding of racing tracks in the summer of 2003 with a standard CSL. Between June and December 2003, BMW "published" a special edition of 1400 vehicles. *Sport auto* pitted a Porsche 911 GT3 against the CSL on the Ring, but lost to the hot BMW by four seconds. The CSL managed a

time of 7.50 minutes, although it is much heavier than the ultra light prototype, and possesses a weight to performance ratio of 8.49 lbs (3.85 kg)/bhp.

The powerhouse of the CSL, a 6-cylinder serial engine with two variably steered overhead camshafts for the 24 valves, produces a rich 360 bhp, which it proudly displays acoustically. It really roars its potential out of its four tailpipes when driven sportily at its sound barrier of 8000 rpm. Its SMG transmission with rocker switching enables a lightning switching time of roughly 0.08 seconds. No act of strength is needed to tame the Bavarian lion, on condition that one possesses a fine touch and is used to dealing with such a high-powered package. The CSL allows itself to be steered in a well-behaved fashion, for the rack-and-pinion steering reacts extremely precisely, and the chassis layout is by all means convincing.

The Michelin tires also make their contribution. The Michelin Pilot Sport Cup that BMW entrusts to its CSL customers, with 235 rollers at the front and 265/30 ZR 19 at the rear, behave like racing tires. Their profile is not particularly deep, apart from which, the tire surface has to build up a certain operating temperature. Cold, wet weather conditions are to be avoided. On the other hand, these tires enable unbelievable driving characteristics. Horst von Saurma who tested the CSL on the Ring for his readers makes the point: "The performance that the BMW M3 CSL with this tire setup displays in the driving dynamism test is no less than breath taking." From 0 to 62 mph (100 kph) in 4.9 seconds, and to 124 [200] in 16.8 seconds, are uplifting acceleration experiences. The CSL would easily reach 175 mph (280 kph) if it were not for the electronic cut off at 155 mph (250 kph).

Attribute wie „Fahrdynamik pur, intelligente Leichtbauweise" oder „Rennsport-Technologie in Reinkultur" begleiten den auf der IAA 2001 als Concept Car vorgestellten BMW M3 CSL. Viel Motorleistung und drastische Gewichtsreduzierung resultieren in 3,5 Kilo pro PS – 4,36 sind es beim Serien-M3. Das Leichtbau-Konzept, dem die BMW M GmbH zunehmend Bedeutung beimisst, beinhaltet einige gut sichtbare CFK-Komponenten: Flaps in der Frontschürze, versehen mit einem gewaltigen Lufteinlass, Außenspiegel und sogar das Dach. Ebenfalls aus Kohlefaser-Struktur, wenngleich lackiert, bestehen die Frontschürze selbst, Türen, Heck-Diffusor und die Kofferraumklappe mit einer ausgeprägten Abrisskante. Viele Karbon-Teile auch im Innenraum, in dem zwei Renn-Schalensitze verankert sind. Die Orgie leichter, aber stabiler Materialien umfasst auch die Motorhaube aus Aluminium oder den Instrumententafel-Träger aus Magnesium. Spezial-Stahl bei der Rohkarosse und eine Sandwich-Bauweise der Bodenbleche verleihen dem Gefährt die nötige Verwindungsfestigkeit. Da es konsequent ums Gewicht geht, besteht die Heckscheibe aus Dünnglas.

„Mit deutlich weniger als acht Minuten Fahrzeit auf der Nürburgring-Nordschleife schlägt das M3 CSL Concept Car sein Serienpendant um fast 30 Sekunden", so ein schriftliches BMW-Statement auf der IAA. Quod erat demonstrandum! Diesen Härtetest auf der anspruchsvollsten Rennstrecke unternimmt im Sommer 2003 die Fachzeitschrift *sport auto* mit einem Serien-CSL. Von Juni bis Dezember 2003 wird nämlich eine Edition von 1400 Exemplaren aufgelegt. Als Referenz-Auto zum CSL hetzt *sport auto* einen Porsche 911 GT3 um den Ring, doch der verliert vier Sekunden auf den heißen BMW. 7:50 Minuten werden für den CSL gestoppt, obwohl er viel schwerer als der superleichte Prototyp ist und sein Leistungsgewicht analog nur noch 3,85 kg/PS beträgt.

Das Kraftwerk des CSL, ein 6-Zylinder-Reihenmotor mit zwei variabel steuerbaren oben liegenden Nockenwellen für die 24 Ventile, produziert satte 360 PS, auf die er stolz akustisch aufmerksam macht. Bei sportlicher Gangart an der Schallgrenze von 8000 Touren brüllt er sein Potential förmlich durch die vier Auspuffendrohre hinaus. Ein SMG-Getriebe mit Wippenschaltung ermöglicht blitzschnelle Schaltzeiten von etwa 0,08 Sekunden. Um den bayerischen Löwen bändigen zu können, bedarf es keiner Kraftakte, vorausgesetzt man besitzt das nötige Fingerspitzengefühl und Routine im Umgang mit derartigen Hochleistungspaketen. Brav lässt sich der CSL dirigieren, denn die direkte Zahnstangenlenkung reagiert außerordentlich präzise und das Fahrwerks-Layout ist ohnehin überzeugend.

Dazu tragen die Michelin-Pneus bei. Die Michelin Pilot Sport Cup, vorn 235-er Walzen, hinten 265/30 ZR 19, die BMW den CSL-Kunden anvertraut, verhalten sich wie Rennreifen. Ihr Profil ist nicht sonderlich tief, und außerdem muss die Reifenoberfläche eine gewisse Betriebstemperatur aufbauen. Nasskalte Witterung ist also tunlichst zu meiden. Andererseits ermöglichen diese Reifen unglaubliche Fahreigenschaften. Horst von Saurma, der den CSL für seine Leser auf dem Ring getestet hat, konstatiert: „Die Leistungen, die der BMW M3 CSL in den Fahrdynamiktests mit diesem Reifensetup zeigt, sind schlicht atemberaubend." 4,9 Sekunden von 0 auf 100 Stundenkilometer, deren 16,8 auf 200 sind erhebende Beschleunigungs-Momente. Ohne elektronische Sperre bei 250 km/h dürfte der CSL locker 280 Stundenkilometer erreichen.

Des attributs tels que une « dynamique de conduite à l'état pur » ou une « construction allégée intelligente » ont ponctué la présentation, à l'IAA 2001, de la BMW M3 CSL qualifiée de *concept-car*. Un moteur d'une puissance exubérante et une réduction draconienne du poids se traduisent par un rapport poids/puissance de 3,5 kg/ch – contre 4,36 pour la M3 de série. Le concept de construction allégée, qui a de plus en plus d'importance pour BMW Motorsport GmbH, comporte quelques composants en fibre de verre bien visibles : flaps dans le tablier avant qui est caractérisé par une gigantesque prise d'air, rétroviseurs extérieurs et même panneau de toit. Le tablier avant lui-même, les portières, le diffuseur à l'arrière et le couvercle de la malle avec une arête de décrochement très marquée ont également une structure en fibre de carbone, qui est toutefois peinte. Les pièces en carbone abondent dans l'habitacle également où – comme seuls sièges – sont boulonnés deux sièges baquet de course. Des aciers spéciaux pour la carrosserie blanche et une construction en sandwich des tôles du plancher confèrent à l'engin l'indispensable rigidité à la torsion.

« Avec nettement moins de huit minutes au tour sur la boucle Nord du Nürburgring, le *concept-car* M3 CSL bat son homologue de série de près de trente secondes », déclare non sans satisfaction un communiqué de BMW publié à l'IAA. « C.Q.F.D. » ! Ce test à la limite de l'extrême a été accompli, durant l'été 2003, par la revue spécialisée *sport auto* avec une CSL de série sur le circuit le plus technique au monde. De juin à décembre 2003, une édition limitée à 1400 exemplaires est, en effet, lancée. Comme voiture de référence pour la CSL, *sport auto* cravache sur le Ring une Porsche 911 GT3 ; mais celle-ci perd quatre secondes sur la bouillon-

nante BMW. Les chronométreurs mesurent un temps de sept minutes et demie pour la CSL bien qu'elle soit beaucoup plus lourde que l'ultraléger prototype et que son rapport poids/puissance ne soit plus que de 3,85 kg/ch.

L'usine à gaz de la CSL, un six-cylindres en ligne à deux arbres à cames en tête à distribution variable pour les vingt-quatre soupapes, ne développe pas moins de 360 ch, sur lesquels le moteur attire avec fierté l'attention par son acoustique. Lorsque l'on adopte une conduite sportive à la limite du mur du son de 8000 tr/min, il hurle littéralement son potentiel à travers les quatre pots d'échappement. Une boîte SMG avec basculeurs au volant permet des changements de rapport à la vitesse de l'éclair d'environ 0,08 seconde. La CSL se laisse piloter avec docilité, car la direction à crémaillère directe réagit avec une précision extrême.

Mais les pneus Michelin y contribuent aussi. Les Michelin Pilot Sport Cup, des gommes de 235 à l'avant et de 265/30 ZR 19 à l'arrière que BMW confie aux clients qui se sont offert une CSL, affichent un comportement typique de pneu de course. Leurs rainures ne sont pas particulièrement profondes et, en outre, la surface de roulement doit avoir atteint une certaine température pour fonctionner. Il est donc impératif d'en éviter l'utilisation par temps froid et humide. En revanche, ces pneus offrent un comportement absolument incroyable. 4,9 secondes pour le 0 à 100 km/h et 16,8 secondes pour passer à 200 km/h sont des accélérations que l'on n'oublie pas. Sans le blocage électronique à 250 km/h, la CSL atteindrait avec la plus grande décontraction une vitesse de 280 km/h.

Sporting externally as well: large air intakes, carbon front apron flaps, aerodynamically formed rearview mirrors, CFRP trunk lid with integrated spoiler, and a diffuser with four exhaust pipes.

Auch äußerlich ein Sportler: Großer Lufteinlass, Frontschürzen-Flaps aus Karbon, aerodynamisch geformte Rückspiegel, CFK-Heckklappe mit integriertem Spoiler und ein Diffusor mit vier Auspuffrohren.

Extérieurement aussi, une sportive : grande prise d'air, flaps en carbone sur le tablier avant, rétroviseurs aérodynamiques, hayon en matière plastique renforcée de fibre de carbone avec aileron intégré et un diffuseur avec quatre pots d'échappement.

The 360 bhp-strong six-cylinder with its carbon-fiber intake stroke is embedded from top to bottom in the light-construction concept. Above it arches a front suspension brace. The cockpit is also sporty: the most important instrumentation lays, framed in matt black, and in full field of view between the rocker switches.

In das Leichtbau-Konzept vom Scheitel bis zur Sohle ist ein 360 PS starker Sechszylinder mit Kohlefaser-Ansaugtrakt eingebettet. Darüber wölbt sich eine Domstrebe. Sportlich auch das Cockpit: Genau im Blickwinkel zwischen den Schaltwippen liegen, mattschwarz eingerahmt, die wichtigsten Armaturen.

Un six-cylindres de 360 ch avec collecteur d'aspiration en fibre de carbone fait partie intégrante du concept de construction allégée poussée au paroxysme. Une barre antirapprochement se tend au-dessus du moteur. Le cockpit est lui aussi sportif : les cadrans les plus importants, cernés d'un noir mat, se trouvent exactement dans le champ de vision, entre les basculeurs.

BMW Z8

The Bavarian vehicle producer presented the Z07 sports car study in distant Tokyo in October 1997 as a conceptional homage to one of the most beautiful vehicles ever built, the BMW 507 of 1956, and harvested much applause. The length and height is almost identical to that of the dream vehicle of the 1950s, and also the sheer endless front construction, the flat BMW kidneys, as well as the side air intakes pick up the design of Count Goertz once again. The pleasing outer skin with short overhangs consists of high stability structured aluminum plates, which fill in the space between the ribs of the extruded profile. This construction of the Dingolfing aluminum experts, a unitized body space frame, bestows upon the roadster the rigidity and torsion stability necessary for high speed driving. 1999 the retro design went into production as the Z8 – almost unchanged.

As with the 507, under the hood beats a V8 engine, positioned so far behind the front axle that the weight ratio to the rear axle lies by a balanced 50:50. The 400 bhp at 6600 rpm and the maximum torque of 500 Newton meters at 3800 rpm is standard for the sporty two-seater. Variable valve control and an induction tract with electronically controlled individual throttle valves bestow a relatively high torque at low engine speed. The engine management MSS 52 can process more than a million control commands per second. But of what use are these giddying dimensions, which we are well used to from Formula 1, when the power and the glory of the engine is suddenly emasculated at 155 mph (250 kph)? At least there is joy to be had with the precise switching of the six gear transmission on sprinting to 62 mph (100 kph) in 4.7 seconds, and opening up a distance a kilometer in only 23.5 seconds.

There is also joy to be had in straining the sporty chassis – at the front completely aluminum, at the rear partially – especially on stretches with a lot of cornering. Especially here is one thankful for the special braking aid CBC (Cornering Brake Control). The power assisted rack-and-pinion steering reacts immediately and directly – as one would expect of a sports car of this caliber – to the classical spoke steering wheel fitted with an airbag. If a slight over steering should creep in despite the dynamic stability control, one has taken the corners a little too vigorously. The Z8 driver is not immobilized by a flat tire: the "Run-flat" tires, 245/45 R 18W at the front, 275/40 R 18W at the rear, have emergency running characteristics that allow a further 185 miles (300 kilometers) of driving at a speed of up to 50 mph (80 kph). For this reason, it is pointless to look for a reserve tire in the luggage compartment.

The cockpit's appearance is factual, almost sober, in which leather and lacquered aluminum dominate. The instrumentation is reduced to the bare essentials, whereby the positioning of the round instruments above the center console – that is, not in the same field of vision as the steering wheel – needs some getting used to and can be irritating when driving more forcefully. A semi automatic material roof with power-assisted closing mechanism or the aluminum hardtop delivered as a Z8 standard can be used according to the time of year and weather conditions prevailing. This coupé top, at the time without a heated rear window, was also available for the 507 – more filigree in design and so harmoniously integrated by Goertz that he still prefers today the closed version to the open-air model.

Als konzeptionelle Verbeugung vor einem der schönsten jemals gebauten Autos, dem BMW 507 von 1956, präsentiert der bajuwarische Fahrzeughersteller im Oktober 1997 im fernen Tokio erstmals die Sportwagen-Studie Z07 und erntet viel Beifall. Länge und Höhe sind nahezu identisch mit dem Traumauto der fünfziger Jahre, und auch der schier endlos lange Vorderbau, die flachen BMW-Nieren sowie die seitlichen Lufteinlässe greifen den Entwurf des Grafen Goertz wieder auf. Die gefällige Außenhaut mit kurzen Überhängen besteht aus hochfesten Aluminium-Strukturblechen, die die Räume zwischen dem Gerippe aus Strangpress-Profilen füllen. Dieser Aufbau der Dingolfinger Alu-Experten, ein selbsttragender Spaceframe, verleiht dem Roadster die nötige Steifheit und Verwindungs-Stabilität selbst für rasanten Fahrbetrieb. 1999 geht das Retro-Design – nahezu unverändert – als Z8 in Serie.

Wie beim 507 pulsiert unter der Haube ein V8-Triebwerk, das so weit hinter der Vorderachse positioniert ist, dass die Gewichtsverteilung zur Hinterachse in einem ausgeglichenen Verhältnis von 50:50 ausfällt. Standesgemäß für den sportlichen Zweisitzer sind die 400 PS bei 6600/min und das maximale Drehmoment von 500 Newtonmetern bei 3800/min. Variable Nockenwellen-Verstellung und ein Ansaug-Trakt mit elektronisch gesteuerten Einzel-Drosselklappen bescheren schon im unteren Drehzahlbereich ein relativ hohes Drehmoment. Mehr als eine Million Steuerkommandos kann das Motormanagement MSS 52 pro Sekunde umsetzen. Doch was nützen diese schwindelerregenden Dimensionen, die man ja aus der Formel 1 kennt, wenn Kraft und Herrlichkeit des Motors bei 250 Stundenkilometern „einen auf den Deckel" bekommen. Zumindest macht das Beschleunigen mit dem präzise schaltbaren 6-Gang-Getriebe Spaß, denn in 4,7 Sekunden wird auf Tempo 100 gesprintet und nach 23,5 Sekunden ist bereits ein Kilometer zurückgelegt.

Auch beim Strapazieren des sportlichen Fahrwerks – vorn ganz, hinten teilweise aus Aluminium – kommt Freude auf, besonders auf kurvenreichen Straßen. Gerade hier ist man für die spezielle Bremshilfe CBC (Cornering Brake Control) dankbar. Auf Lenkeinschläge des klassischen Speichen-Volants, in dem sogar ein Airbag untergebracht ist, reagiert die servo-unterstützte Zahnstangenlenkung direkt und genau – wie man es von einem Sportwagen dieses Kalibers erwartet. Sollte sich freilich trotz der dynamischen Stabilitäts-Kontrolle ein leichtes Untersteuern einschleichen, ist man in der Kurve wohl zu forsch unterwegs. Immer noch unterwegs ist der Z8-Fahrer nach einer Reifenpanne: die „Run-flat"-Reifen, vorn 245/45 R 18W, hinten 275/40 R 18W, besitzen Notlauf-Eigenschaften, die bei gemäßigter Geschwindigkeit bis zu 80 km/h noch für eine 300-Kilometer-Distanz reichen.

Sachlich, fast ernüchternd wirkt das Cockpit, in dem Leder und lackiertes Aluminium dominieren. Das Instrumentarium beschränkt sich auf das Wesentliche, wobei die Positionierung der Rundinstrumente über der Mittelkonsole – also nicht in Blickrichtung Lenkrad – gewöhnungsbedürftig ist. Je nach Jahreszeit und Wetterlage bedient man sich beim Z8 eines halbautomatischen Stoffverdecks mit einem servo-unterstützten Schließmechanismus oder des serienmäßig mitgelieferten Aluminium-Hardtops. Diesen Coupé-Aufsatz, seinerzeit ohne Heckscheiben-Beheizung, gab es auch beim 507 – filigraner gestaltet und von Goertz so harmonisch integriert, dass ihm noch heute die geschlossene Version besser als die offene gefällt.

Pour rendre hommage à l'une des plus belles voitures jamais construites, la BMW 507 de 1956, BMW présente en première mondiale, en octobre 1997, à Tokyo, une étude de style de voiture de sport, la Z07. Le succès est immédiat. Sa longueur et sa hauteur sont pratiquement identiques à celles de la voiture mythique des années 1950 et son capot avant semble ne jamais vouloir finir. Les naseaux BMW à l'horizontale ainsi que les sorties d'air latérales sont une réminiscence de l'esquisse réalisée par le comte von Goertz. La gracile carrosserie aux courts porte-à-faux consiste en tôles d'aluminium structurelles à grande résistance qui habillent avec élégance le squelette en profilés extrudés. Cette robe réalisée par les spécialistes de l'aluminium de Dingolfing, une carrosserie *spaceframe* autoporteuse, confère au roadster la rigidité nécessaire et la stabilité torsionnelle indispensable pour rouler à grande vitesse. Et c'est bien là, *a priori,* sa mission d'origine quand le modèle au design néo-rétro est fabriqué en série – pratiquement sans changements – en 1999 sous l'appellation Z8.

Comme avec la 507, un V8 palpite sous le capot, mais placé si loin derrière le train avant que la répartition du poids est parfaitement équilibrée à raison de 50 % pour chaque essieu. La puissance de la sportive biplace est digne de son rang avec 400 ch à 6600 tr/min pour un couple maximum de 500 Nm à 3800 tr/min. Les arbres à cames à distribution variable et un collecteur d'aspiration avec six vis papillons individuelles à commande électronique garantissent déjà un couple relativement élevé à bas régime. La gestion moteur MSS 52 est capable de répondre à plus d'un million d'instructions par seconde. Au moins appréciera-t-on les accélérations avec la précise boîte manuelle à six vitesses, car la Z8

bondit en 4,7 secondes de 0 à 100 km/h et abat le kilomètre départ arrêté en 23,5 secondes seulement.

Même si l'on pousse dans ses derniers retranchements le châssis sportif – tout en aluminium à l'avant et partiellement à l'arrière –, le plaisir est toujours au rendez-vous, en particulier sur routes sinueuses. C'est là, précisément, que l'on apprécie l'assistance de freinage CBC *(Cornering Brake Control)* spéciale. La direction à crémaillère assistée réagit avec spontanéité et précision aux ordres de braquage que transmet le volant classique, qui héberge même un airbag – comme on est en droit de l'attendre d'une voiture de sport de ce calibre. Un léger sous-virage s'est-il manifesté malgré le contrôle de stabilité dynamique ? Cela signifie que vous avez abordé la courbe trop rapidement. Et ce n'est pas une crevaison qui contraindra le conducteur de Z8 à l'arrêt : les pneus « run-flat », de 245/45 R 18W à l'avant et 275/40 R 18W à l'arrière possèdent un dispositif anti-crevaison qui permet, à la vitesse modérée de 80 km/h au maximum, de couvrir encore 300 km.

Sobre et presque spartiate est le cockpit, où dominent le cuir et l'aluminium vernis. L'instrumentation se circonscrit à l'essentiel. Selon la saison et le temps, on peut ouvrir la capote en tissu semi-automatique de la Z8 avec un mécanisme à assistance ou la coiffer du hard-top en aluminium livré en série. Ce toit coupé, mais alors sans lunette dégivrante, était aussi proposé pour la 507. Plus mince, le comte von Goertz l'avait intégré si harmonieusement qu'aujourd'hui encore, la version fermée lui plaît davantage que son homologue décapotée.

The retro-design of the Z8 is reminiscent of Count Goertz's BMW 507, a homage to one of the most beautiful of sports cars. The flat BMW kidneys are not be forgotten, neither are the side air vents.

Das Retro-Design des Z8 erinnert an den BMW 507 des Grafen Goertz, Hommage an einen der schönsten Sportwagen. Da dürfen die flachen BMW-Nieren ebenso wenig fehlen wie die seitlichen Lüftungsschlitze.

Le design néo-rétro de la Z8 rappelle la BMW 507 du comte von Goertz – ce qui n'est pas fortuit, mais un hommage à l'une des plus belles voitures de sport de tous les temps. Bien évidemment, les plats naseaux de BMW ne doivent pas briller par leur absence, aussi peu que les fentes d'aération latérales.

The classical side profile of the Z8 embodies the BMW roadster tradition. The V8 with 400 bhp is positioned behind the front axle.

Das klassische Seitenprofil des Z8 verkörpert die BMW-Roadster-Tradition. Hinter der Vorderachse positioniert ist der V8 mit 400 PS.

BMW Z8

Le profil latéral classique de la Z8 incarne à la perfection la tradition du roadster selon BMW.
Le V8 de 400 ch est positionné à l'arrière du train avant.

BMW X5 1999

Although it was built in Spartanburg, South Carolina, it was a German car that was the highlight of the North American International Auto Show 1999, right in the Mecca of the US automobile industry, Detroit. The search for new market niches – something which BMW was pursuing as long as 30 years ago with the 02 series – produced the so-called SAV (Sports Activity Vehicle) segment, resulting in the BMW X5.

The X5 was neither intended as competition for the Range Rover within the BMW group, nor represented a "tuned" 5 series touring. On the sidelines at the debut of the X5 BMW announced: "Like other BMW automobiles, the X5 is defined by well-known classic BMW characteristics, such as aesthetics, dynamism and safety. But the X5 in addition places great emphasis on a completely new feel for the driver, produced in particular through the high seating and the excellent road-holding on all the highways and byways of this world."

The most modern all-wheel drive technology with anti-skid regulation by brake action, as well as some BMW high-tech goodies such as automatic and dynamic stability control, lend the X5 on-road qualities which allow for an emphatically sporty drive. But off-road the X5 also makes a strong impression – a powerful mountaineer which has no difficulties with returning to earth due to "hill descent control".

The range of engines for the X5 contains not only the well-known eight-cylinder V-engines, but also offers six-cylinder inline petrol and diesel engines with direct fuel injection. On the subject of safety, BMW powers ahead too with its "F.I.R.S.T." safety package. Strong beams, well-designed crumple zones, and up to ten airbags provide protection in a crash.

As far as equipment and driver comfort is concerned, the range stretches from a sports package via a multi-function steering wheel to a great many items that are electrically controlled, plus diverse seating "furniture" alternatives on to a navigation system and practical roof and rear rack storage systems.

There is enough space between the beefy 19-inch wheels for excursions into uneven countryside. On the other hand there is calculated ground clearance to prevent aerobatics during cornering. As the 23/1998 edition of *auto motor und sport* stated, this BMW, in meeting the dynamic requirements for this brand of car, was designed to lap the north loop of the Nürburgring in less than nine minutes.

At the Frankfurt IAA in 2003, the X5 presents itself thoroughly revamped, optically and technically, and in possession of three new engines. The off-road sportsman from Spartanburg achieves a top speed of 153 mph (246 kph) when fitted with the 4.4-liter V8, and its 320 bhp.

The "xDrive" four-wheel drive, that enables a stepless and variable distribution of driving power between the front and rear axles at incredible speed, is also new.

Ausgerechnet ein deutsches Auto, wenngleich in Spartanburg, South Carolina, gebaut, ist das Highlight der „North American International Auto Show 1999" im US-Automobil-Mekka Detroit. Das Entdecken neuer Marktnischen – von BMW schon vor mehr als 30 Jahren mit der 02er Serie propagiert – brachte das sogenannte SAV-Segment (Sports Activity Vehicle) hervor und resultiert im BMW X5.

Am Rande der Premiere dieses Wagens, der weder innerhalb des Konzerns dem Range Rover Konkurrenz machen soll, noch einen „aufgebockten" 5er Touring darstellt, lässt BMW verlauten: „Der X5 definiert sich wie die anderen BMW-Automobile über die bekannten klassischen BMW-Eigenschaften wie Ästhetik, Dynamik und Sicherheit. Im Falle des X5 ist darüber hinaus ein völlig neues Fahrgefühl, insbesondere durch die hohe Sitzposition und das exzellente Fahrverhalten auf allen Straßen und Wegen dieser Welt stark ausgeprägt."

Modernste Allradtechnologie mit Schlupfregelung durch Bremseingriff sowie einige High-Tech-„Bonbons", zu denen auch eine automatische und dynamische Stabilitätskontrolle gehört, verleihen dem X5 On-Road-Qualitäten, die eine durchaus sportliche Fahrweise ermöglichen. Aber auch im Off-Road-Betrieb hinterläßt der X5 einen starken Eindruck – ein kräftiger Bergsteiger, dem der Abstieg dank „hill descent control" leicht gemacht wird.

Die Motorenpalette für den X5 sieht nicht nur die bekannten Achtzylinder-V-Motoren vor, sondern umfasst auch den Reihensechszylinder als Benziner und als Diesel mit Direkteinspritzung. Auch beim Thema Sicherheit rüstet BMW mit dem „F.I.R.S.T."-Safety-Paket auf. Starke Holme, gut angelegte Knautschzonen und bis zu zehn Airbags bieten bei einem Crash Schutz.

Hinsichtlich Ausstattung und Fahrkomfort reicht das Angebot vom Sportpaket über ein Multifunktionslenkrad, vielen elektrisch verstellbaren Komponenten und diversen Sitzmöbeln bis zum Navigationssystem oder praktischen Dach- und Heck-Trägersystemen.

Zwischen den bulligen 19-Zoll-Rädern befindet sich genügend Freiraum für Exkursionen in unebene Botanik. Andererseits reicht der Bodenabstand noch aus, um in Kurven nicht abzuheben. Denn – so *auto motor und sport* 23/1998 – sollte dieser BMW in Erfüllung markentypischer Dynamikanforderungen in der Lage sein, die Nordschleife des Nürburgrings in weniger als neun Minuten zu umrunden.

Bei der IAA 2003 in Frankfurt präsentiert sich der X5 optisch und technisch gründlich überarbeitet und erhält drei neue Motoren. Mit dem 4,4-Liter-V8, der 320 PS leistet, erzielt der Offroad-Sportler aus Spartanburg eine Spitzengeschwindigkeit von 246 Stundenkilometern.

Neu ist auch das Allradsystem „xDrive", das eine stufenlose und variable Verteilung der Antriebskräfte zwischen Vorder- und Hinterachse in unglaublicher Schnelligkeit ermöglicht.

C'est le monde à l'envers : c'est une voiture allemande, construite à Spartanburg, en Caroline du Sud, qui est la vedette du North American International Auto Show 1999 à Detroit, la capitale nord-américaine de l'automobile. Le segment des SAV (Sports Activity Vehicle) a permis de découvrir de nouvelles niches – un exercice que BMW avait déjà pratiqué il y a plus de trente ans avec la série 02. Le résultat en est la BMW X5.

En marge du lancement de cette voiture, qui n'est pas appelée à concurrencer le Range Rover au sein du groupe et n'est pas non plus une touring série 5, BMW déclare : « La X5 se définit, au même titre que les autres automobiles de BMW, par les caractéristiques classiques bien connues de BMW, telles l'esthétique, la dynamique et la sécurité. Dans le cas de la X5, les sensations de conduite sont absolument différentes, caractérisées, en particulier, par la position élevée du conducteur et son excellent comportement sur la totalité des routes et des chemins du monde. »

Une technologie de traction intégrale ultramoderne avec régulation antipatinage par intervention sur les freins ainsi que quelques perfectionnements dus à la haute technologie, chère à BMW, parmi lesquels figure également un contrôle automatique et dynamique de la stabilité, confèrent à la X5 des qualités qui autorisent parfaitement un style de conduite sportif. Mais, en tout-chemin aussi, la X5 fait forte impression. C'est un véritable « chamois », qui n'a pas de problèmes dans les descentes grâce au « hill descent control ».

La gamme de moteurs pour la X5 ne comporte pas seulement les huit-cylindres en V bien connus, mais aussi le six-cylindres en ligne en version essence et diesel à injection directe. Sur le plan de la sécurité, BMW ne lésine pas avec son pack de sécurité « FIRST ». De solides longerons, des zones de déformation programmée bien calculées et jusqu'à dix airbags offrent une protection optimale en cas de collision.

Dans le registre de l'aménagement et du confort, on n'a que l'embarras du choix : du pack sport au système de navigation ou aux systèmes de portage sur le toit et à l'arrière en passant par un volant multifonctions, de nombreux accessoires électriques et un choix de fauteuils.

Entre les larges roues de 19 pouces, on dispose de suffisamment de marge pour sortir des sentiers battus. D'un autre côté, l'adhérence est suffisante pour conserver sa stabilité dans les virages. En effet, comme le constate le numéro 23/1998 d'*auto motor und sport*, cette BMW, pour respecter les propriétés dynamiques typiques de sa catégorie, devrait être en mesure de couvrir la boucle Nord du Nürburgring en moins de neuf minutes. Moins de huit minutes, c'est le temps que mettra sans aucun doute le nouveau roadster Z7 que BMW a dévoilé à l'automne 2000.

Pour les habitants de Spartanburg, la X5 est, après la Z3, une deuxième bonne nouvelle : les capacités de l'usine ont été multipliées par deux et les effectifs majorés de 50 % en janvier 1999. Avec cet engagement aux États-Unis, BMW considère avoir franchi une nouvelle étape en consolidant la position du groupe dans le monde grâce à sa politique de globalisation.

An extensive range of equipment with up to ten airbags and many extras is as much a part of the X5's SAV (Sports Activity Vehicle) segment as are the BMW engines for the different markets. The X5 performs well on dirt tracks due to its ultra-modern four-wheel drive technology. It is exemplary with regard to driving dynamics and safety.

Eine reichhaltige Ausstattung mit bis zu zehn Airbags und viele Extras gehören ebenso zum SAV-Segment (Sports Activity Vehicle) des X5 wie die BMW-Motoren für die jeweiligen Märkte. Auf unbefestigtem Untergrund macht der X5 dank modernster Allradtechnologie eine gute Figur. Hinsichtlich der Komponenten Fahrdynamik und Sicherheit ist er vorbildlich.

Un équipement presque parfait avec jusqu'à dix airbags et de nombreuses options qui caractérisent le segment de la SAV (Sports Activity Vehicle) auquel appartient la X5, au même titre que les moteurs BMW sur ses marchés respectifs. Sortie des sentiers battus, la X5 fait bonne figure grâce à la technologie ultramoderne de sa traction intégrale. Elle est une référence en termes de dynamique et de sécurité.

Unusual sounds for an autumn day force their way through the open kitchen window of Spielberg 1, the castle of Barons Karl Arbesser. It is the whining of a Formula 1 engine echoing from the Arbesser woods above the A1 Ring. The Spielbergers are amazed, how were they to know that in the appointments calendar of BMW and Williams the following entry has been made for October 5, 1999: first test on a Grand Prix track of the BMW 10-cylinder in a Williams chassis. It is six months to the first race in Australia, during which the technical problems swallowing several motors must be solved. Gerhard Berger, who together with Dr. Mario Theissen forms the BMW Motor sport management, states his opinion: "The requirements of innovative technology and reaction times for further development are unique. Until we can add a current success story to the 1983 World Championship Title difficult years will come and go."

The first is got through in style, with Ralf Schumacher gaining third place at the Williams-BMW FW22 debut in Melbourne, and his young team colleague Jenson Button, occupying fourth place as his engine suddenly strikes and that despite starting in 21st position.

Even so, Dr. Theissen sums up with mixed feelings: "I am visibly surprised how well we have gained a foothold." At the Hungarian GP his motor specialists from Munich break through what had, until then, been the "sound barrier" of 800 bhp. Ralf and Jenson collect their points until the season's end with such vigor that third position in the engine designers' competition is gained at the first go. The prize entices a relieved smile from the rather reticent Frank Williams who values the engine designers' trophy more than the drivers' championship title.

Despite four victories, an equal number of pole positions, and eight fastest circuit times bringing with them once again in 2001 the third position in the designers' world championship, the FW23 is ten times affected by technical defects, six of them in the vicinity of the engine. Gerhard Berger is however confident: "we have come unmistakably nearer the summit." With the target for 2001 achieved, the Berger-Theissen duo's goal for the 2002 season was, as a Bavarian-English liaison, to leave the Swabian-British partnership of Mercedes and McLaren far behind them, by means of a new engine, the P80, a new Williams' chassis, the FW24, and a new tire partner. In this they succeed with 92 points to 65 – but Ferrari remains in a class of its own with 221 points. In reliability, the Williams-BMW beats even the Maranello reds with 1963 circuits from a possible 2180. The next hundred hurdle is taken by the P82 extended engine in action from Monza onward: 900 hp at 19,000 rpm. With it Juan Pablo Montoya roars to the fastest qualifying round in contemporary Formula 1 history in the grounds of the royal park at Monza. Only a few days later the P83, the engine for 2003, has its testing debut.

Dr. Theissen can in 2003 draw the best balance so far, despite a weak season's prelude and some bad luck at the final: "We have fought to the end for the title, and were, with 1800 racing circuits, once again the most reliable team." Four victories, including two doubles, and 144 Points in the designers' championship fill him with pride. Gerhard Berger, who has departed from motor sport for an unspecified period, also congratulates. Williams-BMW actually have a four point lead before the last two races. At the final in Suzuka of all places a leak in the hydraulics lets Montoya's leading FW25

Für einen Herbsttag ungewöhnliche Klänge dringen durch das geöffnete Küchenfenster von Spielberg 1, dem Schloss des Barons Karl Arbesser. Es ist das Kreischen eines Formel-1-Motors, das aus den Arbesser-Waldungen oberhalb des A1-Rings zurückhallt. Die Spielberger sind erstaunt, woher sollten sie wissen, dass auf dem Terminkalender von BMW und Williams unter dem 5. Oktober 1999 steht: Erster Test des BMW-10-Zylinders in einem Williams-Chassis auf einer Grand-Prix-Strecke. Bis zum ersten Renneinsatz in Australien sind es noch sechs Monate, in denen technische Probleme, die einige Triebwerke verschlingen, gelöst werden müssen. Gerhard Berger, der zusammen mit Dr. Mario Theissen das Direktorium von BMW-Motorsport bildet, gibt zu bedenken: „Die Ansprüche an innovativer Technik und an die Reaktionszeiten für die Weiterentwicklung sind einzigartig. Bis wir an den Formel-1-Weltmeistertitel von 1983 ein aktuelles Erfolgskapitel anhängen können, werden schwierige Jahre vergehen."

Das erste wird mit Bravour überstanden, denn bereits beim Debüt des Williams-BMW FW22 in Melbourne belegt Ralf Schumacher den dritten Platz, und der blutjunge Team-Kollege Jenson Button, als 21. gestartet, rangiert auf Position vier, als plötzlich der Motor streikt.

Dennoch resümiert Dr. Theissen mit einem lachenden und einem weinenden Auge: „Ich bin sichtlich überrascht, wie gut wir Fuß gefasst haben." Seine Münchener Motoren-Spezialisten durchstoßen bereits beim GP von Ungarn die damalige „Schallmauer" von 800 PS. Ralf und Jenson punkten bis zum Saisonende so emsig, dass auf Anhieb der dritte Platz in der Konstrukteurswertung herausspringt. Dem eher verschlossenen Frank Williams, der den Konstrukteurs-

BMW Williams FW22–FW26

Pokal über den Fahrer-Titel stellt, entlockt die Ausbeute ein befreites Lächeln.

Vier Siege, ebenso viele Pole-Positionen und acht schnellste Rennrunden bringen 2001 erneut den dritten Rang in der Konstrukteurs-WM, doch zehnmal werden die FW23 von technischen Defekten, davon sechsmal im näheren Umfeld des Motors, heimgesucht. Gerhard Berger gibt sich dennoch zuversichtlich: „Wir sind der Spitze deutlich näher gekommen." Ziel für 2001 erreicht, und so avisiert das Duo Berger-Theissen mit einem komplett neuen Motor, dem P80, einem neuen Williams-Chassis, dem FW24, und einem neuen Reifenpartner eine Saison 2002, in der die bayerisch-englische Liaison die schwäbisch-britischen Partner Mercedes und McLaren hinter sich lassen will. Das gelingt auch mit 92 zu 65 Punkten – doch Ferrari ist mit 221 Zählern eine Klasse für sich. In puncto Zuverlässigkeit liegen die Williams-BMW mit 1963 von 2180 möglichen Rennrunden sogar vor den Roten aus Maranello. Die ab Monza eingesetzte Motoren-Ausbaustufe des P82 überspringt die nächste Hunderter-Barriere: 900 PS bei 19 000 Umdrehungen pro Minute. Damit knallt Juan Pablo Montoya die schnellste Qualifikationsrunde der bisherigen F1-Historie auf das Parkett des königlichen Parks von Monza. Einige Tage später debütiert bei Tests bereits der P83, das Triebwerk für 2003.

Trotz schwachen Saisonauftaktes und etwas Pech beim Finale, kann Dr. Theissen 2003 seine bislang beste Bilanz ziehen: „Wir haben bis zum Schluss um den Titel gekämpft und waren mit 1800 Rennrunden erneut die zuverlässigste Mannschaft." Vier Siege, darunter zwei Doppelerfolge, und 144 Punkte in der Konstrukteurs-WM erfüllen ihn mit Stolz. Gerhard Berger, der sich auf unbestimmte Zeit vom

Un bruit vraiment inhabituel pour une journée d'automne pénètre par la fenêtre ouverte de la cuisine de Spielberg 1, le château du baron Karl Arbesser. C'est le vrombissement d'un moteur de Formule 1 qui résonne dans les futaies d'Arbesser, près du circuit du A1-Ring. A Spielberg, c'est l'étonnement. Comment pourrait-on, en effet, savoir que, sur l'agenda de BMW et de Williams, à la date du 5 octobre 1999, figure la mention : « Premier test du dix-cylindres BMW dans un châssis Williams sur un circuit de Grand Prix. » D'ici à sa première course en Australie, six mois vont encore s'écouler durant lesquels il va falloir résoudre des problèmes techniques qui sonneront le glas de quelques moteurs. Gerhard Berger, membre du directoire de BMW-Motorsport avec Mario Theissen, objecte : « L'innovation technique et la rapidité de réaction qu'implique le perfectionnement d'un tel moteur sont absolument stupéfiantes. Nous allons vivre des années difficiles avant de pouvoir ajouter un chapitre supplémentaire à notre saga après le titre de champion du monde de Formule 1 de 1983. »

Les débuts sont encourageants. En effet, à Melbourne, avec la Williams BMW FW22, Ralf Schumacher termine d'emblée troisième et son tout jeune coéquipier, Jenson Button, parti de la vingt-et-unième place, est déjà quatrième quand, soudain, le moteur s'arrête.

Ce qui n'empêche pas Mario Theissen de faire contre mauvaise fortune bon cœur : « Je suis réellement surpris de voir avec quelle rapidité nous avons pris pied. » Dès le Grand Prix de Hongrie, ses motoristes franchissent le « mur du son » de cette époque, les 800 ch. Jusqu'à la fin de la saison, Ralf et Jenson accumulent les points, tant et si bien que BMW termine troisième au classement des constructeurs.

Le taciturne Frank Williams, pour qui le titre des marques a toujours eu la primauté sur celui des pilotes, se fend même d'un sourire libérateur.

Quatre victoires, quatre pole positions et huit meilleurs tours en course classent de nouveau BMW au troisième rang du championnat du monde des constructeurs 2001. Mais, dix fois, les FW23 sont immobilisées à cause d'une défaillance technique, dont six fois par un incident dans la périphérie immédiate du moteur. Gerhard Berger ne désarme pas pour autant et reste confiant : « Nous nous sommes considérablement rapprochés des meilleurs. » L'objectif atteint pour 2001, Berger-Theissen annoncent un moteur inédit, le P80, un nouveau châssis Williams, la FW24, et un nouveau partenaire pour les pneumatiques pour la saison 2002 au cours de laquelle l'alliance Bavière-Angleterre entend laisser derrière elle la coalition Stuttgart-Woking de Mercedes et McLaren. Objectif atteint avec 92 points contre 65 – mais Ferrari joue dans une catégorie à part avec 221 points. En terme de fiabilité, Williams-BMW fait même mieux que les Rouges de Maranello avec 1963 sur 2180 tours possibles en course. L'évolution P82, qui apparaît à Monza, franchit un nouveau seuil avec 900 ch à 19 000 tr/min. Avec un tel bolide, Montoya grave le tour de qualification le plus rapide dans l'histoire de la Formule 1 sur le bitume du parc royal de Monza. Quelques jours plus tard, l'évolution P83, le moteur pour 2003, fait déjà ses débuts en essais.

Malgré un début de saison mitigé et un peu de malchance lors de la finale, Theissen peut, en 2003, dresser le bilan de sa meilleure saison à ce jour : « Jusqu'à la fin, nous nous sommes battus pour le titre et, avec 1800 tours en course couverts, nous avons de nouveau été l'écurie la down. Maddening, when one considers that the P83 was the object of no less than 1388 changes for ongoing development and optimization during the season.

For 2004, the FW26 is presented with a prominent characteristic: the front spoiler, whose wavy structure is supposed to minimize air turbulence, is positioned in front of the vehicles nose, and held by two protruding arms. Could it be a bad omen not to have the nose ahead of all else? Also the slim down of the side cases of the carbon fiber-aramid-epoxy composite chassis is a result of extensive wind tunnel experiments. Sam Michael, the new young chief engineer, in whose hands Patrick Head has laid his responsibility, performs a great deal of detail work. The P84 from Munich offers a completely reworking of those sections especially put under thermal and mechanical pressure, and that for a reason: from 2004 onwards an engine has to last the entire racing weekend.

Already the season's prelude points clearly to a Ferrari-Schumacher-Bridgestone hegemony and with the BAR-Honda a further component steps to the fore. The Japanese engine genius Takeo Kiuchi has bestowed a further 160 bhp since 2002 on the BAR of the rising sun, triggering at the same time an unbelievable engine arms-race, which FIA President Max Mosley will not condone for long, in the interest of all concerned. At first only Ferrari can keep up with this show of strength, but from Montreal onward BMW also enters the competition. Everything is sweetness and light for the Munich team, they had just snatched a double victory at the hardest 24 hour race at the Nürburgring. Ralf Schumacher in pole position in Canada and second behind his brother, points also for Juan Pablo, but then a justified thunderstorm from the FIA commissioners under the leadership of Jo Bauer from Germany breaks over their heads. Because the cool air inlets do not conform to the regulations, Williams and Toyota (the same misdemeanor) are stripped of all points from this Grand Prix. Sam Michael, overcome with remorse, takes the blame wrangles with his fate: "that it had to happen to me of all people!" Bad luck comes seldom alone: Ralf Schumacher's accident in Indianapolis and Montoya's belated change to the reserve vehicle at the Mecca of American motor sports and disqualification which followed much too late, allow only one conclusion: It really cannot get worse – now things are really going to start moving!

Motorsport verabschiedet hat, gratuliert. Vor den letzten beiden Rennen führt Williams-BMW sogar noch mit vier Punkten Vorsprung. Ausgerechnet beim Endlauf in Suzuka lässt ein Leck in der Hydraulik den in Führung liegenden FW25 von Montoya im Stich. Ärgerlich, wenn man bedenkt, dass dem P83 während der laufenden Saison nicht weniger als 1388 Änderungen zur ständigen Weiterentwicklung und Optimierung zuteil wurden.

Für 2004 präsentiert sich der FW26 mit einem hervorstechenden Merkmal: Von zwei ausladenden Bügeln gehalten, ist der Frontspoiler, dessen gewellte Struktur Luftverwirbelungen minimieren soll, vor der Fahrzeugnase positioniert. Ein schlechtes Omen, die Nase nicht vorn zu haben? Auch die Schlankheitskur der Seitenkästen des aus einem Kohlefaser-Aramid-Epoxy-Verbundes bestehenden Chassis ist das Ergebnis ausgedehnter Windkanalversuche. Sam Michael, der junge neue Chef-Ingenieur, in dessen Hände Patrick Head seinen Aufgabenbereich gelegt hat, leistet viel Detailarbeit. Der P84 aus München wartet mit einer Komplettüberarbeitung der thermisch und mechanisch besonders belasteten Teile auf, denn schließlich muss ab 2004 ein Triebwerk das gesamte Renn-Wochenende halten.

Schon der Saisonauftakt deutet eine Hegemonie der Kombination Ferrari-Schumacher-Bridgestone an, und mit dem BAR-Honda tritt eine weitere Komponente in den Vordergrund. Mit einer Mehrleistung von 160 PS seit 2002 hat das japanische Motoren-Genie Takeo Kiuchi BAR die aufgehende Sonne beschert und gleichzeitig ein unglaubliches Motoren-Wettrüsten ausgelöst, das FIA-Präsident Max Mosley im Interesse aller Teams nicht lange billigen will. Zunächst kann nur Ferrari bei diesem Kraftakt mithalten, doch ab Montreal bietet auch BMW paroli. Bei den Münchnern herrscht eitel Sonnenschein, zumal man gerade beim härtesten 24-Stunden-Rennen auf dem Nürburgring einen Doppelsieg verbucht hat. Ralf Schumacher in Kanada auf Pole und Zweiter hinter seinem Bruderherz, Punkte auch für Juan Pablo, doch dann kommt das berechtigte Donnerwetter der FIA-Kommissare unter Leitung von Jo Bauer aus Deutschland. Da die Kühllufteinlässe der Bremsanlage nicht regelkonform sind, werden Williams und Toyota (gleiches Delikt) alle Punkte dieses Grand Prix aberkannt. Sam Michael, völlig zerknirscht, nimmt die Schuld auf sich und hadert mit seinem Schicksal: „Dass das ausgerechnet mir passieren musste!" Ein Unglück kommt selten allein: Der Unfall von Ralf Schumacher in Indianapolis und das zu späte Umsteigen von Montoya in das Reserve-Auto im Mekka des US-Motorsports mit einer viel zu spät erfolgten Disqualifikation lassen nur noch ein Fazit zu: Schlimmer kann es nicht kommen – jetzt geht es erst richtig los!

plus fiable. » Quatre victoires, dont deux doublés, et 144 points au championnat des constructeurs l'emplissent de fierté. Gerhard Berger, retraité jusqu'à nouvel ordre de la compétition automobile, le félicite. Avant les deux dernières courses, Williams-BMW est même encore en tête du championnat avec quatre points d'avance. Comme par hasard, lors de l'ultime manche, à Suzuka, une fuite d'hydraulique contraint Montoya à abandonner alors qu'il était en tête au volant de sa FW25. Ce qui est vraiment rageant quand on sait que, tout au long de la saison, le P83 a reçu pas moins de 1388 modifications pour le perfectionner en permanence et l'optimiser.

Pour 2004, la FW26 se démarque totalement du reste du plateau par son design : soutenu par deux « défenses de morse », l'aileron avant, dont la structure ondulée minimise les tourbillons, est positionné loin en avant du nez de la voiture. De même, la « cure de minceur » des pontons latéraux du châssis en fibre de carbone-aramide-résine-époxy-matériaux composites est le fruit d'innombrables heures de travail en soufflerie. Sam Michael, le jeune et nouveau directeur technique auquel Patrick Head a cédé une bonne part de ses prérogatives, n'a pas chômé. Le P84 de Munich a donné lieu à une refonte complète des pièces les plus sollicitées au niveau thermique et mécanique. En 2004, un moteur devra, en effet, tenir tout le week-end.

L'ouverture de la saison, déjà, laisse entrevoir une hégémonie du trio Ferrari-Schumacher-Bridgestone, mais, avec BAR-Honda, un nouvel acteur vient se battre pour les premiers rangs. Avec 160 ch de plus depuis 2002, le génial motoriste japonais Takeo Kiuchi a fait se lever le soleil sur l'empire de BAR et, simultanément, déclenché une incroyable course à la puissance, que Max Mosley, le président de la FIA, dans l'intérêt de toutes les écuries, entend ne plus tolérer longtemps. Dans un premier temps, seule Ferrari est capable de répliquer, avant d'être rejointe, à Montréal, par BMW. À Munich, l'humeur est à l'optimisme, d'autant plus que BMW vient de signer un doublé lors de la plus éprouvante course de 24 heures, sur le circuit du Nürburgring. Ralf Schumacher est en pole position au Grand Prix du Canada et arrive deuxième derrière son frère Michael et néanmoins rival ; Juan Pablo Montoya aussi engrange des points. Mais c'est alors que la décision – justifiée, il est vrai – des commissaires de la FIA sous la direction de l'Allemand Jo Bauer éclate comme un coup de tonnerre. Les écopes de freins ne sont pas conformes, Williams et Toyota (même faute, même punition) se voient retirer tous les points obtenus lors de ce Grand Prix. Sam Michael, bourrelé de remords, assume, mais il a le plus grand mal à accepter son destin : « Il a fallu que ce soit à moi que cela arrive ! » Un malheur n'arrive jamais seul : à Indianapolis, Ralf Schumacher est victime d'un accident et Montoya est disqualifié – beaucoup trop tard – pour changement de monture sur la grille de départ en dehors du temps, dans le saint des saints de la compétition automobile américaine. Le verdict est amer : BMW boit le calice jusqu'à la lie, mais ne s'avoue jamais vaincue !

Five generations of Williams-BMW: from the FW22 of 2000 to the FW26 of the 2004 racing season. While the front spoiler is pushed further and further to the fore, the side components increasingly take on an aerodynamic function.

Fünf Generationen Williams-BMW: vom FW22 von 2000 bis zum FW26 der Rennsaison 2004. Während sich der Frontspoiler immer weiter vorschiebt, übernehmen die Seitenteile zunehmend eine aerodynamische Funktion.

Cinq générations de Williams-BMW : de la FW22 de l'an 2000 à la FW26 de la saison 2004. Tandis que l'aileron sous le museau migre toujours plus vers l'avant, les pontons latéraux assument de plus en plus une fonction aérodynamique.

With its four victories in 2001 and already third in the Formula 1 team evaluation, the BMW-Williams combination took a place of honor behind Ferrari in 2002, and only just missed winning the title in 2003. The double keel of the 2004 FW26 is obviously the subject of a run of bad luck.

Mit vier Siegen 2001 bereits Dritter der Konstrukteurswertung der Formel 1, belegte die Kombination BMW-Williams 2002 den Ehrenplatz hinter Ferrari und verfehlte 2003 nur knapp den Titel. Am Doppelkiel-FW26 von 2004 haftete offenbar eine Pechsträhne.

Avec quatre victoires en 2001, déjà troisième au classement Constructeurs de la Formule 1, la combinaison BMW-Williams a occupé en 2002 la place d'honneur derrière Ferrari et n'a raté que d'un rien le titre en 2003. La FW26 à double quille de 2004 n'a, apparemment, pas la baraka.

BMW 745i

Although the form language of BMW designer Christopher Bangle takes some getting used to, and especially the rear of the BMW 7 of 2001 has heartily rubbed conservative aesthetes up the wrong way, the top class limousine convinces skeptics by its exceedingly good engine technology, dynamism, and many driving comforts. The extent of BMW's involvement in this luxury segment of the market is demonstrated by the 5½-inch (14-centimeter) longer Li version with its feudal rear seating area presented at the same time at the 2001 IAA, and the announcement that a 12-cylinder 760 would be on offer from 2002. In 2003, every 18th BMW bought in China was a 760 Li; possessing almost everything that is to be had, cost what it may, as a standard fitting. That the abbreviation "Li" – previously "iL" – sounds Chinese is pure coincidence.

The upper crust 7 from BMW has a choice of six engines. The unusual running characteristics of the great V8 engine (333 bhp) has not been left to chance, as all the relevant parameters – such a engine valve timing, valve stroke, and intake pipe length – are regulated in a stepless manner. Due to the fully variable intake system, the throttle valve is no longer needed, for a longer intake enables a greater torque at lower rpm, and reciprocally, a shorter intake enables an extra burst of power at higher rpm levels. The 445-bhp V12 can make do without an intake pipe fitted as it is with valvetronic and direct gas injection.

Before the world's first standard 6-gear automatic transmission with electrical switching, in short "Drive-by-wire," can transfer power to the rear axle a somewhat tedious start procedure must be carried out. Instead of simply turning the ignition key, the remote control must first be placed in the ignition, and only then can the start button be pressed. The automatic can be activated in the usual manner ("D" for drive) by using the gear stick, or, alternatively, the steptronic

switches on the upper section of the steering wheel can be used. Manual switching is rewarded with better acceleration: from 0 to 62 mph (100 kph) in only 6.3 instead of 7.5 seconds.

That one simply glides along in the 7 is certainly only secondarily due to the lavishly upholstered seating. The extravagant aluminum chassis with a bi-articulated telescopic-legged front axle and an integrated rear axle ensure comfort per se. Help is given by the level adjustment – ensuring a constant distance to the road surface irrespective of load – and, available as an extra on payment of a surcharge, the electronic shock absorber control. Thanks to "Dynamic Drive" – only available as a standard in the 760, as is the case with the pneumatic suspension – wobble during cornering can be reduced to a minimum. Despite the long version of the 7's massive appearance its road handling is exemplary, a plus point for the whole range.

Also intended as a plus point but unfortunately not well accepted, is the "Benchmark" (BMW's favorite word) in driver orientation and comfort, the "i-Drive" concept. To bring together in a round switch eight main computer menus, arranged compass-like, with over 700 subsidiary functions, is definitely a masterly performance, but one that also completely overstretches the driver when driving. Luckily the really important elements needed for driving, such as blinkers, headlights, and windshield wipers can be operated by the usual switches on the steering wheel. Simple functionality can also be a "Benchmark"!

Wenn auch die progressive Formensprache von BMW-Designer Christopher Bangle gewöhnungsbedürftig ist und besonders das Heck des 7er-BMW, Jahrgang 2001, bei konservativen Automobil-Ästheten kräftig aneckt, überzeugt die Oberklassen-Limousine durch souveräne Motorentechnik, Dynamik und sehr viel Fahrkomfort. Wie weit dieses Luxus-Segment bei BMW reicht, demonstriert auf der IAA 2001 auch die gleichzeitig vorgestellte, 14 Zentimeter längere Li-Version mit einem feudalen Fondbereich und die Ankündigung, ab 2002 einen 760 mit 12-Zylinder-Motor anzubieten. 2003 ist jeder 18. in China verkaufte BMW ein 760 Li, bei dem so ziemlich alles, was gut und teuer ist, zur Serienausstattung gehört. Dass das Kürzel „Li" – früher „iL" – chinesisch klingt, ist reiner Zufall.

Insgesamt stehen der 7er-Hautevolee von BMW sechs Motoren zur Auswahl. Nicht von ungefähr kommt die außergewöhnliche Laufkultur dieses Triebwerkes (333 PS), da alle relevanten Parameter – wie Ventil-Steuerzeiten, Ventilhub und Saugrohrlängen – stufenlos reguliert werden. Durch die vollvariable Sauganlage entfällt die Drosselklappe, denn ein langer Ansaugweg ermöglicht ein hohes Drehmoment bei niedrigen Drehzahlen, und reziprok sorgt ein kürzerer Ansaugweg für einen Leistungsschub auch im oberen Drehzahlbereich. Positiver Nebeneffekt: geringerer Treibstoff-Verbrauch und weniger Emissionen. Ohne Saugrohre kommt der 445-PS-V12 aus, da er mit einer Valvetronic und einer Benzin-Direkteinspritzung versehen ist

Ehe das erste serienmäßige 6-Gang-Automatik-Getriebe der Welt mit elektrischer Schaltung, kurz und präzise (Drive-by-wire) den Krafttransfer zur Hinterachse übernehmen kann, muss die etwas umständliche Startprozedur eingeleitet werden. Statt einer simplen Zündschlüssel-Drehung steckt man zunächst die Funkfernbedienung in die Zündanlass-Buchse, und dann erst darf der Start-Knopf gedrückt werden. Über einen Lenkstock-Schalter kann die Automatik im herkömmlichen Verfahren („D" wie Drive) aktiviert werden, oder man schaltet über die Steptronic-Tasten am oberen Lederlenkradkranz. Das manuelle Schaltvergnügen wird mit besserer Beschleunigung belohnt: Von 0 auf 100 Stundenkilometer sind es 6,3 statt 7,5 Sekunden.

Dass man im 7er wie in einer Sänfte dahingleitet, liegt sicherlich nur sekundär an den üppig gepolsterten Sitzmöbeln. Das aufwändige Aluminium-Fahrwerk mit einer Doppelgelenk-Federbein-Vorderachse und einer Integral-Hinterachse bietet Fahrkomfort per se. Hilfestellung leisten die Niveauregulierung – gleich gleibender Bodenabstand unabhängig von der Beladung – und, gegen Aufpreis, die elektronische Dämpfer-Kontrolle. Dank „Dynamic Drive" – wie die Luftfederung nur im 760 serienmäßig – können Wankbewegungen bei Kurvenfahrten auf ein Minimum reduziert werden. So wuchtig gerade die Lang-Version des 7er wirken mag, ihr Fahrverhalten ist vorbildlich, ein Pluspunkt der gesamten Reihe.

Als Pluspunkt gescheitert ist die „Benchmark" (was bei BMW so viel wie Messlatte heißt) in Fahrerorientierung und Komfort, das „i-Drive"-Konzept. Acht Hauptmenüs eines Computers mit über 700 Nebenfunktionen in einem runden Schaltknopf zu vereinen, ist technisch gewiss eine Meisterleistung, überfordert aber den Autofahrer völlig. Zum Glück sind wirklich wichtige Elemente wie Blinker, Licht und Scheibenwischer noch über herkömmliche Schalter am Lenkrad zu bedienen. Einfache Funktionalität kann auch eine „Benchmark" sein!

Même s'il faut être habitué au langage formel très autoritaire de Christopher Bangle, le styliste en chef de BMW, même si la poupe de la BMW Série 7 millésime 2001 a choqué certains esthètes de l'automobile à l'esprit conservateur, la limousine de luxe du constructeur bavarois séduit par sa motorisation souveraine, son dynamisme et son remarquable confort de conduite. Ce segment du luxe est très large chez BMW. Preuve en est lorsque le constructeur présente aussi, à l'IAA 2001, la version Li, dévoilée simultanément, avec un empattement allongé de 14 centimètres et des fauteuils arrière au confort somptueux. Mais, surtout, BMW annonce la commercialisation, en 2002, d'une 760 à moteur V12.

Au total, la luxueuse Série 7 de BMW est proposée avec un choix de six moteurs. Mais l'exceptionnelle souplesse de fonctionnement de ce moteur (V8, 333 ch) n'a, elle, rien à voir avec le hasard. En effet, tous ses paramètres importants – par exemple la distribution et la course des soupapes ou la longueur des tubulures d'aspiration – sont régulés en continu. Le collecteur d'aspiration à longueur variable dans son intégralité rend superflues les vis papillons : une longue tubulure d'aspiration engendre, en effet, un couple élevé à bas régime et, inversement, une courte tubulure d'aspiration, un pic de puissance à haut régime.

Avant que la première – courte et précise (Drive-by-wire) – boîte automatique à six rapports avec commande électrique commercialisée dans le monde puisse assurer le transfert du couple au train arrière, il faut bien s'imprégner de la procédure de démarrage, il est vrai un peu complexe. Au lieu de se contenter de tourner la clé de contact, il faut tout d'abord insérer la télécommande-radio dans la prise de l'allumage et, ensuite seulement, on peut appuyer sur le starter. Le levier sur la colonne de direction permet d'actionner la transmission automatique selon la procédure usuelle (« D » pour Drive), à

moins que l'on ne veuille changer soi-même de vitesse avec les touches Steptronic sur le haut du volant gainé de cuir. La procédure de changement de vitesse à la main est récompensée par de meilleures accélérations : 6,3 secondes au lieu de 7,5 secondes pour le 0 à 100 km/h.

Si, dans la Série 7, on a l'impression de planer sur un nuage, ceci n'est assurément pas dû au seul capitonnage très généreux des fauteuils. Très sophistiquées, les liaisons au sol en aluminium avec un train avant à jambes élastiques à double articulation et un essieu arrière intégral offrent un confort de conduite difficile à égaler. Grâce au « Dynamic Drive » – comme la suspension pneumatique, offerte en série uniquement sur la 760 –, la prise de roulis est réduite au strict minimum.

Ce qui était considéré comme l'un de ses grands avantages et n'a, pourtant, malheureusement pas reçu l'accueil escompté, c'est le « benchmark » (terme de prédilection de BMW qui signifie aune) pour l'information du conducteur et le confort avec le concept « i-Drive ». Combiner huit menus principaux d'ordinateur, à plus de 700 fonctions secondaires dans un bouton de commande circulaire est assurément une prouesse technique. Mais l'utiliser en conduisant excède la capacité de concentration de tout automobiliste.

Par bonheur, on continue de manier les éléments réellement importants pour la conduite, par exemple les clignotants, les phares et les essuie-glaces, à l'aide de commandes conventionnelles. Une fonctionnalité toute simple peut aussi être un « benchmark » !

BMW 745i

BMW turns to a new direction in automobile architecture with the design of the 7 range: unusual and innovative, but the rear section takes some getting used to.

Eine neue Auto-Architekturrichtung schlägt BMW mit dem Design des 7er ein: außergewöhnlich und innovativ, aber auch gewöhnungsbedürftig, was die hintere Region angeht.

Avec le design de la Série 7, BMW s'est engagée dans une nouvelle direction de l'architecture automobile : sortant de l'ordinateur et novatrice, elle demande aussi une certaine accoutumance, notamment en ce qui concerne la poupe.

A challenge: the rear of the 7 range and central control of the i-Drive, a dial and button combination between the comfortable seating. The source of power: a refined V8 with 333 bhp.

Herausforderungen: das 7er-Heck und das zentrale i-Drive-Eingabe-Element, ein Dreh- und Druckknopf zwischen den komfortablen Sitzen. Kraftquelle: kultivierter V8 mit 333 PS.

Défis : la poupe de la Série 7 et le *joystick* de commande centrale du i-Drive, un bouton que l'on fait tourner et sur lequel on appuie entre les confortables sièges. Propulsion : un V8 très raffiné de 333 ch.

BMW 745i

The spiritual father of the Mini, Sir Alexander Arnold Constantino Issigonis, the son of a Greek father and Bavarian mother, would definitely have been greatly pleased by the rebirth of already legendary cult vehicle. The BMW Group has produced the successor to the original Mini in Oxford since 2001 – as an autonomous and unmistakable mark. As was the case with its predecessor, the Mini is characterized by its long wheelbase with extremely short wheel overhangs, while the wheels together with their typical small wing extensions form the corner stone, as it were. The roof contour and the wide stocky rear, under which the trunk nestles, are also reminiscent of the Mini of 1959. A modern stylistic contrast: with all struts and beams concealed behind glass, the green toned window surface of this two-door vehicle gives the impression of a continuous glass band around the automobile.

The Cooper and its powerful S-version's option for roof and exterior mirrors to be in black or white irrespective of the body color distinguish it optically from the normal Mini. Alloy wheels, front spoiler lip, roof spoiler, and the air inlet on the hood, all belong to the deportment of a vehicle whose predecessors have won no less than 19 major international rally events between 1962 and 1967– including three times the "Monte".

The basis of the modern Mini's motorization is provided by the jointly designed by BMW and Chrysler "Pentagon" standard engine with its 1.6-liter capacity, an engine that needing neither secondary air injection nor exhaust gas recirculation. Correspondingly modest is the starting potential of the Mini One with 90 bhp and of the Mini Cooper with 115 bhp. A supercharger was needed. As the Mini Cooper S

it brings 163 bhp to the front wheels, and since 2004 it even achieves 170 bhp. One is served well by the sprint time of 0 to 62 mph (100 kph) in 7.2 rather than in 7.4 seconds and a top speed in the meantime of 141 mph (227 kph), even though the engine is somehow lacking the right bite. This is present in the "Works" edition with modified supercharger that brings the power of 200 horses into play.

Unusual for its class are the technically advanced common denominators of all Mini models: 6-gear transmission, McPherson struts, drive shafts of equal length that ensure a symmetrical feedback effect of the driven front wheels to the steering on cornering, acceleration, and braking, and a multi-link rear suspension with an additional stabilizer. The standard fittings of the Mini Cooper S, already lowered at the factory, also include the "Automatic Stability Control + Traction" (ASC+T) system, a central double piped exhaust system, and alloy wheels fitted with the 195 "Run-flat"-tires.

The large round display over the center console, flanked by two amply dimensioned ventilation vents, dominate the cockpit of the Cooper S. The rev counter and speedometer stare out of the dashboard, well in view of the driver, but with a somewhat forlorn appearance. The adjustable height and good grip of the steering wheel, foot pedals and rests in stainless steel, in addition to the various interior elements with aluminum patina, impart a hint of a sporting atmosphere. However, the interior is not without a certain pep, corresponding to the general impression of the Mini. This has already been enriched by the Mini-Design-Studio, Munich, with a racy cabriolet, further evolution, also in detail, is being prepared.

Der geistige Vater des Mini, Sir Alexander Arnold Constantino Issigonis, Spross eines griechischen Vaters und einer bayerischen Mutter, hätte an der Wiedergeburt seines mittlerweile schon legendären Kult-Autos gewiss seine Freude gehabt. Seit 2001 lässt die BMW Group den Nachfolger des Ur-Mini in Oxford produzieren – als eigenständige, da unverwechselbare Marke. Wie sein Vorgänger wird der Mini von einem langen Radstand mit extrem kurzen Überhängen geprägt, und die Räder samt ihren typischen kleinen Kotflügel-Verbreiterungen bilden sozusagen die Eckpfeiler. Auch die Dachkontur und das breite, gedrungene Heck, unter dem sich das Kofferräumchen einigelt, erinnern an den Mini von 1959. Neuzeitlicher stilistischer Kontrast: Die grün getönten Fensterflächen des Zweitürers vermitteln den Eindruck eines durchgehenden Glasbandes rund ums Auto, denn alle Säulen sind hinter Glas verborgen.

Optisch unverwechselbar mit dem Normal-Mini macht den Cooper und seine kraftvolle S-Version die Option, Dach und Außenspiegel unabhängig von der Wagenfarbe in Schwarz oder Weiß erhalten zu können. Leichtmetallräder, Frontspoiler-Lippe, Dachspoiler und der Luftschacht auf der Motorhaube gehören zum sportlichen Gehabe eines Fahrzeugs, dessen Vorfahren zwischen 1962 und 1967 nicht weniger als 19 große internationale Rallye-Veranstaltungen – darunter dreimal die „Monte" – gewonnen haben.

Basis der neuzeitlichen Mini-Motorisierung ist der von BMW und Chrysler gemeinsam entwickelte „Pentagon"-Grundmotor mit 1,6 Litern Hubraum, ein Triebwerk, das weder Sekundärluft-Zufuhr noch eine Abgas-Rückführung nötig hat. Entsprechend bescheiden ist das Anfangspotential mit 90 PS für den Mini One und 115 PS für den Mini Cooper,

Mini Cooper S

und deshalb musste ein Kompressor her. Als Mini Cooper S bringt er 163 PS und seit 2004 sogar 170 PS auf die Vorderräder. Mit 7,2 statt 7,4 Sekunden von 0 auf 100 und einer Spitzengeschwindigkeit von inzwischen 227 km/h ist man gut bedient, wenngleich dem Triebwerk irgendwie der richtige Biss fehlt. Diesen hat die „Works"-Ausgabe mit modifiziertem Kompressor, der 200 Pferdestärken aktiviert. Klassen-unüblich ist der technisch hochangesiedelte gemeinsame Nenner aller Mini-Modelle: 6-Gang-Getriebe, McPherson-Federbeine und gleich lange Achswellen, die für einen symmetrischen Rückkopplungseffekt der angetriebenen Vorderräder auf die Lenkung beim Kurvenfahren, Beschleunigen oder Bremsen sorgen, und eine Multilenker-Hinterachse mit zusätzlichem Stabilisator. Beim Mini Cooper S, von Haus aus tiefer gelegt, umfasst die Serienausstattung auch die „Automatische Stabilitäts-Control + Traktion" (ASC+T), eine zentrale Doppelrohr-Auspuffanlage und Leichtmetallräder mit 195er „Run-flat"-Reifen.

Im Cockpit des Cooper S dominiert das große Runddisplay über der Mittelkonsole, flankiert von zwei wohldimensionierten Belüftungs-Düsen. Gut im Blickfeld des Fahrers, aber etwas verloren wirkend, äugen Drehzahlmesser und Tacho aus dem Armaturenbrett. Griffiges, höhenverstellbares Leder-Volant, Pedalerie und Fußstütze in Edelstahl sowie Interieur-Elemente mit Alu-Patina vermitteln auch im Innenraum einen Hauch von Sportlichkeit, was man von den in der Seitenführung laschen Sitzen nicht behaupten kann. Dennoch mangelt es dem Interieur nicht an einem gewissen Pep, passend zum gesamten Erscheinungsbild des Mini. Dieses hat das Mini-Design-Studio, München, bereits um ein flottes Cabrio bereichert und bereitet weitere Evolutionen – auch im Detail – vor.

Le père spirituel de la Mini, Sir Alexander Arnold Constantino Issigonis, fils d'un père grec et d'une mère bavaroise, aurait sans aucun doute été ravi de voir la voiture de légende qu'il a créée renaître avec le statut de voiture culte. Depuis 2001, le BMW Group assemble, à Oxford, l'héritière de la mythique Mini – qui est maintenant une marque indépendante et, donc, plus unique que jamais. Comme son ancêtre, la Mini se distingue par un empattement long avec des porte-à-faux extrêmement courts et des roues repoussées, avec leurs typiques petits élargisseurs d'aile, aux quatre coins de la voiture. De même, les contours du toit et la poupe large et râblée sous laquelle se dissimule un petit coffre modulable rappellent, eux aussi, la Mini de 1959. Les jantes en alliage léger, la lèvre d'aileron avant, le becquet de toit et la prise d'air sur le capot moteur sont les attributs sportifs justifiés d'un modèle dont les ancêtres ont remporté pas moins de dix-neuf grands rallyes internationaux – dont le « Monte » à trois reprises – entre 1962 et 1967.

La motorisation de base de la Mini des temps modernes est le moteur « Pentagon » de 1,6 litre de cylindrée mis au point conjointement par BMW et Chrysler, qui respecte d'emblée la norme de dépollution UE4 et n'a besoin ni d'une alimentation en air secondaire ni d'un recyclage des gaz d'échappement. Il ne faut donc pas s'attendre à une puissance exubérante avec 90 ch pour la Mini One et 115 ch pour la Mini Cooper. Un peu plus de cavalerie s'imposait donc, raison pour laquelle BMW a décidé de lui greffer un compresseur. En version Mini Cooper S, elle développe 163 ch et, depuis 2004, même 170 ch, qui entraînent les roues avant. Avec 7,2 secondes au lieu de 7,4 secondes pour le 0 à 100 km/h et une vitesse de pointe d'entre-temps de

227 km/h, on n'a plus aucune raison de se plaindre, même si le moteur donne bizarrement l'impression de manquer de punch. La version « Works », avec un compresseur modifié qui libère 200 chevaux, pallie ce défaut.

La dotation technique de toutes les versions de la Mini, déjà très relevée, est inhabituelle dans cette catégorie : boîte manuelle à six vitesses, jambes élastiques McPherson et demi-arbres de longueur identique garantissant une remontée de couple symétrique des roues avant motrices à la direction dans les courbes ainsi qu'à l'accélération et au freinage, sans oublier un essieu arrière multibras avec barre anti-roulis supplémentaire. Dans le cas de la Mini Cooper S, à l'assiette abaissée départ usine, la dotation de série s'enrichit du dispositif de « Traction + Contrôle de Stabilité Automatique » (ASC+T), d'une sortie d'échappement centrale à double pot et de jantes en alliage léger chaussées de pneus « run-flat » de 195.

Dans le cockpit de la Cooper S, le premier rôle est joué par le grand écran circulaire au-dessus de la console médiane. Un volant cuir tombant bien en mains et réglable en hauteur, un pédalier et un repose-pied en acier inoxydable ainsi que des éléments de cockpit avec une patine aluminium diffusent, dans l'habitacle aussi, une aura de sportivité. Mais l'intérieur possède bel et bien une incontestable originalité qui s'inscrit dans le droit-fil de la généalogie de la Mini. Le studio de design de la Mini lui a déjà donné une petite sœur, un adorable cabriolet dont le succès est assuré et qui annonce d'autres évolutions – notamment sur des points de détail.

The charm and compactness of the original Mini is also expressed in the design lines of the new edition. The sporting attributes of the Mini Cooper S: air scoop, roof spoiler, light alloy wheels under the widened fenders, and double exhaust pipe.

Charme und Kompaktheit des Ur-Mini drücken sich auch in der Linienführung des neuen Mini aus. Sportliche Attribute des Mini Cooper S: Lufthutze, Dachspoiler, Leichtmetallräder unter den Kotflügelverbreiterungen und Doppelrohr-Auspuff.

Le charme et la compacité de la Mini originelle s'expriment aussi au travers des lignes de la nouvelle Mini. Ingrédients sportifs de la Mini Cooper S: prise d'air sur le capot, aileron de toit, jantes alliage sous de volumineux élargisseurs d'ailes et double sortie d'échappement.

The Mini Cooper S's supercharger engine produces 170 bhp.
Classical round instrumentation: rev counter and Tachometer.
Elliptical forms: The interior door paneling with a handle
combination in anthracite, and the rearview mirrors.
Stainless steel entree: the entry baseboard.

170 PS produziert der Kompressor-Motor des Mini Cooper S.
Klassische Rundinstrumente: Drehzahlmesser und Tacho.
Elliptische Gebilde: Die Türinnenverkleidungen mit einer
Griffkombination in Anthrazit und die Außenspiegel.
Edelstahl-Entree: die Einstiegsleiste.

170 chevaux piaffent sous le capot du moteur à compresseur
de la Mini Cooper S.
Cadrans circulaires classiques : compte-tours et tachymètre.
Coup de griffe en ellipse : contre-porte avec combinaison de
poignée anthracite et rétroviseur extérieur.
Entrée en beauté : enjoliveur de seuil de portière chromé.

Mini Cooper S

Typical of the Mini: a long wheelbase and an extremely short overhang.
Classically Mini: the chrome framed rear lights.
Modern Mini: the ribbon of glass practically running through the side and rear windows, and the exhaust covering to be found in the middle.

Typisch Mini: Langer Radstand und extrem kurze Überhänge.
Mini klassisch: Die Heckleuchten mit Chrom-Einfassung.
Mini modern: das virtuell durchgezogene Glasband von Seitenscheiben und Heckfenster und die mittige Auspuffblende.

Typiquement Mini : empattement long et porte-à-faux réduits à leur plus simple expression.
Mini classique : feux arrière cernés de chrome.
Mini moderne : bandeau vitré virtuel qui ceint la voiture et enjoliveur d'échappement au centre.

Mini Cooper S

The classical and the modern Mini combine in the front section of the Cooper S, for which an additional engine tuning is on offer ex works.

Mini-Klassik und -Moderne vereinen sich auch in der Frontpartie des Cooper S, für den auch ein zusätzliches Motor-Tuning ab Werk angeboten wird.

Mini classique et Mini moderne fusionnent aussi dans la partie avant de la Cooper S pour laquelle une préparation moteur additionnelle est proposée départ usine.

One should imagine a large "Z," swinging over the front wing of a classical sports car with a long hood, falling downward at an angle at the A pillar, and carrying the door threshold contour with it gently upward at the rear. This is how to describe the unconventional design of the Z4's flanks through to the rear wheels. On looking the front of the Z4 deep in the slit eyes of its headlights, the brave form innovation of BMW's chief designer Chris Bangle even appears beautiful. It is only at the rear that the harmony of style once again falls by the wayside. Actually, a repetition of the finely beveled swage line of the lower fender area readily presents itself for the trunk lid, instead of which one is confronted with a "duck's tail" à la Marcos for the integrated additional rear lighting. There can be no aerodynamic grounds for this stunted trailing end.

Since the 2003 IAA, a smaller and less expensive 2.2-liter engine has been added to the tried and tested 6-cylinder in-line engines with their 2.5 and 3-liter capacities. It produces 170 bhp, enough to accelerate to a speed of 62 mph (100 kph) in 7.7 seconds. The 3.0i with its 231 bhp on the other hand, thunders past this mark in only 5.9 seconds, and is only electronically tamed when it reaches its supposed top speed of 155 mph (250 kph). Irrespective of whether fitted with an automatic or the standard 6-gear switching transmission, the power of the 3.0i provides endless driving enjoyment. It is only when faced with bumps and ruts that the sporty chassis behaves like an ill-mannered clumsy oaf. As so beautifully put in the Z4 brochure: "never before has one had the impression of so experiencing the road so directly." The Z4 hardly notices a quick change of load. The wide chassis (front track width 4 ft 10 in [1473 mm], rear 5 ft

[1523 mm]), the low center of gravity, and the almost optimal weight distribution between front and rear axles of 50.6 and 49.4 percent, turn the vehicle into easily controlled instrument of joy, helped by many various driving aids.

Maximal safety in case of overturning is ensured by the two steel roll bars behind the headrests – connected to an extremely stabile frame crossbeam – and a bar running through the A pillar and windshield frame. The airbags react independently according to direction of impact and passenger seat occupancy. The powerful ventilated disk brakes, supported by a very sensitive Anti-locking Brake System, deserve special praise. As with the Z8, emergency running tires make the carrying of a spare tire in the luggage compartment superfluous, allowing 8.5 cubic feet (240 liters) of luggage space with folded top, or 9.2 cubic feet (260 liters) without.

The dashboard and instrument panels of the Z4's interior appear almost modest – in view of the large aluminum trim – and yet are both orderly and functionally laid out. The sports' steering wheel equipped with multifunctional or with switches for the sequential manual transmission (SMG) – for an additional 1250 Euro – lies comfortably in the hand. The seating is also above all criticism, leather upholstery being the standard for the 3.0i. Optional extras such as heated seats, or the luxury of electrical seat adjustment with memory function for the passenger seat, let the BMW cash registers ring. If a professional navigation system, whose display folds up from the dashboard at the press of a button, is also desired, then the Z4's price reaches the 50,000 Euro mark.

Man stelle sich ein großes „Z" vor, schwinge es über den vorderen Kotflügel eines klassischen Sportwagens mit langer Motorhaube, lasse es in Verlängerung der A-Säule schräg nach unten fallen und ziehe es mitsamt Türschwellen-Kontur sanft nach hinten hoch. So lässt sich das eigenwillige Design des Z4-Flanken-Verlaufs bis zu den Hinterrädern beschreiben. Der Z4-Front tief in die Schlitzaugen der Scheinwerfer geschaut, wirkt das mutige Linienspiel von BMW-Chefdesigner Chris Bangle sogar schön. Nur beim Heck bleibt die Harmonie des Stylings einmal mehr auf der Strecke. Eigentlich bietet sich eine Wiederholung der fein gewölbten Sicke im unteren Stoßfänger-Bereich auf dem Kofferraumdeckel an, doch stattdessen sieht man sich mit einem „Entenbürzel" à la Marcos für die integrierte Heck-Zusatzleuchte konfrontiert. Aerodynamische Zwänge für diese verkümmerte Abrisskante gibt es wohl kaum.

Neben den bewährten 6-Zylinder-Reihen-Motoren mit 2,5 und knapp drei Litern ist seit der IAA 2003 eine kleinere, preiswertere Motorisierungsstufe mit 2,2 Litern dazugekommen. Sie bringt es auf 170 PS, genug für eine Beschleunigung auf Tempo 100 in 7,7 Sekunden. Der 3.0i hingegen donnert mit seinen 231 PS in 5,9 Sekunden bis zu dieser Marke und wird erst bei seiner Soll-Spitzengeschwindigkeit von 250 km/h elektronisch gebändigt. Ganz gleich, ob mit einer Automatik oder dem serienmäßigen 6-Gang-Schaltgetriebe ausgerüstet, bereitet die Kraft des 3.0i unendliches Fahrvergnügen. Nur bei unangenehmen Bodenwellen oder Spurrillen gebärdet sich das sportliche Fahrwerk wie ein ungezogenes Trampeltier. Wie heißt es doch so schön im Z4-Prospekt: „Noch nie hatte man den Eindruck, eine Straße

BMW Z4 3.0i

so unmittelbar zu erfahren." Schnelle Lastwechsel nimmt der Z4 kaum zur Kenntnis. Das breite Fahrwerk (Spur vorn 1473 mm, hinten 1523 mm), der niedrige Schwerpunkt und die fast optimale Gewichtsbalance von 50,6 und 49,4 Prozent, verteilt auf Vorder- und Hinterräder, machen ihn zu einem leicht beherrschbaren Instrument der Freude.

Im Falle aller Fälle gewährten die zwei Stahl-Überrollbügel hinter den Nackenstützen – verbunden mit einem äußerst stabilen Karosserie-Querträger – sowie ein Bügel, der sich durch A-Säulen und Windschutzscheiben-Rahmen zieht, maximale Sicherheit bei einem Überschlag. Die Airbags reagieren einzeln, je nach Aufprallrichtung und Belegung des Beifahrersitzes. Besonderes Lob verdienen die innenbelüfteten Scheibenbremsen, die kräftig zupacken können und von einem sehr sensiblen Antiblockier-System unterstützt werden. Wie schon beim Z8 erübrigen Reifen mit Notlaufeigenschaften das Mitführen eines Reserverades im Gepäckraum, der mit versenktem Verdeck 240, ansonsten 260 Liter fasst.

Fast bescheiden – angesichts einer großen Aluminium-Blende –, doch aufgeräumt und funktionell gut gegliedert geben sich Armaturenbrett und Bedienelemente im Innenraum des Z4. Das Sportlenkrad, ob nun multifunktional oder mit Wippen für das sequenzielle manuelle Getriebe (SMG) – für zusätzlich 1250 Euro – bestückt, liegt gut in der Hand. Auch die Sitze, beim 3.0i serienmäßig mit Leder überzogen, sind über jede Kritik erhaben. Sitzheizung oder elektrische Sitzverstellung mit Memory-Funktion für den Beifahrersitz lassen die BMW-Kasse zusätzlich klingeln. Will man dann vielleicht sogar ein professionelles Navigationssystem, dessen Monitor auf Knopfdruck aus der Armaturentafel klappt, ist der Z4 3.0i in einer Preisregion von 50 000 Euro angelangt.

Imaginez-vous un immense « Z ». Gravez-le sur les ailes avant d'une voiture de sport classique avec un long capot moteur. Modelez, avec ce « Z », les flancs de la voiture en lui donnant une légère ascendance vers l'arrière. Ainsi peut-on décrire le design, très original, des flancs de la Z4 jusqu'aux roues arrière. Si l'on regarde l'avant de la Z4 aux yeux bridés, on en vient même à concéder une certaine beauté au jeu courageux des lignes auquel se prête Chris Bangle, le chef designer de BMW. Il n'y a que pour l'arrière que, une fois de plus, l'harmonie du style n'échappe pas à toute critique. Alors que l'on s'attendait, en effet, à une poursuite du coup de crayon au galbe élégant dans l'entourage du pare-chocs, on découvre au contraire un arrière tronqué à la Marcos avec un troisième feu de frein intégré au becquet. Pourtant, aucune contrainte aérodynamique ne semble justifier une poupe aussi torturée.

Outre les six-cylindres en ligne éprouvés de 2,5 et 3 litres de cylindrée, BMW propose, depuis l'IAA 2003, une motorisation plus modeste et moins coûteuse de 2,2 litres. Elle développe 170 ch, suffisamment pour couvrir le 0 à 100 km/h en 7,7 secondes. Avec ses 231 ch, la 3.0i accomplit, en revanche, cette discipline en 5,9 secondes et ne voit son élan jugulé électroniquement qu'à une vitesse de pointe de 250 km/h. Que l'on ait opté pour la transmission automatique ou la boîte manuelle à six vitesses de série, la montée en puissance de la 3.0i procure un agrément de conduite infini. Il n'y a que sur mauvaise route ou en présence d'ornières que le châssis sportif se comporte comme un mauvais garçon. Les transferts de charge rapides laissent la Z4 de marbre. Les larges liaisons au sol (voies de 1473 mm à l'avant et de 1523 mm à l'arrière), le centre de gravité très bas et la répartition

presque optimale du poids de respectivement 50,6 % et de 49,4 % pour les trains avant et arrière font d'elle un instrument de plaisir qu'il est toujours facile de maîtriser.

En cas de tonneau, les deux arceaux de sécurité en acier derrière les appuie-tête – qui sont reliés à une poutre transversale extrêmement solide – ainsi que les renforts de la baie de pare-brise offrent une sécurité maximum. Les airbags réagissent individuellement en fonction du sens de la collision et de l'occupation du siège passager. Les freins à disque ventilés méritent des éloges : ils attaquent avec beaucoup de mordant et ils sont soutenus par un système d'antiblocage très sensible. À l'instar de la Z8, des pneus anti-crevaison rendent superflue toute roue de secours dans le coffre, qui, lorsque la capote est repliée, offre une capacité de 240 litres contre 260 litres capote fermée.

Le tableau de bord et les manettes de commande dans le cockpit de la Z4 frisent la sobriété – malgré un vaste panneau en aluminium – mais ils sont bien agencés et d'une grande fonctionnalité. Le volant sport, qu'il soit multifonctionnel ou comporte les palettes de la boîte de vitesses manuelle séquentielle (SMG) – pour un supplément de 1250 euros – tombe bien en mains. Les sièges aussi, gainés de cuir en série dans le cas de la 3.0i, sont au-dessus des critiques. Le chauffage des sièges ou le luxe d'un réglage des sièges avec fonction « Memory » pour le passager font tomber quelques billets supplémentaires dans l'escarcelle de BMW. Si on le souhaite même, on peut se procurer un système de navigation professionnel, dont l'écran sort du tableau de bord en appuyant sur un bouton : la Z4 3.0i flirte alors avec les 50 000 euros.

BMW Z4

The Rear of the Z4 with its brake light hump has more of a baroque appearance in contrast to the harmonious line forms of the front. The material roof is manually stowed away into the variable roof compartment in 22 seconds, electrically – standard with the 3.0i – it disappears in only 10 seconds.

Im Gegensatz zum harmonischen Linienspiel der Z4-Front wirkt das Heck mit dem Bremslicht-Buckel eher barock. Manuell betätigt, ist das Stoffverdeck in 22 Sekunden im variablen Verdeckkasten zwischen Sitzen und Kofferraum verstaut, elektrisch – beim 3.0i serienmäßig – verschwindet es in nur 10 Sekunden.

Contrairement au jeu harmonieux des lignes de la proue de la Z4, la poupe paraît plutôt baroque avec son ébauche de becquet intégrant le troisième feu de frein. La capote en tissu à commande manuelle disparaît en 22 secondes dans le compartiment variable entre les sièges et le coffre ; avec la commande électrique – de série sur la 3.0i – elle se replie comme par magie en 10 secondes seulement.

The cockpit of the roadster concentrates on the essential.
The BMW emblem is the focal point of the curvaceous "Z"
contour. Well braced: the tidy engine compartment of the
6-cylinder in-line engine.

Auf das Wesentliche beschränkt sich das Cockpit dieses
Roadsters. Das BMW-Emblem ist der zentrale Punkt der
geschwungenen „Z"-Kontur. Gut verstrebt: der aufgeräumte
Motorraum des 6-Zylinder-Reihenmotors.

Le cockpit de ce roadster se limite à l'essentiel. L'emblème
BMW est le point central de la griffe en Z. Bien renforcé :
le compartiment moteur du six-cylindres en ligne.

BMW Z4

BMW 530d

The new BMW 5 range of 2003 was due, for its four predecessor generations (E12, E28, E34 and E39) had needed an average production time of seven and a half years, which in itself speaks for their qualities. "As the representative of the dynamic business class," as BMW describes the visual offspring of the 7 series in its business report, the new 5 has five 6-cylinder engines at its disposal, with performance ranging from 170 bhp (520i) to 231 bhp (530i), and even to the 333 bhp of the 545i's V8 engine. The 530d, with its 218 bhp at 4000 rpm, is a common-rail aggregate with a sense of rhythm, for diesel fuel is injected in to the six cylinders under a pressure of 1600 bar up to four times per firing stroke. Quietness of running and only a very subtle diesel smell at low revolution, really recommend the 530d as a business vehicle in which long distances can be covered comfortably, quickly, and economically. Nimbly it accelerates from 0 to 62 mph (100 kph) in 7.1 seconds, reaches a top speed of 151 mph (243 kph), and is suitable for more lengthy non-stop tours due to its 30 mpg (7.8 liter) consumption and 18.5 gallon (70 liter) tank volume.

This success has only been made possible by subjecting the empty weight to a fundamental diet. The new 5 range lies with 3680 lbs (1670 kilograms) under the level of its predecessors and competitors. That is why the entire front end including side panels and hood are of aluminum, and also the double-cardan universal joint telescopic front axle and the integrated rear axle are produced from the non rusting light metal. The balance of material used, aluminum and high-strength steel, leads to a corresponding 50:50 axle load distribution, which makes itself noticeable in the vehicle's excellent handling.

To improve cornering even more, BMW offers for a 1200 Euro surcharge active steering, for which a planetary transmission with electric motor is crucial. This connects the bipartite steering column, and is electronically controlled. The lower the speed the more direct and lighter the steering reaction. The steering angle is reduced at increased speed, with the effect that the steering required also increases and the steering becomes less direct, reacting in a good-natured manner. When used hand in hand with the equally active "Dynamic Drive" chassis system it transforms the man or woman behind the 5 range's steering wheel into an "easy-going-manager".

The new, compact, and well-graded 6-gear transmission – available as an automatic with steptronic for an additional 2000 Euros – has proven itself to be dynamic, while the individual gears can be engaged butter smoothly without any sticking whatsoever. The interior is fitted out conveniently and comfortably. There is a lot on offer for the basic price of 42,600 Euros, including automatic air conditioning, onboard music, computer, electric window lifts, multifunction steering wheel, and electrically adjustable seating.

Never tiring of packing ever more technology into the vehicles of the blue and white brand, even a head-up display similar to that of a modern fighter jet is offered for the 5 range. Important information or navigational directions are projected onto the windshield. A sensor matches the brightness to the surrounding environment.

As of 2005, a "business airplane on wheels" is at the disposal of managers in a hurry: the M5 with 507 bhp.

Er war fällig, der neue 5er-BMW im Jahre 2003, denn seine vier Vorgänger-Generationen (E12, E28, E34 und E39) hatten es auf eine durchschnittliche Produktionszeit von siebeneinhalb Jahren gebracht, was durchaus für ihre Qualitäten spricht. „Als Repräsentant der dynamischen Business-Klasse", wie BMW den optischen Ableger des 7ers im Geschäftsbericht bezeichnet, verfügt der neue 5er über fünf 6-Zylinder-Motoren von 170 PS (520i) bis 231 PS (530i) sowie das 333 PS starke V8-Triebwerk im 545i. Mit 218 PS bei 4000/min ist der 530d ein Common-Rail-Aggregat mit viel Taktgefühl, denn bis zu viermal pro Arbeitstakt wird mit einem Druck von 1600 bar Diesel-Kraftstoff in die sechs Zylinder eingespritzt. Laufruhe und nur ganz dezente Dieselgeräusche in unteren Drehzahlen empfehlen den 530d wirklich als ein Business-Fahrzeug, in dem auch größere Distanzen bequem, schnell und sparsam überbrückt werden können. Hurtig beschleunigt er von 0 bis 100 Stundenkilometer in 7,1 Sekunden, erreicht eine Spitzengeschwindigkeit von 243 km/h und ist mit einem durchschnittlichen Verbrauch von 7,8 Litern – bei 70 Litern Tankinhalt – für längere Non-Stop-Touren geeignet.

Um derart glänzen zu können, ist das Leergewicht einer gründlichen Diät unterzogen worden. Mit 1670 Kilo liegt der neue 5er deutlich unter dem Niveau seines Vorgängers und der Konkurrenz. Deshalb besteht der gesamte Vorderbau einschließlich Seitenwänden und Motorhaube aus Aluminium, und auch Doppelgelenk-Federbein-Vorderachse und Integral-Hinterachse sind aus diesem nicht rostenden Leichtmetall gefertigt. Die Ausgewogenheit der Materialien Aluminium und hochfester Stahl führen zu einer entsprechenden Achslastverteilung von 50:50, was sich letztlich auch in einem hervorragenden Handling bemerkbar macht.

Um noch besser die „Kurve kriegen" zu können, bietet BMW für 1200 Euro Aufpreis eine Aktiv-Lenkung an, deren Dreh- und Angelpunkt ein Planetengetriebe mit Elektromotor ist. Dieses verbindet die zweigeteilte Lenksäule und wird elektronisch dirigiert. Je niedriger die Geschwindigkeit, desto direkter und leichter fällt das Lenkverhalten aus. Bei zunehmendem Tempo reduziert sich der Lenkwinkel mit dem Effekt, dass der Lenkaufwand steigt und die Lenkung indirekter und damit gutmütig reagiert. In Verbindung mit dem ebenfalls aktiven Fahrwerk-System „Dynamic Drive" wird der Mann oder die Frau am 5er-Volant zum „Easy-Going-Manager".

Das neue, kompakte und gut abgestufte 6-Gang-Getriebe – für 2000 Euro extra auch als Automatik mit Steptronic im Angebot – erweist sich als dynamisch, und die einzelnen Gänge lassen sich ohne Hakelei butterweich einlegen. Bequem und komfortabel ist der Innenraum eingerichtet. Für den Grundpreis von 42 600 Euro wird Einiges geboten. Dazu zählen Klima-Automatik, Bordmusik, Computer, elektrische Fensterheber und das Multifunktions-Lederlenkrad ebenso wie elektrisch verstellbare Sitze.

Nimmermüde, immer mehr Technologie in die Wagen der weiß-blauen Marke zu stecken, wird für den 5er sogar ein „Head-Up-Display" wie in einem modernen Kampfflugzeug angeboten. Wichtige Informationen oder Navigationshinweise werden von einem Projektor im Armaturenbrett auf die Windschutzscheibe übertragen. Ein Sensor passt die Leuchtstärke den Lichtverhältnissen des Umfeldes an.

Die „Business-Class" von BMW – besonders eiligen Manager-Typen steht ab 2005 ein „Geschäftsflugzeug auf Rädern" zur Verfügung: der M5 mit 507 PS.

Il était temps qu'elle arrive, la BMW Série 5, en 2003. En effet, les quatre générations précédentes (E12, E28, E34 et E39) pouvaient se prévaloir d'une durée de production moyenne de sept ans et demi, ce qui est une belle preuve de leurs qualités. « En tant que représentante de la classe Business dynamique », comme BMW qualifie dans son rapport d'activités la copie conforme sur le plan esthétique de la Série 7, la nouvelle Série 5 est proposée avec cinq moteurs à six-cylindres allant de 170 ch (520i) à 231 ch (530i) sans oublier le V8 de 333 ch de la 545i. Avec ses 218 ch à 4000 tr/min, la 530d possède un moteur à rampe commune qui sait respecter la cadence, car il reçoit jusqu'à quatre fois par temps de travail du gazole injecté à une pression de 1600 bars dans les six-cylindres. En effet, 7,1 secondes lui suffisent pour abattre le 0 à 100 km/h et elle atteint une vitesse de pointe. de 243 km/h, le tout pour une consommation moyenne de 7,8 litres aux 100 km/h qui lui donne une autonomie enviable grâce à son réservoir de 70 litres.

Pour pouvoir afficher de tels chiffres, le poids à vide a été soumis à une diète sévère. Avec 1670 kg, la nouvelle Série 5 est nettement plus légère que sa devancière et ses concurrentes. C'est pourquoi toute la proue, y compris les parois latérales et le capot moteur, est en aluminium, le train avant à jambes élastiques à double articulation et l'essieu arrière intégral étant fabriqués, eux aussi, dans le même métal inoxydable. L'équilibre des matériaux, aluminium et acier à grande résistance, entraîne une répartition, elle aussi, parfaitement équilibrée du poids entre les deux essieux, ce qui se traduit en dernier ressort par un comportement absolument remarquable.

Afin de faire encore meilleure figure dans les virages, BMW propose une direction active facturée 1200 euros, dont le joyau mécanique est une boîte universelle à moteur électrique. Celle-ci relie les deux éléments de la colonne de direction et est commandée électroniquement. Plus la vitesse est faible, plus la direction est directe et légère. Au fur et à mesure que le rythme augmente, l'angle de braquage se réduit. Par conséquent, l'énergie à exercer au volant augmente elle aussi et la direction devient plus indirecte et, donc, plus tolérante.

La nouvelle boîte à six vitesses, compacte et bien étagée – avec, en option, une transmission automatique avec mode Steptronic pour 2000 euros – s'avère dynamique et permet des changements de rapport à la volée et en douceur. L'habitacle est aménagé selon toutes les règles du confort. Pour un prix de base de 42 600 euros, l'acheteur en a vraiment pour son argent. Il se voit, en effet, offrir une climatisation automatique, une chaîne hi-fi, un ordinateur, des vitres électriques et le volant cuir multifonctions de même que des sièges électriques réglables.

Infatigable quand il s'agit d'offrir toujours plus de technologie dans les voitures de la marque à l'hélice blanche et bleue, BMW propose même pour la Série 5 un « head-up-display » digne d'un avion de chasse moderne. Les informations importantes ou les conseils de navigation sont transmis sur le pare-brise via un projecteur intégré au tableau de bord.

Ceux qui veulent jouer les managers pressés pourront s'offrir, à partir de 2005, un « avion à quatre roues » : la M5 de 507 ch.

The light construction body of the new 5 range appears as a scaled down edition of the 7 range, albeit less bulky. The 530d is the economist of the series, thanks to its low fuel consumption.

Äußerlich wie eine verkleinerte Ausgabe des 7er – aber weniger massig – wirkt die Leichtbau-Karosse des neuen 5er. Dank seines niedrigen Verbrauchs ist der 530d der Ökonom seiner Baureihe.

Extérieurement, on dirait une copie conforme – raccourcie, mais moins massive – de la Série 7 : la carrosserie en construction allégée de la nouvelle Série 5. Grâce à sa faible consommation, la 530d est la championne de l'économie dans sa gamme.

BMW 530d

Internally, the 530d convinces by means of its modern cockpit containing a reworked i-Drive with reduced functions, and by an extraordinary smooth running common-rail diesel engine that deploys 218 bhp.

Innerlich überzeugt der 530d durch sein modernes Cockpit mit einem überarbeitetem i-Drive, dessen Funktionen reduziert wurden, und durch einen ungemein laufruhigen Common-Rail-Dieselmotor, der 218 PS entfaltet.

Intérieurement, la 530d séduit par son cockpit moderne avec un i-Drive revu et corrigé, dont le nombre des fonctions a été revu à la baisse, et par un moteur diesel à rampe commune étonnamment soyeux qui développe 218 ch.

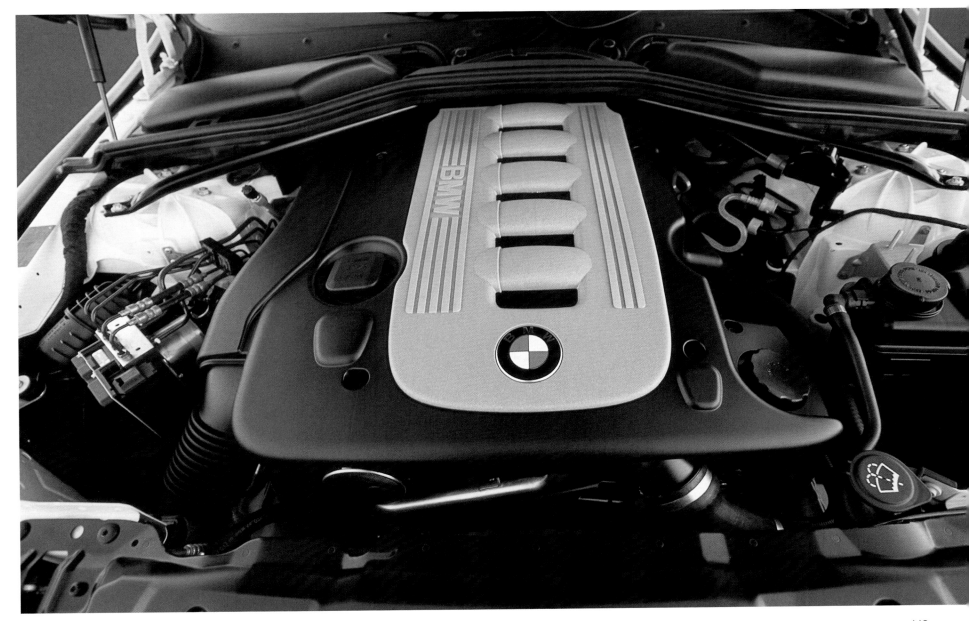

BMW 530d

The M5 is the world's first series limousine to have a 507-bhp V10 engine at its disposal, whose 8250 rpm verge on the engine speed of motor sport. New: a 7-gear SMG switching transmission with extremely short switching times as in Formula 1. A further superlative: The performance to weight ratio is about only 7.7 lbs (3.5 kilograms) per bhp.

Als erste Serien-Limousine der Welt verfügt der neue M5 über ein 507-PS-V10-Triebwerk, das mit 8250 Touren in die Drehzahlregionen von Rennmotoren vorstößt. Neu: ein 7-Gang-SMG-Schaltgetriebe mit extrem kurzen Schaltzeiten wie in der Formel 1. Und noch ein Superlativ: das Leistungsgewicht liegt bei nur 3,5 Kilo pro PS.

La nouvelle M5 est la première limousine de série au monde à être propulsée par un V10, en l'occurrence de 507 ch, qui atteint des régimes de moteur de course : la zone rouge débute à 8250 tours. Nouveauté : la boîte manuelle SMG à sept vitesses avec changements de rapports aussi rapides qu'en Formule 1. Et encore un superlatif : le rapport poids/puissance n'est que de 3,5 kg par ch.

BMW 645Ci

The Coupé 6 of the E24 range was the most successful of the many beautiful coupés that have been a tradition at BMW since October 1938. 86,216 vehicles were constructed between its presentation in Geneva in 1976 and the end of production in the spring of 1989.

A picture book beauty based on the new BMW 5 range and fitted with the 333-bhp V8 presents itself with a long engine hood and a flat elongated roof contour that allows one to forget the small "Bangle-hump" at the rear. Overall, the 6 is 3¾ inches (9.5 centimeters) lower than the 5, whose lightweight front construction it had borrowed. The coupé's doors are also of aluminum, while thermoplastic is used for the sides and the trunk lid is of robust plastic. The light weight of 3725 lbs (1690 kilograms) achieved by these tricks enable a lively acceleration. If the whole six-gear palette of possibilities is used – manual, automatic, and sequential – The smooth 4.4-liter engine expresses its thanks with a powerful forward propulsion accompanied by a pleasant engine sound. Unfortunately, the fun with speed comes to an abrupt end at 155 mph (250 kph).

Pressing the "sport" button in front of the gear leaver produces even more spontaneity from the power source, the automatic transmission is coaxed in to its sport program, and the switching time shrinks to milliseconds with the sequential gear switching. Now the high engine speed can be fully enjoyed. In addition, the steering support is reduced allowing the contact with the road to be felt in the fingertips. All the electronically steered stability systems that BMW has to offer supplement the balanced chassis of the 6, constructed completely of aluminum. It hardly needs to be said that the weight distribution of this vehicle is also optimal. Active

steering and "Dynamic Drive" to compensate for wobble on tight cornering are available at a hefty surcharge to the basic price of 72,000 Euros. The standard emergency-running tires can hardly be noticed despite their strongly pronounced flanks, except that is on already rough road surfaces. The behavior of the 645Ci on tight corners or at fast changes of direction is fascinating. Driving enjoyment at its best!

This can also be enjoyed open air, for the cabriolet appeared only a few months after the coupé with a thermally isolated and sound absorbing material top that sinks electrically into a compartment within 25 seconds, even while driving at slow speed. The side struts of the closed top, described as "fins" by BMW, take up the coupé's Silhouette in a masterly fashion. Chief designer Christopher Bangle demonstrates his passion for practical detail with the vertically arranged rear window which can be independently retracted or if necessary used as a windshield for rear passengers of smaller build. A useful side effect: a lot of fresh air circulates through the cabriolet when driven with a closed top and the rear open. Heated seats and – with a surcharge – a heated steering wheel ensure the right, somewhat homely thermal conditions in the cockpit.

The interior of the BMW 6 not only underlines the elegance of the exterior, but also spoils the occupants with many small details that make touring more pleasant. The price of the cabriolet lies only 8000 Euro above that of the coupé. Both 645Ci's offer more room than two golf bags, obligatory in upper circles, require. Even with lowered top, the cabriolet still has a 10.6-cu.ft. (300-liter) capacity, while the coupé offers half as much again.

Erfolgreichstes Modell unter den vielen schönen Coupés, die bei BMW schon seit Oktober 1938 Tradition besitzen, war das 6er-Coupé der Baureihe E24. Von der Präsentation in Genf 1976 bis zum Produktions-Ende im Frühjahr 1989 wurden 86 216 Exemplare gefertigt.

Auf Basis des neuen 5er-BMW und ausgerüstet mit dem 333-PS-V8 präsentiert sich ein bildhübsches Auto mit langer Motorhaube und flacher, gestreckter Dachkontur, die den kleinen „Bangle-Buckel" am Heck vergessen lässt. Insgesamt fällt der 6er 9,5 Zentimeter niedriger aus als der 5er, von dem er die Leichtbauweise des Vorderwagens übernommen hat. Beim Coupé sind die Türen ebenfalls aus Aluminium, während an den Seitenwänden Thermoplast verwendet wird und die Heckklappe aus stabilem Kunststoff besteht. Das mit diesen Kunstgriffen erzielte Leergewicht von 1690 Kilo lässt sich munter auf 100 km/h beschleunigen. Wird die Bandbreite der sechs Gänge voll genutzt – manuell, automatisch oder sequenziell – bedankt sich das geschmeidige 4,4-Liter-Triebwerk mit kraftvollem Vortrieb, der von einem angenehmen Sound begleitet wird. Leider findet der Speed-Spaß bei 250 Stundenkilometern ein jähes Ende.

Die Betätigung des Druckschalters „Sport" vor dem Schalthebel löst beim Gasgeben noch mehr Spontaneität der Kraftquelle aus, das Automatik-Getriebe wird zu seinem Sportprogramm animiert, und beim sequenziellen Schalten schrumpfen die Schaltzeiten zu Millisekunden. Jetzt werden auch höhere Drehzahlen voll ausgekostet. Zusätzlich reduziert sich die Lenkkraft-Unterstützung, und der Straßenkontakt macht sich in den Fingerspitzen bemerkbar. Fast sämtliche elektronisch gesteuerten Stabilitäts-Systeme, die

BMW zu bieten hat, ergänzen das ausgewogene 6er-Fahr-werk ganz aus Aluminium. Dass die Gewichtsverteilung auch bei diesem Auto optimal ist, sei nur am Rande vermerkt. Aktiv-Lenkung und „Dynamic Drive" zum Ausgleich von Wank-Bewegungen der Karosserie bei scharfen Kurven-fahrten verlangen natürlich einen kräftigen Obolus zum Grundpreis von 72 000 Euro. Die serienmäßigen Reifen mit Notlauf-Eigenschaften machen sich trotz ihrer stärker ausgeprägten Flanken kaum bemerkbar, hauptsächlich auf ohnehin rauen Straßenbelägen. Faszinierend ist das Verhal-ten des 645Ci in engen Kurven oder bei schnellen Rich-tungswechseln. So macht Fahren Spaß!

Diesen kann man auch offen genießen, denn nur wenige Monate nach dem Coupé erscheint das Cabriolet mit einem wärme- und schalldämmenden Stoffverdeck, das sich elek-trisch innerhalb von 25 Sekunden in ein Abteil versenken lässt – sogar bei langsamer Fahrt. Die Seitenteile des geschlossenen Verdecks, von BMW als „Finnen" bezeichnet, greifen die Coupé-Silhouette gekonnt auf. Auch mit der senkrecht angeordneten Heckscheibe, die separat einge-fahren werden kann oder notfalls auch als Windschott für Fondpassagiere nicht allzu großen Körperwuchses dient, demonstriert Chefdesigner Christopher Bangle sein Faible für praktische Details. Nützlicher Nebeneffekt: Gibt man sich oben bedeckt und doch nach hinten offen, zirkuliert viel frische Luft durch das Cabrio. Das Cabriolet liegt im Preis nur 8000 Euro über dem des Coupés. Beide 645Ci bieten im Kofferraum mehr Platz als nur für die, in besseren Kreisen obligatorischen, zwei Golfausrüstungen. Selbst bei versenk-tem Cabrio-Verdeck beträgt das Volumen noch 300 Liter, und das Coupé fasst noch einmal die Hälfte mehr.

Le modèle qui a remporté le plus de succès, parmi les nombreux et magnifiques coupés qui ont une longue tradition chez BMW depuis octobre 1938 déjà, a été le coupé de la Série 6 de la gamme E24. Depuis sa pré-sentation à Genève en 1976 jusqu'à l'arrêt de la production au printemps 1989, 86 216 exemplaires ont, en effet, été fabriqués.

Sur la base de la nouvelle Série 5 et avec, comme moto-risation, le V8 de 333 ch, BMW présente une jolie voiture au long capot moteur et aux contours de toit plats et étirés qui font oublier le petit « becquet Bangle » à l'arrière. Au total, la Série 6 est 9,5 centimètres plus basse que la Série 5, dont elle a repris la proue à la construction allégée. Les portières du coupé sont également en aluminium tandis que les flancs sont en thermoplast et que le couvercle de malle est fabriqué dans une solide matière plastique. Ces quelques astuces ont permis de contenir à 1690 kg le poids à vide de la voiture qui accélère allègrement jusqu'à 100 km/h. Si l'on flirte avec la zone rouge de chacun des six rapports — en mode manuel, automatique ou séquentiel —, le soyeux moteur de 4,4 litres vous récompense par des accélérations énergiques qui sont accompagnées d'une sonorité des plus agréables. Malheureusement, l'ivresse de la vitesse est brutalement « castrée » à 250 km/h.

Actionnez la touche « Sport » qui se trouve devant le pommeau de vitesses : les accélérations sont alors encore plus spontanées, la boîte automatique est gérée par son programme Sport et, avec la commande séquentielle, il suffit de quelques millisecondes pour passer d'un rapport à l'autre. Maintenant, on peut aussi savourer à fond les régimes supé-rieurs. De plus, la démultiplication est réduite et le contact avec la route s'exprime jusqu'au bout des doigts. La quasi-totalité de l'arsenal de systèmes de stabilité à commande électronique que propose BMW complète le châssis équi-libré tout en aluminium de la Série 6. Il est superflu de préci-ser que la répartition du poids est optimale sur cette voiture. La direction active et le « Dynamic Drive », qui réprime la prise de roulis dans les virages franchis trop rapidement, entraînent naturellement un supplément substantiel au prix de base, qui est de 72 000 euros. Les pneus « run-flat », qui équipent la voiture en série, savent se faire oublier malgré leurs flancs plus rigides qui se manifestent essentiellement sur un mauvais revêtement.

Un agrément que l'on peut aussi savourer les cheveux au vent, car, quelques mois plus tard seulement après le coupé, apparaît le cabriolet avec une capote en tissu bien isolée sur le plan thermique et acoustique et qui s'escamote électrique-ment en 25 secondes – même lorsque l'on roule lentement. Les pans latéraux de la capote fermée, appelés « nageoires » par BMW, reprennent avec maestria la silhouette du coupé. Avec la lunette verticale, que l'on peut déplacer séparément et qui sert aussi, en cas de besoin, de coupe-vent pour les passagers des fauteuils arrière (si tant est qu'ils ne soient pas de trop grande taille), le designer en chef Christopher Bangle donne une nouvelle preuve de son penchant pour les détails pratiques. Le cabriolet est facturé seulement 8000 euros de plus que le coupé. Les deux 645Ci possèdent un coffre permettant de transporter plus que deux équipe-ments de golf. Même lorsque la capote est escamotée, la capacité du coffre est encore de 300 litres, le coupé en offre 150 de plus.

BMW 645Ci

A picture of beauty: the elongated roof contour leaves only a horizontal air trailing edge remaining of the trunk lid. The cockpit presents itself as sporty and luxurious. Powerful: the V8 engine of the 645 Ci.

Bildhübsch: die lang gestreckte Dachkontur lässt vom Kofferraumdeckel nur noch eine waagerechte Luft-Abrisskante übrig. Sportlich und luxuriös präsentiert sich das Cockpit. Kraftvoll: der V8-Motor des 645 Ci.

Beauté sculpturale : les contours étirés du toit ne laissent plus place, à hauteur du couvercle de malle, qu'à une arête de décrochement horizontale. Sportif et luxueux : le cockpit. Puissant : le moteur V8 de la 645 Ci.

The long, gently falling-away hood of the vehicle's weight-reduced aluminum front flows into a kidney-shaped configuration set with aperture covers whose lines are continued in the glazing of the upper headlights.

Die lange, sanft abfallende Haube des gewichtsreduzierten Vorderwagens aus Aluminium mündet in einer Nieren-Konfiguration mit aufgesetzten Blenden, deren Linienführung sich in der oberen Scheinwerfer-Verglasung fortsetzt.

Le long capot moteur légèrement plongeant selon les principes de la construction allégée en aluminium débouche sur des naseaux surmontés par un jonc chromé dont la ligne se poursuit, tel un sourcil, au-dessus des phares.

The cabriolet fans of this four-seater are not encased by a collapsible coupé roof, but rather by a thermal material lid, fully retractable in 25 seconds, with a separately operable rear windshield.

Kein zusammenklappbares Coupé-Dach, sondern ein in 25 Sekunden voll versenkbares Thermo-Stoffverdeck mit separat bedienbarer Heckscheibe erschließt die Cabrio-Freuden dieses Viersitzers.

Ce n'est pas un toit coupé repliable, mais une capote parfaitement isolée qui s'escamote en 25 secondes, avec une lunette arrière à commande séparée permettant aux passagers de cette quatre-places de profiter sans regrets des joies du cabriolet.

BMW X3 3.0i

The smaller brother of the X5 is not that much smaller: only 4 inches (10 centimeters) difference in length, and a mere ¾ inch (two centimeters) in width. X5 and X3 are not separated by their technology but rather by geography, for the X3 is not produced parallel to the X5 in Spartanburg, USA. It is constructed by Magna Steyr, Graz, where BMW has had engines built since 1982. As with Steyr-Daimler-Puch AG, the home of the Mercedes G, Germans and Austrians have successfully moved jointly into terrain known in the case of the X3 only by the American term "Sports Activity Vehicle" (SAV). At first glance, this multi-purpose vehicle for road and, when necessary, off road driving, only differs from the X5 by a bend. This stylistic element which slightly bevels the rearmost side windows is known by BMW internally as the "Hofmeisterknick" and has appeared occasionally since the 1970s – for example the M1 designed by Giugiaro. The reversible plastic fenders, fixed to the bodywork at different heights, are not completely in unison with the homogeneity of double kidney headlight section and curved roof contour. This slight deficit in design integration, to which the positioning of the fog lights also belongs, is of less weight when one considers the potential of the X3.

The "xDrive" (BMW's spelling) of this beefy four-wheel drive vehicle sets new standards. It enables a smoothly variable distribution of the propulsion between the powered axles by means of a multi-plate clutch. The system reacts immediately to changes in the road and ground surface conditions, transferring propulsion force to the axle that has the best ground contact at the time. "xDrive" is especially welcome by snow and ice, but it also limits the on-road

tendency to over or under steer when corning at speed. The "Hill Descent Control" (HDC) springs into action should a steep descent occur when off-road, gliding the X3 and its passengers slowly and safely to the bottom at a speed of between 4 and 16 mph (6 and 25 kph) depending on the button pressed. The HDC only takes its leave after the gas pedal has been operated.

Additional security on all surfaces is naturally provided by the tried and tested BMW dynamic stability control, which includes all previously presented regulatory aids such as Anti-lock Braking System, dynamic and cornering brake control, and the automatic differential lock. In order to achieve a relative low center of gravity despite the 8 inch (201 millimeter) ground clearance – measured with only the driver onboard – the drive shaft for the front wheels runs through the oil pan.

The 3.0i engine's four valve technology with double variable valve timing control mobilizing 231 bhp at 5900 rpm, is a BMW standard. With it the X3 can accelerate from 0 to 62 mph (100 kph) in 7.8 seconds like a roadrunner, while the top speed of 130 mph (210 kph) – or even 139 mph (224 kph) with the sport package – is remarkable for a SAV. In contrast to the 3.0d diesel variation with 204 bhp, the EU4 exhaust category 3-liter engine develops a considerable thirst for fuel when driven in a mixture of freeway and city conditions. In open country a little extra gas is in order, for here too the X3 proves its capabilities: it manages mud to a depth of 20 inches (50 centimeters) at 4.5 mph (7 kph), masters diverse gradients, and has an enormous climbing capability where many of its competitors would simply give up and overturn.

Viel fehlt ihm nicht, dem kleinen Bruder des X5: nur zehn Zentimeter Differenz in der Länge und lediglich deren zwei in der Breite. X5 und X3 trennen keine technischen Welten, sondern geographische, denn der X3 läuft nicht parallel zum X5 in Spartanburg, USA, vom Band. Ihn fertigt Magna Steyr, Graz, wo BMW schon seit 1982 Motoren bauen lässt. Wie bei der Steyr-Daimler-Puch AG, Heimstätte des Mercedes G, begeben sich Deutsche und Österreicher gemeinsam erfolgreich auf ein Terrain, das im Falle des X3 nur die amerikanische Bezeichnung „Sports Activity Vehicle" (SAV) kennt. Dieses Mehrzweck-Mobil für befestigte und – wenn es sein muss – auch unbefestigte Pfade unterscheidet sich vom X5 auf den ersten Blick nur durch einen Knick. Dieses stilistische Element, das die hinterste Seitenscheibe leicht abschrägt, wird BMW-intern „Hofmeisterknick" genannt und taucht schon seit den siebziger Jahren vereinzelt auf – sogar beim von Giugiaro entworfenen M1. Nicht ganz im Einklang zur Homogenität von Doppelniere und Scheinwerfer-Partie und der geschwungenen Dachkontur einschließlich Spoiler stehen die reversiblen Kunststoff-Stoßfänger, in unterschiedlicher Höhe an die Karosserie angeflanscht. Diese Marginalien mangelnder gestalterischer Integration, zu der auch die Positionierung der Nebelscheinwerfer gehört, fallen angesichts des X3-Potentials weniger ins Gewicht.

Bei dem bulligen Allradler setzt „xDrive" (so die BMW-Schreibweise) neue Maßstäbe. Es ermöglicht eine stufenlos variable Verteilung der Antriebskräfte zwischen den angetriebenen Achsen durch eine Lamellenkupplung. Das System reagiert sofort auf wechselnde Straßen- und Gelände-Gegebenheiten und überträgt das Antriebsmoment auf die Achse, die gerade die beste Haftung findet. Besonders positiv macht sich „xDrive" bei Schnee und Eis bemerkbar, aber auch bei schnellen Kurvenfahrten im Onroad-Betrieb minimiert es die Tendenz zum Unter- oder Übersteuern. Geht es im Offroad-Bereich einmal steil bergab, springt die „Hill Descent Control" (HDC) ein und geleitet den X3 samt Passagieren langsam und sicher zu Tal – je nach Tastendruck zwischen 6 und 25 km/h. Erst wenn man auf das Bremspedal tritt, verabschiedet sich HDC.

Zusätzliche Geborgenheit auf allen Pfaden vermittelt natürlich die bei BMW erprobte dynamische Stabilitäts-Kontrolle, die alle vorgelagerten Regulative wie Anti-Blockier-System, dynamische sowie Kurven-Bremskontrolle oder die automatische Differenzialsperre mit einbezieht. Um trotz 201 Millimeter Bodenfreiheit – gemessen nur mit dem Fahrer an Bord – einen relativ niedrigen Schwerpunkt erzielen zu können, führt die Antriebswelle für die Vorderräder durch die Ölwanne.

Die Vierventil-Technik mit doppelt variabler Nockenwellen-steuerung des 3.0i-Triebwerkes, das bei 5900/min 231 PS mobilisiert, ist BMW-Standard. Damit beschleunigt der X3 in 7,8 Sekunden von 0 auf 100 Stundenkilometer wie ein Road-runner, und auch die Spitze von 210 km/h – mit Sportpaket sogar 224 km/h – ist beachtlich für einen SAV. Im Gegensatz zur Diesel-Variante, 3.0d mit 204 PS, entwickelt das in der Schadstoffklasse EU4 angesiedelte 3-Liter-Aggregat ziemlich viel Spritdurst im gemischten Fahrbetrieb von Stadt und Autobahn. Im Gelände darf es ein Schluck Benzin zusätzlich sein, denn auch hier stellt der X3 sein Können unter Beweis: 50 Zentimeter Wattiefe bei 7 km/h, das Meistern von diversen Böschungswinkeln und eine enorme Steigfähigkeit, bei der so mancher Konkurrent andächtig nach hinten kippen würde.

Il ne lui manque pas grand-chose au petit frère du X5 : dix centimètres de différence en longueur et seulement deux en largeur. Ce n'est pas un monde mécanique, mais géographique qui sépare le X5 du X3. En effet, le X3 n'est pas construit sur les mêmes chaînes que le X5 à Spartanburg, aux États-Unis. Il est, en effet, fabriqué par Magna Steyr, à Graz, où BMW fait déjà assembler les moteurs depuis 1982. Comme avec la société Steyr-Daimler-Puch AG, le berceau de la Mercedes G, Allemands et Autrichiens s'engagent conjointement, et avec succès, sur un terrain qui, dans le cas du X3, ne connaît que la désignation américaine « Sports Activity Vehicle » (SAV). Au premier coup d'œil, le petit X3, tout aussi polyvalent que le X5, se distingue surtout de celui-ci par sa custode à la base légèrement oblique, figure de style qui était en quelque sorte la griffe de Wilhelm Hofmeister, un ancien designer de BMW qui a eu, dans les années 1960, cette idée qui a caractérisé ponctuellement plusieurs voitures dans les années 1970, dont, notamment, la M1 dessinée par Giorgio Giugiaro.

Avec ce tout-terrain musclé, la transmission « xDrive » (selon la logique de BMW) pose de nouveaux jalons. Elle permet une répartition variable en continu du couple entre les essieux moteurs grâce à un embrayage à lamelles. Le système réagit immédiatement aux changements de la route et selon la nature du terrain, transmettant de manière optimale le couple à l'essieu qui a respectivement la meilleure adhérence. La transmission « xDrive » s'avère particulièrement efficace sur la neige et le verglas, mais lors des virages franchis rapidement sur route asphaltée elle aussi réprime la tendance au sous-virage ou au survirage. Au moment d'aborder une pente escarpée en tout-terrain, le « Hill

Descent Control » (HDC) intervient, garantissant au X3 et à ses passagers une descente lente et en toute sécurité. Il suffit ensuite de donner un léger coup de frein pour que le HDC se déconnecte.

Un confort et une sécurité supplémentaires dans toutes les situations sont, naturellement, garantis par le contrôle de stabilité dynamique, qui a fait ses preuves chez BMW et intègre toutes les assistances à la conduite, telles que le système anti-blocage, le contrôle de freinage dynamique et en virage ou le différentiel autobloquant. Afin d'obtenir un centre de gravité relativement bas malgré une garde au sol de 201 millimètres – mesurée uniquement avec le conducteur à bord –, l'arbre de transmission menant aux roues avant franchit de part en part le carter d'huile.

La technique de culasse à quatre soupapes avec la distribution variable des arbres à cames double-Vanos du moteur 3.0i développant 231 ch à 5900 tr/min est standard pour cette BMW. Avec ce moteur, le X3 réalise le temps flatteur de 7,8 secondes pour le 0 à 100 km/h et atteint une vitesse maximum de 210 km/h – et même de 224 km/h avec le pack Sport – chiffre remarquable pour un SAV. Contrairement à la version Diesel, 3.0d de 204 ch, le moteur à combustion de 3 litres qui respecte la norme de dépollution UE4 s'avère plutôt glouton en consommation mixte (ville et autoroute). En tout-terrain, il s'octroie même une gorgée d'essence supplémentaire. En effet, ici aussi, le X3 administre la preuve de son savoir-faire : avec une profondeur de gué de 50 centimètres à 7 km/h, la maîtrise d'angles d'attaque et de fuite importants ainsi qu'un angle de rampe si remarquable que certains de ses concurrents risqueraient de faire la galipette.

The dominant figure among the compact all-rounders is the BMW X3 produced in Austria, a multi-purpose vehicle that feels at home on the road or in open country. Unfortunately, the very functional cockpit is somewhat soberly designed.

Platzhirsch unter den kompakten Allroundern ist der in Österreich gefertigte BMW X3, ein Mehrzweck-Mobil, das sich auf der Straße und im Gelände wohl fühlt. Leider ist das zwar sehr funktionelle Cockpit etwas nüchtern ausgefallen.

Le seigneur parmi les SUV compacts polyvalents est le BMW X3 fabriqué en Autriche, qui se sent aussi bien sur la route qu'en tout-terrain. Malheureusement, le cockpit certes très fonctionnel s'avère un peu sobre.

BMW X3

Reversible plastic bumpers encase the under section of the X3 with a ground clearance of 8 inches (20 centimeters) and mud manageability to a depth of 20 inches (50 centimeters). The four-wheel drive system enables a smoothly variable dispersion of propulsion power.

Reversible Kunststoff-Stoßfänger umschließen das Unterteil des X3 mit 20 Zentimetern Bodenfreiheit und einer Wattiefe von 50 Zentimetern. Das Allrad-System ermöglicht eine stufenlos variable Verteilung der Antriebskräfte.

Les pare-chocs réversibles en matière plastique cernent la partie inférieure du X3, dont la garde au sol est de 20 centimètres et qui offre une profondeur de gué de 50 centimètres. Le système de traction intégrale permet de répartir le couple en continu entre les deux essieux.

BMW 120i

Although a newcomer to the closely fought over compact class, the 1 has what it takes to become top of the: Strength, modern engines, well thought-out rear-wheel drive principle instead of the usual front-wheel drive, lavish technical detail, extremely long wheelbase with short overhangs, not with a high build but rather a vehicle whose air resistance coefficient of 0.29 would do a sports car proud. "In order not to impinge on the 3, we have transferred the Z4 design philosophy to the 1 which should have an alert appearance, with friendly eyes," that is how BMW design director Christopher Bangle described his compact creation.

This five-door vehicle's luggage room, variable according to rear seat position to between 11.5 and 40.5 cubic feet (330 and 1150 liters), is really pretty mediocre, but having said that, we have dealt with the vehicle's only weak point. Four four-cylinders form the basic motorization at its introduction to the market in early fall 2004. The most powerful of the gasoline variations, the 120i with its variable valve train and continuously variable camshaft adjustment develops 150 bhp, sufficient to achieve an orderly acceleration to 62 mph (100 kph) in 8.7 seconds, and a top speed of 135 mph (217 kph). The 116i with its 115 bhp also breaks through the 125 mph (200 kph) barrier. The 120d with its common-rail injector of the second generation and turbocharger really understands power harnessing: 163 bhp at 4000 rpm, an ample torque of 340 Nm at 2000 rpm, from 0 to 62 mph (100 kph) in 7.9 seconds, as well as a top speed of 137 mph (220 kph). The 118d makes its mark as a consumption ascetic, swallowing an average of 42 miles per gallon (5.6 liters per 100 km) of diesel.

BMW also sets new standards for the compact class with its 6-gear transmission, optionally available, on surcharge, as

an automatic with manual steptronic. Only the 116i has to make do with a 5-gear transmission. The balanced weight distribution of the chassis with a newly conceived five-link rear suspension and double-cardan universal joint with diagonal beams and telescopic legs built of aluminum at the front is also a challenge for the competitors, particularly as the dynamic stability control is standard as is the electronic differential lock. A shining example is the two-step brake light, which warns the following traffic by a more intensive light of possible danger situations arising from hard braking or the use of the ABS and other braking aids. If for some reason the brake light fails, the Light Control Module (LCM) comes into action and utilizes the rear lights as a substitute.

The 8'9" (2.66 meter) wheelbase by a total length of 13'10" (4.22 meters) and its unloaded weight, despite the steel body, of between 2820 lbs (1280 kilograms, 116i) and 3120 lbs (1415 kilograms, 120d), predestine the 1 to become a "cornering weasel," considering that the chassis is extra class anyway. As the world wide largest supplier of "Run-Flat" tires integrated into the production, BMW also lets the 1 travel a gasping further 150 kilometers without air in case of emergency. To safeguard the occupants from being "flattened" in case of an accident, BMW has drawn up realized a comprehensive safety concept. Contributions to reducing the risk of harm have been made by a special seat belt and airbag system, fold away pedals, and a deformable steering column on the one hand, and the cutting off of the electrical components and the activation of the emergency blink system on the other. Much of the interior belongs to the standard outfit, and almost everything that is "in" in the BMW top class can be additionally fitted.

Kaum eingezogen in die heiß umkämpfte Kompaktklasse, besitzt der 1er das Zeug zum Klassen-Primus: Starke, moderne Motoren, ausgewogenes Heckantriebs-Prinzip statt des üblichen Frontantriebs, aufwändige Technik bis ins Detail, extrem langer Radstand mit kurzen Überhängen, kein Hochbau, sondern ein Fahrzeug, dessen Luftwiderstands-Beiwert von 0,29 einem Sportwagen zur Ehre gereichen würde. „Um nicht zu nah an den 3er zu kommen, haben wir die Design-Philosophie des Z4 auf den 1er übertragen. Der 1er soll wach wirken, mit freundlichen Augen", so BMW-Designdirektor Christopher Bangle.

Mit einem Gepäckraum-Volumen, das je nach Rückbank-Position zwischen 330 und 1150 Litern variiert, ist der Fünftürer zwar nur Mittelmaß, doch damit wäre der einzige Schwachpunkt schon abgehakt. Vier 4-Zylinder bilden die Basis-Motorisierung bei Markteinführung im Frühherbst 2004. Der stärkste Benziner, der 120i mit variablem Ventiltrieb und stufenloser Nockenwellen-Verstellung, entwickelt 150 PS, ausreichend für eine recht ordentliche Beschleunigung von 8,7 Sekunden auf Tempo 100 und eine Höchstgeschwindigkeit von 217 Stundenkilometern. Die 200-km/h-Barriere durchbricht sogar der 116i mit 115 PS. Richtig Power aktiviert der 120d mit Common-Rail-Einspritzung der zweiten Generation und Turbolader: 163 PS bei 4000/min, ein fülliges Drehmoment von 340 Nm bei 2000/min, 7,9 Sekunden Spurt von 0 auf 100 km/h sowie 220 km/h Spitze. Als Verbrauchs-Asket profiliert sich der 118d, der durchschnittlich 5,6 Liter Diesel schlürft.

Neue Maßstäbe bei den Kompakten setzt BMW auch mit dem 6-Gang-Getriebe, gegen Zuzahlung optional als Automatik mit manueller Steptronic. Nur der 116i muss sich mit einem 5-Gang-Getriebe bescheiden. Auch das paritätisch belastete Fahrwerk mit neu konzipierter Fünf-Lenker-Hinterachse und einer Doppelgelenk-Zugstreben-Federbeinachse in Aluminium-Bauweise vorn fordert die Konkurrenz, zumal die dynamische Stabilitäts-Kontrolle ebenso serienmäßig ist wie die elektronische Differenzialsperre. Leuchtendes Vorbild ist das zweistufige Bremslicht, das bei Vollbremsungen oder der Inanspruchnahme von ABS und weiteren Bremshilfen durch intensiveres Licht dem nachfolgenden Verkehr eine Gefahrensituation signalisiert. Fällt das Bremslicht einmal aus, springt sofort das Licht-Control-Modul (LCM) dafür ein und lässt ersatzweise das Rücklicht aufleuchten.

2,66 Meter Radstand bei einer Gesamtlänge von 4,22 Metern und ein Leergewicht, das sich trotz Stahl-Karosserie zwischen 1280 Kilo (116i) und 1415 Kilo (120d) bewegt, prädestinieren den 1er zum „Kurven-Wiesel", da das Fahrwerk ohnehin Extra-Klasse ist. Als weltweit größter Anbieter von „Run-Flat"-Bereifung ab Werk lässt BMW auch den 1er im Notfall noch 150 Kilometer ohne Luft durch die Gegend japsen. Um bei einem Unfall nicht „platt gemacht" zu werden, hat BMW für die 1er-Insassen ein umfangreiches Sicherheitskonzept ausgearbeitet und realisiert. Dabei leisten ein spezielles Gurt- und Airbag-System, wegklappende Pedale und eine verformbare Lenksäule ebenso ihren Beitrag zur Reduzierung des Verletzungsrisikos wie die Abschaltung elektrischer Komponenten einerseits und die Aktivierung der Warnblinkanlage andererseits. Alle wichtigen Funktionen gruppieren sich um den Fahrer, während der Beifahrer sich dem Entertainment widmen kann. Vieles im Interieur gehört zur Serienausstattung, und fast alles, was in der Upperclass von BMW „in" ist, kann nachgerüstet werden.

À peine arrivée dans le segment, âprement discuté, des compactes, la Série 1 a tout pour être le meilleur élève de la classe : des moteurs puissants et modernes, une chaîne cinématique équilibrée à propulsion à la place de l'habituelle traction avant, une technique sophistiquée jusque dans les moindres détails. Un empattement extrêmement long avec de courts porte-à-faux, pas de toit surélevé, mais un véhicule dont le coefficient de résistance aérodynamique de 0,29 ferait honneur à une voiture de sport.

Avec un coffre dont la capacité varie, selon la position de la banquette arrière, entre 330 et 1150 litres, la cinq-portes ne bat, certes, pas de record, mais c'est là son seul point faible. Quatre moteurs à quatre-cylindres constituent la motorisation de base lors de sa commercialisation au début de l'automne 2004. Le plus puissant des moteurs à essence, le 120i à distribution variable des soupapes et décalage en continu de l'arbre à cames, développe 150 ch, ce qui suffit pour des accélérations flatteuses avec un temps de 8,7 secondes pour le 0 à 100 km/h et pour une vitesse de pointe de 217 km/h. La 116i de 115 ch franchit même le seuil des 200 km/h. La 120d, à injection par rampe commune de la deuxième génération et turbocompresseur, est même vraiment puissante : 163 ch à 4000 tr/min, un couple généreux de 340 Nm à 2000 tr/min, 7,9 secondes pour le 0 à 100 km/h ainsi que 220 km/h en vitesse de pointe.

BMW pose aussi des jalons chez les compactes avec une boîte manuelle à six vitesses, et, en option et contre supplément de prix, une boîte automatique avec Steptronic manuelle. Seule la 116i doit se contenter d'une boîte manuelle à cinq vitesses. Le châssis à répartition équilibrée du poids, aussi, avec un train arrière absolument inédit à cinq

bras et un essieu à jambes élastiques et tirants à double articulation tout en aluminium à l'avant place la barre très haut pour ses concurrents. D'autant plus que le contrôle de stabilité dynamique équipe la voiture en série au même titre que le blocage de différentiel électronique. Un exemple qui mérite d'être copié est donné par les feux de frein à deux niveaux d'intensité qui, en cas de freinage d'urgence ou lors de l'intervention de l'ABS et d'autres assistances de freinage, signalent une situation dangereuse aux automobilistes qui suivent grâce à une lumière plus intensive. Si les feux de frein devaient tomber en panne, le module de contrôle de la lumière (LCM) prendrait immédiatement le relais et allumerait, en remplacement, le feu de recul.

Un empattement de 2,66 mètres pour une longueur totale de 4,22 mètres et un poids à vide qui, malgré la carrosserie tout en acier, est compris entre 1280 kg (116i) et 1415 kg (120d) prédestine la Série 1 à être sacrée reine des virages, d'autant que ses liaisons au sol sont d'une classe à part. En tant que constructeur qui offre le plus grand nombre de montes pneumatiques « run-flat » départ usine, BMW permet aussi à sa Série 1 de continuer à rouler pendant 150 km sans air dans les pneus.

Pour offrir la meilleure protection possible en cas d'accident, BMW a élaboré et réalisé pour les occupants de la Série 1 un concept de sécurité sans faille. À cette occasion, un système spécial de ceintures de sécurité et d'airbags, un pédalier escamotable et une colonne de direction déformable contribuent à réduire le risque de blessures au même titre que la mise hors circuit des composants électroniques, d'une part, et l'activation des signaux de détresse, d'autre part.

Smiling, BMW design boss Christopher Bangle justified the relatively low 4' 8"- (1.43-meter-) height of the compact 1 range BMW in an interview with the renowned specialist publication *auto motor und sport:* "after all, one is not supposed to stand in the vehicle."

Dass der kompakte 1er-BMW mit 1,43 Metern relativ niedrig ausgefallen ist, begründet BMW-Design-Chef Christopher Bangle in einem Interview mit der renommierten Fach-Publikation *auto motor und sport* lächelnd: „Man soll in dem Auto schließlich nicht stehen."

Si la compacte BMW Série 1 est, avec 1,43 mètre, relativement basse, Christopher Bangle, le chef du design chez BMW, l'explique dans un sourire lors d'une interview accordée à la fameuse revue spécialisée *auto motor und sport :* « Il n'est pas prévu de rester debout dans la voiture. »

BMW 120i

BMW 120i

Special requests such as for leather seating are met promptly. The journey from supplier to incorporation at the Regensburg works takes only a few hours. One searches for the oil-level dipstick in the engine compartment in vain, for the oil level is recorded by an electronic sensor.

Sonderwünsche wie Ledersitze werden prompt erledigt. Der Weg vom Lieferanten bis zum Einbau im Werk Regensburg dauert nur wenige Stunden. Vergeblich wird man im Motorraum den Öl-Messstab suchen, denn den Pegelstand erfasst ein elektronischer Sensor.

Des options telles qu'une sellerie cuir sont disponibles presque instantanément. Le trajet entre le fournisseur et l'usine de montage de Ratisbonne ne prend que quelques heures. C'est en vain que l'on recherchera une jauge à huile dans le compartiment moteur, car le contrôle est désormais assuré par un capteur électronique.

BMW has kept its powder dry for the brilliance of the 1 range's
outer skin: it is covered by an innovative powder clear-lacquer.

Das letzte Pulver, das BMW beim 1er verschießt, dient der Brillanz
der Außenhaut, die ein innovativer Pulver-Klarlack bedeckt.

La dernière poudre que BMW jette aux yeux avec la Série 1
a pour but de donner son brillant à la carrosserie, qui est revêtue
d'un vernis transparent innovant.

		Wartburg Motorwagen	Dixi 3/15 PS
Baureihe			
Baujahre		1898–1900	1927–1929
Modell		Wartburg Kutschierwagen 1898	DA1
Motor	Konfiguration	2-Zylinder (luftgekühlt)	4-Zylinder in Reihe
	Hubraum	479 ccm	748,5 ccm
	Bohrung x Hub	66 x 70 mm	56 x 76 mm
	Kraftstoffversorgung	Oberflächenvergaser	1 Solex-Flachstromvergaser
	Leistung	3,5 PS bei 1100/min	15 PS bei 3000/min
Getriebe		2-Gang	3-Gang
Chassis	Rahmen	Stahlrohrrahmen	U-Profilrahmen aus Pressstahl
	Aufhängung vorn	Einzelradaufhängung mit gekapselten Schraubenfedern und hoch liegender Querfeder	Starrachse mit Querfeder
	Aufhängung hinten	ungefederte Starrachse	Starrachse mit Ausleger-Viertelfedern
Maße	Radstand	1600 mm	1905 mm
	Länge x Breite x Höhe	2300 x 1250 x 1450 mm	2800 x 1170 x 1625 mm
	Gewicht	315 kg	440 kg
Fahrleistung	Höchstgeschwindigkeit	40–45 km/h	75 km/h

		Wartburg	3/20 PS
Baureihe			
Baujahre		1930–1931	1932–1934
Modell		DA3 Sport-Zweisitzer	AM 4
Motor	Konfiguration	4-Zylinder in Reihe	4-Zylinder in Reihe
	Hubraum	748,5 ccm	782 ccm
	Bohrung x Hub	56 x 76 mm	56 x 80 mm
	Kraftstoffversorgung	1 Solex-Flachstromvergaser	1 Solex-Flachstromvergaser
	Leistung	18 PS bei 3500/min	20 PS bei 3500/min
Getriebe		3-Gang	4-Gang
Chassis	Rahmen	U-Profilrahmen, Karosserie in Holz-/Stahlbauweise	Zentralkasten-Niederrahmen
	Aufhängung vorn	Starrachse mit Querfeder	achslos, Querfeder
	Aufhängung hinten	Starrachse mit Ausleger-Viertelfedern	Pendelachse mit 2 Querfedern
Maße	Radstand	1905 mm	2150 mm
	Länge x Breite x Höhe	3100 x 1150 x 1400 mm	3200 x 1420 x 1550 mm
	Gewicht	410 kg	650 kg
Fahrleistung	Höchstgeschwindigkeit	90 km/h	80 km/h

Baureihe		303	315
Baujahre		1933–1934	1934–1936
Modell		303	315/1 Sport-Zweisitzer
Motor	Konfiguration	6-Zylinder in Reihe	6-Zylinder in Reihe
	Hubraum	1173 ccm	1490 ccm
	Bohrung x Hub	56 x 80 mm	58 x 94 mm
	Kraftstoffversorgung	2 Solex-Vertikalvergaser	3 Solex-Flachstromvergaser
	Leistung	30 PS bei 4000/min	40 PS bei 4300/min
Getriebe		4-Gang	4-Gang
Chassis	Rahmen	Leiterrahmen, Stahlrohrlängsträger, 4 Kastenquerträger	Leiterrahmen, Stahlrohrlängsträger, 4 Kastenquerträger
	Aufhängung vorn	Querlenker unten, Querfeder oben	Querlenker unten, Querfeder oben
	Aufhängung hinten	Starrachse mit Halbfedern	Starrachse mit Halbfedern
Maße	Radstand	2400 mm	2400 mm
	Länge x Breite x Höhe	3900 x 1440 x 1550 mm	3800 x 1440 x 1350 mm
	Gewicht	820 kg	780 kg
Fahrleistung	Höchstgeschwindigkeit	90 km/h	130 km/h

Baureihe		326	328
Baujahre		1936–1941	1936–1939
Modell		326 Cabriolet	328 Roadster
Motor	Konfiguration	6-Zylinder in Reihe	6-Zylinder in Reihe
	Hubraum	1971 ccm	1971 ccm
	Bohrung x Hub	66 x 96 mm	66 x 96 mm
	Kraftstoffversorgung	2 Solex-Vertikalvergaser	3 Solex-Fallstromvergaser
	Leistung	50 PS bei 3750/min	80 PS bei 5000/min
Getriebe		4-Gang	4-Gang
Chassis	Rahmen	Tiefbett-Kastenrahmen	Rohrrahmen mit Kastenquerträger
	Aufhängung vorn	Querfeder unten, Querlenker oben	Einzelradaufhängung, Querlenker unten, Querblattfeder oben
	Aufhängung hinten	Starrachse mit Halbfedern	Starrachse
Maße	Radstand	2750 mm	2400 mm
	Länge x Breite x Höhe	4600 x 1600 x 1500 mm	3900 x 1550 x 1450 mm
	Gewicht	1100 kg	830 kg
Fahrleistung	Höchstgeschwindigkeit	115 km/h	150 km/h

Baureihe		327	335
Baujahre		1937–1941	1939–1943
Modell		327 Cabriolet	335 Cabriolet Graber
Motor	Konfiguration	6-Zylinder in Reihe	6-Zylinder in Reihe
	Hubraum	1971 ccm	3485 ccm
	Bohrung x Hub	66 x 96 mm	82 x 110 mm
	Kraftstoffversorgung	2 Solex-Vertikalvergaser	2 Solex-Vertikal-Doppelregistervergaser
	Leistung	55 PS bei 4500/min	90 PS bei 3500/min
Getriebe		4-Gang	4-Gang
Chassis	Rahmen	Tiefbett-Kastenrahmen	Tiefbett-Kastenrahmen
	Aufhängung vorn	Querfeder unten, Querlenker oben	Querlenker und Querfeder oben
	Aufhängung hinten	Starrachse mit Halbfedern	Starrachse, 2 Längsfederstäbe
Maße	Radstand	2750 mm	2984 mm
	Länge x Breite x Höhe	4500 x 1600 x 1420 mm	4988 x 1700 x 1685 mm
	Gewicht	1100 kg	1300 kg
Fahrleistung	Höchstgeschwindigkeit	125 km/h	145 km/h

Baureihe		328 Mille Miglia	325
Baujahre		1940	1937–1940
Modell		Roadster	Leichter Einheits-Pkw, 3türig mit Gerätekasten
Motor	Konfiguration	6-Zylinder in Reihe	6-Zylinder in Reihe
	Hubraum	1971 ccm	1971 ccm
	Bohrung x Hub	66 x 96 mm	66 x 96 mm
	Kraftstoffversorgung	3 Solex-Fallstromvergaser 30 IF, auf 32 mm aufgebohrt	2 Solex-Steigstromvergaser 26 BFLV
	Leistung	130 PS bei 5750/min	50 PS bei 3750/min
Getriebe		4-Gang	5-Gang
Chassis	Rahmen	Rohrrahmen, Kastenquerträger	Kastenrahmen mit Ganzstahlkarosserie
	Aufhängung vorn	Querlenker unten, Querfeder oben	Doppelquerlenker mit 2 Schraubenfedern pro Rad
	Aufhängung hinten	Starrachse mit Halbfedern	Doppelquerlenker mit 2 Schraubenfedern pro Rad
Maße	Radstand	2400 mm	2400 mm
	Länge x Breite x Höhe	3850 x 1490 x 1060 mm	3900 x 1690 x 1900 mm
	Gewicht	700 kg	1775 kg
Fahrleistung	Höchstgeschwindigkeit	200 km/h	80 km/h

Baureihe		Veritas Rennsportwagen	502
Baujahre		1949	1954–1956
Modell		Veritas RS	502 Cabrio 2/2 (Baur)
Motor	Konfiguration	6-Zylinder in Reihe	8-Zylinder V 90°
	Hubraum	1971 ccm	2580 ccm
	Bohrung x Hub	66 x 96 mm	74 x 75 mm
	Kraftstoffversorgung	3 Solex-Vergaser 32 PBIC	Zenith-Doppel-Fallstromvergaser 32 NDIX
	Leistung	125 PS bei 5500/min	100 PS bei 4800/min
Getriebe		4-Gang	4-Gang
Chassis	Rahmen	Gitterrohrrahmen, Kastenquerträger	Kastenrahmen mit Längs- und Rohrquerträgern
	Aufhängung vorn	Einzelradaufhängung, Dreieckslenker unten, Querblattfeder oben	Doppelquerlenker und Längslenker
	Aufhängung hinten	Starrachse, Längsblattfeder	Banjo-Achse an Federhebeln und Dreieckslenker
Maße	Radstand	2250 mm	2835 mm
	Länge x Breite x Höhe	4200 x 1430 x 1030 mm	4720 x 1780 x 1530 mm
	Gewicht	800 kg	1400 kg
Fahrleistung	Höchstgeschwindigkeit	200 km/h	170 km/h

Baureihe		502	Isetta
Baujahre		1957–1961	1956–1962
Modell		502 3,2 Liter Super	Isetta 300
Motor	Konfiguration	8-Zylinder V 90°	1-Zylinder Viertakt
	Hubraum	3168 ccm	298 ccm
	Bohrung x Hub	82 x 75 mm	72 x 73 mm
	Kraftstoffversorgung	2 Zenith-Doppel-Fallstromvergaser	1 Bing-Schiebervergaser
	Leistung	140 PS bei 4800/min	13 PS bei 5200/min
Getriebe		4-Gang	4-Gang
Chassis	Rahmen	Kasten-, Längs- und Rohrquerträger, mit Karosserie verschweißt	Stahlrohr mit Ganzstahlkarosserie
	Aufhängung vorn	Doppelquerlenker, Längsfederstäbe	geschobene Längsschwingen, Schraubenfedern
	Aufhängung hinten	Starrachse, Dreieck-Schublenker, Längsfederstäbe	Starrachse (Schmalspur), Viertelelliptik-Auslegerblattfedern
Maße	Radstand	2835 mm	1500 mm
	Länge x Breite x Höhe	4730 x 1780 x 1530 mm	2285 x 1380 x 1340 mm
	Gewicht	1500 kg	360 kg
Fahrleistung	Höchstgeschwindigkeit	175 km/h	85 km/h

Baureihe		507	503
Baujahre		1956–1959	1956–1959
Modell		507	503
Motor	Konfiguration	8-Zylinder V 90°	8-Zylinder V 90°
	Hubraum	3168 ccm	3168 ccm
	Bohrung x Hub	82 x 75 mm	82 x 75 mm
	Kraftstoffversorgung	2 Zenith-Doppel-Fallstromvergaser	2 Zenith-Doppel-Fallstromvergaser
	Leistung	150 PS bei 5000/min	140 PS bei 4800/min
Getriebe		4-Gang	4-Gang
Chassis	Rahmen	Kasten-, Längs- und Rohrquerträger, mit Karosserie verschweißt	Kasten-, Längs- und Rohrquerträger, mit Karosserie verschweißt
	Aufhängung vorn	Doppelquerlenker, Stabilisator, Längsfederstäbe	Doppelquerlenker, Längsfederstäbe
	Aufhängung hinten	Starrachse	Starrachse, Dreieck-Schublenker, Längsfederstäbe
Maße	Radstand	2480 mm	2835 mm
	Länge x Breite x Höhe	4380 x 1650 x 1300 mm	4750 x 1710 x 1440 mm
	Gewicht	1330 kg	1500 kg
Fahrleistung	Höchstgeschwindigkeit	200 km/h	190 km/h

Baureihe		700	3200CS
Baujahre		1962–1965	1962–1965
Modell		700LS Luxus	3200CS
Motor	Konfiguration	2-Zylinder Boxer	8-Zylinder V 90°
	Hubraum	697ccm	3168 ccm
	Bohrung x Hub	78 x 73 mm	82 x 75 mm
	Kraftstoffversorgung	Solex-Fallstromvergaser 34 PCI	2 Zenith-Doppel-Fallstromvergaser
	Leistung	30 (32) PS bei 5000/min (ab 1963)	160 PS bei 5600/min
Getriebe		4-Gang	4-Gang
Chassis	Rahmen	selbsttragende Ganzstahlkarosserie	Kasten-, Längs- und Rohrquerträger, mit Karosserie verschweißt
	Aufhängung vorn	geschobene Längsschwingen, Schraubenfedern	Doppelquerlenker, Längsfederstäbe, Stabilisator
	Aufhängung hinten	Schräglenker, Schraubenfedern, Gummihohlfedern	Starrachse
Maße	Radstand	2280 mm	2835 mm
	Länge x Breite x Höhe	3860 x 1480 x 1360 mm	4830 x 1720 x 1460 mm
	Gewicht	680 kg	1500 kg
Fahrleistung	Höchstgeschwindigkeit	120 km/h	200 km/h

Baureihe		1500	502
Baujahre		1962–1964	1963
Modell		1500	3200S (Staatslimousine)
Motor	Konfiguration	4-Zylinder in Reihe, um 30° geneigt	8-Zylinder V 90°
	Hubraum	1499 ccm	3168 ccm
	Bohrung x Hub	82 x 71 mm	82 x 75 mm
	Kraftstoffversorgung	Solex-Fallstromvergaser	2 Doppel-Fallstromvergaser
	Leistung	80 PS bei 5700/min	160 PS bei 5600/min
Getriebe		4-Gang	4-Gang
Chassis	Rahmen	selbsttragende Ganzstahlkarosserie	Kasten-, Längs- und Rohrquerträger, mit Ganzstahlkarosserie verschweißt
	Aufhängung vorn	McPherson-Federbeine, Schraubenfedern	Doppelquerlenker, Längsfederstäbe
	Aufhängung hinten	Schraubenfedern, Schräglenker	Starrachse, Dreieck-Schublenker, Längsfederstäbe
Maße	Radstand	2550 mm	2835 mm
	Länge x Breite x Höhe	4500 x 1710 x 1450 mm	4870 x 1780 x 1530 mm
	Gewicht	1060 kg	1490 kg
Fahrleistung	Höchstgeschwindigkeit	148 km/h	190 km/h

		2000	02
Baureihe		2000	02
Baujahre		1965–1970	1971–1975
Modell		2000CS	2002tii
Motor	Konfiguration	4-Zylinder in Reihe, um 30° geneigt	4-Zylinder in Reihe, um 30° geneigt
	Hubraum	1990 ccm	1990 ccm
	Bohrung x Hub	89 x 80 mm	89 x 80 mm
	Kraftstoffversorgung	2 Solex-Doppel-Flachstromvergaser	Kugelfischer-Einspritzpumpe
	Leistung	120 PS bei 5500/min	130 PS bei 5800/min
Getriebe		4-Gang	4-Gang (5-Gang gegen Aufpreis)
Chassis	Rahmen	selbsttragende Ganzstahlkarosserie	selbsttragende Ganzstahlkarosserie
	Aufhängung vorn	McPherson-Federbeine, Schraubenfedern, Stabilisator	McPherson-Federbeine, Schraubenfedern, Drehstab-Stabilisator
	Aufhängung hinten	Schraubenfedern, Stabilisator, Schräglenker	Schraubenfedern, Drehstab-Stabilisator, Schräglenker
Maße	Radstand	2550 mm	2500 mm
	Länge x Breite x Höhe	4530 x 1675 x 1360 mm	4230 x 1590 x 1410 mm
	Gewicht	1200 kg	1010 kg
Fahrleistung	Höchstgeschwindigkeit	185 km/h	190 km/h

		02	2500 (E3)
Baureihe		02	2500 (E3)
Baujahre		1973	1968–1977
Modell		2002 turbo	2500
Motor	Konfiguration	4-Zylinder in Reihe mit Abgas-Turbolader	6-Zylinder in Reihe, um 30° geneigt
	Hubraum	1990 ccm	2494 ccm
	Bohrung x Hub	89 x 80 mm	86 x 71,6 mm
	Kraftstoffversorgung	mechanische Kugelfischer-Benzineinspritzung	2 Fallstrom-Registervergaser
	Leistung	170 PS bei 5800/min	150 PS bei 6000/min
Getriebe		4-Gang	4-Gang
Chassis	Rahmen	selbsttragende Ganzstahlkarosserie	selbsttragende Ganzstahlkarosserie
	Aufhängung vorn	Einzelradaufhängung an Federbeinen und Querlenkern, Stabilisator	McPherson-Federbeine, Schraubenfedern, Gummizusatzfedern, Drehstab-Stabilisator (ab 1971)
	Aufhängung hinten	Einzelradaufhängung an Schräglenkern, Schraubenfeder mit Gummizusatzfeder	Federbeine, Schraubenfedern, Gummizusatzfedern, Boge-Nivomat mit Stabilisator
Maße	Radstand	2500 mm	2692 mm
	Länge x Breite x Höhe	4220 x 1620 x 1410 mm	4700 x 1750 x 1450 mm
	Gewicht	1080 kg	1360 kg
Fahrleistung	Höchstgeschwindigkeit	210 km/h	190 km/h

		3.0CS	3.0CS
Baureihe		3.0CS	3.0CS
Baujahre		1971–1975	1975
Modell		3.0CSi	3.0CSL (IMSA)
Motor	Konfiguration	6-Zylinder in Reihe, um 30° geneigt	6-Zylinder in Reihe
	Hubraum	2985 ccm	3498 ccm
	Bohrung x Hub	89 x 80 mm	94 x 84 mm
	Kraftstoffversorgung	elektronische Bosch-Einspritzung	elektronische Einspritzung
	Leistung	200 PS bei 5500/min	430 PS bei 8500/min
Getriebe		4-Gang	5-Gang
Chassis	Rahmen	selbsttragende Ganzstahlkarosserie	Stahlrahmen mit Überrollkäfig, Aluhauben/-türen, Kunststoff-Aerodynamikteile
	Aufhängung vorn	McPherson-Federbeine, Schraubenfedern, Drehstab-Stabilisator	Magnesium-Radträger für Federbeine, Gelenklager, verstellbarer Stabilisator
	Aufhängung hinten	Federbeine, Schraubenfedern, Drehstab-Stabilisator, Schräglenker	Dreieckslenker, verstellbarer Stabilisator
Maße	Radstand	2625 mm	2625 mm
	Länge x Breite x Höhe	4630 x 1730 x 1370 mm	4630 x 1730 x 1366 mm
	Gewicht	1400 kg	1062 kg
Fahrleistung	Höchstgeschwindigkeit	220 km/h	280–300 km/h (je nach Übersetzung)

Baureihe		5er Reihe (E12)	3er Reihe (E21)
Baujahre		1972–1977	1978–1982
Modell		520	323i
Motor	Konfiguration	4-Zylinder in Reihe, um 30° geneigt	6-Zylinder in Reihe, um 30° geneigt
	Hubraum	1990 ccm	2315 ccm
	Bohrung x Hub	89 x 80 mm	80 x 76,8 mm
	Kraftstoffversorgung	1 Fallstromvergaser	Bosch-Saugrohr-Einspritzung
	Leistung	115 PS bei 5800/min	143 PS bei 6000/min
Getriebe		4-Gang	5-Gang
Chassis	Rahmen	selbsttragende Ganzstahlkarosserie	selbsttragende Ganzstahlkarosserie
	Aufhängung vorn	McPherson-Federbeine, Schraubenfedern, Drehstab-Stabilisator	McPherson-Federbeine, Schraubenfedern, Gummizusatzfedern, Drehstab-Stabilisator
	Aufhängung hinten	Federbeine, Schraubenfedern, Drehstab-Stabilisator, Schräglenker	Federbeine, Schraubenfedern, Gummizusatzfedern, Drehstab-Stabilisator, Schräglenker
Maße	Radstand	2636 mm	2563 mm
	Länge x Breite x Höhe	4620 x 1690 x 1425 mm	4355 x 1610 x 1380 mm
	Gewicht	1275 kg	1180 kg
Fahrleistung	Höchstgeschwindigkeit	175 km/h	192 km/h

Baureihe		7er Reihe (E23)	6er Reihe (E24)
Baujahre		1979–1986	1983–1989
Modell		728i	M 635CSi
Motor	Konfiguration	6-Zylinder in Reihe, um 30° geneigt	6-Zylinder in Reihe, um 30° geneigt
	Hubraum	2788 ccm	3453 ccm
	Bohrung x Hub	86 x 80 mm	93 x 84 mm
	Kraftstoffversorgung	elektronische Bosch-Einspritzung	elektronische Bosch-Einspritzung
	Leistung	184 PS bei 5800/min	286 PS bei 6500/min
Getriebe		4-Gang (5-Gang ab 1982)	5-Gang
Chassis	Rahmen	selbsttragende Ganzstahlkarosserie	selbsttragende Ganzstahlkarosserie
	Aufhängung vorn	McPherson-Federbeine, Schraubenfedern, Drehstab-Stabilisator	McPherson-Federbeine, Schraubenfedern, Drehstab-Stabilisator
	Aufhängung hinten	Federbeine, Schräglenker, Schraubenfedern	Federbeine, Schraubenfedern, Drehstab-Stabilisator, Schräglenker
Maße	Radstand	2795 mm	2626 mm
	Länge x Breite x Höhe	4860 x 1800 x 1430 mm	4755 x 1725 x 1354 mm
	Gewicht	1530 kg	1510 kg
Fahrleistung	Höchstgeschwindigkeit	200 km/h	250 km/h

Baureihe		M1 (E26)	Brabham BMW
Baujahre		1978–1981	1983
Modell		M1	BT52
Motor	Konfiguration	6-Zylinder in Reihe	4-Zylinder in Reihe mit Turbolader
	Hubraum	3453 ccm	1499 ccm
	Bohrung x Hub	93,4 x 84 mm	89,2 x 60 mm
	Kraftstoffversorgung	mechanische Kugelfischer-Einspritzung	elektronische Einspritzung
	Leistung	277 PS bei 6500/min	bis 790 PS bei 3,5 bar
Getriebe		5-Gang	6-Gang
Chassis	Rahmen	Stahlrohr-Gitterrahmen mit Kunststoffkarosserie	Monocoque aus Kohlefaserplatten und Alulegierung
	Aufhängung vorn	Doppelquerlenker, Schraubenfedern, Drehstab-Stabilisator, Gasdruckdämpfer	innenliegende Feder-/Dämpfereinheit, zwei Dreieckslenker mit Doppelquerlenkern
	Aufhängung hinten	Doppelquerlenker, Schraubenfedern, Drehstab-Stabilisator, Gasdruckdämpfer	innenliegende Feder-/Dämpfereinheit, zwei Dreieckslenker
Maße	Radstand	2560 mm	2860 mm
	Länge x Breite x Höhe	4360 x 1824 x 1140 mm	4323 x 2108 x 990 mm
	Gewicht	1440 kg	540 kg
Fahrleistung	Höchstgeschwindigkeit	260 km/h	325–350 km/h (je nach Übersetzung)

Baureihe		3er Reihe (E30)	3er Reihe (E30)
Baujahre		1985–1991	1990–1993
Modell		325iX touring	318i Cabrio (Kat)
Motor	Konfiguration	6-Zylinder in Reihe, um 20° geneigt	4-Zylinder in Reihe, um 30° geneigt
	Hubraum	2494 ccm	1796 ccm
	Bohrung x Hub	84 x 75 mm	84 x 81 mm
	Kraftstoffversorgung	elektronische Bosch-Einspritzung	elektronische Bosch-Einspritzung
	Leistung	171 PS bei 5800/min	113 PS bei 5500/min
Getriebe		5-Gang	5-Gang
Chassis	Rahmen	selbsttragende Ganzstahlkarosserie	selbsttragende Ganzstahlkarosserie
	Aufhängung vorn	McPherson-Federbeine, Schraubenfedern, Drehstab-Stabilisator	McPherson-Federbeine, Schraubenfedern, Drehstab-Stabilisator
	Aufhängung hinten	Schräglenker, Schraubenfedern, Drehstab-Stabilisator	Minibloc-Schraubenfedern, Schräglenker, Drehstab-Stabilisator
Maße	Radstand	2570 mm	2570 mm
	Länge x Breite x Höhe	4325 x 1645 x 1400 mm	4325 x 1645 x 1380 mm
	Gewicht	1330 kg	1230 kg
Fahrleistung	Höchstgeschwindigkeit	210 km/h	190 km/h

Baureihe		3er Reihe (E30)	Z1
Baujahre		1990	1988–1991
Modell		M3 Sport Evolution	Z1
Motor	Konfiguration	4-Zylinder in Reihe, um 30° geneigt	6-Zylinder in Reihe, um 20° geneigt
	Hubraum	2467 ccm	2494 ccm
	Bohrung x Hub	95 x 87 mm	84 x 75 mm
	Kraftstoffversorgung	elektronische Bosch-Einspritzung	digitale Bosch-Motronic
	Leistung	238 PS bei 7000/min	170 PS bei 5800/min
Getriebe		5-Gang	5-Gang
Chassis	Rahmen	selbsttragende Ganzstahlkarosserie	verzinktes Stahlblechgerüst mit Kunststoff- und Verbundstoffteilen
	Aufhängung vorn	McPherson-Federbeine, Schraubenfedern, Drehstab-Stabilisator	McPherson-Federbeine, Schraubenfedern, Drehstab-Stabilisator
	Aufhängung hinten	Schräglenker, Schraubenfedern, Drehstab-Stabilisator	Z-Achse (zentralpunktgeführte sphärische Doppelquerlenker-Achse) mit Längs- und Querlenkern, Schraubenfedern, Drehstab-Stabilisator
Maße	Radstand	2565 mm	2450 mm
	Länge x Breite x Höhe	4345 x 1680 x 1370 mm	3925 x 1690 x 1248 mm
	Gewicht	1200 kg	1290 kg
Fahrleistung	Höchstgeschwindigkeit	248 km/h	220–225 km/h

Baureihe		7er Reihe (E32)	5er Reihe (E34)
Baujahre		1987–1994	1988–1995 (ab 1992*)
Modell		750iL	M5
Motor	Konfiguration	12-Zylinder V 60°	6-Zylinder in Reihe, um 30° geneigt
	Hubraum	4988 ccm	3535 ccm (3795 ccm*)
	Bohrung x Hub	84 x 75 mm	93,4 x 86 mm (94,6 x 90 mm*)
	Kraftstoffversorgung	elektronische Bosch-Einspritzung	digitale Bosch-Motronic
	Leistung	300 PS bei 5200/min	315 PS (340 PS*) bei 6900/min
Getriebe		4-Gang Automatik	5-Gang
Chassis	Rahmen	selbsttragende Ganzstahlkarosserie	selbsttragende Ganzstahlkarosserie
	Aufhängung vorn	McPherson-Federbeine, Schraubenfedern, Drehstab-Stabilisator	Doppelgelenk-Federbeinachse mit Querkraft- und Bremsnickausgleich, Querstabilisator
	Aufhängung hinten	Federbeine, Präzisions-Schräglenkerachse, Drehstab-Stabilisator, Niveauregulierung	Schräglenkerachse mit Anfahrtauchreduzierung und Bremsnickausgleich, Querstabilisator
Maße	Radstand	2947 mm	2761 mm
	Länge x Breite x Höhe	5024 x 1845 x 1400 mm	4720 x 1751 x 1396 mm
	Gewicht	1930 kg	1720 kg
Fahrleistung	Höchstgeschwindigkeit	250 km/h	250 km/h

Baureihe		8er Reihe (E31)	3er Reihe (E36)
Baujahre		1989–1992	1993–1998
Modell		850i	318i Cabrio
Motor	Konfiguration	12-Zylinder, V 60°	4-Zylinder in Reihe
	Hubraum	4988 ccm	1796 ccm
	Bohrung x Hub	84 x 75 mm	84 x 81 mm
	Kraftstoffversorgung	elektronische Bosch-Einspritzung	elektronisches Motormanagement BMS 43
	Leistung	300 PS bei 5200/min	115 PS bei 5500/min
Getriebe		6-Gang/4-Gang Automatik	5-Gang
Chassis	Rahmen	selbsttragende Ganzstahlkarosserie	selbsttragende Ganzstahlkarosserie
	Aufhängung vorn	Doppelgelenk-Federbeinachse, Querstabilisator, Querkraftausgleich	Eingelenk-Federbeinachse mit Vorlaufversatz, Querkraftausgleich, Bremsnickreduzierung
	Aufhängung hinten	Integralachse mit fünf Lenkern, Querstabilisator	Zentrallenkerachse mit Längslenker und Doppelquerlenker, Anfahr- und Bremsnickausgleich
Maße	Radstand	2684 mm	2700 mm
	Länge x Breite x Höhe	4780 x 1855 x 1340 mm	4433 x 1710 x 1348 mm
	Gewicht	1840 kg	1370 kg
Fahrleistung	Höchstgeschwindigkeit	250 km/h	194 km/h

Baureihe		M3 (E36)	3er Reihe (E36)
Baujahre		1992–1999	1994–1998
Modell		M3 Cabrio	318ti compact
Motor	Konfiguration	6-Zylinder in Reihe	4-Zylinder in Reihe
	Hubraum	3201 ccm (ab 1995)	1895 ccm (ab 1996)
	Bohrung x Hub	86,4 x 91 mm	85 x 83,5 mm
	Kraftstoffversorgung	elektronisches Motormanagement MSS 50	elektronisches Motormanagement M 5.2
	Leistung	321 PS bei 7400/min	140 PS bei 6000/min
Getriebe		6-Gang	5-Gang
Chassis	Rahmen	selbsttragende Ganzstahlkarosserie	selbsttragende Ganzstahlkarosserie
	Aufhängung vorn	Eingelenk-Federbeinachse mit Vorlaufversatz, Querkraftausgleich, Bremsnickreduzierung	Eingelenk-Federbeinachse mit Vorlaufversatz, Querkraftausgleich, Bremsnickreduzierung
	Aufhängung hinten	Zentrallenkerachse mit Längslenker und Doppelquerlenker, Anfahr- und Bremsnickausgleich	Einzelradaufhängung an Schräglenker, getrennte Feder und Dämpfer, Anfahr- und Bremsnickausgleich
Maße	Radstand	2710 mm	2700 mm
	Länge x Breite x Höhe	4433 x 1710 x 1355 mm	4210 x 1698 x 1393 mm
	Gewicht	1460 kg	1200 kg
Fahrleistung	Höchstgeschwindigkeit	250 km/h	209 km/h

Baureihe		3er Reihe (E36)	McLaren F1
Baujahre		1995–1999	1994–1998
Modell		320i touring	McLaren F1
Motor	Konfiguration	6-Zylinder in Reihe	BMW 12-Zylinder V 60°
	Hubraum	1991 ccm	6064 ccm
	Bohrung x Hub	80 x 66 mm	86 x 87 mm
	Kraftstoffversorgung	elektronisches Motormanagement MS 41.0	elektronisches Motormanagement
	Leistung	150 PS bei 5900/min	ca. 600 PS bei 7000/min
Getriebe		5-Gang	6-Gang
Chassis	Rahmen	selbsttragende Ganzstahlkarosserie	Kohlefaser-Monocoque
	Aufhängung vorn	Eingelenk-Federbeinachse mit Vorlaufversatz, Querkraftausgleich, Bremsnickreduzierung	Einzelradaufhängung, Dreiecksquerlenker oben und unten, Stabilisator
	Aufhängung hinten	Zentrallenkerachse mit Längslenker und Doppelquerlenker, Anfahr- und Bremsnickausgleich	Einzelradaufhängung, Dreiecksquerlenker oben und unten
Maße	Radstand	2700 mm	2718 mm
	Länge x Breite x Höhe	4433 x 1698 x 1391 mm	4287 x 1920 x 1120 mm
	Gewicht	1365 kg	1016 kg
Fahrleistung	Höchstgeschwindigkeit	230 km/h	bis 370 km/h (je nach Übersetzung)

Baureihe		7er Reihe	5er Reihe (E39)
Baujahre		1996–2001	1996–2003
Modell		740i	540i
Motor	Konfiguration	8-Zylinder V 90°	8-Zylinder V 90°
	Hubraum	4398 ccm	4398 ccm
	Bohrung x Hub	92 x 82,7 mm	92 x 82,7 mm
	Kraftstoffversorgung	elektronisches Motormanagement M 5.2	elektronische Benzineinspritzung M 5.2
	Leistung	286 PS bei 5700/min	286 PS bei 5700/min
Getriebe		6-Gang	6-Gang
Chassis	Rahmen	selbsttragende Ganzstahlkarosserie	selbsttragende Ganzstahlkarosserie
	Aufhängung vorn	Doppelgelenk-Federbeinachse mit Vorlaufversatz, Querkraftausgleich und Bremsnickreduzierung	Druckstreben-Doppelgelenk-Federbeinachse (Aluminium), Querkraftausgleich, Bremsnickreduzierung
	Aufhängung hinten	Integralachse, räumlich wirkende Radaufhängung mit Anfahr- und Bremsnickausgleich	Integralachse (Aluminium), räumlich wirkende Aufhängung mit Anfahr- und Bremsnickausgleich
Maße	Radstand	2930 mm	2830 mm
	Länge x Breite x Höhe	4984 x 1862 x 1435 mm	4775 x 1800 x 1435 mm
	Gewicht	1800 kg	1585 kg
Fahrleistung	Höchstgeschwindigkeit	250 km/h	250 km/h

Baureihe		5er Reihe (E39)	Z3 (E36-7S)
Baujahre		1998–2003	1996–2002
Modell		M5	M roadster
Motor	Konfiguration	8-Zylinder V 90°	6-Zylinder in Reihe, 4-Ventil
	Hubraum	4941 ccm	3201 ccm
	Bohrung x Hub	94 x 89 mm	86,4 x 91 mm
	Kraftstoffversorgung	elektronische Benzineinspritzung MSS 52	elektronisches Motormanagement MSS 50
	Leistung	400 PS bei 6600/min	321 PS bei 7400/min
Getriebe		6-Gang	5-Gang
Chassis	Rahmen	selbsttragende Ganzstahlkarosserie	selbsttragende Karosserie
	Aufhängung vorn	Druckstreben-Doppelgelenk-Federbeinachse (Aluminium), Querkraftausgleich, Bremsnickreduzierung	Eingelenk-Federbeinachse, Querkraftausgleich, Bremsnickreduzierung
	Aufhängung hinten	Integralachse (Aluminium), räumlich wirkende Aufhängung mit Anfahr- und Bremsnickausgleich	Einzelradaufhängung am Schräglenker, getrennte Feder und Dämpfer, Anfahr- und Bremsnickausgleich
Maße	Radstand	2830 mm	2459 mm
	Länge x Breite x Höhe	4784 x 1800 x 1432 mm	4025 x 1740 x 1266 mm
	Gewicht	1720 kg	1350 kg
Fahrleistung	Höchstgeschwindigkeit	250 km/h	250 km/h

Baureihe		Z3 (E36-7)	BMW V12 Le Mans
Baujahre		1998–2002	1998
Modell		Z3 coupé 2.8	BMW V12 Le Mans (LMP1)
Motor	Konfiguration	6-Zylinder in Reihe	12 Zylinder V 60°
	Hubraum	2793 ccm	5990,5 ccm
	Bohrung x Hub	84 x 84 mm	86 x 85,94 mm
	Kraftstoffversorgung	elektronisches Motormanagement MS 41.0	elektronische Einspritzung, eine Einspritzdüse pro Zylinder
	Leistung	192 PS bei 5300/min	550 PS bei 4500/min
Getriebe		5-Gang	6-Gang, sequentiell
Chassis	Rahmen	selbsttragende Karosserie	Kohlefaser-Monocoque mit Aluminium-Befestigungsblöcken
	Aufhängung vorn	Eingelenk-Federbeinachse mit Vorlaufversatz, Querkraftausgleich, Bremsnickreduzierung	Doppel-Querlenkerachse, Feder-/Dämpfereinheit, über Kipphebel und Schubstangen betätigt
	Aufhängung hinten	Einzelradaufhängung an Schräglenker, getrennte Feder und Dämpfer, Anfahr- und Bremsnickausgleich	Doppel-Querlenkerachse, Feder-/Dämpfereinheit, über Kipphebel und Schubstangen betätigt
Maße	Radstand	2446 mm	2790 mm
	Länge x Breite x Höhe	4025 x 1740 x 1293 mm	4650 x 2000 x 1020 mm
	Gewicht	1280 kg	875 kg
Fahrleistung	Höchstgeschwindigkeit	231 km/h	ca. 350 km/h

Baureihe		3er Reihe (E46)	3er Reihe (E46)
Baujahre		1998 →	6/2003–12/2003
Modell		328i	M3 CSL
Motor	Konfiguration	6-Zylinder in Reihe	6-Zylinder in Reihe, 4-Ventil, 2 obenliegende Nockenwellen
	Hubraum	2793 ccm	3246 ccm
	Bohrung x Hub	84 x 84 mm	87,0 x 91,0 mm
	Kraftstoffversorgung	elektronisches Motormanagement	elektronische Einspritzung MSS 54HP
	Leistung	193 PS bei 5500/min	360 PS bei 7900/min
Getriebe		5-Gang	6-Gang-Schaltgetriebe, sequenziell
Chassis	Rahmen	selbsttragende Ganzstahlkarosserie	selbsttragende Leichtbau-Stahlkarosserie mit CFK-Komponenten
	Aufhängung vorn	Eingelenk-Federbeinachse mit Bremsnickausgleich und Stabilisator	Eingelenk-Federbeinachse mit Vorlaufversatz, Querlenker, Stabilisator, Bremsnickreduzierung
	Aufhängung hinten	Zentrallenkerachse mit Längslenker und Doppelquerlenker, Anfahr- und Bremsnickausgleich	Zentral-Lenker-Achse mit Längslenker und Doppelquerlenker, Anfahr- und Bremsnickausgleich
Maße	Radstand	2725 mm	2729 mm
	Länge x Breite x Höhe	4471 x 1932 x 1415 mm	4492 x 1780 x 1365 mm
	Gewicht	1470 kg	1385 kg
Fahrleistung	Höchstgeschwindigkeit	240 km/h	250 km/h, abgeriegelt

Baureihe		Z8 (E52)	X5 (E53)
Baujahre		1999–2003	1999 →
Modell		Z8 Roadster	X5 3.0i
Motor	Konfiguration	8-Zylinder V90°, 4-Ventil	6-Zylinder in Reihe, 4-Ventil
	Hubraum	4941 ccm	2979 ccm
	Bohrung x Hub	94,0 x 89,0 mm	84,0 x 89,6 mm
	Kraftstoffversorgung	elektronische Benzineinspritzung MSS 52	elektronische Einspritzung Siemens MS43
	Leistung	400 PS bei 6600/min	231 PS bei 5900/min
Getriebe		6-Gang-Schaltgetriebe	6-Gang-Schaltgetriebe
Chassis	Rahmen	Leichtmetall-Space-Frame, PU-Stoßfänger	selbsttragende Ganzstahlkarosserie
	Aufhängung vorn	Doppelgelenk-Federbeinachse mit Querlenker und Zugstrebe	Zugstreben-Doppelgelenk-Federbeinachse, kleiner, negativer Lenkrollradius
	Aufhängung hinten	Integral-Mehrlenkerachse, Schraubenfedern, Stabilisator	Integralachse, räumlich wirkende Radaufhängung mit Anfahr- und Bremsnickausgleich
Maße	Radstand	2505 mm	2820 mm
	Länge x Breite x Höhe	4400 x 1830 x 1317 mm	4667 x 1872 x 1715 mm
	Gewicht	1690 kg	2070 kg
Fahrleistung	Höchstgeschwindigkeit	250 km/h, elektronisch abgeriegelt	210 km/h

Baureihe		7er Reihe (E65)
Baujahre		2001 →
Modell		745i
Motor	Konfiguration	8-Zylinder V90°, 4-Ventil
	Hubraum	4398 ccm
	Bohrung x Hub	92,0 x 82,7 mm
	Kraftstoffversorgung	elektronische Benzineinspritzung ME9
	Leistung	333 PS bei 6100/min
Getriebe		6-Gang Automatik mit Steptronic
Chassis	Rahmen	selbsttragende Ganzstahlkarosserie
	Aufhängung vorn	Doppelgelenk-Zugstreben-Federbeinachse in Aluminium-Bauweise, Querkraftausgleich, Bremsnickreduzierung
	Aufhängung hinten	Integral-4-Mehrlenkerachse in Aluminium-Bauweise, räumlich wirkende Radaufhängung mit Anfahr- und Bremsnickausgleich
Maße	Radstand	2990 mm
	Länge x Breite x Höhe	5029 x 1902 x 1492 mm
	Gewicht	1945 kg
Fahrleistung	Höchstgeschwindigkeit	250 km/h, elektronisch abgeriegelt

Baureihe		Mini	Z4 (E85)
Baujahre		2001→	2002→
Modell		Mini Cooper S	Z4 3.0i
Motor	Konfiguration	4-Zylinder in Reihe, quer liegend, 4-Ventil	6-Zylinder in Reihe, 4-Ventil, 2 oben liegende Nockenwellen
	Hubraum	1598 ccm	2979 ccm
	Bohrung x Hub	77,0 x 85,8 mm	84,0 x 89,6 mm
	Kraftstoffversorgung	elektronische Benzineinspritzung Siemens EMS 2000	elektronische Benzineinspritzung MS45
	Leistung	163 PS bei 6000/min	231 PS bei 5900/min
Getriebe		6-Gang-Schaltgetriebe	6-Gang-Schaltgetriebe
Chassis	Rahmen	selbsttragende Ganzstahlkarosserie	selbsttragende Ganzstahl-Karosserie
	Aufhängung vorn	Eingelenk-McPherson-Federbeinachse mit Bremsnickausgleich, Stabilisator	Ein-Gelenk-Federbeinachse mit Vorlaufversatz, Querkraftausgleich und Bremsnickreduzierung
	Aufhängung hinten	Multilenker-Hinterachse, Federn, Dämpfer, Stabilisator	Einzelradaufhängung, Zentrallenkerachse mit Alu-Querlenkern, Dämpfer, Federn, Stabilisatoren, Anfahr- und Bremsnickausgleich
Maße	Radstand	2467 mm	2495 mm
	Länge x Breite x Höhe	3665 x 1688 x 1416 mm	4091 x 1781 x 1299 mm
	Gewicht	1140 kg	1365 kg
Fahrleistung	Höchstgeschwindigkeit	218 km/h	250 km/h

Baureihe		5er Reihe (E60)	6er Reihe (E63)
Baujahre		2003→	2003→
Modell		530d	645Ci Coupé
Motor	Konfiguration	6-Zylinder in Reihe, 4-Ventil	8-Zylinder V90°, 4-Ventil
	Hubraum	2993 ccm	4398 ccm
	Bohrung x Hub	90,0 x 84,0 mm	92,0 x 82,7 mm
	Kraftstoffversorgung	Common-Rail-Einspritzung Bosch DDE 5 (CR)	elektronische Einspritzung Bosch ME 9.2.1
	Leistung	218 PS bei 4000 km/h	333 PS bei 6100/min
Getriebe		6-Gang-Schaltgetriebe oder 6-Gang-Automatik mit Steptronic	6-Gang-Schaltgetriebe oder 6-Gang-Automatik mit Steptronic
Chassis	Rahmen	selbsttragende Leichtbau-Stahlkarosserie mit Aluminium-Vorderbau	selbsttragende Stahlkarosserie mit Aluminium- und Kunststoff-Komponenten
	Aufhängung vorn	Doppelgelenk-Zugstreben-Federbeinachse in Aluminium-Bauweise, Querkraftausgleich, Bremsnickreduzierung	Doppelgelenk-Federbeinachse mit Querlenker und Zugstrebe
	Aufhängung hinten	Integral-4-Mehrlenkerachse in Aluminium-Bauweise, räumlich wirkende Radaufhängung mit Anfahr- und Bremsnickausgleich	Integralachse in Aluminium-Bauweise
Maße	Radstand	2888 mm	2780 mm
	Länge x Breite x Höhe	4841 x 1846 x 1468 mm	4820 x 1855 x 1373 mm
	Gewicht	1670 kg	1690 kg
Fahrleistung	Höchstgeschwindigkeit	245 km/h	250 km/h, elektronisch abgeriegelt

Baureihe		X3 (E83)	1er Reihe (E87)
Baujahre		2003→	2004→
Modell		X3 3.0i	120i
Motor	Konfiguration	6-Zylinder in Reihe, 4-Ventil	4-Zylinder in Reihe, 4-Ventil
	Hubraum	2979 ccm	1995 ccm
	Bohrung x Hub	84,0 x 89,6 mm	90,0 x 84,0 mm
	Kraftstoffversorgung	elektronische Benzineinspritzung Siemens MS45	Saugrohreinspritzung
	Leistung	231 PS bei 5900/min	150 PS bei 6200/min
Getriebe		6-Gang-Schaltgetriebe	6-Gang-Schaltgetriebe
Chassis	Rahmen	selbsttragende Ganzstahlkarosserie	selbsttragende Stahlkarosserie
	Aufhängung vorn	Zugstreben-Doppelgelenk-Federbeinachse, kleiner, negativer Lenkrollradius, Querkraftausgleich, Bremsnickreduzierung	Doppelgelenk-Zugstreben-Federbeinachse in Aluminium-Bauweise
	Aufhängung hinten	Zentral-Lenker-Achse mit Längslenker und Doppelquerlenker, Anfahr- und Bremsnickausgleich	Fünf-Lenker-Achse in Stahl-Leichtbauweise
Maße	Radstand	2795 mm	2660 mm
	Länge x Breite x Höhe	4565 x 1853 x 1674 mm	4227 x 1751 x 1430 mm
	Gewicht	1835 kg	1335 kg
Fahrleistung	Höchstgeschwindigkeit	224 km/h	217 km/h

Glossary · Glossaire

English	Allgemein	Généralités
General	**Allgemein**	**Généralités**
since	ab	depuis
on	an	à
on	auf	sur
made of	aus	en
twin	Doppel-	double
electronic	elektronisch	électronique
for	für	pour
rear	hinten	arrière
per	je	par
no	kein/e	aucun(e)
with	mit	avec
above	oben	supérieur
per	pro	par
see above	s. o.	voir ci-dessus
via/by	über	par
below	unten	inférieur
adjustable	verstellbar	réglable
front	vorn	avant
Series	**Baureihe**	**Gamme**
Years of Production	Baujahre	Millésimes
Model	Modell	Modèle
light standard-type passenger vehicle, 3-door with tool box	Leichter Einheits-PKW, 3türig mit Gerätekasten	VP légère standard, 3 portes avec malle à équipements
state limousine	Staatslimousine	limousine de représentation
Engine	**Motor**	**Moteur**
Configuration	Konfiguration	Configuration
exhaust gas turbocharger	Abgas-Turbolader	turbocompresseur entraîné par les gaz d'échappement
direct fuel injection	Direkteinspritzung	injection directe
inclined block	geneigt	bloc incliné
in-line	in Reihe	en ligne
air-cooled	luftgekühlt	refroidi par air
in-line six-cylinder engine	6-Zylinder in Reihe	six-cylindres en ligne
six-cylinder diesel	6-Zylinder-Diesel	six-cylindres en version diesel
turbocharger	Turbolader	turbocompresseur
four-stroke	Viertakt	à quatre temps
optional	wahlweise	à titre alternatif
cylinder	Zylinder	cylindre
Cubic capacity	Hubraum	Cylindrée
cc	ccm	cm³
Bore x stroke	Bohrung x Hub	Alésage x course
Fuel supply	Kraftstoffversorgung	Alimentation en carburant
fuel injection	Benzineinspritzung	injection d'essence
digital engine electronics	digitale Motorelektronik	électronique du moteur
dual-throat downdraft carburetors	Doppel-Fallstromvergaser	double carburateurs inversés
injector	Einspritzdüse	buse d'injection
injection pump	Einspritzpumpe	pompe d'injection
injection	Einspritzung	injection
electronic engine management	elektronisches Motormanagement	gestion moteur électronique
downdraft register carburetor	Fallstrom-Registervergaser	carburateur inversé à registre
downdraft carburetor	Fallstromvergaser	carburateur inversé
sidedraft carburetor	Flachstromvergaser	carburateur horizontal
mechanical	mechanisch	mécanique
surface carburetor	Oberflächenvergaser	carburateur à surface
inlet pipe injection	Saugrohr-Einspritzung	injection dans les tubulures d'aspiration
sliding carburetor	Schiebervergaser	carburateur à coulisse
updraft carburetor	Steigstromvergaser	carburateur vertical ascendant
vertical double register carburetor	Vertikal-Doppelregistervergaser	carburateur vertical à double registre
vertical carburetor	Vertikalvergaser	carburateur vertical
Output	Leistung	Puissance
bar	bar	bar
at	bei	à
to	bis	jusqu'à
bhp	PS	ch
at … rpm	bei …/min	à … tr/min
Transmission	Getriebe	Boîte de vitesses
2-stage	2-Stufen	à deux rapports
4-speed	4-Gang	à quatre vitesses
four-wheel drive	Allradantrieb	traction intégrale
automatic	Automatik	automatique
at extra cost	gegen Aufpreis	contre supplément
sequential	sequentiell	séquentielle
Chassis	**Chassis**	**Châssis**
Frame	Rahmen	Cadre
aerodynamic parts	Aerodynamikteile	éléments aérodynamiques
aluminum tops and doors	Aluhauben/-türen	capots et portières en aluminium
aluminum alloy	Alulegierung	alliage d'aluminium
aluminum fastening blocks	Aluminium-Befestigungsblöcke	blocs de fixation en aluminium
all-steel body	Ganzstahlkarosserie	carrosserie tout acier
multi-tubular spaceframe	Gitterrohrrahmen	châssis tubulaire
bodywork	Karosserie	carrosserie
box-section cross beams	Kastenquerträger	poutres transversales
box-type frame	Kastenrahmen	châssis à caisson
carbon fiber	Kohlefaser	fibre de carbone
carbon fiber panels	Kohlefaserplatten	panneaux en fibre de carbone
plastic	Kunststoff	matière plastique
plastic and composite material parts	Kunststoff- und Verbundstoffteile	matières plastiques et composites
longitudinal beam	Längsträger	poutre longitudinale
ladder frame	Leiterrahmen	châssis en échelle
pressed steel	Pressstahl	acier embouti
cross beam	Querträger	poutre transversale
tubular frame	Rohrrahmen	cadre en tube
integral	selbsttragend	autoporteuse
sheet steel frame	Stahlblechgerüst	squelette d'acier
steel tube	Stahlrohr	tube d'acier
steel frame	Stahlrahmen	châssis en acier
tubular steel spaceframe	Stahlrohr-Gitterrahmen	châssis en tube d'acier
steel tubular frame	Stahlrohrrahmen	cadre tubulaire en acier
drop base box frame	Tiefbett-Kastenrahmen	châssis surbaissé à caisson
rollovercage	Überrollkäfig	arceau de sécurité
U-section	U-Profil	profilé en U
welded	verschweißt	soudé
galvanized	verzinkt	galvanisé
central box-section low frame	Zentralkasten-Niederrahmen	châssis surbaissé à caisson central
two	zwei	deux
Suspension front/rear	**Aufhängung vorn/hinten**	**Suspension avant/arrière**
axle	Achse	essieu
four-wheel drive	Allradantrieb	traction intégrale
aluminum	Alu / Aluminium	aluminium
anti-dive mechanism	Anfahrtauchreduzierung	réduction de la plongée au démarrage
anti-squat and anti-dive mechanism	Anfahr- und Bremsnickausgleich	compensation du tangage au démarrage et au freinage
cantilever quarter-spring	Ausleger-Viertelfeder	quart de ressort cantilever
banjo axle	Banjo-Achse	essieu en banjo
controlled	betätigt	actionné
anti-dive mechanism	Bremsnickreduzierung	diminution du tangage au freinage
absorber	Dämpfer	amortisseur
double-jointed McPherson strut axle	Doppelgelenk-Federbeinachse	essieu à jambes élastiques à double articulation
double control rods	Doppelquerlenker	double bras transversaux
anti-roll bar	Drehstab-Stabilisator	stabilisateur à barre de torsion
wishbone	Dreieckslenker	bras triangulaire
wishbone	Dreieck-Schublenker	poussoir triangulaire
wishbone	Dreiecksquerlenker	triangle transversal
constant velocity double-jointed McPherson strut axle	Druckstreben-Doppelgelenk-Federbeinachse	essieu à jambes élastiques à double articulation et bras de pression
single-joint McPherson strut axle	Eingelenk-Federbeinachse	essieu à jambes élastiques à une articulation
independent suspension	Einzelradaufhängung	suspension à roues indépendantes
strut	Federbein	jambe élastique
spring/absorber unit	Feder-/Dämpfereinheit	unité ressorts/amortisseurs
spring lever	Federhebel	levier de ressort
five	fünf	cinq
pressurized gas shock absorber	Gasdruckdämpfer	amortisseur à gaz
wishbone	Gelenklager	levier triangulé
enclosed	gekapselt	encapsulé
slide-action longitudinal swing axle	geschobene Längsschwingen	bras oscillants longitudinaux poussés
separate	getrennt	séparé
rubber hollow spring	Gummihohlfeder	ressort creux en caoutchouc
auxiliary rubber spring	Gummizusatzfeder	ressort supplémentaire en caoutchouc
semi-elliptic spring	Halbfeder	ressort semi-elliptique
integral axle	Integralachse	essieu intégral
rocker arm	Kipphebel	culbuteur
longitudinal leaf spring	Längsblattfeder	ressort à lames longitudinaux
longitudinal spring bars	Längsfederstäbe	barres de torsion longitudinales
longitudinal swing arm	Längslenker	bras longitudinal
arm	Lenker	bras
McPherson strut	McPherson-Federbein	jambe élastique McPherson
magnesium wheel bearing	Magnesium-Radträger	palier de roue en magnésium
Minibloc coil spring	Minibloc-Schraubenfeder	ressort hélicoïdal Minibloc
level control	Niveauregulierung	correction d'assiette
swing axle	Pendelachse	essieu oscillant
precision angled control bar axle	Präzisions-Schräglenkerachse	bras oblique à haute précision
transverse leaf spring	Querblattfeder	ressort à lames transversal
transverse spring	Querfeder	ressort transversal
lateral force compensation	Querkraftausgleich	compensation des accélérations latérales
transverse arm	Querlenker	bras transversal
transverse antiroll bar	Querstabilisator	barre stabilisatrice transversale
wheel	Rad	roue
spatially effective	räumlich wirkend	agissant dans l'espace
narrow track	Schmalspur	à voie étroite
diagonal arm	Schräglenker	bras diagonal
diagonal control arm axle	Schräglenkerachse	essieu à bras diagonal
coil spring	Schraubenfeder	ressort hélicoïdal
connecting rod	Schubstange	poussoir
spherical	sphärisch	sphérique
antiroll bar	Stabilisator	barre antiroulis
rigid	starr	rigide
rigid axle	Starrachse	essieu rigide
adjustable	verstellbar	réglable
quarter elliptic cantilever leaf spring	Viertelelliptik-Ausleger-Blattfeder	ressort à lames à quart d'ellipse cantilever
tracking offset	Vorlaufversatz	déport de chasse négative
Z-axle	Z-Achse	essieu en Z
centrally articulated axle	Zentrallenkerachse	essieu en guidage central
centrally articulated	zentralpunktgeführt	guidage par point central
Dimensions	**Maße**	**Dimensions**
Wheelbase	Radstand	Empattement
Length x width x height	Länge x Breite x Höhe	Longueur x largeur x hauteur
100 mm = 3.937 inches	mm	mm
Weight	Gewicht	Poids
1 kg = 2.205 lbs	kg	kg
Performance	**Fahrleistung**	**Performances**
Maximum speed	Höchstgeschwindigkeit	Vitesse de pointe
depending on engine up to c.	je nach Motorvariante bis ca.	selon les options du moteur jusqu'à
depending on ratios	je nach Übersetzung	selon rapport de pont
1 km/h (kph) = 0.622 mph	km/h	km/h

Bibliography · Bibliographie

Jürgen Lewandowski: *BMW Typen und Geschichte,* Augsburg 1998

Horst Mönnich: *BMW, eine deutsche Geschichte,* München 1991

Werner Oswald: *Alle BMW-Automobile seit 1928,* Stuttgart 1993

Halwart Schrader: *BMW,* 2 Bde., Gerlingen 1994

Usines & Industries 85/1989, Bayerische Motoren Werke, Brüssel

Auto und Sport

auto motor und sport

BMW-Magazin

rallye racing

Acknowledgments

I would like to express my thanks to everyone who made it possible for this book to happen by allowing their cars to be used: Hans-Friedrich Andexer, Udo Beckmann, Jochen Burgdorf, Helmut and Thomas Feierabend, Baldur Glaas, Gunter Herz, Dr. August Kau, Dr. Jürgen and Brigitte Klöckner, Michael Knittel, Prof. Dr. Gerhard Knöchlein, Dr. Bernhard Knöchlein, Sepp Mayer, Yvonne Mittler, Jürgen Pollack, Karl Heinz Wedel.

I would also like to thank the members of the press department of BMW AG, BMW Mobile Tradition, BMW Motorsport Ltd. and the BMW office in Frankfurt/Main: Franz Joseph Bötsch, Christian W. Eich, Richard Gerstner, Thomas Giuliani, "Bepi" Grassl, Helmut Grünwald, Franz Inzko, Fred Jakobs, Raimund Kupferschmid, Klaus Kutscher, Uwe Mahla, Joachim Pietzsch, Bruno Santic, Christian Stockmann, Ali Strasser, Dirk-Henning Strassl, Walter Zeichner, Axel Zimmermann.

My gratitude to all those in positions of responsibility at Egelsbach, Michelstadt, Lauf-Lillinghof and Siegerland airports for their kind support when I was photographing there.

And finally, thanks are due to Hartmut Lehbrink and Jochen von Osterroth for their texts, as well as Christian Maiwurm, Monika Dauer, Sabine Gerber and the Könemann team for the inspired way in which they handled the project.

Rainer W. Schlegelmilch

Danksagung

Ich danke allen, die mir die Verwirklichung dieses Buches durch die Bereitstellung ihrer Fahrzeuge ermöglicht haben: Hans-Friedrich Andexer, Udo Beckmann, Jochen Burgdorf, Helmut und Thomas Feierabend, Baldur Glaas, Gunter Herz, Dr. August Kau, Dr. Jürgen und Brigitte Klöckner, Michael Knittel, Prof. Dr. Gerhard Knöchlein, Dr. Bernhard Knöchlein, Sepp Mayer, Yvonne Mittler, Jürgen Pollack, Karl Heinz Wedel.

Ich bedanke mich ebenso bei den Mitarbeitern der Presseabteilung der BMW AG, der BMW Mobile Tradition, der BMW Motorsport Ltd. und der BMW Niederlassung Frankfurt am Main: Franz Joseph Bötsch, Christian W. Eich, Richard Gerstner, Thomas Giuliani, „Bepi" Grassl, Helmut Grünwald, Franz Inzko, Fred Jakobs, Raimund Kupferschmid, Klaus Kutscher, Uwe Mahla, Joachim Pietzsch, Bruno Santic, Christian Stockmann, Ali Strasser, Dirk-Henning Strassl, Walter Zeichner, Axel Zimmermann.

Für die freundliche Unterstützung bei meinen Aufnahmen danke ich den Verantwortlichen der Flugplätze Egelsbach, Michelstadt, Lauf-Lillinghof und des Flughafens Siegerland.

Und zu guter Letzt gilt mein Dank Hartmut Lehbrink und Jochen von Osterroth für ihre Texte sowie Christian Maiwurm, Monika Dauer, Sabine Gerber und dem Könemann-Team für die geniale Realisation.

Rainer W. Schlegelmilch

Remerciements

Je remercie tous ceux qui m'ont permis de réaliser ce livre en mettant leurs voitures à ma disposition : Hans-Friedrich Andexer, Udo Beckmann, Jochen Burgdorf, Helmut et Thomas Feierabend, Baldur Glaas, Gunter Herz, Dr. August Kau, Dr. Jürgen et Brigitte Klöckner, Michael Knittel, Prof. Dr. Gerhard Knöchlein, Dr. Bernhard Knöchlein, Sepp Mayer, Yvonne Mittler, Jürgen Pollack, Karl Heinz Wedel.

Je remercie tout autant les collaborateurs de BMW AG, de BMW Mobile Tradition, de BMW Motorsport Ltd. et de la succursale de BMW de Francfort/Main : Franz Joseph Bötsch, Christian W. Eich, Richard Gerstner, Thomas Giuliani, « Bepi » Grassl, Helmut Grünwald, Franz Inzko, Fred Jakobs, Raimund Kupferschmid, Klaus Kutscher, Uwe Mahla, Joachim Pietzsch, Bruno Santic, Christian Stockmann, Ali Strasser, Dirk-Henning Strassl, Walter Zeichner, Axel Zimmermann.

Je tiens à remercier les responsables des aéroports d'Egelsbach, Michelstadt, Lauf-Lillinghof et de l'aéroport du Siegerland pour leur aide.

Et, enfin, je dois aussi remercier Hartmut Lehbrink et Jochen von Osterroth pour leurs textes ainsi que Christian Maiwurm, Monika Dauer, Sabine Gerber et l'équipe de Könemann pour la qualité de leur travail.

Rainer W. Schlegelmilch

Photography: Rainer W. Schlegelmilch
Text: Hartmut Lehbrink, Jochen von Osterroth

Art direction: Peter Feierabend
Project manager: Sally Bald, Joachim Schwochert (new edition)
Drawings: Jochen von Osterroth
Layout: Christian Maiwurm, Oliver Hessmann
Cover: Oliver Hessmann
Photos p. 8–35: BMW AG
Translations into English: Christian von Arnim, Stephen Hunter, Paul Motley, Russell Cennydd
Translation into French: Jean-Luc Lesouëf

*KÖNEMANN is a registered trademark of Tandem Verlag GmbH

Printed in Germany

ISBN 3-8331-1059-7

10 9 8 7 6 5 4 3 2 1
X IX VIII VII VI V IV III II I